"This is the best of guides to the world of
novel, exciting, detailed, reliable account of how monastic life developed
over twelve centuries and of the many paths to perfection and salvation it
created for both women and men. Medieval monasticism had its failures,
but it also never ceased to surprise by its capacity to adjust to complex,
changing circumstances, to establish itself as a fundamental element
of medieval economy and society, and to cater for the whole spectrum
of religious life from eremitical withdrawal to firebrand preaching.
Here is an exceptionally rich mine of materials drawn from all kinds of
historical sources and thoughtfully presented in the light of an exceptional
understanding of structures and ideals by a wonderful scholar."

> —David Luscombe
> Fellow of the British Academy
> Emeritus Professor
> The University of Sheffield

"The fruit of long study of medieval monks, ascetics, mystics, and the
rules that they lived by, *The World of Medieval Monasticism* is a lively
and erudite companion for any reader interested in exploring the many
astonishing forms of Western religious life."

> —Barbara H. Rosenwein
> Loyola University

"*The World of Medieval Monasticism* is the crowning achievement of the
decades Professor Melville has devoted to the relentless study of medieval
religious life in the West. Marked by a wealth of sources and shaped by
the influential Research Center for the Comparative History of Religious
Life at the University of Dresden, *The World of Medieval Monasticism* is
an essential source in its own right for all those interested in the cultural
history and spiritual inheritance of medieval religious life."

> —Timothy J. Johnson
> Flagler College

"With this splendid translation, English readers have access to a lifetime of scholarly thought and reflection on medieval monastic and mendicant life offered as a coherent narrative. Gert Melville has long been one of the leading interpreters of monastic life in Germany and, at present, perhaps the foremost sponsor of probing new scholarship. This book shows him at his best as a sympathetic student of medieval religious life set, as a good historian would, in its social and material contexts."

> — John VanEngen
> University of Notre Dame

"The doyen of monastic history has poured learning hitherto scattered among innumerable papers into the form of an elegant synthesis—a path-breaking sociological analysis of one of the most interesting medieval forms of life. Decades of scholarships and accumulated insights have been distilled into this volume."

> — David d'Avray
> University College London
> Fellow of the British Academy

CISTERCIAN STUDIES SERIES: NUMBER TWO HUNDRED SIXTY-THREE

The World
of Medieval Monasticism
Its History and Forms of Life

Gert Melville

Translated by
James D. Mixson

Foreword by
Giles Constable

Cistercian Publications
www.cistercianpublications.org

LITURGICAL PRESS
Collegeville, Minnesota
www.litpress.org

Cistercian Publications
Editorial Offices
161 Grosvenor Street
Athens, Ohio 54701
www.cistercianpublications.org

This work was originally published in German as *Die Welt der Mittelalterlichen Klöster. Geschichte und Lebensformen* © Verlag C.H. Beck oHG, München 2012.

The translation of this work was funded by Geisteswissenschaften International— Translation Funding for Humanities and Social Sciences from Germany, a joint initiative of the Fritz Thyssen Foundation, the German Federal Foreign Office, the collecting society VG WORT and the Börsenverein des Deutschen Buchhandels (German Publishers & Booksellers Association).

Scripture texts in this work are taken from the *New Revised Standard Version Bible*, © 1989, Division of Christian Education of the National Council of the Churches of Christ in the United States of America. Used by permission. All rights reserved.

Unless otherwise indicated, quotations from the *Rule of St. Benedict* are taken from *RB 1980: The Rule of St. Benedict in English*, copyright © 1981 by Order of Saint Benedict, Collegeville, Minnesota.

1   2   3   4   5   6   7   8   9

Library of Congress Cataloging-in-Publication Data

Names: Melville, Gert.
Title: The world of medieval monasticism : its history and forms of life / Gert Melville ; translated by James Mixson.
Other titles: Welt der mittelalterlichen Kloster. English
Description: Collegeville, Minnesota : Cistercian Publications, 2016. I Series: Cisterican studies series ; no. 263 I Includes bibliographical references and index.
Identifiers: LCCN 2015034630 I ISBN 9780879072636 I ISBN 9780879074999 (ebook)
Subjects: LCSH: Monasticism and religious orders—Europe—History—Middle Ages, 600–1500. I Monastic and religious life—Europe—History—Middle Ages, 600–1500. I Monks—Europe—Social conditions. I Europe—Church history— 600–1500.
Classification: LCC BX2590 .M45813 2016 I DDC 271.009/02—dc23
LC record available at http://lccn.loc.gov/2015034630

For Marlen, Maximilian, and Niels

Contents

Foreword by Giles Constable   xi

Preface   xiii

List of Abbreviations   xv

Translator's Note   xvii

1. **The Beginnings**   1
   Retreat from the World   1
   The Establishment of Monastic Communities   7
   The First Monasteries in Europe   13

2. **The Benedictine Rule and Its Longevity**   24
   Benedict as "Textual Trace"   24
   The Rule of Saint Benedict   29
   The Career of Benedict and His Rule   34
   The Second Benedict and the Reform
      of the Frankish Monasteries   38

3. **The Flowering of the Benedictines**   50
   A New Beginning in Lotharingia   50
   Cluny: The Establishment of Monastic Liberty   54
   The "Cluniac Church": A Congregation of Monasteries   63
   Ordo Cluniacensis   67
   Church for the World   72
   Monastic Life in Service of King and Nobility,
      Pope and Bishop   80

4. **Return to the Desert**   89
   The New Hermits   89

To Live by One's Own Law   94
Charismatic Preaching and Religious Movements   109
A Return to the Institutions of the Church   120

5. **The Regular Canons: The Clergy's
   New Self-Understanding**   125

6. **The Cistercians: Collegiality Instead of Hierarchy**   136
   Robert's Path from Molesme to Cîteaux and Back   136
   The Measure of the Pure Rule   141
   The *Charter of Charity* and the Invention of the "Order"   146

7. **The Success of the Cistercian Model**   158

   From the Premonstratensians to the Gilbertines
      and the Carthusians   158
   Cluny, Knights, and Hospitals: The Reform of
      Older Congregations and the Creation of
      New "Functional" Orders   166

8. **Diversity and Competition**   180

9. **New Concepts of Belief**   186
   The Search for Religious Identity   186
   Beguines and *Humiliati*: A New Lay Piety   193
   "Holy Preachers" and "Lesser Brothers"   200

10. **The Franciscans: A Mendicant Order with the Whole World
    as Its Monastery**   206
    Francis of Assisi and His Community   206
    The Legacy of Francis   216
    Clare of Assisi   225

11. **The Dominicans: Holy Preaching and Pastoral Care**   232
    Dominic and the Building of a New Order   232
    Rationality and Constitution in the Service of the
       Salvation of Souls   239

12. **Transformations of Eremitical Life**   249
    The Carmelites: From the Mountain into the Cities   250
    The Augustinian Hermits   256

13. **A New Chapter in the Story of the *Vita Religiosa*** 263
The Three Ages of Salvation History 263
Eremitical Congregations and the Work of Peter of Morrone 267
Devotio Moderna 276
The Revelations of Birgitta 280

14. **Mendicant Orders in Conflict: Struggles over Poverty
and Observance** 286

15. **Reformers and Reforms at the End of the Middle Ages** 298
Reform from Above: Pope Benedict XII 298
Reform from Below: The Rise of the Observants 306

16. **A Look Back** 313

17. **Fundamental Structures of the *Vita Religiosa*
in the Middle Ages** 316
The Individual and the Community 318
The Monastery and the Law 332
Institutional Forms: Establishment and Preservation 342
Constructing Particular Pasts 349
Cloister and World 353
Temporalia 359
On the Search for God toward Knowledge of the World 364

Chronology 373

Map 382

Bibliography 384

Image Credits 432

Index of People and Places 433

Index of Monasteries, Congregations, and Orders 440

Foreword

This book will introduce English-speaking readers to the work of Professor Gert Melville, who has for many years played a leading role as a writer and educator in the field of medieval church history. As a lecturer at Munich, Frankfurt am Main, Tübingen, Paris, and Passau and a professor at Münster, Dresden, and Eichstätt, he has influenced countless students. He has organized many scholarly meetings and directed the publication of the proceedings, often in the series *Vita regularis* (which now numbers over sixty volumes) and Norm und Struktur (with over forty volumes). He has edited, or helped to edit, thirty-nine volumes of collected essays. He took the initiative in the creation of the Forschungsstelle für Vergleichende Ordensgeschichte (FOVOG)—the Research Center for the Comparative History of Religious Orders—which promotes the comparative study of the forms of medieval religious life. At the same time, Professor Melville has pursued his own research and published several volumes and well over a hundred articles on topics from Late Antiquity to the Early Modern period, concerned with the church and religious life not only in Europe but also in the Near East and America.

The present work distills a lifetime of study of medieval Christianity and covers an impressive range of material on religious life all over Europe for more than a thousand years. It concentrates on monasticism and other forms of religious life, including hermits as well as monks and nuns, canons and canonesses, and the mendicant orders. Professor Melville maintains a delicate balance between institutions and spirituality, between texts and charisma, and between rules and reality in religious communities, including the relation with the outside world of groups and individuals who have in principle withdrawn from secular society. In the late Middle Ages, the essentially personal element in religious life—the desire "to seek a direct encounter of the individual soul with God," as Professor Melville puts it—inspired the new apostolic orders, communities of hermits, and lay associations of women as well as men. The older institutions lost much of their appeal, though they still attracted new members.

Along the way the reader meets a number of influential religious leaders and develops a sense of the personal and spiritual as well as the institutional side of religious life. The text illuminates the tension between individuals and institutions and contributes to an understanding of the real life in different religious communities, how they were organized and governed, and why they flourished at some times and declined at others.

Giles Constable
Professor Emeritus
School of Historical Studies
Institute for Advanced Study, Princeton

Preface

This book concerns those who sought the perfection of their souls and who were prepared, for that reason, to leave the earthly world behind. They retreated into a monastic community that to them seemed a safe haven amid the futile storms of the world, and there they subjected themselves to the strict regulation of every aspect of life in prayer, ascesis, and work. Such a way of life laid claim to the whole person. It required the absolute faith of approaching God in a way that secured spiritual salvation in the world beyond.

This book traces, from the earliest days of Christianity to the end of the Middle Ages, the many paths that men and women took to achieve this end—a journey that was an all-consuming struggle to adapt to changing spiritual needs and shifting cultural conditions. The history of monastic ways of life thus reveals itself as a multifaceted interweaving not only of experiments, of bold new beginnings and persistent reforms, but also of decline and failure. But in the end, it is the story of remarkable success, one set in a time when the Christian faith, as the bearer of hope for salvation from the afflictions of the world, was the foundation and measure of culture. The women and men of the monastery stood as a model for those who remained "in the world," a model that revealed to all that salvation was actually possible.

The book shows, from the perspective of the monastery, how such a way of life concretely influenced politics, society, economy, and the intellectual world. Monasteries offered themselves as a secure kind of investment, whether spiritual, political, or economic, and they often thereby fell into a dangerous dependence on earthly powers and into worldly temptations. On the other hand, the monastic world saw itself in principle as responsible for the salvation of mankind, and it performed fundamental services in that regard. It understood itself as a relay station, so to speak, between God and the world. Through prayer, preaching, and the communication of knowledge, it sought to bring God and humankind closer together. Through care for the sick, the poor, and the forgotten, those in the monastery sought to follow Christ and to proclaim the message of love of neighbor through their own prominent example. Monasteries were an efficient, fundamental element of a medieval culture that nourished the roots of modernity.

The book paints in broad strokes across long stretches of time, traces particular ramifications, and ends with a presentation of the basic structural elements of monastic forms of life. In this wide thematic field, some things can only be treated briefly; the references to literature in the footnotes thus serve primarily to provide suggestions for further reading.

The book is the result of decades of engagement with the monastic world of the Middle Ages. In the course of writing it, I have enjoyed the support of numerous colleagues and friends. I would like to recognize two people in particular: my wife gave me strength, encouraging criticism, and room for quiet reflection, and Mirko Breitenstein accompanied the entire project with prudent patience, countless suggestions, and knowledgeable references. I also offer most sincere thanks to my coworkers in the Research Center for the Comparative History of Religious Orders (FOVOG), established under my direction at the University of Dresden (Germany). My esteemed colleague James Mixson (The University of Alabama) has prepared the competent and careful translation of this book. I owe a special thanks to him as well.

Gert Melville

Abbreviations

CCCM   Corpus Christianorum, Continuatio Mediaevalis

CCM   Corpus consuetudinum monasticarum

CF   Cistercian Fathers series

CS   Cistercian Studies series

CSEL   Corpus scriptorum ecclesiasticorum laatinorum

Customs   *From Dead of Night to End of Day: The Medieval Customs of Cluny = [Du cœur de la nuit à la fin du jour. Les coutumes clunisiennes au Moyen Âge]*. Edited by Susan Boynton and Isabelle Cochelin. Turnhout: Brepols Publishers, 2005.

Ep(p   Epistola(e

Fontes   *Fontes Franciscani*. Edited by Enrico Menestò and Stefano Brufani. Assisi: Edizioni Porziuncola, 1997.

MGH   Monumenta Germaniae Historica

MGHSS   MGH Scriptores

PG   Patrologia Graeca, ed. J.-P. Migne

PL   Patrologia Latina, ed. J.-P. Migne

SBOp   Sancti Bernardi Opera. Edited by Jean Leclercq and H. M. Rochais. Rome: Editiones Cistercienses, 1957–77.

SCh   Sources chrétiennes

Schriften   *Franziskus-Quellen. Die Schriften des heiligen Franziskus, Lebensbeschreibungen, Chroniken und Zeugnisse über ihn und seinen Orden*. Edited by Dieter Berg and Leonhard Lehmann. Kevelaer: Butzon & Bercker, 2009.

Translator's Note

The basis of this translation is the edition of Professor Melville's book as it was published in 2012 by C. H. Beck. I have translated the text and notes of that edition into English, but Professor Melville has also expanded or otherwise considerably revised certain passages to better suit an Anglophone audience. The notes and bibliography have been considerably revised as well to accommodate an Anglophone readership and to reflect the latest scholarship. In many instances, English titles and translations have replaced or been added to titles appearing in the original work. Formatting has also been altered to reflect the conventions of Cistercian Publications and Liturgical Press.

I am grateful to the Department of History and the College of Arts and Sciences of the University of Alabama for their support of my work on this translation, as well as to Hans Christoffersen, Marsha Dutton, and the editorial staff at Cistercian Publications and Liturgical Press for their kindness, efficiency, and hard work in helping bring this project to conclusion. As ever, I am grateful to my wife for her faithful support and encouragement of my work. But above all I am grateful to Professor Melville himself, who entrusted me with the task of this translation. He has encouraged me, challenged me insistently, and worked with me at every step, line by line. His is a very refined and carefully crafted style, and I am grateful that he was not only thorough enough to save me from my worst mistakes in translating it but also patient enough to help me get it just right. Nevertheless, any shortcomings or errors that remain in the translation itself are of course my responsibility alone.

James D. Mixson
The University of Alabama

1

The Beginnings

Retreat from the World

"You should see it with your own eyes." With these words John Chrysostom (344/49–407), one of the greatest Doctors of the Church in the East, invited his reader to imagine the world of the monastery, where monks lived in the blessedness of Paradise:

> Their work is the same as that of Adam, when in the beginning, before the Fall, clothed in majesty, he communed intimately with God in that most blessed land that he lived in. How could our monks be worse off than Adam before the Fall, since he was entrusted with the building of Paradise? He knew no worldly troubles. Nor do they know them. He came before God with a pure conscience. They do the same. Indeed, they approach God with even more trust, because they are blessed with greater grace by the Holy Spirit.[1]

In these lines Chrysostom had already in Late Antiquity outlined the most important elements of a form of life that would come to shape medieval Christendom in so many ways. In a culture that both alienated and opposed humankind, and in which humankind could only hope to overcome the world through belief in salvation, these words were not to be taken lightly: "You should see it with your own eyes." They suggested that there were those who, though still

---

[1] Johannes Chrysostomus, *In Matthaeum homiliae* 68.3; PG 58:643ff; Johannes Chrysostomus Baur, trans., *Des heiligen Kirchenlehrers Johannes Chrysostomus ausgewählte Schriften*, 7 vols., Bibliothek der Kirchenväter 1:26 (Kempten and Munich: Kösel, 1916), 3:374.

living, had already entered the realm of Paradise and who, because of the power granted to them there, stood closer to God than all others. And to be close to God meant salvation. One could thus see monks as points on a moral compass, as exemplary figures, and as models for the fact that the hope of salvation could be realized. Yet the Paradise of the monks was attainable only through *anachoresis*, the renunciation of the mundane world. Only then could one lead an unconditionally religious life—a *vita religiosa*—that was both ultimately fulfilling and lived to the exclusion of all else. Thus the life of these figures—early on described, fittingly, as *religiosi*, "religious"—both provided a certain orientation for those who remained behind in the world and represented an unattainable world beyond.

The historical roots of this way of life are to be found among those who first sought to be radically free from earthly entanglement, as they stood ready to cross a decisive threshold. It had happened already in Egypt in the third century, when for many men and women it was no longer enough to lead an ascetic life devoted to God while also remaining tied to their families and communities. Longing to be set free from those bonds, they fled into the deserts beyond the banks of the Nile.[2] Liberated from worldly affairs, from the concerns of the church and their obligations to the overseers of their communities, the bishops, they retreated to caves, huts, or ruins in the desert, where they lived lives of contemplation, of penitence and bodily chastisement, of sexual continence and manual labor. They were clothed with cloaks, often made of animal hide. They wanted to be "angels on earth," and ultimately they followed a single commandment. It was soon captured, with enormous existential force, in one pithy phrase: "Wherever you go, above all have God before your eyes."[3] The hermit Anthony (ca. 251–356) is said to have offered up that expression,

---

[2] Martin Krause, "Das Mönchtum in Ägypten," in *Ägypten in spätantikchristlicher Zeit*, ed. Martin Krause (Wiesbaden: L. Reichert, 1998), 149–74; Susanna Elm, *Virgins of God* (Oxford: Oxford University Press, 1994); William Harmless, *Desert Christians* (Oxford: Oxford University Press, 2004); Claudia Rapp, "Early Monasticism in Egypt," in *Female* vita religiosa *between Late Antiquity and the High Middle Ages: Structures, Developments, and Spatial Contexts*, ed. Gert Melville and Anne Müller (Berlin: LIT, 2011), 21–42.

[3] Jean-Claude Guy, ed., *Les Apophtegmes des Pères. Collection systématique* (Paris: Éditions du Cerf, 1993–2005), chaps. 1–9, 1:102; Bernard Lohse, *Askese und Mönchtum in der Antike und in der alten Kirche* (Munich: Oldenbourg,

as the story survives in the *Apophthegmata patrum*, the "Sayings of the Fathers," a collection that was probably first written down in the fifth century in order to hand down his teachings and those of his like-minded contemporaries to their successors. That intention in fact yielded unimaginable fruit, since for the whole of the Middle Ages, the collection would be used as an introduction to monastic life.[4]

Anthony came from a wealthy household in Middle Egypt, and as a youth he had both administered the estate of his deceased parents and raised his younger sister.[5] One day he became fully aware of the meaning of Matthew 19:21 for anyone who sought unconditionally to follow the counsels of the gospel: "If you would be perfect, go and sell all that you have, and give to the poor." Around 270 or 275, he gave away all of his property and retreated first into the Nitrian Desert west of Alexandria and then later to a mountain called Pispir near the Nile and finally to a deserted mountain called Qolzum near Zaafarana on the Gulf of Suez. His contemporaries perceived him as an excellent model of the new kind of eremitical life, and an account of his life written by Athanasius, patriarch of Alexandria, did its best to preserve that image for centuries.[6] But Anthony was not the first, and he was not alone. Well before him, many who longed to flee to God had sought solitude. And among them the archetype of the hermits, according to the tradition handed down by Jerome,[7] was Paul of Thebes, who during the persecution of Christians under Decius (ca. 249–251) had fled to the deserts of Upper Egypt, where he embraced a life of strictest asceticism and supposedly lived to be 113 years old.[8]

Like-minded followers quickly gathered around Anthony and soon formed a colony of hermits inspired by his charismatic leadership. In

---

1969); John Wortley, ed., *The Anonymous Sayings of the Desert Fathers* (Cambridge, UK: Cambridge University Press, 2013).

[4] Lucien Regnault, *Les pères du désert à travers leurs apophthegmes* (Solesmes: Abbaye Saint-Pierre, 1987).

[5] Louis Bouyer, *La vie de S. Antoine*, 2nd ed. (St-Wandrille: Editions de Fontenelle, 1997).

[6] Gerhardus J. M. Bartelink, *Athanase d'Alexandrie: Vie d'Antoine* (Paris: Éditions du Cerf, 2011).

[7] See below, p. 14.

[8] Stefan Rebenich, "Der Kirchenvater Hieronymus als Hagiograph. Die Vita Sancti Pauli primi eremitae," in *Beiträge zur Geschichte des Paulinerordens*, ed. Kaspar Elm (Berlin: Duncker & Humblot, 2000), 23–40.

the broad ring of deserts surrounding Egypt, and soon all throughout Asia Minor, Syria, and Palestine, charismatically gifted men and women offered their leadership as spiritual fathers and mothers (the *Apophthegmata* called them *abba*, "Father," or *amma*, "Mother") to the hermits who flocked around them. Most, whether male or female, did not live entirely alone. They needed their neighbors, as the words of Anthony suggest: "Life and death come to us from our neighbors. For if we win our brother, we win God. But if we offend our brother, we sin against Christ."[9] They did not live in spatially enclosed communities, however, since every hermit, male or female, lived alone, or perhaps in twos or threes, in dwellings they called *kellion* ("cells"). They had no need of a properly formed religious rule to bind them together. The gifts of the Holy Spirit were enough, as Chrysostom had already emphasized. What mattered was an inner consciousness of right, as well as the word and living example of an *abba* or *amma*. Here they could find support for the mighty struggle in which they saw themselves compelled continually to engage, a fight for which they had to make themselves strong through asceticism and prayer: the fight to turn away the demons who so relentlessly attacked them but who in fact were nothing more than the temptations of the hermits' bodily and spiritual passions, which sought to draw them back into the mundane world. Hieronymus Bosch portrayed that temptation masterfully on the eve of modernity in his triptych "The Temptation of Saint Anthony."[10]

Most contemporary observers of this image may have recognized—perhaps fearfully—that Anthony personified not only the fear of losing one's soul but also the overcoming of that fear. Anthony must have stood for them as a hero of the faith, because he had dared to cross the threshold that led him out of the world and into the desert.

But had these observers of the late Middle Ages turned their view from Bosch's image to look out on their own contemporary world, they would surely still have seen those who were thought, rightly, to have had a powerful faith in the world beyond. Yet the so-called desert had become something fundamentally different. The desert had

---

[9] Guy, ed., *Les Apophtegmes des Pères*, 3:12; Bonifaz Miller, trans., *Weisung der Väter*, 8th ed. (Trier: Paulinus, 2009), 16.

[10] *Schrecken und Lust. Die Versuchung des Heiligen Antonius von Hieronymus Bosch bis Max Ernst*, ed. Michael Philipp (Munich: Hirmer, 2008), 106–11.

Demons, as the embodiment of his soul's temptations, threaten Anthony, in an image by Hieronymus Bosch (1450–1516).

become a landscape of monasteries—some still quite poor, but most provided with opulent buildings and fruitful estates, and most now banded together into orders that were present in every locale. And those who had lived in the desert had now become—whether enclosed in cloisters or moving about in cities and towns, in universities and in palaces—monks and canons, bishops, popes, scholars, and heretics. All of them would have assumed, in the depths of their hearts, that they still lived in the desert—in that other world, unreachable for most, beyond the decisive threshold between the mundane and the spiritual.

For the world of monasteries and orders that had grown up in the Middle Ages drew its legitimacy and its meaning from the very fact that it represented the world beyond that threshold. One could thus with justification cite the Scripture, "In the house of my father are many mansions" (John 14:2). From its beginnings among the Desert Fathers, not only through flexibility and eagerness for enrichment via the adoption of new elements but also through a desire for renewal and reform that explicitly reached back to original models or that boldly laid hold of innovative ways of life, through all of the Middle Ages and beyond, the *vita religiosa* developed across a broad spectrum into a diversity that was soon hardly comprehensible—one that continually wove itself together organically into a braid and then divided itself anew.[11]

The sons of the Desert Fathers would soon be called to find new followers in the forests of Europe or to go back out into the world, preaching and teaching. They would come to terms with the representatives of the secular church hierarchy either by installing in its ranks members of their own circles or by getting out of the way. They would form various new kinds of community, follow their charismatic leaders, or allow themselves to be led through written rules and statutes. And they would argue among themselves over the best path to salvation.

Looking back on nearly twelve hundred years of history, it might seem astonishing that such complexity and diversity had already begun to set in from the earliest beginnings of the *vita religiosa*.[12] In the first

---

[11] For an overview of medieval religious life, see David Knowles, *From Pacho-mius to Ignatius* (Oxford: Clarendon Press, 1966); Patrick J. Greene, *Medieval Monasteries* (London: Leicester University Press, 1992); Clifford Hugh Law-rence, *Medieval Monasticism*, 3rd ed. (London: Longman, 2003); Gudrun Gleba, *Klosterleben im Mittelalter* (Darmstadt: Wissenschaftliche Buchgeschellschaft, 2004); Edeltraud Klueting, *Monasteria semper reformanda* (Münster: LIT, 2005); Karl Suso Frank, *Grundzüge der Geschichte des christlichen Mönch-tums*, 6th ed. (Darmstadt: Wissenschaftliche Buchgesellschaft, 2010). Dictionary overviews are found in *Dizionario degli istituti di perfezione*, ed. G. Pelliccia and G. Rocca, 10 vols. (Rome: Editrice Paoline, 1974–2003); Georg Schwaiger, ed., *Mönchtum, Orden, Klöster* (Munich: C. H. Beck, 2003); Isnard W. Frank, *Lexikon des Mönchtums und der Orden* (Stuttgart: Reclam, 2005). Systematic overviews and introductions to sources are found in André Vauchez and Cécile Caby, eds., *L'histoire des moines, chanoines et religieux au moyen âge: Guide de recherche et documents* (Turnhout: Brepols, 2003).

[12] On the early phases of religious life, see Lohse, *Askese und Mönchtum*; Susanna Elm, *Virgins of God*; Martin Krön, *Das Mönchtum und die kulturelle*

third of the fourth century, again in Egypt—as we will see—men began to gather together in monasteries, and alongside the hermits monks lived coenobitically, with common property and in individual poverty. The first monastic rules emerged around the same time. In the fourth and fifth centuries, these religious communities began to be integrated into the episcopal structures of the church hierarchy. The roots of the process would establish themselves in North Africa at the turn from the fourth to the fifth century, when clerics living in the circles of bishops became so-called regular canons who lived in community like monks.

Communities of ascetics thus emerged in Europe (somewhat later than in the East) in Gaul during the fourth and fifth centuries. There, two different fundamental principles of monastic life developed: on the one hand a loose, charismatically inspired community that renounced every kind of material profit, and on the other a community that was well ordered, strictly organized, and economically successful. Finally, as will be seen below, another brand of monastic life was imported from Ireland at the end of the sixth century, and in remarkably successful ways it became tied to the interests of the powerful of this world. Thus already on the first stage of the journey through the Middle Ages, at least the nucleus of nearly every shape and form of religious life had already appeared.

The Establishment of Monastic Communities

A monastic way of life for those who had retreated from the world but who also gathered together in strict community is clearly discernible for the first time around 318/325. They sought to combat, as well as possible, the same danger that had especially confronted the hermits, who were in the end lone warriors against demons. The initiator of this communal ("cenobitic") way of life and the founder of a place in which to live it—a cloister in Tabennisi, a village near Thebes in upper Egypt—was the Egyptian Pachomius (292/298–346), who by that time already had rich experience in the eremitical life.[13]

Tradition des lateinischen Westens (Munich: Tuduv, 1997); Marilyn Dunn, *The Emergence of Monasticism* (Oxford: Blackwell, 2000); Henrik W. Dey and Elizabeth Fentress, eds., *Western Monasticism* ante literam (Turnhout: Brepols, 2011).

[13] Philip Rousseau, *Pachomius* (Berkeley, CA: University of California Press, 1985).

His sister Mary, similarly inspired, founded a women's community, since the cenobitic life had from the beginning been a safe haven for all who sought God, both male and female. Nine more male and two more female communities followed. Contemporaries reported that their members numbered in the thousands, since in those stirring times the desire for salvation was as great as it had been under Emperor Constantine (306–337), when Christianity had been able to emerge into public life.

With the strongest of ties to the Gospel, Pachomius wrote a rule (he called the text "rules," in the plural) for such a life, one that was to be led in strictest community and under absolute obedience to the authority of an abbot.[14] The aim was to provide a secure refuge for those who were too weak for the eremitic life but who nevertheless wanted to live as ascetics. The text is the oldest surviving rule for cenobitic monasticism. The core ideals it recorded—poverty, contemplation, and chastity—were modeled after the example of the hermits. But in the foreground of the rule stood a life lived in community.[15] All of the cells were to be found under one roof, and all who lived there ate together, prayed together, and worked together. The community lived in a strictly enclosed complex of buildings with a gate guarded both from without and from within—in other words, in a cloister in the actual sense of the word, a *claustrum*, a place "enclosed." Its way of life was regulated precisely. The order of the day was firmly established, alternating between periods of prayer, work, eating, and sleeping. And so that these crowds of monks and nuns (as they can now be called) could be directed in an organized way, they were divided into groups (with allegorical reference to the tribes of Israel), each with its various tasks and with a designated leader.

Those who lived in these early communities worked hard, so that from the proceeds of their labor they might uphold the commandment to have charity toward their neighbor. And because they worked with increasing efficiency, already in the lifetime of Pachomius himself incomes surpassed expenses and property holdings grew enormously.

[14] Armand Veilleux, ed., *Pachomian koinonia*, 3 vols., CS 8 (Kalamazoo, MI: Cistercian Publications, 1980–1982); Heinrich Bacht, ed., *Pachomius, Klosterregeln* (St. Ottilien: EOS, 2010).

[15] Terrence G. Kardong, "The Monastic Practices of Pachomius and the Pachomians," *Studia Monastica* 32 (1990): 59–77.

The individual monk remained completely poor even as each community became exceedingly rich—and thus entangled once again in the earthly affairs that the monks had wanted to escape.

To consider the eremitical and the coenobitic forms of life together makes clear how remarkably they capture, in embryonic form, all that the medieval monastic life would then repeatedly take up, test, and adapt in new circumstances.

On the one hand, there were the principles of monastic life's organization: a strict claustration, based on the text of a rule, that sharply cut off the outside world, and a uniform, precisely ruled daily life of manual labor, personal poverty, common worship, eating, and sleeping, all guided by the unassailable authority of the community's superior—as well as an economic strength that could make a monastery into an important institution—and thus an envied one—in the world beyond its walls.

On the other hand, there were the basic elements of eremitic life: charismatic leaders whose aphorisms came to be written down, individualized internalization of the values of religious life, the absence of a written rule and of an organized order, spatially open forms of community with individual cells, and renunciation of, or at least total lack of interest in, economic success.

Another patriarch of coenobitic life was Basil the Great (330–379), archbishop of Caesarea.[16] He saw true Christianity as fulfilled above all through the ascetic life, a life he himself had practiced for decades. As a guide to the common life in a monastery he wrote in dialogue form the texts of rules that were shaped in a deeply theological way by both a call to ascetic renunciation of the world and strict adherence to the norm of the Gospel. At the same time, however, as a bishop he understood the need to integrate monastic life into the structures of ecclesiastical hierarchy within his jurisdiction. Already here an entirely new chapter in the history of the *vita religiosa* had been introduced. Whereas both the communities of hermits and the monasteries of Pachomius had stood at a certain distance from the hierarchical structures of the bishops' regulations, among the monasteries founded by Basil that relationship was of an entirely different nature. Two formerly distinct spheres of influence now came into relationship with

---

[16] Philip Rousseau, *Basil of Caesarea* (Berkeley, CA: University of California Press, 1994).

one another: on the one hand, those active in the world and officially responsible for the growth of Christianity, that is, the bishops as representatives of the established church, and on the other, those who had recently retreated from such a world. Basil sought here to balance tensions that admittedly would never find a definitive solution, even across the coming centuries of the Middle Ages.

In 451, the Council of Chalcedon established a key legal principle: every monastery was to be under the direct supervision of the local bishop, and only the bishop's express authority could allow new foundations.[17] Later generations would continually appeal to these regulations, especially when they needed to arrest the powerful forces working against them. The "paradise of the monks" was difficult to reconcile with the burdens of this world.

In North Africa at the turn to the fifth century, alongside the eremitic and monastic patterns of life, a third lasting form of the *vita religiosa* began to take on its normative shape: the cloistered life of clerics. Augustine (354–430), the most important church father of Late Antiquity,[18] retreated soon after his baptism in Milan in 387 to a small family estate in Thagaste. There with his friends—among them his old and most trusted companion Alypius—he lived in a cloistered community of "servants of God" (*servi Dei*). In the following years he and his circle began to produce several religious rules. They would endure over time and would have a remarkable impact. Despite their diversity, by the Middle Ages all of them were drawn together and circulated in manuscript under the single title of the Rule of Saint Augustine. The complex origins of these texts are in part responsible for that unique reception.[19]

In 391 Augustine was consecrated as a priest in Hippo in North Africa; there he eventually founded another community for pious lay brothers. After being elected bishop of the city in 395/97, around 400 he wrote (probably for that second community) a short rule that was later called *Praeceptum* ("Precept") or *Regula ad servos Dei* ("Rule for the Servants of God"). A somewhat divergent recension of the text, also circulated under the title *Regularis Informatio* ("Regular Instruction"),

[17] Birgitta Meinhardt, *Fanatiker oder Heilige?* (Frankfurt: Peter Lang, 2001).

[18] Wilhelm Geerlings, *Augustinus* (Paderborn: Schöningh, 2002).

[19] Here I follow the foundational work of Luc Verheijen, *La regle de saint Augustin*, vol. 2, *Recherches historiques* (Paris: Études augustiniennes, 1967).

Augustine teaches his circle of students.

survives from that time, in connection with a letter of the bishop called *Obiurgatio* ("Reprimand"), directed to a rebellious convent of religious women.[20] It can no longer be said with certainty which recension—for men or women—served as the basis for the other.

[20] On the women's communities surrounding Augustine, see Georg Jenal, "Frühe Formen der weiblichen vita religiosa im lateinischen Westen (4. und Anfang 5. Jahrhundert)," in Melville and Müller, *Female* vita religiosa, 43–77, here 60–64.

In the meantime, the first community had received its own rule. Alypius, who had remained in Thagaste and became bishop there in 394, had returned home from a journey to Bethlehem with a collection of normative texts on religious life. In 395 he developed these into a rule—the so-called *Ordo Monasterii* ("Order of the Monastery")—and had them recognized by Augustine, who had of course been the founder of the community. From this text another version survives that was intended for women. On a later visit to Hippo, Alypius also learned of the *Praeceptum*, and by combining that text with his *Ordo Monasterii* he developed still another version of the text of the rule.

The *Praeceptum* and the *Ordo Monasterii* differ in both content and function. The latter text provided quite strict instructions for the course of daily life in the monastery and thereby regulated the times for prayer and work, the obligation to obedience, the importance of personal poverty, diet, departure from the cloister, and correction of faults. It was a disciplinary text aimed at the moral formation of humankind, in order to secure (as it says in the closing passages of the text) salvation in Christ. The text of the *Praeceptum* also of course contained practical regulations for the course of the day, food and clothing, property, obedience, and so on, but it tied these patterns of relationship to the obligation of cultivating community, of being "one heart and one soul"[21] like the Christians of the early church, who had all in common (Acts 4:32). A spirit of brotherhood, powerful enough to overcome differences of status between poor and rich, along with mutual reliance on God, forgiveness, and love, stood in the forefront.

As Augustine himself bears witness, the community revealed in these regulations came together after his elevation to the office of bishop, and its members were clergy of his church: "As all of you know, or almost all of you, our way of life in the house called the bishop's is such that we, insofar as we are able, imitate those saints

---

[21] On the later impact of this important phrase, see Klaus Schreiner, "Ein Herz und eine Seele. Eine urchristliche Lebensform und ihre Institutionalisierung im augustinisch geprägten Mönchtum des hohen und späten Mittelalters," in *Regula Sancti Augustini*, ed. Gert Melville and Anne Muller (Paring: Augustiner-Chorherren-Verlag, 2002), 1–47.

of whom the Acts of the Apostles says, 'No one considered anything that he possessed as his own, but all had everything in common.'"[22]

Any knowledge of the texts written by Augustine or those authored in his circle was almost entirely lost over the coming centuries. Already in the first centuries of the Middle Ages, the *Praeceptum* was cited only very rarely, and never in any prominent place—in the Rule of Caesarius of Arles, for example, in the Rule of Saint Benedict, or in the Rule of Ferreolus of Uzès.[23] Yet the reputation of this renowned father of the church as founder of a model community remained intact, and from the eleventh century on it led in fact to a new and special kind of cloistered life—the *vita canonica*, the regular life of canons, as those were called who lived in the service of a bishop's church. As distinct from the eremitical life (*vita eremitica*) and the monastic life (*vita monastica*)—both of which, although in different ways, concerned laymen who had crossed over to religious life to seek God in asceticism, poverty, and inner contemplation—here it was clerics who had also retreated from the world to live in a religious community shaped by asceticism and poverty but who nevertheless remained active in the world through pastoral care. The society of the Middle Ages would come to have great need of such men.

The First Monasteries in Europe

The story thus far has focused only on the Christian regions of the Middle East and of North Africa, a focus justified because the establishment of religious communities in the West was remarkably delayed. It is true that very early—decades before even Augustine—Eusebius (ca. 283–371), who was from 340 on the bishop of Vercelli (Piedmont), had drawn together a community of clerics at his episcopal court and lived with them in a kind of monastic community.[24]

---

[22] Augustine, *Sermones de vita et moribus clericorum*, PL 39:1569 (with citation from Acts 4:32).

[23] Vincent Desprez, "La 'Regula Ferrioli.' Texte critique," *Revue Mabillon* 60 (1982): 117–48.

[24] Enrico Dal Covolo, ed., *Eusebio di Vercelli e il suo tempo* (Rome: LAS, 1997). For the development of monastic life in the broader context of religious and cultural history, see Peter Brown, *The Rise of Western Christendom: Triumph and Diversity, AD 200–1000* (Malden, MA: Wiley-Blackwell, 2013).

Ascetic ways of life of a certain permanence, however, emerged only from the first half of the fourth century. In Italy, for example, aristocratic women who lived ascetic lives on family estates were guided by the *vitae* of the Egyptian fathers of the desert.[25]

The church father and translator of the Bible into Latin, Jerome (331/48–419/20),[26] played an important mediating role in this context. During the years 382–385, he wrote persuasively about the ascetic religious life of *virgines sacrae*, of saintly virgins and widows whom he actively supported in Rome. He maintained close personal relationships with many women—especially the widow Marcella (ca. 325–410),[27] who was from an ancient Roman noble family—and also maintained an active correspondence with them. He knew the eremitic life of Syria from his own experience, and he also wrote a life of Paul of Thebes, the model Desert Father. Drawing from this background but now tailoring it to the Italian setting, he wrote a long treatise on the preservation of virginity.[28] In it he warned of the serious dangers that so clearly could arise from the fact that the ascetic life was lived in a context surrounded by the world, with all of its social entanglements and temptations.

Other anchor points for a cloistered life set apart from the world had also begun to take shape very early on in Gaul. Taking the lead in developing a new model was Martin of Tours (316/17–397),[29] who after breaking off his military career had retreated with a crowd of like-minded followers to the desolation of the forests near Poitiers. Elected bishop of Tours, around 375 he founded communities in Marmoutier for both women and men to live a strongly eremitical life inspired by the model of the early church. The office of bishop, which in Gaul at that time was still overwhelmingly occupied by charismatic "men of God" (Martin was called *vir Dei*), had begun to

---

[25] Griet Petersen-Szemerédy, *Zwischen Weltstadt und Wüste* (Göttingen: Vandenhoeck & Ruprecht, 1993); Jenal, "Frühe Formen." On later development, see Albrecht Diem, *Das monastische Experiment* (Münster: LIT, 2005).

[26] John Norman Davidson Kelly, *Jerome*, 2nd ed. (London: Duckworth, 1998).

[27] Jenal, "Frühe Formen," 49–53.

[28] *De conservanda virginitate*; Jenal, "Frühe Formen," 65–67.

[29] Friedrich Prinz, *Frühes Mönchtum im Frankenreich*, 2nd ed. (Darmstadt: Wissenschaftliche Buchgesellschaft, 1988), 19–46; Régine Pernoud, *Martin de Tours* (Paris: Bayard, 1996).

reconcile itself institutionally with the life of an ascetic hermit who had renounced the world.

The deserts of the East became the forests of Europe. And from the Loire region to the Iberian Peninsula, the number of monasteries that venerated Martin grew rapidly—surely not least because at the end of the fifth century the first Frankish king, Clovis, helped to establish Martin's cult and promoted him as a kind of "royal saint."[30] These "Martinian" monasteries were long left to a certain disordered spontaneity, shaped by the movements of wandering monks who left behind crowds of their followers in various places. Already the first church council in the young Frankish kingdom, held in Orléans in 511, demanded "stability of place" (*stabilitas loci*) of those who lived in these kinds of communities, which in the future could only be established with the permission of the appropriate bishop.[31]

Also in the fifth century, a number of communities both in the lower Rhône valley and on the cluster of islands around the abbey of Lérins (offshore from modern Cannes) turned the highly cultured Provence into another center of monastic life.[32] Above all at Lérins itself, founded between 405 and 410 by Honoratus of Arles, eremitical and coenobitic patterns had been innovatively linked in a stable form of organization. In contrast to the Martinian monasteries, this form offered an alternative monastic world[33] that later spread far into the Burgundian-Frankish north, to Lyon and the Jura. After its foundation, Lérins attracted the aristocratic elite of the region, as well as those from the northern regions of Gaul that had been lost to the Germans. Roman patterns of economic administration quickly turned the monastery into a prosperous concern, as had happened with similar success among the foundations of Pachomius. Here in a fully developed form was that pattern of development of monastic life that in the course of the Middle Ages would transform religious communities into centers of economic wealth and agricultural cultivation, and eventually even into focal points of power. This model was something other than the *vita religiosa* as the arduous way into

---

[30] Prinz, *Frühes Mönchtum*, 22–46.

[31] Prinz, *Frühes Mönchtum*, 91.

[32] Prinz, *Frühes Mönchtum*, 47–87; Yann Codou and Michel Lauwers, eds., *Lérins, une île sainte dans l'Occident médiéval* (Turnhout: Brepols, 2009).

[33] Prinz, *Frühes Mönchtum*, 88–94.

the desert or the forests, and the two models would eventually come into sharp conflict.

Lérins also provided fertile ground for the careers of future bishops, including Caesarius of Arles (470–542),[34] who became a monk at Lérins at the end of the fifth century and who then in the course of an energetic career as archbishop of Arles wrote two rules that had a lasting influence on the future of monastic life, one for the women's monastery in Arles of Saint-Jean, a community that he himself had founded and that his sister Caesaria led.[35] It is one of the oldest surviving rules for women. Particularly striking about it is that on the one hand it requires all of the nuns, regardless of their social rank, to live as equals and without personal property and on the other that the women remain enclosed—the insistence on enclosure not entirely new, but here remarkably strict, and combined with a rigorous insistence on remaining in one place (*stabilitas loci*) that was obligatory even for the abbess.[36] This kind of enclosure of nuns served to preserve the nuns' safety in those unstable times, but it was surely also meant above all as a preemptive measure to guard against sexual temptation.

Early on, the Frankish queen Radegundis established a community according to Caesarius's precepts at Sainte-Croix, which she founded in 558 in Poitiers and which was also easily one of the most renowned women's communities of its time.[37] Admittedly, the founder herself did not entirely adhere to its regulations. She never thought

[34] W. E. Klingshirn, *Caesarius of Arles* (Cambridge, UK: Cambridge University Press, 1994).

[35] Anne-Marie Helvétius, "L'organisation des monastères féminins à l'époque mérovingienne," in Melville and Müller, *Female vita religiosa*, 151–69, here 157–58. On the later development of Frankish women's communities see Franz Felten, "Frauenklöster im Frankenreich. Entwicklungen und Probleme von den Anfängen bis zum frühen 9. Jahrhundert," in *Vita religiosa sanctimonialium*, ed. Christine Kleinjung (Korb: Didymos, 2011), 71–92.

[36] Adalbert de Vogüé, "Caesarius of Arles and the Origin of the Enclosure of Nuns," *Word and Spirit* 11 (1989): 16–29.

[37] Josef Pilvousek and Klaus-Bernward Springer, "Caesarius von Arles und die Klostergründung der heiligen Radegunde," in *Radegunde—ein Frauenschicksal zwischen Mord und Askese*, ed. Hardy Eidam and Gudrun Noll (Erfurt: Druck und Reproverlag, 2006), 79–95; Helvétius, "L'organisation des monastères féminins," in Melville and Müller, *Female vita religiosa*, 158–59.

to renounce her noble customs but instead lived in keeping with her status in a few rooms in the monastery, receiving guests in majestic style. She also involved herself continually in the business of high politics. In that way she was a forerunner of a pattern of relationships that, despite all of the rules to the contrary, became common over the coming centuries, especially in women's religious houses.

John Cassian (ca. 360–430/35)[38] is also worthy of mention as an author of a rule. After living for years in Bethlehem and the monastic communities of Egypt, he arrived around 415 in the still-thriving port city of Massalia (Marseille). There he founded a community for women, as well as one for men. The latter, established under the patronage of Saint Victor, came over the next centuries to be numbered among the most important religious communities in Western Christendom. Cassian recorded his guidelines for monastic life in two works: *On the Fundamentals of the Coenobitic Life* (*De institutis coenobiorum*) and *Conversations with the Fathers* (*Collationes Patrum*).[39] Both were among the most important channels for the transmission of the foundational ideas of the Egyptian hermits to the West.[40]

The starting point for Cassian, as with Augustine, was "to be of one heart and one soul," as in the early church—and as he saw it monks were the only ones who still lived out that ideal. Led by the model of the early Desert Fathers, he was convinced that it was possible to find one's innermost life (and there alone to find God) by turning away from the institutional church and the earthly entanglements of the world—"avoid the bishop and the woman," he said, perhaps with a sense of irony. In pursuit of such spiritual work, which could only be carried out with fraternal assistance, Cassian introduced as an aid to meditation the so-called praying of the hours,

---

[38] Columba Stewart, *Cassian the Monk* (New York: Oxford University Press, 1998).

[39] Johannes Cassian, *De institutis coenobiorum et de octo principalium utiorum remediis libri XII*, in Iohannis Cassiani Opera, vol. 1, ed. Michael Petschenig (Vienna: Austrian Academy of Sciences, 2004), 1–231; *Collationes xxiiii*, in Iohannis Cassiani Opera, vol. 2, ed. Michael Petschenig, CSEL 13 (Vienna: Austrian Academy of Sciences, 2004).

[40] Andreas E. J. Grote, *"Anachorese" und "Zönobium." Der Rekurs des frühen westlichen Mönchtums auf monastische Konzepte des Ostens* (Stuttgart: Thorbecke, 2001), 193–329, 337–40; Thomas Merton and Patrick F. O'Connell, eds., *Cassian and the Fathers*, MW 1 (Kalamazoo, MI: Cistercian Publications, 2005).

the responsive recitation of the Psalms, which for Cassian was to be done in the morning and evening. These precepts, shaped with great spiritual depth, are not to be thought of as a rule in a strict sense; rather, they represent a kind of normative writing that would play an important role in monastic life precisely during its periods of reform and renewal—writing that offered spiritually oriented admonitions, or *paraenesis*.

Another early focal point for monastic life emerged on the westernmost borders of Europe, beyond the farthest borders of the disintegrating Roman Empire—in Ireland. This island, long cut off culturally from the European continent, not least because of the Germanic invasions in Britain, was Christianized through the work of the Welsh missionary Patrick (who died, it is thought, ca. 463/93). Thereafter, a landscape of richly endowed monasteries quickly emerged.[41] The most important links in this long chain were the double monastery of Kildare, founded in 470 by Bridget, daughter of a king; Clonmacnois, founded around 543 by Ciarán; Doire (later Derry), founded around 546 by Columba the Elder; Finnian's community of Clonard, also founded in the sixth century; the monastery of Bangor, founded around 558 by Comgall; and the community of Clonfert, founded by Brendan around 560. These communities nourished the ecclesiastical elite of Ireland and helped shape the fundamentals of its political, economic, and cultural life. Clonmacnois, in fact, was for many centuries the spiritual and intellectual center of the entire island.[42]

What made these many monasteries distinct, scattered as they were across the entire island, was that they also became actual centers for the general organization of the church. In the largest monasteries there usually lived not only an abbot or an abbess but also a bishop. The office of abbot usually remained in the hands of a wealthy family, on whose estates the monastery was located. The abbots and abbesses

[41] John Ryan, *Irish Monasticism* (Dublin: Four Courts Press, 1986); Catherine Thom, *Early Irish Monasticism* (London: T & T Clark, 2006); Stephanie Haarländer, *"Innumerabiles populi de utroque sexu confluentes . . . .* Klöster für Männer und Frauen im frühmittelalterlichen Irland," in Melville and Müller, *Female* vita religiosa, 137–50.

[42] Annette Kehnel, *Clonmacnois—the Church and Lands of St. Ciarán* (Münster: LIT, 1998).

were the guardians of traditions that went back to the founding and preserved the charisma of the founder. The office of abbot was the highest instance of jurisdiction and administration. The power of consecration, however, lay with the bishop, who himself had often been called to his office by an abbot from within the ranks of the monks.

This surely remarkable variant of the mutual exchange between the worlds of monastery and bishop—an exchange that, as has already been shown so often, shaped the *vita religiosa* from the beginning—emerged from the idea that monks (especially if, as in Ireland, they were also ordained as priests) could be of more service to God than those who merely held an office in the church. The often extraordinarily stern ascetic life lived in Irish monasteries, as well as the systematic penitential exercises embraced there, conveys the image of the personal sanctity of the monk as a "man of God" (*vir Dei*). This monastic form of charisma reveals itself to have far surpassed that inherent in the office of the bishop. In Ireland monasteries thus became focal points for pastoral care, in turn requiring of their monks an adequate education—and thereby helping the island, with its broader regional connections to Northumbria, to become home to a vibrant and interwoven culture of the book that, for a time, far outshone that of the continent.[43]

Irish monasticism was also characterized by the particular ascetic practice of voluntary exile, of "wandering for Christ" (*peregrinatio pro Christo*).[44] It inspired individual monks to bring the life of Ireland's monasteries—and with it, by way of mission, the Christian faith—to parts of the British Isles that had remained pagan. An outstanding example of this dynamic is the career of Columbanus the Elder (532/33–597).[45] Born in Ireland and descended from the high nobility, he founded a few monasteries there, among them Daire Calcaich, today Londonderry in Northern Ireland. But he had soon to flee Ireland because of a feud that he himself had caused and that led to a war between noble clans. He made his way with a small

---

[43] Otto Karl Werckmeister, *Irisch-northumbrische Buchmalerei des 8. Jahrhunderts und monastische Spiritualität* (Berlin: de Gruyter, 1967).

[44] Arnold Angenendt, "Charisma und Eucharistie—oder: Das System Cluny," in *Institution und Charisma. Festschrift für Gert Melville zum 65 Geburtstag*, ed. Franz J. Felten, et al. (Cologne: Böhlau, 2009), 331–40.

[45] Brian Lacy, *Saint Columba* (Blackrock: Columba Press, 2013).

group of followers to Pictish Scotland. There, south of the Hebrides, he founded a monastery on the island of Iona around 563 or 564. The community would become a leading center of missions to the pagan Picts and Scots, and also a royal mausoleum.[46] The monastery's influence, however, reached far to the south, into the lands of the Saxons, where Christianity had for the most part died out as a result of the pagan invasions. The impetus came from King Oswald of Northumbria (ca. 604–642), who in his childhood as an exile had been baptized at Iona and raised as a Christian.[47] Seeking to re-Christianize his kingdom, the king turned to that community shortly before 634. After a failed first attempt he soon received the monk Aidan, who founded a new cloister and a successful center for missions on the island of Lindisfarne on the coast of the North Sea.[48] A number of future foundations then allowed the influence of this community to reach into the kingdom of Mercia.

These missions, exports of the world of the monastery across northeastern England, had a certain parallel in the southeast. There the impulses came not from a largely autonomous Irish monasticism but rather by way of the Franks and directly from a mission initiated by the papacy. Its leader was Augustine, longtime prior of the papal abbey of St. Andrew's in Rome and now sent out as a missionary by Pope Gregory (I) the Great.[49] In 597, after a first failure only two years before, he landed on the coast of the kingdom of Kent and made his way to King Aethelbert in Canterbury. The king's wife Bertha was a Frank and a Christian; she had certainly lent her support to the mission, if she had not in fact encouraged it. Aethelbert was himself baptized and tasked Augustine with systematically leading his kingdom—now the most powerful in southern England—to the Christian faith. The pope supported that mission through numerous letters of

[46] Máire Herbert, *Iona, Kells, and Derry* (Oxford: Clarendon Press, 1988).

[47] Clare E. Stancliffe and Eric Cambridge, eds., *Oswald: Northumbrian King to European Saint* (Stamford, UK: Watkins, 1995).

[48] Fiona L. Edmonds, "The Practicalities of Communication between Northumbrian and Irish Churches, c. 635–735," in James A. Graham-Campbell and M. Ryan, eds., *Anglo-Saxon/Irish Relations before the Vikings* (Oxford: Oxford University Press, 2009), 129–50.

[49] Robin Mackintosh, *Augustine of Canterbury* (Norwich: Canterbury Press, 2013).

instruction, through the provision of liturgical objects, books, and reliquaries, and through the sending of further missionaries. He also elevated Augustine to the status of archbishop of Canterbury, with future suffragans in London and Rochester.

Despite these pastoral tasks, Augustine did not forget his roots in monastic life. He founded the abbey of Peter and Paul just outside the gates of his city, thereby establishing a symbolic tie to the princes of the apostles in Rome and also consequently expressing the nature of his program. It remains unclear which rule guided the life of these and later monasteries. In any case the life of these communities was not, as one so often reads, a Benedictine tradition. The monks did follow a Roman rite for their liturgy, however, and thereby distinguished themselves sharply from the inhabitants of the Irish, Scottish, and Northumbrian monasteries.

The Irish monks' embrace of pilgrimage had a key consequence: from the sixth century on, the religious culture of the island established lasting bridges to the continent, above all in what had become an increasingly powerful and large Frankish kingdom led by the Merovingians. The earliest and also the most successful representative of this way of life was Columbanus the Younger (540–615).[50] Around the year 590 he departed from the northern cloister of Bangor with twelve followers. His arrival as a charismatic "man of God" immediately earned him the support of the Frankish king and nobility. It was thus possible for him to establish for the rapidly growing group of monks who followed him first the monastery of Annegrey, on the western slopes of the Vosges Mountains, and shortly thereafter, nearby to the south, the communities of Luxeuil and Fontaines in Dijon.

For these three monasteries Columbanus wrote a single rule that was based above all on acts of penance.[51] It envisioned a monastic life lived according to the strict Irish expectations of chastity and obedience, expectations that had as their goal the imitation of the

[50] Knut Schäferdiek, "Columbans Wirken im Frankenreich (591–612)," in *Die Iren und Europa im früheren Mittelalter*, ed. Heinz Löwe (Stuttgart: Klett-Cotta, 1982), 1:171–201; Yaniv Fox, *Power and Religion in Merovingian Gaul* (Cambridge, UK: Cambridge University Press, 2014).

[51] Adalbert de Vogüé, *Saint Columban. Règles et pénitentiels monastiques* (Bellefontaine: Abbaye de Bellefontaine, 1989).

suffering, humiliated Christ. Its communities were expected to live in almost uninterrupted prayer, and with prayer they would open the way, so to speak, for their ascent to heaven. In addition, Columbanus authored two so-called penitentials. These formally laid out what punishments and acts of penance were appropriate for particular lapses.

Such a harsh form of piety, one focused externally and driven by submission, was in its day quite clearly attractive, because monasteries recruited heavily from the ranks of upper nobility and, like Lérins, were fertile ground for cultivating the careers of future bishops, who also came from the aristocracy.[52] The aristocratic laity who supported and patronized these monasteries were certain that they had made a good investment in their own salvation, sustained as it was by the prayers of these strictly obedient monks. For premodern societies, proper form was often important as a guarantee of content.

Columbanus was exiled after a lengthy struggle with Theoderic II (king of the Burgundian region of the Frankish kingdom from 596–613), whom he accused of an immoral way of life. Columbanus then made his way to Metz, in Austrasia (in the eastern regions of the kingdom), and found acceptance at the court there. But he traveled further to Alemannia, worked there as a missionary, and then came to the Lombard court in Milan. There, in 612, on the northern fringes of the Apennines, he at last founded the monastery of Bobbio,[53] a community that later became a renowned center of education in the West.

After Columbanus's death in 615, his conception of monastic life lived on. Numerous monastic communities shaped by his tradition appeared across Francia, whether with the support of both the secular and the episcopal nobility or through their direct initiative—thereby revealing with remarkable clarity what would become a long-lived, essential element of the *vita religiosa* of the Middle Ages: the close relationship between monastery and political power, a relationship that often took on an almost symbiotic character and that was often expressed as domination over religious communities.

The seventh century thus saw an increase in the number of monasteries that remained, in terms of property law, in the hands of those who had founded them—whether kings, bishops, nobility, or

[52] Prinz, *Frühes Mönchtum*, 121–51.

[53] Michael Richter, *Bobbio in the Early Middle Ages* (Dublin: Four Courts Press, 2008).

sometimes even members of other monasteries—and who provided the appropriate resources, especially land and estates. The individual lords of each of these churches could dispose of the wealth of a so-called proprietary monastery in any way that did not interfere with its religious activity. They could even give their monastery away, leave it as an inheritance, or appoint its abbot, largely without regard to the rights of the local bishop. This institutional dynamic is visible as far back as the fifth century but saw its fullest expansion in the Carolingian era. In fact the church officially recognized it at a Roman synod in 826: "A monastery or a chapel that has been founded correctly according to the law of the church should not be removed from the lordship of the founder [*dominium constructoris*]."[54]

On the other hand, Columbanus's monasteries were able to free themselves from those ecclesiastical structures that had already begun to emerge in his day. Inspired by the Irish ideal of the cloister-bishop, monasteries could free themselves from both the local bishop's oversight and his prerogatives over the consecration and installation of abbots, even though the Council of Chalcedon[55] had granted that right unconditionally. Such monasteries were "exempt," that is, no longer subject to the power of their respective bishops. In principle, an exempt monastery might then be placed directly under the authority of the papacy—as happened for example with Luxeuil, or later, in 628, with the monastery of Bobbio in the Apennines. And with these events there again began to emerge entirely new conditions for the world of the monastery, conditions that would shape the future in essential ways.[56]

With Bobbio the story returns again to Italy and thus to a region that had prepared the ground for one of the most important turning points in the history of monastic life, even if it would be some two centuries more before it came to fruition. The story now turns to an abbot named Benedict.

---

[54] Peter Landau, "Eigenkirchenwesen," in *Theologische Realenzyklopädie* (Berlin: de Gruyter, 1982), 4:399–404.

[55] See p. 10.

[56] Markus Meumann, "Exemtion," in *Handwörterbuch zur deutschen Rechtsgeschichte* (Berlin: Schmidt, 2008), 1:1451–52.

2

The Benedictine Rule and Its Longevity

Benedict as "Textual Trace"

In the last decade of the sixth century, Pope Gregory the Great (590–604) wrote a text in Rome that would soon be comparable to only a few others in its importance for shaping the development of monastic life in the West. The text concerns the origins of Benedictine life.

In four books entitled *Dialogues on the Life and the Miracles of the Italian Fathers* (*Dialogi de vita et miraculis patrum italicorum*),[1] Gregory aimed to prove that the Italian peninsula had nurtured an asceticism equal in standing to that of the East.[2] One of its protagonists was Benedict, from the central Italian city of Nursia (today Norcia), who for decades was the abbot of a monastery on Monte Cassino. The pope, as he admitted, did not know the abbot personally but had only heard of him through contemporary witnesses. Among them were even two of Benedict's successors as abbot. Gregory seems to have seen in Benedict—who was "blessed in grace as well as in name" (*Dialogues* 2. Prologue)[3]—a particularly powerful model character, one worthy of the entire second book of his *Dialogues*.

---

[1] Umberto Moricca, ed., *Gregorii Magni Dialogi libri IV* (Rome: Tipografia del Senato, 1924).

[2] On early religious life in Italy, see Georg Jenal, *Italia ascetica atque monastica. Das Asketen- und Mönchtum in Italien von den Anfängen bis zur Zeit der Langobarden (ca. 150/250–604)*, 2 vols. (Stuttgart: Hiersemann, 1995).

[3] Here and below, translated from *Dialogorum Libri IV de miraculis Patrum Italicorum*, vol. 2, *Kommentar zur "Vita Benedicti": Gregor der Große: das zweite Buch der Dialoge—Leben und Wunder des ehrwürdiger Abtes Benedikt,*

The Abbey San Benedetto near Subiaco. It is also called *Sacro Speco*, the Holy Cave. Here, according to Pope Gregory I, was Benedict's first residence.

---

ed. Michaela Puzicha (St. Ottilien: EOS, 2008). For an English translation, see John Zimmerman, *Saint Gregory the Great: Dialogues* (Washington, DC: Catholic University of America Press, 1983).

Gregory's treatment of the life and work of an abbot who had previously inspired no written record should not be understood as a biography in any modern sense. The work was instead intended to convey an ideal image of an ascetic and a charismatic leader of a monastic community. Consequently, the author was less interested in historical facts than in their power to serve as examples. These bore witness to the abbot's divine gifts, to the sanctity of his conversion and his ability to work miracles, and to his extraordinary power to communicate norms and values.

At the beginning of the text stands Benedict's turn from the world of late antique Rome, which to him now seemed to be completely corrupt: "But as he saw many sink into the abyss of vice, he pulled back the foot that he had placed on the threshold of the world, so that he himself would not also fall into that horrible abyss, had he tasted something of worldly knowledge" (*Dialogues* 2. Prologue). His resolve led him first to the loneliness of a hidden cave near Subiaco on the slopes of the Apennines, where he aimed to live "alone in himself, under the eyes of the heavenly watchman" (*Dialogues* 2.3). But after a time he left this dwelling (over which was eventually built the imposing abbey of San Benedetto, which still stands today) to settle in the valley and to try to live a life of asceticism in community. He took over the leadership of one monastery, where he was almost poisoned by his own monks, and thereafter founded his own. Finally he set out from that region, heading to the south, and settled at Monte Cassino, where with his followers he established a monastery on the site of a ruined ancient temple.

Clearly Gregory's text stylized Benedict's life to this point as the narrative of his gradual steps toward redemption in order to bring him all the more powerfully to his destination. The story goes on to emphasize how Benedict set about fighting with the devil to establish his community, and how through his miracles he established not only its inner stability but also its social moorings in the world around it. The text then places special emphasis on the fact that Benedict wrote a rule there, one that "was excellent in its measured discernment [*discretio*], illuminating in its exposition." "If one should want to learn of his life and his nature more precisely," Gregory wrote, "he can find it all in the prescriptions of this rule, whose discipline he taught through deeds. For the holy man could not teach in any other way than the way he lived" (*Dialogues* 2.36).

Benedict reached the pinnacle of his ascent (a worldly ascent, if considered superficially, but in reality a spiritual one) one night as he stood high above in the window of his tower, in prayer. There, as the text relates (*Dialogues* 2.35), he saw a light as bright as day, and "the whole world" stood before his eyes, "drawn together as in a single ray of sunshine." The scope of his life expanded from the narrows of the first cave near Subiaco to encompass the breadth of the whole world, and even at his death that same ascension was rendered visible one last time: where once his body had been hidden in the walls of caves, separated from all, he now died at Monte Cassino supported by his crowd of followers, lifted high and with his hands raised to heaven.

With this symbolically rich performance, the stage was set for Benedict's future veneration not only as the paternal leader of a community but also, far beyond that, as a mediator between the narrowly bound earthly matters of this world and God's boundlessness in heaven. That kind of message was about far more than any mere historiographical effort to communicate the facts. Without question it provided the foundation for a veneration of Benedict that later earned him the designation "Father of the West" or, as the 1964 papal expression put it, the "Patron of Europe."[4]

All the more striking is that such a grand impact depends on a single text. What Gregory's contemporaries knew of Benedict, what many generations afterward knew, and indeed what we know of Benedict today we know from this one text alone. That includes even Benedict's very existence, since had Gregory not written a second book of the *Dialogues*, no "Benedictine" monasticism could ever have been established. From the point of view of historical criticism, therefore, the text itself becomes a problem.[5] What, after all, guarantees its accuracy? For those in search of historical facts, the panegyric of

---

[4] Filips de Cloedt, ed., *Benedictus. Eine Kulturgeschichte des Abendlandes* (Geneva: Weber, 1980); Adalbert de Vogüé, "Benedikt von Nursia," *Theologische Realenzyklopädie* (Berlin: de Gruyter, 1980), 5:538–49. See James G. Clark, *Benedictines in the Middle Ages* (Woodbridge, UK: Boydell, 2011).

[5] Note here the controversial arguments of Johannes Fried, *Der Schleier der Erinnerung* (Munich: C. H. Beck, 2004); Joachim Wollasch, "Benedikt von Nursia. Person der Geschichte oder fiktive Idealgestalt?" *Studien und Mitteilungen zur Geschichte des Benediktinerordens und seiner Zweige* 118 (2007): 7–30. On the same issue see also Gert Melville, "Montecassino," in *Erinnerungsorte*

the text both clouds the subject matter and in equal measure idealizes it in ways that move beyond history. Gregory provided no chronology anchored in specific years, because he needed nothing of that sort for his purpose. The dates of Benedict's life must be extrapolated from other events or people known from the historical record—480 for his birth, 529 for the foundation of the community at Monte Cassino, and 547 for his death.

Gregory's text was an orphan in its day, moreover, not only because it stood as a single textual witness.[6] Behind it stood not even a contemporary physical monument that might have spoken to the abbot's institutional impact. Gregory himself in fact mentions that the monastery at Monte Cassino had since Benedict's time been destroyed by the Lombards (*Dialogues* 2.17)—an event that would seem to be well placed in the year 577, when forces led by Duke Zotto laid waste to wide stretches of the countryside, but which must date in any case to some point in the broad span of time between the 570s and 580s. A much later and uncertain source, the history of the Lombards written by Paul the Deacon in the 780s, suggests that some of the surviving monks fled to Rome. At the time of the composition of the *Dialogues*, no reliable trace of Benedictine life was to be found anywhere.

Any later impact Benedict might have had as a model of ascetic leadership in a community of monks thus clearly depended on how widely Gregory's *Dialogues* were received. Gregory did nothing worthy of mention to publicize the text, though his name alone carried sufficient renown. The first mention of the work appeared in 613/14, far to the north among the Franks, in an explicit citation. In the course of the seventh century the work then came to be read all over southern and western Europe. Its reading thus allowed Benedict to become quite a familiar figure from an early date,[7] and yet it took until the first decade of the eighth century—so far as we know—for anything about Benedict as a saint worthy of veneration to be written

---

des Christentums, ed. Christoph Markschies and Hubert Wolf (Munich: C. H. Beck, 2010), 322–44.

[6] On the following remarks concerning Benedict's impact, see in more detail Melville, "Montecassino."

[7] Adalbert de Vogüé, "Benedikt von Nursia," *Theologische Realenzyklopädie* 5:549.

down outside of the *Dialogues*, in an entry in the calendar of the Northumbrian and Frisian missionary Willibrord.[8]

The Rule of Saint Benedict

Benedict's actual appearance took place in a different way. It came about earlier, and in the end it had more of an impact than the hagiography. In the year 625 Venerandus, abbot of the Provençal monastery of Hauterive (*Alta Ripa*), wrote to the bishop of Albi that his community followed the Rule *sancti Benedicti abbati Romensis*—of the "Roman" abbot Saint Benedict.[9] The text of the Rule itself prepared the way for the growth of the reputation of Benedict and the power of Benedictine monasticism.

Gregory had written that the Rule of Saint Benedict was filled with the spirit of discernment—*discretio*. The oldest surviving witness of the text that coalesced under the name of Benedict is from early eighth-century England, followed by a somewhat different version from the first third of the ninth,[10] commissioned by Charlemagne. The text, along with others before it, is in fact shaped by the ideal of discernment (*discretio*).[11] Through his normative power, the leader of the community—the abbot—was obligated to righteousness: "He must know," says the text of the Rule, "what a difficult and demanding burden he has undertaken: directing souls and serving a variety of temperaments, coaxing, reproving and encouraging them as appropriate."

---

[8] Pius Engelbert, "Neue Forschungen zu den 'Dialogen' Gregors des Großen. Antworten auf Clarks These," *Erbe und Auftrag* 65 (1989): 376–93, here 381.

[9] Joachim Wollasch, "Benedictus abbas Romensis. Das römische Element in der frühen benediktinischen Tradition," in *Tradition als historische Kraft*, ed. Joachim Wollasch (Berlin: de Gruyter, 1982), 119–37; Pius Engelbert, "Regeltext und Romverehrung. Zur Frage der Verbreitung der Regula Benedicti im Frühmittelalter," in *Montecassino della prima alla seconda distruzione*, ed. Faustino Avagliano (Montecassino: Pubblicazioni Cassinesi, 1987), 133–62.

[10] Georg Holzherr, ed., *Die Benediktsregel: Eine Anleitung zu christlichem Leben* (Fribourg: Paulus, 2007), 37.

[11] Adalbert de Vogüé, *Reading Saint Benedict*, CS 151 (Kalamazoo, MI: Cistercian Publications, 1994). See also the concise treatment of Mirko Breitenstein, "Die Regel—Lebensprogramm und Glaubensfibel," in *Macht des Wortes*, ed. Gerfried Sitar and Martin Kroker (Regensburg: Schnell und Steiner, 2009), 23–29.

He must "accommodate and adapt himself to each one's character and intelligence" (RB 2.31-32). He is to take heed of "this and other examples of discretion, the mother of virtues" (RB 64.19).[12]

These principles guided the allotment of necessities among all in common, the distribution of clothing, food, and drink or the assignment of work on particular tasks, the care of the old, children, and the ill, or the carrying out of punishment. The justification was found in this sentence from the Rule: "Everything he teaches and commands should, like the leaven of divine justice [*divina iustitia*], permeate the minds of his disciples" (RB 2.5). In this way the abbot was positioned to serve as a bridge between the monastery's immanence and divine transcendence. Only by virtue of this double relationship was the abbot to be understood as the representative of Christ in the monastery, as the very beginning of the Rule emphasizes. The same relationship explains both the tremendous responsibility of the abbot with respect to his community and the fact that he alone is responsible for them before God.

The Rule is a spiritual text. Its opening words—"Listen, my son, to the master's instructions, and attend to them with the ear of your heart" (RB Prol. 1)—indicate an inner, spiritual listening, one that should make the "heart wide" and that should make it possible to "run on the path of God's commandments," in "the inexpressible delight of love" (RB Prol. 49). The Rule's admonitions, such as "Let us open our eyes to the divine light and let us hear with a startled ear what the voice of God calls us and urges us to do: 'Today, if you hear his voice, do not let your heart be hardened'" (RB Prol. 9-10), are directed to those who strive for the highest possible perfection of their souls, which they seek to embed within the divine order.

Yet the Rule is also an organizational text. It assumes that the individual remains imperfect, and therefore endangered, and that a life in community, in a monastery cut off from the world, is the best safeguard in the struggle for perfection. In that respect the monastery is to be understood as a "school for the Lord's service" (RB Prol. 45)

---

[12] Rudolf Hanslik, ed., *Benedicti Regula* (Vienna: Hoedler-Pichler-Tempsky, 1977); Latin/German trans. *Die Benediktusregel* (Beuron: Salzburger Äbtekonferenz, 1992); numerical annotations indicate chapter and line. English translations here from *RB 1980: The Rule of St. Benedict in English*, ed. Timothy Fry, et al. (Collegeville, MN: Liturgical Press, 1981).

and is presented as a "workshop" (RB 4.78) in which, with the help of the "tools for good works" (RB 4, heading), the soul is shaped for God. In this school every desire for the love of God and neighbor would be established, as well as the avoidance of moral vices like pride, contentiousness, and idleness.

But beyond that, certain monastic virtues of ascetic life are also important: to love fasting, to chastise the body, to deny fleshly desires, to practice silence, and to renounce personal property. Common prayer and liturgical celebration, common eating, sleeping, and manual labor establish the rhythms of the day. Regarding the last of these, the Rule says, "When they live by the labor of their hands, as our fathers and the apostles did, then they are really monks" (RB 48.8). This sentence had revolutionary potential in the best sense, because it reinterpreted the meaning of manual labor; once an activity that in the ancient tradition was appropriate for a slave but not for a free man, here it appeared as an activity that allowed access to heaven. Work was *ascesis*, and it had the power to ennoble all Christians, regardless of their status.

The Rule lays out in painstaking detail the norms that are to guide all of these relationships, and it thereby lays claim to the whole person, both inwardly and outwardly. At the same time it is a pragmatically oriented text that is able to organize daily life. As a set of legal instructions,[13] it regulates the acceptance of new members, the division of labor among the offices of the monastery, the administration of economic resources, the duties of almsgiving to the poor at the gate, the provision of clothing and tools, and so on. It seeks to forestall deviance, sets out the conditions through which guilt can be acknowledged and atoned for, and lays out guidelines for punitive measures ranging from corporal punishment to exile from the community for serious infractions. The Rule envisions an enclosed community, one whose economy and organization are autarchic and one largely untouched by the interference of outside ecclesiastical authorities. The local bishop is to be called in only when the community's priest has blatantly failed or when the abbot has tolerated moral decline.

---

[13] Uwe Kai Jacobs, *Die Regula Benedicti als Rechtsbuch* (Cologne: Böhlau, 1987).

The text of the Rule itself rests on the foundations of what was already a rich monastic tradition. It depends above all on the so-called Rule of the Master,[14] composed around 500, a text whose strict asceticism and discipline it somewhat relaxed, and it also uses (as the text itself reveals) the "Rule of our Holy Father Basil" (d. 379), thus bringing together the intellectual legacy of Eastern and Western monasticism. It was thus probably the Rule's humane balance between strictness and mercy, as well as its calculated syncretism, that especially contributed to the excellent quality of the text's content and thus to its success. The Rule was exemplary in its moderation, seeking to bring spiritual challenges into harmony with the limits of bodily strength, so that the ascetic world of the monastery might be bearable—not a prison, but a joyful place whose inhabitants were set free to pursue their ultimate end.[15]

And yet it can nowhere be clearly shown that this fascinating text is identical to that which Gregory mentions in his *Dialogues*. When the pope wrote that the Rule written by Saint Benedict was shaped by *discretio*, that in itself was no sufficient basis for forming a judgment about it; the same could have been said, for example, of the Rule of Cassian.[16]

Even if Gregory made it clear that Benedict taught exactly as he lived, the Rule could thereby only give information about the way of life of its author, and not vice versa. The text offers not the slightest hint of biographical evidence. The attribution of the text to a Benedict appears quite early, however, and presumes as accepted fact that the Benedict of the *Dialogues* and the Benedict of the Rule are the same person. The fact that this Benedict was named the "Roman abbot" early on by Venerandus (in the case noted above), and more frequently still in later decades, was—according to the evidence of the *Dialogues*—historically inaccurate; questions thus arise about whether Gregory's text had been understood very well.

---

[14] *La Règle du maître*, ed. and trans. Adalbert de Vogüé (Paris: Éditions du Cerf, 1964); *Die Magisterregel: Einführung und Übersetzung*, trans. Karl Suso Frank (St. Ottilien: EOS, 1989).

[15] Gregorio Penco, "Monasterium—Carcer," *Studia monastica* 8 (1966): 133–43.

[16] See chap. 1, p. 17.

Yet the Rule's very orientation toward Rome—probably because the text was first identified in a remark by a Roman bishop—contributed to its success among those who were at the time predisposed to give it a warm reception: the Franks. In the seventh century a network of Gallo-Frankish patrons gathered around the Merovingian court were committed to founding and supporting monasteries; they had a clear interest in promoting the Rule of Saint Benedict, not least because the text was understood to be "Roman" in a normative sense.[17] Benedict's Rule thus gained in authority and at the same time presented itself as an ideal bridge to Rome, home to the prince of the apostles.

A growing interest in Rome and the life of its monasteries is also discernible in England. From there the Northumbrian abbot Benedict Biscop (629–690), among others, had several times traveled through the western Frankish kingdom and to Rome, in order to study monastic life and its texts in general. He also encountered the Rule of Saint Benedict in Lérins and then introduced it (in the form of a hybrid text) in his monasteries, Wearmouth and Jarrow, on the Northumbrian coast.[18] It is also possible that his travels produced what remains the oldest surviving manuscript of the Rule of Saint Benedict, found today in Oxford (Bodleian Library, Hatton 48). At times Benedict Biscop was accompanied by his friend Wilfrid (ca. 634–709/10), a monk from the community of Lindisfarne.[19] After Wilfrid had returned to his Northumbrian home in 661, he received from Ealhfrith, the son of the king, the abbey of Ripon (today in North Yorkshire). There he introduced both the Roman Rite and the Rule of Saint Benedict, albeit probably in a mixed form, with regional customs. This signaled the start of what would be a strong retreat of the Irish-Scottish traditions of monastic life in central England—a development only strengthened by the subsequent decrees of an Anglo-Saxon council held in Whitby in 664 under the growing influence of southern England.[20]

---

[17] Wollasch, "Benedictus abbas Romensis"; Engelbert, "Regeltext und Romverehrung."

[18] David Knowles, *The Monastic Order in England* (Cambridge, UK: Cambridge University Press, 1950), 21–22.

[19] David Peter Kirby, ed., *Saint Wilfrid at Hexham* (Newcastle upon Tyne: Oriel Press, 1974).

[20] Sarah Foot, *Monastic Life in Anglo-Saxon England c. 600–900* (Cambridge, UK: Cambridge University Press, 2006), 24ff.

The Career of Benedict and His Rule

This phase of the "discovery" of Benedict's Rule, which lasted well into the eighth century, fell within a multifaceted and lively epoch of Latin monasticism.[21] It was an age shaped by the brisk pace of new foundations, especially those of kings and the upper nobility. Some significant examples, among many, include the male monastery of Corbie in the Somme Valley and the women's monastery of Chelles near Paris, both founded by the Frankish queen Balthild (d. 680),[22] and the women's monastery of San Salvatore in Brescia, established in 753 by the Lombard king Desiderius.[23] Also characteristic for the time, however, were the important missionary efforts that had their origins in the Irish, and later in the Anglo-Saxon, ideal of *peregrinatio* noted above and that found both organizational and spiritual manifestation in the founding of numerous new monasteries. Early examples include the foundations of the missionary bishop Pirmin, for example, the monastery of Reichenau, founded in 724.[24] Women's monasticism also found notably strong expression in the form not only of women's communities but also in the rise of double monasteries,[25] in which women and men lived separately yet together as one community. In England, Whitby,[26] founded in 657, stood out

[21] Prinz, *Frühes Mönchtum*, 263–92.

[22] Jacques Dubois, "Sainte Bathilde et les fondations monastiques à l'époque mérovingienne," *Chelles notre ville, notre histoire. Bulletin de la société archéologique et historique de Chelles*, New Series 14 (1995/96): 283–309.

[23] Giancarlo Andenna, "San Salvatore di Brescia e la scelta religiosa delle donne aristocratiche tra età longobarda ed età franca (VIII–IX secolo)," in *Female* vita religiosa *between Late Antiquity and the High Middle Ages: Structures, Developments and Spatial Contexts*, ed. Gert Melville and Anne Müller (Berlin: LIT, 2011), 209–33.

[24] Arnold Angenendt, *Monachi peregrini* (Munich: Wilhelm Fink, 1972); Peter Classen, ed., *Die Gründungsurkunden der Reichenau* (Sigmaringen: Thorbecke, 1977).

[25] Prinz, *Frühes Mönchtum*, 658–63.

[26] Dagmar Beate Baltrusch-Schneider, "Die angelsächsischen Doppelklöster," in *Doppelklöster und andere Formen der Symbiose männlicher und weiblicher Religiosen im Mittelalter*, ed. Kaspar Elm and Michel Parisse (Berlin: Duncker & Humblot, 1992), 57–79; Isabelle R. Odile Charmantier, "Monasticism in Seventh-Century Northumbria and Neustria. A Comparative Study of the Monasteries

as an example here, and in France the monastery of Remiremont in Alsace, founded in 620.[27]

In this era of new beginnings, the text of the Rule that was coming together under the name of Benedict began its career as part of the so-called mixed rules—that is, the textual products of a selective reading of a variety of surviving rules by various authors, shaped not least by local customs or the decisions of local abbots. Normative guidelines that one might call a "religious rule" were at that time not bound to unalterable texts.

One widespread combination blended the Rule of Saint Benedict with that of the Irish missionary Columbanus, who (as was noted above) had founded the monasteries of Luxeuil and Bobbio. Already under the second successor to Columbanus at Luxeuil, Waldebert (629–679), the community began to depart from strict adherence to Columbanus's norms, taking up additional stipulations from the Benedictine rule.[28] Such changes spread quickly. Evidence suggests that already by around 640, life at the new abbey of Fleury (today Saint-Benoît-sur-Loire) was lived "according to the Rule of most holy Benedict and lord Columbanus,"[29] and that this normative guide was quickly passed on to Lérins, the renowned ancient Gallic monastery off the coast of Provence. The focal point of the spread was in Gaul, where up to the end of the seventh century, at least in the northern regions, almost every monastery was more or less strongly influenced by the Benedictine rule. Adding nuance to the pattern is the fact that new rules were also composed at the time using Benedict's text. So, for example, Donatus, bishop of Besançon from 624–660 and strongly influenced by Luxeuil, composed a rule for nuns from texts of Caesarius of Arles and Columbanus as well as from the Benedictine rule.[30] An anonymous author (probably from Luxeuil)

---

of Chelles, Jouaree, Monkwearmouth/Jarrow, and Whitby," PhD dissertation, University of Durham, 1998.

[27] Michel Parisse, ed., *Remiremont, l'abbaye et la ville* (Nancy: Université de Nancy II, 1980).

[28] Prinz, *Frühes Mönchtum*, 270–72.

[29] Maurice Prou and Alexandre Vidier, *Recueil des chartes de l'abbaye de Saint-Benoît-sur-Loire*, 2 vols. (Paris: Picard, 1900–1907), 1:1, 5.

[30] Michaela Zelzer, "Die 'Regula Donati,' der älteste Textzeuge der Regula 'Benedicti,'" *Regulae Benedicti Studia* 16 (1987): 23–36.

was similarly inspired, composing a "rule for virgins" that survives as *regula cuiusdam ad virgines*, a text strongly (though not exclusively) based on the Rule of Saint Benedict.[31]

Yet for all of the places where the Benedict of the *Dialogues* had been active, early on he could be remembered nowhere—there was no Benedictine life in either Subiaco or Monte Cassino. Already in the second half of the seventh century it was believed that Benedict's body had come to rest in the monastery of Fleury on the Loire. Italy seems to have simply forgotten the "humble provincial abbot"[32] who had been stylized in the *Dialogues* as a saintly model.

The situation changed dramatically in 717. Looking back at around the end of the eighth century, the monk Paulus Diaconus wrote in his *History of the Lombards*[33] that Petronax, a leading citizen of the city of Brescia, had moved first to Rome and then—at the insistence of Pope Gregory II (715–731)—to the "fortress" of Cassino, "to the holy body of the blessed father Benedict." There he came upon a few simple men who chose him as their master (*Senior*). After attracting more monks, Petronax came to see himself as compelled to begin a life in community and to found the monastery anew, "under the yoke of the holy rule and according to the model of blessed Benedict." Somewhat later Petronax is said to have received from Pope Zachary (741–752) the more substantial collection of books that was so essential for monastic life, among them the rule that the blessed father Benedict had supposedly written with his own hand. A genuine monastery had now been established, a visible and fixed monument, where previously there had been only the letters of a written report. That it should have turned out this way was certainly because of the personal commitment of Gregory II, who consciously sought to attach himself to the pontificate of his namesake and predecessor—and who wanted to develop good relations with the Franks in order to establish a certain counterbalance to the political and religious influence of the Byzantines.

---

[31] Albrecht Diem, "Das Ende des monastischen Experiments. Liebe, Beichte und Schweigen in der *Regula cuiusdam ad virgines* (mit einer Übersetzung im Anhang)," in Melville and Müller, *Female vita religiosa*, 80–136.

[32] Vogüé, "Benedikt von Nursia," 5:549.

[33] Paulus Diaconus, *Historia Langobardorum*, ed. Georg Waitz, MGH, *Scriptores rerum Langobardicarum* (Hannover: Hahn, 1878), 6:230–31. On the later history of Monte Cassino see the detailed treatment of Melville, "Montecassino."

A succession of visitors quickly began to arrive from the Frankish kingdom. Particularly frequent as guests were the students and associates of Winfrid Boniface of Wessex, whom Gregory II had consecrated as a missionary bishop. Among the first of those, arriving around 730, was Willibald, later bishop of Eichstätt, who had already lived according to the "institution of the regular life of holy Benedict" and who now passed on his experience to the new community at Monte Cassino. In 747 and 748 Sturmius followed, the abbot of Fulda, the community he had founded under the direction of Boniface, which already lived exclusively according to the Rule of Saint Benedict.[34] That rule had certainly found in Boniface an early supporter with widespread influence. Under his direction, in 742/43 a reform synod had prescribed that the Rule of Saint Benedict should be the only authoritative guide for all Frankish monasteries.[35]

And yet something was still missing on Monte Cassino: the body of Benedict. Here too Pope Zacharias offered help, together with another esteemed guest at Monte Cassino: Carloman, the now resigned brother of Pippin, who with the aid of Pope Zacharias had become the Frankish king. In 750/51, Zacharias gave Carloman a letter to take with him to the Frankish kingdom. The letter asked that Benedict's body (which was firmly believed to be at Fleury) be brought back to Monte Cassino. The effort was not very successful: Monte Cassino eventually received only a few bones. In his history (cited above), Paul the Deacon later offered the community the consolation that because no one would have been able to steal any decaying body parts immediately after Benedict's death, they were surely still to be found at the place where he had died. Consequently, Paul said, he could rightly assert—as cited above—that Petronax "was drawn to the holy body of the blessed father Benedict."

More and more Monte Cassino grew "into the role of a monastic model."[36] Abbot Theodomarus (778–797) soon sent a lengthy letter to Count Theodoric, a relative of Charlemagne, in which he wrote out

---

[34] Dieter Geuenich, "Bonifatius und 'sein' Kloster Fulda," in *Bonifatius— Leben und Nachwirken*, ed. Franz J. Felten, et al. (Mainz: Gesellschaft für mittelrheinische Kirchengeschichte, 2007).

[35] Winfried Hartmann, *Die Synoden der Karolingerzeit im Frankenreich und in Italien* (Paderborn: Schöningh, 1989), 47–63.

[36] Pius Engelbert, "Regeltext und Romverehrung," 133–62, here 157.

and explained the customs of Monte Cassino for the use of certain brothers in Gaul.[37] Charlemagne himself visited the abbey in 787, on the occasion of a campaign against the Duchy of Benevento, and asked for a copy of the version of the Rule that Pope Zachary had brought there. Charlemagne, who was generally concerned for the *norma rectitudinis*, for ordering his kingdom according to what was right, valued what he saw as the unadulterated text—a text that in his eyes, of course, stood as the autograph it was claimed to be. As the so-called Aachener Normalkodex, this version of the Rule lived on.

The Second Benedict and the Reform of the Frankish Monasteries

Yet the spread of the text of the Rule, and above all the recognition of the text as the normative standard for monastic life, unfolded more slowly than decrees—for example, the synod of 742/43 noted above— might suggest. Without doubt, in view of the challenge of holding the empire together, the Carolingians had a political interest in having the most uniform rule possible for their monasteries. The Benedictine rule, for both its inner balance and—as has been emphasized—its supposedly Roman origins, seemed best suited in this regard. The decrees of the synods and imperial diets presumed from 789 forward that monastic life should be exclusively Benedictine. Delegates to the diet held in Aachen in autumn of 802 brought with them from all parts of the empire letters reporting how matters stood regarding the recognition and implementation of the Benedictine rule.[38]

In light of their scandalous deficiencies, all monasteries were now strictly commanded to order their liturgical practices according to this rule. The monasteries, each one calling on local traditions foundational to their identity, resisted strongly. The renowned community of Corbie, for example, followed customs that had nothing to do with either the text or the spirit of the Benedictine rule, and at Saint Gall and Reichenau the story was no different. Moreover, especially

---

[37] "Theodomari abbatis Casinensis epistola ad Theodoricum gloriosum," ed. Jacob Winandy and Kassius Hallinger, in *Initia consuetudinis Benedictinae. Consuetudines saeculi octavi et noni*, ed. Kassius Hallinger, CCM 1 (Siegburg: Schmitt, 1963), 125–36.

[38] MGH, *Concilia aevi Karolini [742–842]*, Teil 1 [742–817]: 230.

during the reign of Charlemagne, other renowned male and female monasteries—for example, Saint Denis near Paris, Saint Bénigne in Dijon, Saint Victor in Marseille, Chelles near Paris, and Nivelles in Brabant—gave up their monastic observance and turned to the easier way of life lived by canons and canonesses.

At least in some regions, the measures of 802 were not without results. Archbishop Leidrad of Lyon (d. 813), for example, undertook a massive attempt to enforce the Rule of Saint Benedict in his diocese.[39] But the broader breakthrough of enforcement came under the son of Charlemagne, Louis the Pious, who embraced comprehensive reforms on the political, social, and ecclesiastical levels in order to ensure the unity of his kingdom. One of his most important supporters was Benedict of Aniane (ca. 750–821),[40] born as Witiza, son of the Count of Maguelonne. Already in the late eighth century he had shaped the life of the southern French monastery of Aniane, which he had founded, into a strict Benedictine community guided by a blended, especially stern observance based on particular prescriptions from Basil and Pachomius.

Later he sent monks from Aniane to reform other monasteries across Aquitaine and Languedoc, gave these communities the Rule of Saint Benedict along with other written customs (*consuetudines*), and visited them. From these emerged a loose, nonhierarchical congregation of Benedictine houses. In 814 Benedict of Aniane was called to the side of Louis the Pious, and in 815/16, after a stay in the Alsatian monastery of Maursmünster, with Louis's support he founded the abbey of Inden (later Kornelimünster) near Aachen. He developed that community into a kind of center for training personnel

---

[39] Otto Gerhard Oexle, *Forschungen zu monastischen und geistlichen Gemeinschaften im Westfränkischen Bereich* (Munich: Wilhelm Fink, 1978), 134–57.

[40] Emmanuel von Severus, "Benedikt von Aniane," in *Theologische Realenzyklopädie* (Berlin: de Gruyter, 1980), 5:535–38; Pius Engelbert, "Benedikt von Aniane und die karolingische Reichsidee: Zur politischen Theologie des Frühmittelalters," in *Cultura e spiritualità nella tradizione monastica*, ed. Gregorio Penco (Rome: Pontificio Ateneo S. Anselmo, 1990), 67–103; Walter Kettemann, "Subsidia Anianensia. Überlieferungs- und textgeschichtliche Untersuchungen zur Geschichte Witiza-Benedikts, seines Klosters Aniane und zur sogenannten 'anianischen Reform,'" PhD dissertation, Duisburg, 1999; Online: http://duepublico .uni-duisburg-essen.de/servlets/DocumentServlet?id=18245.

for other monasteries that wanted to embrace the observance of the Benedictine rule.

The remark in the Rule of Saint Benedict (61.2) that each monastery had a certain "local custom" (*consuetudo loci*) was for Benedict of Aniane the key provision that allowed him to assume a twofold normative guide, one based on the Rule as well as on custom—and thus to develop, on the basis of a single valid rule, a single custom for the entire kingdom. In a way consistent with the motto "one rule and one custom" (*una regula et una consuetudo*)[41] and using Inden as a model for monastic life—with the help of royal assurance of immunity from the interference of other sovereigns, assurance of free abbatial elections, and assurance of royal protection even in matters that did not concern royal monasteries—Benedict sought to enforce a uniform monastic life across the Frankish kingdom.

In an unprecedentedly radical way—though the results only emerged after a long process—three synods (held at Aachen in 816, 817, and 818/19) commanded monastic communities to adhere exclusively to the dictates of the Benedictine rule. And as an aid to putting the new policy into practice, Benedict of Aniane himself authored a series of *consuetudines* that served as a kind of guide to implementation. Their guidelines were equally valid for both male and female monasteries, as the anonymous biographer of Louis the Pious emphasized: "the uniform and unchanging custom of life according to the rule of holy Benedict was carried to the monasteries, to men as well as to holy female nuns" (*sanctis monialibus feminis*).[42]

The decrees were broadcast throughout the kingdom by royal ambassadors—*missi*. Yet Benedict of Aniane admittedly did not use every opportunity to achieve as one possible aim of his measures the institutional incorporation of every monastery in the empire under a

[41] On the following, see Josef Semmler, "Benedictus II. Una regula—una consuetudo," in *Benedictine Culture 750–1050*, ed. Willem Lourdaux (Leuven: Leuven University Press, 1983), 1–49; Semmler, "Benediktinische Reform und kaiserliches Privileg. Zur Frage des institutionellen Zusammenschlusses der Klöster um Benedikt von Aniane," in *Institutionen und Geschichte*, ed. Gert Melville (Cologne: Böhlau, 1992), 259–93. For corrections of past research and for further starting points, see Kettemann, "Subsidia Anianensia," 1–32.

[42] Reinhold Rau, ed., "Anonymi vita Hludowici," in *Quellen zur karolingischen Reichsgeschichte* 1 (Darmstadt: Wissenschaftliche Buchgesellschaft, 1977), 1:302–3.

common Benedictine observance. The one binding *consuetudo* was insufficient, not least because it had not been established in a strictly monolithic form. There was no comprehensive cohesion within prayer confraternities, as might have been established according to the Irish/ Anglo–Saxon mode,[43] nor were the monasteries subordinated legally and hierarchically to Benedict of Aniane's leadership, since he was concerned on principle to preserve the autonomous position of each monastery in the Benedictine sense. He sought much more to ensure the continuity of his reforms through the power of the Frankish ruler and the efficacy of his legal ordinances, which were aimed at the establishment and preservation of monasteries guided by the Bene- dictine rule and by a "regular" abbot (*abbas regularis*).

At the same time, and motivated by the same idea of the political unity of the realm, in 816 the Synod of Aachen reformed the clergy by giving them their own way of life alongside the monks—the *ordo canonicus*. Building on regulations that Bishop Chrodegang of Metz[44] (ca. 715–766) had already developed for clergy in his diocese, as well as on the relevant decrees of councils held under Charlemagne (especially that of the year 794), the synod completed a "book on the establishment of the canons" (*Liber de institutione canonicorum*).[45] It set out in detail how the clergy was to lead a life in community—a *vita communis*—in an enclosed, monastic space, whether within a bishop's court or as an independent community; it further required that a *praepositus*—a "su- perior"—should stand at the head of such communities (called "foun- dations"), and finally that the canons were to have a common refectory and dormitory and were to pray and work together.

It can rightly be said that the intention of this legislation was thus to "monasticize" the clergy, but with two very important differ- ences: there was no life-long commitment to membership, and the use of property was allowed. In all events, since from the time of the

---

[43] Dieter Geuenich, "Gebetsgedenken und anianische Reform. Beobachtungen zu den Verbrüderungsbeziehungen der Äbte im Reich Ludwigs des Frommen," in *Klöster und Bischof in Lotharingien*, ed. Raymund Kottje and Helmut Maurer (Sigmaringen: Thorbecke, 1989), 79–106.

[44] Martin Allen Claussen, *The Reform of the Frankish Church* (Cambridge, UK: Cambridge University Press, 2004).

[45] Albert Werminghoff, "Die Beschlüsse des Aachener Concils im Jahre 816," in *Neues Archiv der Gesellschaft für ältere deutsche Geschichtskunde* 27 (1902): 605–75.

Carolingian reforms the *vita canonica* had always also been understood as the *vita apostolica*, the personal poverty of the now-regulated lives of the canons nevertheless remained one of their most essential founding ideals. This set of tensions would eventually nurture a number of later conflicts, each of which would inspire further efforts at reform.

The synods made parallel efforts to regulate the lives of canonesses—women who lived together in communities but who were not bound to a strict vow of poverty or lifelong membership.[46] The 816 synod promulgated the *Institutio Sanctimonialium*, a statute that regulated the life in community of these women. Here too, as among the men, the daily life of community with its obligations of prayer, meals, and sleep in common rooms stood in the forefront. According to this legislation, canonesses were obligated to obedience to an abbess, though they could retain their own personal property (including the ownership of land), employ servants, and use private rooms for retreats within their strictly guarded enclosures. Social differences and sensibility to differences in rank were not denigrated, though no member was to be disadvantaged because of them.

The nature of the surviving sources, however, allows for neither proof of the immediate realization of the *Institutio* or even for the possibility of making a clear distinction over the next two centuries between which houses were occupied by canonesses and which by nuns of some form of Benedictine observance—in later terminology, whether the community was a "foundation" (*Stift*) or a monastery. The boundaries were fluid. This was especially true for the great wave of new women's communities established from the ninth to the early eleventh century in the region of the duchy of Saxony—a wave that began in 800 with Herford, reached its first high point with the establishment of Essen before 850 and Gandersheim in 852, and then continued in the following century with Quedlinburg in 936 and others, eventually encompassing some sixty-four houses.[47]

---

[46] Franz J. Felten, "Auf dem Weg zu Kanonissen und Kanonissenstift. Ordnungskonzepte der weiblichen *vita religiosa* bis ins 9. Jahrhundert," in *Vita religiosa sanctimonialium*, ed. Christine Kleinjung (Korb: Didymos, 2011), 71–92. On the following, see Felten, "Wie adelig waren Kanonissenstifte (und andere weibliche Konvente) im (frühen und hohen) Mittelalter?" in *Vita religiosa sanctimonialium*, 93–162, here 128–32.

[47] Jan Gerchow and Thomas Schilp, eds., *Essen und die sächsischen Frauenstifte im Frühmittelalter* (Essen: Klartext-Verlag, 2004).

Yet in the era that followed the Synod of Aachen—an era that saw the severe endangerment of monastic life across wide stretches of Europe through the destructive power of external invasions—the lifestyle of the canon provided for many monastic communities a kind of refuge from the strictness of their rules. Since Aachen's prescriptions for canons or canonesses had been seen as less strict than the requirements for monks and nuns, from the eleventh century on they would become the object of strong attacks from reformers of the *vita religiosa*. As a consequence it would not be long before at least the elite among the clergy, with the support of the church hierarchy, actually embraced the monastic way of life and remembered the text that had not yet been rediscovered in the time of the Aachen Synod: the Rule of Augustine, with its command of personal poverty in keeping with the spirit of the apostolic community.[48]

But because monastic life in Western Christendom was so deeply embedded in the politics of the Frankish kingdom, it began slowly to change. Because of those political connections, Benedictine life—though with certain delays here and there—finally broke through against all of its competitors some 350 years after Gregory the Great told of its beginnings in the *Dialogues* and retained its dominant position for another 250 years. But the same politics also ensured that the monastic world became more strongly bound to earthly affairs and that it had to be acknowledged to a significant degree as both a provider of services and a source of power. By the time of Charlemagne and Louis the Pious at the latest, a political and also a politicized monastic life had fully developed.

Although Louis the Pious may also have seen his monastic reforms as a matter of serving the reputation (*honor*) of the church and of raising it up (*exaltatio*),[49] monasteries had long since become notable centers of economic activity and focal points for the development of infrastructure. For the eastern regions of the empire, it is enough to cite by way of example older foundations such as Reichenau (founded in 724), Fulda (founded in 744), Tegernsee (founded in the middle of the eighth century), Lorsch (founded in 764), and the women's community on the Odilienberg in Alsace (founded in the seventh

[48] See chap. 1, p. 10.
[49] Semmler, "Benediktinische Reform," 274.

century). But the same was true for more recent foundations like Corvey (founded, after its predecessors, in 822).[50]

All of these communities enjoyed extensive landed estates. Fulda, founded in 744 by Sturmius under the direction of Winfrid Boniface, by 800 had estates and monastic cells that reached as far to the south as the Danube.[51] Such wealthy monasteries, moreover, were a European-wide phenomenon, within what were at that time the boundaries of Christendom. In Italy, for example, Nonantola was founded in the middle of the eighth century, Pomposa was founded in the middle of the ninth century, and Farfa,[52] the imperial abbey in the Sabine country, was founded at the beginning of the eighth century, its wealth soon so enormous that the abbey had its own tax-exempt commercial ship. An idealized plan of the monastery of Saint Gall (presumably drawn up between 820–830 at Reichenau) reveals the new, now architecturally tangible schemes of spatial organization that, though absent from the Rule of Saint Benedict, were being imagined for such massive abbeys.[53] Centered on the church building, the plan was arranged to ensure economic independence, to meet the needs of the abbey's guests (from the most renowned to the simple pilgrim), to ensure the integrity of its insulation from the world (only the abbot, by means of his own house, served as a link to the outside), and to provide for medical care and the education of the next generation. The layout thereby corresponded to the essential decrees of the reform synod at Aachen.

Charlemagne in particular—and his successors followed his lead—knew how to enlist monasteries to meet his kingdom's various needs, whether in technical matters concerning the logistics of provision, in military affairs, or for the formation of a political elite. Most of these monasteries had been granted immunity and were thereby protected

---

[50] For an overview, see Prinz, *Frühes Mönchtum*, 185–262.

[51] Berthold Jäger, "Zur wirtschaftlichen und rechtlichen Entwicklung des Klosters Fulda in seiner Frühzeit," in *Hrabanus Maurus in Fulda*, ed. Marc-Aeilko Aris and Susana Bullido del Barrio (Freiburg im Breisgau: Knecht, 2010), 81–120.

[52] Cosimo Damiano Fonseca, "Farfa abbazia imperiale," in *Farfa abbazia imperiale* (Negarine di S. Pietro in Cariano: Il Segno dei Gabrielli Ed., 2006), 1–17.

[53] Konrad Hecht, *Der St. Galler Klosterplan* (Sigmaringen: Thorbecke, 1983). See p. 46 and the website http://www.stgallplan.org/en/index_plan.html.

from interference by royal officials. They had also been granted sovereign jurisdictional rights. Many of them, moreover, because they had been handed over (*traditio*) to the ruler by a noble founder, had in fact become royal monasteries and thereby enjoyed both the king's protection and the right of free abbatial election.[54] Nearly all of them were also endowed with rich agricultural estates and their appropriate dependent farmers (*socmen*). The varying degrees of attention these monasteries received were thus not always oriented toward the realization of monastic ideals but rather toward political goals, dynastic ties, and the potential for service to the king (*servitium regis*), which included the obligation to provide lodging and provision for the king and to provide a military contingent drawn from the nobility tied to the household.[55] More and more the abbots were able to articulate their concerns (these, too, often shaped by political interests) at the imperial synods. They were at the same time entangled more tightly than ever in the political struggles and rivalries of the day.

And yet this structure certainly had two sides. Charlemagne and his successors had already shown their great interest in upholding proper discipline and piety in the monastery. Encyclicals (capitularies) issued at imperial diets and the decrees of synods all spoke the same language: monasteries were (or at least should be), as it were, extraordinary places for connecting to God, places where one could expect the establishment of peace, the stability of sound royal rule, and protection from overpowering enemies, whether from hell or on earth, as well as the gift of good harvests and reward for good deeds on earth and in heaven. An old obligation of the monastery, well established by long tradition, now came to the fore: to "pray for the salvation of the emperor and his sons and the stability of the empire," as was still said in 819, in the time of Louis the Pious.[56]

These external expectations about the proper relationship to God corresponded to a development within the monastery that was of overwhelming importance: the clericalization of the monks. Chapter 62 of

---

[54] Josef Semmler, "Traditio und Königsschutz," *Zeitschrift der Savigny-Stiftung für Rechtsgeschichte: Kanonistische Abteilung* 45 (1959): 1–34.

[55] For an overview, see Carlrichard Brühl, *Fodrum, gistum, servitium regis* (Cologne: Böhlau, 1968).

[56] "Notitia de servitio monasteriorum," ed. Petrus Becker, in *Initia consuetudinis Benedictinae*, ed. Hallinger, 483–99.

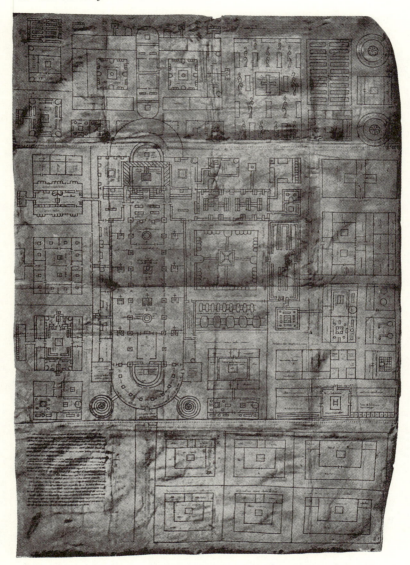

This plan of an ideal monastery (112 x 77.5 cm) was drawn up in the first third of the ninth century on the island of Reichenau. It is preserved in the library of Saint Gall Abbey. See also the web-based project at www.stgallplan.org.

the Rule of Saint Benedict had spoken of only a single priest in the monastic community, one whose task was to ensure against violations of obedience and to enforce the discipline of the Rule. Monks were laymen. Of course there were always a few among them who had been ordained as priests. But by the eighth and ninth centuries, this situation had fundamentally changed: members of the monastic community were now overwhelmingly also priests. It did not come about as a matter of pastoral care for the monks' neighbors, because even when monasteries were responsible for parishes, those parishes were in principle cared for by secular priests who had been assigned to them. "Ordination was the crowning and the completion of spiritual life" and "a call to the holy altars,"[57] in whose service one was more likely to merit a hearing before God than in the corporate prayer of the community.

Moreover, an office had in the meantime emerged that was to protect a monastery from unjust interference, to represent it in legal matters, and to dispense justice in its name within the boundaries of its immunities: the office of the advocate (derived from the Latin *advocatus*), held by a secular lord who was at first usually appointed by the king.[58] This office too was intended to free the monastic community from worldly matters and thereby allow monks to focus on spiritual concerns. Yet from the beginning the danger was clear: the advocates themselves would strive, in the interests of advancing their own power, to assert lordship over the monasteries, especially when the advocate was also—as was usually the case—the owner of the monastery or when (as was more and more the case from the ninth century on) the office of the advocate became inheritable within a particular noble family, thereby depriving the monastery of the possibility of itself choosing the advocate.

How strongly monasteries, despite all of their inner discipline, were shaped by the world around them—a world for whose stability

---

[57] Arnold Angenendt, *Das Frühmittelalter* (Stuttgart: Kohlhammer, 2001), 403–6, here 403, 405.

[58] For brief treatments in English see the articles "Advocatus/Avoué," in *Medieval France: An Encyclopedia*, ed. William W. Kible, et al. (New York: Routledge, 1995), 9; and "Advocate," in *Encyclopedia of the Middle Ages*, ed. André Vauchez (Chicago: Fitzroy Dearborn Publishers, 2000), 1:20. See also Hans-Joachim Schmidt, "Vogt, Vogtei," in *Lexikon des Mittelalters* (Munich and Zurich: Artemis & Winkler, 1997), 8:1811–14.

the monasteries prayed in their own self-interest—became clear at the latest by the time of the Carolingian decline, when it did so in a remarkably dramatic way. The external attacks of the Northmen, Magyars, and Saracens, against whom the Frankish kings at first offered little resistance, began in the ninth century and reached far into the tenth. These attacks had fatal consequences for monastic life in central Europe. The Magyars destroyed a number of monasteries along and south of the Danube in the first half of the tenth century; in 926 they advanced as far as Saint Gall and pillaged it. In 883 the Saracens had already destroyed the abbey of Monte Cassino, so that the mountain remained a wasteland for decades. The Saracens also plundered the Burgundian royal abbey of Saint Maurice on Lake Geneva in 939, and in 940 they destroyed the Alpine monastery of Disentis.

The Northmen, too, left behind scorched earth. Most monasteries near the Atlantic coast—whether in Britain or on the continent—were abandoned, and many women's houses retreated to seek new settlements farther east. So, for example, the members of Saint-Saveur (Redon), in the diocese of Vannes, resettled in the area of Auxerre in Burgundy in 921. But it was no more secure there than in its original site, as the two-time capture of the Eifel community of Prüm in 882 and 892 reveals, along with the plundering of the nearby monastery of Disibodenberg, also in 882—a community that would endure yet another round of destruction at the hands of the Avars in the first half of the tenth century. No cycle of wartime atrocities ever had such a cataclysmic impact on Europe's landscape of monasteries as this series of annihilations.

The weakening of centralized royal power, and the breakdown of order within the empire that followed, had a destructive impact on the life of the monastery. The consequence, especially in the western Frankish kingdom, was the widespread transfer of the royal monasteries' rights of ownership into the hands of the nobility, which thereby often led to a corrosion of monastic discipline, to exploitation, and to the ruin of the monasteries' economic capacity. What the destructive force of external enemies could not accomplish, the private feuds and plundering expeditions of the regional nobility did, in a time whose transformations of power had brought about something close to anarchy.[59]

---

[59] Hartmut Hoffmann, *Gottesfriede und Treuga Dei* (Stuttgart: Hiersemann, 1964), 11–14.

A serious consequence of this general political circumstance then appeared in the western Frankish kingdom: the renewed fragmentation of monastic life into a multiplicity of *consuetudines*, for which the word *Benedictine* was little more than a label. Countless monasteries lost their populations entirely and transformed themselves into canonries without even attempting to uphold the standards of the Aachen decrees.[60] Especially disadvantageous in that day, moreover, were the nearly unbroken traditions of the proprietary church, through which (as has been noted) monasteries became a marker of a founder's wealth and through which the protection and defense of a monastery's rights were subordinated to the interests of a secular (though also often an ecclesiastical) owner—including the appropriation of the office of abbot by a noble layman, who was empowered by rights of ownership to dispose of the material resources of the community and who installed a prior to take care of religious matters. All of these changes fundamentally contradicted the spirit of the Rule of Saint Benedict, to be sure, but they need not in principle have had a negative impact on the welfare of a community. For, as has often been shown, even a "lay abbot"[61] could take good care of both the spiritual and the material affairs of his monastery. In a time of generally weakened structures of order and values, however, such a betrayal of the actual spirit of monastic life had a powerfully threatening potential. It is thus revealing that when in 909, the provincial Synod of Trosly near Laon explicitly recognized laity as the owners of monasteries, it nevertheless emphatically noted that in view of the resulting abuses one could no longer speak of the condition of the monasteries, but only of their decline. To drive home the point, the synod noted that lay abbots (*abbates laici*) now lived in the monasteries with their wives, sons, and daughters, their vassals and hunting dogs.[62]

[60] Elmar Hochholzer, "Die lothringische (Gorzer) Reform," in *Die Reformverbände und Kongregationen der Benediktiner im deutschen Sprachraum*, ed. Ulrich Faust and Franz Quarthal (St. Ottilien: EOS, 1999), 45–87, here 45–46.

[61] Franz J. Felten, *Äbte und Laienäbte im Frankenreich* (Stuttgart: Hiersemann, 1980).

[62] Johannes Dominicus Mansi, *Sacrorum Conciliorum Nova Amplissima Collectio*, vol. 18.1 (Venice, 1773), 271; Felten, *Äbte und Laienäbte*, 9, 303.

3

The Flowering of the Benedictines

A New Beginning in Lotharingia

In both the kingdom of Burgundy (established in 888) and the German kingdom (established in 911 in the eastern regions of the Frankish realm), monastic life stabilized after the coming to power of Otto I in 936, and it did so more quickly than in the politically fragmented western Frankish kingdom. Many of the largest old abbeys continued as royal monasteries, while some among those—like the monastery of Corvey in Saxony, for example—were brought to a great flowering, even expanding the circle of successful communities through additional foundations (the monastery of Saint Maurice in Magdeburg, for example, in 937). Under Otto I the concept of "royal freedom" (*libertas regia*)[1] was invoked again to designate the legal status of the royal monastery, and in keeping with Carolingian traditions that status encompassed (as has been noted) royal protection, immunity, and free elections—thereby designating the monastery's place in the imperial church as well as its relationship to the king. A legal decision (*Weistum*) from the year 951 guarded against the greed of outsiders (especially bishops or the nobility) by articulating the principle that royal monasteries could not be donated to anyone.[2] The measure concerned well over fifty abbeys. Of course these mon-

---

[1] Josef Semmler, "Traditio und Königsschutz," *Zeitschrift der Savigny-Stiftung für Rechtsgeschichte: Kanonistische Abteilung* 45 (1959): 1–34, here 25–33; Hubertus Seibert, "Libertas und Reichsabtei," in *Die Salier und das Reich*, vol. 2, *Die Reichskirche in der Salierzeit*, ed. Stefan Weinfurter (Sigmaringen: Thorbecke, 1991), 503–69, here 505–6.

[2] MGH, *Concilia* 6.84.

asteries were obligated to serve the king in return, and thus the old Carolingian principle of mutuality lived on uninterrupted—although the balance of that mutual relationship, as will be seen, would later shift considerably.

Those Saxon women's communities noted above—their status as foundations of canonesses or as (Benedictine) nuns often difficult to assess—also now rose to special prominence.[3] Taking as examples those foundations (*Stifte*) that were under royal influence, communities like Essen, Gandersheim, or Quedlinburg, their function is easily outlined in terms of two primary concerns: first, the prayer of the community's members for their founders, their king, and the kingdom, and second, the education of and provision for the female members of the royal family and its close associates in the upper nobility. Such houses also served as both burial places and as meeting places for representative assemblies, especially on high church feast days, and were thus political centers of the empire. Here again, as was already noted for the community of the Merovingian queen Radegundis[4] in the sixth century, the interests of lordship were tightly interwoven with devotion and service to the faith, yet in a way that at the time did not necessarily entail a fundamental contradiction.[5]

Yet no account of these structural continuities should ignore the fact that across wide stretches of even the new German kingdom monastic life was in decline—for example in Bavaria, a region that had been particularly devastated by raids from Hungary, and in the regions of the upper Rhine. Efforts to reestablish life according to a monastic rule were undertaken in these regions in the first half of the tenth century, and they were often led by bishops. And bishops could in turn rely on those who, precisely because of such difficult times, were in search of religious fulfillment and who wanted to cross over the threshold, turning from the world and toward a place that could secure their salvation. That kind of place had only to be created once again.

---

[3] Michel Parisse, "Die Frauenstifte und Frauenklöster in Sachsen vom 10. bis zur Mitte des 12. Jahrhunderts," in Weinfurter, *Die Salier und das Reich*, 465–501.

[4] See chap. 1, p. 16.

[5] Gerd Althoff, "Ottonische Frauengemeinschaften im Spannungsfeld von Kloster und Welt," in *Essen und die sächsischen Frauenstifte im Frühmittelalter*, ed. Jan Gerchow and Thomas Schilp (Essen: Klartext, 2001), 29–44.

For that purpose, the upper-Lotharingian region (which belonged to the German kingdom and was bounded by the central Mosel in the north, the upper Maas in the west, and Alsace in the east)[6] proved itself especially fruitful. Here in the early years of the 930s the bishop of Toul, Gozelinus, filled the monastery of Saint-Evre in his city with pious men and placed it under the leadership of an abbot who had come from the already-reformed community of Fleury. This act had an impact on a wider circle of men seeking salvation, those who had personal contacts with Toul, among whom were many who had gained firsthand experience of an exemplary monastic life on journeys that reached Monte Cassino and the monasteries of Basil in southern Italy. Early in 934, with the help of Adalbert, the bishop of Metz, they took over the dilapidated cloister of Gorze.[7] At the same time, authentic monastic life again returned to the abbey of Saint Maximin in Trier, a community that had until that time been governed by a lay abbot, Duke Giselbert of Lotharingia. King Otto I worked immediately to turn these beginnings into a sustained monastic reform by conferring royal *libertas* on Saint Maximin and, a decade later, by solemnly confirming the consolidated properties of both Gorze and Saint Evre. From Saint Maximin the monastery of Saint Maurice in Magdeburg, noted above, was settled with monks. That community was chosen as the burial place of the Ottonians; it would soon become an archbishopric.

At the same time there had also been a wave of new women's foundations, since the monastic life of women had also been in need of renewal—and their way of life should no longer be ignored as part

[6] On the following, see Egon Boshof, "Klöster und Bischof in Lotharingien," in *Monastische Reformen im 9. und 10. Jahrhundert*, ed. Raymund Kottje and Helmut Maurer (Sigmaringen: Thorbecke, 1989), 197–245; Josef Semmler, "Das Erbe der karolingischen Klosterreform im 10. Jahrhundert," in Kottje and Maurer, *Monastische Reformen*, 22–77; Elmar Hochholzer, "Die lothringische (Gorzer) Reform," in *Die Reformverbände und Kongregationen der Benediktiner im deutschen Sprachraum*, ed. Ulrich Faust and Franz Quarthal (St. Ottilien: EOS, 1999), 45–87. In lower Lotharingia the Benedictine abbey of Brogne—founded in 914 by Gerard of Brogne—emerged as another important center of reform. See Steven Vanderputten, "Gérard de Brogne en Flandre. État de la question sur les réformes monastiques du Xᵉ siècle," *Revue du Nord* 92 (2010): 271–97.

[7] Michel Parisse and Otto Gerhard Oexle, eds., *L'abbaye de Gorze au Xᵉ siècle* (Nancy: Presses Universitaires de Nancy, 1993).

of the later story of Lotharingian reform. Bishop Gozelinus founded the women's community of Bouxières-aux-Dames near Nancy, and following the model of Fleury he established it on solid material foundations. Bishop Adalbert of Metz founded the communities of Sainte-Marie-aux-Nonnaines in Metz, Saint Goeric in Epinal, and Neumünster near Ottweiler. Existing women's communities, like the double monastery of Remiremont or St. Pierre-en-Nonnains, were reformed insofar as the strict observance of the Benedictine rule was introduced among them. Other women's communities followed.[8]

The text of the Benedictine rule had to be made known to each of these communities all over again.[9] Bishop Gozelinus obtained it from the monastery of Fleury, which also observed the customs of Benedict of Aniane. The precise observance of these norms led to a strict observance of monastic vows (personal poverty, obedience, and remaining bound to the monastery of one's profession), a renewal of liturgy, balanced asceticism, strict compliance to the rhythms of the monastic day, care for outward appearance in clothing, and above all the banishment of noble influence by means of free abbatial elections. These elements of renewed monastic life were the essential corner-stones of the Lotharingian reform movement[10] that was established across the region in communities such as Saint-Arnoul in Metz and Moyenmoutier on the eastern slopes of the Vosges and that then took root in other monasteries across wide stretches of the German realm. The establishment of this reform depended on two factors: on the one hand, the cohesion of reforming monasteries, sustained by a network

---

[8] Parisse, "Der Anteil der lothringischen Benediktinerinnen an der monastischen Bewegung des 10. und 11. Jahrhunderts," in *Religiöse Frauenbewegung und mystische Frömmigkeit im Mittelalter*, ed. Peter Dinzelbacher and Dieter R. Bauer (Cologne: Böhlau, 1988), 83–97; Hedwig Röckelein, "Frauen im Umkreis der benediktinischen Reformen des 10. bis 12. Jahrhunderts. Gorze, Cluny, Hirsau, St. Blasien und Siegburg," in *Female* vita religiosa *between Late Antiquity and the High Middle Ages: Structures, Developments and Spatial Contexts*, ed. Gert Melville and Anne Müller (Berlin: LIT, 2011), 275–327, here 279–82.

[9] Here and above all for a view of women's communities see Katrinette Bodarwé, "Eine Männerregel für Frauen. Die Adaption der Benediktsregel im 9. und 10. Jahrhundert," in Melville and Müller, *Female* vita religiosa, 235–72, here 246–51.

[10] Boshof, "Klöster und Bischof," 225–45; Hochholzer, "Die lothringische (Gorzer) Reform," 55–66.

(admittedly not exclusive) of affiliations through prayer, and, on the other, the security provided by royal and episcopal privileges— resulting in a distinct harmony with an Ottonian ecclesiastical policy that drew its monasteries into imperial service.

How difficult it could be in that day to bring all religious foundations across the land to live under the guidance of one set of norms (assuming for a moment that they were not already guided by deeply embedded local customs) is made clear from the example of circumstances in tenth-century Anglo-Saxon England. There from 950 on King Edgar sought—with the help of Archbishop Dunstan of Canterbury and his suffragan bishops Aethelward of Winchester (909–84) and Oswald of Worcester († 972)—to revive monastic life after the Viking invasions and other internal disruptions. An intense wave of new foundations resulted, and the two bishops, both of whom were in close contact with reformed monasteries on the continent (especially Fleury), were its main architects. To master so much diversity in monastic life and to lend still more strength to monastic discipline, the king called a synod in Winchester in 970. There, with the aid of learned monks from Fleury and Ghent, and with an eye to the Rule of Saint Benedict, a series of common statutes was crafted to govern everyday life in the monastery (clothing, mealtimes, silence, fasting, choir, and so on). Titled *Regularis Concordia Angliae nationis*, it was promulgated as a text that was binding on all communities. But its goal was achieved to only a very limited degree, since a leading and coordinating figure like Benedict of Aniane was notably absent.[11]

Cluny: The Establishment of Monastic Liberty

Yet the reawakening of monastic life according to the Benedictine rule and the articulation of its practice under Benedict of Aniane could have taken on quite a different and essentially more radical form. Beyond a freedom that was protected and deployed by kings, there was an unconditional freedom from any kind of external power. This earthly autonomy actually accorded with the essence of the *vita*

---

[11] Thomas Symons, "Regularis Concordia: History and Derivation," in *Tenth-Century Studies*, ed. David Parsons (London: Phillimore, 1975), 37–59, 214–17; Semmler, "Das Erbe der karolingischen Klosterreform im 10. Jahrhundert," 44–50.

religiosa in a fundamental way, because it sought a retreat from the world and a complete freedom from it for the sake of an encounter with God.

In a region almost entirely without rulers and a time of one of monastic life's worst degradations, that possibility now became a reality. In 910 there emerged a Benedictine way of life free from every kind of lordly power. And perhaps precisely for that reason—although in a way that could have never been anticipated at the outset—it developed into a self-confident monastic church within the church universal, one that inspired all of Western Christendom and presented itself as the center of Benedictine life, one that soon would far outshine even Monte Cassino, and one that over the next two centuries would ultimately build around one monastery the largest monastic congregation Christendom had ever seen: Cluny, near Mâcon in Burgundy, the "light of the world" as it was later called,[12] broke free from every boundary that had ever been set for monastic life.[13]

Cluny's liberty was born of the explicit intentions of its founder, Duke William of Aquitaine and Count of the Mâconnais.[14] As the duke emphasized in the foundation charter,[15] in what was at first quite conventional language, he established the monastery for the love of God and out of concern for both his own salvation and that of his family. But the duke then included provision for the souls of his dead king Odo and his followers, and he also emphasized that his founding act was intended to strengthen the standing and the integrity of the Catholic religion (*pro statu etiam ac integritate catholicae religionis*). In the same breath, with the establishment of an independent abbatial election in keeping with the Rule of Saint Benedict, William appointed the first abbot and confirmed that the

---

[12] Bull of Urban II from 1097, in *Bullarium sacri ordinis Cluniacensis*, ed. Pierre Symon (Lyon, 1680), 30; Joachim Wollasch, *Cluny—"Licht der Welt." Aufstieg und Niedergang der klösterlichen Gemeinschaft* (Düsseldorf and Zurich: Artemis & Winkler, 1996), 12–13.

[13] On these beginnings in the context of the monastic life of the time, see Giles Constable, "Cluny in the Monastic World of the Tenth Century," in *The Abbey of Cluny*, ed. Giles Constable (Berlin: LIT, 2010), 43–77.

[14] Wollasch, *Cluny*, 19–29.

[15] Auguste Bernard and Alexandre Bruel, *Recueil des chartes de l'abbaye de Cluny*, 6 vols. (Paris, 1876–1903; re-ed. Frankfurt am Main: Minerva, 1974); here vol. 1, no. 112, with citations following.

monastery was from that point forward to be free from the yoke of any earthly power (*cuiuslibet terrenae potestatis iugo*)—including that of his own family. At the same time he handed over his new foundation and all that pertained to it to the Roman apostles Peter and Paul. William also enjoined the pope, as the monastery's future protector and defender (*tutor et defensor*), to use his canonical and apostolic authority to excommunicate all who tried to deprive Cluny of its property. Anyone who presumed to assail the content of the charter was to fall into eternal damnation as a companion of Judas Iscariot, and God was to erase his name from the book of life—so read the stern final closing lines of the charter's penalty clause.

William was a pious man but also a powerful one; he ruled as if he were a king, and he was the undisputed overlord of almost all of southern France—a region that, unusually for his time, remained almost entirely at peace.[16] Surely no one underestimated the provisions of his charter. And yet he had thrust Cluny into a state of freedom that was without any protective authority. The papacy had been invoked but found itself—and William himself was probably not fully aware of this—in one of its greatest crises, morally and politically beaten down in its power struggles with the urban nobility in Rome.[17] Thus the papacy would in fact be able to provide no protection, at least in the near future. Moreover, the Carolingian kings were not only geographically distant from Cluny's region, a borderland between the West Frankish kingdom, the kingdom of Burgundy, and the cultural zones of Aquitaine and the north. They were also worn down from confrontations with the new and increasingly powerful Robertine dynasty, whose descendants, the Capetians, later became the lasting heirs of the West Frankish/French throne. From its beginnings, Cluny was thus in danger of falling victim to a regional power vacuum. While that circumstance could be useful to the abbey, it could also fuel the avarice of powerful secular figures nearby.

Only in retrospect does it become clear how William's foundation charter, crafted with such impressive care, nevertheless opened up so many chances for the future—and how well Cluny was able to

---

[16] Karl Ferdinand Werner, *Die Ursprünge Frankreichs bis zum Jahr 1000* (Stuttgart: Deutsche Verlags-Anstalt, 1989), 464–70.

[17] Harald Zimmermann, *Das dunkle Jahrhundert. Ein historisches Porträt* (Graz: Styria, 1971).

exploit the opportunities. Liberty without protection—when used properly—offered more opportunities for expansion than protection without liberty, since Cluny's liberty was founded on a great idea, one that stretched beyond the monastery itself and that could inspire both monks and laity. This idea found expression in the words of the foundation charter: "to strengthen the standing and the integrity of the catholic religion."

The young abbey of Cluny built itself up on these essentials, and through wise integration of both organization and spirituality it was able not only to guard against the dangers of its unprotected status but also to make the improbable a reality: its rapid rise to a monastic "world power" for the preservation of the Christian faith.[18]

To meet these challenges the abbey had capable leaders from the beginning and well into the twelfth century. Moreover, the earliest abbots, carefully chosen by their predecessors and then unanimously elected by the community, enjoyed unusually long tenures in office. They were therefore able to make the most of the long stretches of time that were strategically necessary to pursue their far-reaching aims.[19] The series of abbots was as follows: Odo (927–942), Aymardus (942–964), Maiolus (964–994), Odilo (994–1049), and Hugh I (1049–1109).

The founding abbot, Berno,[20] already had considerable leadership experience when he came to office, having been an abbot (quite out

---

[18] For a comprehensive overview of the historical development of Cluny, see Guy de Valous, *Le monachisme clunisien des origines au XVᵉ siècle*, 2 vols. (Paris: Picard, 1970); Marcel Pacaut, *L'ordre de Cluny (909–1789)* (Paris: de Boccard, 1986); Wollasch, *Cluny*; Gert Melville, "Cluny und das französische Königtum. Von 'Freiheit ohne Schutz' zu 'Schutz ohne Freiheit,'" in *Die Cluniazenser in ihrem politisch-sozialen Umfeld*, ed. Giles Constable, et al. (Münster: LIT, 1998), 405–68; Dominique Iogna-Prat, *Order and Exclusion: Cluny and Christendom Face Heresy, Judaism, and Islam, 1000–1150* (Ithaca, NY: Cornell University Press, 2002); Odon Hurel and Denyse Riche, *Cluny. De l'abbaye à l'ordre clunisien. Xᵉ–XVIIIᵉ siècle* (Paris: Armand Colin, 2010).

[19] Franz Neiske, "Charismatischer Abt oder charismatische Gemeinschaft? Die frühen Äbte Clunys," in *Charisma und religiöse Gemeinschaften im Mittelalter*, ed. Giancarlo Andenna, Mirko Breitenstein, and Gert Melville (Münster: LIT, 2005), 55–72.

[20] Semmler, "Das Erbe der karolingischen Klosterreform," 30–33, 74–77; Wollasch, *Cluny*, 30–36.

of keeping with the Benedictine norm) in other monasteries—Gigny, which he founded in Burgundy's Jura, and its subsequent affiliate Baume, later destroyed by the Normans. At the same time, however, from his earliest days in monastic life, Berno had been steeped in the worldview of Benedict of Aniane[21] and committed to reforming spirituality. After the founding of Cluny, a follower of Duke William entrusted Berno with the monastery of Déols on the Indre—in this case, revealingly, using the same words as the charter of 910—as well as the abbey of Massay in Berry. Even though Berno bequeathed Gigny and Baume to his brother in his will, here in embryo was one strand of a Cluniac strategy that, while not new, was increasingly pursued with incomparable consistency: to gather together, under the overall leadership of the abbey of Cluny, monasteries that were widely scattered across distant regions yet bound together by a common spirit—thereby not only exponentially enhancing Cluny's spiritual power but also rendering the community itself (because it was anchored in so many centers of worldly power) virtually unassailable. That Berno came from a noble family and had the best of relationships not only with the Duke of Aquitaine but also with the royal families of Provence and upper Burgundy only enhanced Cluny's strong beginnings. Successive abbots, by virtue of their own nobility, were able to maintain a similar framework of contacts to the world of the nobles and to the great worldly powers.

Under Berno's disciple and successor Odo, a mechanism developed that in turn grew stronger under Odo's successor, Abbot Aymardus, and that established itself as a key element in Cluny's preservation: at first the nearby nobility but soon more and more even those from distant regions invested considerable wealth in the abbey through their donations.[22] That it happened during a time when the "Christianization of the feudal nobility"[23] remained a key task—especially for Cluny—strongly suggests that such donations (at least of land and people) were for the time being offered quite pragmati-

---

[21] See p. 39.

[22] Johannes Fechter, *Cluny, Adel und Volk (910–1156)* (Stuttgart: Schwedtner, 1966).

[23] Theodor Schieffer, "Cluny und der Investiturstreit," in *Cluny, Beiträge zu Gestalt und Wirkung der Cluniazensischen Reform*, ed. Helmut Richter (Darmstadt: Wissenschaftliche Buchgesellschaft, 1975), 226–54, here 233.

cally for a purpose that could make an impression on even the most hardened warrior:[24] genuine fear of eternal damnation.

These kinds of gifts, soon appearing in remarkable numbers, were explicitly made *ad sepulturam*—to secure both a burial place in the consecrated ground of the cloister and the prayers that would preserve the donor's memory after death.[25] Often accompanying the donation was a promise that allowed the founder to join the monastery if death was near. If that was not possible, a clause ensured that the donor could at least be buried as a member of the community.

In the course of later abbacies, which in many respects worked to civilize the nobility, the bond between Cluny and the laity was further strengthened by the consolidation of bonds of fraternity (*fraternitas*) between the community and a founder or a founder's family, sealed again through memorial prayer. One particularly effective method at Cluny for satisfying the demands of their associates was used from the time of the abbacy of Maiolus: to lend donated land back to noble castellans in the region at a nominal rate of interest, thereby ensuring that they remained strongly invested in preserving Cluny's status. Indeed there was even a kind of pride associated with being a vassal of the abbey—a *fidelis S. Petri*—as Cluny came to enjoy increasing renown throughout Christendom.[26]

Moreover, since monastic recruits (often already given to the monastery as children) frequently came from these familiar circles of donors, the resulting interplay of mutual gifts—the exchange of material goods for spiritual—helped to develop a protective zone around Cluny. Since Cluny belonged to no one, all took care to ensure that it not fall victim to any one individual.

This mechanism required only one constant: belief in the spiritual power of Cluniac prayer and in the integrity of those who prayed as mediators of salvation. The future would reveal that in the eyes of its

---

[24] Georges Duby, *La société aux XIe et XIIe siècles dans la région mâconnaise* (1971; repr. Paris: Armand Colin, 1982), 173–201.

[25] Dietrich W. Poeck, "Laienbegräbnisse in Cluny," *Frühmittelalterliche Studien* 15 (1981): 68–179.

[26] Fechter, *Cluny, Adel und Volk*, 26; Barbara Rosenwein, *To Be the Neighbor of Saint Peter* (Ithaca, NY: Cornell University Press, 1989); Dominique Iogna-Prat, ed., *Cluny: les moines et la société au premier âge féodal* (Rennes: Presses Universitaire de Rennes, 2013).

founders, Cluny had fulfilled that expectation for centuries and that it would even deepen its spiritual foundations in unimagined ways, thereby expanding its protective mechanism to encompass the grand political stage of kings and dukes in distant lands.

Abbot Odo was able to acquire two charters whose immediate pragmatic benefit, while seemingly meager because of Cluny's place within larger structures of power, had a symbolic value that can hardly be overstated—especially since the privileges the charters contained were used as building blocks for consolidating the legal position of the abbey. The first came in 927, when Rudolf I became the first West Frankish king to confirm the terms of foundation set out by Duke William and to extend them to the royal level, thereby renouncing any rights of lordship over the abbey.[27] Then in 931, Pope John XI issued a papal bull that for the first time confirmed both the assumption that Cluny had been handed over to the prince of the apostles and its freedom from every kind of secular lordship.[28] Moreover, this bull explicitly declared Cluny's immunity from external interference—the status conferred, notably, not by the king as patron and protector, as was customary, but by the pope. Long passages of this bull took their wording from Rudolf's document; in turn many of its formulations appeared again in later royal charters. Like almost no other European monastery, Cluny was for centuries able to draw from a treasury of privileges like these, granted by the highest worldly and spiritual powers.

The most important privilege of these papal bulls, however, was the permission not only to accept into the community monks from foreign monasteries who wanted to enter Cluny in order more properly to fulfill their vows but also to take over entire monasteries for the purpose of reform: "If you consent to take on a monastery in order to improve it, and it is the will of those who have the proper authority that it be given to Cluny, then you should receive our permission to do so."[29] The right to take in foreign monks also appeared elsewhere in

[27] Bernard and Bruel, *Recueil des chartes*, no. 285; Melville, "Cluny und das französische Königtum," 413.

[28] Symon, *Bullarium*, 1–2; Barbara Rosenwein, "Cluny's Immunities in the Tenth and Eleventh Centuries. Images and Narratives," in Constable, et al., *Die Cluniazenser*, 133–63, here 135–39.

[29] Cited from Wollasch, *Cluny*, 50.

monastic privileges, but at that time the reform passage was unprecedented. The fact that the text of the charter was surely formulated by the Cluniacs themselves reveals the uncommon self-confidence of the young abbey.

But in fact Cluny could already look back on some striking successes:[30] in 928/29 the kings of Burgundy had, for the salvation of their souls, handed over their monastery Romainmôtier, an ancient abbey dating back to the early seventh century. The community was thereby reformed and elevated to a priory. In 930 Odo had assumed the office of abbot at Fleury in order to enforce a reform of discipline there as well.[31] Aurillac and Tulle are further notable examples. In 932—a year after the great papal privilege—John XI confirmed Cluny's possession of the abbey of Charlieu to the south, a community that had stood for decades under papal protection. And a short time later, Odo found himself in Italy, where he was active in (among other places) the monasteries of Rome as well as in Farfa and even Monte Cassino—even though he did not seek to affiliate any of those communities with Cluny.[32]

Abbot Odo understood the work of monastic renewal at Cluny as "the starting point of a comprehensive reform of church and world."[33] The weakening of ecclesiastical authority he had observed—driven by embarrassing abuses among even those who were supposed to represent the elite of the faith and who for that reason were expected to stand as exemplars—must in his eyes have had "fatal consequences for the fate of the whole world."[34] His concern was a reflection of Cluny's goal, articulated in its founding charter, of benefiting the "standing and the integrity of the catholic religion." From the earliest days of its growth Cluny thus took upon itself a responsibility not only for the salvation of its own monks but also for the salvation of all of Christendom, and in this apostolic ideal it found an as yet incomparably powerful driving force.

---

[30] On the following, see Wollasch, *Cluny*, 43–48.

[31] Joachim Wollasch, "Mönchtum, Königtum, Adel und Klöster im Berry während des 10. Jahrhunderts," in *Neue Forschungen über Cluny und die Cluniacenser*, ed. Gerd Tellenbach (Freiburg im Breisgau: Herder, 1959), 17–165.

[32] Wollasch, *Cluny*, 58–60.

[33] Poeck, *Cluniacensis Ecclesia*, 216.

[34] Poeck, *Cluniacensis Ecclesia*, 216.

Cluny found continual support for its initiatives in the papacy, which from the bull of John XI from 931 onward described the abbey as "forever subject" (*subjectum*) to the Holy Roman Church. The community thus enjoyed a freedom guaranteed by Rome—a *libertas Romana*, in the words of the soon-customary phrase.[35] From a privilege of Pope Benedict VII in 978, the corresponding curial formula became customary: Cluny was entrusted with the defense and expansion of the Roman church (*commissum ad defendendum et dilatandum*).[36] Cluny also sought to win the goodwill of the bishops and their cathedral chapters across different regions from the tenth century on, primarily through the establishment of confraternal ties.[37] But above all, the exemption of the abbey from the authority of the diocesan bishop of Mâcon was an especially important step toward Cluny's independent expansion. At the end of the tenth century (in 998), Pope Gregory V allowed Cluny freely to choose the bishop who was to consecrate its abbot,[38] and a few decades later Pope John XIX freed the abbey from every jurisdiction of the bishop—though that principle was difficult to enforce in practice and was in any case valid only in very restricted ways for the houses that belonged to Cluny.[39] A similarly constructed policy of protection found particularly significant expression in the era of the Peace of God movement, as especially in southern France bishops—faced with an onslaught of minor and middling nobility who had begun to assault church prop-

---

[35] On precursors, see Egon Boshof, "*Traditio Romana* und Papstschutz im 9. Jahrhundert. Untersuchungen zur vorcluniazensischen *libertas*," in *Rechtsgeschichtlich-diplomatische Studien zu frühmittelalterlichen Papsturkunden*, ed. Egon Boshof and Heinz Wolter (Cologne and Vienna: Böhlau, 1976), 1–100.

[36] Symon, *Bullarium*, 6.

[37] Joachim Wollasch, "Die mittelalterliche Lebensform der Verbrüderung," in *Memoria. Der geschichtliche Zeugniswert des liturgischen Gedenkens im Mittelalter*, ed. Karl Schmid and Joachim Wollasch (Munich: Wilhelm Fink, 1984), 215–32, here 221–22.

[38] Symon, *Bullarium*.

[39] Georg Schreiber, *Kurie und Kloster im 12. Jahrhundert*, 2 vols. (Stuttgart: Enke, 1910), 1:75–78; Gaston Letonnelier, *L'abbaye exempte de Cluny et le Saint-Siège* (Paris: Picard, 1923); Jörg Oberste, "Contra prelatos qui gravant loca et personas Ordinis. Bischöfe und Cluniazenser im Zeitalter von Krisen und Reformen (12./13. Jahrhundert)," in Constable et al., *Die Cluniazenser*, 349–92, here 353–54.

erty, merchants, and unarmed peasants—sought to establish measures that ensured peace and military protection.[40] Around 1021–1023, at the request of the abbot of Cluny as well as the French King Rudolf, Pope Benedict VIII drafted a widely circulated bull in which he called nineteen archbishops and bishops from across all of southern France, listed by name, and seven noble laymen and charged them explicitly with the protection of Cluny and its communities scattered across Burgundy, Aquitaine, and Provence.[41]

The "Cluniac Church": A Congregation of Monasteries

After some 180 years, a broad expansion of the congregation of Cluniac monasteries had made clear the success of the central idea that Cluny was a source of overflowing renewal and strength for all of Christendom. If the first list of the monasteries belonging to its congregation, drawn up by Pope Gregory V in 998, was already impressive (there were thirty-eight),[42] by the year 1109 Abbot Hugh I could happily say that God had spread the influence of Cluniac monks "in their region, but also in Italy, in Lotharingia, in England, in Normandy, in Francia, in Aquitaine, in Gascony, in Provence, and in Spain."[43]

Up to this high point of consolidation under Hugh I, "the Great," Cluny had successfully drawn the monasteries handed over to it together with those it had founded into a transregional alliance of abbeys and priories, which had further organized themselves into affiliations of priories. The groundwork, as noted above, had surely been laid already by the time of Berno, and from there a new practice was quickly developed and preserved, in its essentials, for long afterward: to establish ties of community with those monasteries that were to be reformed by means of a mutual prayer confraternity, including mutual intercession for the dead. Under Abbot Odilo (994–1049), the technicalities of such arrangements were soon refined, perfected,

---

[40] Adriaan H. Bredero, *Christenheit und Christentum im Mittelalter* (Stuttgart: Franz Steiner, 1998), 90–108.

[41] Symon, *Bullarium*, 6–7.

[42] Symon, *Bullarium*, 10–11.

[43] *Imprecatio beati Hugonis abbatis*, ed. M. Marrier and A. Duchesne (Paris, 1614), col. 495. On the spread of the congregation under Hugh I, see Armin Kohnle, *Abt Hugo von Cluny (1049–1109)* (Sigmaringen: Thorbecke, 1993), 135–240.

and extended to the monasteries that had institutional ties to Cluny. The Cluniacs thereby made use of an already well-known means of communication, while deploying it so broadly that its very nature began to change. Cluny became the center—as far as we can reconstruct the matter today—of the production of what were known as "books of the dead."[44] In these were entered, alongside the names of other benefactors from among the laity and clergy (including popes, emperors, and kings), primarily the names of deceased Cluniac brothers—around 48,000 monks from the tenth through the twelfth centuries.[45] On the one hand, this practice from day to day created what became an almost impossible obligation for intercessory prayer. On the other hand, it bound the congregation together in a powerful way, as messengers divided the lists of names among Cluniac monasteries wherever they existed, and in turn these communities, which kept their own books of the dead, sent back to Cluny the names of their own dead. The practice thus nurtured a community not only of those who prayed among the living but also of those among the dead for whom the monks prayed—a community, in other words, that seemed to transcend time and place.

By the middle of the twelfth century, the northernmost monastery of the Cluniac congregation (Paisley) was in Scotland near Glasgow, the southernmost (Polirone) in Italy, and the southwesternmost (Pombeiro) in Portugal. Across such a broadly dispersed region could be found monasteries of quite different status: grand and absolutely confident abbeys with a long prehistory, such as Saint-Martial in Limoges or Moissac in southwestern France, for example; grand priories that had other priories under them (some at quite a distance), such as La Charité-sur-Loire on the Loire or Saint-Martin-des-Champs (today in Paris), with important daughter houses in England (e.g., Lewes in East Sussex); and finally small cells, even the smallest, often little more than administrative posts on agricultural estates, staffed with two or three monks.[46] Altogether around seven hundred Cluniac communities existed by the first half of the twelfth century.

---

[44] Joachim Wollasch, "Totengedenken im Reformmönchtum," in *Monastische Reformen*, ed. Kottje and Maurer, 147–66, here 161–65.

[45] Wollasch, *Cluny*, 130.

[46] On the inner structure of the Cluniac congregation, see Dominique Iogna-Prat, "Cluny comme 'système ecclesial,'" in Constable et al., *Die Cluniazenser*, 13–92; Poeck, *Cluniacensis Ecclesia*.

For all of the effort toward a certain kind of planned procedure, this diversity was also the result of contingent events centered on individual foundations, reforms, or takeovers and was thus in no way the result of anything like a linear process. Especially under Abbot Odilo, as the expansion of Cluny's congregation crossed into northern France and after Cluny in 1027 again received a royal confirmation charter[47] for the first time in seventy-two years (not least because of the close relationship of the abbot with King Robert II), resistance suddenly broke out. It came from the ranks of the French bishops and directed itself—soon finding a satirical spokesman in bishop Adalbert of Laon—against the monastic power of Odilo, now portrayed as a king who had supposedly turned the divinely ordained order upside down.[48]

But attacks like these were merely a reflection of Cluny's attraction. It was under Odilo, in fact, that the number of Cluny's communities doubled, in part because now even the least of the nobility might feel motivated to found a modest monastery and then hand it over to Cluny. Furthermore, Cluny was able to integrate the community of Moissac, noted above, with a network of daughter houses. The foothold in southern France opened up an entirely new dimension to the possibilities of expansion. Under Hugh I, with the support of the papacy as well as an array of regional powers both secular and ecclesiastical, Cluny expanded beyond the boundaries of France.

A certain solidarity began thereby gradually to take hold, one that by the time of the abbacy of Hugh I took the form of a legally established bond between the abbey of Cluny as head (*caput*) and its houses as corresponding members (*membra*). The new name for the organization, and certainly a proud one, was *Cluniacensis ecclesia*, the "Cluniac church."[49] With respect to property law it was subject to the administrative authority (*dispositio*) of the abbot of Cluny, as was expressly emphasized in an 1109 charter of Pope Paschal II.[50] In the background stood the idea of a kind of enormous but "trans-local" community,[51] so

---

[47] Melville, "Cluny und das französische Königtum," 416.

[48] Wollasch, *Cluny*, 133–37.

[49] See Iogna-Prat, *Order and Exclusion*.

[50] Symon, *Bullarium*, 36–37, here 36.

[51] Stefan Weinfurter, "Norbert von Xanten und die Entstehung des Prämonstratenserordens," in *Barbarossa und die Prämonstratenser* (Göppingen: Gesellschaft für staufische Geschichte, 1989), 67–100, here 74.

that in theory every monk newly accepted into a Cluniac priory made his profession at Cluny, the center, alone. This construction conformed perfectly to what had been known from the Rule and the life of Saint Benedict. His rule, too, presumed the community of a single abbey, yet Benedict had also referred allegorically to the whole world, "bathed in a single ray of sunlight," as it had appeared to him one day in a vision.

An achievement like this had of course not come about without setbacks or problems. On many occasions powerful houses (for example, the pilgrimage monastery of Saint Gilles in Provence and the monastery of Saint Cyprian in Poitiers) turned against the prospect of joining Cluny, choosing instead to preserve their old privileges and their particular customs or to cultivate the strongest of ties with local powers and their particular interests.[52] Nor should it be overlooked that the very structure of the congregation—divided between individual abbeys, on the one hand, and priories directly subject to Cluny, on the other—was in many respects anything but unified. An 1107 charter of Pope Paschal II, for example, differentiated precisely between a right to rule (*regimen*), on the one hand, which the abbot of Cluny had over its priories and which gave him the right to install and depose priors at his will, and on the other hand, Cluny's right of arrangement (*ordinatio*) with respect to its abbeys, which needed only to have Cluny confirm their independently elected abbots.[53]

The size that the congregation ultimately reached, of course, showed the power of the Cluniac model of Benedictine life. But that same size also concealed considerable points of weakness. These were notably recognizable, for example, in the fact that while the abbot of Cluny had the personal right to visitation in all of his houses, which in this respect were exempt from the power and control of the local bishop, in reality, because of the increasing distance of those houses over the course of the eleventh century, the abbot could no longer exercise that right comprehensively, even though supervision certainly remained absolutely necessary. The larger the congregation became, the more difficult it was for Cluny to use its central authority to organize its affairs.[54]

[52] Poeck, *Cluniacensis Ecclesia*, 84–128.

[53] Symon, *Bullarium*, 34–35.

[54] Giles Constable, "Cluniac Administration and Administrators in the Twelfth Century," in Constable, *The Abbey of Cluny*, 131–41.

Yet the task of caring for all of Christendom was one to be carried out not only through the organization of now ubiquitous monastic settlements, and not even by means of a monastic congregation the likes of which had never before been seen. There was also a need to present and spread those forms of community that, by virtue of their spiritual power, made the impact of their care for Christendom credible and that could lead other monastic communities to emulate the Cluniac way of life. The task was not limited institutionally to the Cluniac congregation. It was in fact open to all kinds of religious establishments. Cluny thus became the greatest exporter, to that point, of a monastic model.

Ordo Cluniacensis

The texts of religious rules had always provided only a framework for monastic life. In practice, daily routines had continually produced customs that either became normative for the particular circumstances of a given convent or addressed in detail matters not clearly established through the rule. These customs could be handed down from generation to generation and for the most part changed through practice, or they were written down—designated as *consuetudines*—in order to make available a handy set of reference points for orientation. Benedict of Aniane, as was noted, had already produced one great work of *consuetudines* in order to achieve his goal of sustaining proper order in the houses he sought to reform. For the Cluniacs, who themselves made use of Benedict of Aniane's provisions, such a structured extension of the norms of their rule was not unfamiliar. Their customs of liturgical and ritual practice, of prayer, of interacting with one another in obedience and discipline, of ascesis and work, and the effort to overcome the material and the bodily aspects of their existence—all became an expression of their very specific monastic profile. They coalesced over time into a "Cluniac way of life," an *Ordo cluniacensis*, one that not only was standard (albeit with many variations, given the nature of *consuetudines*) for their own congregation, the *Cluniacensis ecclesia* itself, but also, in principle, stood ready as a model for all monastic communities.

The writing down of customs[55] began in Cluny around 990 under Abbot Maiolus with the text of the later so-called *Consuetudines*

---

[55] Isabelle Cochelin, "Évolution des coutumiers monastiques dessinée à partir de l'étude de Bernard," in *From Dead of Night to End of Day: The Medieval*

antiquiores.[56] They concerned liturgical practice alone. A subsequent
work incorporated a much broader range of material, including even
policies and procedures for technical matters of administration. This
was the so-called *Liber tramitis* (the *Book of the Way*),[57] whose textual
foundations had been set down in the 1020s during the abbacy of
Odilo with reference to the collection noted above and which was
then revised, after 1033 and once again between 1050 and 1060, at
the time of Abbot Hugh. At the end of the 1020s, John (a disciple of
Romuald, the founder of the Camaldolese[58] and reforming supporter
of the abbot of Farfa) brought the first version of this collection to
the Italian abbey of Farfa, where it came to serve as a new normative
guide. John had first made a synoptic redaction of two versions of
the text that were available at Cluny, where he had also familiarized
himself with the customs by reading them with his own eyes.[59]

Presumably in the 1070s, Bernard, a monk in Cluny, completed a
new copy of the Cluniac customs.[60] In the midst of a controversy over
proper forms of ritual that was especially unsettling to the novices,
Abbot Hugh I charged Bernard to record the procedures as they had
come to be actually practiced. He thus wanted to capture the "true"

Customs of Cluny (hereafter *Customs*), ed. Susan Boynton and Isabelle Cochelin
(Turnhout: Brepols, 2005), 29–66; Gert Melville, "Action, Text, and Validity: On
Re-examining Cluny's *Consuetudines* and Statutes," in Boynton and Cochelin,
Customs, 67–83.

[56] *Consuetudines Cluniacensium antiquiores cum redactionibus derivatis*, ed.
Kassius Hallinger, CCM 7.2 (Siegburg: Schmitt, 1983).

[57] *Liber tramitis aevi Odilonis abbatis*, ed. Peter Dinter, CCM 10 (Siegburg:
Schmitt, 1980); prologue newly edited in Boynton and Cochelin, *Customs*,
319–27.

[58] See p. 92.

[59] Susan Boynton, "Uses of the 'Liber Tramitis' at the Abbey of Farfa," in
Studies in Medieval Chant and Liturgy in Honor of David Hiley, ed. Terence
Bailey and Láslo Dobszay (Ottawa: Institute for Musicology, 2007), 87–104.

[60] Bernhard, "Ordo Cluniacensis," in M. Herrgott, ed., *Vetus disciplina monastica* (Paris, 1726), 133–364; Joachim Wollasch, "Zur Verschriftlichung der
klösterlichen Lebensgewohnheiten unter Abt Hugo von Cluny," *Frühmittelalterliche Studien* 27 (1993): 317–49, here 339–40; Anselme Davril, "Coutumiers
directifs et coutumiers descriptifs d'Ulrich à Bernard de Cluny," in Boynton and
Cochelin, *Customs*, 23–28. On the contested date of Bernard's work (as well
as that of Ulrich following), see Isabelle Cochelin, "Évolution des coutumiers
monastiques," in Boynton and Cochelin, *Customs*, 52–62.

normative circumstance "in a single volume" and thereby to leave behind for the next generation of monks knowledge of the Cluniac way of life. To that end he made use—as he emphasized—of older records, reports of knowledgeable eyewitnesses, and earlier decrees of the abbots of Cluny, as well as his own knowledge of practice and careful observations.

A little later, perhaps shortly after 1079, Ulrich, another monk of Cluny, began to write down its customs. He did so at the request of William, reforming abbot of the community of Hirsau in the Black Forest, who wanted (as will be discussed below) to introduce them to his monastery.[61] Ulrich too made use of written records, asked his fellow monks for their observations, and drew exhaustively from his own experience. What he provided was not enough, however, and Hirsau thus later sent its own monks to Cluny to be properly trained.

These writings served as a condensation, so to speak, of the *Ordo cluniacensis*, a kind of ready-made form that could now be distributed across broader regions. But at least as important as the written text itself were the people involved, those who learned from Cluny and then passed on or further developed its customs themselves. To note only one example: William, son of the Count of Volpiano (today in Piedmont), was a monk for thirteen years under Abbot Maiolus and then in 990 became abbot of Saint-Bénigne in Dijon, in order to reform it along Cluniac lines.[62] He was successful, and after his community became a widely influential center of monastic spirituality and education, around the year 1000 he was called to renew the foundation of the abbey of Fécamp in Normandy. This region was an entirely new area of cultivation for monastic life. The Normans had at first left only wasteland behind them. But then, as new lords of the

[61] *Udalrici Consuetudines Cluniacenses*, PL 149:635–778. Dedicatory letter and prologue ed. after MS Paris, Bibl. Nationale de France, lat. 18353 (II), fol. 1ʳ–3ʳ, in Boynton and Cochelin, *Customs*, 329–47; Burkhardt Tutsch, *Studien zur Rezeptionsgeschichte der Consuetudines Ulrichs von Cluny* (Münster: LIT, 1998). Isabelle Cochelin, "Customaries as Inspirational Sources. Appendix: The Relation between the Last Cluniac Customaries, Udal and Bern," in *Consuetudines et regulae: Sources for Monastic Life in the Middle Ages and the Early Modern Period*, ed. Carolyn M. Malone and Clark Maines (Turnhout: Brepols, 2014), 27–72.

[62] On the following, see Neithard Bulst, *Untersuchungen zu den Klosterreformen Wilhelms von Dijon, 962–1031* (Bonn: Röhrscheid, 1973).

duchy now named after them and as baptized Christians, they quickly recognized the spiritual as well as the material, political, and military worth of monasteries and now supported them with considerable energy. Within a few generations, there had emerged across the duchy a flowering landscape of monasteries influenced by the Cluniac spirit, with outstanding theology and literature.[63] Notable alongside Fécamp, for example, were Bec, Caen, Évreux, and Jumièges.

After 1066, through the military and political success of Duke William in conquering England, Normandy in turn became the launching point for the expansion of Cluniac-inspired Benedictine monasticism into England. There it was possible to bring about a fundamental renewal of monastic life, since with the exception of the Anglo-Saxon abbeys of Winchester and Glastonbury,[64] the remaining monasteries of England, a mere forty in number, faced desolate circumstances. In particular, they no longer served the key interest of political unification, since their loyalty to their new overlord was suspect. The leader of the effort both to coordinate reform (a reform that the Normans now strictly enforced) and to found new monasteries was the highly learned Lanfranc (1010–1089), who had come originally from Pavia and who had been prior of the monasteries of Bec and of Saint-Étienne in Caen.[65] William the Conqueror, now as king of England, had elevated Lanfranc to archbishop of Canterbury. Among his many accomplishments, he crafted from a range of surviving sources a normative text entitled the *Decreta Lanfranci*. It was intended as a guide for his monks in the cathedral chapter of Canterbury, but in its strictness it came to serve as a model for all the monasteries of England.[66] In the same years the Normans also promoted the cultivation of a comparable Benedictine landscape in the lands they had conquered across southern Italy.[67]

---

[63] Geneviève Nortier, *Les bibliothèques médiévales des abbayes bénédictines de Normandie* (Paris: P. Lethielleux, 1971).

[64] Stephan Albrecht, *Die Inszenierung der Vergangenheit im Mittelalter* (Munich and Berlin: Deutscher Kunstverlag, 2003), 20–42.

[65] Herbert Edward John Cowdrey, *Lanfranc: Scholar, Monk, and Archbishop* (Oxford: Oxford University Press, 2003).

[66] "Decreta Lanfranci," ed. David Knowles et al., in *Corpus Consuetudinum Monasticarum*, vol. 3 (Siegburg: Schmitt, 1967).

[67] Hubert Houben, *Die Abtei Venosa und das Mönchtum im normannisch-staufischen Süditalien* (Tübingen: Niemeyer, 1995).

In 1003 William of Volpiano founded a monastery of his own in Piedmont, Fruttuaria, for which he received (through privileges of King Arduin of Ivrea and Pope John XVIII) the right both freely to elect an abbot and to choose an advocate, as well as the right to choose the consecrating bishop. The monastery was handed over to the papacy and was thereby exempt from the supervising authority of the local bishop. It was soon to be a community of very broad influence.[68]

In all three of the abbeys noted here, a way of life was introduced that was built on the foundations of the customs of Cluny. They thereby not only came to enjoy great renown and to carry the banner of Cluny's aims and influence but also to spread their way of life still further by passing it along to other monasteries. For many years between 1012 and 1031, for example, with great influence on the landscape of monasteries in the German Empire, William also served as leader of the abbey of Gorze in Metz. The customs of Fruttuaria came to influence the reform network of the communities of Siegburg and Saint Blaise.[69]

These monasteries thus followed the *Ordo cluniacensis* in a way that was mediated by and adapted to their circumstances, but they were not part of the *Cluniacensis ecclesia*. The Cluniac idea of a life consecrated to God was larger than its institutional concentration in a legally defined alliance of monasteries. Yet that concentration itself was proof of the power of the ideal.

The breadth of the ideal also encompassed the lives of women consecrated to God. As is recorded in his *Vita*,[70] Abbot Hugh felt obligated to guide Cluny as the ship of Peter (the usual metaphor for the whole church), just as Noah had steered the ark through the flooded world—and in that spirit he believed that God had called him to make room for both sexes. Thus in 1055, for the first time in

---

[68] Mariano Dell'Omo, "L'abbazia medievale di Fruttuaria e i centri della Riforma fruttuariense," *Monastica* 5 (1985): 185–201.

[69] Monica Sinderhauf, "Die Reform von St. Blasien," in *Die Reformverbände und Kongregationen der Benediktiner im deutschen Sprachraum*, ed. Ulrich Faust and Franz Quarthal (St. Ottilien: EOS, 1999), 125–40; Stefan Weinfurter, "St. Blasien—seine Frühzeit und das Aufblühen in der jungcluniazensischen Klosterreform," in *Macht des Wortes*, ed. Holger Kempkens et al. (Regensburg: Schnell & Steiner, 2009), 1:195–202.

[70] Wollasch, *Cluny*, 152; Iogna-Prat, "Cluny comme 'système ecclesial,'" 13–92, here 37–38.

Cluny's history, a women's monastery was founded, established as a priory in Marcigny, in Semur, southwest of Cluny, with which the women enjoyed community of property.[71] Under the leadership of a prioress, with the spiritual and administrative assistance of two priors, ninety-nine noble women—with Mary as the hundredth—were to live in strict enclosure, their lives filled with prayer and contemplation. Along with Mary and Martin of Tours, the patronage of the community was held by Saint Agnes, oldest of the martyrs and patroness of Rome—thereby constructing a meaningful parallel to Cluny's patronage under Peter and Paul as Roman princes of the apostles.

Many members of the female branches of Hugh's family, the counts of Semur, entered Marcigny, including his mother, three sisters, and two nieces. From the beginning their presence nurtured the community's powerful appeal and also established it on a firm financial foundation. As further noble women from distant regions also became members of the community, handing over the property they held in their homelands, already before the end of the eleventh century sub-priories had emerged that were subject to Marcigny and that spread from France to modern Belgium, Castille, England, and Italy.[72] Because of the institutional unity of Marcigny and the abbey of Cluny, there was no need to make a distinct confederation of these women's monasteries.

Church for the World

Cluny impressed contemporaries beyond all measure. Pope Urban II, himself once prior of the abbey, described the Cluniacs in 1097 in the words of Matthew 5:14 spoken to the apostles, as the "light of the world," a place that, he emphasized, lit up the earth like a second sun. Urban spoke here not of cloistered retreat from the world but rather of something typically Cluniac and tied back to the community of the first apostles in Jerusalem: the ideal of reaching out into the world, in order to make it "bright and new."[73]

---

[71] Else Marie Wischermann, *Marcigny-Sur-Loire* (Munich: Wilhelm Fink, 1986).

[72] Röckelein, "Frauen im Umkreis," 275–327, here 287–91. On one exemplary region, see Giancarlo Andenna, *"Sanctimoniales Cluniacenses"*: *Studi sui monasteri femminili di Cluny e sulla loro legislazione in Lombardia (XI–XV secolo)* (Münster: LIT, 2005).

[73] Wollasch, *Cluny*, 13.

And yet Cluny could only shine out into the world because it lived the ideal that inspired it inwardly, in the cloister of contemplative separation from the world. And in order to render God's greatness and magnificence visible to those on earth, Cluny praised these as well in all magnificence, in its celebration of the Eucharist,[74] in the liturgy, in the common prayer life of the community, and in the love of neighbor. This daily spiritual action in turn slowly took on—as did everything in Cluny, in principle—enormous dimensions, forcing certain aspects of monastic life (manual labor, for example) to retreat into the background.[75]

The historian Rudolf Glaber (d. 1047), who dedicated his work to Abbot Odilo, outlined Cluny's spiritual life by way of a measure that was in his day especially impressive: the ability to drive away demons: "Know that of all monasteries in the Latin world Cluny's power to free souls from the power of demons is the strongest. The frequency of the performance of the Mass is so powerful there that hardly a day goes by on which their sacred business does not tear souls away from the power of evil spirits. . . . It was in fact the custom of that monastery, as we ourselves have seen, by virtue of the great number of (priest-) monks, to celebrate Mass continuously, from the first light of day all the way through breakfast."[76]

Cluny also impressed Peter Damian (to note another example), who stayed at Cluny as a papal legate in 1062. Although given to a very different understanding of monastic life, Peter still deeply admired "the order of the holy way of life" that was inspired by the "teaching authority of the Holy Spirit" (*sancti Spiritus magisterium*) as it was found at Cluny. In fact, he said that the duration of the spiritual work of the community and its liturgy was so long that hardly half an hour a day remained as time for the brothers for an ordinary conversation. And even this was a good thing, because such long and disciplined exercise shored up the frailty of the lax and weak

---

[74] Angenendt, *Charisma und Eucharistie.*

[75] With critical observations, see Jean Leclercq, "Zur Geschichte des Lebens in Cluny," in *Cluny,* ed. Richter, 254–318.

[76] Rodulfus Glaber, *Historiarum libri quinque* V.13, in *Rodulfi Glabri Historiarum libri quinque*; Rodulfus Glaber, *The Five Books of the Histories,* ed. Neithard Bulst, trans. John France and Paul Reynolds (Oxford: Clarendon Press, 1993), 234–36; cited from Wollasch, *Cluny,* 121.

brothers and so deprived them of the occasion for lapses that they could hardly have sinned even if they wanted to. Yet care was taken to guard against the instability of the frail, Damian noted, as long as the demands of the community's continuously practiced way of life laid claim to every hour of the day and night.[77] Under Abbot Hugh I, in theory every monk in the Cluniac church had to pray 215 psalms daily, with the greatest of discipline, even though the Rule of Saint Benedict prescribed only thirty-seven.

At the many altars of the churches, passed by long processions of singing and praying monks, the priests who celebrated the Masses constantly changed. In each monastery the monks tirelessly remembered their own dead as well as their deceased benefactors and allies, working through the long lists noted above, calendar entry by calendar entry. Moreover, Abbot Odilo then added a feast for all of the deceased souls in the world on November 2, a feast still celebrated today. The greatness of the Christian faith could also be shown through compassion for the needy, however, and God could thereby also be praised. Hundreds, at times thousands, of the poor were cared for daily by the abbey of Cluny. One trustworthy source reveals that on one occasion some 250 sides of bacon were provided for those who were starving.[78] All was worship: liturgy, psalmody, and love of neighbor.

Under Hugh I the number of monks at the abbey of Cluny had climbed to 300. To praise God in such numbers required space, and thus the building of a new church began in 1088. It was to be the third, a monumental church some 613 feet long with a 252-foot transept, the largest sacred building in all of Western Christendom.[79] It was later seen as a wonder of the world, and at the same time it meant much more: it was the tangible symbol of the Temple of the Lord,

---

[77] Petrus Damiani, *Epistola 5* (to the Cluniacs), PL 144:378–86; Philibert Schmitz, "La liturgie de Cluny," in *Spiritualità Cluniacense, 12–15 ottobre 1958* (Todi: Presso l'Accademia tudertina, 1960), 85–99. In English, see the translations of Owen J. Blum and Irven M. Resnick: Peter Damian, *Letters*, 7 vols. (Washington, DC: The Catholic University of America Press, 1989–2005).

[78] Wollasch, *Cluny*, 118.

[79] Kenneth John Conant, *Cluny. Les églises et la maison du chef d'ordre* (Cambridge: Medieval Academy of America, 1968).

whose precisely cut stones, in keeping with the allegory of the first letter of Peter, represented monastic community itself.[80]

Already around the year 1000 the Cluniacs had begun to embrace with special intensity the cult of Mary in the form of elaborately staged festivals, the composition of prayers, and so on. In Mary the monks saw a mirror of their own virginity, and they also believed themselves to draw from its heavenly purity their own exceptional strength, one that could elevate them to a special status between humans and angels. It was a model possessed of enormous political power. It offered a transcendent justification for the claim that Christendom should be led by those who were the most pure.[81] To bear spiritual responsibility for making the world "bright and new" created a consciousness that the true leadership of the church was to be found in monastic life, with monks as a Christian elite possessed of a virtuosity of faith—a consciousness that was not always easy to reconcile with the hierarchical models of the secular clergy and the institutional church.[82]

Despite such a claim to apostolic authority, or perhaps precisely because of it, the powerful of the world flocked to Cluny: well into the twelfth century, a long series of popes supported the Cluniacs.[83] At the Lateran Synod of 1080, Gregory VII dramatically acknowledged that thanks to God's mercy the monks of Cluny had surpassed all in their service to God and their spiritual zeal.[84] In 1095 Pope Urban II had come personally to dedicate the altar of the new church while it was still under construction.[85] The abbots of Cluny enjoyed a similar affinity with the German kings and emperors, although the abbey itself lay beyond their borders.

[80] Gilo, "Vita sancti Hugonis abbatis," in *Two Studies in Cluniac History (1049–1126)*, ed. Herbert Edward John Cowdrey, *Studi Gregoriani* 11 (1972): 90.

[81] Dominique Iogna-Prat, "Politische Aspekte der Marienverehrung in Cluny um das Jahr 1000," in *Maria in der Welt*, ed. Claudia Opitz et al. (Zürich: Chronos, 1993), 243–51.

[82] On Cluny's ecclesiology, see Iogna-Prat, *Order and Exclusion*, 99–261.

[83] Neiske, "Charismatischer Abt," 55–72.

[84] On the political context of this eulogy, see Armin Kohnle, *Abt Hugo von Cluny*, 109.

[85] Wollasch, *Cluny*, 188–90.

The ruined church of Cluny—even in its side towers—still bears witness to the former majesty of the monastic life that was active there.

These secular rulers, by virtue of their universal claims to spiritual power and governance, ranked alongside the popes,[86] and the head of the Cluniacs, by virtue of his religious status, was on equal footing with them. From the time of Otto I, their close relationship remained unbroken.[87] It was shaped by counsel, spiritual encouragement, intercession, and gifts, as well as other aspects: the probable confraternal bond with Emperor Henry II (d. 1024), or in any case his sending an imperial *globus cruciger*, a scepter and crown to the abbey, the acceptance of Henry III (d. 1056) into the abbey's rounds of liturgical memory, and Hugh I's status as godparent of Henry IV. Hugh then proved himself to be the king's accessible and intercessory ally through all the dangers of the Investiture struggle, and Hugh's sovereignty also allowed him both to stay in contact with Henry and to have liturgical prayers said for the emperor at Cluny long after he had been excommunicated by the pope.

In the thick of events, in 1077, as Abbot Hugh sat between Henry IV and Gregory VII, as it were,[88] the symbolism of that moment revealed a fundamental shift. The changes of the era of the Investiture struggle meant that Cluny's time would soon be over.[89] As has been noted, Cluny understood itself as *ecclesia*, as a monastic church that encompassed all of Christendom and that aimed to make all the world "bright and new." The division of that world into clergy and laity robbed Cluny of the foundation of its impact. And within a Roman church that had now begun slowly to transform itself into an institution claiming to be the only mediator of salvation, there could be no other "light of the world" with claims to its own apostolic validity.

Urban II's dictum of 1097 was to be one of the last great conferrals of honor before Cluny's decline. It is true that soon afterward, in 1119, yet another pope, Gelasius II, sought out Cluny in order to die there and that his successor Calixtus II was elected there.[90] But deeply

---

[86] Schieffer, "Cluny und der Investiturstreit," 235–37.

[87] Sébastien Barret, "Cluny et les Ottoniens," in *Ottone III e Romualdo di Ravenna* (Negarine di S. Pietro in Cariano [Verona]: Il segno dei Gabrielli Ed., 2003), 179–213.

[88] Kohnle, *Abt Hugo von Cluny*, 110–15.

[89] Herbert Edward John Cowdrey, *The Cluniacs and the Gregorian Reform* (Oxford: Clarendon Press, 1970); Schieffer, "Cluny und der Investiturstreit," 250–53.

[90] Wollasch, *Cluny*, 196.

rooted structures change only slowly. At times the pace quickens, at times it slows—as was revealed at Cluny in dramatic fashion. An abbatial schism erupted there in 1122 when Abbot Pons, successor of Hugh I, was deposed and replaced by the aged Hugh II, who died after only three months.[91] Peter, known as the Venerable (*Venerabilis*), followed him (1122–1156). Pons contested the affair but was in the end taken prisoner by the papacy in 1126. Peter proved to be yet another distinguished abbot.[92] Above all he worked to reform Cluny, and not without success, as he rearranged its financial and administrative affairs,[93] wrote a book of miracles for the spiritual instruction of his monks,[94] and produced a comprehensive collection of statutes.[95]

Moreover, Peter too embraced a certain sense of responsibility for all of Christendom. He was impressed by the success of the First Crusade, and he had the Koran translated with the aim of bringing the "Sect of Mohammed" back into the Christian fold, thereby breaking with a centuries-old tradition of ignorance and prejudice.[96] Finally, he also possessed the pastoral magnanimity and the confidence—or perhaps simply the breadth of vision—in 1141 to give refuge at Cluny to a theologian and philosopher whom the church had recently condemned as a heretic: Peter Abelard, who in hindsight came to be seen as the most progressive thinker of his era.[97] When Peter the Venerable died in 1156, Cluny found no successor of his caliber.

[91] Adriaan Bredero, "A propos de l'autorité de Pons de Melgueil et de Pierre le Vénérable dans l'ordre de Cluny," in Adriaan Bredero, *Cluny et Cîteaux au douzième siècle* (Amsterdam/Maarsen: APA - Holland University Press, 1985), 95–113; Joachim Wollasch, "Das Schisma des Abtes Pontius von Cluny," *Francia* 23 (1996): 31–52.

[92] Giles Constable and James Kritzeck, eds., *Petrus Venerabilis, 1156–1956* (Rome: Pontificum Institutum S. Anselmi, 1956); Jean-Pierre Torrell, *Pierre le Vénérable et sa vision du monde* (Leuven: Spicilegium Sacrum Lovaniense, 1986).

[93] Constable, "Cluniac Administration."

[94] *Petri Cluniacensis abbatis de miraculis libri duo*, ed. Denise Bouthillier, CCCM 83 (Turnhout: Brepols, 1988).

[95] "The Statutes of Peter the Venerable," ed. Giles Constable, in *Consuetudines Benedictinae Variae*, CCM 6 (Siegburg: Schmitt, 1975), 19–106; Melville, "Action, Text, and Validity," 67–83.

[96] Iogna-Prat, *Order and Exclusion*, 323–57.

[97] In this regard it should not be forgotten that Abelard himself wrote a rule for Heloise and her Paraclete. See Peter von Moos, "Abaelard, Heloise und ihr

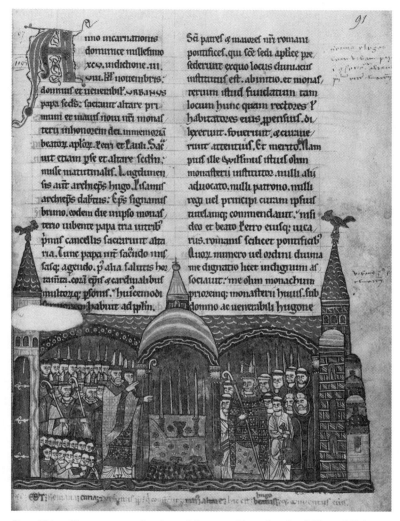

Pope Urban II consecrates the altar of the new abbey church of Cluny. Miniature from the twelfth century.

Paraklet. Ein Kloster nach Maß, zugleich eine Streitschrift gegen die ewige Wiederkehr hermeneutischer Naivität," in Peter von Moos, *Abaelard und Heloise. Gesammelte Studien zum Mittelalter*, ed. Gert Melville (Münster: LIT, 2005), 1:233–301.

Never before, and never after, was the monastic way of life so free and independent as in the great age of Cluny, when it needed only its own power to work for the benefit of all Christendom. But that time now came to an end. Monastic life had been able to become "Cluny" because, on the one hand, it was independent of the powers of the world (even as it understood how to integrate those powers into its own purposes), and on the other hand, because it communicated by every possible means that it had thereby won the power to serve exclusively the glory and the honor of the highest Lord of Christendom, wholly undisturbed by anyone in this world. Its monks served God alone.

Monastic Life in Service of King and Nobility, Pope and Bishop

The German kingdom did not provide fertile ground for Cluny's expansion. Cluniac monasteries were found only in lower and upper Lotharingia, in Alsace, and in the former kingdom of Burgundy, which from 1033 had been ruled through a personal union with the German king.[98] Cluny's settlements were thus in most cases found in regions that were distant from any royal power. The special agreement that the abbots of Cluny had long cultivated with the German kings (all of whom, from Otto I in the tenth century to Lothar III in the twelfth, had also been emperors) reflected Cluny's place in the universal order of salvation. On the institutional level of monastic settlements, Cluny's freedom was not to be confused with the freedom of the imperial monastery described above—neither with respect to the relationship with the king himself nor with respect to the ties inherent within that relationship to the imperial bishops, who themselves consistently sought to expand their power as ecclesiastical princes with the help of additional monasteries inherited through royal ties.[99] In

---

[98] Armin Kohnle, "Cluniazenserklöster und ihre Stifter in Deutschland, der Schweiz und im Elsaß," in Constable et al., *Die Cluniazenser*, 469–84; Florian Lamke, *Cluniazenser am Oberrhein* (Munich: Alber, 2009); Steven Vanderputten, *Reform, Conflict, and the Shaping of Corporate Identities: Collected Studies on Benedictine Monasticism in Medieval Flanders, c. 1050–c. 1150* (Berlin: LIT, 2013).

[99] On the following discussion of imperial monasteries, see Seibert, "Libertas und Reichsabtei," 503–69.

Abbot Hugh I of Cluny in Canossa, with Emperor Henry IV before him and Mathilda of Canossa to the right. Manuscript illumination, before 1144.

that era, the giving of imperial monasteries to bishops wove itself like a chain throughout royal policy. They might be conferred as property or as fiefs, but in both cases the conferral was a flagrant defiance of the decree of 951 noted above.

Henry II, who reigned as the last Ottonian king from 1002 to 1024, was deeply devoted to Saint Benedict, and in his early years, while at the abbey of Saint Emmeram in Regensburg, he had been able to experience monastic life lived perfectly according to the principles of Benedict's Rule. He advanced an intentional monastic policy whose aim was a "program of formation"[100] according to the Rule, one that led to a strengthening of monasticism under royal authority and that served the stability of the empire. Henry supported already-established imperial monasteries, tore older ones away from the power of bishops and especially of dukes, and established them with the privileges of royal freedom. Yet he also rid himself, so to speak, of seventeen weaker imperial monasteries by giving them to the bishops, thereby improving the balance sheet of the imperial monasteries.[101]

Under the Salian Henry III,[102] king from 1039 to 1056, imperial monasteries were no longer used as discretionary instruments within a royal policy of distribution. Rather, they came to be seen, in imitation of the Carolingian model, as places serving something larger than the king's personal utility—namely, the reputation and stability of the realm. Yet under Henry III, bishops nevertheless made notable attempts to bring imperial monasteries under their influence, particularly coveting Benediktbeurn, Disentis, and Fulda. The monasteries involved, however, assertively fended off these efforts, increasingly recognizing the attraction of royal liberty, especially in view of the ever stronger pull of episcopal greed. In 1040, for example, Henry III even granted to the abbey of Pfäfer near St. Gall a privilege of royal liberty (*libertas regia*) set out in almost Cluniac terms: the abbey was to be free from any external and unjustified power (*potestas*), and it was not to be given away by its heirs. Of course the difference from Cluny did not concern the *potestas* of the king himself, since he himself was the source of the *libertas*.

In 1095, however, Henry III's son and successor Henry IV handed Pfäfer over to the bishopric of Basel.[103] For him, imperial monasteries had once again become an asset to be disposed of at will. In 1065, for example, in the face of heavy resistance from those concerned, he had already handed over twelve at once to both spiritual and worldly magnates, thereby shoring up his still notably weak position. Yet over

[100] Stefan Weinfurter, *Heinrich II. Herrscher am Ende der Zeiten* (Regensburg: Pustet, 2002), 178.

[101] Weinfurter, *Heinrich II*, 168–85.

[102] Seibert, "Libertas und Reichsabtei," 524–35.

[103] Seibert, "Libertas und Reichsabtei," 535–67.

the course of his reign, from 1065 to 1105, the structural basis of monastic life in the German realm—and, in view of the flare-ups of the Investiture struggle, not only these—began to shift fundamentally.

At Gorze, things had already fallen quiet around the end of the tenth century.[104] Other centers of reform had meanwhile been active and had begun to grow in importance—for example, the abbey of Niederaltaich on the Donau under Abbot Godehard (960–1038), later bishop of Hildesheim,[105] and the community of Saint Maximin[106] in Trier, influenced by Gorze. Maximin's advocate was Count Siegfried of Luxembourg, whose support bolstered the community's reforming power. With Siegfried's consent, Bishop Wolfgang of Regensburg, who had spent a certain amount of time in Trier, arranged in 974 to have the remarkably energetic monk Rambold come from Saint Maximin to Saint Emmeram, thereby ensuring that the latter house would become one of the most important spiritual and intellectual centers in Bavaria. The daughter of the count, Kunigunde, married Henry II (the later German king) shortly before 1000 and was therefore able to strengthen the bonds between Maximin and Emmeram still further.[107]

Yet soon Gorze, a monastery that had remained subject to the bishop of Metz, itself experienced a period of renewal. Between 1012 and 1031, at the instigation of the bishop of Metz, the former Cluniac monk William of Volpiano[108] took over the leadership of that community. The customs of his home community of Fruttuaria thus came into force in Gorze, and Cluny became an influence on Gorze, however indirectly and faintly.[109] The reform so reawakened Gorze's reputation that in the following decades it was able to install abbots in many episcopal monasteries, some as far away as Kremsmünster in the east.[110]

---

[104] See pp. 52–54.

[105] Christel Jung, "L'abbaye de Niederaltaich, centre de réforme monastique au Xe et XIe siècle," PhD dissertation, Université de Paris, 1988.

[106] Franz-Josef Heyen, "Trier, St. Maximin," in *Die Männer- und Frauen-klöster der Benediktiner in Rheinland-Pfalz und Saarland*, ed. Friedhelm Jürgensmeier (St. Ottilien: EOS, 1999), 1010–88.

[107] Stefan Weinfurter, "Kunigunde, das Reich und Europa," in *Kunigunde, consors regni*, ed. Stefanie Dick (Paderborn: Wilhelm Fink, 2004), 9–27.

[108] See p. 69.

[109] Hochholzer, "Die lothringische (Gorzer) Reform," 81–82.

[110] Hochholzer, "Die lothringische (Gorzer) Reform," 83–85.

Still another network of reforming monasteries established by a bishop, one that also spread over wide stretches of the empire, was established in these years. Archbishop Anno II of Cologne (1056–1075), one of the most prominent figures among the princes of the imperial church in his era,[111] founded the abbey of Siegburg near Cologne in 1064. There he established the customs of Fruttuaria, now modified in certain respects so as to render them more rigorous. The reforming aims that thereby emerged were shaped by the tightest of bonds between the power of the lord bishop and his monastery, which was governed strictly by the Rule of Saint Benedict. This was a matter of a "purely episcopal reform,"[112] one in which any supposed reverence toward the papacy, possibly mediated by Cluniac influence, played almost no role. And yet Cluny's characteristic right of the free election of abbots, so decisive for a monastery's right to self-determination, was not at all restricted.

Also of concern here—thoroughly in keeping with Cluniac traditions but now adapted to the interests of episcopal power—was how best to limit the possibilities of noble interference, insofar as the so-often-powerful position of the monastery's advocate was weakened. That office was now to be conferred by the archbishop only with the consent of the abbot, so that the procedure would ultimately ensure a free abbatial election. Under the aegis of its episcopal owner (at first in the person of Anno II), Siegburg became the center of a widespread monastic reform, one that spread far beyond the archdiocese of Cologne to exert its influence as far as (among others) Thuringia (Saalfeld) and Bavaria, even though these monasteries failed to form a comprehensive and legally established congregation. Rather, groups began to form around bonds of affiliation, including many female monasteries,[113] organized according to the principle of mother houses

---

[111] Georg Jenal, *Erzbischof Anno II. von Köln (1056–75) und sein politisches Wirken* (Stuttgart: Hiersemann, 1974). Especially for matters of monastic politics, see Josef Semmler, *Die Klosterreform von Siegburg. Ihre Ausbreitung und ihr Reformprogramm im 11. und 12. Jahrhundert* (Bonn: Röhrscheid, 1959); Semmler, "Die Klosterreform von Siegburg (11. und 12. Jahrhundert)," in *Die Reformverbände und Kongregationen der Benediktiner im deutschen Sprachraum*, ed. Ulrich Faust and Franz Quarthal (St. Ottilien: EOS, 1999), 141–51.

[112] Semmler, *Die Klosterreform von Siegburg*, 255.

[113] Semmler, *Die Klosterreform von Siegburg*, 337–39; Röckelein, "Frauen im Umkreis," 298–302.

and cells (called "Propsteien"), as was the case in 1071, with Saalfeld's women's monasteries at Coburg and Probstzella.

Alongside these developments, which took shape under the direction of the imperial bishops, who ultimately thereby strengthened their position over against the king, a fundamental shift also took place in the dynamics surrounding the nobility's founding of monasteries. It had been customary for nobility who wanted to secure the greatest possible protection for a community they had endowed to transfer it to the king. In 1039/40 the last such act for some time took place when Count Adalbert of Ebersberg sought to secure the freedom of an imperial monastery for his foundation there.[114] As part of a process of emancipation from royal power, but surely also because of growing skepticism about the durability of this kind of liberty, noble founders of new monasteries increasingly turned to the one who now claimed to represent the proper ordering of the world: the pope. Another form of Benedictine life, one entirely new for Germany, soon emerged from this relationship.

On the basis of the more recent model of reform advanced from Gorze, the abbey of Hirsau[115] in the northern Black Forest was refounded in 1059 by Count Adalbert II of Calw. Thereafter, Abbot William (1069–1091), who had come to the community from Saint Emmeram, established a Cluniac way of life through a modified adaptation of the customs of the Burgundian abbey. The Cluniac monk Ulrich had written these customs down explicitly for this purpose, and they later informed the so-called *Constitutiones Hirsaugienses*.[116] At the center of this text, which outlined the daily life of the monastery

---

[114] Seibert, "Libertas und Reichsabtei," 533.

[115] On the following, see Hermann Jakobs, *Die Hirsauer. Ihre Ausbreitung und Rechtsstellung im Zeitalter des Investiturstreites* (Cologne: Böhlau, 1961); Klaus Schreiner, "Hirsau und die Hirsauer Reform. Spiritualität, Lebensform und Sozialprofil einer benediktinischen Erneuerungsbewegung im 11. und 12. Jahrhundert," in *Hirsau St. Peter und Paul 1091–1991*, vol. 2, *Geschichte, Lebens- und Verfassungsformen eines Reformklosters*, ed. Klaus Schreiner (Stuttgart: Konrad Thiess, 1991), 59–84; Klaus Schreiner, "Hirsau und die Hirsauer Reform. Lebens- und Verfassungsformen einer Reformbewegung," in *Die Reformverbände und Kongregationen der Benediktiner im deutschen Sprachraum*, ed. Ulrich Faust and Franz Quarthal (St. Ottilien: EOS, 1999), 89–124.

[116] *Willehelmi Abbatis Constitutiones Hirsaugienses*, ed. Pius Engelbert and Candida Elvert, 2 vols., CCM 14 (Siegburg: Schmitt, 2010).

in every detail, was a strict liturgical regimen, as in Cluny. Even the clothing was adapted from Cluny.

One divergence in Ulrich's *Constitutiones*, however, was the introduction of the so-called *conversi*, the *fratres barbati*, who as lay brothers were exclusively responsible for manual labor so that the monks could be free to devote themselves entirely to their liturgical duties. In a community shaped by the ideals of the nobility, the practice was justified by the assertion that the "true crown of the monk is not the 'work of the hands [*labor manuum*]' but 'sacred service at the holy altar [*sanctum sacri altaris officium*].'"[117] Moreover the monks of Hirsau renounced the acceptance of children handed over to the monastery by their parents (so-called oblates);[118] the community wanted mature men in their ranks, those who had entered by virtue of a fully free decision. From the beginning women had also been a part of monastic life at Hirsau. Some ten years after Abbot William became abbot, the women's community established at Hirsau relocated to the somewhat more distant community of Kentheim.[119]

From 1079 on, Hirsau grew to become the center of a broad, independent reform movement led overwhelmingly by the nobility. It soon encompassed more than 120 monasteries, above all in the southern regions of the German kingdom but also in the regions around the Weser and the Saale. The Hirsau reform also spread to include women's *vita religiosa*, as witnessed by a number of foundations including many double monasteries[120]—for example, the monasteries of Saint Agnes in Schaffhausen and Lippoldsberg on the Weser, founded in 1080 and 1086, respectively. The monasteries remained bound together only loosely, however, on the level of their common observance; they were unable to form a more strictly organized congregation.

Cluniac influence notwithstanding, Hirsau was strongly shaped by the ideals of a reforming papacy caught in the Investiture struggle. When Hirsau's new founder, Count Adalbert II of Calw, transferred

---

[117] Schreiner, "Hirsau und die Hirsauer Reform," 75.

[118] In opposition to the Cluniacs; see Mirko Breitenstein, "Das Noviziat im hohen Mittelalter," in *Zur Organisation des Eintrittes bei den Cluniazensern, Cisterziensern und Franziskanern* (Münster: LIT, 2008), 39.

[119] Röckelein, "Frauen im Umkreis," 293.

[120] Röckelein, "Frauen im Umkreis," 292–96.

it not to the king but to the Holy See (*traditio Romana*), it stood on the side of the opponents of Henry IV. In that position it was able to foster a certain interweaving both of efforts at emancipation and of movements of piety among the nobility (to the extent that it offered a form of monastic life independent from a kingship whose aims were now desacralized). Hirsau also offered—here like Cluny—an investment in a free and therefore spiritually more consequential monasticism. The latter meant in principle that a noble founder would for the most part renounce any claim to direct influence through the exercise of lordship.

Thus, concretely, already in the so-called Hirsau Formulary[121] of 1075, Adalbert II had given up any claim to the monastery as his own and conferred upon it the "right of full liberty" (*ius totius libertatis*). This included freedom of abbatial election and the appointment of an advocate who was himself to be a member of the founder's family—and to come from another only in the case of an unsuitable candidate. The advocate was also to have the right to exercise justice, a right conferred upon him by the king. The bishop's rights were similarly limited: henceforth successive abbots would receive their insignia through the independent action of the monastery; the bishop could only consecrate. That this arrangement was no longer thought to be "anti-episcopal," as one might have said with regard to the Cluniac congregation, is revealed not only in the fact that the rigid rituals of monastic self-assertion soon softened but also in that the Hirsau movement soon enjoyed the support of the reform-minded bishops themselves, such as famous figures like Otto I of Bamberg (1102–1139).[122]

The powerful attraction of these Benedictine networks—Gorze, Siegburg, and Hirsau, to which Saint Blaise could also be added—lay in an absolute commitment to live out Christian perfection through the spiritual fulfillment of the Benedictine calling. Yet at the same time they stood, as the Bible said, as "among the people" (1 Pet 2:12), among those who across the full spectrum of their activity were woven tightly into the political and social networks of their time,

---

[121] MGH, *Urkunden der deutschen Könige und Kaiser*, 6 vols., *Die Urkunden Heinrichs IV.*, 1:359–62.

[122] Heimo Ertl, ed., *Otto von Bamberg (1102–1139). Vorträge zum Jubiläumsjahr* (Nürnberg: Pirckheimer, 1989).

through intercession both for the welfare of the realm and for their founders and supporters, as well as through the support of growing episcopal power and partisan intervention on behalf of the papacy and its reforming aims. Alongside the imperial abbeys, they advanced the old tradition of political and politicized monasteries. Cluny too involved itself at the highest levels of politics and stood in the political crossfire of the greatest powers, yet it was much more immune to daily disruptions than these monastic centers in Germany, not least because of its exceptional authority. The monasteries influenced by Gorze, Hirsau, or Siegburg, as well as the imperial abbeys, were unable to form themselves into an *ecclesia* like Cluny. They had therefore either to invest the greater part of their energy in protecting their economic and legal resources from the disruptive interventions of powerful worldly outsiders or always to be careful to find a protective authority that would not become an oppressor.

But the expansive power of these monasteries gave out, after a brief time, over the course of the twelfth century. They could not find the strength to maintain their leading position in the face of the new monastic foundations, which grew from quite different spiritual roots and which sought, by means of innovative forms of organization, to secure a more durable stability. Perhaps in view of the dangers to monastic existence posed by the struggle for earthly preservation, they needed to learn that it was all but impossible to realize a life completely devoted to God while remaining "among the people." That insight is hardly pure speculation. The ancient words of Anthony, "Wherever you go, have God always before your eyes," had never been forgotten—especially not in the one place where life could be lived according to that principle: the desert.

4

Return to the Desert

The New Hermits

The eleventh century witnessed the remarkably sudden outbreak of a form of religious life that felt itself drawn beyond the boundaries of traditional Benedictine community and toward the full renunciation of all earthly ties. This new form of life had no concern to strive for monastic self-assertion through legal claims, no concern for political influence or for economic resources. It was not concerned with monastic freedom in the world but with freedom from the dangers of the world.

This new way of life was an eremitical one, and it was fundamentally distinct from that of individual anchorites and anchoresses that had long been realized among monks and nuns living in community—in southern Italy, for example, thanks to the long-lived influence of Basil.[1] The possibility of withdrawing from community and of closing oneself off, all alone with God, in a hermitage, had been part of even the Benedictine tradition from the beginning. The Rule of Saint Benedict said that "the anchorites, that is the hermits," were "taught by the daily life of the monastery" and that they had "learned to fight against the devil" and were therefore "well prepared

---

[1] Vera von Falkenhausen, "Il monachesimo italo-greco e i suoi rapporti con il monachesimo benedettino," in *L'esperienza monastica benedettina e la Puglia*, ed. Cosimo Damiano Fonseca (Galatina: Congedo Ed., 1983), 1:119–35. On the exemplary figure of Nilus von Rossano, who also met with the emperor Otto III, see Giorgio D. Gallaro, "Revisiting the Saintly Founder of Grottaferrata: Nilus the Calabrian," *Nicolaus. Rivista di teologia ecumenico-patristica* 37 (2010): 293–300.

for individual combat" (RB 1.1-5). The image of Anthony threatened by demons stood clearly before their eyes. In this sense the eremitical life was the life of those who were qualified for it only because they had first prepared themselves in the monastery and who then lived as hermits for the most part in the vicinity of their community (a great many of them, for example, lived near the abbey of Cluny).[2] A distinctly female form of the eremitical life was that of the so-called recluse, who was completely enclosed in an individual cell within the monastery precincts, never to leave until death, with only one window for access to the outside world, often with a view of the altar.[3]

The new understanding of eremitical life, however, had as its starting point not training in a well-ordered monastery, but the way of life of the Desert Fathers.[4] That way of life was interpreted as an immediate retreat from all worldly affairs (these now seen as something to be despised) and as a new discovery of self in a place undisturbed by earthly concerns (the "desert"). There, in a community of kindred spirits, hermits would follow the charisma of a model ascetic and, with the help of that person's spiritual support, find a reliable way to God. The concern was to locate the core of religious life in the "inner house of the soul" and not to live, as was said polemically, by means of ritual forms that turned piety into something mostly superficial. Such a way of life was far removed from institutional frameworks. Indeed it had the potential to foster hostility toward institutions, or at least to be seen as doing so by those who wanted to cling conservatively to all that had grown from tradition.

In fact, inherited forms of coenobitic life soon found themselves more and more in crisis.[5] A revolution was imminent, one that would

[2] Dominique Iogna-Prat, *Order and Exclusion: Cluny and Christendom Face Heresy, Judaism, and Islam, 1000–1150* (Ithaca, NY: Cornell University Press, 2002), 46–52.

[3] Jean Sainsaulieu, "Ermites," in *Dictionnaire d'Histoire et de Géographie Ecclésiastiques* (Paris: Letouzey et Ané, 1963), 15:766–87.

[4] See Regnault, *Les pères du désert à travers leurs apophthegmes.*

[5] Jean Leclercq, "La crise du monachisme aux XIe et XIIe siècles," *Bulletino dell'Istituto storico italiano per il medio evo* 70 (1958): 19–41; John Van Engen, "The 'Crisis of Cenobitism' Reconsidered: Benedictine Monasticism in the Years 1050–1150," *Speculum* 61 (1986): 269–304; Cristina Sereno, "La 'crisi del cenobitismo': un problema storiografico," *Bullettino dell'Istituto storico italiano per il Medio Evo* 104 (2002): 32–83.

overshadow everything that to that point had been advanced in the name of reform. It was no longer a matter of merely improving what had been long established but of a completely new start, inspired by a return to the fundamentals of religious life in community.

Such a new beginning had of course to develop slowly at first. The new eremitism[6] was a religious form of seeking, of experiment. Often there was an attempt, for example, to bring individual ascetics living in one small area into a single larger community, as in the case of the monastery that emerged in 1023 from the anchorites gathered together on the mountain of Montserrat in Catalonia, at the behest of the bishop of Vic and Abbot Oliba of Ripoll.[7] Most communities, however, had their beginnings in the retreat of a group gathered around a charismatic leader. Valid among them were only the word and the actions of the leader, along with his admonitions, based on revealed texts such as the gospels, the Acts of the Apostles, or the lives of the Desert Fathers. But because one had to account for the transient nature of those words, it often happened that (analogously to the gospels themselves) they came to be written down, either by their author or by someone recording the author's way of life after his death. There was also a distinct possibility that an existing rule might be adapted (most often the Rule of Saint Benedict or the Rule of Augustine) along with other normative writings; these were then quickly brought together with particular *Consuetudines*. All these affairs reflect a protracted struggle that sought to preserve the power of both content and formlessness, even though content could actually only be preserved through form. It would in the end become clear, of course, that new religious movements might succumb to that struggle, since history unfolded not only as a revolution against institutionalized traditions but also as a development that could lead new movements to be once again institutionalized across a spectrum of traditional forms.

---

[6] For an overview, see *L'eremitismo in Occidente nei secoli XI e XII* (Milan: Vita e pensiero, 1965); Henrietta Leyser, *Hermits and the New Monasticism* (London: St. Martin's, 1984); André Vauchez, ed., *Eremites de France et d'Italie (XIe–XIIe siècle)* (Rome: École française de Rome, 2003); Cécile Caby, *De l'érémitisme rural au monachisme urbain* (Paris: École française de Rome, 1999).

[7] Stefan Petzolt, "Montserrat," *Lexikon für Theologie und Kirche* (Freiburg: Herder, 1998), 7:448.

The first eremitical movements were still strongly shaped by their ties to the traditional monastic world, yet they were able to free themselves from those ties in a variety of ways. Because they had at their respective origins such strikingly charismatic personalities, the sketches that follow develop their respective points of emphasis along biographical lines.

An early example from Italy was the community of Camaldoli, founded by Romuald (951–1027) in the solitude of the Tuscan Apennines.[8] Romuald is known above all from the *Vita* written by the renowned Peter Damian (1006/7–1072), a like-minded hermit, prior of the nearby monastery of Fonte Avellana, and later Cardinal Bishop of Ostia.[9] The nobleman Romuald at first entered the Benedictine abbey of Sant'Apollinare near Ravenna in 972. He left there after three years, however (even though it had just been reformed by Maiolus of Cluny), because it seemed too relaxed and because he had been unable to impose a more rigorous form of life upon its brothers. For a time afterward he retreated to various hermitages, and by 978 he had come as far as the Pyrenees, where in affiliation with the Benedictine monastery of Cuxa he founded his first community of hermits. Nevertheless, he returned to Italy, and in the late 990s, under pressure from Emperor Otto III, he even accepted the office of abbot at Sant'Apollinare. He resigned that position after a year, however, and took up a life of erratic wandering that took him, along with a crowd of followers, to Istria, among other places, and to what was still an almost entirely pagan Hungary.

Amid a life shaped by a restless drive for moral perfection, asceticism, and penance, Romuald focused rather late on one remaining task. In central Italy around the turn of the millennium, he had begun to draw together eremitical communities in various places. A few years before his death he founded one of these in Camaldoli, in the Tuscan Apennines. There, as in other settlements, a group of individ-

---

[8] On the following, see Giuseppe Vedovato, *Camaldoli e la sua congregazione dalle origini al 1184. Storia e documentazione* (Cesena: Badia di S. Maria del Monte, 1994); *San Romualdo. Storia, agiografia e spiritualità* (Negarine di San Pietro in Cariano [Verona]: Il Segno dei Gabrielli Ed., 2002).

[9] Nicolangelo D'Acunto, "Un eremita in movimento: il Romualdo di Pier Damiani," in *L'età dell'obbedienza. Papato, impero e poteri locali nel secolo XI*, ed. Nicolangelo D'Acunto (Naples: Ligouri, 2007), 327–54.

ual houses was built, one for each member of the community. Each member was thus isolated, left to inward contemplation in direct communication with God. Three miles away was a building that was designated a *monasterium*, but it was not a monastic enclosure. Rather, it was a place of rest for guests, a place to provide care for the sick, and a place for administration. But above all it served to guard the nearby hermits from the world beyond.

Camaldoli grew under the leadership of a general prior—and notably not of an abbot—to become the center of an important congregation of eremitical communities. At first they followed the Rule of Saint Benedict, but already between 1076 and 1081/82 they had received a collection of statutes (*constitutiones*) from the hand of the prior general, Rudolph I.[10] His text recorded the system of norms that guided the congregation in practice, and it was driven by a concern to maintain the eremitical life of the Camaldolese—strict, grounded in poverty and ascetical renunciation, and shaped by a strong turning from the world, so that Camaldoli would not fall off into a traditional cenobitic monastic life shaped by the comforts of property.[11]

When around the middle of the twelfth century even Benedictine communities in Italy were being reformed from Camaldoli, when its renown as a leader of the eremitical movement was enormous, and when it enjoyed the highest esteem of the papacy, Camaldoli received its own rule, the *Liber heremitice regule*.[12] This text offered an opportunity to promote, assertively, the anchorite's new/old way of life: "Among the many forms of religious life through which the one God is served . . . the eremitical life has long held the most prominent place. This way of life, namely, is the one that conquers the world, puts the flesh in its place, drives away demons, erases crimes, tames vice, and hobbles the carnal temptations that war against the soul."[13]

---

[10] Pierluigi Licciardello, ed., *Consuetudo Camaldulensis. Rudolphi Constitutiones. Liber Eremitice Regule* (Florence: Ed. del Galluzzo, 2004), 2–21.

[11] Licciardello, *Consuetudo Camaldulensis*, xlix–l.

[12] Licciardello, *Consuetudo Camaldulensis*, 22–81.

[13] Licciardello, *Consuetudo Camaldulensis*, 22–23. See also the thirteenth-century *Libri tres de moribus*, also ed. Licciardello, *Martino III priore di Camaldoli. Libri tres de moribus* (Firenze: Ed. del Galluzzo, 2013). On the later period of Camaldoli, see Caby, *De l'érémitisme rural au monachisme urbain*.

Two other early examples can be noted briefly here: the Florentine nobleman John Gualbert (ca. 1000–1073) and Gunther of Niederalteich (955–1045), a member of the family of the counts of Schwarzburg in Thuringia.

The first of these had professed as a monk in the Benedictine abbey of San Miniato in Florence but left that community after a short time because he refused to accept its abbot, who had attained his office through simony. With his companions he founded the community of Vallombrosa in 1037, in the secluded forests east of Florence. There they lived according to the Rule of Saint Benedict and their own *Consuetudines*. But unlike other Benedictine abbeys, this one strove for complete poverty not only for its individual members but also for the community as a whole.[14] Around the community at Vallombrosa there developed an important network, which Pope Victor II (d. 1057) soon recognized and granted papal protection.

Gunther of Niederalteich[15] entered the community of Hersfeld (in the north of modern Hesse) as a lay brother (*conversus*) at the age of fifty. He then became a novice in the Bavarian Benedictine abbey of Niederalteich on the Danube. In 1008 he left the monastery and retreated into the Bavarian forest to live as a hermit. Around 1011 he ventured farther still into the desert of the forest and founded the cell of Rinchnach with his followers. From there he went on missionary trips to the borderlands of Bavaria and Bohemia, and by virtue of his personal reputation he came to play a role as a political mediator in the wars of the Salians with the Bohemians. In 1040 he was driven farther still into the uninhabited regions of Bohemia, where after a few years he died in a hermitage near Dobrá Voda. His cell at Rinchnach fell to the abbey of Niederalteich.

To Live by One's Own Law

The discussion thus far has centered on those who were seekers, those who could not be content with the paths to salvation provided

---

[14] Nicolangelo D'Acunto, "Monaci poco obbedienti. Le origini vallombrosane fra estremismo riformatore e normalizzazione pontificia," in *L'età dell'obbedienza*, 135–65.

[15] Jan Royt, "Religiöse Kulte im Kloster Brevnov. Der Einsiedler Günther," in *Tausend Jahre Benediktiner-Kloster in Brevnov. Benediktinerabtei der Hl. Margarethe in Prag-Břevnov* (Prague: Typo plus, 1993), 69–80.

by the traditional monastery. To retreat into the desert with a group of followers was for them a more promising alternative. Yet in the early eleventh century, in an era when the Benedictine monasticism still stood at the pinnacle of religious life, these new followers of the eremitical life seemed not yet to have become generally contemptuous of the life of the monastery. Failing strength and worldliness in the monastery seem not yet to have been understood as a structural weakness, and criticism flared up only around individual cases. This circumstance changed in the next generation. Already in the second half of the eleventh century, and more still by the beginning of the twelfth, the discourse would shift dramatically. The Norman historiographer and Benedictine monk Orderic Vitalis, for example, noted how often his contemporaries could take the liberty of denouncing monks as worldly and as "rule breakers" (*regulae praevaricatores*).[16]

Owing not least to what is now known as the Gregorian reform, with its struggles against simony (the sale of spiritual offices), Nicolaitism (clerical marriage and concubinage), and the disruptions of the Investiture struggle, there was now a keener eye for failures within the institutional framework of the church.[17] The recognition of those failures became all the more fundamental in that they coincided with the emergence of a new quality of religious life—one whose demands many traditional ecclesiastical structures could no longer meet, thereby making the church itself seem all the more deficient. Doubt about the ability of established institutions to secure salvation went hand in hand with contemporary demands for a new religious spirit, one oriented toward the internalization of the faith and grounded in the soul's authentic search for God. The eremitical life now presented the world of monasticism with a powerfully contrasting paradigm: the expectation of a life able to sustain itself alone with God and undisturbed by inherited rules or worldly ways, a life dependent entirely on the inherent strength of the soul. It is almost self-evident that such a new paradigm could also be seen in a negative

---

[16] *The Ecclesiastical History of Orderic Vitalis*, ed. and trans. Marjorie M. Chibnall (Oxford: Clarendon Press, 1973), 4:332–34.

[17] For an overview, see Uta-Renate Blumenthal, *The Investiture Controversy: Church and Monarchy from the Ninth to the Twelfth Century* (Philadelphia, PA: University of Pennsylvania Press, 1988); Werner Goez, *Kirchenreform und Investiturstreit. 910–1122* (Stuttgart: Kohlhammer, 2000).

light, as something novel, indeed revolutionary, and as something that traditionally established powers would resist.

In fact, strong disagreements soon flared up. They were decisive for the coming era and rendered its divergent viewpoints plainly visible. Above all, one fundamental issue was clear from this point forward: a life devoted to God, now in a new form, revealed more sharply the problem of those who found their way to a liminal position—settled at the borders of orthodoxy, of conventional rules or institutionalized regulations.[18] In view of the importance of this discourse, the discussion now turns to explore in more detail one particularly significant case.

One day the renowned canonist and bishop Ivo of Chartres (1040–1115) learned that charismatic figures had sought to persuade the monks of the Benedictine abbey of Coulombs, on the banks of the Eure, to leave their abbey and take up an eremitical life in the forests. One argument among others involved the claim that Coulombs unjustifiably collected the tithe (a tenth of the yield of a given property, given to the church) for the abbey's own enrichment.[19] In a letter to the monks Ivo vehemently denounced any aspiration (which he intentionally equated to that of the Sarabaites)[20] to live separately in individual spaces, according to one's own law (*in privatis locis proprio iure*)[21]—that is, far from the generally accepted laws of the

---

[18] On the following see Gert Melville, *"In privatis locis proprio jure vivere. Zu Diskursen des frühen 12. Jahrhunderts um religiöse Eigenbestimmung oder institutionelle Einbindung,"* in *Kulturarbeit und Kirche. Festschrift für Paul Mai*, ed. Werner Chrobak and Karl Hausbacher (Regensburg: Verein für Regensburger Bistumsgeschichte, 2005), 25–38; repr. in Gert Melville, *Frommer Eifer und methodischer Betrieb. Beiträge zum mittelalterlichen Mönchtum*, ed. Cristina Andenna and Mirko Breitenstein (Cologne, Weimar, and Vienna: Böhlau, 2014), 33–48.

[19] Giles Constable, *Monastic Tithes from Their Origins to the Twelfth Century* (Cambridge, UK: Cambridge University Press, 1964); Giles Constable, "Monastic Possession of Churches and 'Spiritualia' in the Age of Reform," in *Il monachesimo e la riforma ecclesiastica (1049–1122)* (Milan: Vita e pensiero, 1971), 304–35.

[20] RB 1.6: "Third, there are the Sarabaites, the most detestable kind of monks, who with no experience to guide them, no rule to try them as gold is tried in a furnace (Prov 27:21), have a character as soft as lead."

[21] Ivo of Chartres, "Epistola 192," PL 162:198–202, here 200.

church and far from its sacred places—as well as any sinister notion that one could already be a master without ever having been a student. Such monks had cut all ties with the institutional church, so Ivo's accusation continued, and they could thus not even be sure whether their own motives were just. One could never attain salvation merely through an outward change of place, and salvation was never assured just because of the assumption that it was being sought under the inspiration of the Holy Spirit.

Ivo wrote a similar letter[22] to another addressee, a certain Rainald, who was also contemplating a retreat to a hermitage even though he had once professed religious life in a Benedictine community. The argument in this letter ran along similar lines, though Ivo also added another sentiment: that the solitary life (*vita solitaria*) was to be embraced only at one's own discretion (*voluntaria*).

Rainald answered with strong words in two extended letters. In the first,[23] he objected to the assumption that a solitary life, as something embraced voluntarily, was to be thought of as less worthy than coenobitic life. God rejoiced more at a willingly embraced servitude (*spontanea servitus*) than one embraced under compulsion. Moreover, he said, it was known that Jesus Christ went alone to the mountain to pray; thus all who wanted to be perfect were to be naked and follow the naked Christ. Rainald had played the card of inner conviction against the card of an externally set norm, in a way that he hoped would influence Ivo.

He did the same in his second letter. He began with harsh accusations against traditional monastic communities. One might fulfill monastic regulations reasonably enough there, he said—in the manner of the Pharisees (*more Pharisaico*),[24] as was often said at the time—but not the commands of the Lord. Unfortunately, because those who lived in the old monasteries were ravenous for riches, it was impossible for anyone to fight for salvation while living among them. It was thus fully justified in that situation for an individual to

---

[22] Ivo of Chartres, "Epistola 256," PL 162:260–61.

[23] Both texts are edited by Germain Morin, "Rainaud l'ermite et Ives de Chartres. Un épisode de la crise du cénobitisme au XIᵉ–XIIᵉ siècle," *Revue Bénédictine* 40 (1928): 99–115.

[24] Giles Constable, *The Reformation of the Twelfth Century* (Cambridge, UK: Cambridge University Press, 1998), 33, 145.

take appropriate action and to leave such a community, even when one had solemnly professed to remain there (*stabilitas loci*). As an authority in support of his position Rainald cited the renowned Lanfranc of Bec, abbot of Caen and then archbishop of Canterbury, who wrote that he would leave a monastery were he unable to save his soul there, even if he had sworn to stay there forever. Rainald emphasized that those who were bound to God for God's sake would not be separated from God—so long as they changed, out of love for God, from being a son of Satan to a son of freedom.

The battle lines had thereby been clearly drawn, and on both sides the opponents stood firmly on their principled positions.[25] Their irreconcilable differences were rooted not only in the abstract matter of different models for understanding religious practice and its institutional composition but also in concrete historical circumstances. The conflict concerned the opposition of both old and new, of tradition and its rejection. So, for example, Orderic Vitalis could say of the way of life of the hermit Vitalis of Savigny (ca. 1060–1122), "He did not follow the rite of the Cluniacs or of others who have devoted themselves to monastic forms of worship from time immemorial. Rather, he embraced novel ways [*modernae institutiones*] of training neophytes [here he meant those newcomers who strove to prove themselves] in whatever way occurred to him."[26] The difference was rooted in divergent points of view: Integrating order against arbitrary isolation, or pharisaically empty formalism against the inner fullness of piety.

Nearly everywhere across the lands of the Latin church—in the Holy Land as well as in Italy, but especially in France, and there especially in Limousin and along the borders of Brittany in the forests of Craon[27]—in the second half of the eleventh century and deep into the twelfth there emerged communities of hermits who did not shy away from explicitly incorporating this departure from tradition into the principles of their way of life.

---

[25] Jean Leclercq, "La poème de Payen Bolotin contre les faux ermites," *Révue Bénédictine* 68 (1958): 52–86.

[26] *Ecclesiastical History*, 4:312.

[27] Leyser, *Hermits and the New Monasticism*; Vauchez, ed., *Ermites de France et d'Italie.*

One of the most uncompromising representatives of this new way was Stephen of Thiers (or of Muret) (1044/45–1124),[28] who from the 1070s on drew a group of followers around him in the forest wilderness of Limoges in order to live a life in service of God and in complete poverty. Through a bold polemic that sharply distinguished his way of life from the great Benedictine abbeys of his day, Stephen called his novices to avoid the traditional houses because they would find there only buildings, expensive meals, livestock, and large estates, whereas he could offer them the cross and poverty.[29]

Stephen prohibited the keeping of livestock, cultivation of land, parish positions, and pastoral care, tithes, buildings—all but the minimal things absolutely necessary for life. Because his followers were already dead to the world, he emphasized, they needed only a piece of land large enough to bury their bodies. And should they produce anything with the labor of their hands, they were always to exchange it for other wares at a loss, so as not to be mistaken for merchants. Moreover, it was forbidden for them to draw up documents over even the smallest of legal affairs, since they were always to yield to any claim made upon them by an outsider. Should they find themselves close to starvation through this way of life, they were first to ask God to save them, and only then to go to their respective bishops to ask for aid. If such requests were also of no help, they were to fast for two more days still. Only then were they allowed, in pairs, to begin begging in their vicinity—and even then only until they had found nourishment enough for one day.

In light of the fact that Benedictine monks had to observe personal poverty while living in what were usually the best-provisioned of

[28] On the following see Gert Melville, "Von der *Regula regularum* zur Stephansregel. Der normative Sonderweg der Grandmontenser bei der Auffächerung der *vita religiosa* im 12. Jahrhundert," in *Vom Kloster zum Klosterverband. Das Werkzeug der Schriftlichkeit*, ed. Hagen Keller and Franz Neiske (Munich: Wilhelm Fink, 1997), 342–63; Jean Becquet, *Études Grandmontaines* (Ussel: Musée du pays d'Ussel, 1998); Cristina Andenna, "Dall'esempio alla santità. Stefano di Thiers e Stefano di Obazine: Modelli di vita o fondatori di ordini?" in *Das Eigene und das Ganze*, ed. Gert Melville and Markus Schürer (Münster: LIT, 2002), 177–224.

[29] *Liber de doctrina uel Liber sententiarum sev rationvm beati viri Stephani primi patris religionis Grandimontis*, in *Scriptores ordinis Grandimontensis*, ed. Jean Becquet, CCCM 8 (Turnhout: Brepols, 1968), 3–62, here 6.

monasteries, these pious hermits—who emerged from the forests in all humility, trusting in God and seeking through begging to preserve their life only in the greatest necessity—must have made a striking impression on their contemporaries. In the future the authenticity of religious life would be judged by these kinds of manifestations of poverty. Here were already the first appearances of a way of life that, with the coming of the mendicant orders, and especially the Franciscans, would soon conquer Christendom in an array of different forms.[30]

The contrast with traditional monasticism could not have been greater. Stephen's way of life, moreover, had an even deeper dimension. It centered on the difference, noted above, between "integrating order" and "arbitrary isolation."

Steven had drawn essential inspiration from the Greek monks that in his day still existed in great numbers in southern Italy (until not long before under Byzantine rule), where they lived according to the Rule of Basil.[31] They had fled to the region at the beginning of the ninth century, driven from Sicily and Sardinia by the advance of the Saracens. Stephen traveled to see them, seeking to learn from those who had a great reputation for living an exemplary eremitical and ascetic life how best to shape his own life in the future.

Soon afterward, in 1076, he resolved to retreat from all worldly affairs and, in keeping with his newly found sense of autonomy, did something highly symbolic: although a layman, he went completely alone into the forests around Limoges and offered up directly to and exclusively before God a vow for his new way of life. No cleric, no prelate of the institutional church, no abbot of a monastery as representative of a monastic rule was present to approve it—only the one who was decisive in Stephen's eyes: God.

This act was the beginning of a new theology of monastic rules—a vow offered up by a layman, yet one fulfilled (so his *Vita* relates) by the spark of his faith. To his students, who received the norms of their

---

[30] Gert Melville, "In solitudine ac paupertate. Stephans von Muret Evangelium vor Franz von Assisi," in *In proposito paupertatis. Studien zum Armutsverständnis bei den mittelalterlichen Bettelorden*, ed. Annette Kehnel and Gert Melville (Münster: LIT, 2001), 7–30.

[31] Biagio Cappelli, *Il monachesimo basiliano ai confini calabro-lucani* (Naples: Fiorentino, 1963).

life in community directly from their teacher's mouth, he taught that there was no other rule than the Gospel of Christ (*Non est alia regula nisi evangelium Christi*).[32] It was the "rule of rules," because Jesus Christ alone was the path by which one could ascend to the kingdom of heaven. And it was Christ himself who had thereby established monastic life. But it therefore followed that the rules later drawn up by humans were merely the branch, not the root, of religious life. It was beside the point that Pope Gregory had said Saint Benedict had written the Rule for monks, since the Rule could be called such only because it had been crafted from the teaching of the Gospel.

With this return to the first foundations of Christianity, Stephen had set aside all tradition, pressed forward to the original core of the Christian faith, and thereby gained what was in his eyes the pure norm of life.

Obviously, however, this change created problems for Stephen in the context of contemporary monastic life, because he saw himself compelled to provide for his brothers, as if in a kind of testament, the arguments they would need to protect themselves against attacks on their identity. They were to be aware, he said, that they were obligated to follow none of the usual observances, that they wore the habit of no known monastic congregation, and so on—and that they followed, more and better than others, not just any rule, but the true rule.

The world obviously had first to become accustomed to the outward appearance of what was seen as a new kind of monastic life, even though the Roman church, through a visitation of two legates, had recognized Stephen's way of life as legitimate.

After Stephen's death his community's fortunes took off.[33] First, though, it had to move from Muret, because it had originally settled there without permission, on the estates of a Benedictine abbey. The community now settled nearby, in a glade named Grandmont, and took its name from there. The Grandmontines expanded across France and England as well as the Iberian Peninsula. Their 150 houses were highly esteemed from the beginning and enjoyed the support of both French and English kings. They reconstructed in writing the oral traditions of the teaching of their master under the title "Book of

---

[32] Becquet, *Liber de doctrina*, CCCM 8:5.

[33] Carole A. Hutchison, *The Hermit Monks of Grandmont,* CS 118 (Kalamazoo, MI: Cistercian Publications, 1989).

Stephen of Thiers hands on his spiritual legacy in written form to his disciple Hugh de Lacerta—though in reality Hugh was the one who first had it written down. Altarpiece from the monastery of Saint-Michel de Grandmont.

Instruction" *(Liber de doctrina)*,[34] and in the fourth generation of successors, under prior Stephen de Liciaco, between 1150 and 1160, they produced their own rule, written down under the name of their founder.[35]

They also developed a complex organizational structure. They lived in common in small, modest communities with a common dormitory and refectory but far from any habitation. The daily tasks of manual labor and administration were in the hands of lay monks *(conversi)*; ordained monks, in contrast, who early on had come to join the community, were to concentrate on worship, spiritual work, prayer, and contemplation—an arrangement that did not avoid serious internal conflict over the actual leadership of the convent.[36]

Around the same time that Stephen of Thiers was active, in a remote alpine valley near Grenoble, a community emerged whose powerful expansion—through the whole of the Middle Ages and into every region of Western Christendom—would achieve the greatest renown of all the eremitical forms of life and eclipse all inherited traditions. Bruno[37] (ca. 1030–1101), from Cologne, former leader of the cathedral school of Reims and chancellor of the archdiocese of Reims, founded the community in a settlement that would later be known as the Grand Chartreuse. As a supporter of the church reforms of Gregory VII, the pope of the Investiture struggle, Bruno had been deposed from office in 1077 in Reims, an event that only fueled his already long-standing drive for ascetical renunciation. He had begun to seek monastic life and in 1081 had come with his companions to the Lotharingian abbey of Molesme, a community recently established from a congregation of eremitical groups under the leadership of the same Robert who would later found Cîteaux.[38]

---

[34] Becquet, *Liber de doctrina*, CCCM 8:3–62.

[35] *Regula venerabilis viri Stephani Muretensis*, in *Scriptores ordinis Grandimontensis*, ed. Jean Becquet, CCCM 8 (Turnhout: Brepols, 1968), 65–99.

[36] Volkert Pfaff, "Grave Scandalum. Die Eremiten von Grandmont und das Papsttum am Ende des 12. Jahrhunderts," *Zeitschrift der Savigny-Stiftung für Rechtsgeschichte, Kanonistische Abteilung* 75 (1989): 133–54.

[37] On the following, see Bernard Bligny, *Saint Bruno, le premier chartreux* (Rennes: Ouest-France, 1984); Gerardo Posada, *Maestro Bruno, padre de monjes* (Madrid: Ed. Católica, 1980); *San Bruno di Colonia: un eremita tra Oriente e Occidente*, ed. Pietro De Leo (Soveria Mannelli [Catanzaro]: Rubbetino, 2004).

[38] See chap. 6, pp. 136–37.

Bruno had been given shelter in a remote locale north of the abbey, in Sèche-Fontaine. But he soon recognized that life in the vicinity of Molesme, a community that had already become an all-too-active center for its granges and priories, was quite unsuitable for his vision of retreat. Living in solitude from day to day inspired Bruno as the ideal and most demanding form of life, but he now aimed to realize it in community with others who were similarly isolated. He believed that in this way he could bring together coenobitic and eremitical life. He thus left Sèche-Fontaine and sought out a remote locale with harsh living conditions.

In 1084 he and a new group of followers found just such a place, with the support of his former disciple Hugh, bishop of Grenoble. It was a wasteland in the mountain range north of Grenoble, given to him by Seguin, abbot of La Chaise-Dieu in the Auvergne. There the community soon erected for each individual member an enclosure in the form of a small hut, each with a room for sleep, prayer, and work, as well as common rooms and a kitchen. But in contrast to Camaldoli, where the individual lodgings stood in isolation, in the Charterhouse (as this design came to be called, taking its name from the valley), in subsequent years a large cloister tied together all of the buildings. The Benedictine historian Guibert of Nogent, writing around 1104,

The Charterhouse of Pavia, with the individual dwellings of its members distinctly visible.

succinctly described this new kind of arrangement as "cells around the cloister walk" (*cellulae per gyrum claustri*).[39]

In those individual cells, in absolute silence, a daily life of isolation was filled with contemplation, with vigils, with strict fasting and abstinence, and with spiritual and physical labor (especially the copying of manuscripts). In the common rooms, on the other hand— along with the church, the chapter room, and the refectory—were held the common worship service and the divine office, as well as common meals and common readings on high feast days. The architecture of the entire complex was thus the symbolic embodiment of a program that sought to structure the isolation of the individual and the interaction of community in a way that united the two in functional collaboration: in isolation, God would be found in the inner life of the individual soul, and in community, God's majesty would be praised.[40] But all of this was physically possible for only a limited number. The community was to consist of precisely twelve members, a number with obvious allegorical meaning. Moreover, the assistance of *conversi*, the lay brothers, was essential.

At the time there was no rule that could be adopted for this way of life; the community could take inspiration only from the Rule of Saint Benedict, the writings of the Desert Fathers, or Jerome. For the moment, however, they had in any case no need for a written framework of precise regulations, since the charismatic word and exemplary deeds of Bruno himself, as with Stephen of Thiers, were what counted. Once again it was clear that monastic life according to a fixed rule had lost its monopoly.

Problems first arose in 1090 when Bruno was called to Rome by Urban II, who had been his disciple in Reims. Bruno then continued on to Calabria, where he founded a new monastery; he never returned. The community fell apart at first, but it soon found itself partially

---

[39] Guibert de Nogent, *De vita sua*, ed. Edmond-René Labande (Paris: Belles Lettres, 1981), chap. 11, p. 66; In English, Paul J. Archambault, *A Monk's Confession: The Memoirs of Guibert of Nogent* (University Park, PA: Pennsylvania State University Press, 1996).

[40] On this, see Guillaume de Saint-Thierry, *Lettre aux frères du Mont-Dieu*, ed. Jean Déchanet, SCh 223 (Paris: Les Éditions du Cerf, 1975). In English, *The Golden Epistle: A Letter to the Brethren at Mont Dieu*, trans. Theodore Berkeley, CF 12 (Spencer, MA: Cistercian Publications, 1971).

reconstituted at La Chartreuse, this time as a small, elite group of followers, zealots of strictness and self-discipline, gathered under the leadership of a disciple of Bruno's named Landuin. Moreover, they continued to enjoy the support of the bishop of Grenoble and the abbot of La Chaise-Dieu. Bruno, too, had not forgotten his foundation: at his request the pope took it under his protection in 1090. But otherwise Bruno sent only a single letter of edification, one that affirmed the Carthusian way of life and praised and encouraged the community for its zeal.[41]

Obviously a few years of charismatic leadership seem to have been sufficient to create a way of life that could live on without its founder and soon be stabilized. After a short time it even began to spread: Carthusian communities, modeled after the Grand Chartreuse, soon began to emerge in other regions, and a few hermits and *conversi* from the Alpine valley were sent to them in order to teach the novices. Guigo (ca. 1086–1136), fourth leader of the Grand Chartreuse after Bruno, saw himself in the end led to respond not only to the encouragement of the bishop of Grenoble but above all to the request of the new convents for authentic accounts of the way of life at the Grand Chartreuse. Between 1121 and 1127 he wrote down the customs (*Consuetudines*) that had grown up there,[42] and Innocent II approved these in 1133. He thereby created a foundational normative framework for the emerging Carthusian Order.[43]

Both of these communities—the Grandmontines and the Carthusians—make clear, on the one hand, the impact that an early charismatic figure could have and, on the other, what considerable effort was needed to ensure that that impact would be a lasting one. The

---

[41] Bruno, "Ad filios suos cartusienses," in *Lettres des premiers Chartreux*, vol. 1, *Saint Bruno—Guigue—Saint Anthelme*, ed. Maurice Laporte, SCh 88 (Paris: Éditions du Cerf, 1988), 82–89.

[42] *Guigues I er, prieur de Chartreuse. Coutumes de Chartreuse. Introduction, texte critique, traduction et notes par 'un Chartreux,'*" ed. Maurice Laporte, SCh 313 (Paris: Éditions du Cerf, 1984).

[43] Florent Cygler, "Vom 'Wort' Brunos zum gesatzten Recht der Statuten über die 'Consuetudines Guigonis.' Propositum und Institutionalisierung im Spiegel der kartäusischen Ordensschriftlichkeit," in *Schriftlichkeit und Lebenspraxis im Mittelalter*, ed. Hagen Keller et al. (Munich: Wilhelm Fink, 1999), 95–110; Florent Cygler, *Das Generalkapitel im hohen Mittelalter* (Münster: LIT, 2002), 209–14.

distance from established institutions that at first characterized these new religious forms and that put them in opposition to the traditional constitution of monastic life unleashed a powerful creative potential. But it did so at the price of grave uncertainties.

Especially revealing in this regard is the development of a broader eremitical movement, important in its own right, which took shape somewhat later under the leadership of Stephen of Obazine (ca. 1085–1156).[44] Originally a secular priest and an engaged pastor in the ecclesiastical province of Bourges, Stephen abruptly set aside those responsibilities so that he himself—as his *Vita* recorded[45]—could follow "poor and naked . . . the poor Christ." For a certain time thereafter he wandered around southern France, hoping to join what he thought would be the best form of an eremitical, penitential life. After this time of searching (one similar to that of Stephen of Thiers and Bruno) he resolved around 1134 to retreat with a companion into the wilderness along the banks of the Corrèze, north of the Dordogne valley. His *Vita* stylized these events in a way that highlighted his autonomous relationship with God, emphasizing that the Lord had in fact wanted him not to be subject to the authority of any other teacher, so that he could remain free to fulfill what God had planned for the holy man.[46]

Thereafter, events unfolded for Stephen almost as they did for his namesake in Thiers: an ascetic way of life attracted a crowd of disciples, with whom he began a life in community. With episcopal license he was allowed to establish a monastery in Obazine (today Aubazine), as long as the inhabitants "followed the customs handed

---

[44] On the following, see Cristina Andenna, "Dall'esempio alla santità"; Gert Melville, "Stephan von Obazine: Begründung und Überwindung charismatischer Führung," in *Charisma und religiöse Gemeinschaften im Mittelalter*, ed. Giancarlo Andenna et al. (Münster: LIT, 2005), 85–102; Alexis Grelois, "Les origines contre la Réforme: nouvelles considérations sur la 'Vie de Saint Étienne d'Obazine,'" in *Écrire son histoire: les communautés régulières face à leur passé*, ed. Nicole Bouter (Saint-Étienne: Publications de l'Université de Saint-Étienne, 2006), 369–88; György Geréby and Piroska Nagy, "The Life of the Hermit Stephen of Obazine," in *Medieval Christianity in Practice*, ed. Miri Rubin (Princeton, NJ: Princeton University Press, 2009), 299–310.

[45] Michel Aubrun, *Vie de saint Étienne d'Obazine* (Clermont-Ferrand: Institut d'études du Massif Central, 1970), 46.

[46] Aubrun, *Vie de saint Étienne*, 54.

down from the fathers."[47] This command, though nowhere fixed in a specific rule, did not in fact make it possible, as it had with Stephen of Thiers, for him to adopt a stance that explicitly rejected all the norms that had grown up after the gospels. Rather, it established a practice of life grounded in the charisma of the leader. On the question of the legally binding norms of this way of life, his *Vita* reads,

> And because no one had taken on the enacted law [*lex posita*] of any kind of order, the instructions of the master [*instituta magistri*] were the guide, not those of any statute—instructions that taught nothing more than humility, obedience, poverty, discipline, and above all abiding love. Such things were in that day the holy man's true and right teaching, which he handed down both confidentially and openly to those who followed him. This law [*hec lex*] was put in force at that time, and no one was concerned with pharisaical traditions [*pharisaïce traditiones*].[48]

This postscript in particular underscores with unusual precision—as has been noted—Stephen's conscious renunciation of a literal adherence to the inherited regulations of monastic life.

Here again the source of the norms guiding this way of life was the charismatic figure whom God had chosen for that purpose, and here too, as a consequence, everything depended on the living person of that charismatic. Had Stephen decided, like Bruno of Cologne, to leave his community, as he at one time considered doing, the community would certainly have been in danger of disintegrating. A structure like this was all the more palpably in danger as the community grew larger through additional foundations, including those of strictly enclosed women. Contemporaries were notably aware of the problem in Obazine, and Stephen's *Vita* articulated their concern, framing it in biblical terms: "But because the days of mankind are short [Job 14:15] and human learning lasts only as long as the teacher lives and is present, they resolved to recognize one of those orders authorized in the church, so that also after the teacher's passing the authority of the written law would remain behind for them, as something that would never have an end."[49]

---

[47] Aubrun, *Vie de saint Étienne*, 54.

[48] Aubrun, *Vie de saint Étienne*, 70.

[49] Aubrun, *Vie de saint Étienne*, 96.

The norms of life embodied in the charismatic would thus find a transpersonal support that guaranteed the longevity of the community. But they would also thereby be fixed to norms that were precisely defined and for the most part unalterable—fixed, that is, precisely to that which polemics had long denounced as "pharisaical traditions." And in fact, Stephen soon compelled his hermits to accept the guardianship of the nearby cloister of Dalon, which had been founded for other hermits as a Benedictine abbey in 1114. They thereby learned how those who by virtue of their pious way of life were "veterans of the heavenly militia"[50] could still see themselves as the purest of beginners in monastic life. The ironic sentiment of Ivo of Chartres about the arrogance of hermits who already saw themselves as masters here found full expression. The link to Dalon did quickly fall apart, but in 1147 Stephen of Obazine's congregation of monasteries was successfully integrated into an order that was already institutionally established and that followed the Rule of Saint Benedict to the letter: the Cistercians, who will receive extensive treatment below.

Charismatic Preaching and Religious Movements

The eremitical life did not play itself out on the public stage. By virtue of their retreat from the world, hermits avoided life "among the people" (1 Pet 2:12) and sought seclusion. Hermits in principle thus provoked only those who, as their competitors with respect to form, were directly challenged by their ways—the traditional monasteries, for example, whose members had walked away and which were defended by a figure like Ivo of Chartres as visiting bishop. But a completely different situation emerged when individual hermits graced with a special charisma refused to remain in their remote places and chose instead to leave the "forest deserts" in order to wander "through the land, renouncing all possessions in imitation of the apostles, exhorting to penitence and peace, as well as agitating against the sins of the clergy."[51]

A consciousness of apostolic mission had of course long been seen in connection with eremitic life. Romuald (of Camaldoli) and

---

[50] Aubrun, *Vie de saint Étienne*, 106.

[51] Herbert Grundmann, *Religious Movements in the Middle Ages* (Notre Dame, IN: University of Notre Dame Press, 1995), 18.

Gunther of Niederalteich, mentioned above, were two examples, from the late tenth and early eleventh centuries, respectively. In the decades around the turn from the eleventh to the twelfth centuries, however, not only did the number of such "wandering preachers" grow considerably, but the quality of their apostolic engagement changed in fundamental ways.[52] They confronted a new, broad public that cut across social ranks, since their times—an age of dissatisfaction with the social order and of longing for new paths to salvation that were now open to every Christian (even to those who remained in the world)—needed charismatic figures who were able to show the way. These wandering preachers did just that by pointing out obstacles to salvation as well as abuses both among the clergy and within the institutions of the church, by calling for repentance and penance, and sometimes even by promising to open the gates to heaven—a promise open to all who turned from the world, who dissolved social bonds, and who turned within themselves. The eremitical ascetics had already made it to heaven's gates, but they now presented their ideas in the public forum and proclaimed heaven as a goal every Christian could reach. Such a new perspective could be provocative—and for the most part that provocation was quite intentional.

The four most prominent personalities among these wandering preachers were Bernard of Tiron, Vitalis of Savigny, Robert of Arbrissel, and Norbert of Xanten. Their biographies all shared in common one thing that was to be of great significance for their emergence in public, and they shared it with some of the more reclusive hermits—Romuald, for example, Bruno of Cologne, and Stephen of Obazine. Before they renounced the world, they had already put an ecclesiastical career behind them and were priests, whether as secular clerics or monks. Moreover, they had put an end to their restless ways as wandering preachers, turned back to the ways of ecclesiastical institutions, and become founders of monasteries. Precisely because

---

[52] For an overview, see Johannes von Walter, *Die ersten Wanderprediger Frankreichs. Studien zur Geschichte des Mönchtums*, 2 vols. (Leipzig: Dietrich, 1903, 1906); Grundmann, *Religious Movements*, 17–21. For exemplary contexts in Italy, especially concerning John of Matera and his congregation of Pulsano, see Francesco Panarelli, *Dal Gargano alla Toscana. Il monachesimo riformato latino dei Pulsanesi (secoli XII–XIV)* (Rome: Istituto storico italiano per il Medio Evo, 1997).

they all embodied a certain kind of Christian zeal, a brief comparison of their individual careers is worthwhile.

Bernard of Tiron[53] (1046–1117) entered the Benedictine community of Saint-Cyprian in Poitiers at the age of twenty and by 1076 became prior of the tradition-rich abbey of Saint-Savin-sur-Gartempe in Poitou. In 1096 he withdrew to a hermit colony in the forest of Craon and thereafter to the Chausey-Isles off the coast of Normandy. Four years later he returned to the aforementioned abbey to lead it himself as abbot. After he had been unable to bring any fundamental reform to fruition there, he again became a hermit as well as a highly esteemed wandering preacher. In 1109 he received a plot of land in Tiron, west of Paris, and there, with the support of Bishop Ivo of Chartres, he founded a Benedictine monastery that became the center of a large congregation of monasteries.

Vitalis of Savigny (ca. 1060–1122),[54] mentioned above, came from Normandy and after his consecration as a secular priest became the chaplain of the brother of William the Conqueror, Robert of Mortain, who gave Vitalis secure provision in the form of a prebend (a position that secured his livelihood) in the canonry of Saint-Evroul, which Robert had founded. Struck by the shallowness of religious life as it had come to be lived there, and seeing no model way of life in Benedictine communities that had become too wealthy, around 1093 or 1095/96 Vitalis too withdrew into the forests of Craon and became the leader of a group of hermits. He too was drawn again and again back into the world both to preach and to found eremitical communities in other regions, communities that in their turn became important centers for retreat. Vitalis's words, masterfully composed, moved the people because of their honesty, earnestness, and wealth of incorruptible judgment. Nor did he shy away from inserting himself into matters of high politics, working, for example, to establish

---

[53] On the following, see Bernard Beck, *Saint Bernard de Tiron, l'ermite, le moine et le monde* (Cormeilles-le-Royal: Éd. La Mandragore, 1998).

[54] On the following, see Jaap J. van Moolenbroek, *Vital l'ermite, prédicateur itinérant, fondateur de l'abbaye normande de Savigny* (Assen: Van Gorcum, 1990); see also "The Life of Blessed Vitalis of Savigny," trans. Hugh Feiss, in *Lives of the Monastic Reformers, 2: Abbot Vitalis of Savigny, Abbot Godfrey of Savigny, Peter of Avranches, Blessed Hamo*, ed. and trans. Hugh Feiss et al., CS 230 (Collegeville, MN: Cistercian Publications, 2014), 41–94.

peace in the civil war between Henry I, king of England and duke of Normandy, and his brother Robert Curthose. In the end Vitalis also received a plot of land, where in 1113 he founded (becoming sedentary, so to speak) the abbey of Savigny as a double monastery. That community in turn became the center of a large congregation of twenty-five houses in France and England, and in 1147 it was accepted (like the congregation of Stephen of Obazine) into the Cistercian Order.

The life of Robert of Arbrissel[55] (ca. 1045–1116) was undoubtedly the most spectacular of all those hermits who took up residence in the forest of Craon during the last decades of the eleventh century. Robert, son of a parish priest and himself consecrated as a priest, took up his father's position in Arbrissel in Brittany in 1076 and there gained his first experience at preaching. Entangled in the struggles over the simoniacal election of the bishop of Rennes, in 1078 he transferred to Paris to study but was called back in 1088/89 to become bishop of Rennes. In the meantime he had transformed himself from a savvy player within a corrupt system into an advocate of church reform who would now combat Nicolaitism—clerical marriage or concubinage—as well as simony in his bishopric. Yet the reactions to his zeal compelled him after a few years to take up study again in a different place—this time in Angers. His teacher there was Marbod, later bishop of Rennes.

In 1095 Robert finally decided to withdraw in asceticism and solitude, which he hoped to find in the forests of Craon. He quickly made a name for himself there, both as a zealot for austerity and penance and as a gifted speaker and convincing charismatic. At his place of residence, La Roë, he founded a community for clerics, so

---

[55] On the following, see Jacques Dalarun, *Robert of Arbrissel: Sex, Sin, and Salvation in the Middle Ages* (Washington, DC: The Catholic University of America Press, 2006); Jacques Dalarun, ed., *Robert d'Arbrissel et la vie religieuse dans l'ouest de la France* (Turnhout: Brepols, 2004); Jacques Dalarun et al., eds., *Les deux vies de Robert d'Arbrissel, fondateur de Fontevraud* (Turnhout: Brepols, 2006); Hervé Oudart, *Robert D'Arbrissel ermite et prédicateur* (Spoleto: Fondazione Centro Italiano di studi sull'alto Medioevo, 2010). Chronology following Jean Longère, "Robert d'Arbrissel prédicateur," in *Robert d'Arbrissel et la vie religieuse dans l'ouest de la France. Actes du colloque international de Fontevraud à l'occasion du IXe centenaire de la fondation de l'abbaye, 13–16 décembre 2001*, ed. Jacques Dalarun (Turnhout: Brepols, 2004), 87–104.

that they could live there undisturbed and in a regulated way (that is, according to the Rule of Augustine and in the "manner of the early church"). The discussion will later return to this form of community.

In 1096 in Angers Robert met Pope Urban II and was allowed to preach before him. Urban came to realize that the "Holy Spirit had personally opened Robert's mouth."[56] Insofar as the sources allow reconstruction of the events, Robert received from Urban a general license to preach, one not bound to any particular diocese. A period of intense preaching activity followed. As Robert moved from place to place, he gathered unprecedented throngs of followers, with every social status represented among them—poor and rich, men and women, established and marginal. Women above all felt drawn to his message, which appealed to the individual soul of every Christian instead of one or another defined position within the social order, which Robert saw as all too often propped up by simoniacal and morally depraved churchmen.

So much proximity to women and so much criticism of the clergy were bound to incite resistance. Marbod, Robert's former teacher and now bishop, felt compelled to admonish him. The result was a notable written exchange[57] in which Marbod described Robert's public appearance in dramatic terms: he showed himself clothed in a threadbare and torn hooded cloak, with his legs half bare, a long beard, roughly cut hair across his face, and bare feet. Robert answered that his manner of appearance allowed him to win authority among the common folk and to arouse a feeling of compassion among the educated. But Marbod strongly disagreed. He told Robert, not without justification, that his clothing and appearance were not appropriate for a priest: "The wise man will not bring public morals into disorder and draw the people to himself through novelties."[58] He insisted that Robert was misleading the common people and that the learned elite saw him as creating only the appearance of religious passion. Moreover, Marbod claimed, in his sermons Robert criticized the

---

[56] Baudri de Bourgueil, *Historia magistri Roberti*, in *Les deux vies de Robert d'Arbrissel, fondateur de Fontevraud. Légendes, écrits et témoignages. Édition des sources avec introductions et traductions françaises* (Turnhout: Brepols, 2006), 156.

[57] Dalarun et al., *Les deux vies*, 526–57.

[58] Dalarun et al., *Les deux vies*, 540.

clergy heavily before the common people, thereby drawing together such crowds of both women and men that many priests no longer had communities to serve. Robert was, he declared, to return to common sense (*sensus communis*)[59] and to reintegrate himself into the conventions of the church.

In the year 1100 at the Council of Poitiers, assembled in the presence of two legates of Pope Paschal II, Robert was exhorted in all severity to bring stability to his restless band of followers of both sexes in such a way that he could settle them in a lasting community. One year later Robert founded a monastery for women and men in a glade named *Fons Evraldi* (Fontevraud) near Saumur, on a property he had received as a gift from the bishop of Poitiers, Peter II. He gave its leadership over to Hersendis, an administratively experienced noblewoman from the house of Champagne, and placed at her side Petronilla of Chemillé, who was by 1115 already her follower.

Petronilla was more than a mere administrator. She had full power over the women as well as the men of the monastery, and she was revered by both the sisters and the brothers as a "spiritual mother."[60] This kind of prominence for women, which allowed a level of esteem for female independence foreign to the Middle Ages, rested on Robert's vision of his own life—which in Robert's own words was to do everything in the world for the benefit of holy women.[61]

In the wake of the decision to institutionalize what was now an enclosed way of life, Robert sought to make every provision necessary to ensure the stability of his community. Somewhat later he therefore wrote for Fontevraud its own constitutions, which took the place of a formal rule and which Pope Calixtus II confirmed.[62] Robert himself obviously did not feel bound by the command to observe stability

---

[59] Dalarun et al., *Les deux vies*, 544.

[60] Jacques Dalarun, *Gouverner c'est servir: Essai de démocratie médiévale* (Paris: Alma, 2012), 156.

[61] Bruce L. Venarde, "Robert of Arbrissel and Women's *vita religiosa*. Looking Back and Ahead," in *Female* vita religiosa *between Late Antiquity and the High Middle Ages: Structures, Developments and Spatial Contexts*, ed. Gert Melville and Anne Müller (Berlin: LIT, 2011), 329–40.

[62] Jacques Dalarun, "Les plus anciens statuts de Fontevraud," in Dalarun, *Robert d'Arbrissel et la vie religieuse*, 139–72; Dalarun et al., *Les deux vies*, 388–405.

of place, however, since already in 1103 and 1104, and once more thereafter, he went on a series of preaching tours—the last of which took him to Berry, where he died in 1116. From Fontevraud would emerge a congregation of monasteries that came to enjoy the decisive support of the Plantagenet dynasty and that would boast some forty settlements by the middle of the twelfth century.

The life of Norbert of Xanten[63] (1080/85–1134) took sharper turns than those just surveyed, but it nevertheless remained within the boundaries of what was typical for a wandering preacher. Of noble descent, even as a child he held a prebend that secured him a good income from the community of Saint Victor in Xanten on the lower Rhine. At first he reached only to the rank of sub-deacon within the church hierarchy. His political connections, however, were more significant. Through these, by way of the archbishop of Cologne, Frederick I, Norbert won early access to the German royal court, accompanying Henry V to Rome for his coronation as emperor in 1111.

But then suddenly—after a lightning strike, according to the account of his *Vita*—in 1115 Norbert had a complete change of heart: the career clergyman now turned from his former way of life, left Saint Victor, and resolved to live a life of repentance. At first he sought the Benedictine abbey of Siegburg (discussed above) and had himself consecrated by the archbishop of Cologne as deacon and priest on the same day—even though that was against the rules laid out by canon law. But a constant search for salvation drew Norbert, like many, away from his own kind and in rapid succession on to the next stages in his journey: first to the regular canonry of Klosterrath, near Aachen, which had been founded shortly before by the hermit Ailbert as a center of strict discipline, then to the hermit Liudolf,

---

[63] On the following, see Franz J. Felten, "Norbert von Xanten—vom Wanderprediger zum Kirchenfürsten," in *Norbert von Xanten*, ed. Kaspar Elm (Cologne: Wienand, 1984), 67–157; Stefan Weinfurter, "Norbert von Xanten als Reformkanoniker und Stifter des Prämonstratenserordens," in Elm, *Norbert von Xanten*, 159–88; Stefan Weinfurter, "Norbert von Xanten und die Entstehung des Prämonstratenserordens," in *Barbarossa und die Prämonstratenser* (Göppingen: Gesellschaft für staufische Geschichte, 1989), 67–100; Franz J. Felten, "Zwischen Berufung und Amt. Norbert von Xanten und seinesgleichen im ersten Viertel des 12. Jahrhunderts," in *Charisma und religiösen Gemeinschaften im Mittelalter*, ed. Giancarlo Andenna et al. (Münster: LIT, 2005), 103–49.

a relentless critic of negligent office holders in the church. Subsequently Norbert turned to harsh ascetic exercises in a hermitage he had established near Xanten. But clothed in a garment of animal skin he also struck out on what were presumably preaching tours in Hainault and Flanders, where with great rhetorical skill he called his audience to repentance and reform.

These activities roused suspicion. Before a synod in Fritzlar in July 1118, Norbert was not only accused of preaching beyond the boundaries of his diocese but also explicitly charged with accusations that were usually cast against heretics. Why did he wear clothing made of sheep and goat skins? That was a question Robert of Arbrissel had already faced. Another question followed: Why did Norbert pretend to live like one who had embraced religious life while still drawing from his prebend and remaining involved in worldly affairs? The accusation of hypocrisy thus hung in the air, the same accusation that Ivo of Chartres had leveled against others who had fled their monasteries. Norbert defended himself by appealing to both his duties as a priest and—this point made visibly by the way he dressed—the model of John the Baptist. But he found the most fundamental justification for his penitential preaching in a passage from the apostle James: "Whoever turns a sinner from the error of his way will save him from death and cover over a multitude of sins" (Jas 5:20).

The outcome of these accusations is unknown. But they emphatically reveal the liminal position of all of these wandering preachers—a position that, as the fate of others shows, could be most dangerous for those concerned. So it was that contemporaries had seen a figure like Peter of Bruis[64] (d. 1139), a priest from the French Alps, as having crossed a still-permeable boundary when he advanced the call for a purely spiritual church in the area around Embrun—thereby radically renouncing nearly all of the symbolism of sacrament and ritual that sustained the institutional church. Although a synod in Reims in 1119 declared Peter a heretic, he continued to preach until he was lynched by an enraged mob. Henry of Lausanne[65] (d.

---

[64] James V. Fearns, "Peter von Bruis und die religiöse Bewegung des 12. Jahrhunderts," *Archiv für Kulturgeschichte* 48 (1966): 311–35.

[65] Adriaan H. Bredero, *Christenheit und Christentum im Mittelalter* (Stuttgart: Franz Steiner, 1998), 169–80; Monique Zerner, "L'hérétique Henri dans les sources de son temps (1135–1145)," *Revue Mabillon*, n.s. 25 (2014): 79–134.

1145), an ascetic and a highly educated monk who roughly attacked the lifestyle of the clergy in his preaching around Le Mans and later southern France, met a similar fate.

In face of the inquiry at Fritzlar, Norbert took immediate action. He gave up both his prebend and his cell in the abbey of Siegburg and hurried off with two companions on a pilgrimage to southern France—continually preaching, barefoot and in the clothing of a penitent, "without roof or a secure home," with "only Christ as leader," as one of his *vitae* described him.[66] In Saint-Gilles in November of 1118, "through God's providence"[67] he met Pope Gelasius II, who saw the spirit of God (*spiritus Dei*) dwelling in him.[68] Norbert used the occasion to have the pope both free him from the guilt of having received two consecrations on the same day and grant him permission to preach in every place he wished in Christendom (*ubique terrarum*).[69]

At Easter in 1119, after many of his early companions had died, Norbert found a new companion in the cleric Hugh of Fosses, who would soon play an important role in shaping Norbert's legacy. Together they wandered through northern France, trusting (as his *vitae* emphasize) that God would give them what they needed to survive. In a way similar to the experience of the recently deceased Robert of Arbrissel, great crowds of people in cities and towns flocked to Norbert whenever he read Mass, preached penance, and taught his listeners about the way of life of prelates and the obedience of subjects, the temptations of the world, heavenly life, and the happiness of the blessed. It was unavoidable that the success of his teaching inspired envy and animosity. But Norbert did not allow himself to be deterred. Rather, in keeping with the teaching of the Epistle of James, cited above, he instead turned many from their error. And as one of his *vitae* emphasizes[70]—here taking a swipe at established monasteries—Norbert enjoyed much more acceptance and approval than any monk of his era.

---

[66] *Vita Norberti B*, PL 170:1272.
[67] *Vita Norberti B*, PL 170:1272.
[68] *Vita Norberti B*, PL 170:1272.
[69] *Vita Norberti B*, PL 170:1273.
[70] *Vita Norberti B*, PL 170:1277.

In autumn of 1119 Norbert's life witnessed another fundamental turn. At the bidding of Calixtus II, who was holding a synod in Reims that was crucial for the course of the Investiture controversy, Norbert was placed under the guardianship of the bishop of Laon, Bartholomew. He was to arrange for Norbert to settle down, and he secured for him at first the leadership of a canonry in Laon. Norbert was ultimately able to ward off this move, however, by placing extreme demands on the inhabitants. He declared his intention to continue to live a life guided exclusively by the Gospel and the apostles. The canons whom he governed would be thus required to live as imitators of Christ (*imitatores Christi*), to be contemptuous of the world, naked and voluntarily poor while voluntarily embracing hunger, thirst, and insult. Norbert's program crystalized all that his contemporaries typically articulated whenever they sought to live a meaningful Christian life by completely renouncing all worldly things. The same things were said in great detail about Norbert's contemporary Stephen of Thiers, for example, and Norbert lived out the same ideal himself, often to the point of complete bodily exhaustion. But among the canons who were obliged to obey him, as two worlds of religious life clashed irreconcilably with one another, Norbert's ways encountered heavy resistance. The project failed before it had even begun.

Thereafter, in 1120, Bartholomew entrusted to Norbert the glade called Prémontré, east of Laon, leaving it to him as his own without any obligation to pay tithes or other duties, so that he could erect a double monastery there. It came together successfully as a community of women and men, laity and clergy. Through his preaching he was able to win them in large numbers and then to bind them together in spirit into one community.

Surviving evidence from this early community of Prémontré—as from the community of Stephen of Obazine—reveals a sense of complete trust in Norbert's salvation-oriented, charismatic leadership. So one source reports, for example, that whenever Norbert went out to preach, demons always found their way into the monastery—in the metaphorical imagination of the day, his contemporaries thus understood themselves as being completely without protection from the devil. By 1121, according to his *Vita*, Norbert had already gathered thirty new novices around himself, and he "cared for them morning

Augustine gives his Rule to Norbert of Xanten. Manuscript illumination from the twelfth century.

and night with the word of salvation and admonished them with consoling speech not to fall away from the blessed intentions and the voluntary poverty they had taken upon themselves. And what he taught he showed to them through his own example, just as the eagle teaches his young to fly."[71] His followers could thus at first trust that what they heard from his mouth was enough to save them, so that they needed neither a fixed order nor a rule for their way of life. But Norbert taught them a better way, declaring the Rule of Augustine, in the strict form of the so-called *Ordo monasterii*, to be binding upon them. He thus emphasized, as had Stephen of Obazine, that evangelical teaching could not be fulfilled over the long term without written order, without rules or those things established by the fathers.[72]

Norbert was thus able to build a congregation of monasteries that was legally tailored to him. From that congregation grew the Premonstratensian Order, after Norbert's life took one last turn—his elevation to archbishop of Magdeburg in 1126. The Order's emergence will be treated below.

A Return to the Institutions of the Church

All of the careers sketched briefly here, both those of the reclusive hermits and of those who had gone out preaching among people of the world, were shaped by a restless agitation that arose from an almost unquenchable desire to find still better paths to salvation. For some, forms of asceticism, of poverty and chastity, seemed ever more dissatisfying. For others there was hope of finding ever more suitable places to build community, or places to advance the message of the faith, calls to repentance, and critiques of established ways. The measure of such things was no longer to be found automatically in fixed rules, dogmatic formulas, or definitive solutions; it would be found within—in the individual self, through expressions like "a burning fire" (*ignis ardens*), as was said, for example, of Stephen

---

[71] *Vita Norberti B*, PL 170:1291.

[72] Werner Bomm, "Augustinusregel, *professio canonica* und Prämonstratenser im 12. Jahrhundert. Das Beispiel der Norbert-Viten Philipps von Harvengt und Anselms von Havelberg," in *Regula Sancti Augustini. Normative Grundlage differenter Verbände im Mittelalter*, ed. Gert Melville and Anne Müller (Paring: Augustiner-Chorherren-Verlag, 2002), 239–94.

of Obazine.[73] The new measure could seem simply boundless in its desire to be close to God, and precisely for that reason a need arose for radically new points of orientation.

Such figures seemed to capture, as through a magnifying lens, the religious desires of so many Christians in their day. Their appearance, set before the background of the established structures of the church, brought about the clash of two seemingly irreconcilable interpretations of how best to realize Christian faith. Herbert Grundmann has characterized this apparent impasse, the result of a fundamental doubt in the ability of the church to ensure salvation, as follows:

> Out of such questions and doubts arose a religious consciousness which no longer saw the essence of Christianity as fulfilled in the Church alone as an order of salvation or in the doctrine of the Church alone as its dogma and tradition. Instead, this new consciousness sought to realize Christianity as a religious *way of life* immediately binding upon every individual genuine Christian, a commitment more essential to the salvation of his soul than his position in the hierarchical *ordo* of the Church or his belief in the doctrines of the Fathers of the Church and its theologians.[74]

Those who strove for this kind of "realization of Christianity" did not, for all of their retreat from the world, live their lives in hiding, since their way of life was a message and an invitation. Moreover, insofar as they went on pilgrimages of preaching and were endowed with great charisma, almost of necessity they drew together communities that shared a common spirit. But their followers need not always have been of the same mind as the ascetics they took to be their models. Many wanted to retreat again from their positions of leadership—so it was said, at least, of Stephen of Obazine, and Bruno of Cologne in fact turned away from his community. But among the wandering preachers too the same tendency appears after the foundation of their communities: Robert of Arbrissel did not take over as the leader of Fontevraud but continued on his pilgrimage of preaching. Norbert of Xanten's circumstance was similar, until at

[73] *Vie de saint Étienne d'Obazine*, 58.
[74] Grundmann, *Religious Movements*, 7–8.

last he left his monastic community entirely to take up the office of archbishop. These examples capture a particular field of tensions in an exemplary way. It had been established on the basis of a procedural dynamic that emerged from the initial decisions of the ascetics and that unfolded in three steps.

To renounce all ties to earthly concerns in order to come closer to God, whether alone, or perhaps with one or two companions, either by retreating into solitude or by setting out on a wandering pilgrimage, was to make an individually self-responsible decision for one's own soul. This was the first step. The second was to launch a collective religious movement. It entailed taking on responsibility for many souls, who trusted that they were being shown the right way to draw near to God—not through external rules, but through the truth that the charismatic leader embodied in word and deed and sought to pass on "like an eagle to his young."[75] The third and final step was to transform what had begun as a religious movement into an institutional form with precisely articulated rules, with duties of office and precisely outlined rituals, all of which could be followed, when necessary, in the "manner of the Pharisees."

Max Weber seems rightly to have conceptualized this process in speaking of the "routinization of charisma."[76] And yet his phrasing does not fully account for certain essential elements of this process: the grounds for such "routinization" are here not to be found—as Weber generally thought—primarily in the "character" of charismatic domination.

The special "extraordinariness" (to maintain Weber's conceptualization) of the charismatically led religious movements of that time had in general pushed a life consecrated to God into a liminal position, as was noted above. From the church hierarchy's point of view, such movements seemed potentially dangerous, since their claim to be "sustained by the power of the Holy Spirit" might allow them to place their own particular demands ahead of the claims of the institutional church.[77] Those same movements, however, were quite

[75] *Vita Norberti B*, PL 170:1291.

[76] Max Weber, *Economy and Society: An Outline of Interpretive Sociology*, ed. Guenther Roth and Claus Wittich (Berkeley: University of California Press, 1978), 246.

[77] See chap. 9, pp. 186–88.

productive in advancing core ideals about the renewal of the church through a reform of piety and morality. For that purpose there was a special need for precisely those who were able to live out and to model an interiorized and self-responsible faith, a life governed by self-authorized guidelines—*proprio iure*, as it was said.[78]

As a consequence there were bishops everywhere, and indeed popes, who acted in support of any move toward institutional stabilization, including incorporating the self-authorized or even sanctioning those who lived *in privatis locis, proprio iure*. So, for example, Bruno, who had retreated with a few followers into the "mountain wilderness" in search of a life withdrawn from the world, was "inspired by the Holy Spirit," as the surviving account says, to turn to Bishop Hugh of Grenoble, asking him for aid and counsel (*auxilium* and *concilium*). In return, Bruno received every kind of support, including land and estates, for the establishment of his community. A figure so chided by a bishop as Robert of Arbrissel received license to preach from the pope after having preached before him with such power that it was said the Holy Ghost himself had opened his mouth. And it was the bishop of Poitiers, in the end, who helped him found the double community of Fontevraud. Norbert of Xanten too had received a pope's license to preach and was, at a pope's behest, placed under the supervision of the bishop of Laon, Bartholomew. The bishop then granted Norbert a place to establish a monastery. And when Stephen of Obazine fled his parish, seeking around 1130 to settle with two companions in the solitude of Corrèze, he went first to the bishop of Limoges and articulated the aims of his new way of life. He then received a blessing as well as permission to establish a monastery and to hold worship services.

The examples could be multiplied. They bear witness at first glance to a constant episcopal and papal concern to safeguard the free movement of zeal for the faith, as long as that zeal remained far from any appearance of overt heresy. In this regard there had been a certain model to follow: first to secure a legitimation of the deeds

---

[78] On this problem, see the fundamental work of Moos, "Krise und Kritik der Institutionalität. Die mittelalterliche Kirche als 'Anstalt' und 'Himmelreich auf Erden,'" in *Institutionalität und Symbolisierung. Verstetigungen kultureller Ordnungsmuster in Vergangenheit und Gegenwart*, ed. Gert Melville (Cologne, Weimar, and Vienna: Böhlau, 2001), 293–340.

of the charismatic, and then to aid those driven by the Holy Spirit in their search for a secure place to continue to live their religious life by establishing a stable community in a monastery. The institutional church thereby appeared as a supporter of religious movements that in principle could have been a structural threat. The "routinization of charisma" had thus been fostered by the sovereignty of a superior authority, which thereby integrated an institutionally distant "extraordinariness" of hermits and wandering preachers into the institutionality of the hierarchical church. Along with this transformative power came the necessity of securing the community over time after the passing of the charismatic, by way of an organization founded on trans-personal law—as became so clear, for example, in the case of the Carthusians, the Grandmontines, Obazine, and the Premonstratensians.

5

The Regular Canons

The Clergy's New Self-Understanding

With the exception of Norbert of Xanten and his community, the eremitical groups surveyed thus far tended to see themselves either as tied to monastic life (insofar as it had shaped their early development) or primarily as movements oriented toward the laity, although their leaders were most often from the clerical ranks, and they often felt strong affinities to that estate—Robert of Arbrissel, for example, who, as noted above, founded the cloister of La Roë exclusively for clergy. Yet already in the early eleventh century an equally momentous religious awakening led individual clerics scattered across Europe to gather together and to live a common life (*vita communis*) or to transform established houses of canons into the same kinds of cloistered communities that from Late Antiquity had been known only to monks.

From these transformations emerged a central idea, one that went beyond the Aachen regulations of 816 and that sought to regulate the clerical estate (*vita canonica*) by requiring strict personal poverty, obedience, regulated hours of the day, fasting, and silence—all analogous to monastic life. From the middle of the eleventh century this same concern to regulate the clergy was shared among the reforming leaders of the Roman Curia.[1] They would seek to build communities according to the model of the apostles and the first Christians in

---

[1] Cristina Andenna, "Kanoniker sind Gott für das ganze Volk verantwortlich," in *Die Regularkanoniker Italiens und die Kirche im 12. Jahrhundert* (Paring: Augustiner-Chorherren-Verlag, 2004), 16–17.

Jerusalem and would call clerics to imitate Christ—in his absolute poverty, his humility, and the self-renunciation through which he brought about humankind's salvation. To live in this exemplary way came to be understood as an apostolic mission.[2]

The beginnings of this movement were often found in the eremitical life as well, since clerics too at first saw communal retreat from the world as the best possibility for leading a life that was radically centered on God and that would secure salvation. The first-known group that sought to realize such a way of life was a band of four clerics who in 1039 withdrew from the world into the church of Saint Rufus, before the gates of Avignon.[3] But early on, canons in bishops' cathedrals—as happened in Saint Martin of Lucca in the first half of the eleventh century—also transformed themselves into communities that submitted to the rule-governed ways (*regularitas*) of the apostolic life.[4] As opposed to the "secular canons," who were usually part of the Aachen tradition, in the future one would speak self-consciously, and in a way that reflected a distinct identity, of "regular canons" (*canonici regulares*).

The enormous potential of the apostolic ideals of these new clerical communities to shape the political affairs of the church became quickly apparent as the church hierarchy around Gregory VII began to seek a renewed model of ecclesiastical validity. In centuries past, the church hierarchy had sometimes allowed its own identity to yield—sometimes until it was hardly recognizable—to a secular power that was understood to be equally sacral. But it now rose from the ashes like a phoenix with the goal of *libertas ecclesiae*, the freedom of the church, which would seek to break the bonds of secular power—

---

[2] On the following, as an overview, see Charles Dereine, "Chanoines," in *Dictionnaire d'histoire et de géographie ecclésiastiques* (Paris: Letouzey et Ané, 1951), 12:354–405; Cosimo Damiano Fonseca, *Medioevo canonicale* (Milan: Vita e pensiero, 1970).

[3] Ursula Vones-Liebenstein, "Der Verband der Regularkanoniker von Saint-Ruf. Entstehung, Struktur und normative Grundlagen," in *Regula Sancti Augustini. Normative Grundlage differenter Verbände im Mittelalter*, ed. Gert Melville and Anne Müller (Paring: Augustiner-Chorherren-Verlag, 2002), 49–103.

[4] Cosimo Damiano Fonseca, "Il movimento canonicale a Lucca e nella diocesi lucchese fra XI e XII secolo," in *Alluccio da Pescia. Un santo laico dell'età post-gregoriana (1070–1134)*, ed. Cinzio Violante (Rome: Jouvence, 1993), 147–57.

even at the cost of a break with the foundational lines of the established order.[5]

For that aim, as has been emphasized, it needed the energy of those who were driven from within by a religious fire, who put their faith before all worldliness, all earthly power, all material wealth. The church hierarchy needed zealots who were driven to a radical reform of Christian life from below, so to speak, because the hierarchy itself was striving for radical reform. And that same need had given rise to the desire to see so many communities of hermits and wandering preachers integrated once again into the institutional church—communities that were led by charismatics and that in many respects stood on the border between heresy and orthodoxy. Yet precisely here was to be found the use of the emergent movement to redefine the clergy. It could become a powerful instrument of church reform—one that in all events now came not from below but from above.

Yet as had been true of the bands of hermits and wandering preachers, such an option for the reform of the church could be embraced only insofar as its proponents did not shy away from setting themselves apart, deliberately and polemically, from established structures. Already in 1059 the Lateran Synod held by Pope Nicholas II had formulated (with Hildebrand, later Gregory VII, as its spokesman) sharp attacks against the lax ways of clerical communities, as well as of canonesses, with regard to private property, and against their pompous lifestyle. The synod had also sharply criticized the old regulations for canonical life crafted at Aachen.[6] The call now was for the creation of communities of clerics who would take as their example the apostolic life of the early church in Jerusalem, where according to the Acts of the Apostles all were of "one heart and one mind" (Acts 4:32).[7] To pursue and to realize this core aim was to create a renewed clerical

---

[5] On its later impact, see Brigitte Szabó-Bechstein, "'Libertas ecclesiae' vom 12. bis zur Mitte des 13. Jahrhunderts. Verbreitung und Wandel des Begriffs seit seiner Prägung durch Gregor VII.," in *Die abendländische Freiheit vom 10. bis zum 14. Jahrhundert*, ed. Johannes Fried (Sigmaringen: Thorbecke, 1991), 147–76.

[6] Uta-Renate Blumenthal, *Gregor VII. Papst zwischen Canossa und Kirchenreform* (Darmstadt: Primus, 2001), 165–66.

[7] Klaus Schreiner, "Ein Herz und eine Seele. Eine urchristliche Lebensform und ihre Institutionalisierung im augustinisch geprägten Mönchtum des hohen und späten Mittelalters," in Melville and Müller, *Regula Sancti Augustini*, 1–47.

estate, one whose integrity and piety, even in its outward appearance, legitimized the church's movement for independence.

The effort was a success. Apart from canonical life's eremitical beginnings, which had a long-lived impact (not least with respect to the community that formed around Norbert of Xanten), the focal points for its new foundations of regular canons shifted to cathedral chapters, and even more to new settlements that were "established among the people," as it was said,[8] and that could thereby carry out their apostolic mission in the form of pastoral care. These new communities were supported by bishops who acted locally in support of church reform in the Roman spirit. Among them were figures like the already-mentioned Ivo of Chartres,[9] for example, or the bishop of Lucca, Anselm (1035–1086),[10] both of whom, significantly, were also great experts in the law of the church.

In Germany the impetus for new foundations came above all from nobility in search of their independence (as has already been shown in the context of monastic foundations) and who therefore preferred to hand over their foundations to the pope rather than to a royal power. But already in the eleventh century, these initiatives often came directly from clergy, about whom there is for the most part little surviving evidence and who were seldom charismatics—figures like the otherwise almost unknown Adam, for example, who founded a church in Mortara, just south of Novara in northern Italy, and who gathered a community of clerics around him.[11] In doing so he laid the foundation for a congregation of regular canons that would receive strong papal support and that would become, like Cluny, recognized as a kind of church, the *ecclesia Mortariensis*.

---

[8] *Libellus de diversis ordinibus et professionibus qui sunt in aecclesia*, ed. Giles Constable and Bernard S. Smith, 2nd ed. (Oxford: Clarendon Press, 2003), 66–86.

[9] Rolf Sprandel, *Ivo von Chartres und seine Stellung in der Kirchengeschichte* (Stuttgart: Hiersemann, 1962), 139–42.

[10] Cosimo Damiano Fonseca, "Il capitolo di San Martino e la riforma canonicale nella seconda metà del secolo XI," in *Sant'Anselmo vescovo di Lucca (1073–1086) nel quadro delle trasformazioni sociali e della riforma ecclesiastica*, ed. Cinzio Violante (Rome: Istituto Storico Italiano per il Medio Evo, 1992), 51–64.

[11] Cristina Andenna, *Mortariensis Ecclesia: Una congregazione di canonici regolari in Italia settentrionale tra XI e XII secolo* (Münster: LIT, 2007).

Across Europe, communities of clerics emerged that began to lead lives of a kind once led only by monks. They did not stand on the border between heresy and orthodoxy, but they very much stood between reactionary forces hostile to reform and the new avant-garde. The clerical movement, too, was thus shaped at first by a search for the best way, by an experiment that carried with it the possibility of compromise and backsliding into old ways.

The dynamic is revealed clearly in the story of a leading protagonist of reform, Bishop Altmann of Passau (1065–1091).[12] He was a genuine supporter of the reforming papacy, a true ally of Gregory VII. But his diocesan clergy made it hard for him to realize his ideals because they firmly resisted his ban on clerical marriage. Altmann now dared to experiment. Around 1067–1073 he founded in his episcopal city a community under the patronage of Saint Nicholas and staffed it with regular clergy. He thereby laid the foundation for what was at first a remarkable success story. In 1071, he reformed his own tradition-rich community of Saint Florian near Linz, and in 1073 he worked to found the community of Rottenbuch[13] in the so-called Pfaffenwinkel ("priests' corner"), a region in the southwestern reaches of Bavaria. He staffed that community with canons from Saint Nicholas. Rottenbuch then became a center of its own reform circle and a place of refuge for many clergy loyal to the papacy.

Rottenbuch was also home to one of the most important of all medieval regular canons, Gerhoh (1092/3–1169),[14] later prior of Reichersberg and an impressive advocate of an eschatologically oriented church—a zealous teacher, as only the *ecclesia militans* of his era could produce. But Rottenbuch was also a model foundation for other

[12] Egon Boshof, "Bischof Altmann, St. Nikola und die Kanonikerreform. Das Bistum Passau im Investiturstreit," in *Tradition und Entwicklung. Gedenkschrift für Johann Riederer*, ed. Karl-Heinz Pollok (Passau: Passavia, 1981), 317–45.

[13] Jakob Mois, *Das Stift Rottenbuch in der Kirchenreform des 11.–12. Jahrhunderts* (Munich and Freising: Verlag des erzbischöflichen Ordinariats München und Freising, 1953).

[14] Peter Classen, "Gerhoch von Reichersberg und die Regularkanoniker in Bayern und Österreich," in *Ausgewählte Aufsätze von Peter Classen*, ed. Josef Fleckenstein (Sigmaringen: Thorbecke, 1983), 431–60; Reinhold Rieger, "Kirchenreform und Theologiekritik bei Gerhoch von Reichersberg," in *Frömmigkeit und Theologie an Chorherrenstiften*, ed. Ulrich Köpf (Ostfildern: Thorbecke, 2009), 141–56.

communities from a legal point of view. Already a few years after its establishment, its founding family, the Welfs, handed it over to the papacy and placed it under papal protection. As a monastery that was the property of the papacy, Rottenbuch enjoyed the so-called *libertas Romana*. It stood out in combative contrast to the traditional ways of imperial monasteries.[15] Within the universal church, Rottenbuch was thus the embodiment of an institution untouched by the traditions of proprietary churches.

From 1078 Bishop Altmann could no longer enter Passau, his episcopal city. His clashes with the clergy—who were for the most part still not reformed—had become too sharp, and he stood prominently on the front lines against Henry IV. But he continued to establish new communities for the regular clergy. In 1081 he transformed his own community of Saint Pölten, in modern Lower Austria, accordingly. In 1083 he then founded Göttweig (also in modern Lower Austria) as a community of regular canons, though later in the same century that community was transformed yet again into a Benedictine abbey. Altmann failed at only one thing: the transformation of his cathedral chapter into a community of regular canons, through which he could have created a spiritual and administrative center for the reform of the clergy.

Also at work in Altmann's era were Archbishop Gebhard of Salzburg (1060–1088) and Bishop Adalbert of Würzburg (1045–1090) in Franconia.[16] Both were similarly zealous supporters of church reform and opponents of Henry IV. They too made use of the strategy of creating new foundations in seeking to establish anchor points for the development of a reformed clergy. Their most important creations were Reichersberg, on the River Inn, and Heidenfeld, near Schweinfurt.

One milestone in the development of the regular canons, however, owed its existence to the pope and former Cluniac monk Urban II,[17] whom we have already encountered so often in connection with the affairs of the monks and their religious movements. Compactly

---

[15] See pp. 56–57.

[16] Stephan Acht, "Die Bischöfe," in *Die Augustinerchorherren in Bayern*, ed. Paul Mai (Regensburg: Schnell & Steiner, 1999), 19–25.

[17] Horst Fuhrmann, *Papst Urban II. und der Stand der Regularkanoniker* (Munich: Verlag der Bayerischen Akademie der Wissenschaften, 1984).

The Regular Canons 131

formulated for the foundation of Rottenbuch in 1092, Urban's "path-breaking" charter came to serve as a formulary for other houses.[18] In the charter Urban set the regulated common life of the canons (the *vita canonica*) on equal footing with the life of monks (the *vita monastica*) insofar as he designated the *vita canonica* as having been the original form of Christian life—albeit one that had fallen into oblivion in the wake of the growth of the church. Because the regular canons, by virtue of this ancient legacy, had been given the task of the *cura animarum*—pastoral care for the souls of humankind—they could be sure that they held a place superior even to the contemplative lives of the monks. As a text from the following decades put it, Christ himself had provided the *vita canonica* to humankind as a medicine that would save them from damnation.[19]

Papal sources from around this time—preserved in the charters of Alexander II and Urban II—contain a formula that sought more precisely to articulate the normative framework of the regular canons' way of life and to tie the familiar concept *regulariter* to a concrete guideline: they were tasked *secundum regulam beati Augustini vivere* ("to live according to the rule of blessed Augustine"). It has been proven, however, that the rule that had been written especially for the common life of clerics was first adopted in 1107/8 in the communities of Springiersbach, Hamersleben (near Halberstadt), and the Parisian abbey of Saint Victor—that is, the Rule of Augustine. Thus regular canons in German-speaking lands are still today called Augustinian *Chorherren*.[20]

With respect to the authenticity of the tradition of the text that was called the Rule of Augustine, contemporaries held many different views.[21] They had no doubt regarding the authenticity of the text called the *Praeceptum*; there was, however, doubt concerning

---

[18] Stefan Weinfurter, "Reformkanoniker und Reichsepiskopat im Hochmittelalter," *Historisches Jahrbuch* 97–98 (1978): 158–93, here 166.

[19] Weinfurter, "*Vita canonica* und Eschatologie," in *Secundum regulam vivere*, ed. Gert Melville (Windberg: Poppe-Verlag, 1978).

[20] Charles Dereine, "Vie commune, règle de Saint Augustin et chanoines réguliers au 11e siècle," *Revue d'histoire ecclésiastique* 42 (1946): 365–406; Stefan Weinfurter, *Salzburger Bistumsreform und Bischofspolitik im 12. Jahrhundert* (Cologne and Vienna: Böhlau, 1975), 236–38.

[21] See p. 12.

another, stricter work, also believed to be a work of Augustine, the so-called *Ordo monasterii*. From the second decade of the twelfth century, the canonical movement began to divide into two camps: the so-called old order (*Ordo antiquus*), which used the *Praeceptum* as its normative text (for example, in Rottenbuch in Bavaria, Marbach in Alsace, and Saint Rufus in southern France, already discussed above) and the new order (*Ordo novus*), which followed the more strict *Ordo monasterii* (among the Praemonstratensians of Norbert of Xanten, for example, Springiersbach on the Mosel, in Klosterrath [near Aachen], noted already as one of Norbert's many stops, and in St. Victor in Paris, one of the greatest spiritual centers of the twelfth century).[22] Both the old and the new orders developed around centers that drew together dependent monasteries or that spread their spiritual influence to other houses. But no great merger ever encompassed whole regions and wide stretches of Christendom, as had happened with Cluny and later Prémontré, or even (as will be seen) Cîteaux.

The Roman church emerged as victor in the struggle for its freedom. A decisive, symbolic pause in the battle was the so-called Concordat of Worms of 1122, which ended the Investiture Controversy. For the reformist movements in Germany this truce between pope and emperor marked an important step, since from that point forward foundations of regular canons no longer needed to be seen, as had been true at Rottenbuch, for example, only as places of refuge for persecuted reformers. Rather, such foundations could now align themselves with the new political direction of the church, an order whose reforming and indeed in many respects quite revolutionary eleventh-century dynamic would be followed by the transformation into a more and more juristically shaped institution.

Communities of canonesses, already sharply criticized in 1059, came to feel these developments keenly and were now emphatically required to order their affairs properly.[23] The Second Lateran Council of 1139 spoke of the contemptible way in which so many women's communities seemed to live according to no established rule. In 1148, the Synod of Reims, with Pope Eugene III presiding, required that women who called themselves *canonicae* (canonesses) and yet who

---

[22] Weinfurter, *Salzburger Bistumsreform*, 238–40.

[23] Hedwig Röckelein, "Die Auswirkung der Kanonikerreform," in *Institution und Charisma*, ed. Franz J. Felten et al. (Cologne: Böhlau, 2009), 55–72.

lived irregularly, luxuriously, and without strict enclosure be required to adopt either the Rule of Saint Benedict or the Rule of Augustine. Nor did these accusations disappear thereafter; until the Council of Vienne in 1311 there were repeated demands for canonesses to adopt a religious rule and make profession of lifelong vows. The success of these efforts, however, was in the end rather limited.[24]

For the regular canons, in contrast, the new ecclesiastical circumstance after the Concordat of Worms proved to be enormously fruitful. What at first served to establish a religiously and morally renewed clerical estate could now in practice be turned toward increasing the efficiency of pastoral efforts within diocesan structures.

In this respect a virtually model enforcement of the apostolic ideal occurred under the archbishop of Salzburg, Conrad I, who led his ecclesiastical province from 1106–1147. A brief sketch of these events can serve to round out the overall developments among regular canons in this period. To do so admittedly provides only an exemplar in a systematic sense. The historical complexity of episcopal politics with respect to the regular canons could and did take many different forms. But apart from papal support,[25] everything depended on the sustained reforming energy of holders of episcopal office.[26]

With Conrad that energy was unstoppable.[27] After Henry IV had entrusted him, in the old manner, with ring and staff—and thus not only with the worldly goods and rights of the archbishopric of Salzburg (the *temporalia*) but also with its spiritual rights (*spiritualia*)—and after he had clashed with Henry IV in 1111, only in the wake of the Concordat of Worms was Conrad once again able to occupy his archiepiscopal seat.

At once he began to undertake broad measures—freeing church institutions from lay control, improving pastoral care through an emphasis on clerical integrity—intended to realize the principles of

---

[24] Immo Eberl, "Stiftisches Leben in Klöstern. Zur Regeltreue im klösterlichen Alltag des Spätmittelalters und der frühen Neuzeit," in *Studien zum Kanonissenstift*, ed. Irene Crusius (Göttingen: Vandenhoeck & Ruprecht, 2001), 275–315.

[25] Ursula Vones-Liebenstein, "Hadrian IV. *regularis inter primos disciplinae aemulator* und die Regularkanoniker," in *Päpstliche Herrschaft im Mittelalter. Funktionsweisen—Strategien—Darstellungsformen*, ed. Stefan Weinfurter (Ostfildern: Thorbecke, 2012), 97–126.

[26] Weinfurter, "Reformkanoniker."

[27] On the following, see Weinfurter, *Salzburger Bistumsreform.*

church reform in his archdiocese. And religious houses, it seemed to him, were especially promising focal points for his efforts. He was certainly concerned with communities of monks—Benedictines and Cistercians—but above all with communities of clerics, since his aim to improve pastoral care depended on them. In this respect he achieved something that had eluded Altmann of Passau: in 1122 Conrad transformed his own cathedral chapter into a community of regular clerics under vows of personal poverty and the common life. The archiepiscopal clerical community of Reichersberg on the Inn followed, and thereafter Maria Saal in Carinthia, the episcopal chapter in Gurk, the communities of Au and Gars on the Inn, Herrenchiemsee, and a dozen more houses, some of them even in the jurisdictions of his suffragans, or subordinate diocesan bishops.

The instruments of Conrad's influence were nearly always the same. Quite against the rigid proprietary-church policies of some other bishops (above all in the western regions of the empire), who usually disposed of their foundations' properties seemingly at random, Conrad established a special propertied estate from which he secured endowments serving the independent administration of each church. He often also tied these, in the case of new foundations, to lands that had been donated by noble families, who now appeared as founders. Each of these strategies helped to preserve the houses by granting them a degree of institutional permanence.

A second element of Conrad's strategy was to transfer the tithes of the laity to his reformed houses in order to strengthen them further financially. He also often handed the leadership of these houses over to archdeacons, whose office occupied an intermediary position between the archbishop and his churches. In terms of ecclesiastical organization and hierarchy, his churches were to be bound directly to him. A final instrument, adopted in the name of ecclesiastical liberty and in the interest of concentrating the special protection of the archbishop, was to place pronounced limits on the reach of the legal institution known as the advocate—an office that was necessary but still dangerous for the independent development of a monastery.

In Conrad's diocese the regular canons came to occupy a predominant position, one that placed them in a sort of symbiotic relationship with the office of archbishop. It might seem that they had also lost something that sustained monastic life in general and that other alliances of regular canons might to a certain degree have been able to preserve: the fundamental unassailability of a cloistered way of life focused strictly on itself. Yet this reform circle produced the introduction to the Rule of Augustine already noted above. That text reflected on the establishment and aims of the *vita canonica* and in doing so reached the exceptionally confident conclusion that the canons' way of life was superior to all others. It renewed in a modern way the ideal of the common life of the apostles that was understood to lie in the origins of the church, forcing aside an outdated present by way of a newly awakened vigor. This eschatological position could certainly be deployed in the service of episcopal interests, but it was in itself unassailable.[28]

---

[28] Weinfurter, "*Vita canonica* und Eschatologie."

6

The Cistercians
Collegiality Instead of Hierarchy

Robert's Path from Molesme to Cîteaux and Back

At that time another community had emerged from eremitical roots.[1] It not only served as a model of remarkable flowering and lastingly shaped the world of monasticism through its innovative organization. It also made the most of the need to combine reforming energy with institutional stability. That community came to be known as the Cistercians.[2]

In 1098, in a meadow called *Cistercium*, in the middle of a deep forest south of Dijon, in a "place of horror" (as in hindsight it would

---

[1] Gert Melville, "Die Zisterzienser und der Umbruch des Mönchtums im 11. und 12. Jahrhundert," in *Norm und Realität. Kontinuität und Wandel der Zisterzienser im Mittelalter*, ed. Franz J. Felten and Werner Rösener (Berlin: LIT, 2009), 23–43.

[2] On the following, as an overview, Louis Julius Lekai, *The Cistercians: Ideals and Reality* (Kent, OH: Kent State University Press, 1977); Kaspar Elm and Peter Joerissen, eds., *Die Zisterzienser. Ordensleben zwischen Ideal und Wirklichkeit* (Cologne: Wienand, 1982); Immo Eberl, *Die Zisterzienser. Geschichte eines europäischen Ordens* (Stuttgart: Thorbecke, 2003); Felten and Rösener, eds., *Norm und Realität*; Mette Birkedal Bruun and Emilia Jamroziak, eds., *The Cambridge Companion to the Cistercian Order* (New York: Cambridge University Press, 2013); Emilia Jamroziak, *The Cistercian Order in Medieval Europe: 1090–1500* (London: Routledge, 2013); Jörg Oberste, *Die Zisterzienser* (Stuttgart: Kohlhammer, 2014). Limited almost exclusively to English Cistercians: Janet E. Burton, *The Cistercians in the Middle Ages* (Woodbridge, UK: Boydell, 2011).

be called in the writing known as the *Exordium Cistercii*)[3] and of
"deserted isolation," a place that was "quite unpleasant and inaccessible to men of the world," a group of twenty-one men who had left
the community of Molesme in northern Burgundy along with their
abbot Robert (ca. 1028–1111) founded a settlement that they called
the "new monastery" (*novum monasterium*). From there they would
begin to build the largest alliance of monasteries that Christendom
had yet seen. The Rule of Saint Benedict would be realized there in
a way that would powerfully eclipse the Benedictine life of Cluny.

Such success, for what was at first a quite insignificant monastic
foundation, had certainly not been foreseen from the beginning.[4]
The new monastery's early days were quite different from those of
Cluny, which from its very founding charter had enjoyed freedom
from every lordship and thereby had the best chance for expansion;
it was different too from the great number of new foundations discussed above, which had emerged under the pressure of or with the
aid of representatives of the church hierarchy. The monastery in
Cistercium—Cîteaux—at first knew nothing of such massive support, enjoying at best only a certain goodwill toward Robert himself
on the part of the nobility of the region, by virtue of ties of kinship.

On the contrary, the foundation was judged a violation of the
law. Ivo of Chartres had earlier designated those monks from Coulombs who wanted to flee from their monastery into the desert as
"Sarabaites," that is, as representatives of what the Rule of Saint Benedict called the "worst kind of monks" (1.6), and had accused them of
wanting to live "in secluded places, according to their own law." The
group around Robert could now be accused of the same—and worse,
since the head of a monastic community was himself among those
who had fled. Hence there was deep ambivalence surrounding the
name of their settlement. The designation *new monastery* expressed
a vision that captured a sense of the abandonment of and separation
from old ways, as well as the desire to venture out into novelty. An
early Cistercian text, the *Exordium parvum*, saw this vision as already
in the heart of the founder: "they rejoiced in setting aside the old man,

---

[3] "Exordium Cisterciensis coenobii," in *Narrative and Legislative Texts from
Early Cîteaux, Latin Text in Dual Edition with English Translation and Notes*, ed.
Chrysogonus Waddell (Brecht: Cîteaux: Commentarii cistercienses, 1999), 179.
[4] On the following, see Melville, "Die Zisterzienser."

and in having taken up the new."[5] The program was intelligible only to those who saw it in terms of renouncing "the old man" and who followed the path to that goal.

The monks of Cîteaux very soon captured their version of their early history in two texts—the *Exordium parvum* and the *Exordium cistercii*—in which they justified, from their point of view, the reasons for a new beginning. In addition, one particularly reliable external observer of all of the transformations of religious life in his day, the historian Orderic Vitalis, sought an explanation for the establishment of Cîteaux in the early history of the community and felt himself compelled to reflect on it in more detail.[6]

Orderic passed down the notable words of Robert from a time before the founding of Cîteaux, when Robert was still abbot of Molesme: there Robert had explained before his brothers that although they had all made profession to the Rule of Saint Benedict, they did not follow it fully (*non ex integro*) since they did not work with their hands, as the fathers Anthony, Macarius, and others had done—those whose inimitable life as *Aegyptiorum patres* Robert now remembered compellingly. The wealth of the monks of Molesme was abundant, drawn as it was from tithes, and they nourished themselves with the blood of men in whose sins they would thereby now have a share. So as not to be breakers of their oaths, they were now to follow the Rule of Saint Benedict completely (*omnino*); they should earn their food and clothing through their own work, give up their luxurious clothing, and renounce their incomes from tithes. And yet the monks of the now wealthy Molesme—so Orderic reported further—had for the most part abruptly rejected all of these impositions, asserting among other things that they well deserved their tithes, because they were members of the clerical estate and holders of clerical offices.

This struggle over tithes and matters of conscience had in a certain way been orchestrated by Ivo of Chartres and his adversary Rainald; it was also symptomatic of models of reform grounded in that era's ideals of poverty. In the monastery of Molesme there

---

[5] Waddell, *Narrative and Legislative Texts*, 253.

[6] *The Ecclesiastical History of Orderic Vitalis*, ed. Marjorie M. Chibnall (Oxford: Clarendon Press, 1973), 4:310–26, and for the following especially 312, 314; Melville, "Die Zisterzienser," 29–30.

had clearly been exceptionally difficult struggles over the matter, as the *Exordium parvum* reveals, mentioning among other things the sharp mistreatment and imprisonment of the prior Alberic, an ally of Robert's. The later course of events has already been noted: Robert and his like-minded followers retreated from Molesme and, with the help of the Burgundian nobility, settled in Cistercium. There from 1098 on they lived in solitude and resolved (as Orderic put it) "to observe the Rule of Benedict to the letter, as the Jews followed the law of Moses" (*regulam Benedicti sicut Judei legem Moisi ad litteram servare penitus*).[7]

Robert's renunciation of office and community was not his first:[8] after becoming a monk in the monastery of Moûtier-la-Celle in Troyes in 1044, and prior there in 1053, in 1068 he was elected abbot of Saint-Michel de Tonnerre, a community shaped by Cluniac traditions. Yet already in 1071 he resigned from this post because he could not bind his monks to a strict observance of the Rule, and he returned to his home monastery. A little later he became prior of Saint-Ayoul de Provins, a dependent of Moûtier-la-Celle. Yet when he was asked around 1073/74 to lead a group of hermits in the forest of Collan near Tonnerre, he changed his mind again, took over the leadership of that group with papal permission, and with them founded the abbey of Molesme in 1075.

At the beginning life there was shaped by hard work and strict asceticism. Yet after 1080, in the wake of a chastening economic crisis, the abbey's wealth grew considerably through donations and transfers of parishes and their tithes. The abbey became an owner of great estates and founded a number of granges and priories. Ignoring their eremitical origins, one faction of the community now looked to Cluny as the model of monastic life. At this very time, Bruno of Cologne came with his followers to Molesme, as was noted above, and Robert secured for them there a remote settlement suitable for their eremitical life. Yet Bruno could not find the isolation from the world he was looking for, and, as noted above, he did not stay long. Those monks of Molesme whose eremitical sympathies

---

[7] *Ecclesiastical History*, 4:322.

[8] On the following, see Eberl, *Die Zisterzienser*, 19–25; and Thomas Merton, "Saint Robert of Molesme, 1028 to 1111," *Cistercian Studies Quarterly* 46 (2011): 273–76.

had not changed, and who perhaps found themselves encouraged by Bruno's appearance, moved out under the leadership of Guérin, later bishop of Sion, and in 1094 founded the monastery of Aulps in upper Savoy.[9] Already disturbed over the growing wealth of his house, Robert left Molesme, designated the prior, Alberic, as his acting representative, and retreated with the others to Aulps. As the tensions in the community of Molesme rose, however, he was forced by papal command to return there—and from that point the well-known story began to run its course.

Thus it should not seem surprising that one year after the settlement at Cîteaux, a charter of the apostolic legate and archbishop of Lyon, Hugh of Die, accused Robert of *solita levitas*, of an inherent lack of seriousness that threatened to lead to more unpredictability.[10] Well into old age (he was already some seventy years old at the founding of Cîteaux), Robert, along with so many of his contemporaries, nonetheless remained filled with restless energy in the search for the best way to salvation—a search that clearly might require moving from place to place and the breaking of institutional boundaries whenever the demands of his inner life were not met. For Robert understood himself as being true to his vow to uphold the Rule of Saint Benedict, which stood higher than the obligation to discharge duties of an office according to church law. The vow alone showed the way to salvation.

In 1099 an assembly in Port-d'Anselle (on the Saône) called by Archbishop Hugh decided, with the approval of pope Urban II, to recall Robert from his new foundation and to compel him to return to his old position in Molesme.[11] The decision was reached at the instigation of the community at Molesme, faced after the loss of its leader with a suddenly waning influence. Robert's followers were allowed to stay at Cîteaux if they wished and to be freed from their profession of obedience to an abbot who had been sent away. So it happened: Robert yielded and returned to Molesme. The majority of the community followed him. A faction that was deeply disappointed by Robert's actions remained in the forest wilderness, ready

[9] Anselme Dimier, "Saint Guérin. Abbé d'Aulps et évêque de Sion," in *Mélanges à la mémoire du père Anselme Dimier*, ed. Benoît Chauvin (Arbois: B. Chauvin, 1987), 689–92.

[10] Waddell, *Narrative and Legislative Texts*, 242.

[11] On the following, see Eberl, *Die Zisterzienser*, 25–46.

to embrace manual labor, asceticism, and strict poverty, far removed from the secular world.

Already at the time of the implementation of the decisions of Port-d'Anselle, the legate Hugh had designated the settlement in Cîteaux as *Novum monasterium*, thereby recognizing its identity as an independent monastery.[12] In October of 1100,[13] with the bull *Desiderium quod*, Paschal II finally recognized the community as a monastery under its abbot, Alberic (1050–1109), once prior in Molesme and successor of Robert in Cîteaux, thereby taking the community under papal protection and freeing it from any affiliation with Molesme. The new foundation now enjoyed legal recognition at the highest levels. Thus within a short time Cîteaux was no longer a *locus privatus*, where renegade monks lived *proprio iure*. It had become an abbey enjoying the privilege of papal protection, one that could now claim for itself the goodwill of the local nobility as well as the episcopacy.

After these troubled beginnings haunted by accusations of illegality, Cîteaux thus quickly acquired a recognized legal status. On this institutional basis could be built a combination of standards of conduct that Cîteaux, like no other religious community, understood itself to represent convincingly: the principle of rigorous poverty, upheld while following literally the Rule of Saint Benedict. Here lay the foundation for Cistercian success.

The Measure of the Pure Rule

As Orderic rightly observed, Cîteaux had in fact realized what in Molesme had remained only an elusive goal: a commitment to follow the Rule of Saint Benedict with adherence to its every word. In the *Exordium parvum*,[14] the Cistercians underscored that the "rightness of the Rule" (*rectitudo regulae*) was to be the measure of their way of life, and they rejected all that was not to be found there[15]—tithes,

---

[12] Waddell, *Narrative and Legislative Texts*, 139–42.

[13] Chrysogonus Waddell, "Prelude to a Feast of Freedom: Notes on the Roman Privilege *Desiderium quod* of October 19, 1100," *Cîteaux* 33 (1982): 247–303, here 267–69.

[14] Waddell, *Narrative and Legislative Texts*, 235–59.

[15] Maria Pia Schindele, "'Rectitudo' und 'puritas,'" in *Zisterziensische Spiritualität*, ed. Clemens M. Kasper and Klaus Schreiner (St. Ottilien: EOS, 1994),

parishes, villages, and bondsmen, for example. In a notable analogy to their contemporary Stephen of Thiers, with whose later congregation of Grandmont they would soon come into competition, the Cistercians emphasized that, "poor with the poor Christ" (*pauperes cum paupere Christo*), they renounced the riches of this world as well as all adornment, even of their churches, Mass vestments, and altar furnishings. Yet in contrast to the Grandmontines, they appealed in this regard not to the Gospel itself but to the Rule of Saint Benedict, a text that for the former had been only a branch, not the root of the true teaching of Christ.

Also in contrast to the essentially more rigid Grandmontines, the Cistercians resolved to accept goods, vineyards, meadows, and forests from their donors. For the administration of those estates they chose to take on *conversi*—laity bound to the monastery—both because the monks could not otherwise observe the prayer services prescribed by the Rule, and also because it was unfitting for monks to spend their time on granges beyond the monastery walls. But on the basis of their experience in Molesme, they well knew that with that kind of agricultural economy came considerable wealth, and with it the concern that their spiritual energy might wane. So also in the *Exordium parvum*, albeit in an extension written a few years later, they countered vehemently, "In that time the abbey's ownership of land, vineyards, meadows, and farms grew, yet its discipline did not decline. The monks of Cîteaux fought well and bravely against their own mistakes and the temptations of evil spirits, and completed their race."[16] As will become clear, over the course of a century their combination of a strong economy and frugality would lead inevitably to considerable wealth, the effects of which could "tarnish purity,"[17] as Pope Innocent III later warned.

But with poverty and strict adherence to the Rule, the Cistercians in those early days had managed to intertwine two ideals that the adher-

---

53–73; Guido Cariboni, "Il papato di fronte alle crisi istituzionale dell'ordine cistercense nei primi decenni del XIII secolo," in *Il nostro ordine è la Carità. Cistercensi nei secoli XII e XIII*, ed. Guido Cariboni (Milan: Vita e pensiero, 2011), 93–126, here 71–76.

[16] "Exordium parvum," in Waddell, *Narrative and Legislative Texts*, chap. 17, p. 257.

[17] *Innocentii III Romani pontificis Regestorum sive epistolarum liber decimus sextus*, PL 216:826; Cariboni, "Il papato," 103.

The cloister of the Cistercian abbey of Fontenay in northern Burgundy.

ents of other religious movements in the era found incompatible. Both were highly charged with symbolic meaning. Across the whole eremitical movement, longing for poverty was a leitmotif, not only in practice but also symbolically, for retreat from the world and for justifying the turn from inherited institutional forms. Life in voluntary poverty could be understood spiritually as the imitation of the lonely Jesus Christ on the mountain, while the embrace of the outward appearance of poverty was sometimes attacked by contemporary observers as a retreat from the *sensus communis*. A retreat from institutional structures for the sake of poverty was in turn interpreted as a "life after one's own law." But it also informed a sharp and polemically articulated opposition to the following of monastic rules as they that been practiced in the old monasteries—a way of life now critiqued as formalistic and denounced as pharisaical quibbling over words. The dichotomy seemed impossible to reconcile and could be circumvented pragmatically only when new guidelines could be crafted either by calling on primordial norms—whether those of the Gospel, the early church, or the Desert Fathers—or by yielding to norms later introduced.

The Cistercians, however, were able convincingly to resolve this tension. They placed great worth on a strict following of the precept of poverty, for they also understood themselves as "poor with the poor

Christ," who had withdrawn from the world. Yet in order to realize their ideal, they did precisely what had been denounced in traditional monasteries: they obeyed an inherited rule, in the words of Orderic Vitalis, "as the Jews followed the law of Moses."

The monks found success without contradicting their ideals, however, because they believed themselves able to discern in the Rule of Saint Benedict the model of poverty itself. One had only to follow the Rule purely and to the letter, and not to weigh it down with as many customs and usages, relaxations and exceptions, as were supposedly found in the old Benedictine monasteries, above all among the Cluniacs—a position no less full of polemic than had been encountered in other eremitical communities.[18] The Cistercians thus brought together in a powerful way the tensions of two symbolic fields whose polarity had ignited the greatest minds of the day: they transformed the one field, observance of the Rule, into the guarantor of the other, renunciation of the world through poverty. It was already an attractive solution in principle, because it tied a structurally boundless search for salvation through poverty to the measure of an established order now lived correctly. In other words, it brought the renewing power of religious energy into harmony with institutional permanence in a way that did not give up one for the other. When the reconciliation of these two perspectives could be put into practice, it created a considerable advantage over whatever else competing forms of religious life might have to offer. The Cistercians could point to a program that they embraced not as willful innovators, as the eremitical movements had been accused of doing, but rather as the true followers and preservers of a truth that had been handed down to them. They were therefore not forced to abandon ascetic poverty as the spiritual stance of their movement.

In order to have credibility in practice, the Cistercians had to distinguish their observance of the Rule from that of other Benedictine monasteries and to formulate a distinct identity within their community.

On the one hand, they accomplished this task on the level of symbolic self-representation, as is demonstrated in the architecture of

---

[18] Adriaan H. Bredero, "The Early Cistercians and the Old Monasticism," in *Cluny et Cîteaux au douzième siècle* (Amsterdam/Maarsen: APA-Holland University Press, 1985), 351–72.

their monastic buildings and above all in churches closed off from all lay outsiders. Their churches were also characterized by a lack of adornment, recognizable in the absence of a tower and a preference for ridge turrets.[19] The new color of their habit, too, was particularly well chosen to have a special impact, since it so notably set itself apart from the inherited style of the Benedictine monks. Of the Cistercian cloth's color Archbishop Hugh of Rouen said, for example, that it was grayish white (it was, that is, neither bleached nor dyed), either because the Cistercians in the region simply could not have found anything cheaper (and thus could be identified as religious living in poverty) or because white was supposed to epitomize the monks' "bodily purity" (*castitas corporalis*).[20]

On the other hand, in differentiating themselves from other religious communities, it was vital that the Cistercians strengthen themselves organizationally and establish themselves as a distinct legal entity. In this regard, the young community now faced a great challenge. For even its lofty claims of pure adherence to the Rule—a core ideal formulated at the very beginning and imported from Molesme itself—should not conceal the fact that at first the little abbey was forced to fight for its very existence. In fact, it had no clear monopoly even on the ideal of adhering closely to the Rule. The hermit and wandering preacher Bernard of Tiron, who also enjoyed the church's great respect, had a career that in many respects mirrored Robert's—including his holding of leading offices in Benedictine communities. So, for example, at the same time as the New Monastery was begun, Bernard also founded a monastery in the wilderness to bring stability to his crowd of followers, and in 1109 he too prescribed for them the Rule of Saint Benedict.

---

[19] Matthias Untermann, "Gebaute 'Unanimitas': Zu den Bauvorschriften der Zisterzienser," in *Zisterzienser. Norm, Kultur, Reform. 900 Jahre Zisterzienser*, ed. Ulrich Knefelkamp (Berlin: Springer, 2001), 239–66; Carola Jäggi, "Ordensarchitektur als Kommunikation von Ordnung. Zisterziensische Baukunst zwischen Vielfalt und Einheit," in *Die Ordnung der Kommunikation und die Kommunikation der Ordnungen*, ed. Cristina Andenna et al. (Stuttgart: Franz Steiner, 2012), 203–25.

[20] Giles Constable, "The Ceremonies and Symbolism of Entering Religious Life and Taking the Monastic Habit from the Fourth to the Twelfth Century," in *Segni e riti nella chiesa altomedievale occidentale* (Spoleto: Centro italiano di studi sull'alto Medioevo, 1987), 771–834, here 828.

The *Charter of Charity* and the Invention of the "Order"

In contrast to most of the other monasteries and congregations that had emerged from the new religious movements, after Robert's departure the Cistercians could claim no founding charismatic whose word and deed could set the boundaries for everyday life and whose presence would provide the power needed both to hold the group together and to shape its identity. Yet this exceptional circumstance was also to prove a further decisive advantage for the Cistercians in their competition against so many other emerging religious communities. Since from the beginning the monks of Cîteaux were confronted with what charismatic-led bands only faced when their leader died—that is, the absence of norms that had been lived out in a model way for the community and that were thereby secure in their interpretation—as a community these new monks set down in writing how they wished to safeguard an observance of the Rule of Saint Benedict that would ensure the salvation of all of their members. Concretely this meant responding to the fact that after a few years of stagnation, Cîteaux had brought forth four daughter houses, later designated as "primary" abbeys: La Ferté (1113), Pontigny (1114), Clairvaux (1115), and Morimond (1115). The Rule of Saint Benedict had not been written for congregations, but for a single monastery. That it could nevertheless function as a general normative guide, however, had led large groups of monasteries to see themselves as a single "trans-local" community. The Cistercians rejected such a fiction from the beginning, however, because they had learned from the example of Molesme, a rich, well-endowed head of dependent houses. Their new houses were to be tied to one another in a different way.

Thus from 1115 onward they created a text whose renown was to be limitless and which was to augment the Rule of Saint Benedict to meet the demands of a family of monasteries. Under the direction of their third abbot, Stephen Harding, an Englishman remarkably skilled in organizational matters, they wrote the *Charter of Charity*, the *Carta caritatis*.[21] No other monastic organization had yet possessed a text like this. More significantly still, it can well be understood as the first constitutional document of the Middle Ages.[22]

---

[21] "Carta caritatis prior," in Waddell, *Narrative and Legislative Texts*, 274–82.

[22] On the following development in constitutional history, see Jean-Berthold Mahn, *L'ordre cistercien et son gouvernement, des origines au milieu du XIIIe siècle (1098–1265)* (Paris: E. de Boccard, 1982).

In 1119, Pope Calixtus II approved the first version of the *Carta caritatis*, which included the provision that every local bishop, before the founding of a Cistercian abbey in his diocese, was to agree "to avoid every conflict between bishop and monk."[23] This provision represented the basis for the future independence of Cistercian monasteries from episcopal control and jurisdiction.

The prologue to the document explained the core of the program, the unity that was to exist among all Cistercian abbeys:

> In this decree the aforesaid brothers, in order to avoid a future disruption of mutual concord, explained and ordered and established for those to come afterward through what contract and by what means, and indeed all the more by what charity [*qua caritate*] their monks should remain inseparably united in spirit, in abbeys scattered across different parts of the world [*in diversis mundi partibus*]. They desired to call this decree the Charter of Charity because it excludes any burden of financial contributions and thus has as its goal only charity and the welfare of souls in things human and divine.[24]

Only the statutes of the eremitical Vallombrosans from a few years before contained a similar thematization of brotherly love among those living in scattered communities. The Vallombrosans, however, had focused exclusively on maintaining a unity of liturgy among the various houses.[25] It is possible that Stephen Harding learned of those statutes during a trip through Italy.

With the *Carta caritatis*, the Cistercians had set in the place of an individual charismatic founder a comprehensive text whose contents expressed the community's will as law. Here they captured all the validity that was otherwise to be found in the charismatic himself. The text was now the embodiment of the charismatic ideal. Those who were ready to follow could bind themselves to it by virtue of a contract (*pactum*)—one that in turn bound together all who committed themselves to it as equals in love. At the same time, the *Carta caritatis* was to be a guarantor of future concord as well as a means of

---

[23] "Carta caritatis prior," 242.

[24] "Carta caritatis prior," 274.

[25] Nicolangelo D'Acunto, "Vallombrosani," in *Regulae—Consuetudines—Statuta*, ed. Cristina Andenna and Gert Melville (Münster: LIT, 2005), 157–67, here 161–62.

securing salvation. Moreover, it evinced a stunning visionary power: it spoke of communities of monks scattered across different regions, thereby anticipating a potential development that, though hardly foreseeable at the time of the text's composition, was in fact soon to be realized. The document looked consistently toward the future; it was a guide that promised posterity that they could not go astray in the future decisions they might face, whatever the circumstance.

In content, the *Carta caritatis* systematically and comprehensively encompassed all the needs for regulation faced by what was soon a community of abbeys that, though widely dispersed, had its own identity. First, it established that the mother abbey of Cîteaux was not to impose any burdens on its daughter houses but should nevertheless feel responsible for the welfare of the souls in each. It therefore denied any sort of the hierarchical or even proprietary and legal orientation toward a central authority that was true in the congregations of monasteries that already existed. A second aspect of the document concerned equality of life and a sense of unanimity (*unanimitas*). In the foreground stood the Rule of Saint Benedict, to be observed in all points and to the letter, according to the example of Cîteaux itself. Furthermore, patterns of daily life, all liturgical rites, and all of the hourly rhythms of prayer were to be the same in every abbey. A corresponding literature of instruction was to be made everywhere available, with identical content; a prime example of that literature was the "book of customs," the *Officia ecclesiastica* (also called the *Liber usuum*),[26] composed in the 1130s.

The *Carta caritatis* turned next—in its most extensive passage—to matters of organization for the community of monasteries. Key topics included the relationships of the abbeys to one another as well as regulations regarding visitation. The latter were to proceed along lines of filiation and were not to become instruments of lordship but rather a service of love that was to regulate, correct, and improve the circumstances in each daughter house in the interest of the welfare of souls. A revised version of the *Carta caritatis*—the so-called *Summa cartae caritatis* (composed presumably around 1124)—wrote succinctly of the limited power of the abbot visitor: "He can determine

---

[26] *Les "Ecclesiastica officia" cisterciens du XIIème siècle. Texte latin selon les manuscrits edités de Trente 1711, Ljubljana 31 et Dijon 114*, ed. Danièle Choisselet and Placide Vernet (Reiningue: Documentation cistercienne, 1989).

or regulate nothing without the permission of the [visited] abbot, with the exception of those things which concern the care for souls."[27] A few years before the composition of the *Carta caritatis*, a similar structure had already been established between the abbey of Aulps and its daughter house Balerne; it probably served here as a model.[28]

Finally, the *Carta caritatis* turned to the establishment of a body that was truly an innovative achievement: the general chapter, the annual gathering of all abbots as equals and representatives of their houses. Its most important task was to care for the salvation of the souls of all of their members and in that spirit "to make arrangements whenever something concerning the observance of the holy Rule or the statutes of the order is to be improved or encouraged, as well as to reinvigorate harmony and mutual love anew."[29] That is, the general chapter was to react with flexibility to new needs or deviations and, through correction, to preserve whatever seemed worthy of preservation. Regulations oriented toward the future had to be adaptable to new circumstances in a way that did not abandon original principles. Consequently the general chapter was further tasked with the punishment of abbots who broke either already established norms or the Rule. Furthermore, regular participation in the general chapter was required.

The revised edition of the *Carta caritatis*, from 1152, ends with an important stipulation. It can be seen as the capstone of the entire structure, because it not only defined in practice but also symbolized what was to become the Cistercians' distinct way: no position of leadership was to be given to anyone who was not a Cistercian. The one great world of monastic life was no more.[30]

In sum, the absence of a single head for the body of Cistercian monasteries required that the entire body provide balance. But the body allowed itself to take on any given burden only with the consent of all members. One such consensus had first been written down in a foundational contract, the *Carta caritatis prior*. It was first approved

---

[27] Waddell, *Narrative and Legislative Texts*, 183 [*Summa cartae caritatis*, chap. 3, "De generali statuta inter abbates"].

[28] Waddell, *Narrative and Legislative Texts*, 508–10.

[29] Waddell, *Narrative and Legislative Texts*, 278.

[30] Joachim Wollasch, *Mönchtum des Mittelalters zwischen Kirche und Welt* (Munich: Wilhelm Fink, 1973), 180.

by Pope Calixtus II in 1119, and in 1152 the Cistercian pope Eugene III approved a second and definitive version, the *Carta caritatis posterior*, with the bull *Sacrosancta Romana Ecclesia*.[31]

By way of a most refined rationality, the *Carta Caritatis* established a constitution that ensured both cohesion among all Cistercian monasteries and the permanence of their consensus. The abbot of Cîteaux was no overlord of the other Cistercian abbots. Along with the abbots of the other primary communities (which Cîteaux had to visit regularly), he enjoyed a certain influential position of honor whose potential power might manifest itself (now more, now less) depending on circumstance.[32] But the body that represented the community as a whole, legally and practically, was the general chapter.[33] Hierarchy and subordination among the Cistercians were replaced by the unifying bonds of mutual charity and unanimity. Legislative acts, necessary to adapt norms to needs and circumstances as they changed over time, were not decrees from above but measures produced through deliberation, called *definitions* (*definitiones*). These too were the written products of a continual process of legal refinement and adaptation, and they had to be made available equally to all. Legally binding codifications of chosen definitions, the earliest of which were already compiled in 1134 under the designation *Instituta generalis capituli*,[34] could be recognized as valid only if they had been approved by the general chapter.

On this foundation was built a new, more broadly defined understanding of the concept of *ordo*. It transcended the inherited meanings that had been limited to a common way of life, as in the case of the *Ordo Cluniacensis*. Observance of normative structures of behavior was now inseparable from the bonds of corporate law. This legislative structure opened the way to an independent institutionalization of religious life, one sharply differentiated from other forms of religious community. It is captured in the concept of *order* in the legal sense

---

[31] Waddell, *Narrative and Legislative Texts*, 389–94. It is also necessary to note here the controversial book by Constance Berman, *The Cistercian Evolution* (Philadelphia: University of Pennsylvania Press, 2000); see Chrysogonus Waddell, "The Myth of Cistercian Origins: C. H. Berman and the Manuscript Sources," *Cîteaux* 51 (2000): 299–386.

[32] Eberl, *Die Zisterzienser*, 129–30.

[33] Florent Cygler, *Das Generalkapitel im hohen Mittelalter* (Münster: LIT, 2002), 23–118.

[34] Waddell, *Narrative and Legislative Texts*, 319–68.

that is still in use today. The Cistercians invented the order as a form of religious organization.

Other monastic congregations, such as the Cluniacs, had accepted the leadership of a single head, whose position was legitimized by charisma of office or grounded in property rights; the houses in such congregations could differ dramatically in their customs or degrees of independence. With the Cistercians, however, the principles now shifted to collegial collaboration among all abbeys, which did not stand in direct dependence on a mother house, as well as strict unity in legal status, customs, liturgy, and so on. To safeguard these principles, the Cistercians turned to a meticulously enforced practice of visitation, which included Cîteaux and which was carried out autonomously along lines of filiation from Cîteaux and the four primary abbeys, as well as to the annual general chapter.[35]

The Cistercians worked, moreover, to secure freedom for each of their abbeys by both rejecting advocates and restricting episcopal interventions (exemptions). They further rejected any reliance on incomes derived from leases or the work of day laborers. They concentrated their economic efforts on their own potential and in that regard made use of *conversi*, as these had been known among the monks of Hirsau, the Grandmontines, and the Carthusians. These laborers had to secure provision for their communities through work on outlying farms or granges, and from the middle of the twelfth century they had their own statutes, known as the *Usus conversorum*.[36]

The early days of the Cistercians, from the second decade of the twelfth century down to its middle years, were also shaped by a figure who brought the young order a considerable degree of prestige. The Cistercians were able to promote his memory to such a degree that even the Franciscans[37] placed him alongside Augustine and Benedict. They traced the system of foundational norms at Cîteaux back to

---

[35] Jörg Oberste, *Visitation und Ordensorganisation* (Münster: LIT, 1996), 57–159.

[36] *Usus conversorum = Cistercian Lay Brothers. Twelfth-Century Usages, with Related Texts*, ed. Chrysogonus Waddell (Brecht: Cîteaux: Commentarii cistercienses, 2000); see Guido Gassmann, *Konversen im Mittelalter* (Berlin: LIT, 2013).

[37] "Seculum perfectionis," in *Fontes Franciscani* (hereafter *Fontes*), ed. Enricò Menestò and Stefano Brufani (Assisi: Ed. Porziuncola, 1997), 1961.

Bernard of Clairvaux, preaching a sermon in the chapter room, teaches his brothers.
Manuscript illumination, around 1455.

him as author, and in the *Divine Comedy* Dante[38] placed him as their
leader in the highest spheres of heaven. The discussion now turns to

[38] Richard Kay, "Dante in Ecstasy: Paradiso 33 and Bernard of Clairvaux,"
Mediaeval Studies 66 (2004): 183–212.

Bernard of Clairvaux (1090–1153),[39] son of a nobleman from northern Burgundy, who while searching for a strict ascetic life entered Cîteaux in 1113 with thirty of his companions—the number of new members alone helped what was still a small community begin what was to be a remarkable flowering.

Near the end of his life, Bernard described himself as the "chimera of the age."[40] He was neither cleric nor layman, he insisted, and he had long since abandoned being a monk, if not a monk's clothing, even though he had been abbot of Clairvaux continually from 1115. He saw himself, rightly, confronted with the fact that the world perceived him above all as the political conscience of his era, as a preacher of the crusades, as the persecutor of heretics, as a brilliant representative of theology, and even as an instructor of popes. His opponents, all of them more or less defeated, ranked among the greatest intellects of the day (and of the future): Peter Abelard and Gilbert of Poitiers, for example.[41] Bernard's network of communication was formidable. Again and again he crisscrossed the lands of Latin Christendom, and he exchanged letters with meaningful personalities of ecclesiastical and religious life, including even Peter the Venerable, the exceptional twelfth-century Cluniac figure who was almost as important as Bernard.

Bernard was, in an essential way, the personification of the Cistercian Order. He epitomized a way of life that was attractive because it resonated with the time and met contemporary needs. Alongside the actual work that he did for the recognition of the Order, Bernard's symbolic power led to an immense number of new foundations. At the

---

[39] Kaspar Elm, ed., *Bernhard von Clairvaux* (Wiesbaden: Harrassowitz, 1994); Adriaan H. Bredero, *Bernard of Clairvaux between Cult and History* (Edinburgh: Eerdmans, 1996); Peter Dinzelbacher, *Bernhard von Clairvaux. Leben und Werk des berühmtesten Zisterziensers* (Darmstadt: Primus, 1998); Brian Patrick McGuire, ed., *A Companion to Bernard of Clairvaux* (Leiden: Brill, 2011); Alice Chapman, *Sacred Authority and Temporal Power in the Writings of Bernard of Clairvaux* (Turnhout: Brepols, 2013).

[40] Bernard of Clairvaux, Ep 250; SBOp 8:147; *The Letters of St Bernard of Clairvaux*, trans. Bruno Scott James (Stroud, UK: Sutton Publishing Ltd., 1953; Kalamazoo, MI: Cistercian Publications, 1998), #326.

[41] Constant J. Mews, "Bernard of Clairvaux and Peter Abelard," in McGuire, *A Companion*, 133–68; Jean Leclercq, "Textes sur Saint Bernard et Gilbert de la Porrée," *Mediaeval Studies* 14 (1952): 107–28.

same time, that power also kept the rapidly growing Order from flying apart. Bernard served as a kind of anchor for the Order's identity, and he promoted that identity effectively as an author through his texts and letters. His early work *On the Degrees of Humility and Pride* (*De gradibus humilitatis et superbiae*) is an instructional work for a monk called to embrace contemplation and to lead the monastic life in ascetic discipline.[42] In the text known as the *Apologia*,[43] written around 1124/25, he outlined and defended the most important core ideals of Cîteaux, often using strong polemic against the opulent lifestyle of the Cluniacs. Another treatise, *On Precept and Dispensation* (*De praecepto et dispensatione*),[44] from around 1140, concerns the validity of both the norms of a rule strictly observed and norms grounded in self-responsibility. Yet these works—as some five hundred of his letters[45] suggest—were certainly only the vanguard, so to speak, of the much broader influence of his teaching and persuasion.

Emerging from its once problematic beginnings at Cîteaux, the new Order now found itself, in an unexpected way, remarkably empowered, both in terms of its people and as an institution. This was true with respect to the establishment of its core spiritual ideals, which combined the new eremitic ideal of poverty with unadulterated Benedictine loyalty to the Rule. It was also true with respect to the rational arrangements of the Order's legal and organizational affairs, which rested on *caritas*,[46] unanimity, and uniformity. As a

---

[42] *De gradibus humilitatis et superbiae*, SBOp 3:1–59; "The Steps of Humility and Pride," trans. M. Ambrose Conway, in Bernard of Clairvaux, *Treatises* I, CF 13 (Kalamazoo, MI: Cistercian Publications, 1973), 1–82. On Bernard's theology, see Michaela Diers, *Bernhard von Clairvaux. Elitäre Frömmigkeit und begnadetes Wirken* (Münster: Aschendorff, 1991).

[43] *Apologia ad Guillelmum abbatem*, SBOp 3:61–108; "St. Bernard's Apologia to Abbot William," trans. Michael Casey, in *Works of Bernard of Clairvaux*, 1, Treatises 1, CF 1 (Spencer, MA, and Shannon, Ireland: Cistercian Publications, 1970), 1–69.

[44] *De praecepto et dispensatione*, SBOp 3:241–94; "St. Bernard's Book on Precept and Dispensation," trans. Conrad Greenia, in *Works of Bernard* 1, 71–150.

[45] SBOp 7–8; *Letters of St Bernard*.

[46] Mirko Breitenstein, "Is There a Cistercian Love? Some Considerations on the Virtue of Charity," in *Aspects of Charity*, ed. Gert Melville (Berlin: LIT, 2011), 55–98.

consequence, some two decades after the founding of Cîteaux, the Order experienced explosive growth whose unparalleled example drew contemporaries along in its path.

The method of that growth was simple, but effective: if a monastery had grown to such a size that it could accommodate sending out twelve brothers and an abbot to found a new community, then, with the approval of the general chapter, it was expected to do so.[47] The new foundation was to be established in a remote location, with the local bishop recognizing the *Carta caritatis* and local nobility providing appropriate estates while receiving no rights of advocacy in return. When the new monastery in its turn grew large enough, it was expected to found its own daughter house. Adding to this dynamic was the fact that often the nobility transferred their proprietary monasteries to Cîteaux for reform and that sometimes already-established congregations of eremitical communities (after making an appropriate request) were accepted into the Order. So, for example, in 1147 the seven settlements that had been established by Stephen of Obazine and the thirty-two houses in the congregation founded by Vitalis of Savigny were incorporated into the Cistercian Order.[48]

Around the middle of the twelfth century, not least as a consequence of the continued influence of Bernard of Clairvaux, the Order had come to number some 340 abbeys with around 11,000 members. A century later the numbers had doubled. Among the Order's houses were those with more than a hundred monks and *conversi* (including Clairvaux itself, Rievaulx in Yorkshire, and Fontenay in Burgundy). The expansion in fact encompassed all of Latin Christendom and often extended far beyond its borders. The gaps were filled later,[49] and in contrast to the Cluniac expansion, here no region was neglected. The primary abbeys were the initial points of focus, and among them Clairvaux was by far the most successful, though Morimond had the strongest impact in the German realm.[50] The high point of the expansion was reached in the second half of the thirteenth century.

---

[47] Waddell, *Narrative and Legislative Texts*, 330.

[48] See pp. 107, 111.

[49] Felten and Rösener, eds., *Norm und Realität*, 287–54 (with many essays on different regions of expansion).

[50] Nicole Bouter, ed., *Unanimité et diversité cisterciennes* (Saint-Étienne: Publications de l'Université de Saint-Étienne, 2000).

The Order was notably reluctant in its early years to accept women.[51] In this regard it followed a particular tradition among the hermits, who strictly rejected women's communities on principle—as did the Carthusians and Grandmontines, for example—although other eremitically inspired groups at first almost promoted women's houses. The early community around Norbert of Xanten was notable in this regard, as was the congregation around Fontevraud and those groups around Stephen of Obazine, whom the Cistercians therefore only accepted with great reservations, as they were not prepared to take on the pastoral care of nuns (*cura monialium*).

But there were women's monasteries early on that stood in a more or less close relationship with the Cistercians. So, for example, the women's monastery of Le Tart was founded near Clairvaux in the 1120s with the help of Abbot Stephen Harding, and soon an entire congregation of monasteries grew from there. Yet until 1200, there was no discernible institutional tie between Le Tart and the Order. The same is true of many other women's monasteries that stood close to the Cistercians in terms of their core ideals and normative foundations—for example, Jully, founded from Molesme with the aid of Bernard of Clairvaux, or the fifteen German convents known to have already been founded in the twelfth century. But in these cases the Cistercians limited themselves to providing hortatory instruction, leaving pastoral care to others.

At the beginning of the thirteenth century, however, the stance of the Order changed, not least because of pressure from without. Through the legal process of affiliation and incorporation, such women's monasteries with Cistercian ties finally gained access to the Order. As a consequence, their number grew, according to James of Vitry, "like the stars in heaven,"[52] and in certain regions they overtook

---

[51] On the following, see Franz Felten, "Der Zisterzienserorden und die Frauen," in *Vita religiosa sanctimonialium*, ed. Christine Kleinjung (Korb: Didymos, 2011), 199–274; Franz Felten, "Abwehr, Zuneigung, Pflichtgefühl. Reaktionen der frühen Zisterzienser auf den Wunsch religiöser Frauen, zisterziensisch zu leben," in *Female* vita religiosa *between Late Antiquity and the High Middle Ages: Structures, Developments and Spatial Contexts*, ed. Gert Melville and Anne Müller (Berlin: LIT, 2011), 391–415.

[52] John Frederick Hinnebusch, ed., *The Historia Occidentalis of Jacques de Vitry. A Critical Edition* (Fribourg: Fribourg University Press, 1972), 117.

the number of male monasteries. But the opening of the Order to women soon again met sharp limitations. In 1220 the general chapter decided to limit future incorporations of women's communities, so that the flood of women to monastic life soon had to be cared for by the emerging mendicant orders.[53]

---

[53] Brigitte Degler-Spengler, "'Zahlreich wie die Sterne des Himmels.' Zisterzienser, Dominikaner und Franziskaner vor dem Problem der Inkorporation von Frauenklöstern," *Rottenburger Jahrbuch für Kirchengeschichte* 4 (1985): 37–50. See also Anne Lester, *Creating Cistercian Nuns* (Ithaca: Cornell University Press, 2011).

7

The Success of the Cistercian Model

From the Premonstratensians to the Gilbertines and the Carthusians

The Cistercian model of organization had hardly been developed before it had already become an essential element of religious corporations in general. Other religious congregations quickly took over the foundational principles of the Cistercians' innovative structure, and they did so in a variety of different ways. This fact casts a distinctive light on both the flexibility of such rationally formed instruments of organization and on their power of innovation. Only a few examples of the wide range of possibilities can be noted here.

In the forefront of those religious congregations that quickly imitated the Cistercian model was a group that sought in 1142 to diffuse alienating strife among its members by entering into a fraternal relationship of prayer with the Cistercians: the Premonstratensians.[1] Under the charismatic leadership of the wandering preacher Norbert of Xanten, introduced above, an alliance in the old tradition expanded after 1120 from the mother monastery at Prémontré. In legal terms, the members of the new alliance were proprietary monasteries of Norbert's. Its leading houses were Floreffe in Namur and Cappenberg in Westphalia. As the alliance multiplied in the following decades, its monasteries offered themselves, on the basis of their extremely strict

---

[1] See pp. 118–20. On the following, see Stefan Weinfurter, "Norbert von Xanten und die Entstehung des Prämonstratenserordens," in *Barbarossa und die Prämonstratenser* (Göppingen: Gesellschaft für staufische Geschichte, 1989), 67–100; see also, for a general outline, Bernard Ardura, *Prémontrés: histoire et spiritualité* (Saint-Étienne: Publications de la Université de Saint-Etienne, 1995).

way of life according to the *Ordo monasterii*, as an alternative of the *vita canonica* to the monastic tradition of the Cistercians.

In the beginning this alliance understood itself, as a whole, almost like an enclosed community, one in which Norbert took on a role almost like a bishop. But after his departure in 1126 to take his position as archbishop of Magdeburg, the group was forced to orient itself in fundamentally new ways. Although as archbishop Norbert continued to look out for his followers in his old congregation, as the accounts of his life emphasize, and although he established a common life for the clerics in his diocese, the disciples he had left behind remained without a leader. They thus faced the fearful possibility that their cluster of monasteries might be dissolved or at least that the affairs of individual monasteries might become subject to the interventions of local bishops.

The Cistercian model stood ready as a way to counterbalance any loss of leadership and to secure a lasting stability by way of statutes, authorities, and organizations—especially the general chapter—that would be valid apart from personal ties. The driving force behind the congregation's remaking of itself on this model, and in that sense the actual founder of the Order, was Hugh of Fosses, who had so long accompanied Norbert on his preaching tours[2] and whom Norbert had established as abbot of Prémontré when faced with the dissolution (*dissolutio*) of the congregation after his departure for Magdeburg. Shortly thereafter the other monasteries received an abbot and thereby established themselves for the first time as independent corporations. They were able, by means of common statutes that were put in force in 1130, to come together in a new way.[3] The programmatic statements

---

[2] Kaspar Elm, "Hugo von Fosses. Erster Abt von Prémontré und Organisator des Prämonstratenserordens," in *Studien zum Prämonstratenserorden*, ed. Irene Crusius and Helmut Flachenecker (Göttingen: Vandenhoeck & Ruprecht, 2003), 35–55.

[3] On the law governing the Premonstratensian Order, see Bruno Krings, "Das Ordensrecht der Prämonstratenser vom späten 12. Jahrhundert bis zum Jahr 1227. Der liber consuetudinum und die Dekrete des Generalkapitels," *Analecta Praemonstratensia* 69 (1993): 107–242; also Bruno Krings, "Zum Ordensrecht der Prämonstratenser bis zur Mitte des 12. Jahrhunderts," *Analecta Praemonstratensia* 76 (2000): 9–28; Jörg Oberste, "Règle, coutumes et statuts. Le système normatif des prémontrés aux XIIᵉ–XIIIᵉ siècles," in *Regulae—Consuetudines—Statuta*, ed. Cristina Andenna and Gert Melville (Münster: LIT, 2005), 261–76.

recorded in those statutes asserted that there was an indissoluble unity among the abbeys, that the Rule was to be observed by all in a unified manner, and that the same way of life, the same habit, and the same liturgical books were to be common to all.[4] When a second body of statutes was drawn up around the middle of the twelfth century, it recorded the same ideals more firmly still: uniformity both in outward customs (*uniformitas exterius servata in moribus*) and in inward unity of the heart (*unitas, que interius servanda est in cordibus*) were to reign over all.[5]

Even before the completion of the first statutes, the circles of Prémontré had already held general chapters that took on tasks like those found among the Cistercians. These chapters were now established in the statutes as a central authority. The statutes now also regulated visitations, which were both to be carried out with paternal care (*paterna sollicitudine*) among daughter houses and to ensure the observance of a common order. The second redaction of the statutes then established a broader and more expansive practice of visitation, one that was unknown among the Cistercians. It would extend control along lines of filiation—for the first time in the monastic world—by way of building provinces, so-called circaries, in which visitors (*circatores*) were to relieve the father-abbots of the burdens of supervision.[6]

From the alliance of monasteries around Norbert of Xanten, the Premonstratensian Order[7] had thus emerged as an independent legal body. Pope Innocent II confirmed its existence in 1131 and at the same time gave the new Order official papal protection.

From the beginnings of this process of institutionalization, efforts were made to expand the Premonstratensian ranks by taking over

---

[4] *Les premiers statuts de l'Ordre de Prémontré. Le clm 17174 (XIIᵉ siècle)*, ed. Raphaël van Waefelghem (Leuven: Smeesters, 1913), 15–74.

[5] *Les statuts de Prémontré au milieu de XIIᵉ siècle*, ed. Placide Lefevre and Wilfried Marcel Grauwen (Averbode: Praemonstratensia, 1978), 1–52, here 1.

[6] Jörg Oberste, *Visitation und Ordensorganisation* (Münster: LIT, 1996), 160–251.

[7] Gert Melville, "Zur Semantik von *ordo* im Religiosentum der ersten Hälfte des 12. Jahrhunderts. Lucius II., seine Bulle vom 19. Mai 1144, und der 'Orden' der Prämonstratenser," in Crusius and Flachenecker, *Studien zum Prämonstratenserorden*, 201–24.

established monasteries as well as by establishing new foundations. Already the first statutes recorded, under the rubric "On constructing new abbeys" (*de construendis abbatiis*),[8] outlined the process: how at least twelve canons were to be provided with necessities like a copy of the Rule, Mass books, and psalters, how they were to be sent out from an abbey to a suitable locale for the founding of a new settlement, and how they were to establish that settlement promptly. In the second half of the twelfth century the Order already encompassed two hundred abbeys.

Alongside a supportive nobility who were also strongly interested in founding women's communities, it was above all reform-minded bishops who supported male settlements and who sought to integrate those communities into their diocesan organizations. To be sure, an orientation toward pastoral care had to develop first. In the beginning contemporary observers still saw the Premonstratensians as contemplatively oriented hermits,[9] but already by 1123, with the founding of the community of Ilbenstadt in the Wetterau, the archbishop of Mainz had made provision for the enjoyment of parochial rights. The foundation of Varlar near Coesfeld received baptismal, burial, and preaching rights from its beginnings in 1129. In a charter issued in 1144 for the Swabian community of Roggenburg, Pope Lucius II explicitly conferred on the Premonstratensians the right to discharge such duties directly rather than through appointed secular clergy. The cathedral chapters of Havelberg, Ratzeburg, and Brandenburg, too, taken over by the Premonstratensians after Norbert's death, were harnessed for pastoral work within the structures of episcopal organization. The Premonstratensians thus grew slowly, with a force that varied by time and place, into established patterns of pastoral care.

They also changed their stance with regard to their women's communities rather quickly.[10] Around 1146/47 a Benedictine abbot and careful observer of Premonstratensian affairs, Herman of Tournai, described how "Norbert worked to convert not only men but

---

[8] *Les premiers statuts de l'Ordre de Prémontré*, ed. Waefelghem, 33.

[9] *Libellus de diversis ordinibus et professionibus qui sunt in aecclesia*, ed. Giles Constable and Bernard S. Smith, 2nd ed. (Oxford: Clarendon Press, 2003), 56–72.

[10] Bruno Krings, "Die Prämonstratenser und ihr weiblicher Zweig," in Crusius and Flachenecker, *Studien zum Prämonstratenserorden*, 75–105.

also women followers, so that today in various places belonging to Prémontré more than a thousand of them can be seen serving God in such hard discipline and under permanent silence as was hardly ever the case in the strictest of male communities."[11] Yet his view was already outdated: the double monastery in Prémontré itself had already been disbanded by the end of the 1130s, with the women's community then relocated to the somewhat distant house of Fontanelles. Other double monasteries suffered similar fates, although there remained strong legal and pastoral ties between men's and women's convents. In France especially, aversion toward women's monasteries grew so strong that between 1154 and 1176 the Premonstratensian general chapter went so far as to prohibit the founding of any more women's communities. In view of the pressures of a period of remarkably strong growth, the measure was in any case not enforceable, and in the reform statutes of 1236 women were once again quite regularly the subject of legislation, which now also included a distinction between choir nuns (*sorores cantantes*) and *conversae* (*sorores non cantantes*).

Premonstratensian monasteries, like those of the Cistercians, were scattered over all of Latin Christendom, including the Holy Land— though not in a comparably dense network, but rather with a notable concentration in the northern and northeastern regions of modern France, in the region of modern Belgium and the Netherlands, and in the middle and lower Rhine.[12] The three primary abbeys of the Order—Floreffe, Cuissy, and Saint Martin in Laon (the last a community that at first, before the founding of Prémontré, had resisted Norbert's reform)—all lay within the French-speaking region.

The ideal of uniformity (*uniformitas*) had been embraced in all houses recorded in the Premonstratensian statutes from the middle of the twelfth century. But that ideal, in contrast to inner unity (*unitas*), proved difficult to enforce strictly in every house.[13] In this respect

[11] Roger Wilmans, ed., *Ex Heermanni Laudunensis libro III*, MGH 12:657–59, cited from Krings, "Die Prämonstratenser," 75–76n2.

[12] Norbert Backmund, *Monasticon Praemonstratense*, 3 vols. (Straubing: Attenkofer, 1949–1956), vol. 1 (Berlin: de Gruyter, 1983). On one exemplary region of expansion, see Ingrid Ehlers-Kisseler, *Die Anfänge der Prämonstratenser im Erzbistum Köln* (Cologne: Böhlau, 1997).

[13] Jörg Oberste, "Zwischen uniformitas und diversitas. Zentralität als Kernproblem des frühen Prämonstratenserordens (12./13. Jahrhundert)," in Crusius and Flachenecker, *Studien zum Prämonstratenserorden*, 225–50.

the challenge was not with larger and highly ambitious houses, such as Steinfeld in the Eifel, which later had a large and widespread network of daughter houses, including the renowned monastery of Strahov in Prague. Rather, the challenge centered on the divergence between those houses that felt themselves to belong to Prémontré and those founded from Magdeburg that for the most part belonged to a visitation circuit centered in Saxony. That divergence was never quite overcome, even deep into the later Middle Ages. And even though from the 1140s these communities made repeated attempts to find common ground on such things as the habit or norms governing visitation and attendance at general chapter, there always remained a certain degree of difference. In the peripheral regions, especially, a great divergence from the practices of the center persisted regarding the frequency of attending general chapters. Yet the tolerance of such a range of variation clearly diffused many potential tensions within the Order and thus helped to maintain a careful balance.

Not least because of their great success in missionary and colonizing work east of the Elbe among the Wends,[14] within a few years after their appearance among the ranks of the regular canons, the Premonstratensians reached a status similar to that of the Cistercians among the monks.

With a speed similar to the Premonstratensians, the congregation of the canons of Arrouaise[15] also adopted the Cistercian model. Founded in Flanders in 1090, the abbey lived according to the *Ordo novus*, and already in the second quarter of the twelfth century some nineteen foundations belonged to its circle, most established through new foundations, appropriations, or transfers facilitated by founders from among the lesser nobility. Thereafter further foundations were made in England, Scotland, Silesia, and France. By around 1129/32 there is already evidence of a general chapter, charged with supervision of practices of visitation and with making all major decisions regarding matters of supreme judicial authority and legislation. From the end of the twelfth century the abbot of Arrouaise came to occupy

---

[14] Franz Winter, *Die Prämonstratenser des zwölften Jahrhunderts und ihre Bedeutung für das nordöstliche Deutschland* (Aalen: Scientia, 1865).

[15] On the following, see Ludo Milis, *L'ordre des chanoines réguliers d'Arrouaise*, 2 vols. (Bruges: De Temple, 1969). See also *Monumenta Arroasiensia. Textes narratifs et diplomatiques de l'abbaye d'Arrouaise*, ed. Ludo Milis and Benoît-Michel Tock (Turnhout: Brepols, 2000).

a central place, especially given his right to make universal visitation and to confirm all abbatial elections—a remarkable preeminence, one that the Cistercians never granted to the abbot of Cîteaux.

The Englishman Gilbert of Sempringham (ca. 1083/89–1189),[16] who during the 1130s had begun in his hometown in England a religious community specially focused on the salvation of women, also made early use of the Cistercian model of organization. The impetus for his move was precisely a rejection by the Cistercian Order, which had refused the supervision of women. In 1147 he tried to step down from his position of charismatic leadership, asking the Cistercian general chapter to supervise his two monasteries. In contrast to Stephen of Obazine and the congregation of Savigny, he was unsuccessful. Thereafter he undertook considerable changes in organizational structure. He transformed his women's monasteries into double monasteries by adding clerics who were to live according to the Rule of Augustine and by directing the women to live according to the Rule of Saint Benedict.

He also gave to these monasteries statutes that he himself had written, these strongly influenced by the Cistercian *Carta caritatis*. The construction of the Order they outlined was, however, more strongly centralized. Through overseers both male and female (*scrutatores* and *scrutatrices*) who were sent out by the "master" (or prior general), individual houses could be tied in to the strict leadership of the Order. These in turn were limited only by the general chapter, whose participants also included the heads of female religious houses. Around the end of the twelfth century this Order, the only one founded in England, had eleven double monasteries.

After a certain delay on the part of Grand Chartreuse, in 1140/41 the Carthusians,[17] whose houses in the beginning shared "no fixed ties of an institutional nature,"[18] finally held a general chapter that consisted of the priors of all houses. A second general chapter fol-

---

[16] On the following, see Brian J. Golding, *Gilbert of Sempringham and the Gilbertine Order c. 1130–c. 1300* (Oxford: Oxford University Press, 1995); Katharine Sykes, *Inventing Sempringham. Gilbert of Sempringham and the Origins of the Role of the Master* (Berlin: LIT, 2011).

[17] On the following, see Florent Cygler, *Das Generalkapitel im hohen Mittelalter* (Münster: LIT, 2002), 205–313.

[18] Cygler, *Das Generalkapitel*, 210.

lowed a year later, and another in 1155; thereafter, however, one was held every year. Notably, at the 1155 chapter every individual house as well as each local bishop had to declare readiness to renounce any claims to having special rights. The Carthusians had thereby formed themselves into an order.[19] The assembly, as a central organization, occupied a sovereign place, with absolute authority over not only legislation but also visitation, correction, appointments to office, and matters of wealth and economy in all houses. It thus had to fear neither the competing rights of individual charterhouses nor the respective local bishops.

But the general chapter was in turn strongly influenced by the Grand Chartreuse itself, which remained revered as the "mother and nurturer of other houses."[20] Of the eight diffinitors who guided the course of business and crafted the chapter's legislative measures, four were members of the Grand Chartreuse, along with the prior himself. The result was a relation of five to four. Neither Cîteaux nor Prémontré had known such an exalted position, but they were also not motherhouses of an order that remained, with respect to its size, a governable organization, one that at the end of the thirteenth century numbered only sixty settlements.

An unusual formulation gave the Carthusian general chapter a spiritual foundation for its remarkable power to influence affairs, insofar as it was described as acting in the place of God.[21] Even if one could thereby rightly conclude (or at least infer convincingly from the context) that the Carthusian Order never had to be reformed because it was never deformed, the Carthusians not only continually issued corrective legislation but also rapidly and repeatedly expanded and refined their normative frameworks. In the twelfth century alone, by around 1140 extensions (*Supplementa*) had been written for Guigo's *Consuetudines*, and between 1141 and 1151 as well as around 1170 two further statutory texts appeared, to which were appended further *Supplementa* around the end of the century.[22] But as the Carthusians'

---

[19] Cygler, *Das Generalkapitel*, 221.

[20] Cygler, *Das Generalkapitel*, 220.

[21] Cygler, *Das Generalkapitel*, 205.

[22] With detailed evidence, see Florent Cygler, "Ausformung und Kodifizierung des Ordensrechts vom 12. bis zum 14. Jahrhundert. Strukturelle Beobachtungen

extension of these laws did not deprive the older texts of their validity, the scope of their legal corpus was able to grow continually.

In view of such rapid and successful spread of an originally Cistercian principle of organization, it should not be overlooked that after what were very often promising beginnings, many loosely organized reform congregations often stagnated as they moved toward stabilization. This was especially the case among the regular canons, who, except for the Premonstratensians and the Order of Arrouaise, never established transregional orders. A prominent example in this regard is the congregation of regular canons of Springiersbach. It had presumably held a general chapter in the year 1125, even before the Premonstratensians did, but it was hindered from further consolidation and autonomy because of unavoidable entanglements in the tensions of territorial politics between the archbishop of Trier and the Rhineland Count Palatinate—whose "house-monastery" was Springiersbach.[23]

Cluny, Knights, and Hospitals:
The Reform of Older Congregations and the Creation
of New "Functional" Orders

These examples of quick takeovers, or at least attempted takeovers, must be extended to include an analysis of three special structural developments, each of which brought both the old and the very new together with the Cistercian constitutional elements discussed above. That both old and new were possible reveals yet again the power and adaptability of the Cistercians' inventions. These possibilities are here explored first with a consideration of the transformation of the old congregation of Cluny into a religious order, second with the consolidation of the church's military orders, especially the Templars, and third with the establishment of the hospital orders.

To the first point: It was not only the recently founded religious congregations that made use of the new organizational form of an

---

zu den Cisterziensern, Prämonstratensern, Kartäusern und Cluniazensern," in *De ordine vitae*, ed. Gert Melville (Münster: LIT, 1996), 7–58, here 22.

[23] Odilo Engels, "Der Erzbischof von Trier, der rheinische Pfalzgraf und die gescheiterte Verbandsbildung von Springiersbach im 12. Jahrhundert," in *Secundum regulam vivere*, ed. Gert Melville (Windberg: Poppe, 1978), 87–104.

order. The older ones, which were bound together above all by virtue of property rights, also transformed themselves on the Cistercian model over the twelfth and thirteenth centuries. The process was certainly not the result of any automatic adaptation of corresponding institutions but rather something that unfolded often in the face of great difficulty of assimilation and that resulted in a variety of independent institutional forms.

To note only one significant example of such a transformation in the face of difficulty, the venerable and still powerful congregation of Cluny, the *Cluniacensis ecclesia*,[24] had in the year 1200 reshaped itself into an order in the new sense, the *Ordo Cluniacensis*, with all of the usual structures. After decades of serious crisis, in that year a general chapter of the Cluniacs gathered together in the Cistercian manner, including all of the heads of the abbeys and priories subject to Cluny. It is clear from today's perspective that a new Cluny was being built on the foundations of the traditional Cluny,[25] a new creation of remarkable durability.

Under the aegis of Abbot Hugh V of Cluny, this assembly drew up a corpus of statutes that gave the congregation a new constitution. It provided for a regularly held general chapter to serve as the highest judicial and legislative authority, though admittedly it would share that authority with the abbot. It also again regulated practices of visitation. The abbot of Cluny did retain his universal right to visitation, but in practice his place was taken by those known as the *Camerarii*—those who presided over the Order's provinces, which were now established after the model of the Premonstratensians and covered the entire area of Cluniac expansion. But there was also now provision, in the Cistercian manner, for visitation of the abbey of Cluny itself. Moreover, the abbot of Cluny now recognized the absolute authority of these statutes, insofar as he allowed them to include the statement "We also subject ourselves to the law" (*etiam*

[24] See pp. 65–67.
[25] On the following, see Gert Melville, "Cluny après 'Cluny.' Le treizième siècle: un champ de recherches," *Francia* 17 (1990): 91–124; Gert Melville, "Die cluniazensische 'Reformatio tam in capite quam in membris.' Institutioneller Wandel zwischen Anpassung und Bewahrung," in *Sozialer Wandel im Mittelalter*, ed. Jürgen Miethke and Klaus Schreiner (Sigmaringen: Thorbecke, 1994), 249–97.

nos legi subjicimus).[26] A long series of similar statutory texts followed
in the next centuries. The most significant change of the constitution once again concerned practices of visitation. Pope Gregory IX
enforced these practices through a reform bull in 1233, which very
much against the monks' will was aimed at improving what was still a
quite inefficiently functioning Cluniac organization.[27] The *Camerarii*
in the provinces were now replaced by alternating visitors who were
elected anew every year by the general chapter, independently from
the power of the abbot of Cluny.

But whereas the Cistercians were committed from the beginning
to an organization whose leadership was collegial and consensual,
the Cluniacs were compelled laboriously to adapt their older, centralized, monarchical constitution to more contemporary forms of
organization. The result was a compromise that led to quite distinct
structures, in that the general chapter now competed with the abbot of
Cluny over the claim to represent the Order and was able to define the
limits of judicial and executive authority only at the cost of a certain
tension. The Order never truly abandoned the vertical dominion of
the head over its members.

To turn to the second point: in a Jerusalem that had been conquered
by Christians on the First Crusade, high up on the Temple Mount
in the royal palace (which had been transformed into the Al-Aqsa
mosque), presumably from 1118 on there lived a group of knights
who submitted themselves to the Latin Patriarch of the Holy City and
promised to live in a strictly monastic way, serving Christ by offering
protection to pilgrims on the way to visit the sites of the gospels. In
1129 these knights, now called Templars[28] because of their place of
residence, received at a synod in Troyes in France a rule that was
issued because of the appeal of their leader Hugh of Payns.

The rule began with the following words:

---

[26] Gaston Charvin, ed., *Statuts, chapitres généraux et visites de l'Ordre de
Cluny* (Paris: E. de Boccard, 1965), 1:42.

[27] Franz Neiske, "Das Verhältnis Clunys zum Papsttum," in *Die Cluniazenser
in ihrem politisch-sozialen Umfeld*, ed. Giles Constable et al. (Münster: LIT,
1998), 279–320.

[28] On the following, see Alain Demurger, *Die Templer* (Munich: C. H. Beck,
2004).

We turn first to all those who despise following their own will and who are eager to offer knightly service, with a pure heart, to the highest king, and who move themselves, with eager care, to fill out the very noble armor of obedience, and to wear it permanently. And so we admonish you, who have until now lived the life of secular knighthood—the foundation of which was not Jesus Christ, and a way of life you embraced only for the favor of men—that you follow those whom God has chosen from the mass of damnation, and whom he has thereby called through his grace and mercy to the defense of the Holy Church, and that you hasten to join them forever.[29]

This rule further establishes in seventy-two chapters, drawn for the most part from the Rule of Saint Benedict, both the spiritual forms of the common life—such as the scope of worship and prayer and the demands of silence—and instructions on living together that were both practical and shaped by a monastic spirit, for example, the process of admitting novices, the common meal, modest clothing, care of the sick, and condemnation of consorting with women. Yet there are also regulations concerning a wide range of weapons, horses and their equipment, and squires. Other regulations condemned knightly games and entertainments, including hunting, while also allowing the possession of land and people.[30]

At first glance what seems like a strange combination of texts was in fact the complex result of an editorial project whose participants included Bernard of Clairvaux.[31] The document faced the considerable skepticism not only of Bernard but also of many other office holders in the church. But by the time of the synod, it was already a widespread notion that the old concept of the "knight of Christ" (*miles Christi*)[32] no longer needed to be understood as applying only to monks; their

---

[29] "Die Regelfassung von Troyes," in *La Règle du Temple*, ed. Henri de Curzon (Paris: Librairie Renouard, 1886), 11–12; English trans. by J. M. Upton-Ward, *The Rule of the Templars* (Woodbridge, UK: Boydell, 1997, 2008), here 19.

[30] Christian Vogel, *Das Recht der Templer* (Berlin: LIT, 2007), 171–235.

[31] Franco Cardini, *I poveri cavalieri del Cristo* (Rimini: Il Cerchio, 1992).

[32] André Vauchez, "La notion de *Miles Christi* dans la spiritualité occidentale aux XIIe et XIIIe siècles," in *Chevalerie et christianisme aux XIIe et XIIIe*

spiritual fight against evil could now be carried over to designate any struggle with arms against both those who disturbed Christian peace and against enemies of the faith. As early as the time of Augustine (354–430), any war that was justified in this sense had been legitimate. In the eleventh century, the bishops of southern France, during the Peace of God movement, had asked loyal knights to put the violent among them in their place; in 1059 Leo IX had called together an army to fight against the Normans in southern Italy with the promise of spiritual reward, and Gregory VII had developed the concept of the *milites sancti Petri*, the knights of Saint Peter. In this era there even emerged a certain spiritualization of knightly norms of conduct, for example through rituals such as the blessing of swords, already in evidence from 960, that soon cultivated the allure of the idea of crusade.[33]

Totally new, however, was the complete fusion of the life of the monastery with that of the military camp. That fusion required an articulation grounded in the world beyond, one that offered more than the prologue to the Rule quoted above. Armed combat and killing went beyond the furthest conceivable boundary of any actively led *vita religiosa*, for example, that of the regular canons. To save a soul and to kill a body before the soul had been saved seemed all the more mutually exclusive. Bernard of Clairvaux sought to legitimize precisely this kind of activity, however, with his work of 1136/37, *In Praise of the New Knighthood* (*De laude novae militiae*). Taking as his foil an evil, pompous knighthood that strove only for empty renown, Bernard praised those knights who fought for Christ, and he released them from all guilt: "But the knights may fight with good conscience the fight of the Lord and need never again fear either the sin of slaying an enemy, or the danger to their own lives. For the death that one suffers, or causes, for Christ, carries in itself no guilt, and earns the highest praise."[34]

siècles, ed. Martin Aurell and Catalina Girbea (Rennes: Presses universitaires de Rennes, 2011), 67–75.

[33] Carl Erdmann, *Die Entstehung des Kreuzzugsgedankens* (Stuttgart: Kohlhammer, 1935; Reprint Darmstadt: Wissenschaftliche Buchgesellschaft, 1980); *"Militia Christi" e Crociata nei secoli XI–XIII* (Milan: Vita e pensiero, 1992).

[34] *De laude novae militiae*, SBOp 3:205–39; *De laude novae militiae*, in Bernhard von Clairvaux, *Sämtliche Werke*, ed. Gerhard B. Winkler (Innsbruck: Tyrolia, 1990); *In Praise of the New Knighthood*, trans. Daniel O'Donovan, CF

Bernard then turned to panegyric depictions of the way of life of the Knights of the Temple. In characterizing their sense of solidarity, he turned to a well-known passage from Acts 4:32, usually cited to describe monastic communities, about being of "one heart and one soul"; concerning the knights' engagement in warfare, he emphasized that they armed themselves inwardly with faith and outwardly with armor. Comparative readings of the Old and New Testaments aided him in grounding the whole enterprise in the context of salvation history. With care and prudence, Bernard said, the knights enter combat, just as the Israelites were said to have taken calmly to battle. Just as Christ angrily drove the money changers from the temple, the knights now serve as its new guardians. They are like both lambs and lions, so that one actually does not know just what to call them—monks or knights? Yet it is fitting to call them both. "Such as these," he concluded, "God has chosen, and he selects them as servants, from the ends of the earth, from among the strongest of Israel, so that they may guard and truly protect the resting place of the true Solomon, the Sepulcher, all of them entrusted with the sword, trained for battle."

In 1139, shortly after Bernard wrote these lines, Pope Innocent II provided the Templars—or more precisely, as their official designation put it, the "Poor Knighthood of Christ and of Solomon's Temple in Jerusalem" (*Pauperes commilitones Christi templique Salomonici Hierosalemitanis*)—a comprehensive privilege that took them under his protection and confirmed their property. He obligated them to poverty, obedience, and chastity—the evangelical counsels—and to life-long commitment to the Order and gave them the opportunity to adapt their rule to new circumstances by means of a general chapter.[35] Documents from subsequent popes followed. These now also called upon ecclesiastical dignitaries to offer donations in support of the Templars. And in fact the properties of the Order grew considerably, both in the Holy Land and in Europe—a growth that, on the one hand, was at first pressingly necessary in order to meet the high cost

---

19 (Kalamazoo, MI: Cistercian Publications, 2000), here 39. See also Malcolm Barber, *The New Knighthood* (Cambridge, UK: Cambridge University Press, 1994; repr. 2012); and Alan Butler, *The Knights Templar* (New York: Shelter Harbor Press, 2014).

[35] Vogel, *Das Recht der Templer*, 38–40.

of transport for supplies (horses, for example) but that, on the other hand, also led to considerable surpluses.[36]

The organization of the Order was functional, effective, and of remarkable refinement, to a degree that would not be seen again until the advent of the mendicant orders of the thirteenth century.[37] A master of the Order served as head, and until at least 1200 he was represented by a seneschal, who in turn was accompanied by a marshal (and his deputy marshals) charged with provision. Each house was led by a commander (*Komtur*). Collectively the houses (initially those in Europe) organized themselves into provinces, under the leadership of a provincial master. There was a central chapter, with subsidiary provincial chapters. The entire Order organized itself into three groups of members: brothers who fought as knights, brothers who prayed as priests, and brothers who served as laborers.

The Templars' military accomplishments in the Holy Land, despite a relatively small number of knights, were enormous. Among the armies of the kingdom of Jerusalem the Templars were the elite, serving in campaigns most often as both vanguard and rear guard. They were able to build fortifications at strategically critical points, first among them the fortress of Toron des Chevaliers, halfway between the port city of Jaffa and Jerusalem. But above all they truly shared the fate of the Holy Land, especially on the front lines—from the fateful battle at Hattin against Saladin in 1187 to the 1291 fall of Acre as the last bastion, where the fortress of the Templars held out the longest. Thereafter the Order's future lay only in Europe, where its military strongpoints had long been. The knights remained most militarily active in the Iberian Peninsula and most economically significant in France, where they were in fact guardians of the French royal treasure. But their wealth, and the greed of the French king Philip IV, led to their annihilation and to Clement V's dissolution of the Order in 1312.[38]

Other military orders of this kind emerged alongside the Templars in the Holy Land. What made them distinct was that they placed Christian love of neighbor at the core of their ideals and in that spirit

[36] Vogel, *Das Recht der Templer*, 332–42.

[37] Vogel, *Das Recht der Templer*, 237–331.

[38] Jochen Burgtorf et al., eds., *The Debate on the Trial of the Templars: 1307–1314* (Farnham: Ashgate, 2010); Malcolm Barber, *The Trial of the Templars* (Cambridge, UK: Cambridge University Press, 1978).

dedicated themselves to charitable works such as caring for the sick and maintaining hospitals. The first among these associations was the Order of Lazarus, formed in Jerusalem around 1110; its members were lepers who both fought as soldiers and cared for their fellow sufferers.[39] The second was the Hospitalers,[40] who were also at first formed as a charitable community in Jerusalem in the second decade of the twelfth century and who then developed a military branch. The third was the Teutonic Order,[41] founded as a military order in Acre in 1198 after many years of serving a hospital in that city. After the loss of Christian control of the Holy Land, in the first decade of the fourteenth century (after a brief interlude in Hungarian Transylvania), the Teutonic Order, with the castle Marienburg at its center, found a new field of activity against the pagan Prussians. From there the Order was able to build up its own territory.[42] The Hospitalers, after their retreat from the Holy Land, also developed their own territory on the island of Rhodes, soon to become a bastion against the Ottoman Empire. The interweaving of monasticism and knighthood into a coherent way of life was a success story that lasted for centuries.[43]

A third structural development was the creation and institutional support of houses that cared for the sick. In the Middle Ages illness could render people helpless to a degree unimaginable today.[44] For reasons none could explain, diseases (most often seen as the wrath

[39] Kay Peter Jankrift, *Leprose als Streiter Gottes* (Münster: LIT, 1997); David Marcombe, *Leper Knights: The Order of St. Lazarus of Jerusalem in England, c. 1150–1544* (Woodbridge, UK: Boydell, 2003).

[40] Jürgen Sarnowsky, *Die Johanniter* (Munich: C. H. Beck, 2011). The best account in English remains Jonathan Riley-Smith, *The Knights of St. John in Jerusalem and Cyprus, c. 1050–1310* (London: Macmillan, 1967).

[41] Jürgen Sarnowsky, *Der deutsche Orden* (Munich: C. H. Beck, 2007). A reliable account in English for the Holy Land is Nicholas Morton, *The Teutonic Knights in the Holy Land, 1190–1291* (Woodbridge, UK: Boydell, 2009). For northern Europe, see Eric Christiansen, *The Northern Crusades* (Minneapolis: University of Minnesota Press, 1980).

[42] Udo Arnold, "Das Ordensland Preußen," in *Der Deutsche Orden in Europa* (Göppingen: Gesellschaft für Staufische Geschichte, 2004), 219–68.

[43] For general overviews, see *Prier et combattre*, ed. Nicole Bériou and Philippe Josserand (Paris: Fayard, 2009).

[44] Kay Peter Jankrift, *Krankheit und Heilkunde im Mittelalter* (Darmstadt: Wissenschaftliche Buchgesellschaft, 2003).

of God) fell across whole stretches of the landscape. The plague was only one among them. There was also ergotism, known at the time as Saint Anthony's Fire. Those who suddenly discerned the first signs of leprosy knew they were condemned to be lifelong outcasts. Those who suffered accidents might find themselves crippled, condemned to live as beggars. Illness for most thus meant both involuntary ostracism and poverty. Nothing fostered Christian love of neighbor in a more fundamental way than these kinds of calamities, and the response was a matter of both body and soul, since in the gospel of Matthew Christ had said, "I was hungry and you gave me food, I was thirsty and you gave me something to drink, I was a stranger and you welcomed me, I was naked and you gave me clothing, I was sick and you took care of me, I was in prison and you visited me" (Matt 25:35-36).

In obedience to this command of *caritas*, love of neighbor, by the early Middle Ages many monasteries (the Cluniacs, as already noted, first among them) had already established the office of an almoner, who was also in charge of a hospice for strangers.[45] Yet as the population grew in the twelfth century these arrangements were no longer sufficient, since especially in the thriving cities of the day an exploding population also meant a sharpened separation between the few rich and the broader masses—who lived at or below minimum subsistence levels and who were thus defenseless before every illness. This reality led to an "almost revolutionary re-evaluation of Christian *caritas*."[46]

Laity who were both filled with compassion and concerned about their own salvation carried out the work of charity, founding houses where the sick received care and spiritual consolation as well as last rites and Christian burial. Such work required not only capital, caregivers, and priests but also, above all, a grounding in the institutional structures of the church. The church could appoint the necessary

---

[45] Joachim Wollasch, "Eleemosynarius. Eine Skizze," in *Sprache und Recht. Beiträge zur Kulturgeschichte des Mittelalters*, ed. Karl Hauck and Karl A. Kroeschell (Berlin: de Gruyter, 1986), 972–95.

[46] Cristina Andenna, "Neue Formen der Frömmigkeit und Armutsbewegung," in *Verwandlungen des Stauferreichs—Drei Innovationsregionen im mittelalterlichen Europa*, ed. Bernd Schneidmüller et al. (Darmstadt: Wissenschaftliche Buchgesellschaft, 2010), 246–63, here 250. Gert Melville, "'Liebe und tue, was du willst!' Eine Herausforderung für den mittelalterlichen Menschen," in *Sorge*, ed. Gert Melville, Gregor Vogt-Spira, and Mirko Breitenstein (Cologne: Böhlau, 2015), 79–95.

priests, carve out spaces for new institutions, recognize them legally in ways that set them alongside traditional monasteries, and approve the necessary statutes as well as align them with church law in general.[47]

After the military orders had undertaken considerable hospital-oriented work in the Holy Land, the popes, as well as a number of local bishops, also took on the task of creating a legal framework that would give an appropriate foundation for providing service to the ill.[48] In this case that framework could again only be the establishment of an order.

Innocent III emerged as the decisive protagonist.[49] In 1198 he first recognized a hospital that a layman named Guido (ca. 1153–1208) had recently founded in Montpellier and dedicated to the Holy Spirit. Innocent exempted that hospital from the power of the local bishop, allowed outside priests to work there, and obligated the local lay community to take a vow similar to that of monks: to serve the poor and sick and to care for them lovingly (*caritative*). Therefore the hospital and its affiliates, soon to be established, became religious institutions of the church.

Yet the process did not stop there. The establishment of an order also required a well-balanced plan. In 1201 Innocent III gave Guido the church of Santa Maria in Saxia, not far from the Vatican, along with the neighboring and long-established hospital of the English on the Tiber not far from the Castel Sant'Angelo. Before 1204 a new hospital under the patronage of the Holy Ghost had already been established there as a papal foundation. And in that year Innocent III issued a solemn charter of privileges that established statutes for the hospital, placed it under the protection of the Holy See, and granted a number of further rights. But above all the decree established a personal union with the Montpellier hospital of the same name. The core spiritual ideal was to give *hospitalitas*, hospitality toward those

---

[47] Gisela Drossbach, "Das Hospital. Eine kirchenrechtliche Institution? (ca. 1150–ca. 1350)," *Zeitschrift der Savigny-Stiftung für Rechtsgeschichte: Kanonistische Abteilung* 87 (2001): 510–22.

[48] Anna Esposito and Andreas Rehberg, eds., *Gli ordini ospedalieri tra centro e periferia* (Rome: Viella, 2007).

[49] On the following, see Gisela Drossbach, *Christliche* caritas *als Rechtsinstitut. Hospital und Orden von Santo Spirito in Sassia (1198–1378)* (Paderborn: Schöningh, 2004).

in need, which—as the text said—stood alongside those pious works by whose measure God would one day judge the good and the evil. After Guido's death in 1208 the purely personal ties between the two communities and their respective affiliates were dissolved, with all of the communities then drawn together into a single order whose center was thenceforth in Rome and whose head, as *summus rector*, was also leader of the Roman hospital.

With this "Order of the Holy Spirit," Innocent III had created a papal order, the first ever. The statutes he issued in 1204 were approved as a rule by the 1230s at the latest. In the first decades of the Order's existence, there were tensions between Montpellier and Rome. But the energetic interventions of Gregory IX later brought these to an end, and by the second half of the thirteenth century the Order was in a position to spread, developing affiliations across wide areas of Europe. Its inner coherence was built on an organizational scheme modeled after the military orders, though their different missions and visions distinguished the two institutions.

The move from a more or less spontaneous practice of *hospitalitas* to a fully formed hospital order could take an entirely different path, however, albeit with certain structural similarities—as is clear from the example in what would eventually become one of the largest orders of its kind, the Order of Saint Anthony.[50] It primarily took care of those who were severely ill from poisoning by ergot, a fungus often encountered in diets dependent on rye. Since contemporaries knew nothing of its cause, they could not protect themselves. Especially in years of heavy rain, the fungus spread over broad regions whose inhabitants fell ill by the thousands, as if by a plague, and for the most part they died in agony. Since victims felt themselves to be burning from within, they spoke of "holy fire."

At the Benedictine priory of Saint-Didier-de-la-Motte (today Saint Antoine-l'Abbaye), between Grenoble and Valence, a church was believed to guard the bones of the Desert Father Anthony. There, from the eleventh century, great crowds of pilgrims began to gather. Among them were always many who suffered from ergotism and

---

[50] On the following, see Adalbert Mischlewski, *Grundzüge der Geschichte des Antoniterordens* (Cologne and Vienna: Böhlau, 1976); Isabelle Brunet, "Les Institutions charitables de Saint-Antoine. Chef-lieu de l'Ordre Hospitalier des Antonins du XIIᵉ au XVᵉ siècles," PhD dissertation, Université de Lyon, 1991.

who prayed to the saint for healing as a last hope. Around 1096 some ten laymen organized themselves there into the brotherhood of Saint Anthony in order to help those in need. The number of members grew quickly, with women also joining in order to care for other women.

At the beginning this community remained completely independent of the Benedictine priory, which was still the manorial lord and which also guarded the pilgrims' goal, the bones of Anthony. The priory merely tolerated the brotherhood, nothing more—and this, not least, was probably the reason that its leaders from the 1120s on were priests, who held a rank equal to that of the priest-monks of the priory.

The community was remarkably successful, since it aimed at spectacular cures by way of sound care, nourishment, and toxin-removing herbs. Already in 1123 the fraternity had been given hospitals in nearby cities. A hospital was also established at the priory itself, and by the end of the century it possessed over one hundred dependencies in Spain, Italy, Germany, and even the Holy Land. Pilgrims on their way from central Europe to Santiago in Galicia made their detours to visit Saint Anthony. Contemporaries no longer spoke of holy fire, but of Anthony's fire—the place of healing had established the name of the illness.

Yet into the thirteenth century the center of this congregation, which now reached to the borders of Christendom, remained tolerated only as a guest on Benedictine soil. The brotherhood had never been allowed to build even its own church, although by now many of its members were clerics. Only in 1209 were the Benedictines compelled, by the archbishop of Vienne and in the name of the pope, to allow the building of a church. But thereafter the process of institutionalization moved quickly. Statutes were drawn up and approved by papal legates in 1232; in 1245 the entire network of hospitals received the protection of Saint Peter from Pope Innocent IV, who proved himself to be especially generous; and in 1247 came official recognition of an independent order that was to live according to the Rule of Saint Augustine. The struggle over the bones of Saint Anthony, so important symbolically, continued until 1297. But it came to an end in a way that is significant with respect to the era's institutional history: Pope Boniface VIII released the Benedictine priory from its dependency to its mother monastery of Saint Peter in Montmajour near Arles and elevated the community itself to the status of an abbey. This community was then united to the hospital and all of its dependencies. Thereafter the abbey and its abbot were jurisdictionally the head and the center of the Order.

In the end, the success of this hard-fought establishment lay only in the fact that a religious organization was fulfilling one specialized task within the broad spectrum of the *vita religiosa*, that of *hospitalitas*, so perfectly that it became almost indispensable. In a certain analogous way the same was true of the hospitals of the Holy Spirit. A new type of order that can be called a functional order had thus been established in the twelfth century, and there were many more of them. If the phrase from Matthew "I was sick and you visited me" had been taken up by the hospital orders, the phrase "I was in prison and you visited me" became central for another order.

In 1198 John of Matha (1154–1213) and Felix of Valois (1127–1212) established the Trinitarians, an order dedicated to ransoming captive Christians from Muslim hands.[51] The Mercedarians, founded in the first third of the thirteenth century by the Catalan Petrus Nolascus (1182/89–1249/56) with the support of King James I of Aragon and Raymond of Peñaforte, pursued the same goal.[52] To note another example: around the years 1225/27, the priest Rudolf founded in Worms, with papal support, a community that took in repentant prostitutes and developed it into the far-flung Order of the *Reuerinnen* or Magdalens.[53] Its inspiration was the word of Christ in the gospel of Luke: "Her sins, which were many, have been forgiven; hence she

---

[51] Cosimo Damiano Fonseca, "La regola dei Trinitari oltre gli ideali degli ordini religioso-cavallereschi," in *Medioevo, Mezzogiorno, Mediterraneo. Studi in onore di Mario Del Treppo*, ed. Gabriella Rossetti and Giovanni Vitolo (Naples: Liguori, 2000), 1:147–59; James Matthew Powell, "Innocent III, the Trinitarians, and the Renewal of the Church, 1198–1200," in James Matthew Powell, *The Crusades, the Kingdom of Sicily, and the Mediterranean* (Aldershot: Ashgate Variorum, 2007), ix, 245–54.

[52] Anne Müller, "Gefangenenloskauf unter der Augustinusregel. Aspekte institutioneller Entwicklung im Mercedarierorden von den Anfängen bis 1317," in *Regula Sancti Augustini. Normative Grundlage differenter Verbände im Mittelalter*, ed. Gert Melville and Anne Müller (Paring: Augustiner-Chorherren-Verlag, 2002), 477–514. See also James Brodman, *Ransoming Captives in Crusader Spain* (Philadelphia: University of Pennsylvania Press, 1986), as well as his *Charity and Religion in Medieval Europe* (Washington, DC: The Catholic University of America Press, 2009).

[53] Guido Cariboni, "Gregorio IX e la nascita delle 'Sorores penitentes' di Santa Maria Maddalena 'in Alemannia,'" *Annali dell'Istituto storico italo-germanico in Trento* 25 (1999): 11–44.

has shown great love. But the one to whom little is forgiven loves little" (Luke 7:47). New research findings, however, show that the founding's core ideal was out of touch with reality.[54] It is far more accurate to say (as it has now been argued) that the papacy, together with the German bishops, saw that by exploiting Rudolf's charisma they could create a new, independent order, which offered a home exclusively for women—not only for former prostitutes but also for all women who wanted to live a monastic *vita religiosa*.

---

[54] See Jörg Voigt, *Beginen im Spätmittelalter. Frauenfrömmigkeit in Thüringen und im Reich* (Cologne: Böhlau, 2012), 44–63.

8

Diversity and Competition

A wide range of goals, a range of ways of understanding organized community, of negotiating hierarchical structures, and of collegial participation could all be realized and advanced through the distinct form of organization that the Cistercians now called a religious order. In broad terms, it brought to the *vita religiosa* both powerful institutional consolidation and stabilization as well as well-regulated procedural structures that served the interests of reform and renewal.

Although during the pontificate of Alexander III (1159–1181) and Innocent III (1198–1216) sharp accusations of a love of material goods had already been cast against the now-wealthy Cistercians, in 1215 the Fourth Lateran Council (as will be discussed below) gave the Order its due as the creator of new constitutional structures.[1] From Cistercian practices of organization the council developed a legal norm of general church law and prescribed, even for monasteries and canonries that were not part of any order, the observance of a general chapter of all prelates, according to the model of the Cistercians (*iuxta morem Cisterciensis ordinis*). The measure concerned above all individual houses of Benedictines and regular canons. Under Honorius III in the years 1219 and 1225, an analogous command followed, directing Benedictine abbeys in various lands to carry out mutual visitations and to establish provinces for that purpose. Both

---

[1] Jean Leclercq, "Passage supprimé dans une épître d'Alexandre III," *Revue bénédictine* 62 (1952): 149–51; Guido Cariboni, "Il papato di fronte alle crisi istituzionale dell'ordine cistercense nei primi decenni del XIII secolo," in *Il nostro ordine è la Caritá. Cistercensi nei secoli XII e XIII* (Milan: Vita e pensiero, 2011), 93–126.

measures found their way into the latest codification of church law, the *Liber Extra*, and thus became universally valid law.[2]

Each individual case of these orders' institutionalization makes clear, however, that a phenomenon of mutual isolation was under way: the statutes of the orders were valid only within the organization that produced them, the general chapter was responsible only for its own members, and only an order's own members could reach its positions of leadership. A variety of different views on religious life (first articulated with the emergence of new forms of eremitical life in the early eleventh century as a quest for the best path of individual salvation) eventually inspired the monastic world to divide into competing organizational structures, none compatible with the others.

In view of such diversity, the threefold typology that had finally been articulated at the Second Lateran Council (1139) is applicable in only a general way. The council spoke of the life of monks (*vita monastica*), of (regular) canons (*vita canonica*), and of hermits (*vita eremitica*). Each had found its guiding principles, respectively, in the three principal rules (*regulae principales*) of Benedict, Augustine, and Basil.[3]

In the second half of the eleventh and beginning of the twelfth centuries, when the new religious movements had yet to take shape, a differentiating polemic of protest directed itself broadly against older, now supposedly hardened and superficial forms of monastic life. Now, as the twelfth century progressed, a contest developed over which form of religious life was the most attractive. Its purpose, among other things, was to lure new recruits where possible or to convince those already committed elsewhere to transfer. With powerful rhetoric that called forth the full range of religious life's symbolic repertoire—for example, the different positions on the proper material and color of the habit[4]—polemical treatises inspired by competing

---

[2] *Corpus Iuris Canonici, Pars Secunda: Decretalium Collectiones. Decretales Gregorii* 3.35.7 and 8, ed. Emil Ludwig Richter and Emil Friedberg (Leipzig: Tauchnitz, 1881).

[3] Jacques Dubois, "Les ordres religieux au XIIᵉ siècle selon la curie romaine," *Revue Bénédictine* 78 (1968): 203–309, here 287–88.

[4] Peter von Moos, "Das mittelalterliche Kleid als Identitätssymbol und Identifikationsmittel," *Unverwechselbarkeit. Persönliche Identität und Identifikation in der vormodernen Gesellschaft*, ed. Peter von Moos (Cologne: Böhlau, 2004), 123–46.

institutional forms of monastic life fought a battle over who upheld the strictest form of life (the *vita strictior* or *arctior*).[5]

The divisions these conflicts inspired were most unsettling to contemporary observers, because a new multiplicity threatened to overwhelm what had been thought to be the foundations of a shared orientation. Around 1145 the Premonstratensian Anselm of Havelberg captured this widespread anxiety by saying that many of his contemporaries wondered why so many novelties had taken root in God's church, and why so many new regulations had grown up.[6] He reflected further: Who could not lament the Christian religion (so they complained), now subject to so much multiplicity, transformed through so many innovations, hounded by so many new statutes and customs, beleaguered by so many rules and norms, all of them renewed almost yearly. In the church of God, they say, one could now see how many would now rise up, those who lived by their own lights, who wore unusual clothing, who chose a novel way of life, and who saw themselves—whether under the pretense of monastic profession or the vows of canonical discipline—as they wished, who sang the psalms in novel ways, who established novel observances of abstinence and diet, and who modeled themselves neither after the monks who fought under the Rule of Saint Benedict nor after the canons who lived an apostolic life according to the Rule of Saint Augustine.

Anselm argued vehemently against such skepticism. He appealed to the one Holy Spirit, who gave life to the church but also shared its gifts in many ways. The Spirit gave its gifts to humankind in different ways across different ages, he said, in order to preserve the one faith that bound all together. As Klaus Schreiner explains, "'Diversity,' a structural principle of God's creating and ordering action, also justified the plurality of forms of monastic life and community."[7]

---

[5] Giles Constable, *The Reformation of the Twelfth Century* (Cambridge, UK: Cambridge University Press, 1998); Gillian R. Knight, *The Correspondence between Peter the Venerable and Bernard of Clairvaux* (Aldershot: Ashgate, 2002).

[6] Anselm von Havelberg, *Anticimenon (Dialogi)*, PL 188:1141–42; Markus Schürer, "Innovation und Variabilität als Instrumente göttlicher Pädagogik: Anselm von Havelberg und seine Position in den Diskursen um die Legitimität religiöser Lebensformen," *Mittellateinisches Jahrbuch* 42 (2007): 373–96.

[7] Klaus Schreiner, "Dauer, Niedergang und Erneuerung klösterlicher Observanz im hoch- und spätmittelalterlichen Mönchtum. Krisen, Reform- und

A roughly contemporary treatise, revealingly titled the *Little Book on the Diverse Orders and Professions that Are in the Church* (*Libellus de diversis ordinibus et professionibus qui sunt in aecclesia*),[8] also arranged the diversity of the era's religious life within God's plan for salvation. In this text the diversity of the world of monasticism found its parallels in Christ's many different ways of interacting, and in the corresponding interactions and groups in the Old Testament. The diversity of monastic life was thus understood by contemporary thinkers to be a message that promised salvation, and one that Christ had signaled in various ways: by retreating into the desert, by carrying the cross on Calvary, and by praying on the Mount of Olives. The spectrum of these possibilities as they were lived out in the monastery corresponded to the elements of a divine plan for salvation that was unified but that expressed itself in various ways; religious life thereby encompassed things that were diverse (*diversitates*) yet not opposed (*adversitates*).[9]

In these models, which advanced claims of an ontologically fundamental nature, difference provided the building blocks of unity, insofar as unity allowed itself to be captured only through complementary aspects of multiplicity. Difference, in a functional sense, was complementarity. Contemporaries anxious to find stable middle ground had to be reminded that after an age of new beginnings, of reform of the church and religious life, of a drive for a more inward faith, and of reaching out for both new and forgotten models, religious life had by the middle of the twelfth century come to take on a variety of forms. But they had also to be reminded that overall such diversity was of unimaginable value for Christendom.

No one knew how to make this case better than the Cistercian monk and bishop of Freising in Bavaria, Otto (1112–1158).[10] Equipped

---

Institutionalisierungsprobleme in der Sicht und Deutung betroffener Zeitgenossen," in *Institutionen und Geschichte*, ed. Gert Melville (Cologne: Böhlau, 1992), 295–341, here 326.

[8] *Libellus de diversis ordinibus et professionibus qui sunt in aecclesia*, ed. Giles Constable and Bernard S. Smith, 2nd ed. (Oxford: Clarendon Press, 2003).

[9] Hubert Silvestre, *"Diversi sed non adversi,"* *Recherches de théologie ancienne et médiévale* 31 (1964): 124–32.

[10] Hans-Werner Goetz, *Das Geschichtsbild Ottos von Freising* (Cologne: Böhlau, 1984); Joachim Ehlers, *Otto von Freising. Ein Intellektueller im Mittelalter* (München: Beck, 2013).

with a refined learning that had been honed in Paris and building on Augustine's teachings about the City of God, he profoundly explored the course of salvation history. As he came to speak of his own day, he too depicted the various forms of religious life in order to highlight all that the appearance of the religious had in common: "So adorned both inwardly and outwardly, they spread out across the whole world, multiplying fruitfully and richly, and their number and their merits grew astoundingly in just a brief time; now they shine in the brightness of their signs [*signa*], and through their wondrous works they light the way. As their numbers were once greatest in Egypt, so they are now in Germany and France."[11] Following these reflections, he came to his powerful conclusion: "On account of the multiplicity of our sins, and on account of the malodorous sinfulness of this most disturbed time, we believe that the world could not long endure were it not preserved by the merits of the holy [religious], the true citizens of the City of God." No passage could have been a more moving witness for the role of religious working for the salvation of all of humankind.

The Cluniacs had once claimed to bear the spiritual responsibility of making the world "bright and new"—in other words, that was the ambition of this single religious congregation that had served as a model for all others. By the middle of the twelfth century, it was the broad diversity of monastic life that served as a guarantor and symbol for the salvation of the world. "In my Father's house there are many rooms," the Bible taught (John 14:2)—a passage that Stephen of Thiers had also recalled.[12]

Alongside the grand theological concept of a City of God with "many rooms," there was also of course a practical interest in capturing so much multiplicity within available structures. Stripped of its claims to legitimacy within a framework of salvation history, the broad spectrum of religious associations might be understood as the

[11] *Chronica sive Historia de duabus civitatibus*, ed. MGH SS rerum Germ. (Hannover and Leipzig: Hahn, 1912), 372. Cited from Walther Lammers, ed., and Adolf Schmidt and Hans-Werner Goetz, revisers, *Otto Bischof von Freising, Chronik oder die Geschichte der zwei Staaten* (Darmstadt: Wissenschaftliche Buchgesellschaft, 2011), 561; subsequent citations from 559 and 561.

[12] *Regula venerabilis viri Stephani Muretensis*, in *Scriptores ordinis Grandimontensis*, ed. Jean Becquet, CCCM 8 (Turnhout: Brepols, 1968), 66.

result of an all-too-random process. A few decades later, the Roman Curia sought to control that process by channeling initiatives for making new foundations. The Fourth Lateran Council issued the following resolution in 1215:[13] Lest the great diversity of religious forms of life—*religio* was the concept used here—create confusion in the Church of God, it was strictly prohibited that anyone should found a new *religio*. Whoever should wish to do so was to embrace one that had already been established. Anyone who was to found a monastery in the future should also adopt the rule and legal traditions (*institutiones*) of an approved form of religious life.

In this context the only available choice, in principle, was between the rules of Benedict and Augustine. But the expectation was not that there should be strict and exclusive observance of one rule or the other. It was essential that special statutes should also have their place in order to articulate a normative framework suitable to the particular circumstances of each individual monastery, congregation, and order. Far more at issue was a fundamental decision about whether to embrace a tradition oriented more toward contemplation or action. That decision was crucial for the many communities that were to be founded in the coming era—the Dominicans, for example, and the many future communities of hermits.

It should thus be clear that the boundaries of the normative frameworks outlined here in fact remained fluid. But they gave the papacy a means through which to control and to channel initiatives for founding new monasteries and orders, and as will soon become clear, the papacy made use of it.

---

[13] Antonio García y García, ed., *Constitutiones Concilii quarti Lateranensis una cum Commentariis glossatorum* (Vatican City: Biblioteca Apostolica Vaticano, 1981), chap. 13, p. 62; Michele Maccarrone, "Le costituzioni del IV concilio lateranense sui religiosi," in *Nuovi studi su innocenzo III*, ed. Roberto Lambertini (Rome: Istituto storico italiano per il Medio Evo, 1995), 1–45; Pietro Silanos, "'In sede apostolica specula constituti'. Procedure curiali per l'approvazione di regole e testi normativi all'alba del IV concilio lateranense," *Quellen und Forschungen aus italienischen Archiven und Bibliotheken* 94 (2014): 33–93.

9

New Concepts of Belief

The Search for Religious Identity

The world had changed fundamentally since the great era of Cluny, and the changes came in a matter of only a few decades. The drive for a self-responsible interiorization of the search for God, with its sharp break from the bustle of a worldly life of conventions and institutions, had brought forth new religious movements that traced their core ideals back to the roots of Christianity. But these movements, or at least those that survived, had to be fit into existing models of monastic life, their charismatic energy captured in statutes, their pious passions harnessed by the "methodical practices"[1] of a rationally grounded life in community.

The question is whether this integration of early religious energies into renewed institutional frameworks could preserve any of what had inspired so many changes—spiritual self-responsibility, the inner life, the restless search for the salvation of the individual soul. If this question could be answered affirmatively, Otto of Freising's allusion to a new Egypt could be seen as convincingly realized, as the religious of his generation stood "shining in the brightness of their

---

[1] Max Weber, *Economy and Society. An Outline of Interpretive Sociology*, ed. Guenther Roth and Claus Wittich (Berkeley: University of California Press, 1978), 1169: "Asceticism becomes the object of methodical practices as soon as the ecstatic or contemplative union with God is transformed, from a state that only some individuals can achieve through their charismatic endowments, into a goal that many can reach through identifiable ascetic means just as in the charismatic training of the guilds of magical priests." Cf. Otto Gerhard Oexle, "Max Weber und das Mönchtum," in *Max Webers Religionssoziologie in interkultureller Perspektive*, ed. Hartmut Lehmann and Jean Martin Quedraogo (Göttingen: Vandenhoeck and Ruprecht, 2003), 311–34.

signs [*signa*]"[2]—something that (as he saw it) might even delay the downfall of the world. On this point a few observations are in order.

Around the year 1140, Gratian published a collection of canon law that would soon shape the life of the institutional church as hardly any other work did. In that collection is a canon (C. 19, q. 2, c. 2) that begins as follows: "There are two kinds of law: a public law, and a personal law" (*Duae sunt . . . leges: una publica, altera privata*).[3] The *lex publica* was understood to be the canon law as it had been written since the days of the fathers; the *lex privata*, in contrast, was that which had been written in the hearts of the faithful by the inspiration of the Holy Spirit (*instinctu Sancti Spiritus*). Should a cleric wish to enter a monastery to find his personal salvation there, the text continued, he was allowed to do so without asking permission of his bishop. The *lex privata*, that is, was superior to the *lex publica*, since the former was the law of the spirit of God—and who, after all, could resist the Holy Spirit? Where the spirit of God is, there is freedom (*ubi Spiritus Dei, ibi libertas*). Therefore those who were led by the spirit of God were subject to no law of the church. Paul had already used an analogous formulation—*ubi Spiritus Domini, ibi libertas*—in his second letter to the Corinthians (2 Cor 3:17). Gratian cited another revered authority as further evidence of the reception of this law—no less than a decretal of one of the leading popes of church reform, Urban II. The decretal was not authentic, but no one knew it at the time.

Each individual who was convinced that he could call on the inspiration of the Holy Spirit was thus able, in keeping with this text, to dispense with all manner of church regulations—indeed, there was no need to establish norms for spiritual life through the institutional church. In the light of divinely guided decisions, neither the judgments of church officeholders nor the legal claims of a bishop

---

.[2] See p. 184.

[3] On the following, see Gert Melville, "Zur Abgrenzung zwischen Vita canonica und Vita monastica. Das Übertrittsproblem in kanonistischer Behandlung von Gratian bis Hostiensis," in *Secundum regulam vivere. Festschrift für P. Nobert Backmund*, ed. Gert Melville (Windberg: Poppe-Verlag, 1978), 205–44; Peter von Moos, "Krise und Kritik der Institutionalität. Die mittelalterliche Kirche als 'Anstalt' und 'Himmelreich auf Erden,'" in *Institutionalität und Symbolisierung*, ed. Gert Melville (Cologne: Böhlau, 2001), 293–340, 34–44.

counted for anything. Personal convictions and norms rooted in the heart stood firm against the positive law of a church that saw itself as a mediator of salvation, placed in principle between God and humankind. The same church now saw itself confronted by those who claimed direct personal inspiration by the spirit of God. But above all the challenge played out in the monasteries of the day, since the freedom of the Holy Spirit was leading so many, in keeping with this text, to make their way there.

A rationally designed organization became the standard framework not only for the new monasteries that had grown up across the spectrum of the religious movements of the twelfth century[4] but also for the older ones that had opened their doors to the inspiration of reform. Yet principles that could only be anchored in the heart were valued at least as highly. The challenge was to find a balance between the needs of an individual quest for salvation and the demands of the well-ordered community that was once again thought to provide its very foundation.[5]

Thus the protagonists of the reforming spirit, figures like William of Saint-Thierry (1075/1080–1148), Bernard of Clairvaux (1090–1153), Peter the Venerable (1092/94–1156), Aelred of Rievaulx (1110–1167), Hugh of Fouilly (1100–1174), Peter of Celle (1115–1183), Philip of Harvengt (d. 1183), and many others, often anonymous, began around the middle of the twelfth century to write a variety of letters or treatises. Their titles are revealing: "On the status of the virtues" (*De statu virtutum*), "On claustral discipline" (*De disciplina claustrali*), and "On conscience" (*De conscientia*). Each of them sought to pass on core spiritual values as a firm foundation for religious interaction.[6] These works came to complement the legal texts. Their claim to validity rested on the fact that they addressed matters essential to salvation. Accordingly, the force behind their sanctions was transcendent, anchored in divine judgment alone, their

---

[4] Giles Constable, *The Reformation of the Twelfth Century* (Cambridge, UK: Cambridge University Press, 1998).

[5] Gert Melville, "Im Spannungsfeld von religiösem Eifer und methodischem Betrieb. Zur Innovationskraft der mittelalterlichen Klöster," *Denkströme. Journal der Sächsischen Akademie der Wissenschaften* 7 (2011): 72–92, here 76–80.

[6] Caroline Bynum, *Docere verbo et exemplo. An Aspect of Twelfth-Century Spirituality* (Missoula, MT: Scholars Press, 1979).

validity located in the conscience of the individual—that is, it was completely individualized.[7] These texts were thus concerned not only with building an inward, personal acceptance of the monastery's ordering of community life but also with the spiritual formation of the individual and a personal concern for the soul.

Yet the matter could not be left even here. The individual also had to live out the teachings captured in these works. Thus one author asked, "What use are these texts, what is to be read and understood, if you do not read and understand yourself? Move yourself to read inwardly, so that you read, explore, and recognize yourself, and understand."[8] The monasteries of the era fostered, for the first time, a systematic dialogue with one's own psyche.

Expressions like these were unthinkable without some conceptualization of those dimensions of thought that the *lex privata* had brought forth through the impetus of the Holy Spirit. They also show how much individual reflection, or at least reflection on the self, had come to be an essential part of monastic life. To peer into the inner life of a person had a strong legitimizing force, insofar as the "inner house" (*interior domus*)—the title of another prominent text of the twelfth century[9]—was the place that made possible an encounter with God.

The language of the monastery had become something different. It now cut across all of the mutually exclusive legal constructions and across the different observances and loyalties of the various orders. Its texts advanced ideas that were interchangeable, and in fact readers quite often exchanged them. The new discourse sought to articulate what monasteries were now supposed to be: institutionalized places whose community life allowed the embrace and preservation of the core ideals of the religious transformations of the era, which

---

[7] Mirko Breitenstein, "Die Verfügbarkeit der Transzendenz. Das Gewissen der Mönche als Heilsgarant," in Gert Melville, Bernd Schneidmüller, and Stefan Weinfurter, eds., *Innovation durch Deuten und Gestalten. Klöster im Mittelalter zwischen Jenseits und Welt* (Regensburg: Steiner, 2014), 37–56.

[8] *Meditationes piissimae de cognitione humanae conditionis* [a twelfth-century anonymous work], PL 184:508.

[9] *De interiori domo seu De conscientia aedificanda*, PL 184:507–52; Philippe Delhaye, "Domo (de interiori)," *Dictionnaire de spiritualité* (Paris: Beauchesne, 1957), 3:1548–51.

had begun with the reformulation of the eremitical ideal. And only that new discourse could now allow the formulation of the kinds of striking expressions offered up by a figure like Peter the Venerable, who was still head of the monastic community that had stood as the epitome of an outdated monasticism. Speaking of the search for inner solitude within the monastery, Peter wrote,

> And as in the solitude of the mountains, so we have built for ourselves secret places for the solitude of our hearts, where alone the true hermitage is found by those who truly renounce the world, where no distractions are allowed, where the storm and noise of worldly tumult have quieted themselves. . . . Let us always retreat to this silence while we yet live and are away from the Lord and find ourselves in the heart of the crowd, and let us find within ourselves what we would travel to the farthest edges of the world to find.[10]

Reformed communities of that era were thus understood as places of protection for both body and soul. As Hugh of Fouilly explained, to retreat behind the walls of the cloister was to flee the attacks of the ancient enemy, the devil, and all of the uncertainty of earthly life.[11] The reformed houses of the era guarded the spiritual heritage of the new piety, which they deepened through reflection and writing. Otto of Freising was thus able to see them as pure, holy places, where God's plan of salvation became eschatologically realized.[12]

The monastery's traditionally strict separation of inside from outside now came also to represent the differences between starkly opposing worlds—here Jerusalem, there Babylon; here Sinai, there Egypt; here the *civitas Dei*, there the *civitas mundi*; here Paradise, there the horrors of the world.[13] These communities were no longer forums for presenting a public invitation to salvation, of the sort

[10] Ep 58, in *The Letters of Peter the Venerable*, ed. Giles Constable (Cambridge, MA: Harvard University Press, 1967), 1:188.

[11] Hugo de Folieto, *De claustro animae*, PL 176:1019–20.

[12] See p. 184.

[13] Gert Melville, "Inside and Outside. Some Considerations about Cloistral Boundaries in the Central Middle Ages," in *Ecclesia in medio nationis*, ed. Brigitte Meijns and Steven Vanderputten (Leuven: Leuven University Press, 2011), 167–82.

that the wandering preachers of the streets and plazas of growing cities had sometimes depicted. They were now understood as solitary bastions of religious life. The Cistercians' refusal to allow the laity access to their churches captures the symbolism perfectly; the same was even true of the foundations of regular canons with pastoral duties in the parishes of a bishopric. It is also revealed in the very small number of cases in which adherents to monastic life went out into the world to preach, as did Bernard of Clairvaux.

The reformed monasteries of that era did more, however, than merely preserve a spiritual inheritance. They clothed that inheritance in models of order that were obedient to rules and that had firm borders—firm, because beyond them lay only a vast, alien world of secular confusion. In that regard, reformed monasteries can be seen as institutional anchor points in the spread of Christendom as it had emerged from the movement to reform the universal church in the eleventh century—a Christendom whose old unity of priesthood (*sacerdotium*) and kingdom (*regnum*) the church had broken but now saw as its own patrimony, a church unified anew and set apart from the world around it.

In the Middle Ages, the Christian faith was the foundation of culture, and it was ever present, in all areas of life, as a standard measure and source of justification. In that climate, the reformed monasteries' attempts to separate themselves from the world could lead to serious problems. A cloistered life, for example, upheld the core ideal that faith could in fact be lived out by embracing monastic life—in humbly following the poor Christ, in the brotherly love of the original Christian community, and in an inner desire for individual salvation. Yet these were ideals that could also become vital options for meeting the needs of the faithful beyond the walls of the traditional cloister. The danger was that those ideals would no longer be negotiable there, thus compelling a search for new configurations of religious life to aid in their realization.

The second half of the twelfth century witnessed a twofold development. On the one hand, quite new social environments and forms of order shaped by the laity began to emerge,[14] especially in the

---

[14] Hagen Keller, "Die Stadtkommunen als politische Organismen in den Herrschaftsordnungen des 11.–13. Jahrhunderts," in *Pensiero e sperimentazioni istituzionali nella societas Christiana (1046–1250)*, ed. Giancarlo Andenna

comparatively advanced urban communes of northern Italy and lower Lotharingia. In these settings, the structures of the faith established by the church allowed religious identity to find new expression only with great difficulty. On the other hand, heretical currents grew remarkably strong, especially in northern Italy and southern France.[15] In many respects those currents had radicalized the old demands of the church reformers. They also settled along the fault lines established between church and world, whether by articulating new religious concepts or by demanding a different kind of church altogether. The two phenomena—the search for religious identity in the context of social transformation, and new models of faith that shattered established boundaries—were not quite identical. But they often found themselves in a complex mutual relationship.

The Roman church, as would soon become clear, had first to adopt strategies that would best allow it to react to these developments in innovative ways. One possible strategy might have been found in the core religious ideals of the reforming monasteries. Both the ecclesiastical hierarchy and secular rulers in fact saw that chance, and they took it: in 1177 Count Raymond V of Toulouse requested the aid of the Cistercian general chapter against the Cathars, who were being persecuted as heretics in his territory. Pope Alexander III gave his support in the matter, and a short time later the Cistercian abbot Henry of Clairvaux arrived to begin work against a heresy that was already deeply rooted in the faith of the common people.[16] His chief instrument was the sword, and he failed. In 1203 Innocent III charged the Cistercians anew, under the leadership of Abbot Arnold of Cîteaux, and this time the chief instrument was to be preaching. Yet the monks' opulent and lordly appearance again limited their success.[17]

(Milan: Vita e pensiero, 2007), 673–703. For Homobonus von Cremona as a symbolic embodiment, so to speak, of these structures, see André Vauchez, *Les laïcs au Moyen Age. Pratiques et experiences religieuses* (Paris: Éditions du Cerf, 1987), 77–82.

[15] Jörg Oberste, *Zwischen Heiligkeit und Häresie*, 2 vols. (Cologne: Böhlau, 2003).

[16] Beverly Mayne Kienzle, "Henry of Clairvaux and the 1178 and 1181 Missions," *Heresis* 28 (1997): 63–87.

[17] Jörg Oberste, "Prediger, Legaten und Märtyrer. Die Zisterzienser im Kampf gegen die Katharer," in *Beiträge zum klösterlichen Leben im christlichen Abend-*

Such a failure clearly shows the degree to which monasteries could become solitary islands that looked out on the world.

Beguines and *Humiliati*: A New Lay Piety

New circumstances demanded new forms of religious life, and the search for those forms marked the beginning of a new act in the drama of the monastic world. Although its roots reached back to the eleventh century's eremitic wandering preachers, who drew around them large crowds especially of female laity, only in the last years of the twelfth century did a strong movement emerge that focused on pious women (*mulieres religiosae*) from every social rank. The focal point of this movement was the vibrant urban environment of the Low Countries and the Rhineland; it spread from there to northern France and along the Rhine down to Switzerland. At first it had almost no organizational framework, and it never attained anything like the structure of a religious order. The movement belonged to women who wanted to live a life of poverty, penance, humility, chastity, and deeply interior piety but who had no intention of professing vows, observing a traditional rule, or retreating from the world into a monastery. Their designation as Beguines was at first a derogatory term used only by outsiders. In the early years they still lived in their own houses or in those of their families.[18] Often they tied some portion of their wealth to a monastery, and each belonged to it as *conversa a seculo* (a "convert from the world") but did not reside there.

The story again recalled the eleventh and early twelfth centuries: a way of religious life, this one led by women, that resisted being drawn into the hierarchical structures of the church, and one that

---

land während des Mittelalters, ed. Reinhardt Butz and Jörg Oberste (Münster: LIT, 2004), 73–92.

[18] Ernest William McDonnell, *The Beguines and Beghards in Medieval Culture* (New York: Octagon Books, 1969); Ernest William McDonnell, "Beginen/ Begarden," in *Theologische Realenzyklopädie* (Leipzig: de Gruyter, 1980); Martina Wehrli-Johns, "Das mittelalterliche Beginentum. Religiöse Frauenbewegung oder Sozialidee der Scholastik," in *Fromme Frauen oder Ketzerinnen? Leben und Verfolgung der Beginen im Mittelalter*, ed. Martina Wehrli-Johns and Claudia Opitz (Freiburg im Breisgau: Herder, 1998), 25–51; Walter Simons, *Cities of Ladies: Beguine Communities in the Medieval Low Countries 1200– 1565* (Philadelphia: University of Pennsylvania Press, 2001).

when observed from the outside appeared in practice to be entirely unregulated, its religious spirit prompting mistrust and suspicion of heresy. The bishop of Acre, James of Vitry (ca. 1170–1240), a careful observer of religious life in his era and a supporter of the women and their experiments in piety, resented the fact that so many of his contemporaries—high-ranking clerics among them—sought "fraudulently to discredit the spiritual life [of these] women."[19] Because the women lacked any kind of representative body or coordination, their efforts to establish trust worked only on a regional or local level.[20] In the first half of the thirteenth century, in many places a form of community life emerged in which the Beguines lived together under the direction of a mistress (*magistra*). In this case too they renounced lifelong vows, with the result that they could leave the community (to marry, for example), though they had to leave behind the property they had brought when they joined. Scholars thus speak today of these women as representatives of a so-called semireligious life.[21] In a few houses of Beguines the women embraced manual labor to support themselves, for example, in textile work, and devoted themselves in addition to religious exercises and prayer to charitable work such as care for the sick and dying and care for the homeless and the poor. In its outward form their pattern of life thus already had a strong affinity to the world of the monastery, and their houses were not infrequently tied, though without vows, to religious life—for example, to the Cistercian Order. They also often assimilated themselves

[19] McDonnell, "Beginen/Begarden," 405. On James de Vitry, see Franz J. Felten, "Geschichtsschreibung cum ira et studio. Zur Darstellung religiöser Gemeinschaften in Jakob von Vitrys Historia occidentalis," in *Christliches und jüdisches Europa im Mittelalter. Kolloquium zu Ehren von Alfred Haverkamp*, ed. Lukas Clemens and Sigrid Hirbodian (Trier: Kliomedia, 2011), 83–120.

[20] Jörg Voigt, *Beginen im Spätmittelalter* (Cologne: Böhlau, 2012).

[21] On the concept, see Kaspar Elm, "*Vita regularis sine regula*. Bedeutung, Rechtsstellung und Selbstverständnis des mittelalterlichen und frühneuzeitlichen Semireligiosentums," in *Häresie und vorzeitige Reformation im Spätmittelalter*, ed. Elisabeth Müller-Luckner and František Šmahel (Munich: Oldenbourg, 1998), 239–73; James Mixson, trans., *Selected Essays of Kaspar Elm* (Leiden: Brill, 2015), chap. 8. See also the work of Elizabeth M. Makowski, especially *"A Pernicious Sort of Woman": Quasi-Religious Women and Canon Lawyers in the Later Middle Ages* (Washington, DC: The Catholic University of America Press, 2005).

to the mendicant orders by way of the pastoral care offered through those communities.[22]

Slowly the Beguines began to win respect even among those whose recognition was essential for their continued existence—city governments and leading families in urban settings and the French royal household, for example, as well as numerous bishops and the papacy. In 1233, Gregory IX issued a decree that protected German Beguines and confirmed their way of life under a mistress.[23] In Cologne around the middle of the thirteenth century there were around a hundred communities of Beguines, twenty-two in Mainz, and twenty-four in Strasbourg, to name only a few examples. The demand for these communities—above all because they were held together by the deeply interior piety of their members—was thus enormous. In the region of Belgium and the Netherlands in fact there were "Beguine courts"—in the Belgian town of Turnhout, for example—which looked like small, autonomous cities, cut off from the urban landscape by their own walls and trenches.

Yet soon afterward the pendulum slowly began to swing in the opposite direction. At the Ecumenical Council of Vienne, held in 1311/12, the Beguines' way of life was fundamentally condemned, on the grounds that the Beguines followed no rule, professed no vow of obedience, and had not renounced their property. Thus, the council ruled, they could not be seen as religious. Moreover, and above all, they stood under suspicion of heresy whenever they lived freely and spontaneously beyond the structures of established communities.[24] The setback for the Beguines was considerable. But to a certain extent they could make a new start under the right conditions, wherever well-established houses survived and where bishops and orders, especially the Dominicans, could lend their support on questions of

[22] Christian-Frederik Felskau, "Von Brabant bis Böhmen und darüber hinaus. Zu Einheit und Vielfalt der 'religiösen Frauenbewegung' des 12. und des 13. Jahrhunderts," in *Fromme Frauen—unbequeme Frauen? Weibliches Religiosentum im Mittelalter*, ed. Edeltraud Klueting (Hildensheim and Zürich: Olms, 2006).

[23] Amalie Fössel and Anette Hettinger, *Klosterfrauen, Beginen, Ketzerinnen. Religiöse Lebensformen von Frauen im Mittelalter* (Idstein: Schulz-Kirchner, 2000), 137–38.

[24] Fössel and Hettinger, *Klosterfrauen*, 147–49; Voigt, *Beginen im Spätmittelalter*, 171–98.

Beguine orthodoxy. Pope John XXII recognized these structures in two bulls in 1318 and 1319, thereby allowing Beguine communities in general to continue to survive.

The tragedy of these developments lay in the fact that, on the one hand, with a few exceptions for extreme theological positions, the Beguines articulated a religiosity that they championed passionately and that needed no institutionalization within the traditional *vita religiosa*. On the other hand, an entirely independent form of women's piety—one that allowed women to abandon their place in established society and to live together without enclosure or vows—was unthinkable. The power of inherited traditions would not allow itself to yield without contest to the spirit of the age, however compelling—especially when those traditions were supported by a church hierarchy that developed ever-stronger legal frameworks and worked through more strictly differentiated norms. Yet the Beguine way of life remained powerful enough, because of both its strength in numbers and the depth of its faith, to continue to present an alternative path to the monastery's traditional purpose: preparing the way for the individual soul's journey back to God.

Developments on another stage reveal that innovative forms of community among devout laity could in any case find solutions of their own on behalf of the hierarchical church, although here too there were numerous points of contention. During the second half of the twelfth century various northern Italian cities saw the emergence of groups of laity, both men and women, coming from a range of levels across society, including the wealthy. These groups embraced a religious life together but remained in the houses of their families. They sustained themselves with the work of their hands and renounced every kind of deception, contention, and oath. They clothed themselves in a kind of monastic habit made of raw, undyed material and thus self-consciously stood apart symbolically from their fellow citizens. They called themselves the *Humiliati*—those who subjected themselves to humility.[25]

---

[25] Annamaria Ambrosioni, "Umiliati/Umiliate," in *Dizionario degli istituti di perfezione* (Rome: Edizioni paoline, 1997), 9:1489–1507; Maria Pia Alberzoni, "Die Humiliaten zwischen Legende und Wirklichkeit," *Mitteilungen des Instituts für Österreichische Geschichtsforschung* 107 (1999): 324–53; Frances Andrews, *The Early Humilitati* (Cambridge, UK: Cambridge University Press, 1999).

Little evidence of these groups survives from their earliest beginnings. Whether they shared particular forms of charismatic leadership or patterns of foundation remains unclear, as is the degree to which they established translocal organizational structures. Only one historiographical text,[26] unfortunately originating decades later, relates that in 1179 ambassadors of the *Humiliati* made their way to Pope Alexander III and the Third Lateran Council and sought official confirmation of their way of life and their preaching. They were well received and in fact praised for their pious way of life. They were forbidden only from holding secret gatherings (*conventicula*), a move designed to guard against both the formation of stable communities and any potential conspiracies. As laity they were allowed to preach only if they received permission explicitly and for each individual occasion from their local bishops. But they refused to accept that limitation, the text further reported, and had thus been excommunicated.

In 1184, a surviving charter issued by Pope Lucius III named the Humiliati in the same breath as the Cathars, the Waldensians, and other heretical groups. The same charter also excommunicated them for a second time, since as laity—along with the others who stood condemned—they had dared to preach "under the appearance of the virtue of piety" (*sub specie pietatis virtutum*) without having been tasked to do so by any proper authority.[27]

Both the disgrace of having been cast out from the church community and the infamy of heresy long followed the *Humiliati*, although the clerics who in the meantime had flocked to their ranks could not be touched by any prohibition against preaching. The prohibition had been directed only against the laity among their ranks, since by virtue of the judgment of heresy against them they had in principle been forbidden to preach. Yet the actual innovation lay precisely in their combining their status as laity who lived a common life among the urban population with their offering of pastoral service to their neighbor through preaching the word of God. This was an entirely new quality of religious life. That the laity should be so bold as to feel themselves responsible for enriching the religiosity of other laity was, in the eyes of the ecclesiastical authorities, scandalous in principle.

[26] Anonymus of Laon, in Alberzoni, "Die Humiliaten," 333.

[27] *Texte zur Inquisition*, ed. Kurt-Victor Selge (Gütersloh: Mohn, 1967), 26–29 (*Ad abolendam*).

The circumstance was not quite comparable to that of the wandering preachers at the turn from the eleventh to the twelfth century, since they had belonged entirely to the ranks of the clergy and needed a license to preach only beyond the boundaries of their bishoprics. The later figures were also unlike those earlier laity who had gathered around the likes of Stephen of Thiers and had retreated almost without a trace into the forest wilderness. The *Humiliati*, in contrast, were active in the plazas of the cities. Here again a new circumstance had emerged, albeit in an entirely different way, that did not fit (to recall the concept of deviance deployed against Robert of Arbrissel) into the *sensus communis* of the church. Moreover, especially in northern Italy, the church hierarchy saw itself as confronted with a palpable expansion of a heresy whose teaching in fact departed dogmatically from orthodoxy.[28]

Thanks to Innocent III, the *Humiliati* were eventually brought back into the fold of the church. Innocent, like none of his predecessors, possessed the precious gift of discretion in matters of practice for the advantage of the church. He hit hard against the stubborn holdouts among the Cathars in southern France, going so far as to call a crusade against them that would last from 1209–1229. On the other hand, he sought to lead back into the church those whose uncommon depth of faith and distinct practices of piety had made it seem that they departed from church rules—not least because they were self-organized lay communities, free of hierarchical ties, which sought above all for themselves (but also for others) to fill the holes in pastoral care that had opened up in their new urban societies. The pope recognized particularly well, as became clear from his later actions, the benefit of such efforts at integration. It was an insight he also shared with his predecessors from the days of the wandering preachers.

At the beginning of Innocent's pontificate in 1198, there had clearly already been contact between the Curia and the *Humiliati*. In December of 1199 Innocent wrote a harsh letter to the canons and archpriests of Verona admonishing them to exercise discretion (as he had already demanded) in distinguishing between true heretics and those communities of *Humiliati* that had already explicitly pledged obedience to the Roman church through their bishops. The prejudice

---

[28] *Lettres de Jacques de Vitry (1160/1170–1240) évêque de Saint-Jean-d'Acre*, ed. Robert Burchard Constantijn Huygens (Leiden: Brill, 1960), 1:36–37.

against what was for that time such an unusual way of life seems to have been deeply rooted in local society.

In December 1200 the pope instructed the *Humiliati* to bring together their various communities into one congregation. With the help of Albert, bishop of Vercelli and former prior of the congregation of Mortara, as well as two prominent Cistercian abbots, the *Humiliati* were also to draw up the norms of their way of life in a new set of statutes. These leaders of established orders had been chosen with intention because they were particularly experienced in the matter of organizing religious communities. The impulse to more firmly establish emergent forms of lay religious community had thus come directly from the world of the reformed monastery—and in fact from the ranks of both regular canons and monks.

A papal commission and even Innocent himself later edited and revised the early statutes, because the pope discerned a fundamental problem: the *Humiliati* were facing a threefold schism. There were communities of clerics, communities of laity living in ways that imitated monastic life but as yet without any recognized rule, and groups whose members continued to live with their families and who were often married. To create a consolidated corpus of norms binding for all had long been beyond the Curia's innovative power.

The problem was how to combine two largely irreconcilable ways of life: on the one hand, a mutually supportive life of clergy and laity, and on the other, a life that was either cloistered yet also apostolic and open to the world or that remained fully within secular structures. In a clerical church, increasingly consolidated and grounded in law, the life of the laity fit only with difficulty into a legal structure designed around the clerical estate.

June 1201 witnessed the emergence of a notable solution, one that in substance stood as the beacon of a new era: Innocent III issued two distinct decrees in rapid succession. They took up in expanded form the early draft of the statutes.[29] On June 7, 1201, he confirmed the *propositum*—the spiritual intention—of those laity who lived with their families.[30] He especially praised their core ideal of pursuing spiritual perfection within the bond of marriage. Under the name of Third Order

---

[29] Girolamo Tiraboschi, *Vetera Humiliatorum monumenta* (Milan: Galeatius, 1768), 2:139–48.

[30] Tiraboschi, *Vetera Humiliatorum monumenta*, 2:128–34.

they also found an identifiable designation that would later serve as a model for other institutional forms within the *vita religiosa*—among the Franciscans, for example, albeit in a somewhat different way, with the concept of "tertiary" men and women.[31] A few days later, on June 16, 1201, the pope issued the bull *Non omni spiritui credere*, in which he solemnly established the new order of the *Humiliati*, preserving its distinct and internally coherent threefold structure and issuing specific statutes for them that were based on the commission's work.[32] These concerned the Order's inner organization, its general chapter and the hierarchy of its leadership, practices of visitation that were consistent with Cistercian precedents, and the celebration of Mass according to the customs of the congregation of Mortara.[33]

It is remarkable both how rapidly these developments unfolded at the papal court and how personally the pope was engaged in them. But the real innovation was hidden in the text itself: not only did it create an order that had as one of its essential elements a religious corporation made up exclusively of laity, but these laity were even allowed to preach. The content of their preaching, however, was divided into two forms: dogmatic preaching that treated matters of belief and penitential preaching that focused on moral behavior and on admonitions to live a life pleasing to God. Trusted laity among the *Humiliati* were henceforth allowed to preach penitential sermons before Sunday congregations, with the bishops' general understanding that permission to preach would not be withheld.

The church had blazed a new trail. It had begun to occupy a new social space, with the help of the forces that that same space had produced. It had also done so through means that would have an unimagined impact over the coming decades.

"Holy Preachers" and "Lesser Brothers"

Around 1224/25 an anonymous regular canon from the community of Lauterberg near Halle wrote his observations about the impact in

---

[31] Karl Suso Frank, "Tertiarier/Tertiarierinnen I und II," in *Theologische Realenzyklopädie* (Berlin: de Gruyter, 2002), 33:85–93; Alison More, "Institutionalizing Penitential Life in Later Medieval and Early Modern Europe: Third Orders, Rules and Canonical Legitimacy," *Church History* 83 (2014): 297–323.

[32] Frank, "Tertiarier/Tertiarierinnen I und II."

[33] Alberzoni, "Die Humiliaten," 331–38; Andrews, *The Early Humiliati*, 64–98.

his region of two orders with an entirely new way of life (*duo novae conversationis ordines*).[34] One group had only clerics as its members and called itself "the holy preachers" (*sancti praedicatores*); the other, which also accepted lay members, called itself the "lesser brothers" or Minorites (*minores fratres*). Both had been confirmed by Innocent III. In view of such high-ranking approval, the regular canon asked himself what the introduction of such novelties might mean. It could only mean, he answered, that those who lived in religious orders, those the church had so long relied on, had become too negligent. But in the end, it could be said that in light of the standard set by Augustine and Benedict, there was certainly no need for new institutions, since those founders had shown—if one would only follow them in obedience—what heights of holiness could be reached. For those who sought holiness through new institutions, all that these most holy fathers had achieved by means of their rules was surely sufficient. The author found it hard to believe that anyone from the ranks of the Order of Preachers or the Minorites could become more holy than Augustine or Benedict. And he did not say this to deny anyone's genuine zeal. Rather, he found it most painful that the old established orders had become so contemptible by virtue of the undisciplined ways of their members that they were no longer sufficient to save those who wanted to retreat from the world. Had their way of life still remained sufficient, no one would ever have gone chasing after new ones.

This anonymous author was not wrong in his assessment, since what he observed in fact reflected the deeper transformation of religious life's meaning in his day: from the cloistered world of the twelfth century, which had built bastions to protect an interiorized faith, to a new style of religious life that seemed, in its acceptance by both the Roman church and the broader population, to have overrun the old ways. Soon afterward, the same phenomenon astonished another anonymous author from an altogether different region of Europe, Normandy. He described the impact of the new orders with

---

[34] *Chronicon Montis Sereni*, ed. MGH SS 23, 220. On the following, see Gert Melville, "Duo novae conversationis ordines. Zur Wahrnehmung der frühen Mendikanten vor dem Problem institutioneller Neuartigkeit im mittelalterlichen Religiosentum," in *Die Bettelorden im Aufbau*, ed. Gert Melville and Jörg Oberste (Münster: LIT, 1999), 1–23.

these words: "And in a short time they filled the earth, so that hardly any city or renowned fortified settlement could be found in Christian lands that was not home to these orders." To this statement he added, somewhat sharply, that both the Order of Preachers and the Friars Minor were now happily embraced by church and people, and that many nobles and educated youths had been drawn to them because of their unusual novelty (*propter novitatem insolitam*).[35]

Surely the anonymous author from Lauterberg was also not entirely wrong in his attempt to explain this crush of new followers by noting the flagging commitment to monastic and canonical norms in the houses of his day, where the dynamic of religious revival had been set aside in favor of the preservation of stability. Yet his observations captured only part of a complex reality, to the extent that he too looked out on the world from a "solitary island" (to recall the phrase, noted above, that attempts to capture the position of the traditional monasteries). What he could not recognize was the fact that the new way of life of these two orders—the *nova conversatio*, as he called it—represented an institutional response to the new religious needs of the laity.

The Order of Preachers had been founded by Dominic Guzmán (1170–1221), and the Minorites had grown from the circles around Francis of Assisi (1181/82–1226).[36] The way of life these orders modeled and mediated, as well as the way they organized themselves, signaled a new kind of search for the truth of the Christian faith and a desire for an assurance of salvation grounded in the gospels. Yet that life was now not necessarily to be found only in a cloister closed off from the world. It could also be lived "among the people" (1 Pet 2:12). The example of the *Humiliati* had already shown that the laity of Europe's new urban environments knew very well how to articulate that kind of search and desire—and that they saw themselves compelled by their changing social circumstance to embrace it if

---

[35] *Annales Normannici*, ed. MGH SS 26, S. 514; Kajetan Esser, *Anfänge und ursprüngliche Zielsetzungen des Ordens der Minderbrüder* (Leiden: Brill, 1966), 9–11; Clifford Hugh Lawrence, *The Friars* (New York: Longman, 1994).

[36] For a comparison of the two, see Kaspar Elm, "Franziskus und Dominikus. Wirkungen und Antriebskräfte zweier Ordensstifter," in Kaspar Elm, *Vitasfratrum*, ed. Dieter Berg (Werl: Dietrich-Coelde, 1994), 123–41; Mixson, *Selected Essays of Kaspar Elm*, chap. 1.

they were ever to craft an appropriate identity across Christendom's spectrum of possibilities.

The two orders had divergent ideas about how to meet the religious and organizational needs of the day. In many instances they sought entirely new ways, even as they remained grounded in certain continuities of religious forms of life: the beginnings of the Order of Preachers lay in the *vita canonica*, and so they sought to link their distinctive model of care for the salvation of their neighbors' souls to the pastoral office of the regular canons.

Francis and his followers, in contrast, lived out the ideal of voluntary poverty[37] and the imitation of Christ "among the people." They thereby advanced, in their own way, something that for at least two hundred years had been a central focus for anyone who wanted to embrace a pure life according to the gospels. Contemporaries with a broad analytical view—figures like James of Vitry, bishop of Acre and cardinal—recognized this connection and interpreted it as the work of God in the context of salvation history.[38] With the Minorites the Lord had created a fourth institution, one that stood alongside the religious life of hermits, monks, and canons and that with them provided the firm durability of a square foundation. Yet upon closer inspection, James continued, God had in fact not introduced a new rule but only revived from the earliest days of the church an old form of religious life, neglected and almost extinct. It was now embodied in the Order of the Minorites, so that new athletes of God could arise in the dangerous last days of the Antichrist and so that the church could be armed against so many threatening afflictions.

These ties to tradition had remained hidden to the anonymous author from Lauterberg. He saw only the ominous acceptance of the new orders, of "unusual novelty," as the Norman historian put it. These two authors rightly sensed that a new era had arrived for the world of monasticism. A new era had begun, one in which all other religious institutions would be cast into the shadows by the

---

[37] Achim Wesjohann, "Überschüsse an Armut. Mythische Grundlagen mendikantischer Armutsauffassungen," in *In proposito paupertatis*, ed. Gert Melville and Annette Kehnel (Münster: LIT, 2001), 169–201, here 184–96.

[38] John Frederick Hinnebusch, ed., *The Historia Occidentalis of Jacques de Vitry* (Fribourg: Fribourg University Press, 1972), 158–61; Melville, "Duo novae conversationis ordines," 7–9.

mendicant orders. The Order of Preachers and the Friars Minor, both founded in the early thirteenth century, were their two most important representatives. There were also other thirteenth-century institutions, established through the transformation of older communities. Among these, attention will be given here above all to the Carmelites and the Augustinian Hermits. Common to all these mendicant orders were the command to live in absolute poverty and the renunciation of ties to a particular community in favor of membership in the order as a whole. The latter led to what was perhaps the most unsettling novelty: the crumbling away of distinctive old patterns of community formation. The old notion of large "translocal communities" may have been a fiction, but in many congregations, before the establishment of proper orders, that fiction had preserved a high degree of stability of place and thereby cultivated an individual's lifelong identification with a single community.

In any event, what actually played out at the beginning of the thirteenth century, despite the continuities of the older bonds of religious life noted thus far, transformed the framework of the world of monasticism in such fundamental ways that it requires a detailed analysis of its own, and one that like the discussion of the outbreak of the eremitical movement cannot be limited to an explanation of external conditions. Of particular interest, moreover, will be a consideration of the genuine core ideas on which the new orders built their overwhelming power, the way they realized the agendas they themselves developed, and the institutional forms they developed to place their beginnings on a lasting foundation.

If one considers only the Order of Preachers (the *Ordo praedicatorum*, commonly if inaccurately called the Dominicans) and the Order of the Friars Minor (*Ordo minorum*, again commonly if inaccurately called the Franciscans), a sharp difference appears in the fundamentals discussed above. That difference symbolizes two different principal possibilities for forms of organization and two different ways of understanding the formation of an order. The organization developed by the Order of Preachers can be explained as the result of highly rational procedures that looked to organizational patterns found among the regular canons, creatively adapted those patterns in ways that gave them a new quality, and enhanced them with innovative structures. The process among the Friars Minor, in contrast, was something else entirely: its establishment was unthinkable without the particular role of a unique person. Even when taking care not to overestimate the importance of great personalities in shaping history, it is difficult to ignore that Francis of Assisi embodied a way of life whose shape and meaning became a model for centuries to come, and for thousands of people.

10

The Franciscans

A Mendicant Order with the Whole World as Its Monastery

Francis of Assisi and His Community

What was in terms of sheer numbers the largest religious order of the Middle Ages spread out very rapidly from Assisi, across Christendom, and even beyond. Already in the lifetime of Francis himself, his followers had become active in England[1] and Ireland,[2] on the Iberian Peninsula, in France,[3] and even in Muslim North Africa. They appeared early in Germany, too, with the foundation of the first friaries from 1221 (in Augsburg, Worms, and Speyer among others).[4] Provinces—a form of organization that may have had as

---

[1] Annette Kehnel, "Die Formierung der Gemeinschaften der Minderen Brüder in der Provinz Anglia," in *Die Bettelorden im Aufbau*, ed. Gert Melville and Jörg Oberste (Munster: LIT, 1999), 493–524; Michael Robson and Jens Röhrkasten, eds., *Franciscans in Medieval England* (Canterbury: JEM, 2008).

[2] Anne Müller, "Conflicting Loyalties: The Irish Franciscans and the English Crown in the High Middle Ages," *Proceedings of the Royal Irish Academy*, C 107 (2007): 87–106.

[3] For an overview of their expansion in Europe: "Franziskaner. B. Verbreitung in den übrigen Ländern Europas. I–IX," in *Lexikon des Mittelalters* (Zurich: Artemis, 1989), 4:807–19. For an overview in English, see Clifford Hugh Lawrence, *The Friars* (New York: Longman, 1994), and for Germany, John Freed, *The Friars and German Society in the Thirteenth Century* (Cambridge, MA: Medieval Academy of America, 1977).

[4] Kaspar Elm, "'Sacrum Commercium': Über Ankunft und Wirken der ersten Franziskaner in Deutschland," in *Reich, Regionen und Europa in Mittelalter und*

its model the circuits of the Premonstratensians or the provinces of the Cluniacs—were soon organized. By 1230 there were two, for the Rhineland and Saxony, and in 1239 the growing number of communities led to the division of the Rhineland province into the provinces of Upper and Lower Germany.

Soon the Franciscans had made their way beyond the boundaries of the known world: in 1245 on behalf of Pope Innocent IV, John de Plano Carpini (1185–1252) set out for the east to scout the looming threat of the Mongols, who were just then appearing in Europe. He came as far as the center of power held by the heirs of Genghis Khan, near Karakorum, south of Lake Baikal. William Rubruk (1215/20–1270) followed him a little afterward on behalf of the French king Saint Louis IX, who had taken special care to surround himself with many Franciscans.[5] Around the turn from the thirteenth to the fourteenth century the Franciscans began to form a province of their order in China, with an archbishopric in Beijing and a suffragan in Zaytun (today Quanzhou), even though that province was lost with the ascendance of the Ming dynasty in 1368.[6] By the end of the fourteenth century there were in all probably more than fourteen hundred Franciscan communities across all of Latin Christendom.

This unprecedented success had been inspired by one person—the little poor man, the "Poverello," as Francis was called. But from the beginning, and today, those who wanted and who still want to follow him have wrestled with appropriating and interpreting the model of life he created. The reason is perhaps to be found in the fact that Francis's embodiment of a particular way of life and its meaning was to be understood above all as a message, one that had to be embraced individually and thus had always to be realized anew.

In this respect, Francis stood as heir to the tradition of the twelfth century. At that time, the question was how far the process of institutionalization that led to monasteries and orders might simply silence any invitation to embrace an individuality of the soul, not

Neuzeit, ed. Paul-Joachim Heinig et al. (Berlin: Duncker & Humblot, 2000), 389–412.

[5] Raymond C. Beazley, ed., *The Texts and Versions of John de Plano Carpini and William de Rubruquis* (London: Hakluyt Society, 1903).

[6] Christian W. Troll, "Die Chinamission im Mittelalter," *Franziskanische Studien* 48 (1966): 109–50; 49 (1967): 22–79.

The oldest representation of Francis of Assisi: a fresco in the Benedictine abbey of Subiaco. It must have been completed before the canonization in 1228, because Francis has no halo.

least because of the tendency to cloister that kind of invitation. Now in Francis's day, however, new religious communities would remain openly accessible. When in a later allegorical text "Lady Poverty" asked the followers of Francis where their community was to be found, the response was revealing: "They showed her all the world they could see and said: 'This, Lady, is our enclosure!'"[7]

In Francis the layman, a particular form of medieval piety had crystallized into a new focal point for Christianity. The new way of life he represented thus deserves more extensive treatment. A few facts deserve note at the outset, even if they are only external points of reference for the more important story, which was to unfold only in Francis's inner life.[8]

Francis, born around 1181/82, was some twenty-eight years old when he first encountered Innocent III, a moment that signaled a breakthrough for his career. By that point he had already passed through a decisive inner crisis. He had grown up in Assisi, the Umbrian episcopal city on the western slopes of the Apennines, as the son of Giovanni Battista Bernadone, a wealthy cloth merchant. He enjoyed a solid education, including a bit of Latin, the language of the church. But for his intended career—as his father's heir he was destined to lead the life of a long-distance merchant—French was more

---

[7] "Sacrum commercium," in Menestò and Brufani, *Fontes*, 1730; *Franziskus-Quellen: Die Schriften des heiligen Franziskus, Lebensbeschreibungen, Chroniken und Zeugnisse über ihn und seinen Orden* (hereafter *Schriften*), ed. Dieter Berg and Leonhard Lehmann (Kevelaer: Butzon & Bercker, 2009), 683; *Francis of Assisi: The Saint*, ed. Regis J. Armstrong et al., *Early Documents*, vol. 1 (New York: New City Press, 1999), here 552.

[8] On the following, see Raoul Manselli, *San Francesco d'Assisi*, ed. Cinisello Balsamo (Milan: San Paolo Edizioni, 2002); Grado Giovanni Merlo, *Tra eremo e città* (Assisi: Edizioni Porziuncola, 2007); Helmut Feld, *Franziskus von Assisi und seine Bewegung* (Darmstadt: Wissenschaftliche Buchgesellschaft, 2007); Giovanni Miccoli, *Francesco d'Assisi. Memoria, storia e storiografia* (Milan: Biblioteca francescana, 2010); Augustine Thompson, *Francis of Assisi: A New Biography* (Ithaca, NY: Cornell University Press, 2012); André Vauchez, *Francis of Assisi: The Life and Afterlife of a Medieval Saint* (New Haven, CT: Yale University Press, 2012); Michael Robson, *The Cambridge Companion to Francis of Assisi* (Cambridge, UK: Cambridge University Press, 2012). For an overview of the sources, see Roberto Rusconi, *Francis of Assisi in the Sources and Writings* (Saint Bonaventure, NY: Franciscan Institute Publications, 2008).

important; he later used that language often, especially to express his religious sentiments. His charismatic ways won him many followers among those his own age, and as their leader he stood at the center of a group that at first embraced a boisterous and superficial life.

Yet when Francis was hardly twenty years old, he had to go to war for his native city against neighboring Perugia, and he was taken prisoner for a year. The result was a prolonged illness and a profound psychological crisis. Nevertheless, a short time later, around 1204/5, he joined a military expedition to southern Italy, still seeking to achieve his ambitions to become a knight and to climb the ranks of society.

On that journey, while in Spoleto, Francis believed that he heard the voice of the Lord in a dream. The experience broke his resolve and led him back to Assisi. There he began inwardly to turn from the worldly life. He distanced himself from his friends, retreated to a grotto in prayer and penance, and made his way to the slums of his city to care for its lepers. One day, as he prayed before the crucifix of the dilapidated church of San Damiano, he heard the divine voice again. It spoke directly from the cross and commanded him to rebuild the church. Francis took the call literally and sought with his own hands to renovate the building. To finance that renovation and to pay for the priests of San Damiano, he appropriated his father's wealth without permission.

In the same years Francis also set off on a pilgrimage to Rome, where for a short time he exchanged his fine clothes for those of a pauper and begged anonymously before the doors of Saint Peter. Returning to Assisi, he once again embezzled his father's money for the renovation of his church and for feeding the poor. Fearing punishment, he fled to a solitary cave and after a time resolved to confront his father again. When he arrived in Assisi, he was jeered in public for his ragged appearance and pelted with garbage. His father imprisoned him.

This misfortune drove Francis to turn from the world entirely. At the beginning of 1207, after his father had dragged him into episcopal court, in front of Bishop Guido II Francis took off his clothes, gave them back to his father, and announced that from then on he would acknowledge only his heavenly father. Clothed in the rags of a hermit, he devoted himself anew to the renovation of San Damiano. He also took on the renovation of the church of Santa Maria degli Angeli, called the Portiuncula. In February of 1208 in that church he heard the words of the Gospel of Matthew that told of the sending forth of Christ's apostles, who were to have neither gold, silver, nor copper coins in their purses (Matt 10:9). Francis, struck mightily by these words, recognized in them his way forward. He thereafter clothed himself in a beggar's cloak held together by a simple cord and began a life of absolute poverty.

In the same year, three followers joined him—two learned jurists and a craftsman—and Francis was thus able to share his way of life with like-minded peers. For this little community he needed concrete principles as a guide, and he found them in the gospels in the formulations of Matthew and Luke: "If you wish to be perfect, go, sell your possessions, and give the money to the poor, and you will have treasure in heaven" (Matt 19:21); "Take nothing for your journey" (Luke 9:3); "If any want to become my followers, let them deny themselves" (Luke 9:23).

Francis set out from Assisi with his followers and began to call those they encountered to repentance and inner conversion. He soon did the same for himself: in a grotto in Poggio Bustone on the slopes of the Rieti valley, he immersed himself in contemplation, which according to tradition revealed to him not only the assurance of his salvation but also the nature of his divine mission. After the small group had returned to Assisi, a Benedictine abbey handed over to them the Portiuncula, where they could remain without any other means of support. More followers now joined them, and together they cared for the indigent and the sick, begged on their behalf, and admonished the rich to repentance.

Francis and his followers were laymen. It was thus still unclear what exactly was to be done with a community like theirs. There were no normative standards that might have served to identify their religious spirit objectively. There was nothing beyond the charismatic power of Francis himself but key phrases from the gospels, which Francis then crafted by means of other biblical passages into what was still a very simple form for a religious rule. It is true that what had been a sharp skepticism toward Francis and his followers on the part of the leading families of Assisi had slowly evolved, by virtue of such a public, pious passion, into respect, and it is true that the bishop continued to view Francis positively, but there was still no traditional institutional model into which the group could be integrated. In 1209

Francis traveled with twelve followers to Rome, seeking recognition for their undertaking.[9] It can be presumed, though there is no evidence, that Bishop Guido had led the way in arranging the affair. It was surely thanks to his good relationship with John, the cardinal of Saint Paul, that the group was even allowed to see Pope Innocent III.

But Francis had already refused before the cardinal to subject his followers to a stationary, monastic, or eremitic way of life. The cardinal was a Benedictine monk and thus sworn to uphold his Rule's accusation against the life of the Sarabaites, which had already been leveled against so many wandering preachers at the beginning of the twelfth century. But despite a certain level of mistrust from within the College of Cardinals over whether a life lived according to the gospels in strict poverty was even possible, in the end the community around Francis received oral permission from Innocent III to continue to live their way of life and to preach penance—under the condition that they should inform the pope after a time about the fruits of their labor, so that if need be he could entrust them with still greater tasks.

The innovation already deployed on behalf of the *Humiliati*—separating dogmatic from penitential preaching and allowing the latter for the laity—now showed its usefulness once more. Yet this case involved something still more decisive: in contrast to the case of the *Humiliati*, this preaching was not limited to defined urban circles but allowed to laymen who traveled with no geographical limitation. All other laity who had previously done that had been branded as heretics and attacked as such. It speaks to the pope's considerable breadth of vision that he recognized how urgently the church needed precisely these kinds of people, who lived Christianity from its innermost core and who longed to use the world's public spaces as a means of passing on their model of life to others.

From this point forward the sphere of influence of what was at first a small community, for the moment called only a brotherhood (*fraternitas*), quickly grew and multiplied. On the evening of Palm

---

[9] Werner Maleczek, "Franziskus, Innocenz III., Honorius III. und die Anfänge des Minoritenordens. Ein neuer Versuch zu einem alten Problem," in *Il papato duecentesco e gli ordini mendicanti*, ed. Enrico Menestò (Spoleto: Centro italiano di studi sull'alto Medio Evo, 1998), 23–80; Maria Pia Alberzoni, *Santa povertà e beata semplicità. Francesco d'Assisi e la Chiesa romana* (Milan: Vita e pensiero, 2015), 79–108.

Sunday in 1211 (or 1212), a woman came for the first time to the Portiuncula. Persecuted by her family, she sought acceptance into the community. Her name was Clare; she was the eighteen-year-old daughter of the nobleman Favarone di Offreduccio. Francis cut her hair before the altar, thereby performing the ritual for consecrating virgins (*consecratio virginum*). Soon thereafter Clare (1193/4–1253) and a small following of like-minded women would withdraw to San Damiano near Assisi, where they would seek to live an evangelical life in imitation of Christ, in absolute poverty and contemplative retreat. They would also write their own rule as a guide to their way of life, and uphold it even against the pope's reservations. Their way of life became an essential precedent for a distinctly late-medieval form of women's religious life. The discussion will soon return to that later history.

In those years Francis received as a gift the mountain of Alverna (La Verna), which lay at some distance north of Assisi, to serve as a site for contemplative retreat,[10] yet at the same time he also led an intensive preaching campaign in Italy. His followers spread out across its regions, consciously choosing places where they were foreigners and where they could avoid familiar interaction with relatives and friends.

The size of Francis's community grew almost explosively, and when his followers all gathered together for the first time at the Portiuncula on Pentecost in 1217, they could already resolve to send their brothers across the Alps, to the Iberian Peninsula, and even to Muslim lands. Francis himself wanted to go to France, but in Florence he was forbidden to do so by Cardinal Hugolino, who would soon take a leading role in the development of the community (and who would later continue to do so as Pope Gregory IX).[11] In June of 1218 Francis and his community for the first time received, from Honorius III, a written confirmation of the orthodoxy of their way of life and their preaching. Addressing himself to all prelates in Latin Christendom, the pope urged his audience to support and to protect

---

[10] Giovanni Miccoli, "Francesco e La Verna," in *Itinerarium montis Alvernae*, ed. Alvaro Cacciotti (Florence: Studi francescani, 2000), 225–59.

[11] *Gregorio IX e gli ordini mendicanti* (Spoleto: Centro italiano di studi sull'alto Medio Evo, 2011); Alberzoni, *Santa povertà*, 145–68.

these brothers "as they travel from place to place according to the example of the Apostles."[12]

Francis then set out on what would be a yearlong trip to the Orient. On the way he encountered the Sultan Malik al-Kamil and preached the Christian faith to him without harm, though also without result. As a fateful drama would have it, around the same time the first followers of Francis met with martyrdom in Morocco.[13]

In 1220 Francis fell gravely ill and returned to Italy. There he recognized that his former community had grown so rapidly that it had reached an almost unmanageable size. There was no longer merely a small circle of followers gathered around a charismatic leader whose word alone was enough to serve as a guide but now an international order, whose organizations and agencies were staking their claim to institutional validity. Francis successfully asked the pope to name Cardinal Hugolino, mentioned above, as protector of the Order,[14] then stepped down from his position as leader and named as his successor Peter Catanii, one of his oldest and most trusted companions, with these words: "From now on I am dead to you. But here is brother Peter Catanii, whom we all, both you and I, now resolve to obey."[15]

The next year, 1221, was a key year for another important step. Again at Pentecost there was another gathering at the Portiuncula, called the "Mat Chapter" because all who attended sat on straw mats in a broad circle. More than three thousand people gathered there, the new cardinal protector among them. Once again the brothers were sent out across all of Christendom. But, most important, the Order received for the first time a more elaborate rule than the one that had been prepared for presentation to Innocent III. Francis himself had also drafted this new text, since his authority, despite (or perhaps

[12] Bull "Cum dilecti filii," in *Bullarium Franciscanum Romanorum Pontificum*, ed. Giovanni Giacinto Sbaraglia (Rome, 1759), 1:2; Armstrong et al., *Francis of Assisi: The Saint*, 558.

[13] John Victor Tolan, *Saint Francis and the Sultan* (Oxford: Oxford University Press, 2009).

[14] On this office, see Martin Faber, "'Gubernator, protector et corrector.' Zum Zusammenhang der Entstehung von Orden und Kardinalprotektoraten von Orden in der lateinischen Kirche," *Zeitschrift für Kirchengeschichte* 115 (2004): 19–44.

[15] "Compilatio Assisiensis," in Menestò and Brufani, *Fontes*, 1484; Berg and Lehmann, *Schriften*, 1098; *Francis of Assisi: The Founder*, ed. Regis Armstrong et al., *Early Documents*, vol. 2 (New York: New City Press, 2000), 125.

even because of) his formal resignation, remained unquestioned. There was no doubt in this regard, as so many signs of his charismatic attraction suggest—for example, a fascinatingly successful sermon in Bologna in August 1222. As Kaspar Elm has put it, "The saint, who at the Pentecost chapter of 1220 had declared that he was thenceforth dead to the Order, and who was in fact increasingly estranged from the Order's second generation, began for the first time in these years fully to become what he had wanted to be: a *forma*, a *figura*, an *exemplum*, a *regula vitae*."[16]

But Francis's crafting of a rule had never been formally approved by the church—hence the text's designation as *Regula non bullata*.[17] And only two years later, in 1223, the Order received a third rule, again written by Francis, but with the support of Hugolino and his jurists. Pope Honorius III recognized this text and promulgated it officially by inserting it into a bull of confirmation.[18]

With this act the community around Francis had definitively taken on the form of an order, one legally established in every aspect of its organization.[19] All of its affairs, as they were now explicitly recorded, presumed both a functioning general chapter and a graduated hierarchy of leaders who were elected to limited terms, rising from the guardian as leader of a community, to the custodian as leader of a district, to the provincial and general minister. The building of the Order thus took shape not as the gathering together of affiliated monasteries, each of them independent entities (as in the case of the Cistercians, for example), but rather as an organization shaped strictly along regional lines. The focal point of the rule, furthermore, was to

---

[16] Kaspar Elm, "Die Entwicklung des Franziskanerordens zwischen dem ersten und letzten Zeugnis des Jakob von Vitry," in Kaspar Elm, *Vitasfratrum. Beiträge zur Geschichte der Eremiten- und Mendikantenorden des zwölften und dreizehnten Jahrhunderts*, ed. Dieter Berg (Werl: Dietrich-Coelde, 1994), 173–93, here 192. See selections from James of Vitry in Armstrong et al., *Francis of Assisi: The Saint*, 578–89.

[17] "Regula non bullata," in Menestò and Brufani, *Fontes*, 185–212; Armstrong et al., *Francis of Assisi: The Saint*, 63–86.

[18] "Regula bullata," in Menestò and Brufani, *Fontes*, 171–81; *La regola dei Frati Minori* (Spoleto: Edizioni Porziuncola, 2010); Armstrong et al., *Francis of Assisi: The Saint*, 99–106.

[19] On this overall development, see Théophile Desbonnets, *De l'intuition à l'institution. Les Franciscans* (Paris: Editions franciscaines, 1983).

be found in guidelines concerning fasting and penance, in the manner of fraternal correction, in norms regarding preaching authority, and in regulations regarding entry to the Order and the establishment of a novitiate.[20] This last set of regulations explicitly signaled the *de facto* end of charismatic leadership, which usually calls new recruits to be members and then ties them directly into the community of followers.

Ever more strongly afflicted by illness, from this point onward Francis led a more and more withdrawn, in some ways even eremitical, life. To make that way of life more available to his brethren in small groups, he had in fact already written a rule for it. La Verna (among other solitary places) became a place of refuge for him, and after his death the brothers learned that he had received the stigmata there.[21] Upon his return to San Damiano, he dictated his most poignant poetic work, the "Canticle of Brother Sun," a prayer that powerfully embraced God's creation.[22] He died in Assisi, according to his wish, lying naked on the ground, on October 3, 1226. He was barely forty-six years old.

The Legacy of Francis

In order to understand the normative impact of this way of life on future developments—which sometimes took on an obsessive quality, but which seemed to establish an unbreakable bond between Francis and every member of the Order—it is essential to gain deeper access to this extraordinary personality. Francis's own words, and the interpretations they inspired, are the best means to that end.

Apart from the texts of his rules, Francis left little writing behind. Charismatic figures typically do not write; they speak and act and thus require evangelists who seek to immortalize their legacy. Francis found many such figures—from those among his own followers to

---

[20] Mirko Breitenstein, "Das Noviziat im hohen Mittelalter," in *Zur Organisation des Eintrittes bei den Cluniazensern, Cisterziensern und Franziskanern* (Münster: LIT, 2008), 423–28.

[21] André Vauchez, "Autour de la stigmatisation de saint François. Une histoire de textes et d'images," in André Vauchez, *Francesco d'Assisi e gli ordini mendicanti* (Assisi: Edizioni Porziuncola, 2005), 73–80.

[22] "Canticum fratri Solis," in Menestò and Brufani, *Fontes*, 39–41; Armstrong et al., *Francis of Assisi: The Saint*, 113–14.

the authors of what would become official biographies, whose differentiated ways of crafting legend and different ways of representation often give some access to the real, historical Francis and not just to his image. Yet Francis himself also wrote a text that revealed the mission to which he felt God had called him and the path he saw to fulfilling it. A few months before his death he looked back on his life and wrote his spiritual Testament.[23] It is helpful here to fill in the bare chronological outline of his biography with the essentials of this text.

A key sentence in this work reads, "After the Lord had given me some brothers, no one showed me what I had to do. But the Most High himself revealed to me that I should live according to the pattern of the Holy Gospel."[24] So Francis explains that he found himself directly tasked by God to follow the Gospel and to live it out along with his disciples. The consequences were dramatic, since to accept that task meant in the strict sense to follow Christ in every way—in his poverty, his humility and self-denial, his suffering and repentance for the sins of humankind, his obedience to the Father, and his love for people, his preaching and homelessness.[25] In a word, it meant to take on the image of Christ (*Christiformis*).[26] Here was the core of Francis's entire way of life, and here alone was the calling he sought to pass along—both to his followers as a model for a particular way of life and to all humankind around the world as something that could give their life direction and possibility.

Already in the lifetime of Francis and, as we will see, after his death as well, the strictness with which he upheld the imitation of Christ was not uncontested. So, according to the surviving sources,

---

[23] "Testamentum," in Menestò and Brufani, *Fontes*, 227–32; Armstrong et al., *Francis of Assisi: The Saint*, 124–27; Jacques Dalarun, "A dernière volonté de saint François," *Bullettino dell'Istituto storico italiano per il Medio Evo* 94 (1988): 329–66.

[24] Dalarun, "A dernière volonté," 228; Armstrong et al., *Francis of Assisi: The Saint*, 125; Alberzoni, *Santa povertà*, 225–61.

[25] *Dalla "Sequela Christi" di Francesco d'Assisi all'apologia della povertà* (Spoleto: Centro italiano di studi sull'alto Medioevo, 1992); Gert Melville, "What Role Did Charity Play in Francis of Assisi's Attitude Towards the Poor?" in *Aspects of Charity*, ed. Gert Melville (Berlin: LIT, 2011), 99–122.

[26] Raoul Manselli, "La povertà nella vita di Francesco d'Assisi," in *La povertà del secolo XII e Francesco d'Assisi* (Assisi: Società Internazionale di Studi Francescani, 1975), 255–82, here 270.

the cardinal of Saint Paul had emphasized this point when he first introduced Francis to the pope and cardinals: "I have found a most perfect man, who wishes to live according to the form of the holy Gospel and to observe evangelical perfection in all things. I believe that the Lord wants through him to reform the faith of the Holy Church throughout the world."[27] But when, in the wake of Francis's appearance, certain reservations arose among some of the cardinals over whether what Francis proposed was just a bit too novel after all, even overwhelming, the cardinal responded—somewhat apologetically—with remarkable words. Even if invented by later authors, they highlight a paradox deeply embedded in the history of the church, one that Francis was convinced he could resolve: "If we refuse the request of this poor man as novel or too difficult, when all he asks is to be allowed to lead an evangelical life, we must be on guard lest we commit an offense against Christ's Gospel. For if anyone says that there is something novel or irrational or impossible to observe in this man's desire to live according to the perfection of the Gospel, he would be guilty of blasphemy against Christ, the author of the Gospel."[28]

To live a life in accord with the Gospel meant a gradual renunciation of the entanglements of earthly life.[29] Already in the first lines of Francis's Testament that theme becomes clear: "So the Lord gave me, brother Francis, thus to begin doing penance in this way; for when I was in sin, it seemed too bitter for me to see lepers. And the Lord himself led me among them, and I showed mercy to them. And when I left them, what had seemed bitter to me was turned into sweetness of soul and body. Thereafter I delayed a little and left the world."[30] The passage makes clear that for Francis to leave the world meant to

[27] "Legenda trium sociorum," in Menestò and Brufani, *Fontes*, 1421; Armstrong et al., *Francis of Assisi: The Founder*, 61–112, here 96.

[28] Bonaventura de Balneoregio, "Legenda maior," in Menestò and Brufani, *Fontes*, 801; translation from Armstrong et al., *Francis of Assisi: The Founder*, 525–683, here 547.

[29] Oktavian Schmucki, "Schrittweise Entdeckung der evangeliumsgemäßen Lebensform durch den heiligen Franziskus von Assisi," in *Oktavian Schmucki OFM Cap. Beiträge zur Franziskusforschung*, ed. Ulrich Köpf and Leonhard Lehmann (Kevelaer: Butzon und Bercker, 2007), 305–58.

[30] "Testamentum," 227; Armstrong et al., *Francis of Assisi: The Saint*, 124.

reverse the sensibilities of the soul in a life lived between virtue and vice. All that was bitter became sweet, hence his expression. Francis sought out and lived his ascetic deprivations, his self-renunciations, his poverty, and his contemplative immersion with ecstatic passion, and he found his soul's happiness in the fullest possible intensification of those sensibilities of renunciation. One of his biographies handed this inward feeling down to his followers: "Such an overwhelming, heavenly sweetness flowed through him then, as he himself told the story, that he not only had no words to express it but could not even move from where he sat. In that moment, a tremendous energy shot through him and drew him into the realm of things unseen. In its power he came to see all earthly things as not only trivial but totally worthless."[31] This power alone brought him in his own eyes a bit closer to the Christ of the gospels, and his ardent soul became thoroughly obedient to a compelling rational logic.

According to his own testimony Francis had left the world behind and yet still lived in it, without monastery walls and only seldom retreating into eremitical isolation. His protective separation from the world was nothing more than an inward sense of blessedness, which displaced the bitterness felt by those who remained trapped in sin. For this reason it could be said confidently of both Francis and those his spark ignited that the whole world was their monastery. For everywhere they went, in a certain way they took the monastery with them. The structures of that way of life provided a mental framework that supported the powerful mission of brothers who were sent out into all regions of the world and who took shelter wherever they could find it.

The religious spirit of a life that both renounced the world yet also remained open to it was approved by the church hierarchy—albeit with certain later institutional adaptations—and therefore did not fall into suspicion of heresy. And that approach was of decisive importance for the survival of the community. As Francis recorded in his Testament, its origin was to be found again in the insight that God had given him: "Afterwards the Lord gave me and gives me still such faith in priests who live according to the rite of the Holy Roman Church, because of their orders, that were they to persecute me, I

---

[31] Thomas de Celano, "Vita secunda," in Menestò and Brufani, *Fontes*, 449; cf. Armstrong et al., *Francis of Assisi: The Founder*, 72.

would still want to have recourse to them. . . . And I do not want to consider any sin in them, because I discern the Son of God in them, and they are my lords."[32] For him the church was founded by the work of Christ, and its holiness was therefore unassailable.[33] For the sake of Christ he was able even to overlook the sins of its consecrated priests. Thus the church did not need to fear some kind of unsettling way of life from Francis, like those of earlier figures like Robert of Arbrissel, for example, or of so many preachers among Francis's contemporaries who were branded with the verdict of heresy— especially since Francis had developed with Cardinal Hugolino, as the protector of his Order, a personal relationship that according to the *Vitae* was like that of a child seeking the protection of a father,[34] and especially because in his now-approved rule, Francis had explicitly recorded the subjection of his Order to the authority of the Roman church. In return, the church supported the expansion of the Order with every means at its disposal. Already in 1218 Honorius III, as has been noted, had called on all bishops to guarantee the protection and support of the Franciscans.

In a remarkable way, Francis nevertheless saw himself as personally independent from the claims of any outsider who sought to make decisions about the norms that guided his way of life and that of his community. Here again his Testament provides a key insight, this time with the phrase cited above: "The Most High Himself has revealed to me that I should live according to the holy Gospel." Mandate and authority were thus given to Francis as the irrefutable and unquestionable requirements for proper conduct. By virtue of God's revelation, Francis was able as late as the "Mat Chapter" of 1221 confidently to renounce before Cardinal Hugolino every rule that had been established for his Order: "God has called me to follow the way of humility and showed me the way of simplicity. I do not

---

[32] "Testamentum," 227–28; Armstrong et al., *Francis of Assisi: The Saint*, 125.

[33] On the image of the church among the early Franciscans, see Yves Congar, *Die Lehre von der Kirche. Von Augustinus bis zum Abendländischen Schisma*, Handbuch der Dogmengeschichte, 3.3c (Freiburg: Herder, 1971), 142–45.

[34] For critical remarks, see Ulrich Köpf, "Hugolino von Ostia (Gregor IX.) und Franziskus," in *Franziskus von Assisi. Das Bild des Heiligen aus neuer Sicht*, ed. Dieter R. Bauer et al. (Cologne: Böhlau, 2005), 163–82, here 170; Alberzoni, *Santa povertà*, 145–68.

want you to give any rule to me, neither that of holy Augustine nor of holy Bernard nor of holy Benedict."[35]

In the Testament, toward the end of the text, Francis included an analogous passage: "But the Lord has given me to speak and write the Rule and these words simply and purely; may you understand them simply and without gloss and observe them with a holy activity until the end."[36] Through his Testament, by looking back on his life, Francis sketched a broad vision in which the norms of the beginning would be strengthened anew, with great power. The text obligated both the Order as a community and Francis himself to obey the leadership of the minister general and the superiors of the individual communities, the Guardians. But above all, it emphasized that absolute poverty was indispensable: "The brothers should guard themselves against accepting in any way churches, poor dwellings, and anything else that can be built."[37]

Francis understood his Testament to be absolutely binding. Every officer in the Order was to keep the text at his side, along with the Rule itself. All who followed it would be "filled with the blessings of the highest Father in heaven."[38] Everyone who knew Francis must have recognized this turn to the divine as self-evident. But it was also a sign of the last gasp of the passing of an era. The Testament had been written too late.

Hugolino, now as Pope Gregory IX, declared Francis a saint in a bull of July 19, 1228. In it, he wrote these words: "Behold, at the eleventh hour the Lord raised up his servant Francis, a man after His own heart. He was a beacon whom the rich viewed with contempt, but whom God had prepared for the appointed time, sending him into his vineyard to root out the thorns and brambles after having put the attacking Philistines to flight, to light up the path to our homeland, and to reconcile people to God by his zealous admonition and

---

[35] "Compilatio Assisiensis," 1497–98; Berg and Lehmann, *Schriften*, 1105; Armstrong et al., *Francis of Assisi: The Founder*, 132–33.

[36] "Testamentum," 231; Berg and Lehmann, *Schriften*, 62; Armstrong et al., *Francis of Assisi: The Saint*, 127.

[37] "Testamentum," 229; Berg and Lehmann, *Schriften*, 61; Armstrong et al., *Francis of Assisi: The Saint*, 126.

[38] "Testamentum," 231; Berg and Lehmann, *Schriften*, 62; Armstrong et al., *Francis of Assisi: The Saint*, 127.

encouragement."[39] A mere two years later, on September 28, 1230, in another bull (called *Quo elongati*) the same pope nullified the validity of the Testament after the general chapter had complained that the Order could not uphold its severity with respect to the issue of poverty. He grounded the act juristically in these words: "Regarding this *mandatum* [i.e., the Testament], we say to you that you do not need to observe it, because it is not binding without the agreement of those it concerns, namely the brothers, and above all the Ministers. Nor is it binding on your successors, since one equal has no authority to command another."[40] Francis had thereby been invoked, yet in a way that robbed him of his holy reputation as the savior of Christendom in its last, almost apocalyptic hour. He was positioned as "equal among equals," and one moreover who had now been linked to his Order's right to determine its own affairs collectively.

The pope had a plausible reason, however, for contradicting Francis.[41] With the text of *Quo elongati* Gregory IX took away a part of Francis, so to speak—Francis as an official, as an earthly leader of the community that had already decisively distanced itself from him. The pope thereby made it possible to keep pure the other aspect, namely, Francis as a charismatic figure. For what remained of Francis is captured in Gregory's earlier bull, which called him the man of the "eleventh hour," the spiritual leader, the unassailable model of a perfect imitation of Christ. A Francis like this could be divorced from any possible quarrel over his earlier acts and decisions amid the everyday business of running an order. That kind of confrontation might have tarnished his memory. But the normative power of the validity of his former actions now referred exclusively to his

---

[39] Bull "Mira circa nos," *Bullarium Franciscanum Romanorum Pontificum*, ed. Giovanni Giacinto Sbaraglia (Rome: Edizioni Porziuncola, 1759), 1:42–44; Berg and Lehmann, *Schriften*, 1631; Armstrong et al., *Francis of Assisi: The Saint*, 566.

[40] Herbert Grundmann, "Die Bulle 'Quo elongati' Papst Gregors IX," *Archivum Franciscanum Historicum* 54 (1961): 3–25; Berg and Lehmann, *Schriften*, 1637; Armstrong et al., *Francis of Assisi: The Saint*, 571.

[41] On the following, see Gert Melville, "Der geteilte Franziskus. Beobachtungen zum institutionellen Umgang mit Charisma," in *Kunst, Macht und Institution*, ed. Joachim Fischer and Hans Joas (Frankfurt am Main and New York: Campus, 2003), 347–63.

charismatic impact as a figure of salvation history[42]—a validity that allowed Francis to become a myth that was at once otherworldly and yet always captured anew in the present.

Yet even this solution left a number of serious problems unresolved. How fierce the fights now became over the correct image of Francis, and above all how many tried to perpetuate his charisma by capturing it in written texts, is made clear by the great number of lives and collections of legends about him. These works again and again seized on surviving traditions in new ways or sought to invent new ones.[43] Such efforts—at the heart of the seminal study of Paul Sabatier published in 1893—raised the so-called Franciscan question into Francis's own intentions,[44] and they inspire important research still today.[45]

Yet the contradictions were already apparent in the problem of how best to honor Francis's corpse. Planned by the pope immediately after Francis's death, a massive, two-storied burial church—a structure that posed tremendous challenges of architecture and engineering—was erected in Assisi; the building is a marvel still today.[46] It was meant to symbolize for Christendom the glory of the saint and his renown. Yet how could it be fitting as a memorial for a figure who was so steeped in humility, one who had once chided his general minister because he had allowed a small building to be erected for his brothers beside the Portiuncula? One surviving source records how

[42] On the later impact of this eschatological thought in the Franciscan Order, see Hans-Joachim Schmidt, "Legitimität von Innovation. Geschichte, Kirche und neue Orden im 13. Jahrhundert," in *Vita religiosa im Mittelalter*, ed. Franz J. Felten and Nikolas Jaspert (Berlin: Duncker & Humblot, 1999), 371–91, here 378–82.

[43] Roberto Rusconi, *Francis of Assisi in the Sources and Writings* (Saint Bonaventure, NY: Franciscan Institute Publications, 2008).

[44] Paul Sabatier, *Life of St. Francis of Assisi* (New York: Scribner, 1930).

[45] Franz Xaver Bischof, "Der Stand der 'Franziskanischen Frage,'" in *Franziskus von Assisi*, ed. Dieter Bauer et al. (Cologne: Böhlau, 2005), 1–16; Jacques Dalarun, *Vers une résolution de la question franciscaine* (Paris: Fayard, 2007).

[46] Jürgen Wiener, "Kritik an Elias von Cortona und Kritik von Elias von Cortona: Armutsideal und Architektur in den frühen franziskanischen Quellen," in *Frömmigkeitsformen in Mittelalter und Renaissance*, ed. Johannes Laudage (Düsseldorf: Droste, 2004), 207–46; Donal Cooper and Janet Robson, *The Making of Assisi* (New Haven, CT: Yale University Press, 2013).

much this contradiction irritated Giles, one of the oldest companions of Francis.[47] He insisted that it was as impossible to dispense with obligations of poverty as with those of chastity. Then, gesturing to the pompous church building that had grown up on the outskirts of Assisi, he quipped that with the completion of such a building as that, there was also no longer any reason to be concerned with chastity.

A noticeable generational shift took place in the course of the thirteenth century. After the contested resignation of the minister general, Elias of Cortona,[48] from 1239 on the Franciscan community—to that point made up overwhelmingly of laymen—became increasingly clerical.[49] Francis himself had never become a priest. But already in 1224 he had made the Portuguese cleric Antonius (1195–1231), who had achieved great renown at the University of Padua, the first theological teacher in his Order.[50] In the following decades the holy simplicity of the faith, so central to the life of the humble Francis and his early followers, yielded ever more to learned theology.[51]

Although in their rapidly expanding areas of growth the Franciscans at first consciously avoided the establishment of permanent monastic buildings, Franciscan churches and complexes nevertheless soon grew up in countless cities. They had been founded by local citizens who feared for their own salvation in light of the coarse moral climate of the day. Their contemporary Thomas of Celano captured something of that climate in his first *Vita* of Francis. He spoke of the many who "had nothing of the Christian spirit in them, whether in their way of life or in their character; they are Christians in name

[47] Ramona Sickert, *Wenn Klosterbrüder zu Jahrmarktsbrüdern werden. Studien zur zeitgenössischen Wahrnehmung der Franziskaner und Dominikaner im 13. Jahrhundert* (Münster: LIT, 2006), 213.

[48] Ramona Sickert, "'Difficile tamen est iudicare alieni cordis occulta . . .' Persönlichkeit oder Typus? Elias von Cortona im Urteil seiner Zeitgenossen," in *Das Eigene und das Ganze*, ed. Gert Melville and Markus Schürer (Münster: LIT, 2002), 303–38.

[49] Laurentio C. Landini, *The Causes of the Clericalization of the Order of Friars Minor 1209–1260 in the Light of Early Franciscan Sources* (Chicago: Pontifical Gregorian University, 1968).

[50] Jacques Toussaert, *Antonius von Padua* (Cologne: J. P. Bachem, 1967).

[51] Achim Wesjohann, "Simplicitas als franziskanisches Ideal und der Prozeß der Institutionalisierung des Minoritenordens," in Melville and Oberste, *Die Bettelorden im Aufbau*, 107–67.

only."[52] The Franciscans brought hope, because unlike wastrel clerics who lived off of prebends, they sought to set an example according to the Gospel. Moreover, as priests who could administer the sacraments and who had the right to preach, they could aid in the salvation of those entrusted to them.

There was never a doubt that Francis's imitation of Christ in absolute poverty was a powerful model, but considerable discussion took place concerning the proper degree of that imitation. The cancellation of the Testament signaled a symbolic turning point. Only fifteen years later, in 1245, a regulation from the Curia allowed the Franciscans to accept moveable and immoveable property that had been donated to them, though not as their own property but as property to be used. Ownership itself was transferred to the papacy. By means of this legal fiction the vow of poverty remained in force.

Yet almost immediately many attacked it precisely as a fiction. The spirit of the early days of community around Francis, expressed symbolically in the dismay of a figure like Giles, lived on, since there were still texts that captured that spirit, or that were now produced— the Rule, the Testament, the legends—in ever greater numbers.[53] Many later appealed to these texts, often in explicit opposition to prevailing opinion, and consequently the unity of the Order as the ongoing invitation of the Poverello could not be preserved—a point to which the discussion will soon return.

Clare of Assisi

Shortly before his death, Francis also left a bequest for Clare and her sisters in San Damiano, again emphasizing poverty: "And I ask you, my ladies, and give you this counsel, that you live always in

---

[52] Thomas de Celano, "Vita prima," in Menestò and Brufani, *Fontes*, 278; Berg and Lehmann, *Schriften*, 200; Armstrong et al., *Francis of Assisi: The Saint*, 171–310, here 183; Schmidt, "Legitimität von Innovation," 376.

[53] Adriaan H. Bredero, *Christenheit und Christentum im Mittelalter* (Stuttgart: Franz Steiner, 1998), 207–10. For a general overview of the later history of the Franciscans, see Duncan B. Nimmo, *Reform and Division in the Medieval Franciscan Order: From Saint Francis to the Foundation of the Capuchins* (Rome: Capuchin Historical Institute, 1987); Grado G. Merlo, *In the Name of Saint Francis: A History of the Friars Minor and Franciscanism until the Early Sixteenth Century* (Saint Bonaventure, NY: Franciscan Institute, 2009).

Clare of Assisi: Fresco from the years 1317–1319 in the Lower Church of the Basilica of San Francesco in Assisi.

this most holy way of life and in poverty, and that you guard yourself carefully, lest you ever depart from it in any way, regardless of the teaching or counsel of any other."[54] These lines had explosive power, because they highlighted the precarious circumstance of women whose intention to follow Christ in absolute poverty faced an even greater skepticism on the part of the church hierarchy than had the analogous intention of Francis and his followers. From the very moment Clare came to Francis, allowed him to cut her hair, and retreated to San Damiano with a small circle of like-minded women, she strove to realize that ideal. But she would not be allowed to do so without further difficulties.

Because the old tensions between inner spiritual conviction and the demand for formal institutional structures arise here again in an exemplary way, the story as it unfolded must now be followed in more detail.

In the second decade of the thirteenth century—thus around the time of the emergence of the Beguines north of the Alps—in the urban milieu of Italy (in Florence, Milan, Siena, Lucca, and other places) a growing number of women's communities sought to lead a life of poverty and charitable activity according to the Gospel and the model of the early church in a way that reveals certain parallels to the Franciscan tradition. Cardinal Hugolino, seeing the potential threat of their uncontrolled growth, felt himself called to rein them in. In 1219, after Francis had set out for the East, the cardinal wrote for these women a normative text, a *forma vitae* shaped by Benedictine and Cistercian precedents. But the women this way of life addressed now found themselves in circumstances completely at odds with their original intention. All of their charitable activities were forbidden. They were commanded to observe strict enclosure and only allowed to observe personal poverty. Their convents continued to own property, and those resources were intended to maintain a respectable standard of living. These *sorores pauperes inclusae*, "poor enclosed

---

[54] Menestò and Brufani, *Fontes*, 119; Berg and Lehmann, *Schriften*, 200; Schmidt, "Legitimität von Innovation," 63. See Jacques Dalarun, *Francis of Assisi and the Feminine* (Saint Bonaventure, NY: Franciscan Institute Publications, 2006); Alberzoni, *Santa povertà*, 171–93. English translations of main sources are in *The Lady: Clare of Assisi; Early Documents*, ed. Regis J. Armstrong (New York: New City Press, 2006).

sisters," would even have to face the possibility that the circle around Clare in San Damiano would be granted a leading position over them. Hugolino clearly envisioned himself as the founder of a larger order of religious women—one that would be the first of its kind.[55]

After the death of Francis, and after Hugolino's ascent to the papal throne as Gregory IX, in 1227 the new pope issued the bull *Quoties cordis*. This decree placed the *cura*, or the pastoral care, of what he considered his nuns' communities under the authority of the Franciscan general minister.[56] In 1228 Gregory used the occasion of the canonization of the Poverello in Assisi to arrange a meeting with Clare and sought to force her to agree to live under his *forma vitae*. Clare, a remarkably bold woman who was filled, so it was said, with the spirit of the deceased Francis, firmly resisted: "In no way, Holy Father, do I wish to be freed permanently from the imitation of Christ."[57] She was successful. Gregory IX allowed her to live in absolute poverty and granted her autonomy.

Yet it was only a temporary victory. Already in 1230 Gregory sought to deprive the community around Clare of the special place that it held within the Franciscan Order, and he decreed that only papal visitors should now have access to San Damiano. Clare responded to the attack by threatening a hunger strike. In the same years Agnes (1211–1282), daughter of Bohemian King Ottokar I Přemysl, had built up a women's community in Prague that was modeled on Clare's example, and in 1238 she received a papal decree that both prohibited her from observing evangelical poverty and commanded her to take up the *forma vitae* of Gregory IX. Meanwhile the title of

[55] On the general institutional development, see Maria Pia Alberzoni, *Chiara e il papato* (Milan: Edizioni Biblioteca Francescana, 1995); Maria Pia Alberzoni, *Clare of Assisi and the Poor Sisters in the Thirteenth Century* (St. Bonaventure, NY: Franciscan Institute, 2004); Niklaus Kuster, "Quia divina inspiratione . . . ," in *Klara von Assisi: Zwischen Bettelarmut und Beziehungsreichtum. Beiträge zur neueren deutschsprachigen Klara-Forschung*, ed. Bernd Schmies (Münster: Aschendorff, 2011), 193–211.

[56] *Bullarium Franciscanum Romanorum Pontificum*, 1:36–37.

[57] "Legenda Hl. Clara," in *Leben und Schriften der Heiligen Klara von Assisi*, ed. Engelbert Grau and Marianne Schlosser (Kevelaer: Butzon & Bercker, 2001), 133; Maria Pia Alberzoni, "Nequaquam a Christi sequela in perpetuum absolvi desidero," in *Chiara d'Assisi e la memoria di Francesco*, ed. Alfonso Marini (Città di Castello: Petruzzi, 1995), 41–65; Kuster, "Quia divina inspiratione," 198.

Ordo Sancti Damiani, curiously enough, took root for convents of the so-called papal congregation, even though San Damiano itself did not belong to it. The pope even brought forth the deceased Francis as the supposed founder of this "Damianite Order"—thereby, on the one hand, legitimizing it and, on the other hand, strengthening his strategy of attrition against Clare.

Gregory IX had no further success. His last years were consumed with his struggles against Emperor Frederick II. His successor, Innocent IV, did seek at first to adhere strictly to his predecessor's politics, approving in 1245 the existing *forma vitae*. But in 1247 a new formulation called for the adoption of the Franciscan form of profession and for subordination to the general minister, thereby binding the women's communities more strongly to the Franciscan Order.[58] All sides rejected the move, however, and the strategy failed.

The final act had begun. Innocent IV met with Clare in person shortly before her death. Mesmerized by this great personality, in 1253 he approved for her, despite the decrees of the Fourth Lateran Council, a rule that she herself had written.[59] Clare died two days later, undefeated. In 1255 she was canonized by Pope Alexander IV in the cathedral of Anagni.[60] Clare's was the first rule that had been written by a woman for women. It was valid for the monastery of San Damiano alone. It commanded obedience to the pope, as Francis himself had wanted, and to the leaders of the Franciscan Order. An elected abbess was to lead the convent and, in an almost Benedictine sense, to serve as a model for the women entrusted to her. On the other hand, she could be voted out of office if she were to prove unsuitable. The central passages of the Rule, however, concerned what it called "most holy" poverty, a chastening way of life, manual labor, and the kinds of alms that could be sought. In this connection appeared perhaps the text's most spiritually deep and also its most touching passage. Here Clare articulated her profound trust in the

---

[58] Cristina Andenna, "'Secundum regulam datam sororibus ordinis sancti Damiani.' Sancia e Aquilina: due esperimenti di ritorno alle origini alla corte di Napoli nel XIV secolo," in *Franciscan Organisation in the Mendicant Context*, ed. Michael Robson and Jens Röhrkasten (Berlin: LIT, 2010), 139–78, here 149.

[59] Menestò and Brufani, *Fontes*, 2291–307; Armstrong, *The Lady*, 108–26.

[60] Bull "Clara claris praeclara," in Menestò and Brufani, *Fontes*, 2331–37; Armstrong, *The Lady*, 263–71.

way of life that had been given to her and from which she drew an unshakeable power:

> After the Most High Celestial Father saw fit by his grace to enlighten my heart to do penance according to the example and teaching of our most blessed Father Saint Francis, shortly after his own conversion, I, together with my sisters, willingly promised him obedience. When the Blessed Father saw that we had no fear of poverty, hard work, trial, shame, or contempt of the world, but, instead, we held them as great delights, moved by piety, he wrote for us a form of life as follows: "Because by divine inspiration you have made yourselves daughters and servants of the most High, most Exalted King, the heavenly Father, and have taken the Holy Spirit as your spouse, choosing to live according to the perfection of the holy Gospel, I resolve and promise for myself and for my brothers always to have the same loving care and special solitude for you as for them." As long as he lived he diligently fulfilled this and wished that it always be fulfilled by the brothers.[61]

Pope Urban IV established in his 1263 bull *Beata Clara virtute clarens* that all groups within the observance of this *forma vitae* should be drawn together into a newly established *Ordo Sanctae Clarae*. To this end, with the aid of Minister General Bonaventure and other cardinals, he fashioned a new text, one that had nothing to do with the text that Clare herself had written just before her death but instead presented Clare as the model for a new monastic, female sanctity. The Order of the Poor Clares, as it has been called ever since, had thereby been established.[62]

In the later course of their history the Poor Clares would see incomparable success. By the end of the fourteenth century, the Order

---

[61] "Clara Assisiensis, Regula," in Menestò and Brufani, *Fontes*, 2299–2300; Armstrong, *The Lady*, 117–18.

[62] Giancarlo Andenna, "Urbano IV e l'istituzione dell'ordine delle clarisse," in *Regulae—Consuetudines—Statuta*, ed. Cristina Andenna and Gert Melville (Münster: LIT, 2005), 539–68; Lezlie Knox, *Creating Clare of Assisi: Female Franciscan Identities in Later Medieval Italy* (Leiden: Brill, 2008). See also Bert Roest, *Order and Disorder: The Poor Clares Between Foundation and Reform* (Leiden: Brill, 2013).

already consisted of around four hundred convents across Europe, with a notably high number of its foundation initiatives coming from the courtly milieu.[63]

[63] Raphaela Averkorn, "Adlige Frauen und Mendikanten im Spannungsverhältnis zwischen Macht und Religion. Studien zur Iberischen Halbinsel im Spätmittelalter," in *Imperios sacros monarquías divinas*, ed. Carles Rabassa and Ruth Stepper (Castelló de la Plana: Univ. Jaume I, 2002), 219–68; Ingrid Würth, "Altera Elisabeth: Königin Sancia von Neapel (1286–1345) und die Franziskaner," in *Religiöse Bewegungen im Mittelalter. Festschrift für Matthias Werner*, ed. Enno Bünz et al. (Cologne: Böhlau, 2007), 517–42; Andenna, "Secundum regulam."

11

The Dominicans

Holy Preaching and Pastoral Care

Dominic and the Building of a New Order

Despite many structural similarities between the Minorites and the Order of Preachers, to which we now turn, both the founding and the subsequent history of the latter Order differed greatly from those of the former. The Order of Preachers never lost its unity. That does not necessarily mean that it somehow stood on a higher level but rather that its organization managed to achieve a higher degree of coherence. The Order's long-standing unity can also be traced back to the fact that it knew no core ideal, like that of the Franciscans, whose radicalism might have compelled its individual adherents to struggle continually over their obligations to it.

Perhaps a paradigmatic divergence can even be found in the orientations of the orders' respective founders, a divergence that was decisive for the later developments of each order. Thus it was significant that upon the canonization of the cleric Dominic, the founder of the Order of Preachers, Pope Gregory IX summarized his life with the following words: "I knew him as a man who imitated the life of the apostles completely."[1] Here was a contrast with the layman Francis's charisma of the *sequela Christi*, the imitation of Christ.

Born in 1170 of noble lineage in Caleruega (in northern Spain), Dominic de Guzman studied the liberal arts and theology at Palencia and then became a canon at the Cathedral Chapter of Osma, which

---

[1] Ambrosius Esser, "Dominikus," in *Theologische Realenzyklopädie* (Berlin: de Gruyter, 1982), 9:126.

embraced reform in 1198 and established the observance of common property.[2] Dominic at first devoted himself to both contemplation and pastoral care.

That commitment changed dramatically in 1203 when Dominic accompanied his bishop Diego on a diplomatic mission to Denmark. Departing from Castile, they headed north, crossed the Pyrenees, and entered the lands of the Cathars, where they were astounded at how strong and widespread that heretical movement had become.[3] After a first stop in Denmark, they returned there two years later, having learned of the threat the heathen Cumans posed in the Baltic region. Afterward, in 1206, they traveled to Rome, because Diego wanted to be relieved of his duties by Innocent III and to devote himself, together with Dominic, to the conversion of the Cumans.

The pope refused the request but did send both to southern France to combat heresy. There they encountered the already-mentioned Cistercian abbot Arnold of Cîteaux and other papal delegates. In the face of the obvious failure of Arnold's effort, Diego and Dominic developed a new strategy for winning converts:[4] they decided to appear in apostolic poverty themselves, with simple clothing, a modest demeanor, and no pompous retinue. Their intention was thereby to craft for themselves an appearance that was, on the one hand, in sharp contrast to that of the traditional papal delegation yet, on the other, precisely in conformity with that of the Cathar preachers. The assumption was that the best way to disrupt the Cathars' success was by imitating them in appearance. Having confirmed that assumption

---

[2] On the following, see Marie Humbert Vicaire, *Histoire de Saint Dominique*, 2nd ed., 2 vols. (Paris: Éditions du Cerf, 1982); Simon Tugwell, "Notes on the Life of St. Dominic," *Archivum Fratrum Praedicatorum* 65 (1995): 5–169; 66 (1996): 5–200; 67 (1997): 27–59; 68 (1998): 5–116; 73 (2003): 5–141.

[3] Arno Borst, *Die Katharer* (Freiburg im Breisgau: Hiersemann, 1995); Malcolm Lambert, *The Cathars* (Oxford: Blackwell, 1998); Malcolm Barber, *The Cathars* (New York: Longmann, 2000). See also the key historiographical essay by Robert More, "The Cathar Middle Ages as an Historiographical Problem," in *Christianity and Culture in the Middle Ages*, ed. David C. Mengel and Lisa Wolverton (Notre Dame, IN: University of Notre Dame Press, 2014), 58–86.

[4] Wolfram Hoyer, "Der dominikanische Ansatz zum Dialog mit den Religionen in der Gründerzeit des Ordens," in *Das Charisma des Ursprungs und die Religionen*, ed. Petrus Bsteh and Brigitte Proksch (Vienna and Berlin: LIT, 2011), 242–64.

among the papal delegation, they went out two by two across the land and found some early success. In 1207 Diego and Dominic founded a monastery for converted Cathar women at Prouille, west of Carcassonne. At the end of that year Diego died, but Dominic continued to advance "holy preaching" (*sancta predicatio*) as an organized program of conversion.[5] It was based on learned engagement with the text of the Bible and thus took shape as the kind of dogmatic and instructional preaching that was allowed to him as a cleric. At its core was also an intensive pastoral concern for a particular social class, one that had developed here, as in northern and central Italy, in an emerging urban environment.[6]

Innocent then called a crusade against the heretics.[7] In 1215 in Toulouse, the most important city in Languedoc (by then taken back from the Cathars), a clerical community of six members took up *sancta praedicatio* anew, and a new papal delegate immediately approved it. The Fourth Lateran Council began that year, and Dominic traveled immediately to Rome, accompanied by his supporter Bishop Fulco of Toulouse, hoping to win papal protection and recognition for his fledgling community. But the pope disappointed him, refusing to approve a corporation that was independent in terms not only of its organization but also of its norms. Blocking the way was the restriction that the pope himself sponsored at the council prohibiting the foundation of any new orders.[8] Dominic was advised to adopt an already existing rule for his community. In this respect he stood at a disadvantage to Francis, who had already received a verbal confirmation for his community before the council.[9]

As canons in the community of Saint-Romain in Toulouse (which had been given to them by Fulco), they immediately adopted the Rule

---

[5] Tugwell, "Notes on the Life," 5–69.

[6] Jörg Oberste, *Zwischen Heiligkeit und Häresie. Religiosität und sozialer Aufstieg in der Stadt des hohen Mittelalters*, vol. 2, *Städtische Eliten in Toulouse* (Cologne: Böhlau, 2003).

[7] Jörg Oberste, *Der "Kreuzzug" gegen die Albigenser* (Darmstadt: Primus, 2003). See also Mark Pegg, *A Most Holy War: The Albigensian Crusade and the Battle for Christendom* (Oxford: Oxford University Press, 2008).

[8] See p. 185.

[9] Herbert Grundmann, *Religious Movements in the Middle Ages*, trans. Stephen Rowan (Notre Dame, IN: University of Notre Dame Press, 1995), 61–64.

of Augustine and chose the stricter form as it had been modeled by the Premonstratensians. The new pope, Honorius III, confirmed this decision in December 1216.[10] But their goal was to realize a distinct combination of ideals: "holy preaching" in word and deed for the fighting of heresy, an apostolic life lived in poverty, and a concern for spiritual progress. Here was a new concept for the Christian life, one whose organizational implementation required the development of a new framework of fundamental norms.[11]

On January 21, 1217, the papal bull *Gratiarum omnium* was issued for the now rapidly growing community in Toulouse.[12] It was a decisive step, though one hardly noticeable at first glance because it lay hidden in an opening address to the community whose new formulation spoke only of the prior (Dominic) and the brothers of Saint-Romain as "preachers" (*praedicatores*), not as those engaged in preaching (*praedicantes*).[13] Dominic himself had been present at the Roman Curia just before the bull had been drawn up and had insisted on this formulation after *praedicantes* had already been written there. The conceptual shift was profound, because it institutionalized preaching as an office, so to speak, and imposed it (with a certain demanding professionalism) onto the members of the community around Dominic, all of whom were now called the Preachers. Thomas of Cantimpré (1201–1270/72), the renowned encyclopedist and hagiographer of the early Dominicans, underscored the meaning of this designation through a precise explanation: "'Preacher' is the proper name; it is at once a verbal and a personal designation, one in which the name of the office (*nomen officii*) is explained most clearly."[14] He

---

[10] *Monumenta diplomatica s. Dominici*, ed. Vladimir J. Koudelka and Raymond-Joseph Loenertz (Rome: Institutum historicum fratrum praedicatorum, 1966), 71–76 (no. 77).

[11] On the following process of the formation of the Order, see Grado G. Merlo, "Gli inizi dell'ordine dei frati Predicatori. Spunti per una riconsiderazione," *Rivista di storia e letteratura religiosa* 31 (1995): 415–41; Florent Cygler, "Zur Funktionalität der dominikanischen Verfassung im Mittelalter," in *Die Bettelorden im Aufbau*, ed. Gert Melville and Jörg Oberste (Münster: LIT, 1999), 385–428.

[12] Koudelka and Loenertz, *Monumenta diplomatica s. Dominici*, 78–79 (no. 79).

[13] Cygler, "Zur Funktionalität," 392–93.

[14] *Thomae Cantipratani . . . Bonum Universale de apibus* 1.9.5, ed. Georgius Colvenerius (Douai, 1627), 38.

then reflected, in a highly panegyric way, on the aims and character of the community: its members were filled by the fire of Christian love; they were doctors concerned for the welfare of the soul, armed with the sword of faith and the helmet of salvation.

Despite these grand words, the bull was still addressed only to Saint-Romain. But a little later Dominic sent seven brothers to Paris for university study and others to Spain. That move necessitated further papal privileges, and Dominic sought to secure them through direct intervention in Rome.

He was successful. From February 11, 1218, onward, over the course of the next six years, Honorius III issued over forty bulls. In them he turned to all prelates of the church, instructing them to support the Order of Preachers (he already here spoke explicitly of an order) to the best of their ability.[15] The bulls were in a certain sense letters of recommendation that could be given to individual canons and taken along as they now began in ever-greater numbers to move beyond the borders of Toulouse and spread out into all of the lands of Christendom. The anchor points of that movement were the community (presumably founded by Dominic himself) in the Castilian royal city of Segovia as well as those of the university cities of Paris (with its focus on theology) and Bologna (as a center for the study of canon law).[16]

In Bologna in May 1220, Dominic was already able to call a first general chapter, whose leadership, despite his presence, he handed over to a team of diffinitors. A second chapter followed in the same city a year later, attended this time by representatives from more than twenty communities. Among them was the important community of Santa Sabina in Rome, which Honorius III had handed over to the Order. The expansion of the new order had in the meantime reached across France, the Iberian Peninsula, Italy, Germany, and Scandinavia, so that at the general chapter of 1221 it was possible to create eight European provinces and also to send brothers to Hungary, Poland, and England. Like the Franciscans, the Dominicans avoided a system of affiliation. They instead organized their Order according

[15] Cygler, "Zur Funktionalität," 394.

[16] Marie-Humbert Vicaire, "Dominikaner, Dominikanerinnen. A. Allgemeine Struktur des Ordens. V. Ausbreitung des Ordens in Frankreich und Italien," in *Lexikon des Mittelalters* (Munich: Artemis, 1986) 3:1200–1205.

to geographical divisions, quickly adding the remaining regions of Europe a short time later. Already by the 1230s, two settlements had been established in the Holy Land, and by the middle of the century individual brothers, in a way parallel to the Franciscans, were sent to explore the Middle East.[17]

In only six years, from 1215 to 1221, what had begun as a circle of six clerics around Dominic had become an international order whose members enjoyed the rights to preach anywhere and to provide pastoral care. Analogously to the Franciscans, the Dominican Order cut across traditional diocesan structures, and in doing their work the brothers came into competition with secular clergy regionally and locally. That competition was only sharpened by the fact that the Order of Preachers had been concerned from its beginnings to uphold the highest standards of education for its members. It was thus obvious, as with the Franciscans, that the Order as a whole and each of its members should be obligated to obey the pope as head of the universal church. By the middle of the fourteenth century there were supposedly around 21,000 Dominicans in 630 communities.[18]

Already in its first years, however, the Order began to outgrow the normative framework that had been provided by the Rule of Augustine. The model of regular life for canons that had been provided by the Premonstratensians was no longer adequate. It thus seemed to Dominic that the most pressing task was to address the weaknesses arising from the fact that he had been unable in 1215 to give his community its own organizational model. A hundred years earlier that might still have been easy. Dominic used those first general chapters to craft a comprehensive statutory framework, which served as a normative basis tailored to the needs of his community. Thus alongside

---

[17] Berthold Altaner, *Die Dominikanermissionen des 13. Jahrhunderts* (Habelschwerdt: Franke, 1924), 41–141; Anne Müller, "Die dominikanische Mission *inter infideles et scismaticos*. Konzepte, Leitbilder und Impulse bei Humbert de Romanis," in *Die Bettelorden im Aufbau*, 321–82. On the corresponding education, see Anne Müller, *Bettelmönche in islamischer Fremde* (Münster: LIT, 2002). See also Robin Vose, *Dominicans, Muslims, and Jews in the Medieval Crown of Aragon* (Cambridge, UK: Cambridge University Press, 2009).

[18] For a historical overview, see William A. Hinnebusch, *The History of the Dominican Order*, vol. 1, *Origins and Growth to 1500*; vol. 2, *Intellectual and Cultural Life to 1500* (New York: Alba House, 1965, 1973).

regulations regarding visitation, the building of communities, the regular holding of general chapters, and the building of a functional hierarchy of offices, something very specific was decided for the Order: that in the future it was to renounce every kind of ownership and to exempt the superiors of each community from liturgical duties whenever doing so would support them in more engaged study or in their preparations for preaching.

On August 6, 1221, Dominic died in Bologna. He had been a relentless spirit. What was true for Francis was also true for him: without his extraordinarily powerful influence, his Order would never have come into existence. But Dominic's relationship to his work was radically different from that of Francis. Dominic seemed always to be longing to return to those early days of his missionary work with Bishop Diego among the Cumans, and he once even suggested to his brothers that he wanted to set off on a missionary trip. But in reality he remained constantly engaged as the tireless organizer of his grand idea. Alongside his own intense activity as a preacher, he knew, as did almost no one else, how to move a pope and his Curia's bureaucracy to focus within a short time on all that was necessary in the way of privileges to build a highly professional order. Moreover, he understood how best to send his community out into the world with a plan and a purpose—and to begin by establishing a structure strong enough to hold together his far-flung community of brothers. While Francis was increasingly estranged in principle from what grew into a gigantic order bearing his name, Dominic drove the growth of his Order forward with all his strength. He transferred his charisma onto its institutional form, thereby already "routinizing" it (to use Max Weber's word) in his lifetime.

There was thus no lack of clarity after Dominic's death about what was to be done with his legacy. Little was done at first even to commemorate him.[19] His canonization came relatively late, in 1234, and he received his first biographical treatment from one of his brothers, Petrus Ferrandi, between 1234 and 1242.[20] Dominic lived on in a

[19] Achim Wesjohann, "Flüchtigkeit und Bewahrung des Charisma oder: War der heilige Dominikus etwa auch ein Charismatiker?" in *Charisma und religiöse Gemeinschaften im Mittelalter*, ed. Giancarlo Andenna et al. (Münster: LIT, 2005), 227–60.

[20] Simon Tugwell, "Petrus Ferrandi and his *legenda* of St Dominic," *Archivum Fratrum Praedicatorum* 77 (2007): 19–100.

different way: in principle his followers needed only to continue on where he had left off, and they did precisely that.

Rationality and Constitution in the Service of the Salvation of Souls

After further annual chapters held in various places, in 1228 the first master general of the Order, Jordan of Saxony,[21] called together a special assembly of the Order in Paris. Its participants included leaders of houses and provinces as well as elected representatives from each community.[22] The importance of the gathering was registered in its new designation, a shift from *Capitulum generale* to *Capitulum generalissimum*—not a "general chapter," but, as it were, a "most general chapter"—because it was to craft something that would not only shape the entire later history of the Order but also come to stand as a symbol of its identity: the *Constitutiones*, the Order's statutes.[23] They were a masterpiece of rational legislation.

A preamble to the text—like that of the Cistercian *Carta caritatis*[24] before it—noted the act of creating law itself as the foundation of the legitimacy of valid statutes. In the 1228th year of the Lord's incarnation, the provincial priors came together in Paris at the house of Saint James with Master General Jordan (so the difficult, juridical style of the era). Joining them were two diffinitors from each of the provincial chapters, each having been unanimously granted by their brothers the right of voice (*votum*) as well as the full authority (*potestas plenaria*) to make decisions. They could thereby establish, without any outside interference, what was to remain in place for all time by stipulating or omitting, changing, adding, or striking, as they wished. Through the guidance of the Holy Spirit and through careful examination they would unanimously and peacefully craft specific constitutions for the use, renown, and preservation of the Order. They

---

[21] Dieter Berg, "Jordan von Sachsen," in *Verfasserlexikon* (Berlin: de Gruyter, 1983), 4:861–64.

[22] On the following, see Cygler, "Zur Funktionalität," 397–400.

[23] Antoninus Hendrik Thomas, ed., *De oudste constituties van de dominicanen* (Leuven: Universiteitsbibliotheek, 1965), 309–69.

[24] See p. 146.

would in turn implement these, along with other legislative measures, in their particular locales.[25]

With that, many years of work toward a comprehensive body of legislation adapted to the circumstance of the Order of Preachers had provisionally come to a close. It had been decisive to underscore that this work rested on the consensus of the whole Order, as expressed through its elected representatives. The Order had thereby been established as a legal entity from within, of its own accord, apart from the founding achievements of Dominic and the approvals of the papacy. A corporation had been created whose head (much more than in any previous order) represented the body as a whole and that laid claim to the *potestas plenaria*, which drew its legitimacy from itself. The *Constitutiones* were the symbol that established this corporate identity.[26]

The Dominicans had ordered their community in such a way as to ensure that it efficiently supported the religious aims of the Order. The best way to discern what was so special about these arrangements is to investigate the rational structure of their laws and their organization.[27] The following pages will therefore consider the *Constitutiones* somewhat more precisely. To do so offers insight into what would stand as the highest degree of organizational achievement that had ever been possible for the *vita religiosa* in the Middle Ages. In this respect the Dominicans surpassed all other institutions of their era, both secular and spiritual.

The statutory framework of the Order was organized into three registers of validity. A first register concerned principles that were valid for all time, untouchable and unchangeable—so, for example, the prohibition against accepting property and incomes. A second concerned statutes that were unchangeable insofar as they were not changed or abrogated by a *Capitulum generalissimum* in light of new circumstances; these included prohibitions against the eating of meat, for example, or riding horses. Finally, a third kind of statute

---

[25] Thomas, *De oudste constituties*, 309.

[26] Florent Cygler, "Zur institutionellen Symbolizität der dominikanischen Verfassung. Versuch einer Deutung," in *Institutionalität und Symbolisierung*, ed. Gert Melville (Cologne: Böhlau, 2001), 409–24.

[27] Gert Melville, "System Rationality and the Dominican Success in the Middle Ages," in *Franciscan Organisation in the Mendicant Context*, ed. Michael Robson and Jens Röhrkasten (Berlin: LIT, 2010), 377–88.

Dominicans accompany the godly members of all social ranks in the Church Militant of this world on their way to the Church Triumphant in the next. Detail from a fresco in the Spanish Chapel of the convent of Santa Maria Novella in Florence.

could be changed at will after it had been read three times before the general chapter.[28]

Following the preamble came a prologue that sought to explain the nature of the subsequent regulations.[29] The first passage was

[28] Thomas, *De oudste constituties*, 309–10.
[29] Thomas, *De oudste constituties*, 311–12.

taken word for word from the prologue to the statutes of the Premonstratensians, as that text had taken shape by the middle of the
twelfth century.[30] This built a bridge back to the common ground of
the Rule of Augustine, since what followed (so the prologue read) was
meant to foster a more proper observance of Augustine's commands.
The insertion of this Premonstratensian section was wise, because
doing so suggested with great effect (as the future legal practice of
the Dominican Order would make clear) that the *Constitutiones* had
a validity and an authority that was hardly inferior to the Rule itself.
The later master general and commentator of both the *Constitutiones*
and the Rule, Humbert of Romans (ca. 1200–1277), emphasized that
very point (albeit transposing the actual order of the reflections):[31]
a new order like that of the Preachers required new norms, which it
had to craft itself, and for that purpose it was therefore most useful
to adopt a rule that contained nothing that would stand in the way of
innovation. The Rule of Augustine was that kind of rule. Humbert's
observation would play a key role in the development of other orders
as well.

The second section of the prologue, now following its own formulations, established both the goals of the Order and the normative
structures that linked pastorally oriented spirituality with organizational pragmatism. It also made clear that all legislative measures
were to be subordinate to the Order's goals. For that reason, of all the
norms articulated in this document, the first was that it was possible
to be freed from legal norms. The explanation for this approach—
astounding at first glance, indeed seemingly self-contradictory—
followed immediately. It pointed to the extraordinarily functional,
indeed functionalist, understanding that the Order had adopted concerning religious affairs, an understanding discernible not only in
this prologue but also in many of the ways it handled organizational
matters. It made clear, for example, that a superior had the power to
dispense with regulations whenever it seemed advantageous for study,
preaching, or pastoral care, "because from the beginning our Order

---

[30] See pp. 159–60.

[31] "Expositio regulae b. Augustini secundum b. Humbertum, magistrum ordinis fratrum Praedicatorum," in *B. Humberti de Romanis quinti Praedicatorum
magistri generalis opera de vita regulari*, ed. Joachim Joseph Berthier (Rome:
Befani, 1889), 1:50–51.

has been established for preaching and the saving of souls; and therefore our effort must direct our study in principle and with passionate effort, so that we can be useful for the souls of our neighbors."[32] The master general Jordan of Saxony added that in the *Constitutiones* there was hardly anything so serious that it could not be dispensed with.[33] A modern historian has rightly interpreted this model of dispensation as one geared toward "efficiency."[34]

The second legal principle followed immediately, and it is no less remarkable: "we wish and declare that our *Constitutiones* bind [the soul] not with respect to guilt but with respect to penalty"—*non ad culpam, sed ad penam*. Tradition suggests that this principle had been introduced according to Dominic's own wishes so as to relieve his brothers from unnecessary scruples of conscience, thereby freeing them to concentrate all the more intently on saving the souls of their neighbors.[35] But this peace of individual conscience (*pax conscientiarum*) was in turn also useful to the Order as a whole, as Humbert of Romans explained,[36] because it rendered the Order all the more able to function in the service of its aims.

In the context of an overall legal system, however, this division meant the creation of a purely positive law whose sanctions were inherent in the law itself and that needed no transcendent (i.e., divine) justification for its legitimacy. This legislative act was an astounding innovation for a religious order—one that was at first certainly not uncontested and that reveals the earliest origins of what in the modern era would become a division between morality and law. Already in the Middle Ages the Premonstratensians (1236/38), Cluniacs (1289), Augustinian Hermits (1290), and Cistercians (1289/1316) all followed this same principle.

The *Constitutiones* of the Order of Preachers represent a milestone in European legal history. Their perfected rationality—which

---

[32] Thomas, *De oudste constituties*, 311.

[33] Angelus Maria Walz, ed., *Beati Iordani de Saxonia epistulae* (Rome: Institutum Historicum Fratrum Praedicatorum, 1951), 56; Cygler, "Zur Funktionalität," 401.

[34] Marie Humbert Vicaire, *Histoire de Saint Dominique*, 2:203.

[35] Cygler, "Zur Funktionalität," 405–10.

[36] "Expositio magistri Humberti super constitutiones fratrum Praedicatorum," in *B. Humberti de Romanis . . . opera de vita regulari*, 2:48–49.

informed both a legitimizing bond between law and the consent of the community as a whole, as well as a functionality of legal principles—shaped the subsequent division of the text into two large sections of more specific legal provisions.

The structure of the *Constitutiones* was revised only once more, this time by the second master general, Raymond of Peñaforte,[37] the great scholar of church law and editor of the most important collection of canon law in the thirteenth century, the so-called *Liber extra*. His systematic approach had a long future and would serve as a fixed grid for arranging legal materials in a specific sequence, both thematically and textually. Flexibility with regard to inherited legal materials, also accomplished in other orders by way of periodical revision or reissue of collected statutes, was here manifest only in the general chapter's interventions in specific passages in need of revision. An illustration of this quite subtle process (to choose at random only one out of hundreds of similar changes from the thirteenth century alone) is the Dominican initiation in 1240 of a revision and extension of previous provisions for the election of a prior with the following words: "Where it is said in the *Constitutiones* concerning the election of a conventual prior 'he will be elected according to the canonical regulations' should be added 'namely from the greater part of the electors or through compromise or through general inspiration, as happens analogously with the election of the master general and the provincial prior.'"[38] The same example also reveals that such innovations could be undertaken in great number. Already in 1266, and again in 1272, the Dominicans made further changes to the same passage.[39]

The result as a whole was, so to speak, a fluid text that was anchored in a fixed framework. Alongside the rational composition of

[37] Raymond Creytens, "*Les constitutions* des Frères Prêcheurs dans la rédaction de S. Raymond de Penyafort (1241)," *Archivum Fratrum Praedicatorum* 18 (1948): 29–68.

[38] *Acta capitulorum generalium ordinis Praedicatorum*, vol. 1, *ab anno 1220 usque ad annum 1303*, ed. Andreas Frühwirth, Acta capituli generalis Bononiae celebrati anno domini MCCXL (Rome, 1898), 14.

[39] *Acta capitulorum generalium ordinis Praedicatorum*, Acta capituli generalis apud Treverim celebrati anno domini MCCLXVI, 132; Acta capituli generalis apud Florencie celebrati anno domini MCCLXXII, 161–62.

the corpus of laws itself, an extraordinarily refined legal procedure aimed at adapting to new needs and conditions contributed in essential ways to the stability of the Order.

At the time of their composition, the Dominican *Constitutiones* represented the most modern constitutional text anywhere in Europe.[40] They made possible a way of life guided by sophisticated constitutional structures, innovative forms of representation, and legal processes. One of the hallmarks of the text was a deliberate move to limit institutional power, insofar as a "descending chain of command" was held in balance with an "ascending line of control."[41] Overlapping guidelines of responsibility were to bind all members of the Order to a common effort continually to realize their common aims.[42] This effort required, on the one hand, that at every level of authority (the Order as a whole, the province, the community), power from above could be understood only as having been delegated from below, since the most important officeholders in the organization (master general and provincial and conventual priors)—the *prelati*—were of course elected either with the cooperation of or exclusively by ordinary brothers, and, on the other hand, that constitutional bodies based on the composition of conventual, provincial, and general chapters were to have both higher officeholders and ordinary brothers—the *subditi*—as their decision makers and supervisors.

This foundational principle became organized concretely in a way that differed from the conventions found in other orders. The *Constitutiones* declared that for two consecutive years the general chapter would consist of diffinitors chosen anew by the provincial chapters from among the circles of ordinary brothers, the *subditi*; in the third year, the general chapter would consist of the provincial priors, the *prelati*. Characteristically, both types of assemblies enjoyed equal rights with respect to their legislative, administrative, and judicial

---

[40] Léo Moulin, "Le pluricaméralisme dans l'Ordre des Frères Prêcheurs," *Res publica* 2 (1960): 50–66, here 54. For a general introduction to constitutional history, see Hans Vorländer, *Die Verfassung. Idee und Geschichte* (Munich: Beck, 2009), 29–30.

[41] Hinnebusch, *History of the Dominican Order*, 1:170–72.

[42] For an overview of the structures of the constitutions and of the Order, see Georgina R. Galbraith, *The Constitution of the Dominican Order, 1216 to 1360* (Manchester: University Press, 1925).

authority. For this reason every revision of the text of the *Constitutiones* required three consecutive readings, so that both assemblies of the general chapter would thereby be compelled to consider it.

Every group had the right to initiate a revision and to take it up again whenever an initiative failed in the course of the legislative process.[43] It was emphasized that such a procedure contributed greatly to careful deliberation, since often the revision process was thereby drawn out over many years.[44] To avoid the danger of important measures becoming gridlocked, the Dominicans also introduced an additional process, one that anticipated what in the modern era would become a two-tiered legal order.[45] Every general chapter was required to enact individual measures (*admoniciones*) that came into force immediately but that could be rescinded by the next general chapter. That happened very rarely, however, and thus there slowly emerged a considerable collection of regulations that extended the *Constitutiones* with supplemental measures that were quickly adaptable to circumstance.

The Dominicans were keenly aware that the interlocking structures of their general chapter were not only ideal for ensuring the best possible decisions for the Order as a whole, however, but also that those structures held a special symbolism for the Order's institutional principles. When Humbert of Romans was asked whether the Dominicans were wiser than those whose orders recorded their legislation only during a single sitting of their general chapter, he answered by setting down the following basic observations: among the Cistercians and Premonstratensians all the authority of decision making lay with the highest prelates alone; among the Franciscans it was shared between the *prelati* and the *subditi*, but it was put into

[43] Gert Melville, "*Fiat secretum scrutinium*. Zu einem Konflikt zwischen *praelati* und *subditi* bei den Dominikanern des 13. Jahrhunderts," in *Vita Religiosa im Mittelalter*, ed. Franz J. Felten and Nikolas Jaspert (Berlin: Duncker & Humblot, 1999), 441–60.

[44] Gert Melville, "Die Rechtsordnung der Dominikaner in der Spanne von *constituciones* und *admoniciones*. Ein Beitrag zum Vergleich mittelalterlicher Ordensverfassungen," in *Grundlagen des Rechts. Festschrift für Peter Landau zum 65. Geburtstag*, ed. Richard H. Helmholz et al. (Paderborn: Schöningh, 2000), 579–604, here 586.

[45] Melville, "Die Rechtsordnung der Dominikaner," 603.

practice in ways that involved an immense throng of participants. Among the Dominicans, however, both the *prelati* and the *subditi* had independent but equally valid pathways to reaching decisions.[46] Thus the Dominican general chapter was to be understood as the symbolic embodiment of a kind of differentiation specific to the Order. Its cornerstone—as it emphasized—was that both leaders and individual members were bound together harmoniously, in mutual responsibility for the Order as a whole.

The organizational structure of the Dominican Order has received detailed attention here because it reveals, as has already been noted, a very specific Dominican achievement within the broader context of the history of the religious orders: a process shaped by what has been called "system rationality."[47] This was understood as the functional alignment of all elements (whether in relation to one another or to the Order as a whole) to a single goal, which was realized, in practice as well as in principle, without contradiction or conflict. The resulting weave of relationships can be seen as a coherent, self-contained system—something that no other order had yet managed to achieve, at least to this degree, and something that rendered the organization of the Dominicans superior to every other order.

With such refined ways of legislating, of supervision, and of administration, the Dominican Order managed not only to create but also to sustain the best possible conditions for realizing its fundamental concern: the salvation of the souls of all humankind. Preaching served this goal, study in turn served preaching, and the business of daily life in turn served study.[48]

Such an emphasis on structure must not lead to a misappraisal of the Dominicans. The rationality of the Order's "methodical practices"[49] need not be placed in opposition to religious zeal. Rather, it is best to speak of a "spirituality of pragmatism." Even the core religious values of an individual pursuit of salvation—poverty, for example,

---

[46] Melville, "*Fiat secretum scrutinium*," 441–60.

[47] Melville, "System Rationality."

[48] Hinnebusch, *The History of the Dominican Order*, vol. 2, *Intellectual and Cultural Life to 1500*; Marian Michèle Mulchahey, "*First the bow is bent in study. . .*": *Dominican Education before 1350* (Toronto: University of Toronto Press, 1998).

[49] See p. 186.

whose realization among the Grandmontines or the Franciscans was seen as the most profound way to imitate Christ—were subordinate to the all-encompassing principle of pastoral care. Humbert of Romans did emphasize, however, that a preacher of his Order who spoke of the poor Christ and the indigent apostles was more trustworthy when he himself remained poor. Moreover, the poor were more likely to gather around a poor preacher (since like things combined freely with like), and even rich folk would approach him out of respect for his voluntary poverty. From this pragmatic stance Humbert then went on even to argue for the superiority of his Order.[50] In contrast to the others, his was founded not only for the salvation of those who entered it but for the salvation of the whole world.

Through this kind of self-assessment, the Dominicans came early on to an awareness that their Order had a central role in the unfolding of salvation history. In around 1260 the Dominican historian Geraldus de Fracheto (1205–1271/81) wrote about all of the prophecies that pointed to his Order as the moral compass of a church so in need of rescue from its downfall.[51] The Dominicans thus took a leading position in an apocalyptic tradition that Otto of Freising had invoked in the middle of the twelfth century in order to underscore the central role of the religious orders as a whole in the story of salvation, and that James of Vitry had invoked not long afterward to do the same for the Franciscans.[52] At Mary's request, so it was said, God now allowed the Order of Preachers to advance the work of the prophets and apostles. The Dominicans were seen as the "messengers of God," called to their task now because the church's inherited means of grace was no longer sufficient.

[50] "Expositio magistri Humberti super constitutiones fratrum Praedicatorum," in *B. Humberti de Romanis . . . opera de vita regulari*, 2:38–39.

[51] Gerardus de Fracheto, *Vitae Fratrum ordinis Praedicatorum*, ed. Benedikt Maria Reichert (Louvain, 1896), 18–30.

[52] See p. 203; Hans-Joachim Schmidt, "Klosterleben ohne Legitimität. Kritik und Verurteilung im Mittelalter," in *Institutionen und Geschichte*, ed. Franz J. Felten et al. (Cologne: LIT, 2009), 377–400.

12

Transformations of Eremitical Life

In the course of the twelfth century the world of monasticism had institutionalized itself along Cistercian lines in firmly established organizational structures. It had also begun to anchor its innovative potential more and more in the urban milieu. Meanwhile the hermits, who in the eleventh century had still had enough energy to contribute to remarkable renewals in religious life, now disappeared from the limelight and no longer drew the attention of their contemporaries. But their way of life was certainly not extinct. On the one hand, there were still communities of hermits that had organized themselves constitutionally—the Grandmontines, for example, or the Carthusians—whose way of life was in full bloom and whose order boasted fifty-six communities across Europe by the middle of the thirteenth century. On the other hand, individual hermits continued to retreat from the world, setting off with a few followers to find God in solitude. They could be found in forests and mountains across Europe, but especially in Italy, and even in the Holy Land.

In this setting, around the middle of the thirteenth century, something remarkable happened among these eremitical groups. With the support of the papacy, and in one case under papal direction, they transformed themselves into mendicant orders—thereby embracing a form of religious life that in many respects aimed at something other than flight from the world into wastelands of solitude. But as the life of Francis reveals, the mendicant and the eremitical way of life (for any one individual, at least) need not have been wholly incompatible.

The new mendicant orders that emerged in this context were the Carmelites and the Augustinian Hermits. Together with the Franciscans and Dominicans, they represent the four main mendicant orders.

The Carmelites: From the Mountain into the Cities

The beginnings of the Carmelites are poorly documented. The story begins in a lonely valley of the mountain range called Carmel, overlooking the city of Haifa. There, presumably around the end of the twelfth century, near the well that had supposedly been home to the prophet Elijah, a group of hermits had settled and established a chapel in honor of Our Lady.[1] A few decades later, the bishop of Acre, James of Vitry, wrote in his history of Jerusalem about the throng of settlers that had come to the Holy Land. In doing so he characterized the circumstance in Carmel, and, as was the style of his day, he made use of a vivid metaphor: "In imitation of the holy hermit, the prophet Elijah, they lived as hermits on Mount Carmel . . . where they built individual cells like beehives and lived, as it were, like the Lord's bees, making spiritual sweetness, like honey."[2] With this description he hit on two characteristics of the region's eremitical life already encountered among the Camaldolese in the eleventh century: a life enclosed in separate huts, and a binding sense of return to an eremitical tradition that was rooted in the Old Testament.

At the beginning of the thirteenth century, under the leadership of a certain B (only the initial is known for certain from the evidence), the community resolved to live within a more precisely defined normative framework. They turned to Albert, the Latin patriarch of Jerusalem (whose see was in nearby Acre), with a request for the relevant guidelines. Albert had previously been bishop of Vercelli as well as prior of the congregation of the regular canons of Mortara.[3] He had also been numbered among that small group of those who had prepared the statutes of the *Humiliati*. Albert wrote a rule for the hermits of Mount Carmel between 1206 and 1214, calling it a "formula of life" (*vitae formula*), and thereby created for them, through its observance, the possibility of forming their own institutional identity.[4]

---

[1] On the following, see Joachim Smet and Ulrich Dobhan, *Die Karmeliten* (Freiburg im Breisgau: Herder, 1981); Joachim Smet, *The Carmelites*, 2nd ed., vol. 1 (Darien, IL: Carmelite Spiritual Center, 1988); Frances Andrews, *The Other Friars* (Woodbridge, UK: Boydell, 2006), 7–68.

[2] Jacques de Vitry, "Historia Hierosolimitana," ed. Jacques Bongar, in *Gesta Dei per Francos* (Hannover, 1611), 1:1074; Smet and Dobhan, *Die Karmeliten*, 18–19.

[3] See p. 199.

[4] Bede Edwards, ed., *The Rule of Saint Albert* (Aylesford: Carmelite Book Service, 1973); Carlo Cicconetti, *La regola del Carmelo* (Rome: Institutum

The text of this rule established in outline the essentials of the Carmelite way of life. It began with the leadership of the prior and with life in individual cells (which the inhabitants were not to exchange) and then moved from practices of prayer and the establishment of a house of prayer and a chapter of faults (a gathering typical of life in a traditional monastery, in which individuals acknowledged their sins) to practices of common property and individual poverty, fasting, and silence, as well as ascetic practices such as penitential exercises and manual labor—all so that the devil would find the hermits too busy to fall into temptation. The text then emphasized the obligation (a matter that would later prove problematic) to found future settlements only in lonely and isolated locales. Yet it thereby captured in writing only the most important elements of an overall framework. Such formulations diverged from what was becoming typical at the time—grounding every affair in detail and in juridical form, as especially the Dominicans would do so well soon afterward. Here, in contrast, the deeply contemplative piety of the hermits themselves seems to have been enough to guarantee that the spirit of the community's norms would be followed. Albert captured the essentials in the prologue: "True to Jesus Christ, pure in heart, and firm in conscience."[5]

Their political environment, however, did not offer the hermits of Carmel the best of circumstances for an undisturbed observance of religious life.[6] After the defeat at Hattin in 1187 and the loss of Jerusalem, crusaders found themselves forever on the defensive. The last decade of the twelfth century and the gains of the Third Crusade—for example, the recapture of Acre in 1191—had only brought the mild improvements that could make the growth of an eremitical community at Carmel even possible. Emperor Fredrick II was finally able to capture Jerusalem by treaty for the Christians in 1229, but the city fell once more in 1244. Carmel was thus never the most secure place for hermits to retreat to undisturbed from the world or to receive the long-term donations necessary for their basic survival.

Carmelitanum, 1973); Kevin Alban, ed., *The Carmelite Rule 1207–2007* (Rome: Institutum Carmelitanum, 2008); Steven Payne, *The Carmelite Tradition* (Collegeville, MN: Liturgical Press, 2011), 1–9.

[5] Edwards, *The Rule of Saint Albert*, 79.

[6] An overview appears in the classic work of Steven Runciman, *A History of the Crusades*, vols. 2 and 3 (Cambridge, UK: Cambridge University Press, 1952, 1955).

In the years 1226 and 1229, Popes Honorius III and Gregory IX nevertheless confirmed Albert's rule, which had been written just before the decrees of the Fourth Lateran Council already mentioned.[7] Also in 1229 the community in Carmel was forbidden to have common property, a ruling that made the observance of their way of life all the more difficult and that placed them on the same level with the strictest of eremitical groups, such as the Grandmontines. Alongside the command to embrace poverty, Carmel was also placed under the protection of the Holy See. Both papal measures certainly worked to enhance the reputation of the community. It was now able to expand by establishing further settlements in the area immediately around Mount Carmel.

Yet despite the momentum of this expansion, the pervasive threats of the Holy Land seemed to take the upper hand. A slow retreat to Europe was soon under way, with the founding of new settlements above all in coastal cities: 1235 in Valenciennes, 1238 in Cyprus and Messina in Sicily, and 1242 in Hulne and Aylesford in England,[8] as well as Les Aygalades in Marseille, with the parallel establishment of provinces in a way consistent with the conventions of the Dominicans and Franciscans. The rapid expansion of the Order throughout Europe thereafter can to a great extent be traced back to the agency of returning crusaders, who wanted to bring the spiritual power of Mount Carmel home with them.[9] How the Carmelites drew the recruits necessary for such an impressive array of new communities remains unknown, however, because of the lack of source material.

The most serious obstacle to the advance of the Carmelite way of life emerged only at this point. It was a problem with both institutional and spiritual dimensions. The hermits from Carmel had made their way directly into the urban environments of Europe. In Valenciennes, for example, they were granted land in the tanners' quarter with the expectation that they would build a church and a monastery there.[10] How were they to live there, "among the people," while still leading an eremitical life?

---

[7] Smet and Dobhan, *Die Karmeliten*, 25–27.

[8] Richard Copsey, ed., *Carmel in Britain: Essays on the Medieval English Carmelite Province*, vol. 3, *The Hermits from Mount Carmel* (Rome: Edizioni Carmelitane, 2004).

[9] Smet and Dobhan, *Die Karmeliten*, 28–31.

[10] Smet and Dobhan, *Die Karmeliten*, 29.

That question may well have been raised at the first-ever Carmelite general chapter, held in southeastern England in 1247 in Aylesford. The Order elected its first prior general there, and soon afterward its emissaries appeared before Innocent IV, whom they asked for relaxation of their rule.[11] The pope tasked two Dominicans with a review of the text, and on October 1 of the same year he issued a bull in which he promulgated a revised text. It spoke for the first time of an order of Carmelites. The new version at first glance seems to have offered only unremarkable changes.[12] There was now to be a common meal, new foundations no longer had to be located in isolated places, and the observances of silence and of abstinence from meat were relaxed for those who were begging or traveling, so as not to offend their hosts. Closer observation reveals, however, that all of these measures concerned a daily life that approximated common practice among the mendicant orders. It was now possible to establish a cenobitic way of life in urban convents and to practice itinerant begging in absolute poverty.

There was not yet any explicit discussion of taking on pastoral responsibilities as the established mendicant orders had. Simply integrating the Carmelite settlements into the urban environment, however, meant that the issue would become unavoidable. There is no direct evidence of how exactly the clericalization of the Order unfolded, or of how in this early era the Order in fact carried out its pastoral work. But one text from 1270 suggests the nature of that development negatively, by way of its rejection.

Nicholas of Narbonne (called *Gallicus*), general prior of the Order from 1266 to 1271, composed the text and gave it an emphatic title, "The Flaming Arrow" (*Ignea sagitta*).[13] It is the oldest Carmelite

[11] Adrianus Staring, ed., "Four Bulls of Innocent IV, a Critical Edition," *Carmelus* 27 (1980): 273–85.

[12] Edwards, *The Rule of Saint Albert.*

[13] Adrian Staring, ed., "Nicolai Prioris Generalis Ordinis Carmelitarum Ignea Sagitta," *Carmelus* 10 (1962): 237–307; *The Flaming Arrow (Ignea sagitta)* by Nicholas, prior general of the Carmelite Order, 1266–1271, trans. and intro. Bede Edwards (Internet-edition: http://www.carmelitanacollection.com/The Ignea Sagitta.pdf); Smet and Dobhan, *Die Karmeliten*, 40–42; Andrew Jotischky, *The Carmelites and Antiquity* (Oxford: Oxford University Press, 2002), 79–105; Steven Payne, *The Carmelite Tradition* (Collegeville, MN: Liturgical Press, 2011), 10–20.

literary work, and in it Nicholas issued his brothers a sharp demand: to leave the cities again and to retreat anew into the wilderness. For as long as they lived in the cities, he maintained, they could not be true sons of Carmel, but only stepsons. Worse, he accused, they were not even properly suited—let alone properly trained—for the demands of preaching and pastoral care. He emphasized that he had become familiar with the Order's circumstance through his visitations, and he now asked himself why so many unlettered brothers now strove to hear confessions, to pose as doctors of the soul, or—without proper knowledge of the laws—to bind and loose what should not have been bound or loosed. Hardly any words could capture more compellingly, on the one hand, that a transformation into an order that embraced pastoral care was already fully under way and, on the other, that none of the supporting structures of education and regulation was yet in place. Underscoring the spiritual benefits that only an eremitical life of contemplation could bring, Nicholas then concluded his indictment with a song of praise to the nightly heavens, a song whose passionate dialogue with creation recalls the thought of Francis: "In the company of all of creation, which we see and hear in the desert, we find refreshment and encouragement. In their silence they preach a wonderful sermon and compel us to praise the creator."[14]

No formal act—whether an act of the papacy or any kind of internal legislative measure—ever transformed the Carmelites from an eremitical community into a religious order that had the authority and the mandate (like the Franciscans or Dominicans) of preaching and pastoral care. Obviously they evolved only slowly into their apostolic, that is to say, their pastoral, responsibilities. Though the acerbic accusations of a figure like Nicholas regarding the pastoral failures of his day were probably on the mark, the Order had nevertheless successfully organized itself legally and administratively. General chapters, which as a rule met in various places every three years, had by the 1250s produced (according to the Dominican model)[15] constitutions that sought both to render more specific a rule that had been cast in very general terms and also, in a certain way, to expand that rule through regulations focused on implementation.

[14] Staring, "Nicolai Prioris," 298–99; Smet and Dobhan, *Die Karmeliten*, 41.
[15] Smet and Dobhan, *Die Karmeliten*, 37–39.

This legislative work was advanced still more intently over the course of the century, in such a way that a cumulative corpus of statutory legislation, its measures adopted step-by-step, began slowly to emerge. The Order's structure of offices was also organized according to a threefold stratification: the individual house with a prior, the province with a provincial prior and provincial chapter, and the entire Order, with its general prior and general chapter. Diffinitors were chosen from the provinces to serve in this legislative body, the highest within the Order. They codified the decisions of the general chapter, and they bound the general prior to them—as long as he did not abrogate those decisions with the approval of the provincial priors. Here too the desire to establish a balance among competing powers is obvious. The Order's alliance with the Holy See was manifest, among other ways, in that the Carmelites, like the Franciscans, for example, soon enjoyed a cardinal protector.

Nevertheless, the Carmelites never failed to see themselves, and to represent themselves, as contemplative successors to the Old Testament prophets at Carmel. In their constitutions they wrote the following words: "We declare and affirm without any doubt that since the day when the prophets Elijah and Elisha lived piously on Mount Carmel, holy fathers of the Old as well as the New Testament, drawn by the contemplation of heavenly things to the solitude of the same mountain, have lived a successful and edifying life uninterrupted in holy penance there by the well of Elijah." Directly following these words was an explanation that identified the Carmelites as the heirs of this enduring tradition: after the formation of their community had been advanced by Albert and approved by Innocent IV, they now served the Lord, so the text explicitly said, "in different parts of the world up to the present day."[16] To be tied back to Carmel was of utmost importance not only because the Order faced a loss of identity amid its transformations in Europe but also because the Order was thereby allowed to escape the prohibitions of the Fourth Lateran Council against the establishment of new religious orders. Albert's text had been finished just before the establishment of that prohibition, and Elisha's works had stood from time immemorial.

---

[16] Ludovico Saggi, ed., "Constitutiones Capituli Londinensis anni 1281," *Analecta Ordinis Carmelitarum Calceatorum* 15 (1950): 208; Smet and Dobhan, *Die Karmeliten*, 36; Jotischky, *The Carmelites and Antiquity*, 106–49.

We will later encounter the same strategy of argument among the Augustinian Hermits, who faced a similar problem.

A further step in the establishment of the Order's identity was its veneration of Mary, which grew considerably stronger over the course of the thirteenth century. Given the fact that there was already a chapel devoted to Our Lady at Carmel, it also became common in Europe for the Carmelites to choose Mary as the patron of their churches. Marian mysticism, too, increasingly came to the fore-front among those for whom the contemplative life had always been important. In this connection the very name of the Order became linked with Mary: the general chapter of 1294 explicitly expressed its preference for the designation "Order of Our Lady."[17]

Three years before, however, the Carmelite way of life in the Holy Land had been brought definitively to an end with the conquest of Acre by the Mamluks. Henceforth the Carmelites were limited exclusively to Europe.

The Augustinian Hermits

Around the same time that this internal process of transformation unfolded within the Carmelite Order, a similarly strong process transformed another tradition of eremitical life into an apostolic life devoted to pastoral care. Yet here the process was imposed from above and resulted in a decisive crisis whose events unfolded over the course of only a few days.

On April 9, 1256, Alexander IV issued a bull (known from its opening words as *Licet ecclesiae catholicae*) in which he approved the creation of a new order by way of gathering a number of established eremitical congregations into one and giving it a new name: *Ordo fratrum Eremitarum S. Augustini*—abbreviated as the Order of Augustinian Hermits.[18] The Order was to follow both the Rule of Augustine and its own statutes, which were soon to be issued, and its members were to wear a new, uniform habit. Moreover, the Order could enjoy the cumulative privileges, all of them now assembled like building blocks, that its groups had once received individually.

---

[17] Smet and Dobhan, *Die Karmeliten*, 43–45.

[18] Benignus van Luijk, ed., *Bullarium Ordinis Eremitarum S. Augustini. Periodus formationis 1187–1256* (Würzburg: Augustinus, 1964), no. 163, 128–30.

Cardinal Richard Annibaldi became protector of the Order. A prior general was appointed by the pope—in other words, not elected by the Order itself—and granted the wide-ranging powers he would need to break any resistance against the process of unification.

This act of the Great Union (*Magna Unio*), as it would come to be called, was the culmination of a longer and multifaceted history.[19] It involved four congregations or orders, some of them reaching back to the middle of the twelfth century, whose separate communities had at first lived an eremitical life in widely different ways but had then been broken up "among the people."

The largest congregation belonged to the so-called Williamites.[20] It had its beginnings in 1158 around the grave of the hermit William of Malavalle, who did not leave behind a rule but who did have one follower who knew how to give initial guidelines on how best to live the eremitic life to the growing number of those who now sought salvation in the Tuscan solitude of Malavalle near Castiglione della Pescaia. The cult around William was first officially recognized a good twenty years later by Pope Alexander III and then again in 1202 by Innocent III. The community expanded quickly, with new settlements throughout central Italy. In 1244 it established a presence north of the Alps, and in the year of the "Great Union" it already had settlements in northern France, Germany, Bohemia, and Hungary.

Despite this success, however, the congregation was at a great disadvantage: quite against the trend of the day—one that had come to encompass all religious congregations, including eremitical ones—the Williamites' organization remained quite primitive. There was neither a central executive authority nor a general chapter. Although its ascetic

[19] On the following, see Kaspar Elm, "Italienische Eremitengemeinschaften des 12. und 13. Jahrhunderts. Studien zur Vorgeschichte des Augustiner-Eremitenordens," in *L'eremitismo in Occidente nei secoli XI e XII* (Milan: Vita e pensiero, 1965), 491–559; David Gutiérrez, *Geschichte des Augustinerordens*, vol. 1, *Die Augustiner im Mittelalter 1256–1356* (Würzburg: Augustinus-Verlag, 1985); Cristina Andenna, "'Non est haec vita apostolica, sed confusio babylonica.' L'invenzione di un ordine nel secolo XIII," in *Regulae—Consuetudines—Statuta*, ed. Cristina Andenna and Gert Melville (Münster: LIT, 2005), 569–632; Andrews, *The Other Friars*, 69–172.

[20] On the following, see Kaspar Elm, *Beiträge zur Geschichte des Wilhelmitenordens* (Cologne: Böhlau, 1962); Andenna, "'Non est haec vita apostolica,'" 605–8; Andrews, *The Other Friars*, 76–77.

practices were extraordinarily strict, the popes repeatedly intervened to soften them and at the same time to promote unity and uniformity. In place of the old customs that reached back to William of Malavalle himself, Gregory IX prescribed for the Williamites the Rule of Saint Benedict and the normative frameworks of the Cistercians in order to free them from an eremitical stasis. But the strategy could never be successful, because such complex forms of regular life were far too large in scale to impose on small eremitical communities. Innocent IV thus began an energetic attempt to draw the Williamites away from a purely eremitical life and to move them toward the practices of pastoral care and preaching that were customary in the mendicant orders. In 1249 he recognized them as a monastic order and granted them extensive rights. Yet they remained obligated half to an eremitical life and half to a monastic life—and it was in that hybrid position, as will be seen, that the Order became a candidate for the Curia's efforts at union in 1256.

The other three candidates were smaller congregations and never stood in the limelight of church affairs quite like the Williamites. Yet they too would receive powerful support.

The so-called Tuscan Hermits had grown together slowly in the first half of the thirteenth century from many communities scattered across Tuscany, some of them quite long established,[21] before Innocent IV in 1244 prescribed the Rule of Augustine for them as a distinct congregation and required that they develop an overall organizational structure—a process aided by their protector cardinal Richard Annibaldi (noted above) and two Cistercian monks.[22] A year later they received rights of preaching and confession and important exemptions from episcopal power, until they were on nearly equal footing with the Franciscans and Dominicans. In that position they too became candidates for the project of 1256.

The John-Bonites[23] were followers of John Bonus, who until his death in 1249 lived for decades as a hermit on the edge of the Apen-

---

[21] Andenna, "'Non est haec vita apostolica,'" 592–97; Andrews, *The Other Friars*, 72–76.

[22] Bull "Religiosam vitam eligentibus," in *Bullarium Ordinis Eremitarum S. Augustini*, 40–43, no. 46.

[23] Cristina Andenna, "Urbano IV e l'istituzione dell'ordine delle clarisse," in Andenna and Melville, *Regulae—Consuetudines—Statuta*, 600–605; Andrews, *The Other Friars*, 78–81.

nines near Cesena. His asceticism, his deep piety, and his zealous engagement for the integrity of the church made it seem that he was already a saint in his own lifetime. The number of those seeking to share in his eremitical way of life grew rapidly. They founded new communities across the Po valley, typically in the cities, from Venice to Milan. In need of a rule (which in keeping with the decrees of the Fourth Lateran Council could not be a new one), they turned to the Curia and around 1226 received the Rule of Augustine. John Bonus still sought to devote himself entirely to a contemplative life, so in 1238, like Francis, he stepped down from the leadership of a community that was rapidly becoming a more thoroughly organized order. His followers, however, sought to lead a life that reconciled eremitical retreat with pastoral responsibilities, and they received the appropriate privileges from Pope Innocent IV in 1246. But only a few years later the unity of the Order began to crumble. Defenders of the eremitical life and those who embraced pastoral care stood strongly opposed and could not be reconciled. This circumstance, too, made them candidates for the "Great Union."

Finally, the hermits of Brettino[24] emerged from a gathering of a few men who sought to find their way to God together by retreating into the solitude of the mountains around the Adriatic city of Fano, where they lived in strict poverty and asceticism as well as communal harmony. As their way of life drew more and more followers, soon additional communities had to be founded. In 1228 Innocent IV gave them the Rule of Augustine, and five years later papal confirmation of their own constitutions followed, leaving them with a normative structure similar to the Dominicans'. In 1243 they received (again from Innocent IV) rights of confession and preaching, and two years later the remaining privileges of the great mendicant orders—to which they were increasingly similar not in size and scope, but in appearance and aspiration.

Common to all four of these congregations was that through their development they had come to stand on the threshold of a shared status as purely apostolic orders—and in fact they only stood on the threshold, because none had fully renounced its eremitical past, and indeed one had been led to serious conflicts over its eremitical heritage. Seen

---

[24] Andenna, "Urbano IV," 597–600; Andrews, *The Other Friars*, 81–82.

from the other side, however, in their activities, rights, and exemptions they had come more and more to appear and in fact to function like the mendicant orders, especially the Franciscans. The political strategies of the popes in the first half of the thirteenth century, especially Gregory IX and Innocent IV, had already laid the foundations for that transformation. They no longer shied away from lending their powerful support to the old alignments of eremitic life and preaching that had once captivated Christian society—however many in the church hierarchy might have remained suspicious of that old alliance.

In the thirteenth century, eremitic asceticism still symbolized a vital piety, for those who lived both in the cities and in the countryside, and it remained the strongest possible guarantee of the certainty of salvation for those who sought to participate in its charismatic power. The Curia— no doubt influenced by the tireless work of Richard Annibaldi, who could be sure of the support of Alexander IV, his uncle[25]—was interested in the potential of this form of piety (even though the groups mentioned here were still scattered and imperfectly organized) for helping to bring together into more organized structures all of the pastoral work that was still waiting to be carried out more intensively. The best solution was for the popes to compel the last step over the threshold—in this case, by way of the "Great Union," to form a new order dedicated to pastoral care and preaching and to provide for that order the rule that most of its members in any case already observed: the Rule of Augustine.

With this act the papacy once again showed both its desire and its power to intervene decisively in order to shape the world of monasteries and orders. With great flexibility, Innocent III had been able to found new orders, or at least to make their foundation possible. Honorius IV had decisively refined the structures of two of the greatest mendicant orders. And now, from Gregory IX and Innocent IV to Alexander IV, the popes had transformed one fundamental pattern of the *vita religiosa* into another. They had turned an eremitical life into an apostolic life and once again founded a new order.

After 1256, events did not unfold without conflict, to be sure. Distinct traditions and identities were not so easily abandoned. The Williamites managed after a short time to break away from the Union. Another band of hermits intended for the Union, from Monte Favale

---

[25] Francis Roth, "Cardinal Richard Annibaldi: First protector of the Augustinian Order," *Augustiniana* 4 (1954): 5–24.

in the diocese of Pesaro, was never formally integrated.[26] Others, like the congregation of the Poor Catholics (*Pauperes catholici*),[27] declared their allegiance to the act of 1256, but they faced such strong internal opposition that later, in 1272, they actually had to resort to coercion in an attempt to retain their members.

Nevertheless, the Order of Augustinian Hermits, which also developed a female branch, had a successful future before it. Already in 1256, alongside its numerous Italian provinces, the Order founded new ones in western and central Europe.[28] In the German province of the Order alone there were already eighty communities by the end of the thirteenth century.[29] The constitutional structure of the Order was similar in general outline to those of the other established orders,[30] and like the Dominicans, the Augustinian Hermits placed special emphasis on the theological education of their members. For both orders, Paris thus became central for that enterprise.[31]

In the interests of self-preservation, but also to assert themselves against their competitors, the Augustinian Hermits established for themselves a firm identity that was anchored in a past that reached back far beyond 1256, one that could therefore seem magnificent in comparison to those of the other orders. Among the first to articulate an elaborate vision of that past was Henry of Friemar, an Augustinian Hermit from Erfurt, in his work *On the Origins and Growth of the Order of Brother Hermits* (*De origine et progressu ordinis fratrum eremitarum*).[32] This treatise, written in 1334, transformed the church

---

[26] Gutiérrez, *Geschichte des Augustinerordens*, vol. 1, *Die Augustiner im Mittelalter 1256–1356*, 44–45; Andrews, *The Other Friars*, 82.

[27] Andenna, "Urbano IV," 608–10.

[28] Gutiérrez, *Geschichte des Augustinerordens*, vol. 1, *Die Augustiner im Mittelalter 1256–1356*, 50–54; Pierantonio Piatti, *Il movimento femminile agostiniano nel Medioevo. Momenti di storia dell'Ordine eremitano* (Rome: Città nuova, 2007); Eric Saak, *High Way to Heaven: The Augustinian Platform Between Reform and Reformation, 1292–1524* (Leiden: Brill, 2002).

[29] Michael Klaus Wernicke, "Die Augustiner-Eremiten im Deutschland des 13. Jahrhunderts," *Analecta Augustiniana* 70 (2007): 119–32.

[30] Wernicke, "Die Augustiner-Eremiten," 77–101.

[31] Wernicke, "Die Augustiner-Eremiten," 161–96.

[32] Rudolph Arbesmann, ed., "Henry of Friemar's 'Treatise on the Origin and Development of the Order of the Hermit Friars and Its True and Real Title,'" *Augustiniana* 6 (1956): 37–145.

father Augustine himself into a hermit.[33] Henry proposed, among other things, that the Desert Fathers of Egypt had in fact founded the eremitical life, but that Augustine in particular had founded the way of life of the Augustinian Hermits when he had once lived for an extended time among the hermits of Tuscany and had given them a rule:

> And when in the wilderness of Tuscany he had found many hermits with one holy way of life, he came at last to our place, which was called Centumcellae. This was, as it is said [*ut dicitur*], the first community of our order, and Augustine lived among these brothers for two years. After he had then made good progress in the knowledge of the faith, he wrote a rule for their way of life and gave it to them. All of this can be surmised from the old, unabridged legends [*ex antiquis legendis non abbreviatis*].[34]

Henry then developed this basic line of argument further still, claiming, for example, that Augustine had already worn the habit of the Augustinian Hermits in his own day.[35] For Henry it seemed quite clear that the Order of Augustinian Hermits could not only boast of a founder of incomparable rank but also that it was tied to a venerable tradition—one that was far older than those of its competitors, the Dominicans and the Franciscans.[36]

---

[33] On the following, see Kaspar Elm, "Die Bedeutung historischer Legitimation für Entstehung, Funktion und Bestand des mittelalterlichen Ordenswesens," in *Herkunft und Ursprung. Historische Formen der Legitimation*, ed. Peter Wunderli (Sigmaringen: Thorbecke, 1994), 71–90, here 79; Gert Melville, "Knowledge of the Origins: Constructing Identity and Ordering Monastic Life in the Middle Ages," in *Knowledge, Discipline, and Power in the Middle Ages: Essays in Honour of David Luscombe*, ed. Joseph Canning et al. (Leiden: Brill, 2011), 41–62, here 48–51; Achim Wesjohann, *Mendikantische Gründungserzählungen im 13. und 14. Jahrhundert* (Berlin: LIT, 2012), 533–36.

[34] Arbesmann, "Henry of Friemar's 'Treatise,'" 96.

[35] Arbesmann, "Henry of Friemar's 'Treatise,'" 98.

[36] Arbesmann, "Henry of Friemar's 'Treatise,'" 109.

13

A New Chapter in the Story of the *Vita Religiosa*

The Three Ages of Salvation History

Medieval people typically saw themselves as living in an aging world. In the middle of the twelfth century, for example, Otto of Freising saw the world as already at its end, were it not for the monks' appeasing intercessions before God. Around the middle of the thirteenth century, in stark contrast, the Dominican Vincent of Beauvais had a vision of a world rejuvenated, a world to which would be brought new strength through the youthful vitality of its religious orders.[1]

In the epilogue to his encyclopedic history the *Speculum historiale*, completed in 1246, Vincent wrote that in his exegesis of Jeremiah,[2] the *abbas Joachim* spoke prophetically of two orders that would inaugurate a third age.[3] The Lord, according to Joachim's exegesis, had once used Moses and Joshua to defeat the hostile Canaanites, and later Paul and Barnabas to strike down the idolaters. Now finally he would use two orders to subdue an unbelieving people. Vincent thus believed he could discern how in the first age God had once chosen

---

[1] Marco Rainini, "I predicatori dei tempi ultimi. La rielaborazione di un tema escatologico nel costruirsi dell'identità profetica dell'ordine domenicano," *Cristianesimo nella storia* 23 (2002): 307–44, here 335–36.

[2] Marjorie Reeves, *The Influence of Prophecy in the Later Middle Ages: A Study in Joachimism*, 2nd ed. (Notre Dame, IN: University of Notre Dame Press, 1993), 150–53.

[3] Vincentius Bellovacensis, *Speculum historiale* (Douai, 1624; repr. Graz: Akademische Druck- und Verlagsanstalt, 1965), 1324–25.

old men, in the second age young men (the apostles), and now, in the third age, young boys to proclaim the Gospel and the word of God. His talk of new orders was surely a veiled reference to his own Dominicans, and to the Franciscans.

The works of *abbas Ioachim*—as Joachim of Fiore (1130/35–1202) was called here—were alluring to orders that sought (as all sought in principle) to highlight their dignity within salvation history. The Calabrian Joachim, once a hermit, then a Cistercian, and finally in around 1190 the founder of his own Order,[4] had written a number of works of biblical exegesis, though not the one noted here, which was presumably written under his name between 1243 and 1248.[5] In his works he advanced with great vigor the theory that salvation history was unfolding in three stages: the age of the Father, corresponding to the Old Testament; the age of the Son, reaching from the time of Christ to the thirteenth century; and finally the age of the Holy Spirit, which was to supersede the era of the hierarchical, propertied church and to be led by monks, who would usher in an age of perfect peace on earth.[6]

The Franciscans, who were uneasy about their order's departure from its original norms and who longed to return to the authenticity of Francis's message, were especially taken by Joachim's vision of a spiritual church led by monks, as was promised for those still on earth in the third age. Their stance in fact had roots that reached back to the time immediately after the death of the Poverello, but it grew stronger in the second half of the thirteenth century and led to both deep divisions within the Order and sharp conflicts with the hierarchical church. The discussion will later return to that development.

With his reference to Joachimist thought, Vincent of Beauvais had thus touched on a stirring theme of his era, and with its help he had strengthened a fundamental belief in the divinely inspired leadership of religious communities—especially in the two great mendicant orders. That particular stance deserves emphasis, because it signals,

---

[4] Gian Luca Potestà, *Il tempo dell'Apocalisse. Vita di Gioacchino da Fiore* (Rome: Edizioni Laterza, 2004).

[5] On the dating of the "Expositio super Hieremiam," see Reeves, *Influence of Prophecy*, 56. See also Emmett Randolph Daniel, *Abbot Joachim of Fiore and Joachimism: Selected Articles* (Aldershot: Ashgate Variorum, 2011).

[6] Reeves, *Influence of Prophecy*, 133–292.

from the middle of the thirteenth century, a new chapter in the medieval story of the *vita religiosa*. At first glance, quite in contrast to Vincent's projections into the future, it seems that the world of monasticism had passed its zenith.[7] Over the course of the coming centuries no new order would approach the scope, presence, and influence of the four great mendicant orders. And there would only be one—the Birgittines—that would make for itself the same claim that the Franciscans, Dominicans, and earlier established forms of the *vita religiosa* had also made: to fulfill a calling within salvation history, or even to be salvation history institutionalized.

The shaping power of the *vita religiosa*, which had always found a way—whether driven from within or in reaction to ever-changing spiritual and social needs—to create entirely new forms of life, seems to have been extinguished. Soon after Vincent's euphoric reflections, the main concern seems to have been to preserve through reform whatever might be salvaged of discipline and piety, as well as material resources and organizational structure.

Yet this image is deceptive, because it is seen in an unfocused light. Certainly these assessments are not false, but from the thirteenth to the fifteenth century there was vitality enough both to expand and to make new beginnings—a vitality that certainly rested on the kind of confidence that a figure like Vincent of Beauvais so consciously represented. On the one hand, the four major mendicant orders had come to influence every aspect of society: the cities, the nascent universities, courts, and church institutions. They grew to become leaders of the spiritual elite of Christendom, and when all seemed lost after the fall of Acre in 1291, two of them even spearheaded Christian missions to the farthest reaches of Asia.

On the other hand, two main sources for the continued establishment of new forms of religious life proved to be anything but exhausted: first, the lay religious movement that at the opening of the thirteenth century had already been approved (in the form of the *Humiliati*) by a church that was willing to recognize it in principle and that continued to build on that foundation; second, the

---

[7] Kaspar Elm, "Verfall und Erneuerung des Ordenswesens im Spätmittelalter," in *Untersuchungen zu Kloster und Stift* (Göttingen: Vandenhoeck & Ruprecht, 1980), 188–238. English trans. in James D. Mixson, trans., *Selected Essays of Kaspar Elm* (Leiden: Brill, 2015), chap. 4.

timeless impetus to take literally the call to turn from the world and to seek God by retreating into the eremitical solitude of the desert. And finally there was still the traditional world of the Benedictines, Cistercians, and Premonstratensians, the foundations of the regular canons, and the settlements of so many eremitical congregations, such as the Grandmontines and Carthusians, now centuries old—all of which sought not only to preserve their own traditions but also to make room for new impulses.

It is certainly hard to escape the impression that the landscape of Latin Christendom in the later Middle Ages had long been densely packed with monastic institutions. What can at first glance seem like overgrown stagnation can thus perhaps be traced back to nothing other than an overly satisfied demand, or an exhaustion of human and material resources—which would be reduced further still in the age of the Black Death[8] and the Hundred Years' War.[9]

To render an overview of these complex circumstances more manageable, they cannot be confronted comprehensively, in chronological sequence. Rather, we must draw from them a series of contrasts that make it possible to highlight particular developments in the world of late-medieval monasticism.

To that end, the following aspects deserve attention. First, the analysis focuses on circumstances that fostered new institutions. Here the attention is on the phenomenon of the continued growth of eremitical communities and on a novel configuration in the life of religious community among regular canons known as the *Devotio moderna*—the so-called Modern Devotion—as well as the growth of an order that even laid claim to its own rule, the Order of the Savior or the Birgittines. The second theme is the struggle for universal recognition and the formation of institutional identity among recently established institutions, especially the mendicant orders. Third and finally, the analysis turns to reform movements that were

---

[8] On exemplary structures, see Anne Müller, "Managing Crises: Institutional Restabilisation of the Religious Orders in England after the Black Death (1347–1350)," *Revue Mabillon* 16 (2005): 205–19.

[9] On exemplary structures, see Anselme Dimier, "La grande pitié des monastères cisterciens de France pendant la guerre de Cent Ans," in *Mélanges à la mémoire du père Anselme Dimier*, ed. Benoît Chauvin (Arbois: Chauvin, 1982), 1:540–44.

either initiated by the papacy or developed autonomously by individual religious congregations. Of interest here are the reform projects of Pope Benedict XII and especially the Benedictine networks that sought a renewal of discipline in the fifteenth century. Any account of these diverse histories is of course subject to a certain abridgment and generalization.

Eremitical Congregations and the Work of Peter of Morrone

By virtue of its geographical scope, the unification of eremitical communities that established the Order of Augustinian Hermits in 1256 (noted above) encompassed broad sections of Europe, but its starting point was at first concentrated especially in central Italy. Across the broad expanse of Christendom in the same era, however, the eremitical life was lived nearly everywhere, and in a way in keeping with its essence—in groups that were small and scattered and that also stood on the threshold of a more apostolic orientation. Once again, the same challenges in principle remained: how to draw various groups together, and how to integrate them functionally into the church's effort to meet a range of pastoral needs. In thirteenth-century Hungary we find an example of one attempt to meet those challenges—an attempt (despite certain aberrations due to a particular set of circumstances) that ultimately met with success.

Much like the forest of Craon in the late eleventh and early twelfth centuries, as noted above, the Pilis Mountains southwest of the River Donau's turn in Hungary had long been a region especially dense with eremitical communities.[10] There in 1250 Eusebius, a cathedral canon from Esztergom, founded the community of the Holy Cross for various eremitical groups from across his region. He also took over

---

[10] On the following, see Gabor Sarbak, "Entstehung und Frühgeschichte des Ordens der Pauliner," *Zeitschrift für Kirchengeschichte* 99 (1988): 93–103; Beatrix Fülöpp-Romhányi, "Die Pauliner im mittelalterlichen Ungarn," in *Beiträge zur Geschichte des Paulinerordens*, ed. Kaspar Elm (Berlin: Duncker & Humblot, 2000), 143–56; Maria-Elisabeth Brunert, "Die Pauliner. Zu den Ursprüngen ihres Ordens, seiner Geschichte und Spiritualität," in *Klosterforschung: Befunde, Projekte, Perspektiven*, ed. Jens Schneider (Munich: Wilhelm Fink, 2006), 11–39; Gabor Sarbak, ed., *Der Paulinerorden. Geschichte—Geist—Kultur* (Budapest: S. István Társulat, 2010).

a second community, founded under the patronage of Saint James in 1225 by Bishop Bartholomew of Pécs. The bishop had founded this community, near Patacs in the Mecsek Mountains of southern Hungary, for previously scattered eremitical groups in his diocese. Both of these communities, drawn together by personal union and established from what had originally been small communities, presumably had access to a short collection of statutes that Bishop Bartholomew had already written for his community of St. James.

The number of communities grew rapidly. Nevertheless, the pope denied their 1262 petition to be recognized as an independent order. By that time, the Curia was thinking strongly in fiscal terms, and in view of the poverty of these eremitical communities it had no desire to create yet another mendicant order. In the following year the pope's emissary, Bishop Paul of Veszprém, issued the congregation its own set of statutes; further statutes, more fully elaborated, followed in 1297 from the bishop of Esztergom. In 1308[11] a papal legate finally allowed the communities both to adopt the Rule of Augustine and to compose an extended body of statutes. It was here that the communities for the first time formulated what became their lasting designation as *Ordo sancti Pauli primi eremite*, the "Order of St. Paul the First Hermit." In 1328 Pope John XXII confirmed the rule of the newly established order, its property as well as its constitutions. He also exempted the Order from episcopal power and from the obligation to pay tithes; a privilege of Gregory XI in 1377 then established the Order's full exemption. The parallels to the transformations surrounding the Great Union of the Augustinian Hermits are clear.

Although the Paulines, as they are often called, did not expand dramatically from their heartland in greater Hungary, they were soon to be found in Poland, Germany, and by the fifteenth century even Portugal. Their organization was soon almost identical to that of the other mendicant orders, especially the Dominicans. Like them, by the time of their flowering in the fifteenth century, the Paulines took on the duties of pastoral care. They also devoted themselves to scholarship,[12] especially in the old, prescholastic tradition of monastic theology that seemed so natural to them.

---

[11] On the following, with all of the evidence, see Sarbak, "Entstehung und Frühgeschichte," 101–2.

[12] Gabor Sarbak, "Das Buch- und Bibliothekswesen der Pauliner im Mittelalter," in Elm, *Beiträge zur Geschichte des Paulinerordens*, 41–62.

The Paulines shared with the Augustinian Hermits and the Carmelites in particular a bold, sweeping return to an immemorial past. Their model, indeed their supposed founding father, was Paul of Thebes, whom the *Vita* written by Jerome had celebrated in the fourth century as the model desert hermit.[13] Decisive for their self-understanding was that they looked back not to the creator of their rule, Augustine, but rather that they wanted to represent symbolically the archetype, so to speak, of eremitic life. The Paulines formed a community grounded in tradition, one that despite its apostolic mission never lost sight of the eremitic, contemplative life.

But the powerful attraction of the eremitic life also remained undiminished across thirteenth-century Italy. The Great Union of 1256 had in no way absorbed every eremitical community. As a consequence, the unifying framework of the Rule of Augustine, along with its apostolic orientation, did not *de facto* become the main principle of organization.[14]

One case that was normatively established long before 1256 illustrates this point. At the age of fifty, in the wake of a personally tragic experience arising from a bitter fight with his bishop, the priest Silvester Guzzolini (1177–1267) from Osimo in Ancona fled to a cave and lived as a hermit. A circle of companions soon joined him, and in 1231 he established an isolated monastery on the mountain of Fano in the March of Ancona. The community adopted the Rule of Saint Benedict and had their choice confirmed by Innocent IV in 1247. Thereafter further communities were established in the March of Ancona, in Tuscany, and in Umbria, leading to the formation of a transregional congregation, albeit still a small one, that after its founder's death came to be called the Silvestrines.[15] Some significant

---

[13] Kaspar Elm, "Elias, Paulus von Theben und Augustinus als Ordensgründer: Ein Beitrag zur Geschichtsschreibung und der Geschichtsdeutung des Eremiten- und Bettelordens des 13. Jahrhunderts," in *Geschichtsschreibung und Geschichtsbewußtsein im späten Mittelalter*, ed. Hans Patze (Sigmaringen: Thorbecke, 1987), 371–99, here 375–81. In English, "Elijah, Paul of Thebes, and Augustine: *Fundatores Ordinum*: A Contribution to the Historical Self-understanding of Medieval Religious Orders," *Augustinian Heritage* 36 (1990): 163–82.

[14] For an overview, see Giorgio Picasso, ed., *Il monachesimo italiano nel secolo della grande crisi* (Cesena: Badia di Santa Maria del Monte, 2004).

[15] Giovanni Spinelli, "Silvestriner," in *Lexikon des Mittelalters* (Munich: Artemis, 1995) 7:1909–10.

differences distinguish them from the Augustinian Hermits and Pau-lines. Here again at the origins stood a charismatic leading figure (like a Romuald or a Stephen of Obazine in the eleventh century, for ex-ample) from whom the community actually took its name. But there was no mention of the Rule of Augustine. Rather, the Benedictine tradition actually came closest to serving the needs of this eremitical group. And in the end the group remained independent.

A certain compatibility with these structures is notable in the case of a French congregation, whose example shows once again how experimental the eremitical embrace of the *vita religiosa* could be. According to tradition, a certain Gui (or Viard) left the Charterhouse of Lugny in Northern Burgundy in 1184 and retreated into the lonely forests of Châtillon-sur-Seine, between Troyes and Dijon.[16] A short time later—as was common for hermits held in great esteem—a small group of like-minded followers gathered around him. Whatever the reliability of this story of origins, there is evidence that by the end of the twelfth century a settlement of hermits had been established near Châtillon in Val des Choux and that Duke Odo III of Burgundy had provided it with a monastery. In 1205 the hermits, now called Caulites (after the valley that was their home), received confirma-tion of their way of life from Innocent III, with the archbishop of Rheims as mediator.[17] Over the course of the thirteenth century the congregation grew to twenty priories, most of them in Burgundy and the Île-de-France, but many also in the Netherlands and England.

The Caulite constitution was a unique combination of Carthusian and Cistercian elements. On the one hand, the members lived separately in strictest poverty and asceticism, fending for themselves in small huts, their community restricted to no more than twenty members. On the other hand, they took all of their meals in common, and they prayed and worked together. In 1215 they entered into a prayer confraternity with the Cistercians, and in 1224 Honorius III approved for them both

[16] On the following, see Robert Folz, "Le monastère du Val des Choux au premier siècle de son histoire," *Bulletin philologique et historique (jusqu'à 1610) du Comité des Travaux Historiques et Scientifiques. Section de Philologie et d'histoire, année 1959* (1960): 91–115.

[17] Phillip Carl Adamo, "The Manuscript Tradition and Origins of the Cau-lite Customary: An Historiographic Examination," *Revue Mabillon* 72 (2000): 197–220.

an adaptation of their customs and the acceptance of the Benedictine rule but without requiring them to give up their eremitic way of life. By adopting significant portions of the Cistercians' organizational norms, the congregation increasingly took on Cistercian standards, but throughout the Middle Ages it never lost its independence.

In Italy in the thirteenth century, all of Western Christendom experienced, in a literal sense, still another case, this one similarly experimental yet far more prominent. Celestine V (1209/1210–1296)[18]—the only medieval pope ever to have formally renounced his office—was elected in 1294 because the College of Cardinals had sought and then received (through a unanimous election guided by the inspiration of the Holy Spirit) a figure deeply grounded in personal piety. In the decades before his pontificate, Celestine had been the founder of an order.[19]

Peter of Morrone, as he was originally called, came from a rural family in the Abruzzo. He entered a Benedictine abbey as a boy, and after a few years resolved to pursue a quite common path, one for which the Benedictine rule itself had made provision: to retreat to a hermitage without giving up his connection with the monastery. In 1233/34, while in Rome seeking clarity about his future, he was ordained a priest. He then returned to the Apennine Mountains and, with the permission of his abbot, retreated once more to a hermitage, this one on the mountain of Morrone near the episcopal city of Sulmona. His experience there was similar to that of nearly all of his eremitical predecessors. His reputation as an ascetic, as a penitent, and as one who sought God soon spread, and a crowd of followers gathered around him. He created his first community, and though he disbanded it after only a few years, he never lost spiritual contact with its members.

Peter then struck out more deeply into the Apennines, into the mountainous wilds of Maiella. There too a community soon began to gather. They rebuilt an old, isolated church and named it after the Holy Spirit (S. Spirito a Maiella) because a dove had appeared

---

[18] Peter Herde, *Cölestin V. (1294), Peter von Morrone, Der Engelpapst. Mit einem Urkundenanhang und Edition zweier Viten* (Stuttgart: Hiersemann, 1981); Roberto Rusconi, "Celestiniana: dal santo eremita al santo papa," *Sanctorum* 7 (2010): 109–29; Alessandra Bartolomei Romagnoli, *Una memoria controversa. Celestino V e le sue fonti* (Florence: Edizioni del Galluzzo, 2013).

[19] On the following, see Karl Borchardt, *Die Cölestiner* (Husum: Matthiesen, 2006), 13–33.

to its members while they were at work restoring the church. Their choice of the name may very well have resonated with the Joachi-mist vision of a future age of the Holy Spirit. Because Peter was still a Benedictine, he gave his followers the Rule of Saint Benedict as a guide. But their holy way of life, which they had also lived in Morrone, now attracted patrons who wanted to invest in their own salvation. Moreover, the hermits enjoyed the support of the bishop and the commune of Sulmona, as well as of the Count of Manopello, the leading power in the region. Both settlements soon received land and the rights to rivers and forests.

By the 1260s the point had long since been reached that both of these communities, now firmly established both internally and exter-nally, needed legal safeguarding by the papacy. Urban IV provided it in 1263, taking the church of Santo Spirito a Maiella and all of its properties under his protection.[20] He also assigned the Benedictine rule for the hermits, with the mediation of the local bishop of Chi-eti. The foundation had thereby been laid for a growing number of settlements whose network soon reached to Latium, but above all to the south. The kingdom of Sicily, which bordered the Papal States to the south and east, was in many respects the heartland of Peter's community. There, as the Hohenstaufen era came to an end, Charles of Anjou had come to power with papal support in 1266. Peter found strong support in both Charles and his son and successor, Charles II, who would later also even help bring him to the papal throne.

The community, now properly established as a congregation and expanding, had begun to flower. But there soon emerged a danger from quite a different quarter. In Lyon in 1274, a general church council gathered and sought once again to review the implementa-tion of the decrees of Lateran IV that had considerably limited the establishment of new religious foundations. At the center stood the mendicant orders, whose impact among the bishops and the secular clergy had inspired strong discontent.

In its openness to accepting new institutions, Christendom had over time become, as was discussed above, highly saturated with a great many different forms of a *vita religiosa* that still maintained its powerful attraction. Hermits with a strong pastoral presence could

---

[20] Tommaso Leccisotti, *Abbazia di Montecassino. I regesti dell'archivio*, vol. 3, *Fondo di S. Spirito del Morrone* (Rome: Pisani, 1966), 31–32.

also easily inspire a certain degree of reservation and resentment. In that context, the bishop of Chieti took the stage at the Council of Lyon as a spokesman for a number of his episcopal colleagues, advocating that Peter's congregation be disbanded. The reputation of his communities highlighted contrasting ways of life and thus seemed to the bishops to be a thorn in the side of every diocese, since monks still lived from their own manual labor and cultivated a strict ascetic life of fasting and penitential discipline. Moreover, the bishops sought to lay claim to the properties of the various foundations. In response, the elderly Peter of Morrone made his way on foot from central Italy to Lyon, seeking to save his community by appearing there in person. His commitment bore fruit: in March of 1274 he received renewed papal confirmation of his congregation.[21]

Although the churches of Peter's congregation did carry out certain pastoral duties, their hermits remained true in the first instance to their life of retreat and contemplation. Even the administrators, though in a community that would soon take shape as an established order,[22] held office for only a limited time, so that they would be able periodically to return to solitude. When an aging Peter of Morrone was elected pope in 1294 as Pope Celestine V, he had already long since retreated from any kind of leadership in the congregation. He had lived in his cell, turning to God in contemplation—and he now found himself God's representative on earth, in a Curia that had masterfully shaped both a bureaucracy that was impenetrable to outsiders and an intricate web of figures obsessed with power. The "Angelic Pope,"[23] as the Franciscan Spirituals hoped he would be, the hermit of the desert, was destined to fail in that environment, even if he did erect (as tradition has it) a hermit's enclosure in the papal palace. The same had been true for Bruno, who some two hundred years earlier had come to the Roman Curia from the solitude of the mountains and at once discovered that he had to flee once again into the forests of Calabria.

When Peter of Morrone was elected Celestine V, his Order had some thirty-five monasteries and some six hundred members who now called themselves Celestines. To the end of the Middle Ages they

---

[21] Edited in Borchardt, *Die Cölestiner*, 375–77.

[22] Borchardt, *Die Cölestiner*, 171–218.

[23] Peter Herde, "Cölestin V. 'Der Engelpapst,'" in *Gestalten der Kirchengeschichte*, ed. Martin Greschat (Stuttgart: Kohlhammer, 1983), 1:244–46.

would continue to expand throughout all of Italy, as well as north of the Alps as far as Bohemia.

Yet the power of the eremitic life had at this point by no means exhausted itself. On the contrary, the spectrum of small congregations to be established in the future could be surveyed only with difficulty. A few examples can suffice. In 1313 the Sienese city councilman Bernardo Tolomei retreated with two followers to a solitary family estate south of Siena. The community grew rapidly thereafter, changed the name of its settlement to Monte Oliveto (the Mount of Olives), and by 1319 already enjoyed the recognition of the bishop of Arezzo. After the foundation of subsequent communities and the adoption of the Benedictine rule (in a slightly modified form), Pope Clement VI approved the established congregation in 1344, and by the middle of the fifteenth century it had some fifty communities spread across Italy.[24]

Around 1350 in Toledo in Castile, a strong veneration of Jerome and the memory of his time in the desert inspired the formation of the small eremitical order of the Jeronimites, which lived according to the Rule of Augustine and was confirmed in 1373.[25] Its expansion was especially strong across the Iberian Peninsula as well as in Italy, and it was later closely associated with the Spanish crown. Emperor Charles V died in one of its houses.

The Pisan Pietro Gambacorta (1355–1435), similarly inspired by Jerome, created the congregation of the Poor Hermits of St. Jerome, which established close relationships with the Franciscans and lived according to statutes that consisted of norms drawn from (among others) the rules of Augustine and Francis and that prescribed charitable works above all.[26]

---

[24] Giorgio Picasso, "La spiritualità dell'antico monachesimo alle origini di Monte Oliveto," in *Charisma und religiöse Gemeinschaften im Mittelalter*, ed. Giancarlo Andenna et al. (Münster: LIT, 2005), 443–52; Luigi Gioia, *San Bernardo Tolomei e lo spirito della famiglia monastica di Monte Oliveto* (Siena: Abbazia di Monte Oliveto, 2009).

[25] John Roger Loxdale Highfield, "The Jeronimites in Spain, Their Patrons and Success, 1373–1516," *The Journal of Ecclesiastical History* 34 (1983): 513–33; see also Timothy J. Schmitz, "The Spanish Jeronymites and the Reformed Texts of the Council of Trent," *Sixteenth Century Journal* 37 (2006): 375–99.

[26] *Constitutiones oder Satzungen des Eremiten-Ordens S. Hieronymi, Congregationis Des Seeligen Petri von Pisa, Der strengern Observanz* (Munich, 1744).

The former disciple of Franciscan friars, Franz of Paola (1416–1507), joined with his companions in eremitical life to found a community in 1454, in Calabria's Cosenza. In 1474 Pope Sixtus IV recognized it as the Order of the Minims.[27] Although limited at first to Italy, before the end of the century its influence had already spread to Germany and France.[28]

The list of these groups could be extended. And its length is eloquent proof that the drive both to retreat from the world and also, from that place of retreat, to be open to those in need of pastoral care, had hardly faltered—even though the drive itself was increasingly captured in ever smaller, independent institutional formations. In conjunction with the attraction of individual charismatic figures who sought compelling influence through nothing but the extraordinary intensity of their piety, regional conditions, or particular political interests (especially the house of Anjou in southern Italy), often played an important role. But what may often have been just as decisive was that many who sought salvation obviously wanted to keep a certain distance from the great, established orders and to trust more strongly in those more individual avenues to the *vita religiosa* whose turn from the world seemed somehow more authentic. The eremitical life of the day might thereby also be understood as a place of refuge amid the inscrutable ways of the great, established religious corporations—or amid what was perceived as the dying embers of faith. Something similar had already happened in the eleventh and the beginning of the twelfth centuries, but it was now characteristic that new communities could no longer look for normative structures, as they once had, in a new rule or new statutes. Rather, they were forced to choose—and here they did have a certain freedom—one of the established rules, and they were anxious to receive quick approval from the head of the church. Yet it was no longer possible for the popes—though many often had the intention of doing so—to respond (as they had in 1256) by trying to draw together what had become such a bewildering variety of forms of religious life.

---

[27] Alessandro Maria Galuzzi, *Origini dell'Ordine dei Minimi* (Rome: Pontificia Università Lateranense, 1967).

[28] Dominique Dinet, "L'installation et la diffusion des Minimes en France," in *Saint François de Paule et les Minimes en France de la fin du XVᵉ au XVIIIᵉ siècle*, ed. Pierre Benoist and André Vauchez (Tours: Presses universitaires François-Rabelais, 2010), 13–22.

Devotio Moderna

In the last two centuries of the Middle Ages, the search for individual access to an extraordinary life of piety was also realized in a completely different way than through eremitic retreat. This development played itself out in the Netherlands and was at first associated with the strong need of laity to be able to devote themselves to a religious life without having to profess solemn vows. This kind of semireligious life had been known to the region by way of the Beguines, and it was not unfamiliar to the church hierarchy. On the contrary, all of the problems that might arise from unregulated religious communities were very well known.

Almost unmanageable social and religious tensions reigned in this remarkably prosperous region of the Netherlands. Unimaginable luxury stood side by side with the miserable poverty of the broader population. An unsatisfied longing for religious fulfillment often broke the bounds of orthodoxy, at times extending to the rejection of all norms, while a great many of the clergy themselves led a dissolute, worldly life. Social unrest and war aggravated the situation. The desire to retreat into the self, to find a safe haven, was everywhere palpable. The contested ways of the Beguines had already offered one possibility, a way that did not require women to retreat either to the individual solitude of the recluse or to the cloistered life of the nun.

At the origin of this new religious transformation—in a way quite analogous to the eremitic congregations discussed above—stood one particularly charismatic figure: Geert Groote (1340–1384), who like so many earlier leaders of religious movements (Norbert of Xanten, for example) experienced a sharp conversion to a more religious life.[29] As the son of a wealthy cloth merchant in Deventer, he had enjoyed an excellent education and was able at the University of Paris to study deeply in the liberal arts, in law, medicine, and theology, ultimately attaining the rank of Master in the Faculty of Arts. While steeped in this worldly life, he encountered two figures who had embraced the eremitic life and who would change his life dramatically.

The first was Jan van Ruysbroeck (1293/94–1381), the priest, mystic, and author of numerous works of spiritual instruction who

---

[29] On the following, see Georgette Épiney-Burgard, *Gérard Grote (1340–1384) et les débuts de la Dévotion Moderne* (Wiesbaden: Franz Steiner, 1970); Susanne Krauss, *Die Devotio moderna in Deventer* (Münster: LIT, 2007), 40–43.

had retreated with three companions to the solitude of Groenendaal southeast of Brussels and there founded a community that observed the Rule of Augustine.[30] The second was Henry Eger of Kalkar (1328–1408), also a mystic and author of numerous treatises, among them the *Mirror of Sinners* (*Speculum peccatorum*), which was destined to have considerable influence on Groote's new form of piety.[31]

Henry Eger was prior of the Charterhouse of Monnikhuizen near Arnhem. In 1374 he invited Groote to live for a time in his monastery, in the silence of the Charterhouse, but without taking religious vows. Groote gave up his prebends and accepted the invitation, but before doing so he did something unusual: he donated his parents' house in Deventer to a group of God-seeking women as a kind of protective space for a life in community, one also lived without vows. Groote himself stayed for many years in the Charterhouse and while there developed the *leitmotif* he would later hand on to the followers gathered around him. It rested on the opposition between *propositum* and *votum*. Decisive for Groote was the *propositum* alone—the personal intention to devote one's life to God, the single-minded aim of following the "rule of rules," the Gospel. In contrast, the vow—in formal legal terms the eternally binding oath of the religious—was meaningless in Groote's eyes. An inner commitment of the heart stood here against an institutional obligation that was usually binding even when the will to fulfill it had long since faded. Decisive for Groote's model of piety was the struggle for spiritual perfection by way of an inward elevation of the soul to God. In his own day, and especially among his followers as they developed it in the early fifteenth century, this perspective came to be called *Devotio moderna*.[32] Its means were twofold: on the one hand, inner contemplation, meditation, or spiritual consciousness, which cultivated a religious sensibility similar

---

[30] Kurt Ruh, "Jan van Ruusbroec. Versuch einer Würdigung von Person und Werk," *Zeitschrift für deutsches Altertum und deutsche Literatur* 125 (1996): 1–50.

[31] Heinrich Rüthing, *Der Kartäuser Heinrich Egher von Kalkar 1328–1408* (Göttingen: Vandenhoeck & Ruprecht, 1967).

[32] Krauss, *Die Devotio moderna*, 329–93; John van Engen, *Sisters and Brothers of the Common Life: The Devotio Moderna and the World of the Later Middle Ages* (Philadelphia: Pennsylvania University Press, 2008); Dick E. H. de Boer and Iris Kwiatkowski, eds., *Die Devotio moderna. Sozialer und kultureller Transfer (1350–1580)*, 2 vols. (Münster: Aschendorff, 2013).

to mysticism; on the other, training of the soul through a life and labor that were practical and pleasing to God.

This kind of personally shaped piety was not first developed among the Beguines. In principle, it had been a part of every search for individual faith and had already found strikingly analogous expressions both in early Franciscan circles and in the charismatic communities of the eremitic movement of the eleventh and twelfth centuries. So it was that the followers of Stephen of Obazine, who (as was discussed above) lived only by internalizing oral teachings on humility, obedience, poverty, and steadfast love, could see themselves as "veterans of the heavenly militia"—yet with no obligations to vows or other legally established norms.

Nevertheless, Groote sought to give his *Devotio moderna* enough of an institutional form to ensure that his followers could live undisturbed by threats and prohibitions. The recent fate of the Beguines cast a threatening shadow. In 1379 he established at his parents' house a settlement for the "Sisters of the Common Life,"[33] who were to live without vows, observing only the commands of chastity and obedience under the supervision of a prioress, to sustain themselves by the work of their own hands,[34] and to live a pious life of contemplation and prayer. This house in Deventer would soon lead to a number of similar communities.

Groote had himself consecrated as a deacon so that he could preach. He made his way through the cities as a penitential preacher, called for the imitation of Christ, denounced the moral dissolution of his day, and criticized the property of monks and the simoniacal corruption of the clergy. And like so many of the wandering preachers who had been his predecessors, his ways inspired the fierce resistance of the bishop, who in 1383 withdrew Groote's license to preach. But Groote had already found another outlet for his energy, one that would lead incrementally to the foundation of a monastery along the lines of traditional religious life. From around 1380, a group of men—mostly young laymen and clerics—had slowly begun to gather around him, without any organization or episcopal approval, seeking to share in his

[33] On the houses of the sisters, see Krauss, *Die Devotio moderna*, 91–144.

[34] Martina B. Klug, *Armut und Arbeit in der Devotio moderna: Studien zum Leben der Schwestern in niederrheinischen Gemeinschaften* (Munich: Waxmann, 2005).

life of piety. He put them to work, instructing them not only to meditate on spiritual texts but also to copy them and to meet their needs by selling them.[35] Inner self-examination, combined with engaged activity toward that same end, would lead to a deepening of personal piety. Groote also gathered this group into a community without vows, calling them the Brothers of the Common Life.[36]

Shortly before the end of his life, however, Groote resolved to establish a religious community bound by a rule. This was a notable turn that seemed to contradict his previous stance toward an institutionalized *vita religiosa*. His model was the convent of his father figure Jan van Ruysbroeck in Groenendaal, where regular canons lived according to the Rule of Augustine, which had so strongly emphasized daily life in community. But in 1384, the plague carried Groote away. It fell to his friend Florens Radewijns (1350–1400) to realize the plan.

With the help of the brotherhood in Deventer, the construction of a modest monastery was begun in Windesheim near Zwolle in 1387.[37] The first six members, who had solemnly sworn to observe the Rule of Augustine and called themselves regular canons, moved in soon after. In 1395 Boniface IX, the pope of the Roman obedience (in the age of the Great Schism, with an antipope in Avignon), approved the community and two daughter houses. In the following decades, alongside the communities of women and men who lived without vows, the Windesheimers quickly developed a remarkably widespread congregation. At around the middle of the fifteenth century, it numbered thirty houses, and by 1464 some sixty-eight male and thirteen female communities had long since expanded beyond the Low Countries into northern Germany, Alsace, Switzerland, and Bavaria. Their growth involved not only the founding of new houses but also the takeover and reform of old ones, including the venerable

[35] Nikolaus Staubach, "Text als Prozeß. Zur Pragmatik des Schreibens und Lesens in der Devotio moderna," in *Pragmatische Dimensionen mittelalterlicher Schriftkultur*, ed. Christel Meier (Munich: Wilhelm Fink, 2002), 251–76.

[36] On their houses, see Nikolaus Staubach, ed., *Kirchenreform von unten. Gerhard Zerbolt von Zutphen und die Brüder vom gemeinsamen Leben* (Frankfurt am Main: Peter Lang, 2005); Susanne Krauss, *Die Devotio moderna*, 196–228.

[37] On the following, see Stephan Acht, "Die Windesheimer Augustinerchorherren-Kongregation gestern und heute," in *Die Augustinerchorherren in Bayern*, ed. Paul Mai (Regensburg: Schnell & Steiner, 1999), 57–60.

community of Rebdorf near Eichstätt (in modern Upper Bavaria), established in 1156.

The Windesheim congregation was attractive not only because it so strongly embraced the *Devotio moderna* but also because its intensely personal form of piety was now anchored in the stabilizing framework of rule-bound, life-long commitment to religious community.[38] This protected space allowed such great and spiritually strong personalities as Thomas of Kempen (1380–1471) to achieve deep mystical contemplation and to write his *Imitation of Christ* (*De imitatione Christi*)—a book that was long second only to the Bible as the most widely circulated spiritual work in all of Christendom.[39]

Because the Windesheimers also knew how best to make use of all the constitutional tools available since the days of the Cistercians (especially regular general chapters and networks of mutual visitation), in this regard—apart from a few exceptions like the Premonstratensians and the congregation of Arrouaise—they achieved an organizational efficiency far superior to that of the isolated regular canonries of the previous era.

The Revelations of Birgitta

Apart from the movements among communities of hermits and regular canons described thus far, during the later Middle Ages the spirit of the old Benedictine world also found the strength, in a single instance, to produce a form of religious life that was new in both spirit and structure. In this case there was no need for the Rule of Saint Benedict itself but rather for a rule that claimed to bring forth a renewed monastic life. The origin of this remarkable development was along one of the most distant borders of Christendom, in Sweden.[40]

---

[38] Sönke Lorenz, "Zu Spiritualität und Theologie bei der Windesheimer Kongregation," in *Frömmigkeit und Theologie an Chorherrenstiften*, ed. Ulrich Köpf (Ostfildern: Thorbecke, 2009), 169–84.

[39] Thomas à Kempis, *De imitatione Christi libri quatuor*, ed. Tiburzio Lupo (Città del Vaticano: Libreria editrice Vaticana, 1982); Nikolaus Staubach, "Von der Nachfolge Christi und ihren Folgen: Oder warum wurde Thomas von Kempen so berühmt?" in *Kempener Thomas-Vorträge*, ed. Ulrike Bodemann (Kempen: Thomas-Archiv, 2002), 85–104.

[40] Tore Nyberg, "Der Birgittenorden als Beispiel einer Neugründung im Zeitalter der Ordensreformen," in *Reformbemühungen und Observanzbestrebungen*

The noble widow Birgitta (1303–1373) lived for years in the Cistercian abbey of Alvastra (Östergötland) after the death of her husband in 1344.[41] While there, by her own testimony, she began to receive revelations from Christ, which the Cistercians wrote down. Among these revelations was a rule for an order that would consist of double houses dedicated to the Savior. Again and again, for the rest of her life, Birgitta advanced this issue before every figure of authority, all the way to the pope. She later came before Pope Urban V and in 1370 set forth her claim that she was to obey this command of Christ, as it had been recorded in her revelations: "Go there and say to him [the pope] that for my part I [Christ] have given you the rule of the order, which should be established and begun in the place called Vadstena in Sweden."[42]

For Birgitta, all religious rules were divine in origin, as one passage in her *Revelations* makes emphatically clear. In the text Christ himself speaks:

> The Rule that this Francis introduced was not dictated or composed by human intellect and sagacity but by me in accordance with my will. Each word written in it was inspired in him by my spirit, and later he presented and offered the rule to others. So, too, all other rules which my friends have introduced, keeping and observing them themselves, teaching and offering them to others to good effect: they were neither dictated nor composed by their own human intellects and wisdom but by the inspiration of the Holy Spirit.[43]

---

im spätmittelalterlichen Ordenswesen, ed. Kaspar Elm (Berlin: Duncker & Humblot, 1989), 373–96.

[41] On the following, see Günther Schiwy, *Birgitta von Schweden. Mystikerin und Visionärin des späten Mittelalters. Eine Biographie* (Munich: C. H. Beck, 2003).

[42] *Sanctae Birgittae Revelaciones*, ed. Birger Bergh et al. (Stockholm: Almqvist & Wiksell, 1967–2002), here *Revelaciones* 4.137; trans. from *Leben und Offenbarungen der heiligen Brigitta, nach der Übersetzung von Ludwig Clarus* (1888), digitalized and rev. Gertrud Willy; http://www.joerg-sieger.de /isenheim/brigitta/b_03.html; English trans. Denis Michael Searby, *The Revelations of St. Birgitta of Sweden*, 4 vols. (Oxford: Oxford University Press, 2006–2012), here 2:247.

[43] *Revelaciones* 7.20; trans. Searby, 3:247.

Yet Birgitta was convinced that the rule revealed to her had now to be put into practice, in order to hold up a newly flowering religious life before the different forms of the old—all of which seemed defeated and which no longer obeyed their old rules. Only then could religious life set itself aright. Already the prologue of the Rule invoked the biblical allegory of the "Lord's vineyard" (e.g., Isa 5, Matt 20:1-16): the servants of the king had found in his vineyards only weeds and very few vines, so the lord commanded a new vineyard to be built. He himself would "watch over it, so that everything harmful that grew there would wither, decay, rot, and become harmless, and so that the wine would be all the more strong and sweet." "But from this vineyard," the text continued, "many vineyards long barren will be renewed, and each will begin to bear fruit according to the day of its renewal."[44]

In light of such conviction, Birgitta was not to be denied an extraordinary sense of mission. Never before in what had now become the long history of the monastic world had such an exalted and divinely inspired claim to save religious life as this been recorded in the text of a rule itself. Perhaps it was the view from Christendom's borders that fostered this perspective, along with its sharp criticisms of established orders and their observances.[45] Yet Birgitta also knew much of Europe's heartland well, having traveled with her husband as far as Galicia, to the tomb of Saint James. Her experiences from her travels were no doubt decisive in shaping her point of view.

The impulse for shaping Birgitta's rule came from the Benedictine and Cistercian traditions.[46] A monk from Alvastra had accompanied her and her husband on their pilgrimage to Santiago. The rule was written in that monastery, and the prior of Alvastra, Petrus Olavi, later expanded it by way of statutes modeled on the Cistercian tradition. A characteristic element in the rule is the remark that in uncertain

---

[44] *Revelaciones*, Regula I.2; trans. Searby 4:123–47.

[45] Pavlína Rychterová, "Kirchenkritische Visionen der hl. Birgitta von Schweden und ihre Übersetzung von Thomas von Štítný," in *Pater familias: Sborník prispevku k životnímu jubileu Prof. Dr. Ivana Hlaváčka*, ed. Jan Hrdina (Prague: Scriptorium, 2002), 357–80.

[46] Helmut Schatz, "Heimweh nach der Urkirche: Brigitta von Schweden und ihr Orden im Umkreis der Zisterzienser," *Cistercienser Chronik* 110 (2003): 237–42.

circumstances, the Rule of Saint Benedict and the *Carta caritatis*, which contemporaries considered to be a rule written by Bernard, were always to be consulted.

And yet the rule that is woven into Birgitta's revelations has a character all its own. All of its formulations regarding clothing, the Divine Office, silence, enclosure, and fasting reveal both a certain prudence and also the kind of zeal that could only arise from the depths of mystical experience. The high point of the text is its depiction of the way in which the community was to accept a new nun: the bishop was first to consecrate the clothing of the one who was to enter, then to set a crown atop her black veil, put a golden ring on her finger, and hand her over to the abbess.[47]

Birgitta did not seek to establish a convent in the way customary for the mendicant orders or among congregations of hermits. Rather, she sought an enclosed monastery whose members were permanently bound to one place (*stabilitas loci*) and led not by those elected only for limited terms but by an abbess, who in the Benedictine sense held her office from God for life. The monastery sheltered two distinct communities, one of nuns and the other of ordained monks.[48] The latter were led by a "general confessor" (a prior), but all were subject to the ultimate authority of the abbess.

The total number of the community was restricted to the symbolic number of eighty-five: thirteen priests, corresponding to the apostles (counting those later chosen, Matthias and Paul), four deacons, eight lay brothers, and sixty nuns. The last three groups totaled seventy-two— the number of Christ's disciples. The community thus represented the family gathered around the Savior, with the men fulfilling their priestly duties both for the women and for those in the surrounding area, while the women dedicated themselves to prayer, intercession, and domestic work. The local bishop held authority over the community as a whole, because Birgitta never sought episcopal exemption.[49]

The layout of the monastery reflected the nature of the double community. The priests' house (*curia*) was not to be built next to the women's house (*monasterium*). A wall separated the two areas. Into

---

[47] Tore Nyberg, *Birgittinische Klostergründungen des Mittelalters* (Leiden: Sijthoff, 1965), 2–3.

[48] Nyberg, *Birgittinische Klostergründungen*, 32–42.

[49] Nyberg, *Birgittinische Klostergründungen*, 59–63.

it was set a room that allowed the priests to hear the confessions of the strictly enclosed nuns and that also served as a conference room for the coordination of the affairs of the entire complex. Both groups had their own entrances to the church. The nuns' choir was located in an upper gallery and the priests' choir below, by the altar.

Yet a first monastery—as the revelations had foreseen, it was in Vadstena, in southwest Sweden—would only be approved after some time. In 1349 Birgitta set out for Rome to seek approval of the "Rule of the Savior."[50] But the well-known decrees of the Fourth Lateran Council stood against her intentions, and her request was refused. Despite that failure, however, she remained in the Eternal City and there gained in reputation as a holy woman. She became one of the principal voices among those calling for the popes to return from their exile in Avignon to the city of Peter and Paul, and after two decades, in 1370, she finally won at least a partial success. Pope Urban V, who between 1367 and 1370 resided in Rome instead of Avignon, gave her permission to establish two distinct communities in Vadstena—but both were to abide by the Rule of Augustine (which had slowly become something of a wild card in the establishment of institutional norms for religious life) along with further specific guidelines from Birgitta's own pen.[51]

Birgitta died in July 1373. In 1378 her daughter Catherine was able to win approval of the rule from Pope Urban VI, albeit in a modified form, as revised constitutions that were clothed in the mantle of the Augustinian rule.[52] In this version it was no longer Christ himself who spoke; he was only spoken of in the third person. A text of revelation shaped by the deepest piety had evolved into a legal text geared toward practical adaptation to circumstance.

In any case, these legal constructions, which changed nothing essential in the founding concepts of the organization, fostered the emergence of a new monastic congregation, known as the "Order of the Savior" (*Ordo Sanctissimi Salvatoris*) or, as it was often called,

[50] Pavlína Rychterová, *Die Offenbarungen der heiligen Birgitta von Schweden. Eine Untersuchung zur alttschechischen Übersetzung des Thomas von Štítné (um 1330–um 1409)* (Cologne: Böhlau, 2004), 38–43.

[51] Nyberg, *Birgittinische Klostergründungen*, 43–46.

[52] Nyberg, *Birgittinische Klostergründungen*, 49–59.

the "Birgittine Order."[53] Despite the structure of its communities, which was often difficult to realize, by 1500 the Order claimed some twenty-seven houses, most of them concentrated in Germany, and especially in its northwestern territories, in Bavaria, and on the Baltic coast, but with others in England, Norway, Sweden (where Vadstena remained the congregation's center), Finland, Poland, and Italy.[54]

The monastery church of Vadstena is the former center of the Order of the Birgittines.

[53] Tore Nyberg, "Die Entwicklung der Statuten des Brigittenordens bis 1420," *Zeitschrift der Savigny-Stiftung für Rechtsgeschichte: Kanonistische Abteilung* 75 (1989): 202–27.

[54] Nyberg, *Birgittinische Klostergründungen*, 69–222.

14

Mendicant Orders in Conflict

Struggles over Poverty and Observance

Two passages in Birgitta's revelations leveled sharp criticisms against the two largest mendicant orders. Both the Dominicans and the Franciscans faced the accusation that many among them had fallen away from the values of their founders. Mary thus complained to Birgitta that under her broad mantle of protection there had come to be found fewer sons of Dominic than in his lifetime; most had chosen to follow the lax way that led to the devil. Only a few still followed the humble footsteps of Dominic. Pride, lust for honor, and arrogance reigned among them instead. They strove after episcopal office, relaxed the strictures of their fasts, wore refined clothing, and had buildings bathed in splendor, even though their rule prohibited all superfluity.[1] Mary also sternly accused the Franciscans, saying that the devil had turned many of them "from humility to pride, from reasoned poverty to greed, from true obedience to self-reliance." They hoarded gold secretly and against their rule, and they concerned themselves with study so that they could earn "honors and dignities" in the Order, thereby enjoying still more material comforts.[2]

The fact that some one hundred years after the euphoric words of Vincent of Beauvais, noted above, these two orders could be criticized in this way offers an occasion to turn from the story of the rich growth

---

[1] *Sanctae Birgittae Revelaciones*, ed. Birger Bergh et al. (Stockholm: Almqvist & Wiksell, 1967–2002), 3.17–18. English trans. Denis Michael Searby, *The Revelations of St. Birgitta of Sweden*, 3 vols. (Oxford: Oxford University Press, 2006–2012).

[2] *Revelaciones* 7.20.

of new communities in the later Middle Ages to consider the progress of the Franciscans and Dominicans, who at the beginning of the era had transformed the entire framework of the *vita religiosa* in a way that was as full of promise as it was self-confident.

The almost explosive spread of the settlements of these two orders, noted above, is the story of a success that was both immediate and unchecked. From the thirteenth century on, Franciscans and Dominicans were leaders in pressing forward with missions. They served as ambassadors, advisers, confessors, and tutors of the powerful, whether secular and spiritual rulers or rich merchants and patricians,[3] for whom they carried out charitable work and with whose help all might find their way through the famous eye of the needle and on to salvation (Mark 10:25). But above all, both orders served the common people through their preaching and pastoral care in the cities—an activity sustained by their right, as orders exempt from the authority of local bishops, to dispense the sacraments regardless of established parochial structures. Their only competition in that context came after a time from the other mendicant orders, especially smaller ones such as the Carmelites or Augustinian Hermits, as well as from those approved congregations of hermits best described as "urbanites" (*urbanite*), as contemporaries often called them.

Mendicant friars were visible nearly everywhere.[4] Their monastery was the world (so it had been said metaphorically), and they made their way into it, moving beyond the walls of their own communities and churches to beg and to proclaim the word of God in the streets and plazas of the cities. A Franciscan like Berthold of Regensburg (1201–1272), who traveled across Europe, who drew thousands everywhere he went, who preached about the sins of every rank of society, and who called all to contrition and repentance with his sharp words, became a hero to the masses.[5] To Benedictines like

---

[3] Jörg Oberste, "Gesellschaft und Individuum in der Seelsorge der Mendikanten. Die Predigten Humberts de Romanis († 1277) an städtische Oberschichten," in *Das Eigene und das Ganze*, ed. Gert Melville and Markus Schürer (Münster: LIT, 2002), 497–527.

[4] Ramona Sickert, *Wenn Klosterbrüder* (Münster: LIT, 2006), and on the mendicant sermon 87–112.

[5] Peter Segl, "Berthold von Regensburg—Prediger (1210–1272)," in *Berühmte Regensburger. Lebensbilder aus zwei Jahrtausenden*, ed. Karlheinz Dietz and

Richer of Sens, who remained hidden behind monastery walls, such a life lived "among the people" must have seemed perverse. Richer wrote in around 1270, astonished at how the friars could settle in the cities, where immorality and profit reigned and where worldly affairs flourished.[6] But the mendicants went into the cities precisely for that reason, since it was there that so many more sinners could be found and converted by the word of God.[7] City dwellers, in turn, were deeply touched that men of God on that mission would pay them notice and take so much care for their souls—and this, moreover, on behalf of the official church rather than as suspicious, freelance zealots (there were many of these too in the urban environment) on the hunt for heretics.[8]

Dominicans (and to a lesser extent also Franciscans) were deployed as inquisitors against heretics, to be sure.[9] In fact their success was such that soon a play on words came to call them the *domini*

Gerhard H. Waldherr (Regensburg: Universitätsverlag Regensburg, 1997), 79–88; Georg Steer, "Bettelorden-Predigt als 'Massenmedium,'" in *Literarische Interessenbildung im Mittelalter*, ed. Joachim Heinzle (Stuttgart: Metzler, 1993), 314–36.

[6] *Richeri Gesta Senoniensis Ecclesiae von Sens*, MGH SS 25, 306.

[7] Humbert de Romanis, *De eruditione praedicatorum, II. De modo prompte cudendi sermones circa omne hominum et negotiorum genus*, ed. Marguerin La Bigne, Maxima bibliotheca veterum patrum, vol. 25 (Lyon, 1677), no. 72, 491–92.

[8] Bernhard Stüdeli, *Minoritenniederlassungen und mittelalterliche Stadt* (Werl: Dietrich-Coelde, 1969); Norbert Hecker, *Bettelorden und Bürgertum* (Frankfurt am Main: Peter Lang, 1981); Ingo Ulpts, "Die Mendikanten als Konkurrenz zum Weltklerus zwischen Gehorsamsgebot und päpstlicher Exemption," *Wissenschaft und Weisheit* 66 (2003): 190–227; Jacques Le Goff, "Apostolat mendiant et fait urbain dans la France médiévale. L'implantation des ordres mendiants," in Jacques Le Goff, *Héros du Moyen Âge, le saint et le roi* (Paris: Gallimard, 2004), 1207–26; Jens Röhrkasten, "The Early Franciscans and the Towns and Cities," in *The Cambridge Companion to Francis of Assisi*, ed. Michael Robson (Cambridge, UK: Cambridge University Press, 2012), 178–92.

[9] *Praedicatores Inquisitores*, vol. 1, *The Dominicans and the Mediaeval Inquisition: Acts of the 1st International Seminar on the Dominicans and the Inquisition (Rome; 23–25 février 2002)* (Rome: Istituto Storico Domenicano, 2004). See also Christine Ames, *Righteous Persecution* (Philadelphia: University of Pennsylvania Press, 2008), and (for a later period) Michael Tavuzzi, *Renaissance Inquisitors: Dominican Inquisitors and Inquisitorial Districts in Northern Italy, 1474–1527* (Leiden: Brill, 2007).

canes (the "dogs of the Lord"). The phrase is captured visibly on the walls of Santa Maria Novella in Florence, where Dominicans stand guard along the border between the church militant on earth and the church triumphant in heaven.

But there was another side to the story. Success fostered pride and a drive for still more success, as Birgitta's revelations would later lament. Some among the mendicant orders lost their way as they became accustomed to incomes, with money that "was begged for in greed, carelessly accepted, and still more carelessly used," as the Franciscan minister general Bonaventure (1221–1274) warned in light of the behavior of his fellow friars.[10] Above all, success was dangerous because of the envy it fostered. All across Europe, parish clergy increasingly voiced their concerns to their bishops. Priests faced a serious loss of surplice fees—fees charged for marriages, baptisms, and burials. They had also to fight the competition of so many indulgences offered in mendicant churches and saw the testamentary donations of their parishioners lost to Dominicans, Franciscans, and others.[11] More and more the intransigent position became standard: pastoral care was only to be carried out within the jurisdiction of the parish, even if this practice cut against the papacy's policy of promoting the mendicant orders.

These tensions came sharply to the fore in a place where both sides were active: the University of Paris.[12] In 1252 the professors there who were secular clergy sought to revoke the right that the Dominicans and Franciscans had won to occupy two teaching chairs

[10] Max Bierbaum, *BetteLorden und Weltgeistlichkeit an der Universität Paris: Texte und Untersuchungen zum literarischen Armuts- und Exemtionsstreit des 13. Jahrhunderts (1255–1272)*, Ep. Officiales 1.2 (Münster: Aschendorff, 1916), 245.

[11] Sickert, *Wenn Klosterbrüder,* 123–24. For exemplary structures, see Arnold L. Williams, "Relations between the Mendicant Friars and the Regular Clergy in England in the Later Fourteenth Century," in *Annuale Mediaevale* 1 (1960): 22–95; Jens Röhrkasten, *The Mendicant Houses of Medieval London: 1221–1539* (Münster: LIT, 2004), 257–76, 317–30; Robert N. Swanson, "The 'Mendicant Problem' in the Later Middle Ages," in *The Medieval Church: Universities, Heresy, and the Religious Life; Essays in Honour of Gordon Leff,* ed. Peter Biller and Richard B. Dobson (Woodbridge, UK: Boydell, 1999), 217–38.

[12] Bierbaum, *Bettelorden und Weltgeistlichkeit*; Anastasius van den Wyngaert, "Querelles du clergé séculier et des ordres mendiants à l'université de Paris au XIIIᵉ siècle," *La France Franciscaine* 5 (1922): 257–81, 369–97.

each, insisting that each be granted only one. For the mendicant orders it was a call to arms that threatened the core of their existence, because their high standards of pastoral care required a university education. In this respect, the Franciscans had followed the lead of the Dominicans. To limit their access to study undermined their pastoral mission—but that was precisely the intention of their opponents.

In 1255, through the intervention of Alexander IV, the mendicants prevailed. Although the Franciscans gave up the second university chair, the secular clergy's faction fought on. In the following year their spokesman, William of Saint Amour,[13] composed a massive polemic, "On the Dangers of the Last Days." In it he contested any right the mendicant orders claimed to offering pastoral care—and thereby their right to sustain themselves from it. Shortly thereafter William raised the stakes and came to attack begging itself as illegitimate, since religious were to live only from the work of their hands according to the words of Paul: "Anyone unwilling to work should not eat" (2 Thess 3:10). To become poor for the sake of Christ was honorable; to be an able-bodied beggar was despicable and sinful.[14] This attack called the justification for the existence of the Franciscans and Dominicans even more deeply into question. Their leaders therefore rose in opposition, offering up the most spirited defenders they could muster: Bonaventure (1221–1274)[15] for the Franciscans and Thomas Aquinas (1225–1274)[16] for the Dominicans. Convinced by their arguments yet also concerned to preserve established papal

---

[13] Michel-Marie Dufeil, *Guillaume de Saint-Amour et la polémique universitaire parisienne, 1250–1259* (Paris: Picard, 1972); Sita Steckel, "Ein brennendes Feuer in meiner Brust. Prophetische Autorschaft und polemische Autorisierungsstrategien Guillaumes de Saint-Amour im Pariser Bettelordenstreit (1256)," in *Prophetie und Autorschaft. Charisma, Heilsversprechen und Gefährdung*, ed. Christel Meier and Martina Wagner-Egelhaaf (Berlin: de Gruyter, 2014), 129–68.

[14] Ulrich Horst, *Wege in die Nachfolge Christi. Die Theologie des Ordensstandes nach Thomas von Aquin* (Berlin: Akademie, 2006), 57–58.

[15] Christopher M. Cullen, *Bonaventure* (Oxford: Oxford University Press, 2006); Timothy J. Johnson, *The Soul in Ascent: Bonaventure on Poverty, Prayer, and Union with God* (Quincy, IL: Francisco Press, 2001).

[16] Jean-Pierre Torrell, *Saint Thomas Aquinas*, vol. 1, *The Person and His Work* (Washington, DC: The Catholic University of America Press, 2005); Maximilian Forschner, *Thomas von Aquin* (Munich: C. H. Beck, 2006).

policy, Pope Alexander IV condemned William's work and repulsed his attack.

Hardly twenty years later the themes of this "Paris mendicant controversy," as it has come to be called, emerged once again. Papal decrees had been able partially to dampen but not to extinguish the fires of controversy. In 1274, the Council of Lyon was set to begin. In preparation the papal Curia entertained a remarkable number of petitions, many of them concerned with the affairs of the religious orders. Alongside petitions from the former Dominican master general Humbert of Romans (1194–1277)[17] and the Franciscan and Parisian theologian Guibert of Tournais (1200–1284),[18] Bruno of Schauenburg, bishop of Olomouc (in Moravia),[19] offered his own contribution to the discussion surrounding the mendicant orders. He pled anew on behalf of the secular clergy that the mendicants' rights be curtailed and that the bishops take a stronger stand, especially with regard to the founding of new communities. The Franciscans and Dominicans were protected by their strong position with the pope. But since the council was also concerned, as was noted above, to gauge the implementation of the decrees of Lateran IV, other mendicant orders found themselves in great danger. They stood in competition not only with the secular clergy but also with the two great mendicant orders.

One of the most successful of these orders, alongside the Franciscans and Dominicans, was the so-called Friars of the Sack, which had been founded by Raymond Athenulfi in Southern France in 1248.[20] Even though it numbered over one hundred communities by 1274

---

[17] Humbertus de Romanis, "Opusculum Tripartitum," in *Fasciculus rerum expetendarum et fugiendarum*, ed. Ortwin Gratius and Edward Brown (London, 1690), 2:185–29.

[18] Guibert de Tournai, "Collectio de scandalis ecclesiae," ed. Autbert Stroick, *Archivum Franciscanum Historicum* 24 (1931): 36–62.

[19] Bruno von Holstein-Schauenburg, "Relatio de statu Ecclesiae in regno Alemannie," in *MGH Constitutiones III*, 589–94; Sickert, *Wenn Klosterbrüder*, 78–81.

[20] Kaspar Elm, "Ausbreitung, Wirksamkeit und Ende der provençalischen Sackbrüder (Fratres de Poenitentia Jesu Christi) in Deutschland und den Niederlanden. Ein Beitrag zur kurialen und konziliaren Ordenspolitik des 13. Jahrhunderts," in Elm, *Vitasfratrum*, ed. Dieter Berg (Werl: Dietrich-Coelde, 1994), 67–120; Frances Andrews, *The Other Friars* (Woodbridge, UK: Boydell, 2006), 175–223.

and had been both approved and granted preaching rights by Popes Innocent IV and Alexander IV in 1251 and 1255, respectively, it fell victim to episcopal polemic and was disbanded by the council. The Carmelites and Augustinian Hermits remained on the waiting list, so to speak, until the uncertainty over their legal foundations could be clarified. Only in 1298 did Pope Boniface VIII definitively resolve the issues, ruling that both orders would retain their legitimacy because they had been founded before the Fourth Lateran Council.[21] The struggle to construct a deeper past that reached beyond memory had been worthwhile; the spiritual sons of Elijah and Augustine could not be simply wished away.

The Dominicans emerged from this struggle for existence in a stronger position. The situation for the Franciscans, in contrast, was much more precarious—the fundamental question of voluntary poverty had remained unresolved from the Parisian conflict down to the close of the council. The issue was not only essential to their religious identity; during that era it was also more and more a point of constant internal dissension that gravely threatened the Order.

The roots of that conflict had already been laid amid the controversy over Francis's burial and the annulment of his Testament. The first divergences from the Poverello's vision of poverty had already been allowed by then, until Innocent IV clarified the issue in 1245 with the legal fiction that all property of the Order was to be owned by the Roman church.[22] There was opposition to that kind of thinking within the Order from the beginning. It drew from the Joachimite tradition to articulate the ideal of a purity of spirit reached through poverty. Even the Dominican Vincent of Beauvais, as was noted above, had placed his trust in that vision. As a consequence Bonaventure, as minister general at the time of the Parisian controversies, had both to defend Franciscan justifications for poverty and also to fight against those in the Order who believed in a future that was both without a propertied church and led by Franciscans.

---

[21] On the Carmelites, see *Bullarium Carmelitanum* (Rome, 1715), 1:48–49. On the Augustinian Hermits, see *Bullarium eremitarum sancti Augustini* (Rome, 1628), 44.

[22] Bull "Ordinem vestrum," ed. *Bullarium Franciscanum* (Rome, 1754), 1:400–402. On the following, see Helmut Feld, *Franziskus von Assisi und seine Bewegung* (Darmstadt: Wissenschaftliche Buchgesellschaft, 2007), 455–63.

After extended consultation, Pope Nicholas III (earlier cardinal protector of the Franciscans) issued the decree *Exiit qui seminat* in 1279.[23] With it he hoped to bring all of the conflicting positions more closely into harmony. He defended evangelical poverty as an indispensable foundation for the Order and once again differentiated decisively between ownership and rights of use. He thereby allowed the Order moderate use (*usus moderatus*) of what had become its rich accumulation of monasteries, churches, and other properties. The adherents of strict poverty were bitterly disappointed. They feared a further decline in discipline, something that had in fact already been palpable soon after Bonaventure's death.[24]

In the southern French figure Peter John Olivi (1247/48–1298),[25] a disciple of Bonaventure, the Order's greatest theologian, the defenders of poverty found a decisive and intellectually refined advocate. Olivi's spiritual aim was, by way of contemplative immersion in God, to approach the evangelical perfection that the Joachimite tradition said could be realized in the third age of the Holy Spirit. In the poverty of Francis, he saw the possibility of laying the foundations for that age and of being set free from all worldly ties. He called for more than a moderate use of poverty; he required what he called *usus pauper*, a "poor use" that was restricted to only those things most necessary for survival. Because the majority of the Order, the "community," saw his stance as all too extreme, Olivi was forced to defend himself at the general chapter of Montpellier in 1287. But no one was able to bring him to renounce his views. On the contrary, his circle of supporters began to grow rapidly, and soon a transregional

[23] Bull "Exiit qui seminat," *Bullarium Franciscanum* 3:404–17.

[24] On the following, see David Burr, *The Spiritual Franciscans* (University Park: Pennsylvania State University Press, 2003); Feld, *Franziskus von Assisi*, 486–501; Jürgen Miethke, "Der 'theoretische Armutstreit' im 14. Jahrhundert. Papst und Franziskanerorden im Konflikt um die Armut," in *Gelobte Armut*, ed. Heinz-Dieter Heimann (Paderborn: Schöningh, 2012), 243–84. On Franciscan self-understanding in the early years, see Thomas Ertl, *Religion und Disziplin* (Berlin: de Gruyter, 2006); on the juridical discussion over the position of the Minorites in the time thereafter, see Andrea Bartocci, *Ereditare in povertà. Le successioni a favore dei frati minori e la scienza giuridica nell'età avignonese (1309–1376)* (Naples: Jovene editore, 2009).

[25] *Pierre de Jean Olivi—philosophe et théologien*, ed. Catherine König-Pralong (Berlin: de Gruyter, 2010).

movement had taken shape within the Order. Its adherents came to be called the Spirituals.[26]

The election of Peter of Morrone as Pope Celestine V brought hope above all to an Italian faction under the leadership of Angelo Clareno (ca. 1245–1337), who came to be the herald of the movement, so to speak, with his work *On the Seven Tribulations of the Minorites* (*De VII tribulationibus Ordinis minorum*).[27] But Celestine's successor Boniface VIII then revoked Angelo's permission to found his own branch of the Order. Under the designation "The Poor Hermits of Lord Celestine" (*Pauperes Eremiti Domini Coelestini*), Angelo would have established the Testament and the Rule of Francis as the only legitimate normative foundation for the Franciscan life and would have brought about a re-markable, consequential reversal of the usual evolution from hermit to mendicant. Many Spirituals, Angelo Clareno among them, thus chose to retreat into solitude, especially in southern Italy; there, as so-called Fraticelli, they were constantly hounded by inquisition.[28]

Ubertino of Casale (1259–ca. 1328),[29] a disciple of Olivi, took over after his teacher's death in 1298. The tensions in the Order had already begun to sharpen when in 1295 Boniface VIII deposed the minister general and Spiritual sympathizer Raymond Gaufredi. Ubertino depicted the pope as the Antichrist, as the "first beast" of the Apocalypse. Others subsequently declared Nicholas III a heretic because he had interpreted the Rule of Francis, whereas according to the Poverello Francis it was the word of Christ. Even Olivi had already warned against such an extreme position.

But under Clement V, who was already holding court in Avignon, the scales seemed to tip in the direction of the Spirituals, and the pope wanted to move decisively to restore unity to the Order. Ubertino had

---

[26] Dieter Berg, "Spiritualismus und Fundamentalismus," in *Konfessionelle Pluralität als Herausforderung*, ed. Joachim Bahlcke et al. (Leipzig: Leipziger Universitätsverlag, 2006), 35–54; David Burr, *Olivi and Franciscan Poverty: The Origins of the* Usus Pauper *Controversy* (Philadelphia: University of Pennsylvania Press, 1989).

[27] *Angelo Clareno Francescano* (Spoleto: Centro italiano di studi sull'alto Medioevo, 2007).

[28] Gian Luca Potestà, *Angelo Clareno. Dai poveri eremiti ai fraticelli* (Rome: Istituto storico italiano per il Medio Evo, 1990).

[29] Charles T. Davis, "Ubertino da Casale and His Conception of *Altissima Paupertas*," *Studi medievali* 22 (1981): 1–56.

written a treatise on the depraved state of the Order. It brought him into the public fray, and in fact it earned him a papal audience. But since no solution could be reached internally, in 1312 the arguments were aired before the Council of Vienne (the same gathering that later oversaw the dissolution of the Templars).[30] Now the debates over Franciscan poverty had become an affair for all of Western Christendom. The council seems to have decided on a more strict interpretation of the issue. It established explicitly that the brothers, by virtue of their vows, were to be bound to "strict or poor uses [*ad arctos usus seu pauperes*] of those things that are expressly noted in the Rule."[31] Accordingly, the Order's communities were not allowed to accept bequests or own vineyards, and they were to erect only plain buildings. The theological question of how the poverty of the Franciscans related to the poverty of Christ—a point Francis himself would never have even considered worthy of reflection—was excluded, and mutual accusations of heresy were forbidden. But this was precisely the most virulent problem of the day, and what might at first have appeared to the Franciscans as a victory after a brief time suddenly became a tragedy.

Pope John XXII, who came to the papal throne in 1316, took a sharply hostile stance against the Spirituals.[32] When by 1316 tensions had turned to physical altercations between hostile parties in both Provence and eastern Languedoc, the new minister general Michael of Cesena (1270–1342)[33] had a few ringleaders from among the Spirituals brought before the pope in Avignon. They were handed over to inquisitors in Marseilles; four remained firm in their convictions and were burned in 1318.

---

[30] Alain Demurger, *Der letzte Templer: Leben und Sterben des Grossmeisters Jacques de Molay* (Munich: C. H. Beck, 2005); Malcom Barber, *The Trial of the Templars* (Cambridge, UK: Cambridge University Press, 1978).

[31] Josef Wohlmuth, ed., *Dekrete der ökumenischen Konzilien*, vol. 2, *Konzilien des Mittelalters* (Paderborn: Schöningh, 2000), 400.

[32] On the following, see Feld, *Franziskus von Assisi*, 496–501; Jürgen Miethke, "Papst Johannes XXII. und der Armutstreit," in *Angelo Clareno Francescano*, 263–313.

[33] Roberto Lambertini, "Das Geld und sein Gebrauch. Pecunia im Streit zwischen Michael von Cesena und Papst Johannes XXII," in *Geld im Mittelalter. Wahrnehmung—Bewertung—Symbolik*, ed. Klaus Grubmüller and Markus Stock (Darmstadt: Wissenschaftliche Buchgesellschaft, 2005), 216–43.

But the drama did not end there. In 1321 and 1322 the Curia engaged in a debate over the question of Christ's poverty that had been passed over at Vienne. The Franciscan Order as a whole feared a hostile papal decision, and at its general chapter in Rimini in 1322 it therefore adopted the position that the absolute poverty of Christ and the apostles was orthodox Catholic doctrine. The pope saw immediately how that position undermined the legitimacy of both the propertied church and his own position as vicar of Christ. The debate had thus returned to where it had earlier been decided, in favor of the message of Francis: all that was needed to be poor and to follow a poor Christ was to live according to the Gospel. John XXII, however, disagreed with the Poverello. He declared the Franciscan claim that Christ had been without possessions to be heretical. He also now forced the Franciscans to own their property and absolved the Holy See of the responsibility for owning any of the Franciscans' goods. All that Innocent IV's fiction had allowed the Roman church to hold in trust after 1245 now flowed back to the Franciscans, who suddenly found themselves, in legal terms, extremely wealthy.

The struggle continued until the death of John XXII in 1334.[34] Michael of Cesena and other Franciscans, among them the famous scholastic philosopher and theologian William of Ockham, made their way to Munich and gave their allegiance to the most crucial political opponent of the pope, Emperor Ludwig the Bavarian.[35] The overwhelming majority of leading Franciscans, however, submitted themselves to John XXII, and in 1329 they elected a general minister who would be loyal to him.

Despite the reforms undertaken by Benedict XII (a subject to be discussed in the next chapter) a number of forces contributed to a further decline in the Order's discipline: a relaxation of the ideal of

[34] See Filippo Sedda, *Veritatem sapientis animus non recusat. Testo fraticellesco sulla povertà contro Giovanni XXII. Studio ed edizione critica* (Rome: Antonianum, 2008); Melanie Brunner, "Pope John XXII and the Franciscan Ideal of Absolute Poverty," PhD dissertation, University of Leeds, 2010, http://etheses.whiterose.ac.uk./1095.

[35] Michael Menzel, "Weltstadt mit Geist? Marsilius von Padua, Michael von Cesena, Bonogratia von Bergamo und Wilhelm von Ockham in München," in *Bayern und Italien: Kontinuität und Wandel ihrer traditionellen Bindungen*, ed. Hans-Michael Körner and Florian Schuller (Lindenberg: Wilhelm Fink, 2010), 88–102.

poverty, the all-too-powerful influence of local urban environments on the affairs of local communities, and the confusion unleashed on the orders by the Great Schism of the West, which divided both the church and the religious orders for several decades, from 1378 to the Council of Constance in 1414/15. But the ideal of living out the poverty of Christ was never entirely extinguished.[36] From the end of the fourteenth century a movement emerged that sought once again to adhere strictly to the Rule of Francis, thus a movement of strict observance. Under that name, and with the powerful leadership of figures like Bernardino of Siena (1380–1444), a new Franciscan family, the Observants, began to separate itself out and to develop its own hierarchy. Soon its houses numbered in the hundreds. Beginning in the time of the Council of Constance (1414–1418) and later bolstered by the privileges of Eugene IV in 1446, this family won institutional independence from the traditional Franciscan community, the so-called Conventuals.

[36] Duncan B. Nimmo, "The Franciscan Regular Observance: The Culmination of Medieval Franciscan Reform," in *Reformbemühungen und Observanzbestrebungen im spätmittelalterlichen Ordenswesen*, ed. Kaspar Elm (Berlin: Duncker & Humblot, 1989), 189–205. See also Nimmo's full-length study *Reform and Division in the Medieval Franciscan Order: From Saint Francis to the Foundation of the Capuchins*, 2nd ed. (Rome: Capuchin Historical Institute, 1995).

15

Reformers and Reforms at the End
of the Middle Ages

Reform from Above: Pope Benedict XII

The events described above demonstrate once again the strength
that the papacy could by now bring to bear in matters concerning
the religious orders.[1] In the twelfth century the popes had been concerned to provide protection for fledgling congregations and orders,
including the privilege of exemption from local bishops. They also
stood ready to lend their approval whenever circumstances proved
threatening to the orders' progress, as in the case of the Cistercians,
for example, or when an impetus toward consolidation was necessary
in the wake of the loss of a charismatic founder, as in the case of the
Premonstratensians. In the thirteenth century, in contrast, popes like
Innocent III had already begun to create new orders and to exercise
control over new foundations by way of universally valid legislation, such as that of Lateran IV. In relation to the religious orders,
the papacy was no longer merely the highest spiritual authority. It
was also, in an institutional sense, the highest and quite inescapable
authority with regard to approval, correction, and interpretation. A
visible sign of this power was the fact that individual communities
alone were no longer handed over to the See of Saint Peter. Rather,
entire orders (for example, the Franciscans) allied themselves with

---

[1] Paravicini Bagliani, *Il trono di Pietro. L'universalità del papato da Alessandro III a Bonifacio VIII* (Rome: Carocci, 1996), 121.

the pope.[2] Old instruments of monastic exemption were also now deployed to cover entire orders.[3]

Over against the general laws of the church (*ius commune*), individual religious communities naturally preserved their own rights (*ius particulare*) as well as the authority to develop their own laws. In 1245, the canonist Godfrey of Trano correctly characterized the varying subjects of monastic "particularities" that had thereby emerged: "But because different observances and statutes have been established [in the orders], they provide a better guide to the legal circumstance of religious life than the general laws of the church."[4] Regardless of these many different legal situations, the popes nevertheless sought to enforce their power of governance, which rested on the primacy of their jurisdiction, by intervening directly in the particular law of each order.

The Franciscans provided just one illustration of this dynamic. In that instance, popes like Gregory IX and Nicholas III had even nullified the normative text of a founder and subjected another text to a binding exegesis. Yet Gregory IX reformed by decree the constitutional structure of the Cluniacs, the Grandmontines, the Premonstratensians, and the regular canons of Arrouaise; Clement IV did the same with the Cistercians. The list could go on.[5]

None of these congregations and orders, whether in the thirteenth or in later centuries, was ever able to develop the kind of sovereign self-confidence that had characterized the *ecclesia Cluniacensis*—an open model, within a closed world order, that could represent all of monastic life. But many congregations were certainly able to preserve an identity that at its core represented a world distinct from that of

---

[2] *Il papato duecentesco e gli ordini mendicanti*, ed. Enrico Menestò (Spoleto: Centro italiano di studi sull'alto Medioevo, 1998), 23–80.

[3] Michele Maccarrone, "Riforma e sviluppo della vita religiosa con Innocenzo III," *Rivista di storia della chiesa in Italia* 16 (1962): 29–72.

[4] Goffredus da Trani, *Summa super titulis decretalium* (Lyon, 1519; repr. Aalen: Scientia, 1992), fol. 154[V]; Gert Melville, "'Diversa sunt monasteria et diversas habent institutiones.' Aspetti delle molteplici forme organizzative dei religiosi nel Medioevo," in *Chiesa e società in Sicilia. I secoli XII–XVI*, ed. Gaetano Zito (Turin: Società editrice internazionale, 1995), 323–45, here 332.

[5] Jan Ballweg, *Konziliare oder päpstliche Ordensreform. Benedikt XII. und die Reformdiskussion im frühen 14. Jahrhundert* (Tübingen: Mohr Siebeck, 2001), 69–74.

the ecclesiastical hierarchy. Thus while individual orders, such as the Carthusians, sought to distance themselves from every kind of external reform,[6] others delayed or resisted reform, or at least sought to correct it. In 1233 Gregory IX, for example, had to initiate his reform of the Cluniacs a second time after the monks had successfully resisted the implementation of a first bull issued the previous year, one that had placed their old competitors, the Cistercians, in a supervisory role over them.[7] Even confident and legally sophisticated popes, for all their power, recognized that it was best to be diplomatic about such sensitive issues. A figure such as John XXII was in this respect (as in other areas of ecclesiastical politics) probably an exception.

All that has been outlined here provided the essentials of a procedural starting point for the Cistercian monk and pope Benedict XII as he designed a major initiative to reform the religious orders in the 1330s—the most comprehensive initiative of its kind to that point.[8] It was his intention, speaking generally, to arrest a seemingly pervasive decline of morality and discipline through strict statutes, through an emphasis on education, through better regulation of the use of material goods, and through improvement of procedures of oversight and decision making. He pursued these goals with an often obsessive attention to detail. For example, as the texts of the reform decrees make clear, he sought to regulate precisely the length of time that Benedictines studied at the University of Paris.[9] He also sought to combat the Cistercian custom, increasingly common from the thirteenth century, of partitioning the common dormitory into individual cells: "No longer should anyone build individual cells in a dormitory. And those already built should be torn down within

[6] Florent Cygler, "Cartusia numquam reformata? La réforme constitutionelle de l'ordre cartusien au XIIIe siécle," in *Studia monastica. Beiträge zum klösterlichen Leben im christlichen Abendland während des Mittelalters*, ed. Reinhardt Butz and Jörg Oberste (Münster: LIT, 2004), 47–72.

[7] Franz Neiske, "Das Verhältnis Clunys zum Papsttum," in *Die Cluniazenser in ihrem politisch-sozialen Umfeld*, ed. Giles Constable et al. (Münster: LIT, 1998), 279–320.

[8] On the following, see Franz J. Felten, "Die Ordensreformen Benedikts XII. unter institutionsgeschichtlichem Aspekt," in *Institutionen und Geschichte*, ed. Gert Melville (Cologne: Böhlau, 1992), 369–435; Ballweg, *Konziliare oder päpstliche Ordensreform*.

[9] Ballweg, *Konziliare oder päpstliche Ordensreform*, 265.

three months following the promulgation of this apostolic decree. The visitors will oversee the matter."[10] The latter issue seems almost an afterthought; but in reality it represented a breach of norms that symbolized a declining emphasis on values like communal spirit and discipline.

In light of the sheer variety of organizational forms across the orders, a reform project like this was anything but a simple undertaking, even though the pope, with the aid of separate commissions, took counsel from a range of stakeholders:[11] from the abbot of Cîteaux and the three Cistercian primary abbots, for example; from six Benedictines who were also scholars of canon law; from the general minister, six provincial ministers, and the procurator of the Franciscans, as well as other theologians from that Order, and so on. Benedict XII then issued three extensive reform decrees in rapid succession: on July 12, 1335, *Fulgens sicut stella* for the Cistercians, his own Order; on June 20, 1336, *Summi Magistri* for the Benedictines; on November 28, 1336, *Redemptor noster* for the Franciscans; and, after a brief delay, a fourth on May 15, 1339, *Ad decorem* for the regular canons.[12]

In the prologues of these bulls, Benedict was notably concerned to build consensus for his project and to create the impression that he acknowledged the merits of earlier initiatives, even as he now sought to advance his own thoroughgoing reforms. So, for example, his bull for the Cistercians used a text taken from the Old Testament (Sir 50:6) to flatter their order. It opened with the words *Fulgens sicut stella matutina*, "Shining like the morning star among the clouds," and then continued, "the holy Cistercian Order is at work at the heart of the Church Militant through word and example."[13] Pope Benedict in

---

[10] Bull "Fulgens sicut stella," chap. 24; trans. from *Neuerung und Erinnerung, Wichtige Quellentexte aus der Geschichte des Zisterzienserordens vom 12. bis 17. Jahrhundert*, ed. Hildegard Brem and Alberich M. Altermatt (Langwaden: Bernardus-Verlag, 2003), 247.

[11] Felten, "Die Ordensreformen Benedikts XII," 375.

[12] Bull "Summi magistri," ed. *Magnum Bullarium Romanum*, 3.2 (Rome, 1741), 214–40; Bull "Fulgens sicut stella," ed. *Magnum Bullarium Romanum*, 3.2, 203–13; Bull "Ad decorem," ed. *Magnum Bullarium Romanum*, 3.2, 264–86; Bull "Redemptor noster," ed. in Michael Bihl, "Ordinationes a Benedicto XII pro Fratribus Minoribus promulgatae per bullam Nov. 18, 1336," *Archivum Franciscanum Historicum* 30 (1937): 309–90.

[13] Trans. from *Neuerung und Erinnerung*, 217.

turn sought to win over the regular canons by reinforcing their self-understanding of renewal through apostolic community by tying their way of life back to the earliest days of the church and by reassuring them that he would change nothing of the timeless essentials of their institutions, only establishing something new insofar as it might be useful to them. But at the same time, the pope also intentionally pointed them back to the "holiness of their origins"[14] and noted that the distance between those foundations and the present had fostered much that might be in need of reform.

Benedict XII's intentions as a reformer involved no changes that required any fundamental recasting of the orders' core ideals. He sought only to reinforce normative structures, so to speak, in both those places that promised to have direct practical impact and that had special symbolic meaning. Nevertheless, his project often faced fierce resistance. The Carthusians remained inaccessible, because they stood as always on their reputation as the strictest order. But the Dominicans, too, successfully resisted any papal effort at reform. Their arguments rested not on any claim like that of the Carthusians that their order was in no need of reform. Rather, they noted the decree of Pope Alexander IV in 1255 confirming the sovereignty of Dominican legal foundations.[15] Their constitutions, which reflected the identity of the Order, guaranteed an independent enforcement of reform. The Milanese Dominican and historian Galvaneus Fiamma,[16] who was among the sharpest polemicists against the program of Benedict XII, founded his arguments precisely on this principle, declaring that were they to accept interference in their affairs from a papal reform, they would be abdicating their legislative autonomy.

The other orders' reception of Benedict's reform bulls was something less than ideal.[17] The Franciscans, for example, in fact promulgated his decree at their general chapter in 1337 but thereafter allowed it to fall into oblivion. Among the Benedictines—whose history always resists generalization, who aside from Cluny knew

[14] Ballweg, *Konziliare oder päpstliche Ordensreform*, 263.

[15] Ballweg, *Konziliare oder päpstliche Ordensreform*, 236–39.

[16] Volker Hunecke, "Die kirchenpolitischen Exkurse in den Chroniken des Galvaneus Flamma OP (1283–ca. 1344). Einleitung und Edition," *Deutsches Archiv für Erforschung des Mittelalters* 25 (1969): 111–208.

[17] Felten, "Die Ordensreformen Benedikts XII," 411–20; Ballweg, *Konziliare oder päpstliche Ordensreform*, 310–14.

no Europe-wide congregations, and who had to this point never lost their decisive character as independent monasteries—the reforms that provincial chapters (among others) had prescribed for them (as the Fourth Lateran Council had done) met with a widely varied reception. In England, provincial chapters were held steadily over the coming centuries. In Germany they were held continually only in certain regions, though Benedict's initiatives had some impact on the later emergence of reform congregations in the region, as will be discussed below. In France, the outbreak of the Hundred Years' War stopped every reform initiative before it could even begin. Finally, even the Cistercians failed to ensure the lasting success of the reform measures of a fellow Cistercian, since the content of his bull was never taken up in subsequent Cistercian legislative collections.

In light of such a discrepancy between, on the one hand, the effort to prepare for reform, a strong commitment to reform on the part of a pope fully empowered to enact it, and such an evident need for reform, and on the other hand, such disappointing results, questions arise about the failure of the endeavor.[18] The causes can neither be traced in technical details nor pursued in the complexities of the orders' internal lines of communication, where individual communities made all of the important decisions about the adoption of new norms. Rather, the causes of failure can be found in a fundamental miscalculation of the effectiveness of reform "from above" in orders and communities whose oldest houses had developed their own local customs over centuries and even whose youngest organizations had existed for some two hundred years.

Reformers of an earlier era, who had once set the zeal of inner piety against the "pharisaical" ways of traditional Benedictines, had relied on both the power of charismatic leadership and the stabilizing force of external instruments of institutional organization that they themselves had formulated and created. They were convinced that both were necessary to preserve the energy of the early days of their institutions. The reforms of Benedict XII were conceived in a fundamentally different way. Little was expected from within the orders and communities themselves, and the pope had instruments that could only impose order superficially. But above all, reform was no longer driven by a desire to preserve the zeal of new beginnings.

---

[18] Felten, "Die Ordensreformen Benedikts XII," 420–35.

Rather, it aimed to reanimate what had become settled institutions. Only a comparison with later reform movements can clarify whether Benedict failed, whether the orders and communities his reforms addressed were responsible for the failure, or whether they could still be reformed at all. Perhaps many had already long been on the search for new forms of religious life or new content in old forms. The lay movements of the day, the *Devotio moderna*, the variety of independent pursuits of solitude, and the founding of entirely new orders with their own rules, such as the Birgittines—all showed something of the possibilities.

In any case, a reform of long-established structures was once again soon under way. Benedict XII had certainly properly recognized the need, and the vision articulated in Birgitta's *Revelations* of the desolate vineyard of the Lord also had its justification. In the old communities of Benedictine observance, as well as in the orders of the twelfth and thirteenth centuries, discipline had slowly but increasingly faltered. Monasteries no longer stood as representatives of Paradise on earth. They were bound all the more to earthly affairs whenever they failed radically to complete their turn from the world by renouncing all that had come before, whenever they continued to maintain family ties, as was common in both the cities and the countryside, and whenever their members lived more as nobles or patricians than as monks and nuns. Without inner conviction and without the pressure of external sanctions, there could be no progress toward heaven.

On the contrary, worldly ways became comfortably settled in monastic communities as a long-established way of life. Ascetic commitments invariably became somnolent, along with commitments to poverty, prayer, and meditation, as these were displaced by personal property, alienation of corporate goods, abandonment of chastity, pompous lifestyles, revelry, and so on. The stories told by outside observers, the work of satirists, and the relevant reports of the orders' visitations, are legion.[19] Responsible leaders of monas-

---

[19] For abundant material on this development, see Hans-Joachim Schmidt, "Klosterleben ohne Legitimität. Kritik und Verurteilung im Mittelalter," in *Institutionen und Geschichte. Festschrift für Gert Melville zum 65. Geburtstag*, ed. Franz J. Felten et al. (Cologne: LIT, 2009), 377–400; Ramona Sickert, *Wenn Klosterbrüder* (Münster: LIT, 2006).

tic communities, as well as bishops, popes, and holders of secular power in every epoch of the *vita religiosa* had seen such turns toward decay and decline—they were especially visible in the wake of the disintegration of Carolingian power, and then again amid the transformations of church reform unleashed by the Investiture struggle. From the twelfth century on, therefore, the orders used their statutes to establish and demonstrate their embrace of *semper reformare*, a program of perpetual reform.

In the last two centuries of the Middle Ages still more dangers, and new ones, emerged to threaten the life of the old religious houses in particular. As has already been noted, the attracting power of religious life had shifted away from them toward the newer apostolic orders— and also toward forms of life that made it possible for pious laity to gather in communities that rejected the "pharisaical" ways of old norms long since divorced from daily reality and in communities that instead sought God inwardly. Deeply anchored in the legal system of both the world and the church, as well as in regional structures of economy and lordship, the old monasteries were far more vulnerable to worldly influence than flexible lay communities or communities of hermits without property.

The fourteenth and fifteenth centuries brought severe challenges for religious communities—above all the Great Schism, which lasted for decades and unleashed divisions that reached down to the level of individual monasteries, and the Hundred Years' War, whose destruction was particularly devastating for the Cluniacs and Cistercians in France. Yet the reverse was also true: peace and economic prosperity brought dangers all their own. Rich abbeys quickly became coveted treasures. Of course they had always been so, and at the extreme they had even become the property of lay abbots. But now the papacy itself, and to a lesser extent territorial princes as well, had come to see these communities as prebends that they could give as political favors to high-ranking clerics and even to laity. In such cases, the income of a community, whether from landed property or other rights, would be handed over to a third party, designated as a so-called commendatory abbot,[20] who had no particular obligation

---

[20] Giorgio Picasso, "Commenda," in *Dizionario degli istituti di perfezione*, ed. Guerrino Pelliccia and Giancarlo Rocca (Rome: Edizioni Paoline, 1975), 2:1246–50.

toward the community itself—and for the most part no interest in its spiritual reform.

Not even the more structurally coherent orders were insulated from these trends. In fact, such dangers threatened the independent communities of Benedictines and Augustinian canons even more strongly than the other groups, since they were without the mutual support of a general chapter, an effective political center, or even a procurator. As Benedict XII had already noted in his decree for the Benedictines, *Summi magistri*, reform's chance of success was greater to the extent that it was tied to the formation of congregational networks.[21]

Reform from Below: The Rise of the Observants

In the central Italian community of Subiaco—which Gregory the Great had identified in the *Dialogues* as Benedict's first home as both a hermit and a founder of a religious community—one of the first transregional movements for Benedictine reform began in the 1360s. Established from two houses nestled on the slopes of the Apennines, Subiaco had already been reformed by Innocent III in 1202.[22] But the influence of the local nobility soon again turned the monks off of the right path, and by the early fourteenth century it was a completely broken community. After prodding by the papacy, which at first came to take an interest in the community above all because it was economically vital to the Papal States, Subiaco launched a series of reform projects that in the 1370s led finally to restabilization and to the recording of customs strongly rooted in the Benedictine tradition, the *Consuetudines Sublacenses.*[23] Those customs, in a way

[21] Klaus Schreiner, "Reformstreben im spätmittelalterlichen Mönchtum: Benediktiner, Zisterzienser und Prämonstratenser auf der Suche nach strenger Observanz ihrer Regeln und Statuten," in *Württembergisches Klosterbuch*, ed. Wolfgang Zimmermann and Nicole Priesching (Ostfildern: Thorbecke, 2003), 91–108.

[22] Uwe Israel, "Der Papst und die Urkunde an der Wand. Innocenz III. (1198–1216) in Subiaco," *Quellen und Forschungen aus italienischen Archiven und Bibliotheken* 84 (2004): 69–102; Annarita De Prosperis, "Innocenzo III e i monasteri di Subiaco," *Latium. Rivista di studi storici* 25 (2008): 3–30.

[23] Barbara Frank, "Subiaco, ein Reformkonvent des späten Mittelalters. Zur Erfassung und Zusammensetzung der Sublacenser Mönchsgemeinschaft in der Zeit von 1362 bis 1514," *Quellen und Forschungen aus italienischen Archiven*

that recalls Cluny's classical age, became what might be called "export commodities." On the one hand, Subiaco's way of life spread across all of Italy, through both new foundations and the reform of established communities, and on the other, it worked its way north of the Alps, above all into Germany, where at the turn of the fourteenth and fifteenth centuries it established important anchors for further Benedictine reform at both Kastl (Upper Palatinate [Bavaria]) and Melk (Lower Austria). Reform spread through both written texts and knowledge gained from personal experience, just as it had in an earlier era, for example, from Cluny to Farfa or Hirsau.

In 1403, Nicholas Seyringer (1360–1425), originally a canon of Olomouc in Moravia and from 1401 rector of the University of Vienna, had set out with three companions for Subiaco.[24] He hoped to be able to bring his scholarly work into fruitful harmony with a well-ordered ascetic life. After a ten-year stay, he went to S. Anna in Rocca di Mondragone, a dependent of Subiaco in Campania, and became its prior.

Soon afterward, in 1414, the Council of Constance began to work to end the Great Schism, as well as to advance fundamental reforms in the church and in monastic life.[25] The means to that end were different, however, from those used in Benedict XII's grand interventions. The council's reform plan sought to build from the ground up, using small constellations of communities that would serve as catalysts for wider reform. At an important conference held in the monastery of Petershausen[26] near Constance in 1417, the Benedictine abbots gathered there resolved to begin that process through a grandly conceived visitation initiative, its catalogue of mandatory questions formulated according to Benedict XII's *Summi Magistri*. The project enjoyed

---

und Bibliotheken 52 (1972): 526–656; Uwe Israel, "Reform durch Mönche aus der Ferne. Das Beispiel der Benediktinerabtei Subiaco," in *Vita communis und ethnische Vielfalt*, ed. Uwe Israel (Berlin: LIT, 2006), 157–78.

[24] Freimut Löser, "Nikolaus Seyringer von Matzen," *Neue Deutsche Biographie* 19 (1998): 274; Israel, "Reform durch Mönche," 172–74.

[25] Dieter Mertens, "Reformkonzilien und Ordensreform im 15. Jahrhundert," in *Reformbemühungen und Observanzbestrebungen im spätmittelalterlichen Ordenswesen*, ed. Kaspar Elm (Berlin: Duncker & Humblot, 1989), 431–57.

[26] Joseph Zeller, "Das Provinzialkapitel im Stifte Petershausen im Jahre 1417," *Studien und Mitteilungen zur Geschichte des Benediktinerordens und seiner Zweige* 41 (1921–22): 1–73.

the crucial support of the region's territorial princes, above all the Austrian Duke Albert V, not least because reforms always worked in the interests of a monastery's economic stability. The duke's representative was Nicholas of Dinkelsbühl, one of the leading theologians of the day and former rector of the University of Vienna, who had written a treatise (*Reformationis methodus*) on the prospects of reform in Austrian monasteries.[27] He instructed Nicholas Seyringer, whom he knew from Vienna, to take over the visitations in Austria.

Here two important reform initiatives of the fifteenth century had come together: on the one hand, the work of the Council of Constance, which was later continued at the Council of Basel after 1431, resulting in the first consolidation of Benedictine reform in Germany, and, on the other hand, the exemplary renewal of the way of life at Subiaco.

The abbot of the monastery of Melk on the Danube, faced with the demands of reform, resigned in 1418. Nicholas Seyringer was provisionally appointed as the new abbot and resigned his position as visitor. Thereafter began what would be a fifty-year flowering of Benedictine reform that centered on Melk and spread far beyond.[28] The spiritual core of the movement took its inspiration from Subiaco. Its hallmarks were strict preservation of the precepts of the Rule of Saint Benedict, with an emphasis on contemplation, on prayer both in private and in community, and on strict observance of silence, fasting, and total abstinence from meat. Also crucial was the total renunciation of individual ownership, a principle upheld so strictly that priests who entered the community were even required to renounce their prebends. Though at first these precepts were modeled after the customs of Subiaco, they provided a basis, after a period of adjustment, for Melk in 1460 to record its own community's norms: the *Caeremoniae regularis*

---

[27] Alois Madre, *Nikolaus von Dinkelsbühl: Leben und Schriften* (Münster: Aschendorff, 1965).

[28] On the following, see Joachim Angerer, "Reform von Melk," in *Die Reformverbände und Kongregationen der Benediktiner im deutschen Sprachraum*, ed. Ulrich Faust and Franz Quarthal (St. Otttilien: EOS, 1999), 83–95; Meta Niederkorn-Bruck, *Die Melker Reform im Spiegel der Visitationen* (Munich: Oldenbourg, 1994). See also the essays in *Die Benediktinische Klosterreform im 15. Jahrhundert*, ed. Franz Xaver Bischof et al. (Berlin: de Gruyter, 2013). For a thematic study of the tensions of reform, property, and community in this setting, see James D. Mixson, *Poverty's Proprietors* (Leiden: Brill, 2009).

Mellicensium.[29] Crucial as well were the monastery's close ties to the University of Vienna, a relationship that helped revive Melk's culture of writing, its library, liturgy, and theology.

From Melk this way of life spread to several dozen communities of women and men across southern Germany, reaching all the way to the diocese of Constance, where Melk reformers commissioned by the Council of Basel took over the task of visitation. In its ranks were now renowned communities like Tegernsee (in Upper Bavaria), which by that time had become one of the most important focal points for the reception of Italian humanism north of the Alps.[30] Saint Peter in Salzburg, Saints Ulrich and Afra in Augsburg, and the "Schottenstift" of Vienna were all reformed as well, and these monasteries in turn led the reform of others. Yet one thing failed to happen—and here the structural developments recall the story of the Hirsau reform long before: no legally established congregation emerged. The exchange of reform ideas and, building on that exchange, the establishment of networks of communication took place exclusively through time spent in Melk itself or through the sending out of monks from Melk to serve either as abbots in newly reformed communities or as visitors.[31]

The monks of Melk would thus find themselves at a decisive disadvantage with respect to the sustainability of their movement's momentum. The traditional independence of Benedictine houses was certainly at work here, even though after some three centuries of success in building new orders the path to organizational efficiency ought to have been clear. By around 1470 the potential of the Melk reform to influence other communities had already been spent.

The same weakness beset the Benedictine abbey of Kastl in the Palatinate. There a center of reform inspired by Benedict XII's decree *Summi Magistri* had already been established at the end of the fourteenth century, influenced both by reforming currents from

[29] *Caeremoniae regularis observantiae sanctissimi patris nostri Benedicti ex ipsius Regula sumptae, secundum quod in sacris locis, scilicet Specu et Monasterio Sublacensi practicantur*, ed. Joachim F. Angerer, CCM 11.1 (Siegburg: Schmitt, 1985).

[30] Winfried Müller, "Die Anfänge der Humanismusrezeption in Kloster Tegernsee," *Studien und Mitteilungen zur Geschichte des Benediktinerordens und seiner Zweige* 92 (1981): 28–90.

[31] Niederkorn-Bruck, *Die Melker Reform*, 36–40.

Bohemia and, later, by Subiaco. The support of territorial princes was again key in the rapid spread of reform, especially that of the Wittelsbach Count Palatine Rupert II.[32] Kastl's affiliates soon included such prestigious communities as Saint Emmeram in Regensburg, Michelsberg in Bamberg, Münsterschwarzach on the Main, and Saint Gall. Yet the ties among these communities were even looser than those among the communities reformed by Melk.

A more strictly organized congregation, one that approached the character of an order, first emerged in the middle of the fifteenth century from a reform initiative at the Benedictine abbey of Bursfelde on the Weser.[33] Here too reform depended on the support of a territorial prince, the Welf Duke Otto of Brunswick-Göttingen. Later Nicholas of Cusa, the cardinal legate and great humanist scholar, also became a notable supporter. In 1446, the Council of Basel gave its approval for the establishment of a congregation, and in 1453 Pope Nicholas V issued a decree of recognition, followed in 1459 by approval from Pope Pius II.

The core of this reform program, again, was precise observance of the Rule of Saint Benedict as well as a special cultivation of proper liturgy, which was made uniform across all of the monasteries of the congregation. Also central was a high degree of contemplative interiority and strict asceticism that in its details drew inspiration from Carthusian statutes. Trithemius, the renowned humanist and abbot of Sponheim, described the spirituality of Bursfelde in his 1497 work, *De triplici regione claustralium et spirituali exercitio monachorum*,[34] which contributed significantly to the spread of the reform.

Inspired by the ideal of "one body and one [uniting] chapter" (*unum corpus et capitulum*), in a short time a congregation of formerly independent abbeys was established. By 1530 it numbered

---

[32] On the following, see Peter Maier, "Die Reform von Kastl," in Faust and Quarthal, *Die Reformverbände*, 225–67.

[33] On the following, see Hans Walter Krumwiede, "Die Geschichte des Klosters Bursfelde," in *Kloster Bursfelde*, ed. Lothar Perlitt (Göttingen: Göttinger Tageblatt, 1984), 9–24; Walter Ziegler, "Die Bursfelder Kongregation," in Faust and Quarthal, *Die Reformverbände*, 315–407.

[34] Paulus Volk, "Ioannis Trithemii Liber de triplici regione claustralium," *Studien und Mitteilungen zur Geschichte des Benediktinerordens und seiner Zweige* 48 (1930): 446–52.

some ninety-four communities, among them such important houses as Saint Peter in Erfurt and Saint James in Mainz as well as Hirsau, Gembloux, and Corvey. The leadership of the congregation was strong, with a single president, yearly general chapters responsible for judicial affairs and legislation, and a central visitation modeled after (and having the same privileges as) Saint Giustina in Padua, which the Olivetans had reformed in an exemplary way in 1408.[35] Furthermore, over sixty women's communities joined the Bursfelde ranks, albeit without official standing within the congregation.

Yet not only the Benedictine communities embraced reform. The ideal of an inwardly driven return to observance of the earliest forms of religious life came by the end of the Middle Ages to encompass all varieties of the *vita religiosa*.[36]

So, for example, the Council of Basel commissioned the community of Windesheim with the reform of Augustinian canons and canonesses in Germany. Rising to prominence as one of the leaders of that project was John Busch (1399–1479/80), who had been assigned to the task by Nicholas of Cusa. The *Devotio moderna* spread to Italy as well, especially to Saint Salvatore in Laterano in Rome (from 1445/46), where the "Lateran Congregation" emerged and began to build new networks of reform all the way to East Central Europe.[37] Under the influence of the piety of *Devotio moderna*, the Carthusian Order also emerged anew as an attractive community that combined mysticism and learned humanism, its many houses located near the center of cities like Cologne, Basel, and Freiburg im Breisgau.[38]

---

[35] Giorgio Picasso, "La spiritualità dell'antico monachesimo alle origini di Monte Oliveto," in *Charisma und religiöse Gemeinschaften im Mittelalter*, ed. Giancarlo Andenna et al. (Münster: LIT, 2005), 443–52, here 443.

[36] For general orientation to these movements, with further literature, see the essays in Elm, *Reformbemühungen und Observanzbestrebungen*, as well as James Mixson and Bert Roest, eds., *A Companion to Observant Reform in the Late Middle Ages and Beyond* (Leiden: Brill, 2015). For broader contexts, see John Van Engen, "Multiple Options: The World of the Fifteenth-Century Church," *Church History* 77 (2008): 257–84.

[37] Wilhelm Kohl, "Die Windesheimer Kongregation," in Elm, *Reformbemühungen*, 83–106.

[38] Heinrich Rüthing, "Die Kartäuser und die spätmittelalterlichen Ordensreformen," in Elm, *Reformbemühungen*, 35–58; Thomas Woelki, "Die Kartäuser und das Basler Konzil," *Zeitschrift für Kirchengeschichte* 121 (2010): 305–22.

Reform took root in the mendicant orders in the second half of the fourteenth century as well, in a movement understood as a commitment to renewed observance, with essentials again centered on a return to the original ideals of each individual order and its rule. Inspired by the master general Raymond of Capua, Dominican reform began in 1390 and was led, for example, in Germany above all by the theologian John Nider (1385–1438), at the Council of Basel.[39] Among the Franciscans, who remained handicapped by the legacy of the Spirituals, a return to the core ideals of the Order's founder emerged both especially strongly in Foligno under the inspiration of Paolucci Trinci after 1368 and in eremitic retreat. But it was carried forward later in other centers of reform, above all under the leadership of Bernardino of Siena (1380–1444), and by the middle of the fifteenth century it had grown into what was in a certain sense a new order, the Observants.[40]

[39] Bernhard Neidiger, "Selbstverständnis und Erfolgschancen der Dominikanerobservanten. Beobachtungen zur Entwicklung in der Provinz Teutonia und im Basler Konvent (1388–1510)," *Rottenburger Jahrbuch für Kirchengeschichte* 17 (1998): 67–122. For Nider as a reformer, see Michael D. Bailey, *Battling Demons: Witchcraft, Heresy, and Reform in the Late Middle Ages* (University Park: Pennsylvania State University Press, 2003), and for reform of religious life, especially chapter 4. See also James D. Mixson, "The Setting and Resonance of John Nider's 'De reformatione religiosorum,'" in *Kirchenbild und Spiritualität: Dominikanische Beiträge zur Ekklesiologie und zum kirchlichen Leben im Mittelalter. Festschrift für Ulrich Horst O.P. zum 75. Geburtstag*, ed. Thomas Prügl and Marianne Schlosser (Paderborn: Schöningh, 2006), 291–317.

[40] Duncan B. Nimmo, "The Franciscan Regular Observance. The Culmination of Medieval Franciscan Reform," in Elm, *Reformbemühungen*, 189–205, and Nimmo, *Reform and Division in the Medieval Franciscan Order* (Rome: Capuchin Historical Institute, 1987). See also Ludovic Viallet, *Les sens de l'observance. Enquête sur les réformes franciscaines* (Berlin: LIT, 2014).

16

A Look Back

A walk through twelve centuries of history has shown that like the church generally, the world of the medieval monastery emerged from the culture of Late Antiquity and came to be established in every region of Western Christendom. In both monasteries and the church, Christian piety found universal expression. Yet while the church strove for unification, in the *vita religiosa* no single force was able to bind its widely divergent manifestations together coherently. The spectrum of possibilities for the world of monasticism was remarkably diverse. And that diversity had been established from the beginning. The *vita religiosa* had always divided itself along two lines, each corresponding to the fundamental ideals of being free from earthly concerns and of "having God always in view," as it was said, but along different paths: on the one hand, an eremitic life under the leadership of charismatic personalities who established norms by way of word and deed, and on the other hand, a cenobitic life in community, lived in enclosed spaces, that played out within fixed institutional forms grounded in a written rule.

All of this diversity was the result of remarkable flexibility in the face of ongoing changes in ideas and practices of piety, social needs, and conceptualizations of both individuality and community. Moreover, the full spectrum of the *vita religiosa* itself, together with all of the particular forms and institutions within it, was in fact part of the universal church, but as such it was either allowed a certain latitude in its affairs or bound to particular functions in remarkably divergent ways. In view of the constantly changing ecclesiological models of a church that experienced fundamental reform, a church that consolidated itself institutionally as the mediator of salvation, and that began to articulate legal distinctions between clergy and laity, the position of the *vita religiosa* changed considerably.

The changes in the world of medieval monasticism resulted, however, not only from outside influences. Much more decisive was that world's own internal dynamic, which emerged over the course of its many centuries. This dynamic inspired constant innovation in matters of spirituality and organization—in the years around 1200, for example, in the cultivation of lay piety. The same dynamic helped to refine and optimize all that was already to hand, as among the Dominicans, or to cultivate a return to supposedly ideal early forms, such as the apostolic community. In many cases these processes were of a decidedly experimental character, as was true among the new hermits of the eleventh and early twelfth centuries, but the story often enough had its share of failures—as, for example, in the case of the Friars of the Sack.

The world of monasticism appears as a rich and complex braid, one that formed itself from interwoven cycles, for example, the frequent return to specific centers of reform, or from shifting focal points of influence, as in the movement from the monastic community to the mendicant friary, or from the sometimes fierce competition that broke out between orders, as was true of the Cluniacs and Cistercians. There were also peripheral forces, hardly visible at first, that suddenly erupted, seen, for example, in the impact of the Rule of Augustine or the Rule of Saint Benedict, as well as supposedly dead ends that suddenly opened up new paths for development, like the congregation that emerged around Norbert of Xanten and became the Premonstratensian Order. Across a wide chronological span, too, this interweaving witnessed times of rupture (the Carolingian reforms), of transformation (the establishment of the regular canons), of continuation (the flowering of Cluny), and of acceleration, especially during the eleventh and twelfth centuries.

This world of diversity and change built itself up, as it were, from only a few basic but remarkably fruitful elements. To understand each of them is indispensable for a proper understanding of this complex historical braid.

A closing chapter of this book thus outlines its most important contours. It offers a systematically comparative view that focuses on the relationships between individual and community in the spiritual life of the monastery, the legal and normative range of the *vita religiosa*, modes of institutionalization ranging from charismatic leadership to the formal establishment of an order, the orders' historical self-consciousness, the mutual tensions between cloister and world, the worldly economic realities that sustained monastic life, and finally the search for knowledge and faith.

17

Fundamental Structures
of the *Vita Religiosa* in the Middle Ages

Medieval culture viewed the *vita religiosa* as a domain that in its totality was distinct from all other forms of Christian life. Early on, two formulas emerged that came to mark religious life's fundamental difference as an alternative to a worldly life. The first was articulated by Augustine (354–450), who developed the long-influential and biblically based model of the "three kinds of man" (*tria genera hominum*).[1] Typologically, Noah represented the clergy, Job the laity, and Daniel the religious, who like Daniel retreated from the tumult of society to serve God in leisure (*otium*) and who—as the Cistercian bishop Otto of Freising put it in the twelfth century—were "inwardly undisturbed by the ever-changing course of the world."[2]

Ambrose of Milan (339–397) articulated a second model. He was among the first to develop a distinction between the precepts (*praecepta*) and the counsels (*consilia*) of the New Testament.[3] That distinction came to inform assumptions about a fundamental division in Christian society between those who were expected only to follow the precepts (the laity and the clergy) and those who were also called to live out the counsels under vows of obedience, chastity, and poverty (the religious). To be obedient was to imitate Christ, who sub-

---

[1] Otto Gerhard Oexle, "Tria genera hominum. Zur Geschichte eines Deutungsschemas der sozialen Wirklichkeit in Antike und Mittelalter," in *Institutionen, Kultur und Gesellschaft im Mittelalter*, ed. Lutz Fenske et al. (Sigmaringen: Thorbecke, 1984), 488–94.

[2] See p. 184.

[3] Ambrose, *De viduis* 12.72ff., PL 16:243–76.

jected himself unconditionally to the will of the Father and thereby represented a turn to God in a spirit of unconditional love. To live in chastity was to overcome the body as a "grave of the soul,"[4] and to live in poverty in imitation of Christ was to embrace symbolically the contempt of the world. The rules of the orders in the High Middle Ages—for example, those of the Grandmontines and Franciscans, but above all thirteenth-century canon law—saw in the observance of these "evangelical counsels" the core essentials (*substantialia*) of the *vita religiosa*.[5] These concepts allowed the world of monasteries and orders to define itself clearly, to set itself apart, and to form a common identity.

Vita religiosa was understood as a way of life, regulated and lived in community, which led individual souls to holiness through an encounter with and assimilation to God. It thereby presented within broader Christian culture a model that was in principle desirable for all but in practice pursued by only a very few spiritual elite. To realize this way of life, religious houses and orders institutionalized themselves as strongly coherent systems of interaction between individuals and the community that bound them together. Yet for all of their appearance as "total institutions,"[6] it must not be overlooked that their distinctiveness lay precisely in the ways in which they cut across systemic boundaries.

There were two ways in which religious communities were something larger than their institutional framework. First, however strongly monastic life may have been established institutionally, however ordered and organized according to rules, however strictly led by its appointed officeholders, it was also always "institutionally tran-

---

[4] Thomas Füser, "Der Leib ist das Grab der Seele. Der institutionelle Umgang mit sexueller Devianz in cluniazensischen Klöstern des 13. und frühen 14. Jahrhunderts," in *De ordine vitae*, ed. Gert Melville (Münster: LIT, 1996), 187–245.

[5] For example, with Goffredus da Trani (1200–1245), *Summa super titulis decretalium* (Lyon, 1519) (repr. Aalen: Scientia, 1992), fol. 155^r. For an overview, see Gert Melville, "Zum Recht der Religiosen im 'Liber extra,'" *Zeitschrift der Savigny-Stiftung für Rechtsgeschichte. Kanonistische Abteilung* 118 (2001): 169–71, 173, 187–88.

[6] Erving Goffman, "The Characteristics of Total Institutions," in *A Sociological Reader on Complex Organizations*, ed. Amitai Etzioni (New York: Holt, Rinehart and Winston, 1969), 312–38.

scendent."[7] The ultimate aim of this way of life—to seek a direct encounter of the individual soul with God—was essentially impossible to capture definitively within any process of institutionalization, because that encounter had always to be achieved anew, uniquely and individually, through inward desire. No external institution could ever coerce a soul's sacrifice to God, and certainly no institution could offer spiritual fulfillment. The principle of free will was essential, because—as was so often emphasized—it was grounded in the love of the heart.

Second, since the sole function of monastic systems was to lead the individual soul to perfection in God, the ultimate purpose of the *vita religiosa* was not to be found in any aspect of earthly existence. As a result, its institutions had an essentially transitory character.[8] *Vita religiosa*, understood as a *vita perfectionis* (a "life of perfection"), was thus a life of transition, a temporary stopover for the individual soul between earth and heaven. The Rule of Saint Benedict, for example, thus spoke of a monastery as both a "school for the Lord's service" (*dominici schola servitii*) and as a "workshop" (*officina*). The worth of a religious community was not to be found in itself, however, but rather as a means to a higher end. For that reason, the individual could be expected to submit to its discipline for the sake of salvation, to seek freedom from earthly ties through it, and to devote life fully to the spiritual experience of divine transcendence.

That individual members believed in both the transcendent and the transitory character of their community allowed the monastery to serve its pragmatic function as a staging ground for reaching the world beyond, and that same belief thereby contributed in essential ways to keeping the community stable over many generations and eras.

The Individual and the Community

To be a religious was to bring divine transcendence into the individual soul and, through love and obedience, to allow God to dwell

---

[7] Peter von Moos, "Krise und Kritik der Institutionalität. Die mittelalterliche Kirche als 'Anstalt' und 'Himmelreich auf Erden,'" in *Institutionalität und Symbolisierung*, ed. Gert Melville (Cologne: Böhlau, 2001), 293–340, here 301–10.

[8] Gert Melville, "Im Spannungsfeld von religiösem Eifer und methodischem Betrieb. Zur Innovationskraft der mittelalterlichen Klöster," *Denkströme. Journal der Sächsischen Akademie der Wissenschaften* 7 (2011): 72–92, here 76–77.

there.[9] To achieve that goal required a renunciation of the external world and voluntary subjection to the strict rules of life in a monastery.

That monastery was understood, as Benedict's rule formulated it, as a "House of God" (*domus Dei*) (RB 31.19). But even if it provided a physical space for the development of an elite virtuosity in its spiritual encounter with divine transcendence, that space alone was not enough to secure salvation. Contemporaries invoked an often used phrase, "The habit does not make the monk" (*habitus non facit monachum*)—and the truth behind that phrase remained, no matter how often contemporaries tried to weigh down the cut and color of the habit with a symbolism that identified the individual not only as a religious in general but also as a member of a particular observance or monastic organization.[10] Black—so Arno of Reichersberg (1100–1157), who interpreted the colors of the habits typologically—represented the monk, who mourned Christ's death and therefore lived in contemplation, and white the regular canons, who rejoiced in resurrection and therefore lived actively in the world.[11]

The leading thinkers of religious life, particularly in the High Middle Ages, insistently emphasized that the main aim of their way of life was to build up the "inner household" of the soul as a temple of the Lord, as the "soul's cloister" (*claustrum animae*).[12] But the

---

[9] Gert Melville, "Im Zeichen der Allmacht. Zur Präsenz Gottes im klösterlichen Leben des hohen Mittelalters," in *Das Sichtbare und das Unsichtbare der Macht*, ed. Gert Melville (Cologne: Böhlau, 2005), 19–44.

[10] Peter von Moos, "Le vêtement identificateur. L'habit fait-il ou ne fait-il pas le moine?" in *Le corps et sa parure (The Body and Its Adornment)*, ed. Thalia Brero (Florence: SISMEL edizioni del Galluzzo, 2007), 41–60; Jörg Sonntag, *Klosterleben im Spiegel des Zeichenhaften* (Berlin: LIT, 2008), 94–119.

[11] Gerhoh von Reichersberg, *Liber de aedificio Dei*, PL 194:1270. The widespread allegorical typology of Mary (representing contemplation) and Martha of Bethany (representing the active life) was thereby also addressed. See Giles Constable, "The Interpretation of Mary and Martha," in *Three Studies in Medieval Religious and Social Thought* (Cambridge, UK: Cambridge University Press, 1995), 1–141.

[12] Gerhard Bauer, *Claustrum animae. Untersuchungen zur Geschichte der Metapher vom Herzen als Kloster* (Munich: Wilhelm Fink, 1973); Ineke van't Spijker, *Fictions of the Inner Life. Religious Literature and Formation of the Self in the Eleventh and Twelfth Centuries* (Turnhout: Brepols, 2004).

insights were essential and valid for every era and every form of the *vita religiosa*—in fact the texts that articulated those insights were not only shared across the boundaries of order and observance but also rested on traditions that went back to the earliest days of the church fathers and that had been upheld for centuries.[13]

Once a religious house had been established—so these texts concluded—the turn inward could be complete only if the soul was able to cease "from going out through the eyes, ears, and other senses, and from taking joy in external things."[14] God, after all, would not enter in, so went the powerful imagery, where "the walls are damaged and crumbling." It seemed impossible to establish a relationship with God if the soul could not abandon the impressions of the bodily senses and turn from all exterior things (*exteriora*).[15] Unconditional "alienation from the world" (*alienatio a saeculo*) was essential, because "earthly entanglements" (*implicamenta terrena*) kept every soul from turning fully to God.[16]

"Entering into the monastery, he gives skin for skin, and all that he has, his soul, as he puts off the old man and takes up the new, entering into a new form of life." With these words Peter of Celle, twelfth-century abbot of Moûtier-la-Celle, clearly articulated a view of the boundary between monastery and world.[17] The only way for an individual to cross that boundary was through a dramatic "conversion of the whole heart to God" (*conversio totalis ad Deum cordis*):[18] when chastity (*castitas*) became the marker of the unblemished beauty of holiness and demanded ascetic zeal in order to safeguard the health

---

[13] Mirko Breitenstein, "Der Transfer paränetischer Inhalte innerhalb und zwischen Orden," in *Die Ordnung der Kommunikation und die Kommunikation der Ordnungen im mittelalterlichen Europa*, vol. 1, *Netzwerke: Klöster und Orden im 12. und 13. Jahrhundert*, ed. Cristina Andenna et al. (Stuttgart: Franz Steiner, 2012), 37–53.

[14] *De interiori domo seu de conscientia aedificanda*, PL 184:509–10 (with the citation following).

[15] Gert Melville, "Im Zeichen der Allmacht. Zur Präsenz Gottes im klösterlichen Leben des hohen Mittelalters," in *Das Sichtbare und das Unsichtbare der Macht*, ed. Melville, 19–44, here 32–33.

[16] *Epistola cujusdam de doctrina vitae agendae*, PL 84:1187.

[17] *De disciplina claustrali*, ed. Gérard de Martel and Pierre de Celle, *L'école du cloître* (Paris: Éditions du Cerf, 1977), 192, 194.

[18] *Epistola cujusdam de doctrina vitae agendae*, PL 184:1187.

of both soul and body; when there was a call to embrace humility, fasting, and renunciation of meat, to embrace a silence that communicated only through a soundless sign language (*signa loquendi*), or to embrace contemplation and nightly vigils; when pride and arrogance (*superbia*) were denounced as the gravest vice; when humility (*humilitas*), envisioned in the Rule of Saint Benedict (7.7) as a ladder of twelve steps, was upheld as the highest virtue—only then were the essential demands of the new community and its way of life made clear, a way of life that could only be lived in the wake of such a *conversio*.

These were the fundamental patterns of an asceticism that required the commitment of the whole person; at the same time, they were norms that commanded absolute submission to the will of God. To want to be near God and to "assimilate" to him spiritually (as Bernard of Clairvaux put it)[19] could be realized, so it was emphasized, only through absolute acceptance of God's power. Yet at the same time, God was to be obeyed not out of fear, but out of love alone—in keeping with the example of Christ himself, who was obedient to his beloved father unto death. Disobedience, in contrast, was a kind of criminal idolatry, because it set up idols of the heart, insofar as disobedience against God was a lapse into the world that had been overcome—a lapse that turned a religious into a rebel against virtue and truth.[20]

Obedience was submission first to God and then to superiors in the monastery or the order,[21] even if the rhetorical force of most of the relevant didactic works seemed mostly to emphasize obedience to prelates. The justification here was found already in the Benedictine axiom that a religious superior was God's representative on earth. Yet precisely this foundational principle—one also found in other rules, such as the Rule of Augustine—in turn put limits on the power of a superior in decisive ways and required that the demands of obedience respect certain boundaries. Bernard of Clairvaux, for example, clearly articulated in *De praecepto et dispensatione* the principle that no monk professed according to the will of an abbot,

---

[19] Michaela Diers, *Bernhard von Clairvaux* (Münster: Aschendorff, 1991), 45–46.

[20] Melville, "Im Zeichen," 19–20; Sébastien Barret and Gert Melville, eds., *Oboedientia* (Münster: LIT, 2005). For an overview, see Sonntag, *Klosterleben*, 469–526.

[21] Constable, "Authority of Superiors."

but rather according to the Rule. As a consequence, while an abbot might in fact command things that were harsh or difficult to bear, he could in no way command something that was against the Rule and therefore against God.

Those who were subject to such commands, as has been emphasized above, could never be compelled to obey the dictates of communal life only by extrinsic norms and their punitive sanctions or by constant controlling interventions. Rather, obedience also required an inward acceptance of fundamental principles. Thus, despite the fact that an independent will had renounced itself in the service of absolute obedience, there was still an individual will that stood poised to obey.[22] It was a relationship that captured the full range of tensions (typical for religious life) between the intrinsic value of personal salvation and the need to subdue the individual will. And as such, it was a relationship that had to be both learned and continually trained.

It had been common, from the earliest days of monasticism, for parents or guardians to hand over even young children as oblates to a monastic community.[23] By means of a long process, the children would then become accustomed to current local customs and develop an inward disposition to accept their norms. But from the twelfth century on it became increasingly common that only adults entered religious life,[24] with the acceptable age of entry ranging between fourteen and twenty. For that reason, an important concern centered more than ever on how best to transform into monks and nuns those who had already oriented their lives according to their own values. Thus the novitiate, an initiation into daily monastic life whose length had already in Late Antiquity varied from a few days to three years, now took on much greater importance. The novitiate had to be sustainable as a process that would purify prospective monks and nuns not only of sin but also of all their previous ways. The process was also to lead to a willingness to take on the "new yoke of obedience" and the "strictness of discipline," as Peter of Celle had once put it.

---

[22] Gert Melville, "Der Mönch als Rebell," 171–72.

[23] Markus Karl von Pföstl, *Pueri oblati*, 2 vols. (Kiel: Solivagus, 2011).

[24] On the following, see Breitenstein, *Das Noviziat im hohen Mittelalter* (Münster: LIT, 2008).

The conclusion of this process of socialization was marked by a solemn ceremony of profession to the local monastery (in the Cluniac congregation, among others, profession to the monastery was complemented by a subsequent consecration in Cluny itself), while mendicants made their profession to the Order. Such ceremonies were understood symbolically as a kind of second baptism. To become a monk,[25] which was seen as comparable to the beginning of martyrdom, was also understood to be a kind of dying to the world. Thus among the Benedictines it was often common after profession to completely cover the head of the novice with a hood for three days—the length of time Christ spent in limbo.

From the days of the charismatic Desert Fathers of Late Antiquity through all of the later history of the *vita religiosa*, reforming protagonists worked to grant permanence to extraordinary spiritual power through both oral instruction and so-called parenetic texts, or works of exhortation. Notably, however, an anonymous author of the twelfth century recognized the core problem of that kind of model of persuasion when he called out emphatically to the monastic audience of his text, "What use are these writings of exhortation if you do not read and understand within yourself?"[26] Perhaps no expressions capture more forcefully than these the criteria by which the interiorization of monastic norms was measured: conscience (*conscientia*), understood as *cordis scientia*, knowledge from the heart.[27]

Especially in an era of reform like the twelfth century, religious were taught to embrace conscience as an inescapable companion, to encounter the self in the conscience as an individual faced with the commands of religious life, and to have as a partner only God, who sees into the heart. Though it might be possible to conceal behavior from the outside world, it was impossible to do so before the self.

---

[25] On the following, see Sonntag, *Klosterleben*, 120–64.

[26] *Meditationes piissimae de cognitione humanae conditiones*, PL 184:508.

[27] Ermenegildo Bertola, *Il problema della coscienza nella teologia monastica del XII secolo* (Padua: CEDAM, 1970); Melville, "Mönch als Rebell," 172–77. Mirko Breitenstein, "Die Verfügbarkeit der Transzendenz: Das Gewissen der Mönche als Heilsgarant," in *Innovation durch Deuten und Gestalten. Klöster im Mittelalter zwischen Jenseits und Welt*, ed. Gert Melville, Bernd Schneidmüller, and Stefan Weinfurter (Regensburg: Schnell and Steiner, 2014), 37–56.

With slogans like "Take care to know yourself" (*Aude cognoscere te*)[28] or "Follow your conscience and your own law will bind you" (*lex tua te constringit*),[29] religious were trained to rely on their own judgment and not that of others, since keeping company with one's conscience ensured that no one knew one better than oneself.

Such familiarity with the self was deeply internalized spiritually, and it allowed for transcendence directly to God. It was marked by total sacrifice; it was, in the end, at the core of the soul, totally individualized and boundlessly emotional—and therefore inevitably radical and anti-institutional. At the same time, however, it was often institutionally strangled by the pattern of monastic life, subject to discipline and humility, poured out into the molds of a community of peace, and fixed within rational rules that had moderation, measured discretion (*discretio*), and justice as their foundational principles.[30] European culture found in this seeming paradox a model that allowed individual religious devotion to be lived out in tension with rule-bound, practical rationality, in such a way that the two forces did not neutralize but rather strengthened one another.

When women and men of the Middle Ages who had submitted themselves to the *vita religiosa* praised the "delights of Paradise" (*deliciae paradysi*) they found in the monastery—because there alone had they found the possibility of achieving perfection in Christian virtues—or when they spoke of the monastery as a "port of salvation" (*portus salutis*), they outlined the fundamental patterns of a life whose realization was to be found not only by stepping into a "monastery of the soul," a place of individual interiority, but also by entering into an all-encompassing life of community. With a strictness found almost nowhere else, the common life (*vita communis*) of the monastery required religious to subject every aspect of their daily lives (if not

---

[28] *Meditationes piissimae de cognitione humanae conditiones*, PL 184:494.

[29] *De interiori domo seu De conscientia aedificanda*, PL 184:534. Cf. Mirko Breitenstein, "Der Traktat vom 'Inneren Haus.' Verantwortung als Ziel der Gewissensbildung," in *Innovation in Klöstern und Orden des Hohen Mittelalters. Aspekte und Pragmatik eines Begriffes*, ed. Mirko Breitenstein et al. (Berlin: LIT, 2012), 263–92.

[30] Mirko Breitenstein and Gert Melville, "Gerechtigkeit als fundierendes Element des mittelalterlichen Mönchtums," in *Bilder—Sachen—Mentalitäten*, ed. Heidrun Alzheimer et al. (Regensburg: Schnell & Steiner, 2010), 33–42.

The dormitory of the Cistercian abbey of Fontenay in northern Burgundy.

themselves entirely) to a greater purpose. To that end, they both made use of pragmatic regulations and cultivated a symbolic self-assurance regarding proper behavior.[31]

The hope, speaking allegorically, was that the convent would resonate like the harp of David, as the individual strings of its members found their way to the harmony of a melody.[32] Claiming to have seen the ideal of the *vita communis* realized already in the first community in Jerusalem, Augustine adopted for his community of clerics the phrase found in the Acts of the Apostles: "one heart and one soul" (*cor unum et anima una*). He thereby gave the *vita religiosa* a basic norm, one whose impact would reach far beyond the formation of those communities that invoked his name. Mutual complement and mutual love were the pillars of a community of peace, a community that was to support and encourage its individual members not only

---

[31] For an overview, see Melville, "Einleitende Aspekte zur Aporie von Eigenem und Ganzem im mittelalterlichen Religiosentum," in *Das Eigene und das Ganze*, ed. Gert Melville and Markus Schürer (Münster: LIT, 2002), XI–XLI.

[32] *Das Eigene und das Ganze*, XXIII; Sonntag, *Klosterleben*, 90.

throughout an entire life lived on earth as an "angelic existence in God's army"[33] but also through death and beyond. That ideal was valid for every kind of community, whether made up mostly of nobility or dominated by urban burghers.

This function of monastic community is exemplified in the observation that lengthy liturgical-spiritual work and ascetic exercises that demanded great physical stamina (and among some communities, especially the mendicants, intellectual stamina as well)[34] countered the fragility of negligent and weak brothers and indeed almost eliminated occasions for transgression. A strict ordering of monastic life was thus seen as a protective barrier against sinfulness; it strengthened the individual by way of external pressure alone and guarded against transgression even in the face of a will to sin. The Cistercian Bernard of Clairvaux thus located the protection against sinfulness in the "battle lines of so many in the monastery who fight in the same way" (*in acie multorum pariter pugnantium*). With their help, the individual could withstand the attacks of the evil one, since he always had like-minded brothers by his side, and since monks who had been long tested in battle were there to warn of the wiles of the enemy. The only ones in danger were those who fell victim to the vice of self-righteousness (*nequissimum vitium singularitatis*), who retreated into the narrows of self-will (*angulae propriae voluntatis*) and thereby undermined the blessed unity of the community.[35]

The all-encompassing care of community was perhaps never more in evidence, however, than in the fact that while every individual, even in the monastery, died a unique death, it was never experienced alone, but always in the company of fellow religious.[36] Drawn together by the choreography of liturgy, the community surrounded the dying as

---

[33] Sonntag, *Klosterleben*, 87–93. This did not, however, exclude an enjoyment of games: Jörg Sonntag, "Le rôle de la vie régulière dans l'invention et la diffusion de divertissements sociaux au Moyen Âge," *Revue Mabillon* 83 (2011): 79–98.

[34] Klaus Schreiner, "Brot der Mühsal," in *Arbeit im Mittelalter*, ed. Verena Postel (Berlin: Akademie, 2006), 133–70.

[35] Bernard of Clairvaux, *Parabolae 3*, ed. Jean Leclercq and Henri-Marie Rochais, *Sancti Bernardi Opera* 6/2 (Rome: Editiones Cistercienses, 1970), 274–76.

[36] For an overview, see Sonntag, *Klosterleben*, 469–526. See also Frederick S. Paxton, ed., *The Death Ritual at Cluny in the Central Middle Ages / Le rituel de la mort à Cluny au Moyen Âge central* (Turnhout: Brepols, 2013).

The dying Dominic, surrounded by his brethren. The surrounding text reads, "This one, the father of the Preachers and leader of the monks, is led to the choir of royalty and the heights of heaven."

one and bonded with him as if one body—from which the deceased, when finally buried, was not so much released as "enclosed" in another form. Furthermore, the bonds of community did not end after death. Rather, they were immortalized when the names of the dead were written into the community necrology.[37] And it was again a choreographed liturgy that communally and repeatedly called off the name (and all of the other names) of the dead. In doing so, the liturgy re-created, year after year, a timeless body established by memory (*memoria*). With the entry of the name the individual was named as such; that is to say, the distinct identity of one who died a unique death lived on in the recorded name, since the community offered up prayers for the salvation of that individual soul explicitly by name. In its entirety, in all of its hundreds of entries, a monastic necrology

[37] On the following, see Karl Schmid and Joachim Wollasch, eds., *Memoria* (Munich: Wilhelm Fink, 1984).

thus represented a monastic community as a unique whole. But at the same time—and in a way that could hardly be more meaningful—the very series of names stood as a reminder that the community was also understood to have consisted of each of its individual members.

Religious communities claimed to be able to guarantee freedom from earthly mutability by expressing that ideal symbolically. When medieval women and men subjected themselves to a daily rhythm that was forever the same, an ever-repeated daily round of worship, of prayer according to the seven canonical hours, of sleeping and waking, of work and mealtimes, in doing so they lived together in a circle of time that broke from the earthly flow of hours—and they were thus able symbolically to represent timeless eternity.[38] When in liturgy, in the singing of the choir, in psalmody, in rituals like the Benedictines' washing of the feet of the poor,[39] but also in a daily life of work and of hearing and reciting religious texts—when in all these ways what counted as the truth of divine revelation was brought permanently and palpably to mind, the result was the embodiment of monastic life's intention to bring earthly existence into harmony with heavenly order by way of practices that were lived day to day and thereby established institutionally. The same was true of the regular rhythm of chapters of faults, where individuals acknowledged their sin before the community, and which were seen as a representation of the Last Judgment.[40]

When, for example, the four sides of the cloister—that communal monastic space in which contemplative immersion, whispered reading of sacred texts, and communal rituals like shaving took place— were equated allegorically by regular canons like Hugh of Fouilly (ca. 1100–1174) and others with renunciation of self and world and with love of neighbor and love of God, an earthly space thereby became a heavenly one, and fundamental virtues began symbolically to move together in a circular transcendence.[41]

---

[38] Sonntag, *Klosterleben*, 226–44; Jörg Sonntag, "Tempus fugit. La circolarità del tempo monastica nello specchio del potenziale di rappresentazione simbolica," in *Religiosità e civiltà. Le comunicazioni symboliche (secoli IX—XIII)*, ed. Giancarlo Andenna (Milan: Vita e pensiero, 2009), 221–42.

[39] Sonntag, *Klosterleben*, 580–614.

[40] Sonntag, *Klosterleben*, 390–442.

[41] Sonntag, *Klosterleben*, 59–60.

These experiences required in principle a monastic space distinct from the secular world and guarded by a sharp differentiation between inside and outside.[42] As Hugh of Fouilly put it, distinguishing between the spiritual and bodily aspects of human existence, "When they are guarded within the fortress of the monastic walls, the inner and outer man are able to escape the attacks of the ancient enemy and the tumult of temporal affairs."[43] The built environment of the monastery provided a tangible framework in this regard.[44] The cloister was at the center, and all around it were arranged the spaces that shaped a cloistered existence—one set apart from the outside world. The actual arrangements of the buildings varied widely according to the divergent goals of the many forms of religious community. Thus the common dormitory (*dormitorium*) typical of Benedictine community arrangements differed from those of the eremitical Carthusians, who preferred separate apartments, and these in turn differed from the Dominican preference for cells devoted to individual study.[45]

Yet with respect to their core functions and symbolism they were all similar, in a way parallel (as noted above) to the cloister, the refectory (the common meal hall), and the library, whose designation as the *armarium* was a reminder of its function as the arsenal and armory for spiritual warfare.[46] The chapter room was universally recognized as a place not only of communal conversation and counsel but also

---

[42] Gert Melville, "Inside and Outside: Some Considerations about Cloistral Boundaries in the Central Middle Ages," in *Ecclesia in medio nationis*, ed. Brigitte Meijns and Steven Vanderputten (Leuven: Leuven University Press, 2011), 167–82.

[43] Hugo de Folieto, *De claustro animae*, PL 176:1019.

[44] As an overview, Wolfgang Braunfels, *Monasteries of Western Europe: The Architecture of the Orders* (London: Thames and Hudson, 1972); Renate Oldermann, ed., *Gebaute Klausur* (Bielefeld: Verlag für Regionalgeschichte, 2008); Günther Binding and Matthias Untermann, eds., *Kleine Kunstgeschichte der mittelalterlichen Ordensbaukunst in Deutschland* (Stuttgart: Theiss, 2001).

[45] Thomas Lentes, "'Vita perfecta' zwischen 'Vita communis' und 'Vita privata': Eine Skizze zur klösterlichen Einzelzelle," in *Das Öffentliche und Private in der Vormoderne*, ed. Gert Melville and Peter von Moos (Cologne: Böhlau, 1998), 125–64.

[46] Hilmar Tilgner, "Armarium und Bibliotheksbau. Die Bibliotheksräume im Zisterzienserkloster Eberbach vom 12. Jahrhundert bis 1810," *Wolfenbütteler Notizen zur Buchgeschichte* 23 (1998): 132–81.

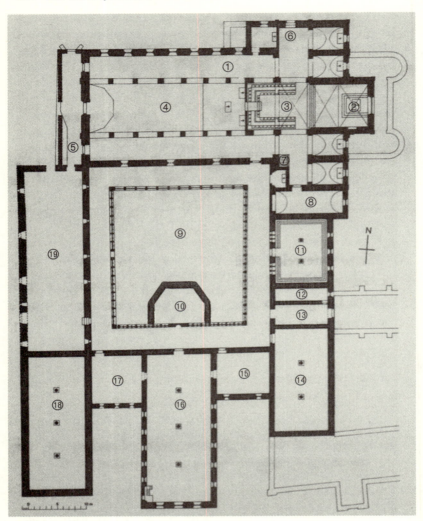

Plan of a Cistercian Monastery

1. Monastery church; 2. Main altar; 3. Monks' choir; 4. Lay brothers' section; 5. "Paradise" (Narthex); 6. Door to cemetery; 7. Night stairs to the *Dormitorium* (second-floor sleeping quarters); 8. Sacristy; 9. Cloister; 10. *Lavabo* (fountain for hand washing before mealtimes); 11. Chapter room (monks' assembly room); 12. Day stairs to dormitory on second floor; 13. *Parlatorium* (conference room); 14. Monks' work-room; over 8–14, on the second floor, the monks' *Dormitorium* (sleeping quarters); 15. *Calcefactorium* (warming room); 16. *Refectorium* (dining hall) of the monks; 17. Kitchen; 18. *Refectorium* (dining hall) of the lay brothers; 19. *Cellerarium* (storeroom). Over 18–19 on the second floor, *Dormitorium* (sleeping quarters) of the lay brothers. This reconstruction follows the outline of the monastery of Wettingen in Aargau/Switzerland, built 1227–1256. It has been slightly modified in order to account for all typical elements. Source: Günther Binding and Matthias Untermann, *Kleine Kunstgeschichte der mittelalterlichen Ordensbaukunst in Deutschland*, 3rd ed. (Darmstadt: Wissenschaftliche Buchgesellschaft, 2001), 225.

The latrine (left) of the Cistercian abbey of Royaumont north of Paris is a monument to mastery over the most earthly aspects of the daily life of the monastery.

of the chapter of faults and its cleansing from sin.[47] The monastic church served the same purpose, regardless of a remarkably varied architecture shaped by the specific needs of the different forms of observance. Among the early Cistercians, for example, who withdrew by way of liturgy to focus only on communication with God, the church was closed to outsiders.[48] But it was easily accessible from the monks' dormitory, allowing them to attend services at night, and was also increasingly divided into distinct areas for *conversi* and choir monks.[49]

The needs of the preaching mendicant orders, in contrast, dictated an almost inviting church, one architecturally broad and open for

[47] Heidrun Stein-Kecks, *Der Kapitelsaal in der mittelalterlichen Kloster-baukunst. Studien zu den Bildprogrammen* (Berlin: Deutscher Kunstverlag, 2004).

[48] Carola Jäggi, "Ordensarchitektur als Kommunikation von Ordnung. Zis-terziensische Baukunst zwischen Vielfalt und Einheit," in Andenna et al., *Die Ordnung der Kommunikation*, 203–21.

[49] Markus Späth, *Zisterziensische Klausurarchitektur als Mittel institutioneller Differenzierung* (Krems: Medium Aevum Quotidianum, 2000).

pastoral offerings, for burials, for the altars of guilds, and so on.[50]
Moreover, these many church buildings could be understood symbolically in a variety of ways. In their size and beauty they could serve
as a manifestation of the heavenly Jerusalem (as in the Benedictine
community of Saint Denis in Paris, for example), or as an expression,
also biblically inspired, of humility and renunciation of earthly treasures—churches without towers (among the Cistercians, for example)
that sought to imitate the straw-covered hut of Abraham,[51] churches
that refused gold and silver (among the Carthusians, for example),
and churches that were built as simple halls with vaulted naves (for
example, among the Franciscans and Dominicans).

The Monastery and the Law

According to the explicit claims of the Rule of Saint Benedict,
but in principle also according to the general understanding of all
those responsible for ensuring the best possible realization of the
vita religiosa, the monastery was a place for the spiritually weak,
those who could not yet stand alone and unprotected in combat with
evil out in the world. "Keep this little rule that we have written for
beginners. After that, you can set out for the loftier summits of the
teaching and virtues we mentioned above, and under God's protection
you will reach them," read the closing words of the Rule of Saint
Benedict (RB 73.8-9).

In light of the resulting transitory nature of the *vita religiosa*,
clearly only a highly rationally formed and institutionally governed
system of order was capable of realizing and preserving such radical
demands and expectations over time. Max Weber long ago pointed
out the paradox of the ambitions of a monastic ascetic who was looking for salvation, on the one hand, and the "rational achievements"
of monasticism, on the other. He resolved the conflict by articulating
that "asceticism becomes the object of methodical practices."[52] These

---

[50] Wolfgang Schenkluhn, *Architektur der Bettelorden* (Darmstadt: Wissenschaftliche Buchgesellschaft, 2000).

[51] Sonntag, *Klosterleben*, 62.

[52] Max Weber, *Economy and Society: An Outline of Interpretive Sociology*,
ed. Guenther Roth and Claus Wittich (Berkeley: University of California Press,
1978), 1169.

concepts of "rational achievement" and "methodical practices" are key to a proper understanding of monasticism's accomplishments in matters of organization, and they once again deserve a systematic treatment here. Pragmatically, it is proper to speak of methodical rationality whenever there is reflective, objectifying treatment of one's own actions or the actions of others, and whenever social action unfolds according to systematic design—a design that in turn manages to grasp the various conditions, modes, and aims of that action in differentiated ways. Faced with the necessity of translating the ideals of their otherworldly way of life into institutional forms, monasteries developed precisely this kind of methodically applied rationality.

In so doing, the world of medieval monasticism realized decisive achievements that were full of innovative power, that in many respects surpassed the techniques of organization found in the cities, at the courts of the nobility, or in the circles of secular clergy and that built institutions whose impact long survived the Middle Ages.

A variety of constituencies helped to establish stability and to preserve it. Here, as has already been noted, the matter depended in a fundamental way on many factors: an inescapable compulsion of the individual conscience, which could be sharpened by the impact of texts of exhortation; also the influence of charismatic personalities who formulated the core ideals of a *propositum* and who through their interaction provided exemplary patterns of life, thereby serving as living rules and ever-present models; and the fraternal bonds of community, which represented a battle line whose closed ranks guarded against spiritual dangers.

No less important was the scaffolding of a legal framework, which structured regulations of daily practice in the form of strict organizations by way of written rules, orally transmitted customs (*consuetudines*), written statutes (*statuta, constitutiones*, etc.), an array of legal decisions and administrative measures (definitions, visitation protocols, property surveys, indices), a turn to the common law of the church (*ius commune*), and authoritative decrees (papal decretals, synodal statutes, etc.). The same legal framework established procedural guidelines, sought to prevent deviation, and made it possible to enforce punishment.[53]

---

[53] For an overview, see Gert Melville, "Zur Funktion der Schriftlichkeit im institutionellen Gefüge mittelalterlicher Orden," *Frühmittelalterliche Studien* 25 (1991): 391–417.

The best articulation of this model came from the Dominican master general Humbert of Romans (ca. 1200–1277), who wrote as the legalism of the church had begun to reach one of its first high points.[54] As Humbert explained, every law that was binding on monasteries, congregations, or orders was integrated into the hierarchy of the legal sources of the church. The highest commands, of course, were those of God. These dwarfed even those of the church or the pope. Smaller still were the rules of church fathers like Augustine, Benedict, and others. Smallest of all were those commands of their successors, that is, of the institutional decisions of the monasteries and orders themselves.

From the early days of monasticism the official church had moved repeatedly to intervene in the internal affairs of religious communities. On one hand, it did so through both universal and local synods—Chalcedon in 451, for example, and the Lateran Synod of 1059, and the Fourth Lateran Council of 1215.[55] On the other, individual popes sought from early on and by various means to lay their protective and controlling hand on the affairs of monasteries. By way of individual privileges they granted exemptions from episcopal power, as, for example, in 628 at Bobbio.[56] Other privileges provided papal protection or claimed a monastery as the papacy's own, as at Cluny at the beginning of the tenth century.[57] Others confirmed properties and legal rights, such as the election of an abbot or an advocate, and approved new organizations along with their founding documents and their forms of observance, such as the Cistercian *Carta caritatis* in 1119 or the institutional form of the congregation of Mortara in 1130.[58] Still others established new orders, like the Hospitalers of Santo Spirito in 1204 or the Augustinian Hermits in 1256.[59]

Another strategy involved the so-called *Litterae de gratia*, by means of which from the thirteenth century on the papacy sought to

---

[54] "Expositio magistri Humberti super constitutiones fratrum Praedicatorum," in *B. Humberti de Romanis quinti Praedicatorum magistri generalis opera de vita regulari*, ed. Joachim Joseph Berthier (Rome: Befani, 1889), 2:16.

[55] See pp. 10, 127, 180.

[56] See p. 23.

[57] See p. 60.

[58] See pp. 128, 146.

[59] See pp. 175, 256.

confirm summarily all rights, privileges, indulgences, and properties granted by any predecessor, including even secular powers. The popes also issued reform decrees or mandates that in the High and late Middle Ages came to encompass entire orders, including, for example, the Cistercians in 1169 and 1265, the Premonstratensians in 1232, the Cluniacs in 1233, and nearly every transregional order in the context of the reform policies of Benedict XII.[60]

The Roman Curia's interventions in the affairs of religious communities grew stronger in ways proportional to the growth of papal monarchy in the wake of the church reforms of the eleventh and twelfth centuries and the centralization of ecclesiastical power in the Roman Curia. From then on, the curial administration sought to structure the most important communications between the papacy and the religious orders by means of a more uniform discourse and conceptual framework. Already in the twelfth century, a so-called *clause de régularité*[61] had been developed, obligating all newly emergent congregations to observe a specific rule and commanding each not to alter either the order that rule had established or the rule's specific religious intention (*propositum*).[62] So, for example, the Premonstratensians were said to live *secundum beati Augustini regulam* ("according to the Rule of Augustine"). From the beginning of the thirteenth century, these and other turns to properly documentary formulas came to be developed for the individual orders and kept in the records of the papal chancellery.[63]

Between 1247 and 1264, moreover, some five orders (Franciscans, Camaldolese, Augustinian Hermits, Dominicans, and Cluniacs) established their own procurators, through whom they were able to

---

[60] Jan Ballweg, *Konziliare oder päpstliche Ordensreform. Benedikt XII. und die Reformdiskussion im frühen 14. Jahrhundert* (Tübingen: Mohr, 2001); Franz J. Felten, "Die Ordensreformen Benedikts XII. unter institutionsgeschichtlichem Aspekt," in *Institutionen und Geschichte*, ed. Gert Melville (Cologne: Böhlau, 1992), 369–435.

[61] Jacques Dubois, "Les ordres religieux au XIIᵉ siècle selon la curie romaine," *Revue Bénédictine* 78 (1968): 283–309.

[62] Markus Schürer, "Das 'propositum' in religiös-asketischen Diskursen. Historisch-semantische Erkundungen zu einem zentralen Begriff der mittelalterlichen 'vita religiosa,'" in *Oboedientia*, ed. Sebastien Barret and Gert Melville (Münster: LIT, 2006), 99–128.

[63] *Die päpstlichen Kanzleiordnungen von 1200–1500*, ed. Michael Tangl (Aalen: Scientia, 1959), 221–360.

have their interests represented amid the routine business of the curial courtrooms and the papal chancellery.[64] Around the same time, the institution of the cardinal protector emerged, providing a crucial link between the papacy and the orders.[65]

Nevertheless, from the thirteenth century on, most orders knew how to set themselves against the all-too-persistent interventions of the papacy, as did the Cluniacs in 1231/33, how to modify them, like the Premonstratensians in 1246, or how to flatly reject them, as the Carthusians did continually.[66] In this context, there was an almost universal and strict prohibition—though it was by no means always enforced—against individual religious who attempted to appeal directly to the Holy See, bypassing the usual authorities within their own order.[67] Monasteries had otherwise almost nothing at their disposal to resist the Curia's late-medieval practice of seeking to hand them over to so-called commendatory abbots, thereby putting them in danger of economic exploitation.

Religious communities—individual monasteries as well as entire congregations and orders—were, however, always in principle tied back into the general framework of the ecclesiastical *ius commune*.[68] That framework grew in importance in the wake of the systematic articulation of church law as a scholarly discipline, at the latest from the time of Gratian's *Concordia discordantium canonum*. That text, completed around 1140 and thereafter a fundamental compilation for canon law, was the basis for a subsequent juridification of legal

---

[64] Andreas Sohn, "Mittler zwischen Papsttum und Orden: Zu den Generalprokuratoren in Rom," in *Rom und das Reich vor der Reformation*, ed. Nikolaus Staubach (Frankfurt am Main: Peter Lang, 2004), 71–90.

[65] Martin Faber, "Gubernator, protector et corrector. Zum Zusammenhang der Entstehung von Orden und Kardinalprotektoraten von Orden in der lateinischen Kirche," *Zeitschrift für Kirchengeschichte* 115 (2004): 19–44.

[66] Gert Melville, "Ordensstatuten und allgemeines Kirchenrecht. Eine Skizze zum 12./13. Jahrhundert," in *Proceedings of the 9th International Congress of Medieval Canon Law*, ed. Peter Landau and Jörg Müller (Vatican City: Biblioteca Apostolica Vaticana, 1997), 691–712, here 700–702. For an example of a strong papal politics with respect to the orders, see Franz J. Felten, "Abwehr, Zuneigung, Pflichtgefühl," in *Female* vita religiosa *between Late Antiquity and the High Middle Ages: Structures, Developments and Spatial Contexts*, ed. Gert Melville and Anne Müller (Berlin: LIT, 2011), 391–415.

[67] Guido Cariboni, *"Non ut liceret, sed an liceret,"* in Barret and Melville, *Oboedientia*, 305–34.

[68] Melville, "Ordensstatuten," 706–11.

process in church politics, administration, and economy that monasteries and orders also came to feel acutely. An early high point in these developments was the so-called *Liber extra*, a compilation of papal decrees created by the Dominican master general, Raymond of Peñaforte, promulgated by Gregory IX in 1234. It presented for the first time, and systematically, legal materials concerning religious life, arranged as chapters and as the law of an "estate" (*status*). The *Liber* thus represented a kind of legislative framework, the template of a rich catalogue of normative guidelines for the *vita religiosa*—including materials on renunciation of ownership and abstinence from meat, for example, as well as technical organizational matters such as the procedures guiding the governance of the monastery, provisions for entry, and measures concerning punishment and discipline.[69]

The study of canon law, alongside Roman law, was often condemned in many orders because of the lucrative and worldly careers that it made available.[70] But those who wished to study it could often find ways around the normative strictures of such prohibitions, not least through papal dispensation.

With regard to the creation of their own law, that is, the establishment of a *ius particulare*, most religious organizations were granted a wide-ranging autonomy from the outset. Writing in the thirteenth century, Hostiensis, the great scholar of the church's *ius commune*, stood speechless before the diversity of the many particular forms of law within the *vita religiosa*. He noted, however, that it was difficult to articulate the legal status of monasteries within the general laws of the church, because there were so many different kinds of monasteries, and because they had all been established in different ways (*diversa sunt monasteria et diversas habent institutiones*).[71]

Like no other way of life, the *vita religiosa* had from its ancient beginnings been bound to written guidelines, all of them adapted to a particular set of core ideals (*proposita*) and organizational structures.[72] The ability of the written word to endure across time and

---

[69] For an overview, see Lars-Arne Dannenberg, *Das Recht der Religiosen in der Kanonistik des 12. und 13. Jahrhunderts* (Berlin: LIT, 2008).

[70] Melville, "Ordensstatuten," 706.

[71] *Summa aurea* (Venice, 1574), 1144.

[72] Klaus Schreiner, "Observantia regularis—Normbildung, Normkontrolle und Normwandel im Mönchtum des frühen und späten Mittelalters," in *Prozesse der Normbildung und Normveränderung im mittelalterlichen Europa*, ed. Doris

space was crucial for the institutional stability of monastic communities beyond the early days of their founding. All recognized that writing made possible the authentic preservation of a full range of early traditions, and such knowledge was preserved even in times when literacy had almost totally disappeared across Europe— thereafter to be innovatively deployed, from the eleventh century, in all areas of pragmatically oriented literacy.[73]

The most important products of this literacy across the spectrum of the *vita religiosa* were rules, customs, and statutes.[74] In these texts, more than anywhere else, the foundations of the normative structure of a religious community become visible—albeit in sharply divergent forms and functions, since these three genres of text themselves differ strongly not only in their claims to validity but also in their respective intentions. By no means did every religious community always have a rule, customs, and statutes all at once. To note only three representative examples: the Carthusians had no rule, the Grandmontines no *Consuetudines*, and until the end of the twelfth century the Cluniacs no constitutional statutes. And long-term developments suggest (speaking generally) that in the first phase of religious life, through the early Middle Ages, rules were predominant; an age characterized by written customs followed, and then, from the twelfth century on, a period dominated by statutes.

Because the categories for these kinds of texts overlap, it is impossible to construct a single typology. It is possible to read the historical evidence of the texts themselves comparatively, however, and thereby to draw a series of representative distinctions. To that end we can offer the following conclusions, here formulated very generally.[75]

Ruhe and Karl-Heinz Spiess (Stuttgart: Franz Steiner, 2000), 275–313; Mirko Breitenstein et al., eds., *Rules and Observance: Devising Forms of Communal Life* (Berlin: LIT, 2014).

[73] Melville, "Zur Funktion der Schriftlichkeit"; Klaus Schreiner, "Verschriftlichung als Faktor monastischer Reform," in *Pragmatische Schriftlichkeit im Mittelalter*, ed. Hagen Keller et al. (Munich: Wilhem Fink, 1992), 37–75.

[74] On the following see Cristina Andenna and Gert Melville, eds., *Regulae— Consuetudines—Statuta* (Münster: LIT, 2005).

[75] On the following, see Gert Melville, "Regeln—Consuetudines—Texte— Statuten. Positionen für eine Typologie des normativen Schrifttums religiöser Gemeinschaften im Mittelalter," in Andenna and Melville, *Regulae—Consuetudines—Statuta*, 5–38, with full documentation. For a particular case of shaping

In principle, a rule is the work of a single author—sometimes written with the advice of others—who seeks to pass on a compelling message about a proper way of life to a community of followers. Analogously, someone might introduce an already established rule into a community, as Norbert of Xanten did with the Rule of Augustine.

Rules originally required no approval from a higher ecclesiastical authority. Only the High Middle Ages saw a change in the legal circumstances, which were intensified by the decrees of the Fourth Lateran Council. From that point forward new rules—like those of Francis, Clare, and Birgitta—always had to be approved by the papacy. Rules originally concerned only the communities of particular monasteries and their dependent houses. At first, however, the same rule could be adopted by numerous monasteries, even if they shared no other legal or institutional ties. Thus from the twelfth and thirteenth centuries on, the Rule of Augustine, with its remarkably general norms, came to serve as a kind of wild card rule for many new congregations. In the same era, specific rules emerged for the first time for individual orders, texts closely tied to a particular institutional identity and therefore in principle not transferable to other orders. Early examples include the rules of the Templars, the Grandmontines, and the Camaldolese, as well as the one Abelard drew up for the women's community of the Paraclete. The most famous example, however, is certainly the Rule of Francis.

In terms of its content, a rule encompassed all fundamental aspects of life—norms of behavior and obligations of prayer and liturgy as well as leadership structures, discipline, economic affairs, daily routines, clothing, eating, and living together. As a consequence, a rule dealt with both matters of the spirit and technical matters of organization. Apart from the fact that rules, especially in the early Middle Ages, were combined with one another and used variously

---

norms in the context of adapting them to the needs of women, see Maiju Lehmijoki-Gardner, "Writing Religious Rules as an Interactive Process: Dominican Penitent Women and the Making of their 'Regula,'" *Speculum* 79 (2004): 660–87. Albrecht Diem, "Inventing the Holy Rule: Some Observations on the History of Monastic Normative Observance in the Early Medieval West," in *Western Monasticism ante Litteram: The Space of Monastic Observance in Late Antiquity and the Early Middle Ages*, ed. Hendrik W. Dey and Elizabeth Fentress (Turnhout: Brepols, 2011), 53–84.

in so-called mixed rules, they were in principle unalterable. Rules came to be shaped ever more strongly by the assumption that they were holy texts and therefore untouchable, founded on the Gospel but ultimately, as figures like Francis or Birgitta of Sweden emphasized, handed down by God.

Consuetudines were established customs already approved by the normative power of practice within a community or order. Thus their various written versions had no real author in the proper sense, and the corresponding texts neither needed to be nor could be approved by an ecclesiastical authority. But they were easily transferrable to other communities, as long as their content was used only as a model. In such cases the text itself was most often changed to adapt it according to local circumstance, as was true of the customaries of the regular canons in the twelfth century.[76] The reception of a customary in this regard was not a marker of legal dependence. A given monastic congregation could have, as distinct from a single rule, a range of sharply divergent customs.

The texts of *Consuetudines* provided both expansions and supporting interpretations of a given rule. In the widest sense, they primarily concerned interactions and patterns of life, forms of common prayer and liturgy, clothing, mealtimes, rituals, daily rhythms, and so on, but they also addressed the organizational system of offices, recruitment of the next generation (for example, the election of an abbot or guidelines on oblates and novices), and the enforcement of discipline. A model in this regard seems to be the Cluniac *Consuetudines*, already noted, which were recorded around 1080 by Bernard and Ulrich.

The texts of *Consuetudines* could also not strictly speaking be changed, because they had captured in retrospect practices that had already been established. Thus they themselves were not bearers of the validity of norms. Nor did they produce or reproduce any validity, because that validity was already to hand in those interactions that had been continually repeated and that continued to be repeated. Acts were valid insofar as they were thought always to have been done. Yet it is possible to discern subtle differences in how these texts communicated validity (though not the validity itself), since some among them are more descriptive and others more directive

---

[76] Stefan Weinfurter, ed., *Consuetudines canonicorum regularium Springirs-bacenses-Rodenses*, CCCM 48 (Turnhout: Brepols, 1978).

in function.[77] In this respect a difference clearly emerges between customary texts intended exclusively for instruction of houses that did not belong to a given congregation (so, for example, the *Consuetudines* of Ulrich of Cluny for Hirsau, noted above) and those that sought through writing to secure and to preserve, through their textuality, a binding set of customs for posterity, as, for example, the *Consuetudines* of the regular canons of Springiersbach/Klosterrath from the 1120s.[78]

Statutes were in principle drawn up with the consent of an entire community or their representatives, and in the case of entire orders, of a central legislative body such as *diffinitors* or a general chapter. Classic examples in this regard are the *Carta caritatis* of the Cistercians and the Dominican *Constitutiones*. Statutes were also composed, whether by the founder of a community, as was true for the congregation of Fontevraud and its founder Robert of Arbrissel, or by representatives of a "second generation"[79] that had begun to pass down established *Consuetudines* as statutes, especially if the founder had left nothing comparable behind, as was true for the Carthusians. An important dimension of such statutes was that while they were derived from the consensus of the community, they were also binding on even the leading officeholders of a monastery or an order.

In principle, statutes were not transferable to other monasteries, congregations, or orders; in legal terms, because religious communities had created them to be legally valid locally—and locally only—statutes were a decisive marker of a community's identity. Within a congregation or an order, in contrast, statutes were binding on every house. The model here was the widely influential *Carta caritatis* noted above, which decisively insisted on normative uniformity in every area of life.

In general, statutes encompassed every area of community life, but they often placed considerable emphasis on matters of organization, hierarchy, and leadership and on daily interaction and matters

---

[77] Anselme Davril, "Coutumiers directifs et coutumiers descriptifs d'Ulrich à Bernard de Cluny," in Boynton and Cochelin, *Customs*, 23–28.

[78] Weinfurter, ed., *Consuetudines canonicorum regularium Springirsbacenses-Rodenses*.

[79] Gert Melville, "Brückenschlag zur zweiten Generation," in *Religiöse Ordnungsvorstellungen und Frömmigkeitspraxis im Hoch- und Spätmittelalter*, ed. Jörg Rogge (Korb: Didymos, 2008), 77–98.

of discipline. For matters concerning liturgy and spiritual practice, however, there were often collections of statutes dedicated to those particular themes—as in the case of the Cistercian *Liber usuum* noted above, for example, which despite its name was not a collection of customs but of enacted statutes. At any time, the authority that created the statutes could change, revise, nullify, or rewrite them, although the Cistercian *Carta caritatis* was an exception to that generalization, as it was often equated to a religious rule. Admittedly, the problem of the mutability of law always presented itself, thereby inspiring critics' denunciations of a novelty that threatened to overwhelm the unchanging truth of virtue.[80] Peter the Venerable, abbot of Cluny, confronted that concern head-on in the prologue to his collection of statutes. He made a distinction between unchanging virtues, on the one hand—love of God and neighbor, humility, righteousness, and the corresponding norms that secured them—and on the other hand, the instruments of the virtues, all of them quite variable, such as ascetic practices, manual labor, prescriptions for fasting, and so on. The latter concerns for Peter could thus easily become a matter of statutory legislation. New texts most often displaced the old (as was true among the Premonstratensians and the Cluniacs from the thirteenth century on), but among some orders they steadily accumulated, leading to an increasingly expansive corpus, as happened among the Carthusians.

Statutes resulted from the writing down of norms that were in principle, from the moment of their publication, to be divorced from the circumstances of the past and to point the way into the future. In this respect, the text itself was the bearer of a forward-looking validity, its very words a binding force.

Institutional Forms: Establishment and Preservation

On the basis of such structures of literacy, certain kinds of "rational-legal" communities emerged (from the earliest era of the *vita religiosa*, though more vigorously from the twelfth century) as a fundamental type of cenobitic monasticism. The legitimacy of this type rested—to frame the issue in the words of Max Weber—"on

---

[80] Andreas Fieback, "Necessitas non est legi subiecta, maxime positivae," in Melville, *De ordine vitae*, 125–51.

a belief in the legality of enacted rules,"[81] because the identity of these kinds of religious communities was bound to a normative text that had been either collectively legislated in the form of statutes or established by a papal decree. The normative text occupied a fundamental position—that is, it constituted a given community in a way both grounded in the present and looking toward the future. In this respect, such a text had both an instrumental and a symbolic dimension. Once again the strong opening words of the Cistercians' *Carta caritatis* are revealing in this regard: "In this decree, then, the aforesaid brethren, taking precaution against future shipwreck of their mutual peace, elucidated and decreed and left for their posterity by what covenant, or in what manner, indeed with what charity their monks throughout abbeys in various parts of the world, though separated in body, could be indissolubly knit together in mind."[82] With these words the Cistercians set down forward-looking norms within the framework of the Rule of Saint Benedict, and those norms were universally valid independent of any particular person. The text looked to a regulated future whose way of life was to be led methodically, even in daily affairs, and which was to be sustained by mutual responsibility. But the text also embodied the guiding ideas that established the community's identity and therefore possessed a symbolic power of tremendous integrative force.

From the earliest days of religious life, the primordial norms of community life could just as easily emerge from the words and deeds of a charismatic founder. Charismatic leadership is thus the second path toward the formation of religious community. In this case, it was not a text but rather a person who served as the symbolic embodiment of common ideals.[83] So it was said, euphorically, of the religious zealot Stephen of Obazine, who in the first half of the twelfth century had gathered a following of hermits around him, "His word is like burning fire, which inflames the souls of his listeners so strongly that their entire lives and mores are changed. His outward

---

[81] Weber, *Economy and Society*, 215.

[82] *Carta caritatis prior*, in *Narrative and Legislative Texts from Early Cîteaux*, ed. and trans. Chrysogonus Waddell (Cîteaux-Commentarii Cistercienses, 1999), 442.

[83] On the following, see Giancarlo Andenna et al., eds., *Charisma und religiöse Gemeinschaften im Mittelalter* (Münster: LIT, 2005).

appearance as well as his demeanor, and everything that he does, are as it were a sermon, and show nothing other than a way of life and disciplined morals and deeds."[84] In principle all leading figures of this kind—Bruno of Cologne, Robert of Arbrissel, Norbert of Xanten, or Francis of Assisi, to name only a few significant examples, already noted above, from the High Middle Ages—positioned their authority beyond the entanglements of daily life and claimed for themselves the power to interpret fundamental principles, which thereby came to be seen as having no alternative. These charismatics often adopted a revolutionary stance, which turned decidedly against tradition and returned to the fundamental structures of the faith. Stephen of Thiers, for example, saw all existing rules as only stems and branches. He called his followers back to the roots, to the Gospel itself. Francis, too, rejected every established rule as a guide for his community, calling instead on the word of God as it had been revealed to him directly as a set of concrete guidelines for his way of life.

The boundaries of embodied norms, however, were set by the corruptibility of the body itself. Stephen of Obazine thus early on subjected his followers to the "authority of written law."[85] For the same reason, Norbert of Xanten vehemently rejected his followers' desire to heed only his words. He knew that no religious goals could be reached without adopting written rules that were valid over the long term.

Only a few examples of the consequences need be noted here. Norbert's community eventually adopted the Rule of Augustine, but Robert of Arbrissel himself provided a collection of statutes for his double community of men and women. Similarly Guigo, the later successor of Bruno of Cologne as leader of the Grand Chartreuse, had the emerging customs of that community written down and established as binding law for all other Carthusian communities. The successor of Stephen of Thiers wrote a rule, naming it after Stephen himself, and last, Stephen of Obazine's monasteries, at Stephen's urging, joined the Cistercian Order.

In the overwhelming number of cases, dynamics like those outlined here played a fundamental role in the formation of religious communities in the Middle Ages. But Weberian models of the transi-

[84] See p. 107.
[85] See p. 109.

tion from "charismatic authority" to the "routinization of charisma"[86] cannot fully explain those dynamics. They were more complex, not least because they either allowed a charismatic leader to set aside charisma in favor of a rational legitimizing force—as is so remarkably visible in the case of Stephen of Obazine—or because a "second generation"[87] built up (in the Weberian sense) a "legal authority" while also forming a myth of origins.[88] A charismatic leader was thus no longer a transitory figure, and the normative power of his memory was now permanently integrated into a written apparatus of justifications for legitimacy—as was the case with the rule ascribed to Stephen of Thiers, for example, or with Francis, whose hagiographies served as a codification of an exemplary and binding way of life.

The successful formation of a religious community proved itself both through long-term survival after a time of beginnings and through lasting pursuit of institutional goals sustained by authorities and organizations that functioned according to expectations. The forward-looking character of early constitutional documents, whether rules or statutes, was first put to the test because of the demands and the resistance of daily life. Thus the process that formed religious communities, whether individual monasteries, congregations, or orders, did not end with a founding act. Rather, that process took place over a long subsequent period of strenuous reform and correction that sought to realize and preserve core essentials.[89] Monastic life achieved much toward that end, and on that basis, over long stretches of the Middle Ages, it took a leading role in the rational formation of organized communities.

In the Rule of Saint Benedict, the abbot was grounded in a spiritual transcendence that framed his duty as Christ's representative in the paternal sense as shepherd. But the abbot was given tasks that above all demanded the art of rational analysis in daily affairs. The abbot was to exercise the art of discretion (*discretio*)—in negotiating

---

[86] Weber, *Economy and Society*, 246–354.

[87] Gert Melville, "Brückenschlag zur zweiten Generation," 77–98.

[88] Achim Wesjohann, *Mendikantische Gründungserzählungen im 13. und 14. Jahrhundert* (Berlin: LIT, 2012).

[89] Karl Augustin Frech, *Reform an Haupt und Gliedern* (Frankfurt am Main: Peter Lang, 1992); Edeltraud Klueting, *Monasteria semper reformanda* (Münster: LIT, 2005).

the demands of others for fair treatment and their various needs and aptitudes, as well as in matters concerning worldly goods and the proper administration of the household.[90] The community elected its abbot in accordance with the Rule, not by a majority but rather by the community's "healthier part" (*sanior pars*). The abbot thereafter enjoyed almost unlimited power; he could not be removed from office, and it was only recommended, but not required, that he take counsel with his brothers. In the end, the abbot alone would render an account before God for each member of the community.

From the eleventh century on, most eremitical reformers of religious life, as well as the later mendicants, set aside the title of abbot in their communities because of its symbolically charged, sacrosanct character. They refused to name their superiors *abba* (father) or *abbatissa*. Instead they chose relatively unencumbered designations such as *prior* or *priorissa* (prior, prioress),[91] *provost* (from *praepositus*), *guardian* (*guardianus*), *minister*, or *master*.

Within the community, a number of officeholders, whom the Cluniacs called *obedientiarii*, ensured the smooth functioning of local affairs. An idealized listing of the most important offices as they were likely to have been encountered in a typical Benedictine abbey provides an overview:[92] from the ninth century on, the designation of prior began to displace the title of *praepositus*, which appears in the Rule as a term for the abbot's representative. A cellarer was responsible for the economic provision of the community, a *camerarius* for the running of the household, a novice master (*magister novitiorum*) for those entering the community, a *hospitarius* (guest master) for guests, an almoner for the distribution of alms, a porter for allowing or preventing entry, a *circator* for oversight of the monks in the dormitory and at work, a librarian for books and archives, an infirmarian for the care of the sick, and a cantor for liturgical chant. Communities in orders with particular aims of course had still more specific offices, such as those of preacher, and master of studies (*magister studiorum*), among the Dominicans. In addition, women's communities

---

[90] Franz J. Felten, "Herrschaft des Abtes," in *Herrschaft und Kirche*, ed. Friedrich Prinz (Stuttgart: Hiersemann, 1988), 147–296.

[91] *Prieurs et prieurés dans l'occident medieval*, ed. Jean-Loup Lemaître (Geneva: Droz, 1987).

[92] Jacques Hourlier, *L'âge classique 1140–1378. Les religieux* (Paris: Cujas, 1971), 311–43.

required a male pastor to be sent to the community from outside. If the community did not belong to an established order, the pope often provided the pastor, who was chosen either from the secular clergy or from Cistercian, Dominican, or Franciscan houses.[93]

The organization of entire congregations and orders, however, was a matter of incomparably greater complexity. In this regard it is important to differentiate, systematically and in a certain sense also chronologically, between two types of organization.

On the one hand, an older form of organization involved congregations that by virtue of property law were personally subject to a head who was the superior of a centrally located community. The model example in this regard, though itself not an early case, is Cluny in its classical era, from around the middle of the tenth century to the end of the twelfth. Its abbot possessed monarchical power over not only the monks subject directly to him but also all of the houses that were his own, that is, whose monks offered their profession to him, whose officeholders he could depose at will, and which in principle he was to visit in person. Scholars have in this regard justifiably spoken of Cluny as a single, large, "trans-local" community.

A more modern, progressive organizational form, on the other hand, involved institutionally consolidated groups of houses that were cooperatively organized and that represented themselves as a transpersonal entity. From the twelfth century onward, this pattern signaled the establishment of an "order" as a totally new form of the *vita religiosa*. But there is yet another distinction to be made here between such corporations, which brought their communities as autonomous units into the whole (here the Cistercians are the prime example and also chronologically the earliest, along with the Carthusians or Premonstratensians), and those that saw their houses as only branches within a more comprehensive system (above all the different branches of the mendicants with their strict provincial divisions).

The general chapter, which usually met once a year, was the representative body of a religious order.[94] It consisted of either the leaders of individual houses, as was true, for example, of the Cistercians,

[93] Klaus Schreiner, "Seelsorge in Frauenklöstern—Sakramentale Dienste, Geistliche Erbauung, Ethische Disziplinierung," in *Krone und Schleier. Kunst aus mittelalterlichen Frauenklöstern* (Bonn and Essen: Hirmer, 2005), 52–65.

[94] Florent Cygler, *Das Generalkapitel im hohen Mittelalter. Cistercienser, Prämonstratenser, Kartäuser und Cluniazenser* (Münster: LIT, 2002).

Premonstratensians, Carthusians, and Cluniacs from the thirteenth century on (to name only a few), or the leaders of provinces or elected delegates from the provinces (the Dominicans, for example, alternated regularly among these groups after every one or two meetings). The task of these gatherings was to ensure the orders' stability in spiritual and temporal affairs (*in spiritualibus et temporalibus*) through judicial, administrative, and reforming legislative measures. To this end an executive council emerged, called the *Definitorium*, which made appropriate "definitions" based on the submission of reports from individual houses and, where necessary, from the provinces. In each case the focal point of the effort could shift in various ways. The Cluniac general chapter, for example, was concerned above all with judicial matters, while that of the Cistercians was more legislative. The decision was then usually handed over to the appropriate members of the order's hierarchy (the superiors of monasteries or provinces) for execution, and in serious cases to a commission, as, for example, among the Cistercians, or even to the head of an entire order, for example, with the Cluniacs or the mendicant orders. Women's communities were usually not represented by a woman at the general chapter.

The coherence of an order was structured either vertically or horizontally and tied to a coherent system of comprehensive visitations[95] that were in principle carried out autonomously, independent of episcopal oversight. Vertical organization was established as a system of filiation among mother- and daughterhouses, with visitors moving from above to below. The model example again comes from the Cistercians, whose hundreds of houses spread out from Cîteaux, which was in turn visited by the abbots of the four primary abbeys. In the horizontal model, an order (in most instances geographically encompassing virtually all of Christendom) was divided up into provinces, each with a superior and answerable to regional visitation. The Premonstratensians were the first to develop such circuits (*circaria*) for visitation. The Cluniacs followed in around 1200, and the mendicant orders (among others) a little after that. In congregations or orders that were exclusively female (the congregation of Prémy,

---

[95] Jörg Oberste, "Institutionalisierte Kommunikation. Normen, Überlieferungsbefunde und Grenzbereiche im Verwaltungsalltag religiöser Orden im hohen Mittelalter," in Melville, *De ordine vitae*, 59–99.

for example) or that were led by women (the congregation of Fontevraud), female superiors personally carried out the visitations.[96]

Typically the information collected by the visitors *in temporalibus et spiritualibus* (encompassing matters of discipline as well as economy, finance, and so on) was sent on to the general chapter, which made decisions regarding those matters that had not been worked out locally. In this way, the general chapter was able to maintain detailed and continual oversight over the overall situation of the whole Order. An ever growing and ever more elaborate corpus of written records served to consolidate lines of communication further.[97] In ways that moved far beyond traditional patterns of record keeping in individual monasteries—rent rolls, customaries, cartularies—the orders now collected and archived records that captured an overall view of their various economies as well as the reports of their members, affidavits of obedience, election reports, and much more. Often duplicate copies of visitation reports were made to allow for a later follow-up. Certified copies of the general chapter's proceedings were always prepared and used to communicate legislation to the members of individual communities. Reports to the leadership of the orders increasingly promoted formal criteria of communication, which were conducive to legibility and especially to rapid categorical classification. The Dominicans, as beneficiaries of this kind of emergent rationality, became masters in these techniques.[98]

Constructing Particular Pasts

Both to establish a particular identity and to attain the external recognition that secured legitimacy, it was not enough to internalize core ideals and to establish an organization that functioned well in all the

---

[96] Franz J. Felten, "Verbandsbildung von Frauenklöstern," in *Vom Kloster zum Klosterverband*, ed. Hagen Keller and Franz Neiske (Munich: Wilhelm Fink, 1997), 277–341.

[97] Oberste, "Institutionalisierte Kommunikation."

[98] Gert Melville, "Die Rechtsordnung der Dominikaner in der Spanne von *constituciones* und *admoniciones*. Ein Beitrag zum Vergleich mittelalterlicher Ordensverfassungen," in *Grundlagen des Rechts. Festschrift für Peter Landau zum 65. Geburtstag*, ed. Richard H. Helmholz et al. (Paderborn: Nomos, 2000), 579–604, here 594.

ways outlined here. Institutional stability, established both inwardly and outwardly, required an explicit symbolic articulation: that the *vita religiosa* could live up to what in essence legitimized its existence (and to what was repeatedly endangered structurally)—namely, its independence from the temporal entanglements of the world.

A text ascribed to the Franciscan minister general Bonaventure captured what can be seen as the ontological core of this problem: "Everything that does not owe its existence to itself tends to decline and to oblivion, unless it is sustained by that which provides its existence; so it is with every person and every order. Thus every order not only of monks but also of bishops, secular priests, and laity, indeed every estate, declines sharply whenever one measures its customary circumstance by its beginnings."[99] With the establishment of this general principle, the author turned to a consideration of five reasons that a religious community such as an order tended to decline (*deficit*) over time. The first, he suggested, was the crowd of new members, who were not so easy to lead as were the few in the early days. The second reason was that the first generation died off or lost strength, their model discipline lost its force, leaving only cheap imitation. Because those who came after the first generation failed to appreciate the Order's virtues as the older ones had upheld them, the Order had everywhere abandoned those virtues. The third reason was the increasing somnolence of later generations, who could only hand down what they themselves had learned imperfectly. The fourth reason was the encroachment of bad customs, the fifth and final reason the all-too-frequent engagement in worldly affairs.

The author here presented in general outline a model of institutional development grounded in the assertion of a primordially established core ideal (*propositum*) and then remarked on its real or supposed loss. As a counterweight, religious congregations crafted their own founding histories, through which they sought to make credible, both inwardly and outwardly, the claim that the legacy of their excellent origins had been realized down to the present.

In a pragmatic way, local communities reached back into their own histories to craft so-called cartulary chronicles or foundation

---

[99] *Determinationes quaestionum circa Regulam Fratrum minorum*, in *Doctoris seraphici S. Bonaventurae . . . opera omnia, Ad Claras Aquas* (Quaracchi, 1898), 8:349.

stories,[100] most of which were bound to sacralizing narratives of a community's origins and to stories of the deeds of the community's leaders (*Gesta abbatum*).[101] As such, these texts sought not only to archive a legal and economic *status quo* for the collective memory of the community, but above all to present an array of traditions that immortalized its past.

In larger religious congregations, a common strategy for securing the legitimacy of a particular identity was to locate the origins of a communal life devoted to God in the early church, the *ecclesia primitiva* of the apostolic community in Jerusalem. The brotherhood and common property shared among those who were individually poor, as related in the book of Acts, served as both a model and a concrete point of historical origin for their particular ways of life.[102] To note only a few examples: around the middle of the twelfth century, the Benedictine author of the chronicle of the Hirsau community of Petershausen (*Casus Monasterii Petrishusensis*) emphasized that the virtues and customs of the apostles—their embrace of the common life, their renunciation of worldly things, their tenacity in the service of God, their uninterrupted praise of God, their unanimity (*unanimitas*), and so on—were also an obligatory model for his particular community.[103] Another example is the Cistercian apologetic text known as the *Exordium magnum*, composed between 1186 and 1221, which tersely asserted that the common life of the monastery was the way of life of the *ecclesia primitiva* itself and that the monastic way of life had its origins there.[104] Alongside these articulations from the

[100] Jörg Kastner, *Historiae fundationum monasteriorum: Frühformen monastischer Institutionsgeschichtsschreibung im Mittelalter* (Munich: Arbeo-Gesellschaft, 1974); Alois Schmid, "Die Fundationes monasteriorum Bavariae: Entstehung—Verbreitung—Quellenwert—Funktion," in *Geschichtsschreibung und Geschichtsbewußtsein im späten Mittelalter*, ed. Hans Patze (Sigmaringen: Thorbecke, 1987), 581–646.

[101] Michel Sot, *Gesta episcoporum, gesta abbatum*, 2 vols. (Turnhout: Brepols, 1981, 1985).

[102] Giovanni Miccoli, "Ecclesiae primitivae forma," *Studi medievali*, series 3.1 (1960): 470–98.

[103] Anonymus Petrishusensis, *Casus monasterii Petrishusensis*, MGH Scriptores 20, 621–83, praefatio.

[104] *Exordium magnum Cisterciense, oder Bericht vom Anfang des Zisterzienserordens*, trans. and commentary by Heinz Piesik, 2 vols. (Langwaden:

monastic milieu, the regular canon Lietbert of St. Ruf also claimed at the beginning of the twelfth century that the rule under which his community lived (*regula . . . qua vivimus*) had been handed down by Christ, who had lived the common life with his disciples, and that they in turn had passed it on to the church.[105]

Just as compelling were the ways in which the story of a particular monastery or order might be woven into the larger tapestry of salvation history.[106] As one example, the Camaldolese were already aware of their transcendent significance in the twelfth century as they composed their rule, the *Liber heremitice regulae*, which opened with these words: "Although there are many forms of religious life, it is the solitary life that stands out among them in an instructive way."[107] As proof the text ran off a distinguished series of exemplary hermits, beginning with Moses and continuing with David, Elijah, Elisha, John the Baptist, Christ, the Desert Fathers, and Benedict of Nursia, ending with Romuald, the founder of Camaldoli. All of them had chosen the

---

Bernardus-Verlag, 2000/2002), 1:12. In English, *The Great Beginning of Cîteaux: A Narrative of the Beginning of Cîteaux; The* Exordium Magnum *of Conrad of Eberbach*, trans. Benedicta Ward and Paul Savage, ed. E. Rozanne Elder, CF 72 (Kalamazoo, MI: Cistercian Publications, 2011), here 49.

[105] PL 157:715–19.

[106] Kaspar Elm, "Die Bedeutung historischer Legitimation für Entstehung, Funktion und Bestand des mittelalterlichen Ordenswesens," in *Herkunft und Ursprung. Historische Formen der Legitimation*, ed. Peter Wunderli (Sigmaringen: Thorbecke, 1994), 71–90; Cécile Caby, "La mémoire des origines dans les institutions médiévales: bilan d'un séminaire collectif," in *Écrire son histoire: les communautés régulières face à leur passé*, ed. Nicole Bouter (Saint-Étienne: Publications de l'Université de Saint-Étienne, 2006), 13–20; Gert Melville, "Knowledge of the Origins: Constructing Identity and Ordering Monastic Life in the Middle Ages," in *Knowledge, Discipline and Power in the Middle Ages: Essays in Honour of David Luscombe*, ed. Joseph Canning et al. (Leiden: Brill, 2011), 41–62; Gert Jäkel, *. . . usque in praesentem diem. Kontinuitätskonstruktionen in der Eigengeschichtsschreibung religiöser Orden des Hoch- und Spätmittelalters* (Berlin: LIT, 2013); Philippe Josserand and Mathieu Olivier, eds., *La mémoire des origines dans les ordres religieux-militaires au Moyen Âge. / Die Erinnerung an die eigenen Ursprünge in den geistlichen Ritterorden im Mittelalter* (Berlin: LIT, 2013).

[107] Pierluigi Licciardello, ed., *Consuetudo Camaldulensis. Rudolphi Constitutiones. Liber Eremitice Regule* (Florence: SISMEL edizioni del Galluzzo, 2004), 22.

life of a hermit either of their own accord or through God's command, and every one of their lives served as proof of the extraordinary profit found in leading an eremitical life. These *exempla*, deeply rooted in salvation history and charged with tremendous allegorical power, certainly provided the Camaldolensian way of life with exemplary standards. These served not only to inspire imitation, however, but also to affirm the Order's distinct religious path and, before the entire world, to clothe that path in a validity that pointed to the world beyond.

Common to all of the strategies of constructing the past outlined here is that they formed for each community a distinct historical memory, with whose help each community was able to confront any doubt about the stability and legitimacy of religious institutions. Such "founding histories"[108] always returned to origins, granted them validity by virtue of their exemplarity, and then made possible the assertion that such validity, as an unchanging continuum, had successfully been carried all the way down to the present.

Cloister and World

Monastic communities saw themselves as institutions standing between heaven and earth. Yet they could only open the way to heaven by living their earthly lives in a way that made heaven accessible. Monasteries were places in which the life of faith was perfectly organized and reserved for only the elite of *religio*, yet at the same time places that served as models for all of the faithful who hoped for heaven. From this coupling of inward faith and perfected organization, the religious found the strength to move beyond the walls of their communities and decisively to influence the world beyond—or to draw their own inspiration from it. The essential needs of medieval society were thus crystalized in the form of religious life. The religious not only set the example for how the ethical principles of the Christian faith were to be realized but also offered the promise of a secure investment, in terms of both piety and the worldly business of economics and politics.

---

[108] On this concept, see Jan Assmann, *Cultural Memory and Early Civilization: Writing, Remembrance, and Political Imagination* (Cambridge, UK: Cambridge University Press, 2011).

From the early Middle Ages on, the nobility had founded monasteries on their own estates, both to exploit their agricultural potential and to establish indivisible anchor points for their power.[109] Later on, when from the beginning of the eleventh century the nobility came to shape itself according to agnatic familial alliances (grounded in the male line), monasteries came to provide symbolic focus for lordship. They served as family burial sites,[110] and they were the institutions through which a dynasty might first be created, so to speak, by way of historiographical works about a founding figure and the growth of his lineage.[111]

But the nobility founded and fostered religious communities for another reason: because of God's good will, the prayers of the religious brought a benefit for the individual soul, a benefit that outlasted even death. Kings supported religious communities in order to secure places where the praise of God would sustain the welfare of both kingdom and people. For those prayers to be heard, the life of the religious community had to be lived spiritually in the best possible way. To that end, those supporters who saw themselves as responsible for a given community—but who were also plagued by fear of damnation—took care to establish it on a firm material foundation and to win recruits who were accomplished virtuosos in the life of the faith. Reform communities like Inden, Cluny, Fruttuaria, Gorze, and Hirsau were widely respected as places for sound investment, where earthly donations could, through appreciation, be transformed into spiritual dividends. Other communities of the strictest discipline—the Grandmontines and the Carthusians, as well as other congregations and orders that also fulfilled their apostolic missions in compelling ways—were similarly renowned.

Well into the High Middle Ages, the nobility had taken exclusive responsibility for the founding of religious communities, but from the thirteenth century on, with the flowering of the cities, new classes

---

[109] Nathalie Kruppa, A*dlige—Stifte—Mönche* (Göttingen: Vandenhoeck & Ruprecht, 2007).

[110] For a famous example, see Renate Prochno, *Die Kartause von Champmol* (Berlin: Akademie, 2002).

[111] Hans Patze, "Adel und Stifterchronik. Frühformen territorialer Geschichtsschreibung im hochmittelalterlichen Reich," in *Ausgewählte Aufsätze von Hanz Patze*, ed. Peter Johanek et al. (Stuttgart: Thorbecke, 2002), 109–49.

of merchants and artisans also emerged as patrons.[112] By drawing together their resources, they were able to found and support mostly mendicant communities in their cities. According to their various means they gave land, vineyards, and fish ponds, whether as property or as a right of use. They donated wax, liturgical objects, altar images, and provisions, and they bequeathed incomes and cash in their wills. Decisive in these arrangements was that they established a lasting structure for the commemoration of the beneficiary, one that would continue to provide intercession long after the death of the donor—*pro remedio animae*, as the foundation documents usually said. Urban women's communities especially, whose inhabitants (in contrast to their male counterparts in mendicant convents) lived stationary lives, often became the focal points of complex spaces of communication between religious houses and the urban environment. The individual nuns' family members (often clergy) were active as patrons and pastors, building up individual networks sustained by emotional bonds and thereby competing with similar networks built up by others.[113]

But a monastery was also a place whose walls could keep out the dangers of the world only with difficulty—as epitomized in the apocalyptic image of Babylon—and its inhabitants often found themselves (in the biblical language of the time) "between hammer and anvil."[114] "The monastery is also a microcosm of the mundane world," as Marie-Dominique Chenu emphasized.[115] External troubles were woven into the fabric of monastic life. The power of the monastery to shape the world around it was of necessity faced with entanglement in the

---

[112] On the most important structures, see Andreas Rüther, *Bettelorden in Stadt und Land. Die Straßburger Mendikantenkonvente und das Elsaß im Spätmittelalter* (Berlin: Duncker & Humblot, 1997).

[113] Christine Kleinjung, *Frauenklöster als Kommunikationszentren und soziale Räume* (Korb: Didymos, 2008).

[114] Gert Melville, "Die 'Exhortatiunculae' des Girardus de Arvernia an die Cluniazenser. Bilanz im Alltag einer Reformierungsphase," in *Ecclesia und regnum. Beiträge zur Geschichte von Kirche, Recht und Staat. Festschrift für Franz-Josef Schmale*, ed. Dieter Berg and Hans-Werner Goetz (Bochum: Winkler, 1989), 203–34, here 211.

[115] Marie-Dominique Chenu, *La théologie au XIIe siècle* (Paris: Vrin, 1966), 230: "Le monastère est en même temps la cellule d'une cité terrestre"; Ludo Milis, *Les Moines et le peuple dans l'Europe du Moyen Âge* (Paris: Belin, 2002).

respective historical structures of its social, political, and economic environment. Those entanglements could not only prove useful for a given religious community; they could also draw the community into an institutionally conditioned dependence on secular powers— for example, when the leadership of a monastery was taken over by laity through a lay abbacy, when the monastery's right to dispose of its goods was granted to outsiders (through proprietary churches or patronage), or when a community was subject to the protection of an advocate or, especially in French territories, the *garde*.[116] Moreover, religious communities were constantly faced with those who, although appointed as protectors, were always gratuitously seizing monastic wealth. Monasteries tried to guard against such aggression through a very specific means: by using their command of literacy to record their rights to properties, at least in such a way as to provide proof of theft. Expressions such as this one from the abbey of Saint-Bertin in Flanders were legion: "We have put together this codex over the course of the years, on parchment and in the form of a book, only so that it can be consulted whenever someone might be greedy enough to try to seize the properties of this place for himself."[117]

The world of the nobility and the world of monasticism could find themselves in a symbiotic relationship, but they disagreed fundamentally over two matters.[118] The first was that life in the monastery served all who were enclosed within its walls equally in their struggle for salvation. There was in principle no place for differentiation according to social status. To point to any special merits was to fall victim to *superbia*, pride, and thus to be guilty of the worst of all vices. Yet the social world of the nobility was driven by public competition over rank and renown. It constituted itself from those who were

[116] Noël Didier, *La garde des églises au XIIIe siècle* (Paris: Picard, 1927).

[117] "Hunc tantummodo codicem de membranulis in unius libri cumulavimus corpus, ut, si forsan quis istius loci possessionum investigandarum fuerit avidus, ad hunc recurrat" (*Gesta abbatum Sithiensium*, MGH SS 13:608).

[118] Klaus Schreiner, *Mönchsein in der Adelsgesellschaft des hohen und späten Mittelalters* (Munich: Oldenbourg, 1989); Christina Lutter, ed., *Funktionsräume, Wahrnehmungsräume, Gefühlsräume. Mittelalterliche Lebensformen zwischen Kloster und Welt* (Vienna: Böhlau, 2011). Christina Lutter, "Social Groups, Personal Relations, and the Making of Communities in Medieval *Vita Monastica*," in *Making Sense as a Cultural Practice: Historical Perspectives*, ed. Jörg Rogge (Bielefeld: Transcript, 2013), 45–61.

born into and belonged to a specific place in the social hierarchy. The second matter over which monastery and nobility disagreed was the view that noble power and lordship rested on personal wealth and that to increase that wealth was crucial not least as a distinctive means of representation. Yet poverty, humility, and chastity, for the individual and often for an entire community, were specific and fundamental requirements for leading the *vita religiosa*.

From Late Antiquity, in Lérins and in the communities of the Rhône, for example, until well into the High Middle Ages, the nobility filled the ranks of most religious communities. Without question, the desire to make salvation more secure was usually the motive for most who entered the monastery. But in many cases, the reasons were also quite practical: membership in a monastic community guaranteed noble families influence in matters of politics and helped to provide for the provision of daughters and second-born sons, as well as (so numerous sources report) the physically handicapped.[119]

Nobles also lived in religious communities—whose spiritual depth was never in doubt—in a way that was in keeping with their status, at least insofar as the norms of the Rule might barely allow. In Cluny, for example, a community that over the course of time was more and more dominated by the nobility, meals were without question extraordinarily sumptuous for a monastic environment—and thus provided the hermits and the Cistercians of the twelfth century with good reason to launch their severe critiques. In Cluny, but also in other communities, for example, in communities of canonesses, the use of servants was also common. Manual labor—an essential element of Benedictine life—was scorned in Cluniac monasteries, and when it was required (even if only as a matter of symbolic interaction) it was not to be done in public view.

Reform-minded communities, above all the Cistercians, sought a return to original ideals of equality. They proclaimed the dissolution of differences according to status as a form of asceticism and a form of self-humiliation, and they were not without success in doing so. As Klaus Schreiner has put it so well and concisely, "the flattening of distinctions of status made clear that in the monastery it was no longer

---

[119] Ulrich von Cluny, *Epistola nuncupatoria*, in Boynton and Cochelin, *Customs*, 329–47.

nobility as merely a nominal title of secular lineage that mattered, but rather the true nobility of the spiritual life."[120]

Reforming orders wanted to accept those who were possessed of a high degree of self-responsibility, and they therefore allowed admission only to adults. But in doing so they thereby accepted women and men who had already experienced a socially stratified world and who brought that memory with them.[121] This in turn fostered its own threats to a spirit of equality. For example, in the thirteenth century the Cistercian Caesarius of Heisterbach told of a formerly noble lay brother (*conversus*) who had long been accustomed only to caring for pigs and who began to brood over his circumstance: "What am I doing here? As a man I am high born, but because of this humble task I am despised by all my friends. I can no longer stay here as a swineherd."[122] The humility that came from conversion, Caesarius concluded, had transformed itself into pride and had turned a God-fearing soul into a rebel against virtue and truth. At around the same time Gerard de Arvernia, the keen observer of the Cluniacs, told how relatives would visit noble monks, approach them with poisonous flattery, and voice their embarrassment over the living conditions in the monastery. He continued by casting the world of the aristocrat, the society of the high born, of private incomes and noble posterity in the harsh light of missed opportunities.[123]

Religious communities shaped by the nobility were also to be found in the late Middle Ages—often as male Benedictine monasteries, but especially as women's communities—and the reform movements that produced the networks of Melk or Kastl still sought to guard against both excesses of lifestyle and the exclusion of those who were not of noble blood. But it was the establishment of the mendicant orders

---

[120] Schreiner, *Mönchsein*, 17. The same point becomes clear by considering the way in which distinguished guests were treated. See Jörg Sonntag, "Welcoming High Guests to the Paradise of the Monks—Social Interactions and Symbolic Moments of Monastic Self-Representation According to Lanfranc's Constitutions," in *Self-Representation of Medieval Religious Communities*, ed. Anne Müller and Karen Stöber (Berlin: LIT, 2009), 45–65.

[121] Jean Leclercq, *L'amour vu par les moines au XIIᵉ siècle* (Paris: Éditions du Cerf, 1979), 16–25.

[122] *Caesarii Heisterbacensis monachi ordinis Cisterciensis Dialogus miraculorum*, ed. Joseph Strange (Cologne, 1851), 1:175.

[123] Melville, "Die 'Exhortatiunculae' des Girardus de Arvernia," 212.

and their integration into structures of urban life that marked a turning point in the social history of monastic community.[124] Mendicant houses were usually filled with representatives of every social rank. The Franciscan call to imitate the poor Christ, especially, was unconcerned with boundaries of status. And such a message could be taken up and interiorized by those who were concerned not to follow rules like Pharisees but instead to embrace a new and open way of life. Beguines and other semireligious women (and men, too) came from every social rank, and where necessary they discounted an aristocratic heritage in favor of service to their neighbors. Already in her own day, Elizabeth of Thuringia was a highly esteemed example of that kind of piety.[125]

Temporalia

In order to preserve the special status of a community set apart from the world, economic self-sufficiency was a fundamental principle of monastic life, even among those who observed the strictest possible measure of poverty. To note one example, the Grandmontines, who lived in solitude and complete poverty, were not allowed to possess livestock, tithes, or prebends and could own only enough land to allow for burial. In cases of absolute necessity they were allowed to go begging but had to cease as soon as they had enough provision to last them one day. "Those who had died to the world," as contemporaries described them, were no longer to entangle themselves in worldly structures. The followers of Francis, to note a second example, were to work above all in order to take care of their necessities.[126] And as the *Regula non bullata* made clear, they were allowed to beg for alms like the rest of the poor only out of necessity. A little later, Innocent IV crafted the fiction that the Franciscans merely used the things they possessed while the church retained ownership of their goods.

---

[124] Dieter Berg, "Zur Sozialgeschichte der Bettelorden im 13. Jahrhundert," *Wissenschaft und Weisheit* 43 (1980): 55–64.

[125] Matthias Werner, "Die heilige Elisabeth in ihrer Zeit—Forschungsstand und Forschungsprobleme," in *Heilige Elisabeth von Thüringen—theologische Spurensuche,* ed. Dieter Wagner (Frankfurt am Main: Knecht, 2008), 14–69.

[126] Dieter Berg, *Armut und Geschichte* (Kevelaer: Butzon & Bercker, 2001); Annette Kehnel and Gert Melville, eds., *In proposito paupertatis* (Münster: LIT, 2001).

Monks build the monastery of Maulbronn in the Kraichgau, in an image from 1450.

In an age whose economy was overwhelmingly agricultural, monastic communities of the Benedictine tradition, along with foundations of regular canons, held their common property mainly in the form of landed estates.[127] The command to observe poverty (quite

___

[127] Cinzio Violante, "Monasteri e canoniche nello sviluppo dell'economia monetaria (secoli XI–XIII)," in *Istituzioni monastiche e istituzioni canonicali in Occidente (1123–1215)* (Milan: Vita e pensiero, 1980), 369–416.

apart from the question of its actual observance) was binding only on the individual. The dictates of religious rules covered the issue in principle—the Rule of Saint Benedict outlined in chapters 31 and 32 the duties of the cellarer and discussed matters like tools and clothing—but the broader structures of ownership were the result of a historical process in which monastic houses came to be seen by the outside world above all as infrastructural nuclei and anchor points for economic expansion. Already from the early Middle Ages, by way of gifts and donations that came to them alongside tithes, parish prebends, and rights to tolls, mines, and markets, monastic communities had become surrounded by often enormous landholdings. These could no longer be directly cultivated but had instead either to be worked by serfs or wage laborers or to be leased—as was the case with the Cluniacs, for example, on a grand scale.[128] The new reform movements of the eleventh and twelfth centuries, and especially the Cistercians, launched their attacks against Benedictine monasticism on precisely this point. They accused the traditional abbeys of living a festive life in pompous buildings, living from the fruits of estates that were worked by "foreign labor" (*labor alienus*).[129] The Cistercians themselves soon possessed extensive properties that had come to them by way of donations and thus moved to embrace as a new norm both their own manual labor and the independent cultivation of their estates. Work, as Bernard of Clairvaux emphasized, purified the heart and disciplined the body.[130] Yet among the priest-monks of the following generation, manual labor was reduced to a token, symbolic gesture. The economic duties of what became a far-flung network of farms (granges) and urban centers of trade[131] were now taken over by lay brothers, *conversi*—a group that in fact belonged to the monastic *familia*, but whose members had only sworn simple vows.

The Cistercians had developed the most advanced system with respect to techniques of economic exploitation. But the agriculturally

<hr>

[128] Georges Duby, "Cluny e l'economia rurale," in *La bonifica benedettina*, ed. Aldo Ferrabino (Rome: Istituto della enciclopedia italiana, 1963), 107–17.

[129] Schreiner, "Brot der Mühsal."

[130] Schreiner, "Brot der Mühsal," 149.

[131] Werner Rösener, "Die Agrarwirtschaft der Zisterzienser. Innovation und Anpassung," in *Norm und Realität. Kontinuität und Wandel der Zisterzienser im Mittelalter*, ed. Franz Felten and Werner Rösener (Berlin: LIT, 2009), 67–95.

oriented communities of every observance faced a serious crisis at the close of the High Middle Ages with the encroachments of a new economy based on currency.[132] While religious houses in urban contexts—specifically, and paradoxically, the mendicants[133]—remained secure by virtue of strong financial support from burghers, those rural communities that continued to rely on leases struggled as funding and provision became more expensive while the financial yields from the leases remained the same. The visitation protocols of the Cluniacs in the thirteenth and fourteenth centuries, for example, recorded hundreds of cases of monasteries massively in debt and confronted with all of its negative consequences—collapsing buildings, community unrest and rebellion, alienation of property, and so on.[134]

Nevertheless, in general the technical achievements designed to improve the monasteries' economic yields were extraordinary.[135] Admittedly, it is difficult precisely to determine the monasteries' concrete roles in spreading specific strategies of crop cultivation, particular kinds of fruit cultivation, or methods of animal breeding. But it is certain that many communities were successful enough at cultivating grain, wine, and fruit and at raising fish, pork, and sheep that they both amassed an agricultural surplus and sought to profit from it. Here too the Cistercians, whose numerous urban houses served as locales for commodity exchange, stood in the forefront.[136]

In maintaining and building up a remarkable network that encompassed both agricultural production and trade, the Celestines accomplished something truly remarkable. They organized an infrastructure of transhumance over enormous stretches across central

---

[132] Violante, "Monasteri e canoniche," 109–250.

[133] Jens Röhrkasten, *The Mendicant Houses of Medieval London, 1221–1539* (Münster: LIT, 2004), 221–78; Nicole Bériou, ed., *Économie et religion* (Lyon: Presses universitaires de Lyon, 2009).

[134] Melville, "Die 'Exhortatiunculae' des Girardus de Arvernia."

[135] Klaus Schreiner, "Technischer Fortschritt als Weg in ein neues Paradies. Zur theologischen und sozialethischen Legitimationsbedürftigkeit technischer Neuerungen im späten Mittelalter und in der frühen Neuzeit," in *Aufbruch im Mittelalter*, ed. Christian Hesse and Klaus Oschema (Ostfildern: Thorbecke, 2010), 125–58.

[136] Wolfgang Bender, *Zisterzienser und Städte. Studien zu den Beziehungen zwischen den Zisterzienserklöstern und den großen urbanen Zentren des mittleren Moselraumes (12.–14. Jahrhundert)* (Trier: Trier Historische Forschungen, 1992), 39–45.

and southern Italy.[137] The Order's settlements, scattered across the Apennines, served as anchor points and centers of communication for the shepherds who made their way across the landscape with great flocks of sheep twice yearly—up into the mountains in spring to summer pastures, and back down in fall to the winter pastures of the plains. The animals were an important element in the provisioning of the cities, but they were also feared by landowners because of the damage they did to the fields. The Celestines, with the help of their widely dispersed settlements, channeled and directed the routes of the sheep drives, cared both materially and spiritually for the shepherds, arranged for financial settlements among the owners of land and sheep, and served as brokers in urban markets.

Among monasticism's particularly beneficial technical achievements were those concerning handicrafts and building[138] (for example, the abbey church of Saint-Bénigne in Dijon, which stands as the beginning of the Romanesque tradition, and Saint-Denis in Paris as the beginning of the Gothic) as well as hydraulic engineering and mining.[139] In the field of water management, canals and tunnels were built to protect monasteries from floods, to acquire fruitful ground, or to increase the speed of flowing water. Notable examples in this regard include the channel known as the Almkanal in Salzburg, cut through the Mönchsberg after 1136, mostly by the *conversi* of the Benedictine abbey of St. Peter, or the so-called Fulbert tunnel, completed under Fulbert, the second abbot of Maria Laach between 1152 and 1170. A description of the abbey of Clairvaux from the beginning of the thirteenth century emphasizes the importance of water management for the proper ordering of daily monastic life. The little River Aube was channeled through the monastery to drive the grain mill and later the fulling mill. The stream also provided for the tannery and the kitchen, among others, before finally leaving the monastery, taking with it the community's refuse.[140] Experience in water

---

[137] See Karl Borchardt, *Die Cölestiner* (Husum: Matthiesen, 2006), 311–18.

[138] Wolfgang Braunfels, "Abendländische Klosterbaukunst," in *Kunstgeschichte, Deutung, Dokumente* (Cologne: DuMont, 1985).

[139] Dieter Hägermann, "Das Kloster als Innovationszentrum. Mühlenbetrieb, Salzproduktion und Bergbau," in *Kloster und Wirtschaftswelt im Mittelalter*, ed. Claudia Dobrinski et al. (Munich: Wilhelm Fink, 2007), 13–23.

[140] Clemens Kosch, "Wasserbaueinrichtungen in hochmittelalterlichen Konventsanlagen. Eine Nachlese," in *Wohn- und Wirtschaftsbauten frühmittelalterlicher*

management and redirection also proved useful in mining. Almost every abbey near the sea made an effort to secure shares of rights in salt works. Others, such as the regular canonry of Berchtesgarden, sought to gain the right to mine salt from the mountains in order to be able to produce, process, and sell the costly mineral as part of their own initiatives. But the Cistercian communities again stood out above all as "cultivators of a new, profitable mining technique."[141] Especially the medieval monasteries' smelting furnaces and forges, many of which still survive today, bear witness to the intensity of monastic mining and metalworking. The Cistercians of the Belgian convent of Val-Saint-Lambert, for example, mined coal so actively that their house came to be called the "coal convent."[142]

Technology allowed for shaping of the world, and Genesis 1:28, which gave the command to "fill the earth and subdue it," provided the appropriate legitimation. For those who lived the *vita religiosa*, such work was not an unfitting forgery of God's creative power but rather a means of ordering the world materially and economically— and thereby a means of being set free from its entanglements. In taking hold of the world, religious saw the possibility of overcoming it.

On the Search for God toward Knowledge of the World

Religious, as they searched for God, both acquired and inquired about knowledge of the world so that they might also find the key to the order of creation.[143] They wrote and handed down texts to guard

---

Klöster, ed. Hans Rudolf Sennhauser (Zurich: VDF Hochschulverlag, 1996), 69–84; Winfried Schich, "Klosteranlage und Wasserversorgung bei den Zisterziensern," in *Wirtschaft und Kulturlandschaft: Gesammelte Beiträge 1977 bis 1999 zur Geschichte der Zisterzienser und der "Germania Slavica,"* ed. Winfried Schich et al. (Berlin: Berliner Wissenschafts-Verlag, 2007), 25–41.

[141] Otto Volk, *Salzproduktion und Salzhandel mittelalterlicher Zisterzienserklöster* (Sigmaringen: Thorbecke, 1984).

[142] Horst Kranz, "Energie für die niederen Lande: Kohlenhandel auf der Maas im 14. Jahrhundert," in *Inquirens subtilia diversa. Dietrich Lohrmann zum 65. Geburtstag*, ed. Horst Kranz and Ludwig Falkenstein (Aachen: Shaker, 2002), 359–74.

[143] Jean Leclercq, *The Love of Learning and the Desire for God: A Study of Monastic Culture* (New York: Fordham University Press, 1982); Martin Kintzinger, "Keine große Stille—Wissenskulturen zwischen Kloster und Welt,"

against forgetting and to preserve knowledge for posterity. They tested the limits of rational understanding through the dialectic of the schools and burst beyond them in their individual mystical experiences.

In a way already articulated after 540 by Cassiodorus (485–580) in the monastery of Vivarium on the eastern coast of Calabria, the study of written texts would remain tied to religious life in a specific way for all of the Middle Ages. Cassiodorus, a Roman senator and highly ranked state official under Ostrogothic King Theoderic, had retreated from the business of politics at the age of fifty-five. As he himself recorded, he then experienced a conversion to a religious way of life and established Vivarium on his inherited estate near Squillace.[144] There he obligated the monks to offer service to God by working with both Christian and pagan texts, whether by revising and improving, copying, or at least collecting excerpts from them. He himself sought to allow for a stronger presence of pagan knowledge in the realm of Christian theology. A similar approach had already been in evidence in the early fifth century in the works of Augustine, especially in his *De doctrina christiana* (On Christian Doctrine),[145] where he explicitly justified Christians—whom he likened to the Jews plundering Egyptian treasures—who used pagan knowledge in the service of the truth of Christianity. Cassiodorus sought to articulate an analogous view in his encyclopedic *Institutiones*.[146] That work offered an invitation to study of the Bible and provided a systematic introduction to divine and human knowledge; it became authoritative for medieval systems of scholarly classification.

Few early developments showed more strikingly than these the consequences that arose from the fact that Christianity is a religion of the book. Precisely for men and women in monastic life, who sought a methodical way to ensure salvation, a sustained interaction with texts was decisive because it led to the proper carrying out of the service of God—whether in the practice of the liturgy and prayer, in

---

in *Monastisches Leben im urbanen Kontext*, ed. Anne-Marie Hecker and Susanne Röhl (Paderborn: Wilhelm Fink, 2010), 109–30.

[144] Fabio Troncarelli, *Vivarium. I libri, il destino* (Turnhout: Brepols, 1998).

[145] Augustine, *De doctrina christiana*, ed. William McAllen Green, CSEL 80 (Vienna: Hoelder-Pichler-Tempsky, 1963), 75–76.

[146] *Cassiodori Senatoris Institutiones*, ed. Roger Aubrey B. Mynors (Oxford: Clarendon Press, 1937, repr. 1961).

the encounter with biblical revelation, or in knowledge of creation. The centrality of books is already in evidence in the Rule of Saint Benedict, a text that raised the reading of sacred texts at mealtime or after Compline, as well as private reading, to an institutional level.

A sophisticated and productive engagement with texts in search of knowledge of God and the world first emerged around the seventh century in Ireland and then in Anglo-Saxon monasteries, before finally being carried over to the continent. There, especially in the wake of the Carolingian Renaissance, which had as its core the establishment of correct biblical texts, monasteries came to hold a virtual monopoly on textual production.[147] The image of a monastic asceticism grounded in the writing of books had now emerged.

The same era also saw the widespread establishment of monastic scriptoria[148] as well as proper monastic schools[149] that were to a limited degree open even to students from outside the monastic community. That tradition of monastic schooling, focused of course on the education of its own recruits but also open to and influential in the world, endured for centuries, though incurring some criticism. It played a partial but decisive role in helping to shape the establishment of universities—for example, in the case of St. Victor in Paris.[150] In the end, however, monastic education was either reduced

---

[147] Pierre Riché, *Education and Culture in the Barbarian West* (Columbia: University of South Carolina Press, 1976); Rosamond McKitterick, *The Carolingians and the Written Word* (Cambridge, UK: Cambridge University Press, 1995).

[148] Guglielmo Cavallo, "Le scriptorium médiéval," in *Lieux de savoir*, vol. 2, *Les mains de l'intellect*, ed. Christian Jacob (Paris: Albin Michel, 2011), 537–55.

[149] Rudolf Freister, "Die Klosterschule," in *Macht des Wortes*, ed. Gerfried Sitar and Martin Kroker (Regensburg: Schnell & Steiner, 2009), 1:235–42. On further developments, see Peter Johanek, "Klosterstudien im 12. Jahrhundert," in *Schulen und Studien im sozialen Wandel des hohen und späten Mittelalters*, ed. Johannes Fried (Sigmaringen: Thorbecke, 1986), 35–68; Nathalie Kruppa and Jürgen Wilke, eds., *Kloster und Bildung im Mittelalter* (Göttingen: Vandenhoeck & Ruprecht, 2006); Frank Rexroth, "Monastischer und scholastischer Habitus. Beobachtungen zum Verhältnis zwischen zwei Lebensformen des 12. Jahrhunderts," in *Innovationen durch Deuten und Gestalten*, ed. Gert Melville et al. (Regensburg: Schnell & Steiner, 2014), 317–33.

[150] Dominique Poirel, ed., *L'école de Saint-Victor de Paris. Influence et rayonnement du Moyen Âge à l'époque moderne* (Turnhout: Brepols, 2010).

to serving only as "preparation for higher study"[151] or transformed (especially in the hands of the mendicants) to serve as a means of educating the children of the urban elite.[152] The elite of the religious orders themselves had in the meantime made their way to the leading universities, where they at first faced strong resistance (especially in Paris around the middle of the thirteenth century) from the secular clergy already established there. But they soon founded their own houses of study, or, in the case of the mendicant orders, established *studia generalia*—advanced schools of theology whose conditions were similar to those of the university.[153]

Given the diversity of the *vita religiosa* and the great expanse of time under consideration here, it is difficult to make general claims about the religious orders' interests in education. Although for centuries religious communities were home to the scholarly elite, and although they shaped European culture in decisive ways, both the content and the methods of education varied considerably.

Reform movements, which throughout the Middle Ages saw ascetic practice as the most important means to spiritual growth, stood at a distance from what today might be called "intellectuality" and quickly tended to stigmatize passion for knowledge as sinful curiosity (*curiositas*).[154] For reformist zealots, it was enough to move along the path of inner contemplation (*contemplatio*)[155] to a mystical "consciousness

---

[151] Rainer A. Müller, "Klosterschulen," in *Enzyklopädie des Mittelalters*, ed. Gert Melville and Martial Staub (Darmstadt: Primus, 2008), 1:417.

[152] Roberto Lambertini, "Il sistema formativo degli studia degli Ordini Mendicanti: osservazioni a partire dai resultati di recenti indagini," in Andenna et al., *Die Ordnung der Kommunikation*, 135–46, here 137.

[153] Dieter Berg, *Armut und Wissenschaft*; Kaspar Elm, "Studium und Studienwesen der Bettelorden. Die 'andere' Universität," in *Stätten des Geistes*, ed. Alexander Demandt (Cologne: Böhlau, 1999), 111–26; Bert Roest, *A History of Franciscan Education (c. 1210–1517)* (Leiden: Brill, 2000); *Studio et studia. Le scuole degli ordini mendicanti tra XIII e XIV secolo. Atti del XXIX Convegno internazionale. Assisi, 11–13 ottobre 2001* (Spoleto: Centro italiano di studi sull'alto Medioevo, 2002).

[154] Richard G. Newhauser, "Augustinian *Vitium curiositatis* and Its Reception," in *Sin: Essays on the Moral Tradition in the Western Middle Ages*, ed. Richard G. Newhauser (Aldershot: Ashgate, 2007), 99–124.

[155] Jean Leclercq, *Otia monastica. Études sur le vocabulaire de la contemplation au Moyen Âge* (Rome: Herder, 1963); Christian Trottmann, ed., *Vie active

of the presence of God."[156] In contrast, orders committed to the task of religious instruction, such as the Dominicans, had to make the study of both Christian and pagan texts their profession—yet without excluding the possibility of mystical experience, as the work of Meister Eckhart (1260–1328), Henry Suso (1295–1366), and John Tauler (1300–1361) reveals.[157]

But in principle, it was decisive for all religious orders that every kind of instruction should serve the acquisition of spiritual wisdom (*sapientia*). Here a passage from Paul quoted by Augustine in the above-mentioned *De doctrina christiana* met with a broad, programmatic reception in medieval religious life: through the contemplation of visible, earthy things (*visibilia*), the ability to discern (*intelligentia*) things unseen (*invisibilia*) in the divine order was enhanced, and the search for the symbols of the divine presence in the created order thus became powerfully attractive.[158] Precisely this kind of education—understood as the formation (*formatio*) of a soul striving for knowledge—was understood in the medieval view as both a guard against the danger of falling into the vanity of worldly entanglements and as a possibility of escaping imprisonment in the mundane. Thus the Dominican encyclopedist Vincent of Beauvais, discussed above, summarized what a deeply Christian Middle Ages believed so emphatically: "Life itself (if it can even be called life) bears witness with

---

et vie contemplative au Moyen Âge et au seuil de la Renaissance (Rome: École française de Rome, 2009).

[156] Hedwig Röckelein, "Mystik," in Melville and Staub, *Enzyklopädie des Mittelalters*, 1:348–51; Kurt Ruh, *Geschichte der abendländischen Mystik*, 4 vols. (Munich: C. H. Beck, 1990–1999); Peter Dinzelbacher, *Christliche Mystik im Abendland. Ihre Geschichte von den Anfängen bis zum Ende des Mittelalters* (Paderborn: Schöningh, 1994); Bernard McGinn, *The Presence of God: A History of Western Christian Mysticism*, 5 vols. (New York: Crossroad Publishing, 1992–2012); Walter Haug and Wolfram Schneider-Lastin, *Deutsche Mystik im abendländischen Zusammenhang* (Tübingen: Niemeyer, 2000).

[157] Marie-Anne Vannier, ed., *Les mystiques rhénans. Eckhart, Tauler, Suso* (Paris: Éditions du Cerf, 2010).

[158] Alois Dempf, *Sacrum imperium. Geschichts- und Staatsphilosophie des Mittelalters und der politischen Renaissance* (Munich: Oldenbourg, 1973), 229–68. For important representatives of this tradition of thought, see Wolfgang Jungschaffer, "Artes liberales und Symbolismus bei Gerhoch von Reichersberg," in *Gerhoch von Reichersberg zu seinem 800. Todestag* (Linz: Bischöfl. Ordinariat, 1969), 46–60; Dale M. Coulter, *Per visibilia ad invisibilia: Theological Method in Richard of St. Victor († 1173)* (Turnhout: Brepols, 2002).

Representation of the Seven Liberal Arts and of Philosophy in the *Hortus deliciarum* of Herrad of Landsberg, an encyclopedia completed around 1170. Reproduction from the nineteenth century.

countless burdensome evils to the fact that from the first moment on, all mortal men were damned. What else could be this horrible fullness of ignorance, out of which every error arises and which ensnares all of the sons of Adam in its dark folds in such a way that mankind cannot be torn from it without instruction that is full of labor, pain, and fear?"[159]

[159] Vincentius Bellovacensis, *Speculum doctrinale* (Douai, 1624; Graz: Akademische Druck- und Verlaganstalt, 1964), 5–6.

Education was thus of central importance to those who lived in monastic community. It was one of the paths that could lead to salvation, and it had to be followed systematically. The system of the seven liberal arts (*septem artes liberales*), inherited from Late Antiquity, showed the way. Its curriculum allowed those who followed it to climb from the basic disciplines of the "threefold way" (*trivium*) of grammar, rhetoric, and logic up to the "fourfold way" (*quadrivium*) of arithmetic, geometry, music, and astronomy, the disciplines that allowed discernment of the harmonious order of creation.[160] In Paris, the regular canon Hugh of St. Victor (ca. 1097–1141) captured the spirit of the curriculum in his didactic work *Didascalicon de studio legendi* (*Instruction in the Study of Reading*). There he opened the way for those in religious orders by outlining appropriate learning techniques, according to this core principle: "There are two things above all through which everyone is brought to wisdom, namely reading and meditation."[161]

This kind of education, one both outwardly receptive and conditioned by reading, as well as inwardly reflective and gained through meditation, was equally valid for both men and women. Women religious took their place at the pinnacle of learning in their day: the canoness Herrad of Landsberg (1125/30–1195), for example, whose *Hortus Deliciarum* (*Garden of Delights*)[162] was the first encyclopedia written by a woman, and the Benedictine Hildegard of Bingen (1098–1179), who was not only renowned for her visionary ability but who also advanced innovative studies of ethics and cosmology, music and medicine.[163]

---

[160] Josef Koch, ed., *Artes liberales. Von der antiken Bildung zur Wissenschaft des Mittelalters* (Leiden: Brill, 1959); *Arts libéraux et philosophie au Moyen Âge* (Montreal: Institut d'Études Médiévales, 1969).

[161] Hugh of St. Victor, *Didascalicon de studio legendi*, ed. Thilo Offergeld (Freiburg: Herder, 1997), 106–7.

[162] Fiona J. Griffiths, "Female Spirituality and Intellect in the Twelfth and Thirteenth Centuries: A Case Study of Herrad of Hohenbourg," PhD diss., Cambridge University, 1998. For the education of women religious in the High and later Middle Ages, see the comprehensive treatment of Katharina Ulrike Mersch, *Soziale Dimensionen visueller Kommunikation in hoch- und spätmittelalterlichen Frauenkommunitäten* (Göttingen: Vandenhoeck & Ruprecht, 2012).

[163] Rainer Berndt, ed., *"Im Angesicht Gottes suche der Mensch sich selbst": Hildegard von Bingen (1098–1179)* (Berlin: Akademie, 2001); Heinrich Schip-

Without the monastic drive for knowledge, many questions might never have been asked, questions that with great anthropological depth explored the relationships between reason and faith and were thus of existential import. On the one hand, they inspired reflection on a human createdness that pointed to the divine, on how humanity was shaped by its primordial sinfulness, and on humankind's consequent existence in the world as foreigners and exiles. The same reflections led to the conclusion that humans were dependent on God's saving grace and on faith as a source of hope. On the other hand, monks sought insight into humankind as made in the image of God, a state that had brought with it the ability to reason.[164] Reason's capacity to learn the truth could itself be seen as an opportunity to escape the miserable conditions of earthly life. But it had also to be reconciled with faith as a source of revealed truth. In good Augustinian fashion, the Benedictine Anselm of Bec (later of Canterbury) already addressed that issue at the end of the eleventh century: "For I do not seek to understand that I may believe, but I believe in order to understand" (*Neque enim quaero intelligere ut credam; sed credo ut intelligam*).[165]

Had an established and continuous tradition of this kind of theological and philosophical discourse not already been in place—a tradition to which the medieval monastic world had contributed in essential ways—thirteenth-century Europe could hardly have experienced its crucial breakthrough into modernity, when the reception of Aristotle forced a new discussion of the relationship between

---

perges, *Die Welt der Hildegard von Bingen: Leben, Wirken, Botschaft* (Erftstadt: Hohe, 2007). See also the essays in *Voice of the Living Light: Hildegard of Bingen and Her World*, ed. Barbara Newman (Berkeley: University of California Press, 1998). On the later Middle Ages, see Eva Schlotheuber, *Klostereintritt und Bildung* (Tübingen: Mohr Siebeck, 2004), and Schlotheuber, "Sprachkompetenz und Lateinvermittlung. Die intellektuelle Ausbildung der Nonnen im Spätmittelalter," in Kruppa and Wilke, *Kloster und Bildung im Mittelalter*, 61–87.

[164] Gert Melville, "Wozu Geschichte schreiben? Stellung und Funktion der Historie im Mittelalter," in *Formen der Geschichtsschreibung*, ed. Reinhardt Koselleck et al., Beiträge zur Historik, vol. 4 (Munich: Deutscher Taschenbuch Verlag, 1982), 91–95.

[165] Anselm of Canterbury, *Proslogion*, ed. Franciscus Salesius Schmitt (Stuttgart-Bad Cannstadt: Friedrich Frommann, 2005), 83, 85. In English, among many available versions, see *Anselm: Basic Writings*, trans. S. N. Deane (La Salle: Open Court, 1962), here 53.

humankind and God. In the vanguard again was a religious, the Dominican Thomas Aquinas,[166] who moved far beyond Augustine in showing the way to a fruitful encounter between human reason and a metaphysically transcending faith.

Religious as individuals taught people how to live in a way pleasing to God, showed the way to an inner life, and at the same time interpreted the meaning of creation, of life, and of heaven in their preaching—a task for which they created specialized orders.

But religious communities, too, were leaders in advances of technology, medicine, agricultural exploitation, architecture, study, and writing. The mendicants dared to go as missionaries into Muslim lands, crossed the boundaries of the known world, brought back the first reports of advancing Mongols, established a new ecclesiastical province in China, and began to write the geography of the world anew.

Through the exemplary development of their own structures, monks and nuns, canons and canonesses, hermits, Beguines, and mendicants all shaped European conceptualizations of the interchange between individual and community. They taught Europe the rationality of planning, setting norms, division of labor, asset allocation, and economic efficiency. They cultivated a sense of the responsible disposition of worldly goods and promoted poverty as a way to be freed from earthly chains. They successfully tested the rational construction of social systems—whether through the statutes of constitutional texts or through the supervision of their leaders—and thereby opened the way to the formation of statehood.

Indeed medieval religious communities were "laboratories of innovation"[167] that laid down essential foundations for modernity.

---

[166] Rolf Schönberger, *Thomas von Aquin zur Einführung* (Hamburg: Junius, 2002). See also Jean-Pierre Torrell, *Saint Thomas Aquinas*, vol. 1, *The Person and His Work*, rev. ed. (Washington, DC: The Catholic University of America Press, 2005).

[167] Melville, "Im Spannungsfeld von religiösem Eifer und methodischem Betrieb," in *Innovationen durch Deuten und Gestalten*, ed. Melville et al. (Regensburg: Schnell & Steiner, 2014).

Chronology

Monastic World		General History
Anthony lives in the Egyptian desert	275–376	
Pachomius	292–346	
	313	Constantine the Great's Edict of Milan
Basil of Caesarea	329/330–379	
Martin of Tours founds the monastery of Marmoutier	375	
	380	Christianity becomes the state religion of the Roman Empire
Jerome in Rome as spiritual leader of ascetic women	382–385	
Baptism of Saint Augustine and growth of a monastic community	387	
Founding of a monastery on the archipelago of Lérins	405/10	
John Cassian dies	430/35	
	451	Council of Chalcedon

Monastic World		General History
	498/99	Baptism of the Frankish king Clovis
According to Gregory I, the founding of Monte Cassino	529	
Founding of Vivarium by Cassiodorus	540/54	
Caesarius of Arles dies	542	
According to Gregory I, the death of Benedict of Nursia	547	
Columbanus travels to the kingdom of the Franks	590/91	
	590–604	Pope Gregory I (the Great)
Augustine, sent by Pope Gregory I, founds the monastery of Peter and Paul in Canterbury	ca. 597	
First mention of the Rule of Saint Benedict	625	
Resettlement of Monte Cassino	ca. 717	
At a reform synod, the Rule of Saint Benedict is prescribed for all monasteries for the first time	742/43	
	800	Charlemagne crowned emperor
Reform synod of Aachen	816–819	

Monastic World		General History
Benedict of Aniane dies	821	
	899	Alfred the Great, king of the Anglo-Saxons, dies
Founding of Cluny	910	
Papal confirmation of Cluny's liberties	931	
Reform of Gorze	934	
	962	Otto I crowned emperor
Reform of Anglo-Saxon monasteries through the *Regularis Concordia*	970	
William of Volpiano becomes abbot of Saint-Benigne (Dijon)	990	
Odilo is abbot of Cluny	994–1049	
	996	Otto III crowned emperor
	997	Hugh Capet becomes king of France
Founding of Fruttuaria	1003	
William of Volpiano is abbot of Gorze for a few years in this time range	1012–1031	
Romuald, founder of Camaldoli, dies	1027	
Beginning of the community of regular canons of St. Ruf	1039	

Monastic World		General History
Hugh I is abbot of Cluny	1049–1109	
Founding of the Cluniac women's community of Marcigny	1055	
Founding of the abbey of Siegburg	1064	
	1066	William, Duke of Normandy, conquers England
William is abbot of Hirsau	1069–1091	
	1073–1085	Pope Gregory VII
Stephen of Thiers begins his eremitical life	1076	
	1077	Henry IV's journey to Canossa
	1088–1099	Pope Urban II
Altmann of Passau (supporter of the regular canons) dies	1091	
Bruno founds the Grande Chartreuse	1094	
Robert of Arbrissel becomes a hermit and wandering preacher	1095	
Beginning of the work of the Antonites	1096	
	1096–1099	First Crusade
Founding of Cîteaux	1098	

Monastic World		General History
Bernard is abbot of Clairvaux	1115–1153	
Papal approval of the Cistercian *Carta caritatis* (*prior*)	1119	
Norbert of Xanten founds the abbey of Prémontré	1120	
	1122	Concordat of Worms
Peter the Venerable is abbot of Cluny	1122–1156	
Norbert of Xanten becomes archbishop of Magdeburg; growth of the Praemonstratensian Order under Hugh of Fosses	1126	
The Templars receive their Rule at the Synod of Troyes	1129	
Stephen of Obazine begins his eremitical life	1130	
Gilbert founds the priory of Sempringham	1131	
Conrad I of Salzburg (supporter of the regular canons) dies	1147	
	1155	Frederick I Barbarossa crowned emperor
Founding of the Teutonic Order	1189	

Monastic World		General History
	1198–1216	Pope Innocent III
Transformation of the Cluniacs into an order	1200	
Papal approval of the Humiliati	1201	
Joachim of Fiore dies	1202	
The Carmelites receive a rule	1206/14	
Francis of Assisi before Pope Innocent III	1209	
Dominic founds the clerical community in Toulouse	1215	Fourth Lateran Council
Regula bullata of the Franciscans	1223	
	1226–1270	Saint Louis IX, king of France
	1227–1241	Pope Gregory IX
Capitulum generalissimum of the Dominicans, with the enactment of the *Constitutiones*	1228	
Papal bull of protection for German Beguines	1233	
	1245	First Council of Lyon
Papal approval of the Silvestrines; first general chapter of the Carmelites	1247	
Mendicant controversy in Paris	1252–1255	

Monastic World		General History
Clare of Assisi dies	1253	
Formation of the Order of Augustinian Hermits	1256	
Papal bull of protection for the eremitical community of Peter of Morrone	1263	
Bonaventure dies; Thomas Aquinas dies	1274	Second Council of Lyon
	1291	Fall of Acre
Peter Olivi dies	1294	
	1309–1377	Papacy in Avignon until the Great Western Schism (1378)
Founding of the monastery of Monte Oliveto	1313	
	1316–1334	Pope John XXII
Franciscans' avowal of poverty at the general chapter of Rimini	1322	
Papal confirmation of the Paulines	1328	Coronation of Ludwig IV the Bavarian as emperor
Reforms of Pope Benedict XII	1335–1339	
Birgitta of Sweden dies	1373	
	1378–1417	Great Western Schism
Geert Groote, founder of the *Devotio moderna*, dies	1384	

Monastic World		General History
Founding of the community of Windesheim	1387	
Death of the reforming abbot Otto Nortweiner of Kastl	1399	
	1414–1418	Council of Constance
Beginning of the Melk reform under Nicholas Seyringer	1418	
	1431–1449	Council of Basel
Approval of the congregation of Bursfelde by the Council of Basel	1446	

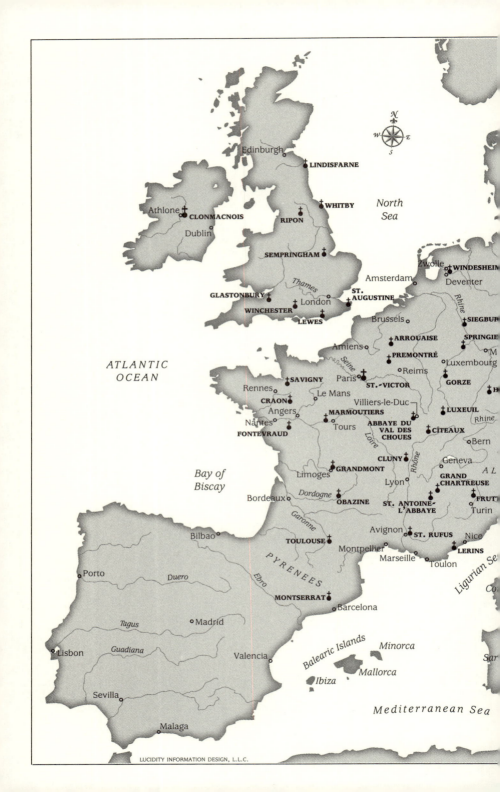

Bibliography

Acht, Stephan. "Die Bischöfe Altmann von Passau, Adalbero von Würzburg und Erzbischof Gebhard von Salzburg als Wegbereiter des regulären Kanonikertums in Bayern." In *Die Augustinerchorherren in Bayern*, edited by Paul Mai. Regensburg: Schnell & Steiner, 1999. 19–25.

———. "Die Windesheimer Augustinerchorherren-Kongregation gestern und heute." In *Die Augustinerchorherren in Bayern*, edited by Paul Mai. Regensburg: Schnell & Steiner, 1999. 56–60.

"Advocate." *Encyclopedia of the Middle Ages*. Edited by André Vauchez. Chicago: Fitzroy Dearborn Publishers, 2000.

"Advocatus/Avoué." *Medieval France: An Encyclopedia*. Edited by William W. Kibler, Grover A. Zinn, John Bell Henneman, Jr., and Lawrence Earp. New York: Routledge, 1995.

Alban, Kevin, ed. *The Carmelite Rule, 1207–2007*. Rome: Edizioni Carmelitane, 2008.

Alberzoni, Maria Pia. *Chiara e il papato*. Milan: Edizioni Biblioteca Francescana, 1995.

———. *Clare of Assisi and the Poor Sisters in the Thirteenth Century*. Saint Bonaventure, NY: Franciscan Institute, 2004.

———. "Die Humiliaten zwischen Legende und Wirklichkeit." *Mitteilungen des Instituts für Österreichische Geschichtsforschung* 107 (1999): 324–53.

———. "Nequaquam a Christi sequela in perpetuum absolvi desidero." In *Chiara d'Assisi e la memoria di Francesco*, edited by Alfonso Marini. Cittá di Castello: Petruzzi, 1995. 41–65.

———. *Santa povertà e beata semplicità. Francesco d'Assisi e la Chiesa romana*. Milan: Vita e pensiero, 2015. 79–108.

Albrecht, Stephan. *Die Inszenierung der Vergangenheit im Mittelalter. Die Klöster von Glastonbury und Saint-Denis*. Munich/Berlin: Deutscher Kunstverlag, 2003.

Altaner, Berthold. *Die Dominikanermissionen des 13. Jahrhunderts. Forschungen zur Geschichte der kirchlichen Unionen und der Mohammedaner und Heidenmission des Mittelalters*. Habelschwerdt: Franke, 1924.

Althoff, Gerd. "Ottonische Frauengemeinschaften im Spannungsfeld von Kloster und Welt." In *Essen und die sächsischen Frauenstifte im Frühmittelalter*, edited by Jan Gerchow and Thomas Schilp. Essen: Klartext-Verlag, 2001. 29–44.

Ambrosioni, Annamaria. "Umiliati/Umiliate." In *Dizionario degli istituti di perfezione*. 10 vols. Rome: Edizioni Paoline, 1997. 9:1489–1507.

Ames, Christine. *Righteous Persecution: Inquisition, Dominicans, and Christianity in the Middle Ages*. Philadelphia: University of Pennsylvania Press, 2008.

Andenna, Cristina. "Dall'esempio alla santità. Stefano di Thiers e Stefano di Obazine: Modelli di vita o fondatori di ordini?" In *Das Eigene und das Ganze*, edited by Gert Melville and Markus Schürer. Münster: LIT, 2002. 177–224.

———. *"Kanoniker sind Gott für das ganze Volk verantwortlich." Die Regularkanoniker Italiens und die Kirche im 12. Jahrhundert*. Paring: Augustiner-Chorherren-Verlag, 2004.

———. *Mortariensis Ecclesia. Una congregazione di canonici regolari in Italia settentrionale tra XI e XII secolo*. Münster: LIT, 2007.

———. "Neue Formen der Frömmigkeit und Armutsbewegung." In *Verwandlungen des Stauferreichs—Drei Innovationsregionen im mittelalterlichen Europa*, edited by Bernd Schneidmüller, Stefan Weinfurter, and Alfried Wieczorek. Darmstadt: Theiss, 2010. 246–63.

———. "'Non est haec vita apostolica, sed confusio babylonica.' L'invenzione di un ordine nel secolo XIII." In *Regulae—Consuetudines—Statuta. Studi sulle fonti normative degli ordini religiosi nei secoli centrali del Medioevo*, edited by Cristina Andenna and Gert Melville. Münster: LIT, 2005. 569–632.

———. "'Secundum regulam datam sororibus ordinis sancti Damiani.' Sancia e Aquilina: due esperimenti di ritorno alle origini alla corte di Napoli nel XIV secolo." In *Franciscan Organisation in the Mendicant Context. Formal and Informal Structures of the Friars' Lives and Ministry in the Middle Ages*, edited by Michael Robson and Jens Röhrkasten. Berlin: LIT, 2010. 139–78.

Andenna, Cristina, and Mirko Breitenstein, eds. *Frommer Eifer und methodischer Betrieb. Beiträge zum mittelalterlichen Mönchtum*. Cologne, Weimar, and Vienna: Böhlau, 2014.

Andenna, Cristina, Klaus Herbers, and Gert Melville, eds. *Die Ordnung der Kommunikation und die Kommunikation der Ordnungen im mittelalterlichen Europa*. Vol. 1, *Netzwerke: Klöster und Orden im 12. und 13. Jahrhundert*. Stuttgart: Franz Steiner, 2012.

Andenna, Cristina, and Gert Melville, eds. *Regulae—Consuetudines—Statuta. Studi sulle fonti normative degli ordini religiosi nei secoli centrali del Medioevo*. Münster: LIT, 2005.

Andenna, Giancarlo. "Sanctimoniales Cluniacenses." *Studi sui monasteri femminili di Cluny e sulla loro legislazione in Lombardia (XI–XV secolo).* Münster: LIT, 2005.

———. "San Salvatore di Brescia e la scelta religiosa delle donne aristocratiche tra età longobarda ed età franca (VIII–IX secolo)." In *Female* vita religiosa *between Late Antiquity and the High Middle Ages: Structures, Developments and Spatial Contexts*, edited by Gert Melville and Anne Müller. Berlin: LIT, 2011. 209–33.

———. "Urbano IV e l'istituzione dell'ordine delle clarisse." In *Regulae— Consuetudines—Statuta. Studi sulle fonti normative degli ordini religiosi nei secoli centrali del Medioevo*, edited by Cristina Andenna and Gert Melville. Münster: LIT, 2005. 539–68.

Andenna, Giancarlo, Mirko Breitenstein, and Gert Melville, eds. *Charisma und religiöse Gemeinschaften im Mittelalter.* Münster: LIT, 2005.

Andrews, Frances. *The Early Humilitati.* Cambridge, UK: Cambridge University Press, 1999.

———. *The Other Friars. The Carmelite, Augustinian, Sack and Pied Friars in the Middle Ages.* Woodbridge, UK: Boydell, 2006.

Angenendt, Arnold. "Charisma und Eucharistie—oder: Das System Cluny." In *Institution und Geschichte. Festschrift für Gert Melville zum 65. Geburtstag*, edited by Franz J. Felten, Annette Kehnel, and Stefan Weinfurter. Cologne: Böhlau, 2009.

———. *Das Frühmittelalter. Die abendländische Christenheit von 400 bis 900.* Stuttgart: Kohlhammer, 2001. 331–39.

———. *Monachi peregrini. Studien zu Pirmin und den monastischen Vorstellungen des Frühen Mittelalters.* Munich: Wilhelm Fink, 1972.

Angerer, Joachim. "Reform von Melk." In *Die Reformverbände und Kongregationen der Benediktiner im deutschen Sprachraum*, edited by Ulrich Faust and Franz Quarthal. St. Otttilien: EOS, 1999. 83–95.

Ardura, Bernard. *Prémontrés: histoire et spiritualité.* Saint-Étienne: Publications de la Université de Saint-Etienne, 1995.

Armstrong, Regis J., J. A. Wayne Hellmann, and William J. Shor, eds. *Clare of Assisi: Early Documents.* New York: New City Press, 2005.

———. *Francis of Assisi: Early Documents.* New York: New City Press, 2000.

Arnold, Udo. "Das Ordensland Preußen." In *Der Deutsche Orden in Europa.* Göppingen: Gesellschaft für Staufische Geschichte, 2004. 219–68.

Averkorn, Raphaela. "Adlige Frauen und Mendikanten im Spannungsverhältnis zwischen Macht und Religion. Studien zur Iberischen Halbinsel im Spätmittelalter." In *Imperios sacros, monarquías divinas. Heilige Herrscher, göttliche Monarchien*, edited by Carles Rabassa and Ruth Stepper. Castelló de la Plana: Univ. Jaume I, 2002. 219–68.

Bacht, Heinrich, ed. *Pachomius, Klosterregeln. Gebote, Gebote und Weisungen, Gebote und Entscheidungen, Gebote und Gesetze.* St. Ottilien: EOS, 2010.

Backmund, Norbert. *Monasticon Praemonstratense.* 3 vols. Straubing: Attenkofer, 1949–56. Vol. 1. Berlin: de Gruyter, 1983.

Bailey, Michael D. *Battling Demons: Witchcraft, Heresy, and Reform in the Late Middle Ages.* University Park: Pennsylvania State University Press, 2003.

Ballweg, Jan. *Konziliare oder päpstliche Ordensreform. Benedikt XII. und die Reformdiskussion im frühen 14. Jahrhundert.* Tübingen: Mohr, 2001.

Baltrusch-Schneider, Dagmar Beate. "Die angelsächsischen Doppelklöster." In *Doppelklöster und andere Formen der Symbiose männlicher und weiblicher Religiosen im Mittelalter,* edited by Kaspar Elm and Michel Parisse. Berlin: Duncker & Humblot, 1992. 57–79.

Barber, Malcolm. *The New Knighthood. A History of the Order of the Temple.* Cambridge, UK: Cambridge University Press, 1994. Reprint, 2012.

―――. *The Trial of the Templars.* Cambridge, UK: Cambridge University Press, 1978.

Barret, Sébastien. "Cluny et les Ottoniens." In *Ottone III e Romualdo di Ravenna. Impero, monasteri e santi asceti. Atti del XXIV convegno del Centro Studi Avellaniti 2002.* Negarine di San Pietro in Cariano (Verona): Il Segno dei Gabrielli Ed., 2003. 179–213.

Barret, Sébastien, and Gert Melville, eds. *Oboedientia. Formen und Grenzen von Macht und Unterordnung im mittelalterlichen Religiosentum.* Münster: LIT, 2005.

Bartelink, Gerhardus J. M. *Athanase d'Alexandrie: Vie d'Antoine.* Paris: Éditions du Cerf, 2011.

Bartocci, Andrea. *Ereditare in povertà. Le successioni a favore dei frati minori e la scienza giuridica nell'età avignonese (1309–1376).* Naples: Jovene Editore, 2009.

Bartolomei Romagnoli, Alessandra. *Una memoria controversa. Celestino V e le sue fonti.* Florence: Edizioni del Galluzzo, 2013.

Bauer, Gerhard. *Claustrum animae. Untersuchungen zur Geschichte der Metapher vom Herzen als Kloster.* Munich: Wilhelm Fink, 1973.

Beck, Bernard. *Saint Bernard de Tiron, l'ermite, le moine et le monde.* Cormelles-le-Royal: Éd. La Mandragore, 1998.

Becquet, Jean. *Études Grandmontaines.* Ussel: Musée du Pays d'Ussel, 1998.

Berg, Dieter. *Armut und Geschichte. Studien zur Geschichte der Bettelorden im Hohen und Späten Mittelalter.* Kevelaer: Butzon & Bercker, 2001.

―――. *Armut und Wissenschaft. Beiträge zur Geschichte des Studienwesens der Bettelorden im 13. Jahrhundert.* Düsseldorf: Pädagogischer Verlag Schwann, 1977.

————. "Spiritualismus und Fundamentalismus: Studien zur Bedeutung der Spiritualen und ihrer Geschichtstheologie im Franziskanerorden im Späten Mittelalter." In *Konfessionelle Pluralität als Herausforderung: Koexistenz und Konflikt in Spätmittelalter und Früher Neuzeit. Winfried Eberhard zum 65. Geburtstag*, edited by Joachim Bahlcke, Karen Lambrecht, and Hans-Christian Maner. Leipzig: Leipziger Universitätsverlag, 2006. 35–54.

Berg, Dieter, and Leonhard Lehmann, eds. *Franziskus-Quellen. Die Schriften des heiligen Franziskus, Lebensbeschreibungen, Chroniken und Zeugnisse über ihn und seinen Orden*. Kevelaer: Butzon & Bercker, 2009.

Bériou, Nicole, ed. *Économie et religion. L'experience des ordres mendiants (XIIIᵉ–XVᵉ siècle)*. Lyon: Presses universitaires de Lyon, 2009.

Bériou, Nicole, and Philippe Josserand, eds. *Prier et combattre. Dictionnaire européen des ordres militaires au Moyen Age*. Paris: Fayard, 2009.

Berman, Constance. *The Cistercian Evolution: The Invention of a Religious Order in Twelfth-Century Europe*. Philadelphia: University of Pennsylvania Press, 2000.

Bernard of Clairvaux. *Epistolae*. Edited by Jean Leclercq and H. M. Rochais. Sancti Bernardi Opera. Vols. 7–8. Rome: Editiones Cistercienses, 1957–1963.

————. *Tractatus et opuscula*. Edited by Jean Leclercq and H. M. Rochais. Sancti Bernardi Opera. Vol. 3. Rome: Editiones Cistercienses, 1957–1963.

Bertola, Ermenegildo. *Il problema della coscienza nella teologia monastica del XII secolo*. Padua: CEDAM, 1970.

Bierbaum, Max. *Bettelorden und Weltgeistlichkeit an der Universität Paris: Texte und Untersuchungen zum literarischen Armuts- und Exemtionsstreit des 13. Jahrhunderts (1255–1272)*. Münster: Aschendorff, 1916.

Binding, Günther, and Matthias Untermann, eds. *Kleine Kunstgeschichte der mittelalterlichen Ordensbaukunst in Deutschland*. Stuttgart: Theiss, 2001.

Bischof, Franz Xaver. "Der Stand der 'Franziskanischen Frage.'" In *Franziskus von Assisi. Das Bild des Heiligen aus neuer Sicht*, edited by Dieter R. Bauer, Helmut Feld, and Ulrich Köpf. Cologne: Böhlau, 2005. 1–16.

Bischof, Franz Xaver et al., eds. *Die Benediktinische Klosterreform im 15. Jahrhundert*. Berlin: de Gruyter, 2013.

Bligny, Bernard. *Saint Bruno, le premier chartreux*. Rennes: Ouest-France, 1984.

Bodarwé, Katrinette. "Eine Männerregel für Frauen. Die Adaption der Benediktsregel im 9. und 10. Jahrhundert." In *Female vita religiosa between Late Antiquity and the High Middle Ages: Structures, Developments and Spatial Contexts*, edited by Gert Melville and Anne Müller. Berlin: LIT, 2011. 235–72.

Bomm, Werner. "Augustinusregel, *professio canonica* und Prämonstratenser im 12. Jahrhundert. Das Beispiel der Norbert-Viten Philipps von

Harvengt und Anselms von Havelberg." In *Regula Sancti Augustini. Normative Grundlage differenter Verbände im Mittelalter*, edited by Gert Melville and Anne Müller. Paring: Augustiner-Chorherren-Verlag, 2002. 239–94.

Borchardt, Karl. *Die Cölestiner. Eine Mönchsgemeinschaft des späteren Mittelalters*. Husum: Matthiesen, 2006.

Boshof, Egon. "Bischof Altmann, St. Nikola und die Kanonikerreform. Das Bistum Passau im Investiturstreit." In *Tradition und Entwicklung. Gedenkschrift für Johann Riederer*, edited by Karl-Heinz Pollok. Passau: Passavia, 1981. 317–45.

———. "Klöster und Bischof in Lotharingien." In *Monastische Reformen im 9. und 10. Jahrhundert*, edited by Raymund Kottje and Helmut Maurer. Sigmaringen: Thorbecke, 1989. 197–245.

———. "*Traditio Romana* und Papstschutz im 9. Jahrhundert. Untersuchungen zur vorcluniazensischen *libertas*." In *Rechtsgeschichtlich-diplomatische Studien zu frühmittelalterlichen Papsturkunden*, edited by Egon Boshof and Heinz Wolter. Cologne/Vienna: Böhlau, 1976. 1–100.

Bouter, Nicole, ed. *Unanimité et diversité cisterciennes. Filiations, réseaux, relectures du XIIᵉ au XVIIᵉ siécle*. Saint-Étienne: Publications de l'Université de Saint-Étienne, 2000.

Bouyer, Louis. *La vie de S. Antoine*. 2nd ed. St-Wandrille: Editions de Fontenelle, 1977.

Boynton, Susan. "Uses of the 'Liber Tramitis' at the Abbey of Farfa." In *Studies in Medieval Chant and Liturgy in Honor of David Hiley*, edited by Terence Bailey and Lásló Dobszay. Ottawa: Institute for Musicology, 2007. 87–104.

Boynton, Susan, and Isabelle Cochelin, eds. *From Dead of Night to End of Day. The Medieval Customs of Cluny [Du cœur de la nuit á la fin du jour. Les coutumes clunisiennes au Moyen Áge]*. Turnhout: Brepols, 2005.

Braunfels, Wolfgang. *Monasteries of Western Europe: The Architecture of the Orders*. London: Thames and Hudson, 1972 .

Bredero, Adriaan H. "À propos de l'autorité de Pons de Melgueil et de Pierre le Vénérable dans l'ordre de Cluny." In *Cluny et Cîteaux au douzième siècle. L'Histoire d'une controverse monastique*, by Adriaan H. Bredero. Amsterdam/Maarsen: APA - Holland University Press, 1985. 95–113.

———. *Bernard of Clairvaux between Cult and History*. Edinburgh: Eerdmans, 1990.

———. *Christenheit und Christentum im Mittelalter: Über das Verhältnis von Religion, Kirche und Gesellschaft*. Stuttgart: Franz Steiner, 1998.

———. "The Early Cistercians and the Old Monasticism." In *Cluny et Cîteaux au douzième siècle. L'Histoire d'une controverse monastique*, by Adriaan H. Bredero. Amsterdam/Maarsen: APA - Holland University Press, 1985. 351–72.

Breitenstein, Mirko. *Das Noviziat im hohen Mittelalter: Zur Organisation des Eintrittes bei den Cluniazensern, Cisterziensern und Franziskanern.* Münster: LIT, 2008.

———. "Der Traktat vom 'Inneren Haus.' Verantwortung als Ziel der Gewissensbildung." In *Innovation in Klöstern und Orden des Hohen Mittelalters. Aspekte und Pragmatik eines Begriffes,* edited by Mirko Breitenstein, Stefan Duchhardt, and Julia Dücker. Berlin: LIT, 2012. 263–92.

———. "Der Transfer paränetischer Inhalte innerhalb und zwischen Orden." In *Die Ordnung der Kommunikation und die Kommunikation der Ordnungen im mittelalterlichen Europa.* Vol. 1, *Netzwerke: Klöster und Orden im 12. und 13. Jahrhundert,* edited by Cristina Andenna, Klaus Herbers, and Gert Melville. Stuttgart: Franz Steiner, 2012. 37–53.

———. "Die Regel—Lebensprogramm und Glaubensfibel." In *Macht des Wortes. Benediktinisches Mönchtum im Spiegel Europas, Essayband,* edited by Gerfried Sitar and Martin Kroker. Regensburg: Schnell & Steiner, 2009. 23–29.

———. "Die Verfügbarkeit der Transzendenz. Das Gewissen der Mönche als Heilsgarant." In *Innovationen durch Deuten und Gestalten. Klöster im Mittelalter zwischen Jenseits und Welt,* edited by Gert Melville, Bernd Schneidmüller, and Stefan Weinfurter. Regensburg: Schnell & Steiner, 2014. 37–56.

———. "Is there a Cistercian Love? Some Considerations on the Virtue of Charity." In *Aspects of Charity. Concern for One's Neighbour in Medieval Vita Religiosa,* edited by Gert Melville. Berlin: LIT, 2011. 55–98.

Breitenstein, Mirko, Julia and Stefan Burkhardt, and Jens Röhrkasten, eds. *Rules and Observance. Devising Forms of Communal Life.* Berlin: LIT, 2014.

Breitenstein, Mirko, and Gert Melville. "Gerechtigkeit als fundierendes Element des mittelalterlichen Mönchtums." In *Bilder—Sachen—Mentalitäten. Arbeitsfelder historischer Kulturwissenschaften. Wolfgang Brückner zum 80. Geburtstag,* edited by Heidrun Alzheimer, Fred G. Rausch, Klaus Reder, and Claudia Selheim. Regensburg: Schnell & Steiner, 2010. 33–42.

Brown, Peter. *The Rise of Western Christendom: Triumph and Diversity, AD 200–1000.* 10th Anniversary Revised Edition. Malden, MA: Wiley-Blackwell, 2013.

Brühl, Carlrichard. *Fodrum, gistum, servitium regis. Studien zu den wirtschaftlichen Grundlagen des Königtums im Frankenreich und in den fränkischen Nachfolgestaaten Deutschland, Frankreich und Italien vom 6. bis zur Mitte des 14. Jahrhunderts.* Cologne: Böhlau, 1968.

Brunert, Maria-Elisabeth. "Die Pauliner. Zu den Ursprüngen ihres Ordens, seiner Geschichte und Spiritualität." In *Klosterforschung: Befunde, Projekte, Perspektiven,* edited by Jens Schneider. Munich: Wilhelm Fink, 2006. 11–39.

Brunet, Isabelle. "Les institutions charitables de Saint-Antoine. Chef-lieu de l'Ordre Hospitalier des Antonins du XIIᵉ au XVᵉ siècles." PhD dissertation, Université de Lyon, 1991.

Bruun, Mette Birkedal, and Emilia Jamroziak, eds. *The Cambridge Companion to the Cistercian Order*. Cambridge, UK: Cambridge University Press, 2013.

Bulst, Neithard. *Untersuchungen zu den Klosterreformen Wilhelms von Dijon, 962–1031*. Bonn: Röhrscheid, 1973.

Burgtorf, Jochen, et al., eds. *The Debate on the Trial of the Templars: 1307–1314*. Farnham: Ashgate, 2010.

Burr, David. *Olivi and Franciscan Poverty: The Origins of the* Usus Pauper *Controversy*. Philadelphia: University of Pennsylvania Press, 1989.

———. *The Spiritual Franciscans. From Protest to Persecution in the Century after Saint Francis*. University Park: Pennsylvania State University Press, 2003.

Burton, Janet E. *The Cistercians in the Middle Ages*. Woodbridge: Boydell, 2011.

Butler, Alan. *The Knights Templar: Their History and Myths Revealed*. New York: Shelter Harbor Press, 2014.

Bynum, Caroline. *Docere verbo et exemplo. An Aspect of Twelfth-Century Spirituality*. Missoula, MT: Scholars Press, 1979.

Caby, Cécile. *De l'érémitisme rural au monachisme urbain. Les camaldules en Italie à la fin du moyen âge*. Paris: École française de Rome, 1999.

———. "Fondation et naissance des ordres religieux. Remarques pour une étude comparée des ordres religieux au moyen âge." In *Mittelalterliche Orden und Klöster im Vergleich. Methodische Ansätze und Perspektiven*, edited by Gert Melville and Anna Müller. Berlin: LIT, 2007. 115–37.

———. "La mémoire des origines dans les institutions médiévales: bilan d'un séminaire collectif." In *Écrire son histoire: les communautés régulières face à leur passé*, edited by Nicole Bouter. Saint-Étienne: Publications de l'Université de Saint-Étienne, 2006. 13–20.

———. "Vies parallèles: ermites d'Italie et de la France de l'Ouest (Xᵉ–XIIᵉ siècle)." In *Robert d'Arbrissel et la vie religieuse dans l'ouest de la France. Actes du colloque international de Fontevraud à l'occasion du IXᵉ centenaire de la fondation de l'abbaye, 13–16 décembre 2001*, edited by Jacques Dalarun. Turnhout: Brepols, 2004. 11–24.

Cappelli, Biagio. *Il monachesimo basiliano ai confini calabrolucani*. Naples: Fiorentino, 1963.

Cardini, Franco. *I poveri cavalieri del Cristo. Bernardo di Clairvaux e la fondazione dell'ordine templare*. Rimini: Il Cerchio, 1992.

Cariboni, Guido. "Gregorio IX e la nascita delle 'Sorores penitentes' di Santa Maria Maddalena 'in Alemannia.'" *Annali dell'Istituto Storico italo-germanico di Trento* 25 (1999): 11–44.

————. "Il papato di fronte alle crisi istituzionale dell'ordine cistercense nei primi decenni del XIII secolo." In *Il nostro ordine è la Caritá. Cistercensi nei secoli XII e XIII*, by Guido Cariboni. Milan: Vita e pensiero, 2011. 93–126.

————. "'Ordo noster est caritas.' Osservazioni su ideali guida, testi normativi e dinamiche istituzionali presso le prime generazioni cistercensi." In *Il nostro ordine è la Caritá. Cistercensi nei secoli XII e XIII*, by Guido Cariboni. Milan: Vita e pensiero, 2011. 59–92.

Chapman, Alice. *Sacred Authority and Temporal Power in the Writings of Bernard of Clairvaux*. Turnhout: Brepols, 2013.

Charmantier, Isabelle R. Odile. "Monasticism in Seventh-Century Northumbria and Neustria. A Comparative Study of the Monasteries of Chelles, Jouaree, Monkwearmouth/Jarrow and Whitby." PhD dissertation, University of Durham, 1998.

Cicconetti, Carlo. *La regola del Carmelo. Origine, natura, significato*. Rome: Institutum Carmelitanum, 1973.

Clark, James G. *Benedictines in the Middle Ages*. Woodbridge: Boydell, 2011.

————. *The Religious Orders in Pre-Reformation England*. Woodbridge, UK: Boydell, 2002.

Classen, Peter. "Gerhoch von Reichersberg und die Regularkanoniker in Bayern und Österreich." In *Ausgewählte Aufsätze von Peter Classen*, edited by Josef Fleckenstein. Sigmaringen: Thorbecke, 1983. 431–60.

Classen, Peter, ed. *Die Gründungsurkunden der Reichenau*. Sigmaringen: Thorbecke, 1977.

Claussen, Martin Allen. *The Reform of the Frankish Church: Chrodegang of Metz and the "Regula canonicorum" in the Eighth Century*. Cambridge, UK: Cambridge University Press, 2004.

Cline, Ruth Harwood. "The Congregation of Tiron in the Twelfth Century: Foundation and Expansion." PhD Dissertation, Georgetown University, 2000.

Cochelin, Isabelle. "Customaries as Inspirational Sources. Appendix: The relation between the last Cluniac customaries, Udal and Bern." In *Consuetudines et regulae: Sources for Monastic Life in the Middle Ages and the Early Modern Period*, edited by Carolyn M. Malone and Clark Maines. Turnhout: Brepols, 2014. 27–72.

————. "Évolution des coutumiers monastiques dessinée à partir de l'étude de Bernard." In *From Dead of Night to End of Day. The Medieval Customs of Cluny [Du cœur de la nuit à la fin du jour. Les coutumes clunisiennes au Moyen Âge]*, edited by Susan Boynton and Isabelle Cochelin. Turnhout: Brepols, 2005. 29–66.

Codou, Yann, and Michel Lauwers, eds. *Lérins, une île sainte dans l'Occident médiéval*. Turnhout: Brepols, 2009.

Conant, Kenneth John. *Cluny. Les églises et la maison du chef d'ordre.* Cambridge, MA: Medieval Academy of America, 1968.

Constable, Giles. "The Authority of Superiors in the Religious Communities." In *La Notion d'autorité au Moyen Âge. Islam, Byzance, Occident,* edited by George Makdisi, Dominique Sourdel, and Janine Sourdel-Thomine. Paris: Presses Universitaires de France, 1982. 189–210.

———. "The Ceremonies and Symbolism of Entering Religious Life and Taking the Monastic Habit from the Fourth to the Twelfth Century." In *Segni e riti nella chiesa altomedievale occidentale.* Spoleto: Centro italiano di studi sull'alto Medioevo, 1987. 771–834.

———. "Cluniac Administration and Administrators in the Twelfth Century." In *The Abbey of Cluny. A Collection of Essays to Mark the Eleven-Hundredth Anniversary of its Foundation.* Berlin: LIT, 2010. 131–41.

———. "Cluny in the Monastic World of the Tenth Century." In *The Abbey of Cluny. A Collection of Essays to Mark the Eleven-Hundredth Anniversary of its Foundation,* by Giles Constable. Berlin: LIT, 2010. 43–77.

———. "The Interpretation of Mary and Martha." In *Three Studies in Medieval Religious and Social Thought,* by Giles Constable. Cambridge, UK: Cambridge University Press, 1995. 1–141.

———. "Monastic Possession of Churches and 'spiritualia' in the Age of Reform." In *Il monachesimo e la riforma ecclesiastica (1049–1122).* Milan: Vita e pensiero, 1971. 304–35.

———. *Monastic Tithes from their Origins to the Twelfth Century.* Cambridge, UK: Cambridge University Press, 1964.

———. *The Reformation of the Twelfth Century.* Cambridge, UK: Cambridge University Press, 1998.

Constable, Giles, and James Kritzeck, eds. *Petrus Venerabilis, 1156–1956. Studies and Texts Commemorating the Eighth Centenary of His Death.* Rome: Pontificum Institutum S. Anselmi, 1956.

Cooper, Donal, and Janet Robson. *The Making of Assisi: The Pope, the Franciscans and the Painting of the Basilica.* New Haven, CT: Yale University Press, 2013.

Copsey, Richard, ed. *Carmel in Britain: Essays on the Medieval English Carmelite Province.* Vol. 3, *The Hermits from Mount Carmel.* Rome: Institutum Carmelitanum, 2004.

Cowdrey, Herbert Edward John. *The Cluniacs and the Gregorian Reform.* Oxford: Clarendon Press, 1970.

———. *Lanfranc. Scholar, Monk, and Archbishop.* Oxford: Oxford University Press, 2003.

Crusius, Irene, ed. *Studien zum Kanonissenstift.* Göttingen: Vandenhoeck und Ruprecht, 2001.

Crusius, Irene, and Helmut Flachenecker, eds. *Studien zum Prämonstratenserorden.* Göttingen: Vandenhoeck and Ruprecht, 2001.

Cygler, Florent. "Ausformung und Kodifizierung des Ordensrechts vom 12. bis zum 14. Jahrhundert. Strukturelle Beobachtungen zu den Cisterziensern, Prämonstratensern, Kartäusern und Cluniazensern." In *De ordine vitae. Zu Normvorstellungen, Organisationsformen und Schriftgebrauch im mittelalterlichen Ordenswesen*, edited by Gert Melville. Münster: LIT, 1996. 7–58.

———. "*Cartusia numquam reformata?* La réforme constitutionelle de l'ordre cartusien au XIIIᵉ siécle." In *Studia monastica. Beiträge zum klösterlichen Leben im christlichen Abendland während des Mittelalters*, edited by Reinhardt Butz and Jörg Oberste. Münster: LIT, 2004. 47–72.

———. *Das Generalkapitel im hohen Mittelalter. Cisterzienser, Prämonstratenser, Kartäuser und Cluniazenser*. Münster: LIT, 2002.

———. "Vom 'Wort' Brunos zum gesatzten Recht der Statuten über die 'Consuetudines Guigonis.' Propositum und Institutionalisierung im Spiegel der kartäusischen Ordensschriftlichkeit." In *Schriftlichkeit und Lebenspraxis im Mittelalter. Erfassen, Bewahren, Verändern*, edited by Hagen Keller, Christel Meier, and Thomas Scharff. Munich: Wilhelm Fink, 1999. 95–110.

———. "Zur Funktionalität der dominikanischen Verfassung im Mittelalter." In *Die Bettelorden im Aufbau. Beiträge zu Institutionalisierungsprozessen im mittelalterlichen Religiosentum*, edited by Gert Melville and Jörg Oberste. Münster: LIT, 1999. 385–428.

———. "Zur institutionellen Symbolizität der dominikanischen Verfassung. Versuch einer Deutung." In *Institutionalität und Symbolisierung. Verstetigung kultureller Ordnungsmuster in Vergangenheit und Gegenwart*, edited by Gert Melville. Cologne: Böhlau, 2001. 409–24.

D'Acunto, Nicolangelo. "Monaci poco obbedienti. Le origini vallombrosane fra estremismo riformatore e normalizzazione pontificia." In *L'età dell'obbedienza. Papato, impero e poteri locali nel secolo XI*, edited by Nicolangelo D'Acunto. Naples: Liguori, 2007. 135–65.

———. "Un eremita in movimento: il Romualdo di Pier Damiani." In *L'età dell'obbedienza. Papato, impero e poteri locali nel secolo XI*, edited by Nicolangelo D'Acunto. Naples: Liguori, 2007. 327–54.

———. "Vallombrosani." In *Regulae—Consuetudines—Statuta. Studi sulle fonti normative degli ordini religiosi nei secoli centrali del Medioevo*, edited by Cristina Andenna and Gert Melville. Münster: LIT, 2005. 157–67.

Dalarun, Jacques. *Francis of Assisi and the Feminine*. Saint Bonaventure, NY: Franciscan Institute Publications, 2006.

———. *Gouverner c'est servir: Essai de démocratie médiévale*. Paris: Alma, 2012.

———. "La dernière volonté de saint François." In *Bullettino dell'Istituto storico italiano per il medio evo* 94 (1988): 329–66.

————. "Les plus anciens statuts de Fontevraud." In *Robert d'Arbrissel et la vie religieuse dans l'ouest de la France. Actes du colloque international de Fontevraud à l'occasion du IXe centenaire de la fondation de l'abbaye, 13–16 Décembre 2001.* Turnhout: Brepols, 2004. 139–72.

————. *Robert of Arbrissel: Sex, Sin, and Salvation in the Middle Ages.* Translated with an introduction and notes by Bruce L. Venarde; with a new preface by the author. Washington, DC: The Catholic University of America Press, 2006.

————. *Vers une résolution de la question franciscaine. La légende ombrienne de Thomas de Celano.* Paris: Fayard, 2007.

Dalarun, Jacques, ed. *Robert d'Arbrissel et la vie religieuse dans l'ouest de la France. Actes du colloque international de Fontevraud à l'occasion du IXe centenaire de la fondation de l'abbaye, 13–16 décembre 2001.* Turnhout: Brepols, 2004.

Dalarun, Jacques, Geneviève Giordanengo, Armelle Le Huërou, Jean Longère, Dominique Poirel, and Bruce Venarde, eds. *Les deux vies de Robert d'Arbrissel, fondateur de Fontevraud. Légendes, écrits et témoignages. Édition des sources avec introductions et traductions françaises.* Turnhout: Brepols, 2006.

Dal Covolo, Enrico, ed. *Eusebio di Vercelli e il suo tempo.* Rome: LAS, 1997.

Dalla "Sequela Christi" di Francesco d'Assisi all'apologia della povertà. Atti del 18 convegno internazionale, Assisi (18–20 ottobre 1990). Spoleto: Centro italiano di studi sull'alto Medioevo, 1992.

Daniel, Emmett Randolph. *Abbot Joachim of Fiore and Joachimism: Selected Articles.* Aldershot: Ashgate Variorum, 2011.

Dannenberg, Lars-Arne. *Das Recht der Religiosen in der Kanonistik des 12. und 13. Jahrhunderts.* Berlin: LIT, 2008.

Davril, Anselme. "Coutumiers directifs et coutumiers descriptifs d'Ulrich à Bernard de Cluny." In *From Dead of Night to End of Day. The Medieval Customs of Cluny [Du cœur de la nuit à la fin du jour. Les coutumes clunisiennes au Moyen Âge]*, edited by Susan Boynton and Isabelle Cochelin. Turnhout: Brepols, 2005. 23–28.

de Boer, Dick E. H., and Iris Kwiatkowski, eds. *Die Devotio moderna. Sozialer und kultureller Transfer (1350–1580).* 2 vols. Münster: Aschendorff, 2013.

de Cloedt, Filips, ed. *Benedictus. Eine Kulturgeschichte des Abendlandes.* Geneva: Weber, 1980.

Degler-Spengler, Brigitte. "'Zahlreich wie die Sterne des Himmels.' Zisterzienser, Dominikaner und Franziskaner vor dem Problem der Inkorporation von Frauenklöstern." *Rottenburger Jahrbuch für Kirchengeschichte* 4 (1985): 37–50.

de Leo, Pietro, ed. *San Bruno di Colonia: un eremita tra Oriente e Occidente.* Soveria Mannelli (Catanzaro): Rubbettino, 2004.

dell'Omo, Mariano. "L'abbazia medievale di Fruttuaria e i centri della Riforma fruttuariense." *Monastica* 5 (1985): 185–201.

Demurger, Alain. *Die Templer, Aufstieg und Untergang, 1120–1314*. Munich: C. H. Beck, 2004.

Dereine, Charles. "Chanoines." In *Dictionnaire d'histoire et de géographie ecclésiastiques*. Paris: Letouzey et Ané, 1951. 12:354–405.

———. "Vie commune, règle de Saint Augustin et chanoines réguliers au 11e siècle." *Revue d'histoire ecclésiastique* 42 (1946): 365–406.

Desbonnets, Théophile. *De l'intuition à l'institution. Les Franciscans*. Paris: Editions franciscaines, 1983.

Desprez, Vincent. "La 'Regula Ferrioli.' Texte critique." *Revue Mabillon* 60 (1982): 117–48.

de Valous, Guy. *Le monachisme clunisien des origines au XVe siècle*. 2 vols. Paris: Picard, 1970.

de Vogüé, Adalbert. "Benedikt von Nursia." *Theologische Realenzyklopädie*. Berlin: de Gruyter, 1980. 5:538–49.

———. "Caesarius of Arles and the Origin of the Enclosure of Nuns." *Word and Spirit* 11 (1989): 16–29.

———. *Reading Saint Benedict: Reflections on the Rule*. Kalamazoo, MI: Cistercian Publications, 1994.

———. *Saint Columban. Règles et pénitentiels monastiques*. Bellefontaine: Abbaye de Bellefontaine, 1989.

Dey, Henrik W., and Elizabeth Fentress, eds. *Western Monasticism ante litteram. The Space of Monastic Observance in Late Antiquity and the Early Middle Ages*. Turnhout: Brepols, 2011.

Dialogorum Libri quattuor de miraculis. Patrum Italicorum. Vol. 2, *Gregor der Große Der Hl. Benedikt. Buch 2 der Dialoge, lateinisch–deutsch*, edited under the direction of the Salzburg Abbot's conference. St. Ottilien: EOS, 2008.

Die Magisterregel: Einführung und Übersetzung. Translated by Karl Suso Frank. St. Ottilien: EOS, 1989.

Diem, Albrecht. "Das Ende des monastischen Experiments. Liebe, Beichte und Schweigen in der *Regula cuiusdam ad virgines* (mit einer Übersetzung im Anhang)." In *Female* vita religiosa *between Late Antiquity and the High Middle Ages: Structures, Developments and Spatial Contexts*, edited by Gert Melville and Anne Müller. Berlin: LIT, 2011. 80–136.

———. *Das monastische Experiment. Die Rolle der Keuschheit bei der Entstehung des westlichen Klosterwesens*. Münster: LIT, 2005.

———. "Inventing the Holy Rule: Some Observations on the History of Monastic Normative Observance in the Early Medieval West." In *Western Monasticism ante Litteram: The Space of Monastic Observance in Late Antiquity and the Early Middle Ages*, edited by Hendrik W. Dey and Elizabeth Fentress. Turnhout: Brepols, 2011. 53–84.

Diers, Michaela. *Bernhard von Clairvaux. Elitäre Frömmigkeit und begnadetes Wirken.* Münster: Aschendorff, 1991.

Dinzelbacher, Peter. *Bernhard von Clairvaux. Leben und Werk des berühmtesten Zisterziensers.* Darmstadt: Primus, 1998.

———. *Christliche Mystik im Abendland. Ihre Geschichte von den Anfängen bis zum Ende des Mittelalters.* Paderborn: Schöningh, 1994.

Dinzelbacher, Peter, and Dieter R. Bauer, eds. *Religiöse Frauenbewegung und mystische Frömmigkeit im Mittelalter.* Cologne: Böhlau, 1988.

Dizionario degli istituti di perfezione. 10 vols. Edited by Guerrino Peliccia and Giancarlo Rocca. Rome: Edizioni Paoline, 1974–2003.

Drossbach, Gisela. *Christliche* caritas *als Rechtsinstitut. Hospital und Orden von Santo Spirito in Sassia (1198–1378).* Paderborn: Schöningh, 2004.

———. "Das Hospital. Eine kirchenrechtliche Institution? (ca. 1150–ca. 1350)." *Zeitschrift der Savigny-Stiftung für Rechtsgeschichte: Kanonistische Abteilung* 87 (2001): 510–22.

Dubois, Jacques. "Les ordres religieux au XIIᵉ siècle selon la curie romaine." *Revue Bénédictine* 78 (1968): 283–309.

———. "Sainte Bathilde et les fondations monastiques à l'époque mérovingienne." *Chelles notre ville, notre histoire. Bulletin de la société archéologique et historique de Chelles.* New Series 14 (1995–1996): 283–309.

Duby, Georges. *La société aux XIᵉ et XIIᵉ siècles dans la région mâconnaise.* Paris: Armand Colin, 1953; reprint Paris; Ed. de l'École des hautes études en sciences sociales, 1988.

Dunn, Marilyn. *The Emergence of Monasticism: From the Desert Fathers to the Early Middle Ages.* Oxford: Blackwell, 2000.

Eberl, Immo. *Die Zisterzienser. Geschichte eines europäischen Ordens.* Stuttgart: Thorbecke, 2003.

———. "Stiftisches Leben in Klöstern. Zur Regeltreue im klösterlichen Alltag des Spätmittelalters und der frühen Neuzeit." In *Studien zum Kanonissenstift*, edited by Irene Crusius. Göttingen: Vandenhoeck & Ruprecht, 2001. 275–315.

Edmonds, Fiona L. "The Practicalities of Communication between Northumbrian and Irish Churches, c. 635–735." In *Anglo-Saxon/Irish Relations before the Vikings*, edited by James A. Graham-Campbell and M. Ryan. Oxford: Oxford University Press, 2009. 129–50.

Edwards, Bede, ed. *The Rule of Saint Albert.* Aylesford: Carmelite Book Service, 1973.

Ehlers, Joachim. *Otto von Freising. Ein Intellektueller im Mittelalter.* Munich: C. H. Beck, 2013.

Ehlers-Kisseler, Ingrid. *Die Anfänge der Prämonstratenser im Erzbistum Köln.* Cologne, Weimar, Vienna: Böhlau, 1997.

Elm, Kaspar. "Ausbreitung, Wirksamkeit und Ende der provençalischen Sackbrüder (Fratres de Poenitentia Jesu Christi) in Deutschland und den Niederlanden. Ein Beitrag zur kurialen und konziliaren Ordenspolitik des 13. Jahrhunderts." In Kaspar Elm, *Vitasfratrum. Beiträge zur Geschichte der Eremiten- und Mendikantenorden des zwölften und dreizehnten Jahrhunderts*, edited by Dieter Berg. Werl: Dietrich-Coelde, 1994. 67–120.

———. *Beiträge zur Geschichte des Wilhelmitenordens*. Cologne and Graz: Böhlau, 1962.

———. "Die Bedeutung historischer Legitimation für Entstehung, Funktion und Bestand des mittelalterlichen Ordenswesens." In *Herkunft und Ursprung. Historische Formen der Legitimation*, edited by Peter Wunderli. Sigmaringen: Thorbecke, 1994. 71–90.

———. "Die Entwicklung des Franziskanerordens zwischen dem ersten und letzten Zeugnis des Jakob von Vitry." In Kaspar Elm, *Vitasfratrum. Beiträge zur Geschichte der Eremiten- und Mendikantenorden des zwölften und dreizehnten Jahrhunderts*, edited by Dieter Berg. Werl: Dietrich-Coelde, 1994. 173–93.

———. "Franziskus und Dominikus. Wirkungen und Antriebskräfte zweier Ordensstifter." In Kaspar Elm, *Vitasfratrum. Beiträge zur Geschichte der Eremiten- und Mendikantenorden des 12. und 13. Jahrhunderts*, edited by Dieter Berg. Werl: Dietrich-Coelde, 1994. 123–41.

———. "Hugo von Fosses. Erster Abt von Prémontré und Organisator des Prämonstratenserordens." In *Studien zum Prämonstratenserorden*, edited by Irene Crusius and Helmut Flachenecker. Göttingen: Vandenhoeck & Ruprecht, 2003. 35–55.

———. "Italienische Eremitengemeinschaften des 12. und 13. Jahrhunderts. Studien zur Vorgeschichte des Augustiner-Eremitenordens." In *L'eremitismo in Occidente nei secoli XI e XII. Atti della seconda Settimana internazionale di studio Mendola, 30 agosto–6 settembre 1962*. Milan: Vita e pensiero, 1965. 491–559.

———. "'Sacrum Commercium.' Über Ankunft und Wirken der ersten Franziskaner in Deutschland." In *Reich, Regionen und Europa in Mittelalter und Neuzeit. Festschrift für Peter Moraw*, edited by Paul-Joachim Heinig, Sigrid Jahns, Hans-Joachim Schmidt, Rainer Christoph Schwinges, and Sabine Wefers. Berlin: Duncker & Humblot, 2000. 389–412.

———. "Studium und Studienwesen der Bettelorden. Die 'andere' Universität." In *Stätten des Geistes. Große Universitäten von der Antike bis zur Gegenward*, edited by Alexander Demandt. Cologne: Böhlau, 1999. 111–26.

———. "Verfall und Erneuerung des Ordenswesens im Spätmittelalter." In *Untersuchungen zu Kloster und Stift*. Gottingen: Vandenhoeck & Ruprecht, 1980. 188–238.

————. "*Vita regularis sine regula*. Bedeutung, Rechtsstellung und Selbstverständnis des mittelalterlichen und frühneuzeitlichen Semireligiosentums." In *Häresie und vorzeitige Reformation im Spätmittelalter*, edited by Elisabeth Müller-Luckner and František Šmahel. Munich: Oldenbourg, 1998. 239–73.

Elm, Kaspar, ed. *Bernhard von Clairvaux. Rezeption und Wirkung im Mittelalter und in der Neuzeit*. Wiesbaden: Harrassowitz, 1994.

————. *Norbert von Xanten. Adliger, Ordensstifter, Kirchenfürst*. Cologne: Wienand, 1984.

Elm, Kaspar, and Peter Joerissen, eds. *Die Zisterzienser. Ordensleben zwischen Ideal und Wirklichkeit*. Cologne: Wienand, 1982.

Elm, Susanna. *Virgins of God. The Making of Asceticism in Late Antiquity*. Oxford: Oxford University Press, 1994.

Engelbert, Pius. "Benedikt von Aniane und die karolingische Reichsidee: zur politischen Theologie des Frühmittelalters." In *Cultura e spiritualità nella tradizione monastica*, edited by Gregorio Penco. Rome: Pontificio Ateneo S. Anselmo, 1990. 67–103.

————. "Neue Forschungen zu den 'Dialogen' Gregors des Großen. Antworten auf Clarks These." In *Erbe und Auftrag* 65 (1989): 376–93.

————. "Regeltext und Romverehrung. Zur Frage der Verbreitung der Regula Benedicti im Frühmittelalter." In *Montecassino della prima alla seconda distruzione. Momenti e aspetti di storia cassinese (secc. VI–IX). Atti del II convegno di studi sul medioevo meridionale (Cassino-Montecassino, 27–31 maggio 1984)*, edited by Faustino Avagliano. Montecassino: Pubblicazioni Cassinesi, 1987. 133–62.

Engels, Odilo. "Der Erzbischof von Trier, der rheinische Pfalzgraf und die gescheiterte Verbandsbildung von Springiersbach im 12. Jahrhundert." In *Secundum regulam vivere. Festschrift für P. Nobert Backmund*, edited by Gert Melville. Windberg: Poppe, 1978. 87–104.

Épiney-Burgard, Georgette. *Gérard Grote (1340–1384) et les débuts de la Dévotion moderne*. Wiesbaden: Franz Steiner, 1970.

Ertl, Thomas. *Religion und Disziplin: Selbstdeutung und Weltordnung im frühen deutschen Franziskanertum*. Berlin: de Gruyter, 2006.

Esposito, Anna, and Andreas Rehberg, eds. *Gli ordini ospedalieri tra centro e periferia*. Rome: Viella, 2007.

Esser, Kajetan. *Anfänge und ursprüngliche Zielsetzungen des Ordens der Minderbrüder*. Leiden: Brill, 1966.

Faber, Martin. "'Gubernator, protector et corrector.' Zum Zusammenhang der Entstehung von Orden und Kardinalprotektoraten von Orden in der lateinischen Kirche." *Zeitschrift für Kirchengeschichte* 115 (2004): 19–44.

Fearns, James V. "Peter von Bruis und die religiöse Bewegung des 12. Jahrhunderts." *Archiv für Kulturgeschichte* 48 (1966): 311–35.

Fechter, Johannes. *Cluny, Adel und Volk. Studien über das Verhältnis des Klosters zu den Ständen (910–1156)*. Stuttgart: Schwedtner, 1966.

Feld, Helmut. *Franziskus von Assisi und seine Bewegung*. Darmstadt: Wissenschaftliche Buchgesellschaft, 2007.

Felskau, Christian-Frederik. "Von Brabant bis Böhmen und darüber hinaus. Zu Einheit und Vielfalt der 'religiösen Frauenbewegung' des 12. und des 13. Jahrhunderts." In *Fromme Frauen—unbequeme Frauen? Weibliches Religiosentum im Mittelalter*, edited by Edeltraud Klueting. Hildesheim and Zürich: Olms, 2006.

Felten, Franz J. *Äbte und Laienäbte im Frankenreich. Studien zum Verhältnis von Staat und Kirche im früheren Mittelalter*. Stuttgart: Hiersemann, 1980.

———. "Abwehr, Zuneigung, Pflichtgefühl. Reaktionen der frühen Zisterzienser auf den Wunsch religiöser Frauen, zisterziensisch zu leben." In *Female* vita religiosa *between Late Antiquity and the High Middle Ages: Structures, Developments and Spatial Contexts*, edited by Gert Melville and Anne Müller. Berlin: LIT, 2011. 391–415.

———. "Auf dem Weg zu Kanonissen und Kanonissenstift. Ordnungskonzepte der weiblichen vita religiosa bis ins 9. Jahrhundert." In Franz J. Felten, *Vita religiosa sanctimonialium. Norm und Praxis des weiblichen religiösen Lebens vom 6. bis zum 13. Jahrhundert*, edited by Christine Kleinjung. Korb: Didymos, 2011. 71–92.

———. "Der Zisterzienserorden und die Frauen." In Franz J. Felten, *Vita religiosa sanctimonialium. Norm und Praxis des weiblichen religiösen Lebens vom 6. bis zum 13. Jahrhundert*, edited by Christine Kleinjung. Korb: Didymos, 2011. 199–274.

———. "Die Ordensreformen Benedikts XII. unter institutionsgeschichtlichem Aspekt." In *Institutionen und Geschichte. Theoretische Aspekte und mittelalterliche Befunde*, edited by Gert Melville. Cologne: Böhlau, 1992. 369–435.

———. "Frauenklöster im Frankenreich. Entwicklungen und Probleme von den Anfängen bis zum frühen 9. Jahrhundert." In Franz J. Felten, *Vita religiosa sanctimonialium. Norm und Praxis des weiblichen religiösen Lebens vom 6. bis zum 13. Jahrhundert*, edited by Christine Kleinjung. Korb: Didymos, 2011. 31–95.

———. "Geschichtsschreibung cum ira et studio. Zur Darstellung religiöser Gemeinschaften in Jakob von Vitrys Historia occidentalis." In *Christliches und jüdisches Europa im Mittelalter. Kolloquium zu Ehren von Alfred Haverkamp*, edited by Lukas Clemens and Sigrid Hirbodian. Trier: Kliomedia, 2011. 83–120.

———. "Gregor IX. als Reformer von Orden und Klöstern." In *Gregorio IX e gli ordini mendicanti. Atti del XXXVIII Convegno internazionale*,

Assisi, 7–9 (Ottobre 2010). Spoleto: Centro italiano di studi sull'alto Medioevo, 2011. 3–71.

———. "Herrschaft des Abtes." In *Herrschaft und Kirche. Beiträge zur Entstehung und Wirkungsweise episkopaler und monastischer Organisationsformen*, edited by Friedrich Prinz. Stuttgart: Hiersemann, 1988. 147–296.

———. "Norbert von Xanten—vom Wanderprediger zum Kirchenfürsten." In *Norbert von Xanten. Adliger, Ordensstifter, Kirchenfürst*, edited by Kaspar Elm. Cologne: Wienand, 1984. 67–157.

———. "Verbandsbildung von Frauenklöstern. Le Paraclet, Prémy, Fontevraud mit einem Ausblick auf Cluny, Sempringham und Tart." In *Vom Kloster zum Klosterverband. Das Werkzeug der Schriftlichkeit*, edited by Hagen Keller and Franz Neiske. Munich: Wilhelm Fink, 1997. 277–341.

———. "Wie adelig waren Kanonissenstifte (und andere weibliche Konvente) im (frühen und hohen) Mittelalter?" In Franz J. Felten, *Vita religiosa sanctimonialium. Norm und Praxis des weiblichen religiösen Lebens vom 6. bis zum 13. Jahrhundert*, edited by Christine Kleinjung. Korb: Didymos, 2011. 93–162.

———. "Zwischen Berufung und Amt. Norbert von Xanten und seinesgleichen im ersten Viertel des 12. Jahrhunderts." In *Charisma und religiösen Gemeinschaften im Mittelalter*, edited by Giancarlo Andenna, Mirko Breitenstein, and Gert Melville. Münster: LIT, 2005. 103–49.

Felten, Franz J., Annette Kehnel, and Stefan Weinfurter, eds. *Institution und Charisma. Festschrift für Gert Melville zum 65. Geburtstag*. Cologne: Böhlau, 2009.

Felten, Franz J., and Werner Rösener, eds. *Norm und Realität. Kontinuität und Wandel der Zisterzienser im Mittelalter*. Berlin: LIT, 2009.

Folz, Robert. "Le monastère du Val des Choux au premier siècle de son histoire." *Bulletin philologique et historique (jusqu'à 1610) du Comité des Travaux Historiques et Scientifiques. Section de Philologie et d'histoire, année 1959* (1960): 91–115.

Fonseca, Cosimo Damiano. "Farfa abbazia imperiale." In *Farfa abbazia imperiale. Atti del Convegno internazionale, Farfa-Santa Vittoria in Matenano, 25.–29.8.2003*. Negarine di San Pietro in Cariano (Verona): Il Segno dei Gabrielli Ed., 2006. 1–17.

———. "Il capitolo di San Martino e la riforma canonicale nella seconda metà del secolo XI." In *Sant'Anselmo vescovo di Lucca (1073–1086) nel quadro delle trasformazioni sociali e della riforma ecclesiastica*, edited by Cinzio Violante. Rome: Istituto storico italiano per il Medio Evo, 1992. 51–64.

———. "Il movimento canonicale a Lucca e nella diocesi lucchese fra XI e XII secolo." In *Alluccio da Pescia (1070 ca.–1134). Un santo laico dell'età postgregoriana*, edited by Cinzio Violente. Rome: Jouvence, 1993. 147–57.

————. "La regola dei Trinitari oltre gli ideali degli ordini religioso-cavallereschi." In *Medioevo, Mezzogiorno, Mediterraneo. Studi in onore di Mario Del Treppo.* Vol. 1, edited by Gabriella Rossetti and Giovanni Vitolo. Naples: Liguori, 2000. 147–59.

————. *Medioevo canonicale.* Milan: Vita e pensiero, 1970.

Foot, Sarah. *Monastic Life in Anglo-Saxon England, c. 600–900.* Cambridge, UK: Cambridge University Press, 2006.

Fössel, Amalie, and Anette Hettinger. *Klosterfrauen, Beginen, Ketzerinnen. Religiöse Lebensformen von Frauen im Mittelalter.* Idstein: Schulz-Kirchner, 2000.

Fox, Yaniv. *Power and Religion in Merovingian Gaul: Columbanian Monasticism and the Formation of the Frankish Aristocracy.* Cambridge, UK: Cambridge University Press, 2014.

Frank, Isnard W. *Lexikon des Mönchtums und der Orden.* Stuttgart: Reclam, 2005.

Frank, Karl Suso. *Grundzüge der Geschichte des christlichen Mönchtums.* 6th ed. Darmstadt: Primus, 2010.

————. "Tertiarier/Tertiarierinnen I und II." In *Theologische Realenzyklopädie.* Vol. 33. Berlin: de Gruyter, 2002.

Freed, John B. *The Friars and German Society in the Thirteenth Century.* Cambridge, MA: Medieval Academy of America, 1977.

Freister, Rudolf. "Die Klosterschule." In *Macht des Wortes. Benediktinisches Mönchtums im Spiegel Europas, Essayband*, edited by Gerfried Sitar and Martin Kroker. Regensburg: Schnell & Steiner, 2009. 1:235–42.

Fried, Johannes. *Der Schleier der Erinnerung. Grundzüge einer historischen Memorik.* Munich: C. H. Beck, 2004.

Fry, Timothy, ed. *RB 1980: The Rule of St. Benedict in English.* Collegeville, MN: Liturgical Press, 1981.

Fuhrmann, Horst. *Papst Urban II. und der Stand der Regularkanoniker (Sitzungsberichte/Bayerische Akademie der Wissenschaften, phil.-hist. Klasse).* Munich: Verlag der Bayerischen Akademie der Wissenschaften, 1984.

Fülöpp-Romhányi, Beatrix. "Die Pauliner im mittelalterlichen Ungarn." In *Beiträge zur Geschichte des Paulinerordens*, edited by Kaspar Elm. Berlin: Duncker & Humblot, 2000. 143–56.

Galbraith, Georgina R. *The Constitution of the Dominican Order, 1216 to 1360.* Manchester: University Press, 1925.

Gallaro, Giorgio D. "Revisiting the Saintly Founder of Grottaferrata: Nilus the Calabrian." *Nicolaus. Rivista di teologia ecumenico-patristica* 37 (2010): 293–300.

Galuzzi, Alessandro Maria. *Origini dell'Ordine dei Minimi.* Rome: Libreria Editrice della Pontificia Università Lateranense, 1967.

Gassmann, Guido. *Konversen im Mittelalter. Eine Untersuchung anhand der neun Schweizer Zisterzienserabteien.* Berlin: LIT, 2013.

Geerlings, Wilhelm. *Augustinus. Leben und Werk. Eine Bibliographische Einführung.* Paderborn: Schöningh, 2002.

Geréby, György, and Piroska Nagy. "The Life of the Hermit Stephen of Obazine." In *Medieval Christianity in Practice*, edited by Miri Rubin. Princeton, NJ: Princeton University Press, 2009. 299–310.

Geuenich, Dieter. "Bonifatius und 'sein' Kloster Fulda." In *Bonifatius—Leben und Nachwirken. Die Gestaltung des christlichen Europa im Frühmittelalter*, edited by Franz J. Felten, Jörg Jarnut, and Lutz E. von Padberg. Mainz: Gesellschaft für mittelrheinische Kirchengeschichte, 2007.

———. "Gebetsgedenken und anianische Reform. Beobachtungen zu den Verbrüderungsbeziehungen der Äbte im Reich Ludwigs des Frommen." In *Monastische Reformen im 9. und 10. Jahrhundert*, edited by Raymund Kottje and Helmut Maurer. Sigmaringen: Thorbecke, 1989. 79–106.

Gleba, Gudrun. *Klosterleben im Mittelalter.* Darmstadt: Wissenschaftliche Buchgeschellschaft, 2004.

Golding, Brian J. *Gilbert of Sempringham and the Gilbertine Order c. 1130–c. 1300.* Oxford: Oxford University Press, 1995.

Greene, Patrick J. *Medieval Monasteries.* London: Leicester University Press, 1992.

Gregorio IX e gli ordini mendicanti. Atti del XXXVIII Convegno internazionale, Assisi, 7–9 (Ottobre 2010). Spoleto: Centro italiano di studi sull'alto Medioevo, 2011.

Gregory the Great. *Dialogues.* Translated by Odo John Zimmerman. The Fathers of the Church. Vol. 39. Washington, DC: The Catholic University of America Press, 2002.

Grélois, Alexis. "Les origines contre la Réforme: nouvelles considérations sur la 'Vie de Saint Étienne d'Obazine.'" In *Écrire son histoire: les communautés régulières face à leur passé*, edited by Nicole Bouter. Saint-Étienne: Publications de l'Université de Saint-Étienne, 2006. 369–88.

Griffiths, Fiona J. "Female Spirituality and Intellect in the Twelfth and Thirteenth Centuries: A Case Study of Herrad of Hohenbourg." PhD dissertation, Cambridge University, 1998.

Grote, Andreas E. J. *"Anachorese" und "Zönobium." Der Rekurs des frühen westlichen Mönchtums auf monastische Konzepte des Ostens.* Stuttgart: Thorbecke, 2001.

Grundmann, Herbert. *Religious Movements in the Middle Ages: The Historical Links between Heresy, the Mendicant Orders, and the Women's Religious Movement in the Twelfth and Thirteenth Century, with the Historical Foundations of German Mysticism.* Trans. Steven Rowan. Notre Dame, IN: University of Notre Dame Press, 1995.

Gutiérrez, David. *Geschichte des Augustinerordens*. Vol. 1, *Die Augustiner im Mittelalter 1256–1356*. Würzburg: Augustinus-Verlag, 1985.

Guy, Jean-Claude, ed. *Les Apophtegmes des Pères. Collection systématique. Chapitres I–IX*. SCh 387, 474, 498. Paris: Éditions du Cerf, 1993–2005.

Haarländer, Stephanie. *"Innumerabiles populi de utroque sexu confluentes . . . .* Klöster für Männer und Frauen im frühmittelalterlichen Irland." In *Female* vita religiosa *between Late Antiquity and the High Middle Ages: Structures, Developments and Spatial Contexts*, edited by Gert Melville and Anne Müller. Berlin: LIT, 2011. 137–50.

Hallinger, Kassius. *Gorze-Kluny. Studien zu den monastischen Lebensformen und Gegensätzen im Hochmittelalter*. 2 vols. Rome: Herder, 1950/1951.

Hamburger, Jeffrey. *The Visual and the Visionary. Art and Female Spirituality in Late Medieval Germany*. New York: Zone Books, 1998.

Hanslik, Rudolf, ed. *Benedicti Regula*. Vienna: Hoedler-Pichler-Tempsky, 1977.

Harmless, William. *Desert Christians. An Introduction to the Literature of Early Monasticism*. Oxford: Oxford University Press, 2004.

Hartmann, Winfried. *Die Synoden der Karolingerzeit im Frankenreich und in Italien*. Paderborn: Schöningh, 1989.

Haug, Walter, and Wolfram Schneider-Lastin. *Deutsche Mystik im abendländischen Zusammenhang: Neu erschlossene Texte, neu methodische Ansätze, neue theoretische Konzepte*. Tübingen: Niemeyer, 2000.

Hecht, Konrad. *Der St. Galler Klosterplan*. Sigmaringen: Thorbecke, 1983.

Hecker, Norbert. *Bettelorden und Bürgertum. Konflikt und Kooperation in deutschen Städten des Spätmittelalters*. Frankfurt am Main: Peter Lang, 1981.

Helvétius, Anne-Marie. "L'organisation des monastères féminins à l'époque mérovingienne." In *Female* vita religiosa *between Late Antiquity and the High Middle Ages: Structures, Developments and Spatial Contexts*, edited by Gert Melville and Anne Müller. Berlin: LIT, 2011. 151–69.

Herbert, Máire. *Iona, Kells and Derry. The History and Hagiography of the Monastic Familia of Columba*. Oxford: Clarendon Press, 1988.

Heyen, Franz-Josef. "Trier, St. Maximin." In *Die Männer- und Frauenklöster der Benediktiner in Rheinland-Pfalz und Saarland*, edited by Friedhelm Jürgensmeier. St. Ottilien: EOS, 1999. 1010–88.

Highfield, John Roger Loxdale. "The Jeronimites in Spain, their Patrons and Success, 1373–1516." *The Journal of Ecclesiastical History* 34 (1983): 513–33.

Hinnebusch, John Frederick, ed. *The Historia Occidentalis of Jacques de Vitry. A Critical Edition*. Fribourg: Fribourg University Press, 1972.

Hinnebusch, William A. *The Dominicans. A Short History*. Dublin: Dominican Publications, 1985.

————. *The History of the Dominican Order.* Vol. 1, *Origins and Growth to 1500.* Vol. 2, *Intellectual and Cultural Life to 1500.* New York: Alba House, 1965, 1973.

Hochholzer, Elmar. "Die lothringische (Gorzer) Reform." In *Die Reformverbände und Kongregationen der Benediktiner im deutschen Sprachraum,* edited by Ulrich Faust and Franz Quarthal. St. Ottilien: EOS, 1999. 45–87.

Holzherr, Georg, ed. *Die Benediktsregel: Eine Anleitung zu christlichem Leben.* Fribourg: Paulus, 2007.

Horst, Ulrich. *Wege in die Nachfolge Christi. Die Theologie des Ordensstandes nach Thomas von Aquin.* Berlin: Akademie, 2006.

Houben, Hubert. *Die Abtei Venosa und das Mönchtum im normannisch-staufischen Süditalien.* Tübingen: Niemeyer, 1995.

Hoyer, Wolfram. "Der dominikanische Ansatz zum Dialog mit den Religionen in der Gründerzeit des Ordens." In *Das Charisma des Ursprungs und die Religionen. Das Werden christlicher Orden im Kontext der Religionen,* edited by Petrus Bsteh and Brigitte Proksch. Vienna/Berlin: LIT, 2011. 242–64.

Hurel, Daniel-Odon, and Denyse Riche. *Cluny. De l'abbaye à l'ordre clunisien. X^e–XVIIIe siècle.* Paris: Armand Colin, 2010.

Hutchison, Carole A. *The Hermit Monks of Grandmont.* CS 118. Kalamazoo, MI: Cistercian Publications, 1989.

Il papato duecentesco e gli ordini mendicanti. Edited by Enrico Menestò. Spoleto: Centro italiano di studi sull'alto Medioevo, 1998. 23–80.

Iogna-Prat, Dominique. "Cluny comme 'système ecclesial.'" In *Die Cluniazenser in ihrem politisch-sozialen Umfeld,* edited by Giles Constable, Gert Melville, and Jörg Oberste. Münster: LIT, 1998. 13–92.

————. *Order and Exclusion: Cluny and Christendom Face Heresy, Judaism, and Islam, 1000–1150.* Ithaca: Cornell University Press, 2002.

————. "Politische Aspekte der Marienverehrung in Cluny um das Jahr 1000." In *Maria in der Welt. Marienverehrung im Kontext der Sozialgeschichte im 10.–18. Jahrhundert,* edited by Claudia Opitz, Hedwig Röckelein, Gabriela Signori, and Guy P. Marchal. Zürich: Chronos, 1993. 243–51.

Iogna-Prat, Dominique, ed. *Cluny: les moines et la société au premier âge féodal.* Rennes: Presses Universitaire de Rennes, 2013.

Innovation durch Deuten und Gestalten. Klöster im Mittelalter zwischen Jenseits und Welt. Edited by Gert Melville, Bernd Schneidmüller, and Stefan Weinfurter. Regensburg: Schnell & Steiner, 2014.

Israel, Uwe. "Reform durch Mönche aus der Ferne. Das Beispiel der Benediktinerabtei Subiaco." In *Vita communis und ethnische Vielfalt. Multinational zusammengesetzte Klöster im Mittelalter,* edited by Uwe Israel. Berlin: LIT, 2006. 157–78.

Jacobs, Uwe Kai. *Die Regula Benedicti als Rechtsbuch. Eine rechtshistorische und rechtstheologische Untersuchung.* Cologne: Böhlau, 1987.

Jäger, Berthold. "Zur wirtschaftlichen und rechtlichen Entwicklung des Klosters Fulda in seiner Frühzeit." In *Hrabanus Maurus in Fulda. Mit einer Hrabanus Maurus-Bibliographie (1979–2009)*, edited by Marc-Aeilko Aris and Susanna Bullido del Barrio. Freiburg am Main: Knecht, 2010. 81–120.

Jäggi, Carola. "Ordensarchitektur als Kommunikation von Ordnung. Zisterziensische Baukunst zwischen Vielfalt und Einheit." In *Die Ordnung der Kommunikation und die Kommunikation der Ordnungen im mittelalterlichen Europa*. Vol. 1, *Netzwerke: Klöster und Orden im 12. und 13. Jahrhundert*, edited by Cristina Andenna, Klaus Herbers, and Gert Melville. Stuttgart: Franz Steiner, 2012. 203–25.

Jakobs, Hermann. *Die Hirsauer. Ihre Ausbreitung und Rechtsstellung im Zeitalter des Investiturstreites*. Cologne: Böhlau, 1961.

Jäkel, Gert. . . . *usque in praesentem diem. Kontinuitätskonstruktionen in der Eigengeschichtsschreibung religiöser Orden des Hoch- und Spätmittelalters*. Berlin: LIT, 2013.

Jamroziak, Emilia, *The Cistercian Order in Medieval Europe: 1090–1500*. London: Routledge, 2013.

Jamroziak, Emilia, and Karen Stoeber, eds. *Monasteries on the Borders of Medieval Europe: Conflict and Cultural Interaction*. Turnhout: Brepols, 2013.

Jankrift, Kay Peter. *Leprose als Streiter Gottes. Institutionalisierung und Organisation des Ordens vom heiligen Lazarus zu Jerusalem von seinen Anfängen bis zum Jahre 1350*. Münster: LIT, 1997.

Jenal, Georg. "Frühe Formen der weiblichen vita religiosa im lateinischen Westen (4. und Anfang 5. Jahrhundert)." In *Female* vita religiosa *between Late Antiquity and the High Middle Ages: Structures, Developments and Spatial Contexts*, edited by Gert Melville and Anne Müller. Berlin: LIT, 2011. 43–77.

———. *Italia ascetica atque monastica. Das Asketen- und Mönchtum in Italien von den Anfängen bis zur Zeit der Langobarden (ca. 150/250–604)*. 2 vols. Stuttgart: Hiersemann, 1995.

Johanek, Peter. "Klosterstudien im 12. Jahrhundert." In *Schulen und Studien im sozialen Wandel des hohen und späten Mittelalters*, edited by Johannes Fried. Sigmaringen: Thorbecke, 1986. 35–68.

Johnson, Timothy J. *The Soul in Ascent: Bonaventure on Poverty, Prayer, and Union with God*. Quincy, IL: Francisco Press, 2001.

Josserand, Philippe, and Mathieu Olivier, eds. *La mémoire des origines dans les ordres religieux-militaires au Moyen Âge./Die Erinnerung an die eigenen Ursprünge in den geistlichen Ritterorden im Mittelalter*. Berlin: LIT, 2013.

Jotischky, Andrew. *The Carmelites and Antiquity. Mendicants and their Pasts in the Middle Ages*. Oxford: Oxford University Press, 2002.

Jung, Christel. "L'abbaye de Niederaltaich, centre de réforme monastique au Xème et XIème siècles." PhD dissertation, Université de Paris, 1988.

Kardong, Terence G. "The Monastic Practices of Pachomius and the Pachomians." *Studia Monastica* 32 (1990): 59–77.

Kasper, Clemens M. *Theologie und Askese. Die Spiritualität des Inselmönchtums von Lérins im 5. Jahrhundert.* Münster: Aschendorff, 1991.

Kastner, Jörg. *Historiae fundationum monasteriorum: Frühformen monastischer Institutionsgeschichtsschreibung im Mittelalter.* Munich: Arbeo-Gesellschaft, 1974.

Kehnel, Annette. *Clonmacnois—the Church and Lands of St. Ciarán. Change and Continuity in an Irish Monastic Foundation (6th to 16th Century).* Münster: LIT, 1998.

————. "Die Formierung der Gemeinschaften der Minderen Brüder in der Provinz Anglia. Überlegungen zum *Tractatus de adventu fratrum minorum in Angliam des Bruders Thomas von Eccleston.*" In *Die Bettelorden im Aufbau. Beiträge zu Institutionalisierungsprozessen im mittelalterlichen Religiosentum*, edited by Gert Melville and Jörg Oberste. Münster: LIT, 1999. 493–524.

Kehnel, Annette, and Gert Melville, eds. *In proposito paupertatis. Studien zum Armutsverständnis bei den mittelalterlichen Bettelorden.* Münster: LIT, 2001.

Kelly, John Norman Davidson. *Jerome: His Life, Writings and Controversies.* 2nd ed. London: Duckworth, 1998.

Kettemann, Walter. "Subsidia Anianensia. Überlieferungs- und textgeschichtliche Untersuchungen zur Geschichte Witiza-Benedikts, seines Klosters Aniane und zur sogenannten 'anianischen Reform.'" PhD dissertation, Universität Duisburg, 1999.

Kintzinger, Martin. "Keine große Stille—Wissenskulturen zwischen Kloster und Welt." In *Monastisches Leben im urbanen Kontext*, edited by Anne-Marie Hecker and Susanne Röhl. Munich: Wilhelm Fink, 2010. 109–30.

————. "Monastische Kultur und die Kunst des Wissens im Mittelalter." In *Kloster und Bildung im Mittelalter*, edited by Nathalie Kruppa and Jürgen Wilke. Göttingen: Vandenhoeck & Ruprecht, 2006. 15–47.

Kirby, David Peter, ed. *Saint Wilfrid at Hexham.* Newcastle upon Tyne: Oriel Press, 1974.

Klingshirn, W. E. *Caesarius of Arles. The Making of a Christian Community in Late Antique Gaul.* Cambridge, UK: Cambridge University Press, 1994.

Klueting, Edeltraud. *Monasteria semper reformanda. Kloster- und Ordensreformen im Mittelalter.* Münster: LIT, 2005.

Klug, Martina B. *Armut und Arbeit in der Devotio Moderna: Studien zum Leben der Schwestern in niederrheinischen Gemeinschaften.* Munich: Waxmann, 2005.

Knowles, David. *From Pachomius to Ignatius. A Study in the Constitutional History of the Religious Orders.* Oxford: Clarendon Press, 1966.

———. *The Monastic Order in England.* Cambridge, UK: Cambridge University Press, 1950.

Knox, Lezlie. *Creating Clare of Assisi: Female Franciscan Identities in Later Medieval Italy.* Leiden: Brill, 2008.

Kohl, Wilhelm. "Die Windesheimer Kongregation." In *Reformbemühungen und Observanzbestrebungen im spätmittelalterlichen Ordenswesen,* edited by Kaspar Elm. Berlin: Duncker & Humblot, 1989. 83–106.

Kohnle, Armin. *Abt Hugo von Cluny (1049–1109).* Sigmaringen: Thorbecke, 1993.

———. "Cluniazenserklöster und ihre Stifter in Deutschland, der Schweiz und im Elsaß." In *Die Cluniazenser in ihrem politisch-sozialen Umfeld,* edited by Giles Constable, Gert Melville, and Jörg Oberste. Münster: LIT, 1998. 469–84.

Köpf, Ulrich. "Hugolino von Ostia (Gregor IX.) und Franziskus." In *Franziskus von Assisi. Das Bild des Heiligen aus neuer Sicht,* edited by Dieter R. Bauer, Helmut Feld, and Ulrich Köpf. Cologne: Böhlau, 2005. 163–82.

Krause, Martin. "Das Mönchtum in Ägypten." In *Ägypten in spätantik-christlicher Zeit,* edited by Martin Krause. Wiesbaden: L. Reichert, 1998. 149–74.

Krauss, Susanne. *Die* Devotio moderna *in Deventer. Anatomie eines Zentrums der Reformbewegung.* Münster: LIT, 2007.

Krings, Bruno. "Das Ordensrecht der Prämonstratenser vom späten 12. Jahrhundert bis zum Jahr 1227. Der *liber consuetudinum* und die Dekrete des Generalkapitels." *Analecta Praemonstratensia* 69 (1993): 107–242.

———. "Die Prämonstratenser und ihr weiblicher Zweig." In *Studien zum Prämonstratenserorden,* edited by Irene Crusius and Helmut Flachenecker. Göttingen: Vandenhoeck & Ruprecht, 2003. 75–105.

———. "Zum Ordensrecht der Prämonstratenser bis zur Mitte des 12. Jahrhunderts."*Analecta Praemonstratensia* 76 (2000): 9–28.

Krön, Martin. *Das Mönchtum und die kulturelle Tradition des lateinischen Westens. Formen der Askese, Autorität und Organisation im frühen westlichen Zönobitentum.* Munich: Tuduv, 1997.

Krumwiede, Hans Walter. "Die Geschichte des Klosters Bursfelde." In *Kloster Bursfelde,* edited by Lothar Perlitt. Göttingen: Göttinger Tageblatt, 1984. 9–24.

Kruppa, Nathalie, ed. *Adlige–Stifte–Mönche. Zum Verhältnis zwischen Klöstern und mittelalterlichem Adel.* Göttingen: Vandenhoeck & Ruprecht, 2007.

Kruppa, Nathalie, and Jürgen Wilke, eds. *Kloster und Bildung im Mittelalter.* Göttingen: Vandenhoeck & Ruprecht, 2006.

Kuster, Niklaus. "Quia divina inspiratione . . . ." In *Klara von Assisi: Zwischen Bettelarmut und Beziehungsreichtum. Beiträge zur neueren deutschsprachigen Klara-Forschung*, edited by Bernd Schmies. Münster: Aschendorff, 2011. 193–211.

Lacy, Brian. *Saint Columba. His Life and Legacy*. Blackrock: Columba Press, 2013.

Lambertini, Roberto. "Il sistema formativo degli studia degli Ordini Mendicanti: osservazioni a partire dai risultati di recenti indagini." In *Die Ordnung der Kommunikation und die Kommunikation der Ordnung im mittelalterlichen Europa*. Vol. 1, *Netzwerke: Klöster und Orden im 12. und 13. Jahrhundert*, edited by Christina Andenna, Klaus Herbers, and Gert Melville. Stuttgart: Franz Steiner, 2012. 135–46.

Lamke, Florian. *Cluniazenser am Oberrhein. Konfliktlösungen und adlige Gruppenbildung in der Zeit des Investiturstreits*. Munich: Alber, 2009.

Landau, Peter. "Eigenkirchenwesen." *Theologische Realenzyklopädie*. Berlin: de Gruyter, 1982. 4:399–404.

Landini, Laurentio C. *The Causes of the Clericalization of the Order of Friars Minor 1209–1260 in the Light of Early Franciscan Sources*. Chicago: Pontifical Gregorian University, 1968.

Lang, Gotthard. *Der selige Gunther der Eremit. Der Heilige des Böhmerwaldes*. Regensburg: Habbel, 1948.

La Règle du maître. Edited and translated by Adalbert de Vogüé. SCh 105, 106. Paris: Éditions du Cerf, 1964.

La regola dei Frati Minori. Atti del XXXVII Convegno internazionale, Assisi, 8–10 ottobre 2009. Spoleto: Centro italiano di studi sull'alto Medioevo, 2010.

Lawrence, Clifford Hugh. *The Friars: The Impact of the Early Mendicant Movement on Western Society*. London: Longman, 1994.

———. *Medieval Monasticism: Forms of Religious Life in Western Europe in the Middle Ages*. 3rd ed. London: Longman, 2003.

Leclercq, Jean. "La crise du monachisme aux XIᵉ et XIIᵉ siècles." *Bullettino dell'Istituto storico italiano per il Medio Evo* 70 (1958): 19–41.

———. *L'amour vu par les moines au XIIᵉ siècle*. Paris: Éditions du Cerf, 1979.

———. *The Love of Learning and the Desire for God: A Study of Monastic Culture*. Translated by Catharine Misrahi. New York: Fordham University Press, 1982.

———. *Otia monastica. Études sur le vocabulaire de la contemplation au Moyen Âge*. Rome: Herder, 1963.

———. "Zur Geschichte des Lebens in Cluny." In *Cluny, Beiträge zu Gestalt und Wirkung der Cluniazensischen Reform*, edited by Helmut Richter. Darmstadt: Wissenschaftliche Buchgesellschaft, 1975. 254–318.

Le Goff, Jacques. "Apostolat mendiant et fait urbain dans la France médié-vale. L'implantation des ordres mendicants." In Jacques Le Goff, *Héros du Moyen Âge, le Saint et le roi*. Paris: Gallimard, 2004. 1207–26.

Lehmijoki-Gardner, Maiju. "Writing Religious Rules as an Interactive Process: Dominican Penitent Women and the Making of their 'Regula.'" *Speculum* 79 (2004): 660–87.

Lekai, Louis Julius. *The Cistercians: Ideals and Reality*. Kent, OH: Kent State University Press, 1977.

Lemaître, Jean-Loup, ed. *Prieurs et prieurés dans l'Occident médiéval*. Geneva: Éditions Droz, 1987.

Lentes, Thomas. "'Vita perfecta' zwischen 'Vita communis' und 'Vita pri-vata': Eine Skizze zur klösterlichen Einzelzelle." In *Das Öffentliche und Private in der Vormoderne*, edited by Gert Melville and Peter von Moos. Cologne: Böhlau, 1998. 125–64.

L'eremitismo in Occidente nei secoli XI e XII. Atti della seconda Settimana internazionale di studio Mendola, 30 agosto–6 settembre 1962. Milan: Vita e pensiero, 1965.

Letonnelier, Gaston. *L'abbaye exempte de Cluny et le Saint-Siège. Étude sur le développement de l'exemption clunisienne des origines jusqu à la fin du XIIIᵉ siècle*. Paris: Picard, 1923.

Leyser, Henrietta. *Hermits and the New Monasticism. A Study of Religious Communities in Western Europe 1000–1150*. London: St. Martin's, 1984.

Libellus de diversis ordinibus et professionibus qui sunt in aecclesia. Edited by Giles Constable and Bernard S. Smith. 2nd ed. Oxford: Clarendon Press, 2003.

Licciardello, Pierluigi, ed. *Consuetudo Camaldulensis. Rudolphi Constitutiones. Liber Eremitice Regule*. Florence: Edizione del Galluzzo, 2004.

———. *Martino III priore di Camaldoli. Libri tres de moribus*. Florence: Edizione del Galluzzo, 2013.

Lohse, Bernhard. *Askese und Mönchtum in der Antike und in der alten Kirche*. Munich: Oldenbourg, 1969.

Longère, Jean. "Robert d'Arbrissel prédicateur." In *Robert d'Arbrissel et la vie religieuse dans l'ouest de la France. Actes du colloque interna-tional de Fontevraud à l'occasion du IXᵉ centenaire de la fondation de l'abbaye, 13–16 décembre 2001*, edited by Jacques Dalarun. Turnhout: Brepols, 2004. 87–104.

Lorenz, Sönke. "Zu Spiritualität und Theologie bei der Windesheimer Kongregation." In *Frömmigkeit und Theologie an Chorherrenstiften*, edited by Ulrich Köpf. Ostfildern: Thorbecke, 2009. 169–84.

Lutter, Christina, ed. *Funktionsräume, Wahrnehmungsräume, Gefühls-räume. Mittelalterliche Lebensformen zwischen Kloster und Welt*. Vienna: Böhlau, 2011.

————. "Social Groups, Personal Relations, and the Making of Communities in Medieval *Vita Monastica*." In *Making Sense as a Cultural Practice: Historical Perspectives*, edited by Jörg Rogge. Bielefeld: Transcript, 2013. 45–61.

Maccarrone, Michele. "Le costituzioni del IV concilio lateranense sui religiosi." In *Nuovi studi su Innocenzo III*, edited by Roberto Lambertini. Rome: Istituto storico italiano per il Medio Evo, 1995. 1–45.

————. "Primato romano e monasteri dal principio del secolo XII ad Innocenzo III." In *Istituzioni monastiche e istituzione canonicali in Occidente (1123–1215)*. Milan: Vita e pensiero, 1980. 49–132.

————. "Riforma e sviluppo della vita religiosa con Innocenzo III." *Rivista di storia della chiesa in Italia* 16 (1962): 29–72.

Mackintosh, Robin. *Augustine of Canterbury. Leadership, Mission and Legacy*. Norwich: Canterbury Press, 2013.

Madre, Alois. *Nikolaus von Dinkelsbühl: Leben und Schriften*. Münster: Aschendorff, 1965.

Mahn, Jean-Berthold. *L'ordre cistercien et son gouvernement, des origines au milieu du XIIIᵉ siècle (1098–1265)*. 2nd ed. Paris: E. de Boccard, 1982.

Mai, Paul, ed. *Die Augustiner Chorherren in Bayern: Zum 25–jährigen Wiedererstehen des Ordens*. Regensburg: Schnell & Steiner, 1999.

Maier, Peter. "Die Reform von Kastl." In *Die Reformverbände und Kongregationen der Benediktiner im deutschen Sprachraum*, edited by Ulrich Faust and Franz Quarthal. St. Ottilien: EOS, 1999. 225–67.

Makowski, Elizabeth M. *"A Pernicious Sort of Woman": Quasi-Religious Women and Canon Lawyers in the Later Middle Ages*. Washington, DC: The Catholic University of America Press, 2005.

Maleczek, Werner. "Franziskus, Innocenz III., Honorius III. und die Anfänge des Minoritenordens. Ein neuer Versuch zu einem alten Problem." In *Il papato duecentesco e gli ordini mendicanti*, edited by Enrico Menestò. Spoleto: Centro italiano di studi sull'alto Medioevo, 1998. 23–80.

Manselli, Raoul. "La povertà nella vita di Francesco d'Assisi." In *La povertà del secolo XII e Francesco d'Assisi*. Assisi: Società internazionale di studi francescani, 1975. 255–82.

————. *San Francesco d'Assisi*. Edited by Cinisello Balsamo. Milan: San Paolo Edizioni, 2002.

Marcombe, David. *Leper Knights: The Order of St. Lazarus of Jerusalem in England, c. 1150–1544*. Woodbridge, UK: Boydell, 2003.

McDonnell, Ernest William. "Beginen/Begarden." In *Theologische Realenzyklopädie*. Leipzig: de Gruyter, 1980. 5:404–11.

————. *The Beguines and Beghards in Medieval Culture, with Special Emphasis on the Belgian Scene*. New York: Octagon Books, 1969.

McGinn, Bernard. *The Presence of God: A History of Western Christian Mysticism*. 5 vols. New York: Crossroad, 1992–2012.

McGuire, Brian Patrick, ed. *A Companion to Bernard of Clairvaux*. Leiden and Boston: Brill, 2011.

Meinhardt, Birgitta. *Fanatiker oder Heilige? Frühchristliche Mönche und das Konzil zu Chalkedon*. Frankfurt: Peter Lang, 2011.

Melville, Gert. "Action, Text, and Validity: On Re-examining Cluny's *Consuetudines* and Statutes." In *From Dead of Night to End of Day. The Medieval Customs of Cluny [Du cœur de la nuit à la fin du jour. Les coutumes clunisiennes au Moyen Âge]*, edited by Susan Boynton and Isabelle Cochelin. Turnhout: Brepols, 2005. 67–83.

―――. "Cluny après 'Cluny.' Le treizième siècle: un champ de recherches." *Francia* 17 (1990): 91–124.

―――. "Cluny und das französische Königtum. Von 'Freiheit ohne Schutz' zu 'Schutz ohne Freiheit.'" In *Die Cluniazenser in ihrem politisch-sozialen Umfeld*, edited by Giles Constable, Gert Melville, and Jörg Oberste. Münster: LIT, 1998. 405–68.

―――. "Der geteilte Franziskus. Beobachtungen zum institutionellen Umgang mit Charisma." In *Kunst, Macht und Institution. Studien zur Philosophischen Anthropologie, soziologischen Theorie und Kultursoziologie der Moderne. Festschrift für Karl-Siegbert Rehberg*, edited by Joachim Fischer and Hans Joas. Frankfurt am Main/New York: Campus, 2003. 347–63.

―――. "Der Mönch als Rebell gegen gesatzte Ordnung und religiöse Tugend. Beobachtungen zu Quellen des 12. und 13. Jahrhunderts." In *De ordine vitae. Zu Normvorstellungen, Organisationsformen und Schriftlichkeit im mittelalterlichen Ordenswesen*, edited by Gert Melvile. Münster: LIT, 1996. 153–86.

―――. "Die cluniazensische 'Reformatio tam in capite quam in membris.' Institutioneller Wandel zwischen Anpassung und Bewahrung." In *Sozialer Wandel im Mittelalter. Wahrnehmungsformen, Erklärungsmuster, Regelungsmechanismen*, edited by Jürgen Miethke and Klaus Schreiner. Sigmaringen: Thorbecke, 1994. 249–97.

―――. "Die Rechtsordnung der Dominikaner in der Spanne von constituciones und admoniciones. Ein Beitrag zum Vergleich mittelalterlicher Ordensverfassungen." In *Grundlagen des Rechts. Festschrift für Peter Landau zum 65. Geburtstag*, edited by Richard H. Helmholz, Paul Mikat, Jörg Müller, and Michael Stolleis. Paderborn: Schöningh, 2000. 579–604.

―――. "Die Zisterzienser und der Umbruch des Mönchtums im 11. und 12. Jahrhundert." In *Norm und Realität. Kontinuität und Wandel der Zisterzienser im Mittelalter*, edited by Franz J. Felten and Werner Rösener. Berlin: LIT, 2009. 23–43.

―――. "'Diversa sunt monasteria et diversas habent institutiones.' Aspetti delle molteplici forme organizzative dei religiosi nel Medioevo." In *Chiesa e società in Sicilia. I secoli XII–XVI*, edited by Gaetano Zito. Turin: Società editrice internazionale, 1995. 323–45.

————. "Duo novae conversationis ordines. Zur Wahrnehmung der frühen Mendikanten vor dem Problem institutioneller Neuartigkeit im mittelalterlichen Religiosentum." In *Die Bettelorden im Aufbau. Beiträge zu Institutionalisierungsprozessen im mittelalterlichen Religiosentum*, edited by Gert Melville and Jörg Oberste. Münster: LIT, 1999. 1–23.

————. *Frommer Eifer und methodischer Betrieb. Beiträge zum mittelalterlichen Mönchtum*, edited by Mirko Breitenstein and Cristina Andenna. Cologne and Vienna: Böhlau, 2014.

————. "Im Spannungsfeld von religiösem Eifer und methodischem Betrieb. Zur Innovationskraft der mittelalterlichen Klöster." In *Denkströme. Journal der Sächsischen Akademie der Wissenschaften* 7 (2011): 72–92.

————. "Im Zeichen der Allmacht. Zur Präsenz Gottes im klösterlichen Leben des hohen Mittelalters." In *Das Sichtbare und das Unsichtbare der Macht. Institutionelle Prozesse in Antike, Mittelalter und Neuzeit*, edited by Gert Melville. Cologne, Weimar, and Vienna: Böhlau, 2005. 19–44.

————. *"In privatis locis proprio jure vivere*. Zu Diskursen des frühen 12. Jahrhunderts um religiöse Eigenbestimmung oder institutionelle Einbindung." In *Kulturarbeit und Kirche. Festschrift Msgr. Dr. Paul Mai zum 70. Geburtstag*, edited by Werner Chrobak and Karl Hausbacher. Regensburg: Verlag des Vereins für Regensburger Bistumsgeschichte, 2005. 25–38.

————. "Inside and Outside. Some Considerations about Cloistral Boundaries in the Central Middle Ages." In *Ecclesia in Medio Nationis: Reflections on the Study of Monasticism in the Central Middle Ages/Réflexions sur l'Étude du Monachisme au Moyen Âge Central*, edited by Steven Vanderputten and Brigitte Meijns. Leuven: Leuven University Press, 2011. 167–82.

————. "In solitudine ac paupertate. Stephans von Muret Evangelium vor Franz von Assisi." In *In proposito paupertatis. Studien zum Armutsverständnis bei den mittelalterlichen Bettelorden*, edited by Gert Melville and Annette Kehnel. Münster: LIT, 2001. 7–30.

————. "Knowledge of the Origins: Constructing Identity and Ordering Monastic Life in the Middle Ages." In *Knowledge, Discipline and Power in the Middle Ages. Essays in Honour of David Luscombe*, edited by Joseph Canning, Edmund King, and Martial Staub. Leiden/Boston: Brill, 2011. 41–62.

————. "'Liebe und tue, was du willst!' Eine Herausforderung für den mittelalterlichen Menschen." In *Sorge*, edited by Gert Melville, Gregor Vogt-Spira, and Mirko Breitenstein. Cologne: Böhlau, 2015. 79–95.

————. "Montecassino." In *Erinnerungsorte des Christentums*, edited by Christoph Markschies and Hubert Wolf. Munich: C. H. Beck, 2010. 322–44.

————. "Ordensstatuten und allgemeines Kirchenrecht. Eine Skizze zum 12./13. Jahrhundert." In *Proceedings of the 9th International Congress of Medieval Canon Law*, edited by Peter Landau and Jörg Müller. Vatican City: Biblioteca Apostolica Vaticana, 1997. 691–712.

————. "Regeln—Consuetudines—Texte—Statuten. Positionen für eine Typologie des normativen Schrifttums religiöser Gemeinschaften im Mittelalter." In *Regulae—Consuetudines—Statuta. Studi sulle fonti normative degli ordini religiosi nei secoli centrali del Medioevo*, edited by Cristina Andenna and Gert Melville. Münster: LIT, 2005. 5–38.

————. "Stephan von Obazine: Begründung und Überwindung charismatischer Führung." In *Charisma und religiöse Gemeinschaften im Mittelalter*, edited by Giancarlo Andenna, Mirko Breitenstein, and Gert Melville. Münster: LIT, 2005. 85–102.

————. "System Rationality and the Dominican Success in the Middle Ages." In *Franciscan Organisation in the Mendicant Context. Formal and Informal Structures of the Friars' Lives and Ministry in the Middle Ages*, edited by Michael Robson and Jens Röhrkasten. Berlin: LIT, 2010. 377–88.

————. "Von der *Regula regularum* zur Stephansregel. Der normative Sonderweg der Grandmontenser bei der Auffächerung der *vita religiosa* im 12. Jahrhundert." In *Vom Kloster zum Klosterverband. Das Werkzeug der Schriftlichkeit*, edited by Hagen Keller and Franz Neiske. Munich: Wilhelm Fink, 1997. 342–63.

————. "What Role Did Charity Play in Francis of Assisi's Attitude towards the Poor?" In *Aspects of Charity: Concern for One's Neighbour in Medieval* Vita Religiosa, edited by Gert Melville. *Vita Regularis* 45. Berlin: LIT, 2011. 99–122.

————. "Zur Abgrenzung zwischen *Vita canonica* und *Vita monastica*. Das Übertrittsproblem in kanonistischer Behandlung von Gratian bis Hostiensis." In *Secundum regulam vivere. Festschrift für P. Nobert Backmund*, edited by Gert Melville. Windberg: Poppe-Verlag, 1978. 205–44.

————. "Zur Funktion der Schriftlichkeit im institutionellen Gefüge mittelalterlicher Orden." *Frühmittelalterliche Studien* 25 (1991): 391–417.

————. "Zur Semantik von *ordo* im Religiosentum der ersten Hälfte des 12. Jahrhunderts. Lucius II., seine Bulle vom 19. Mai 1144, und der 'Orden' der Prämonstratenser." In *Studien zum Prämonstratenserorden*, edited by Irene Crusius and Helmut Flachenecker. Göttingen: Vandenhoeck & Ruprecht, 2003. 201–24.

Melville, Gert, and Anne Müller, eds. *Female* vita religiosa *between Late Antiquity and the High Middle Ages: Structures, Developments and Spatial Contexts*. Berlin: LIT, 2011.

————. *Regula Sancti Augustini. Normative Grundlage differenter Verbände im Mittelalter*. Paring: Augustiner-Chorherren-Verlag, 2002.

Melville, Gert, and Jörg Oberste, eds. *Die Bettelorden im Aufbau. Beiträge zu Institutionalisierungsprozessen im mittelalterlichen Religiosentum*. Münster: LIT, 1999.

Melville, Gert, and Markus Schürer, eds. *Das Eigene und das Ganze. Zum individuellen im mittelalterlichen Religiosentum*. Münster: LIT, 2002.

Menestò, Enrico, and Stefano Brufani, eds. *Fontes Franciscani*. Assisi: Edizioni Porziuncola, 1997.

Merlo, Grado Giovanni. "Gli inizi dell'ordine dei frati Predicatori. Spunti per una riconsiderazione." *Rivista di storia e letteratura religiosa* 31 (1995): 415–41.

————. *In the Name of Saint Francis: A History of the Friars Minor and Franciscanism until the Early Sixteenth Century*. Saint Bonaventure, NY: Franciscan Institute, 2009.

————. *Tra eremo e città. Studi su Francesco d'Assisi e sul francescanesimo medievale*. Assisi: Edizioni Porziuncola, 2007.

Mersch, Katharina Ulrike. *Soziale Dimensionen visueller Kommunikation in hoch- und spätmittelalterlichen Frauenkommunitäten. Stifte, Chorfrauenstifte und Klöster im Vergleich*. Göttingen: Vandenhoeck & Ruprecht, 2012.

Mertens, Dieter. "Reformkonzilien und Ordensreform im 15. Jahrhundert." In *Reformbemühungen und Observanzbestrebungen im spätmittelalterlichen Ordenswesen*, edited by Kaspar Elm. Berlin: Duncker & Humblot, 1989. 431–57.

Merton, Thomas. "Saint Robert of Molesme, 1028 to 1111." *Cistercian Studies Quarterly* 46 (2011): 273–76.

Merton, Thomas, and O'Connell, Patrick F., eds. *Cassian and the Fathers: Initiation into the Monastic Tradition*. MW 1. Kalamazoo, MI: Cistercian Publications, 2005.

Meumann, Markus. "Exemtion." In *Handwörterbuch zur deutschen Rechtsgeschichte*. Berlin: Schmidt, 2008. 1:1451–52.

Miccoli, Giovanni. *Francesco d'Assisi. Memoria, storia e storiografia*. Milan: Biblioteca Francescana, 2010.

Miethke, Jürgen. "Der 'theoretische Armutstreit' im 14. Jahrhundert. Papst und Franziskanerorden im Konflikt um die Armut." In *Gelobte Armut. Armutskonzepte der franziskanischen Ordensfamilie vom Mittelalter bis in die Gegenwart*, edited by Heinz-Dieter Heimann. Paderborn: Schöningh, 2012. 243–84.

Milis, Ludo. *Les Moines et le peuple dans l'Europe du Moyen Âge*. Paris: Belin, 2002.

————. *L'ordre des chanoines réguliers d'Arrouaise. Son histoire et son organisation, de la fondation de l'abbaye-mère vers 1090, à la fin des chapitres annuels (1471)*. 2 vols. Brugge: De Tempel, 1969.

Milis, Ludo, and Benoît-Michel Tock, eds. *Monumenta Arroasiensia. Textes narratifs et diplomatiques de l'abbaye d'Arrouaise*. Turnhout: Brepols, 2000.

Miller, Bonifaz. *Weisung der Väter. Apophthegmata Patrum, auch Gerontikon oder Alphabeticum genannt*. 8th ed. Trier: Paulinus, 2009.

Mischlewski, Adalbert. *Grundzüge der Geschichte des Antoniterordens bis zum Ausgang des 15. Jahrhunderts*. Cologne and Vienna: Böhlau, 1976.

Mixson, James. *Poverty's Proprietors: Ownership and Mortal Sin at the Origins of the Observant Movement.* Leiden: Brill, 2009.

——. "The Setting and Resonance of John Nider's 'De reformatione religiosorum.'" In *Kirchenbild und Spiritualität: Dominikanische Beiträge zur Ekklesiologie und zum kirchlichen Leben im Mittelalter. Festschrift für Ulrich Horst O.P. zum 75. Geburtstag,* edited by Thomas Prügl and Marianne Schlosser. Paderborn: Schöningh, 2006. 291–317.

Mixson, James, and Bert Roest, eds. *A Companion to Observant Reform in the Late Middle Ages and Beyond.* Leiden: Brill, 2015.

Mois, Jakob. *Das Stift Rottenbuch in der Kirchenreform des 11.–12. Jahrhunderts. Ein Beitrag zur Ordens-Geschichte der Augustiner-Chorherren.* Munich and Freising: Verlag des erzbischöflichen Ordinariats München und Freising, 1953.

More, Alison. "Institutionalizing Penitential Life in Later Medieval and Early Modern Europe: Third Orders, Rules, and Canonical Legitimacy." *Church History* 83 (2014): 297–323.

Moricca, Umberto, ed. *Gregorii Magni Dialogi libri IV.* Rome: Tipografia del Senato, 1924.

Mulchahey, Marian Michèle. *"First the bow is bent in study . . .": Dominican Education before 1350.* Toronto: University of Toronto Press, 1998.

Müller, Anne. *Bettelmönche in islamischer Fremde. Institutionelle Rahmenbedingungen franziskanischer und dominikanischer Mission in muslimischen Räumen des 13. Jahrhunderts.* Münster: LIT, 2002.

——. "Conflicting Loyalties: The Irish Franciscans and the English Crown in the High Middle Ages." *Proceedings of the Royal Irish Academy* 107C (2007): 87–106.

——. "Gefangenenloskauf unter der Augustinusregel. Aspekte institutioneller Entwicklung im Mercedarierorden von den Anfängen bis 1317." In *Regula Sancti Augustini. Normative Grundlage differenter Verbände im Mittelalter,* edited by Gert Melville and Anne Müller. Paring: Augustiner-Chorherren-Verlag, 2002. 477–514.

Müller, Winfried. "Die Anfänge der Humanismusrezeption in Kloster Tegernsee." In *Studien und Mitteilungen zur Geschichte des Benediktinerordens und seiner Zweige* 92 (1981): 28–90.

Neiske, Franz. "Charismatischer Abt oder charismatische Gemeinschaft? Die frühen Äbte Clunys." In *Charisma und religiöse Gemeinschaften im Mittelalter,* edited by Giancarlo Andenna, Mirko Breitenstein, and Gert Melville. Münster: LIT, 2005. 55–72.

——. "Das Verhältnis Clunys zum Papsttum." In *Die Cluniazenser in ihrem politisch-sozialen Umfeld,* edited by Giles Constable, Gert Melville, and Jörg Oberste. Münster: LIT, 1998. 279–320.

——. "Reform oder Kodifizierung? Päpstliche Statuten für Cluny im 13. Jahrhundert." *Archivum Historiae Pontificiae* 26 (1988): 71–118.

Newman, Barbara, ed. *Voice of the Living Light: Hildegard of Bingen and Her World*. Berkeley: University of California Press, 1998.

Niederkorn-Bruck, Meta. *Die Melker Reform im Spiegel der Visitationen*. Munich: Oldenbourg, 1994.

Nimmo, Duncan B. "The Franciscan Regular Observance. The Culmination of Medieval Franciscan Reform." In *Reformbemühungen und Observanzbestrebungen im spätmittelalterlichen Ordenswesen*, edited by Kaspar Elm. Berlin: Duncker & Humblot, 1989. 189–205.

————. *Reform and Division in the Medieval Franciscan Order: From Saint Francis to the Foundation of the Capuchins*. 2nd ed. Rome: Capuchin Historical Institute, 1995.

Nortier, Geneviève. *Les bibliothèques médiévales des abbayes bénédictines de Normandie: Fécamp, Le Bec, Le Mont Saint-Michel, Saint-Evroult, Lyre, Jumièges, Saint-Wandrille, Saint-Ouen*. Paris: P. Lethielleux, 1971.

Nyberg, Tore. *Birgittinische Klostergründungen des Mittelalters*. Leiden: Sijthoff, 1965.

————. "Der Birgittenorden als Beispiel einer Neugründung im Zeitalter der Ordensreformen." In *Reformbemühungen und Observanzbestrebungen im spätmittelalterlichen Ordenswesen*, edited by Kaspar Elm. Berlin: Duncker & Humblot, 1989. 373–96.

Oberste, Jörg. "Contra prelatos qui gravant loca et personas Ordinis. Bischöfe und Cluniazenser im Zeitalter von Krisen und Reformen (12./13. Jahrhundert)." In *Die Cluniazenser in ihrem politisch-sozialen Umfeld*, edited by Giles Constable, Gert Melville, and Jörg Oberste. Münster: LIT, 1998. 349–92.

————. *Die Zisterzienser*. Stuttgart: Kohlhammer, 2014.

————. "Gesellschaft und Individuum in der Seelsorge der Mendikanten. Die Predigten Humberts de Romanis († 1277) an städtische Oberschichten." In *Das Eigene und das Ganze. Zum Individuellen im mittelalterlichen Religiosentum*, edited by Gert Melville and Markus Schürer. Münster: LIT, 2002. 497–527.

————. "Institutionalisierte Kommunikation. Normen, Überlieferungsbefunde und Grenzbereiche im Verwaltungsalltag religiöser Orden im hohen Mittelalter." In *De ordine vitae. Zu Normvorstellungen, Organisationsformen und Schriftlichkeit im mittelalterlichen Ordenswesen*, edited by Gert Melville. Münster: LIT, 1996. 59–99.

————. "Prediger, Legaten und Märtyrer. Die Zisterzienser im Kampf gegen die Katharer." In *Beiträge zum klösterlichen Leben im christlichen Abendland während des Mittelalters*, edited by Reinhardt Butz and Jörg Oberste. Münster: LIT, 2004. 73–92.

————. "Règle, coutumes et statuts. Le système normatif des prémontrés aux XIIe–XIIIe siècles." In *Regulae—Consuetudines—Statuta. Studi sulle fonti normative degli ordini religiosi nei secoli centrali del Medioevo*, edited by Cristina Andenna and Gert Melville. Münster: LIT, 2005. 261–76.

————. *Visitation und Ordensorganisation. Formen sozialer Normierung, Kontrolle und Kommunikation bei Cisterziensern, Prämonstratensern und Cluniazensern (12.–frühes 14. Jahrhundert)*. Münster: LIT, 1996.

————."Zwischen uniformitas und diversitas. Zentralität als Kernproblem des frühen Prämonstratenserordens (12./13. Jahrhundert)." In *Studien zum Prämonstratenserorden*, edited by Irene Crusius and Helmut Flachenecker. Göttingen: Vandenhoeck & Ruprecht, 2003. 225–50.

Oexle, Otto Gerhard. *Forschungen zu monastischen und geistlichen Gemeinschaften im Westfränkischen Bereich*. Munich: Wilhelm Fink, 1978.

————. "Max Weber und das Mönchtum." In *Max Webers Religionssoziologie in interkultureller Perspektive*, edited by Hartmut Lehmann and Jean Martin Quedraogo. Göttingen: Vandenhoeck & Ruprecht, 2003. 311–34.

Oldermann, Renate, ed. *Gebaute Klausur. Funktion und Architektur mittelalterlicher Klosterräume*. Bielefeld: Verlag für Regionalgeschichte, 2008.

Oudart, Hervé. *Robert D'Arbrissel ermite et prédicateur*. Spoleto: Centro italiano di studi sull'alto Medio Evo, 2010.

Pacaut, Marcel. *L'ordre de Cluny (909–1789)*. Paris: de Boccard, 1986.

Panarelli, Francesco. *Dal Gargano alla Toscana. Il monachesimo riformato latino dei Pulsanesi (secoli XII–XIV)*. Rome: Istituto storico italiano per il Medio Evo, 1997.

Parisse, Michel. "Der Anteil der lothringischen Benediktinerinnen an der monastischen Bewegung des 10. und 11. Jahrhunderts." In *Religiöse Frauenbewegung und mystische Frömmigkeit im Mittelalter*, edited by Peter Dinzelbacher and Dieter R. Bauer. Cologne: Böhlau, 1988. 83–97.

————. "Die Frauenstifte und Frauenklöster in Sachsen vom 10. bis zur Mitte des 12. Jahrhunderts." In *Die Salier und das Reich*. Vol. 2, *Die Reichskirche in der Salierzeit*, edited by Stefan Weinfurter. Sigmaringen: Thorbecke, 1991. 465–501.

————. *Religieux et religieuses en Empire du Xe au XIIe siècle*. Paris: Picard, 2011.

Parisse, Michel, ed. *Remiremont, l'abbaye et la ville*. Nancy: Université de Nancy II, 1980.

Parisse, Michel, and Otto Gerhard Oexle, eds. *L'abbaye de Gorze au Xe siècle*. Nancy: Presses Universitaires de Nancy, 1993.

Paxton, Frederick S., ed. *The Death Ritual at Cluny in the Central Middle Ages = Le rituel de la mort à Cluny au Moyen Âge central*. Turnhout: Brepols, 2013.

Payne, Steven. *The Carmelite Tradition*. Collegeville, MN: Liturgical Press, 2011.

Penco, Gregorio. "Monasterium—Carcer." *Studia monastica* 8 (1966): 133–43.

Pernoud, Régine. *Martin de Tours*. Paris: Bayard, 1996.

Petersen-Szemerédy, Griet. *Zwischen Weltstadt und Wüste. Römische Asketinnen in der Spätantike. Eine Studie zu Motivation und Gestaltung der Askese christlicher Frauen Roms auf dem Hintergrund ihrer Zeit.* Göttingen: Vandenhoeck & Ruprecht, 1993.

Pfaff, Volkert. "Grave Scandalum. Die Eremiten von Grandmont und das Papsttum am Ende des 12. Jahrhunderts." *Zeitschrift der Savigny-Stiftung für Rechtsgeschichte, Kanonistische Abteilung* 75 (1989): 133–54.

Piatti, Pierantonio. *Il movimento femminile agostiniano nel Medioevo. Momenti di storia dell'Ordine eremitano.* Rome: Città Nuova, 2007.

Picasso, Giorgio, ed. *Il monachesimo italiano nel secolo della grande crisi.* Cesena: Badia di Santa Maria del Monte, 2004.

———. "La spiritualità dell'antico monachesimo alle origini di Monte Oliveto." In *Charisma und religiöse Gemeinschaften im Mittelalter*, edited by Giancarlo Andenna, Mirko Breitenstein, and Gert Melville. Münster: LIT, 2005. 443–52.

Pilvousek, Josef, and Klaus-Bernward Springer. "Caesarius von Arles und die Klostergründung der heiligen Radegunde." In *Radegunde—ein Frauenschicksal zwischen Mord und Askese*, edited by Hardy Eidam and Gudrun Noll. Erfurt: Stadtverwaltung, 2006. 79–95.

Poeck, Dietrich W. *Cluniacensis Ecclesia. Der Cluniazensische Klosterverband (10.–12. Jahrhundert).* Munich: Wilhelm Fink, 1998.

———. "Laienbegräbnisse in Cluny." *Frühmittelalterliche Studien* 15 (1981): 68–179.

Posada, Gerardo. *Maestro Bruno, padre de monjes.* Madrid: Ed. Católica, 1980.

Potestà, Gian Luca. *Il tempo dell'Apocalisse. Vita di Gioacchino da Fiore.* Rome: Edizioni Laterza, 2004.

Powell, James Matthew. "Innocent III, the Trinitarians, and the Renewal of the Church, 1198–1200," in *The Crusades, the Kingdom of Sicily, and the Mediterranean*, by James M. Powell. Aldershot: Ashgate Variorum, 2007. IX, 245–54.

Praedicatores, Inquisitores. Vol 1: *The Dominicans and the Mediaeval Inquisition. Acts of the 1st International Seminar on the Dominicans and the Inquisition (Rome, 23–25 février 2002).* Rome: Istituto storico Domenicano, 2004.

Prinz, Friedrich. *Frühes Mönchtum im Frankenreich. Kultur und Gesellschaft in Gallien, den Rheinlanden und Bayern am Beispiel der monastischen Entwicklung (4. bis 8. Jahrhundert).* 2nd ed. Darmstadt: Wissenschaftliche Buchgesellschaft, 1988.

Rainini, Marco. "I predicatori dei tempi ultimi. La rielaborazione di un tema escatologico nel costruirsi dell'identità profetica dell'ordine domenicano." *Cristianesimo nella storia* 23 (2002): 307–44.

Rapp, Claudia. "Early Monasticism in Egypt. Between Hermits and Ceno-
    bites." In *Female* vita religiosa *between Late Antiquity and the High
    Middle Ages: Structures, Developments and Spatial Contexts*, edited by
    Gert Melville and Anne Müller. Berlin: LIT, 2011. 21–42.

Rebenich, Stefan. "Der Kirchenvater Hieronymus als Hagiograph. Die Vita
    Sancti Pauli primi eremitae." In *Beiträge zur Geschichte des Paulineror-
    dens*, edited by Kaspar Elm. Berlin: Duncker & Humblot, 2000. 23–40.

Reeves, Marjorie. *The Influence of Prophecy in the Later Middle Ages.
    A Study in Joachimism*. 2nd ed. Notre Dame, IN: University of Notre
    Dame Press, 1993.

Regnault, Lucien. *Les pères du désert à travers leurs apophthegmes*. Soles-
    mes: Abbaye Saint-Pierre, 1987.

Rexroth, Frank. "Monastischer und scholastischer Habitus. Beobachtungen
    zum Verhältnis zwischen zwei Lebensformen des 12. Jahrhunderts." In
    *Innovationen durch Deuten und Gestalten. Klöster im Mittelalter zwi-
    schen Jenseits und Welt*, edited by Gert Melville, Bernd Schneidmüller,
    and Stefan Weinfurter. Regensburg: Schnell & Steiner, 2014. 317–33.

Richter, Michael. *Bobbio in the Early Middle Ages. The Abiding Legacy of
    Columbanus*. Dublin: Four Courts Press, 2008.

Robson, Michael. *The Cambridge Companion to Francis of Assisi*. Cam-
    bridge, UK: Cambridge University Press, 2012.

Robson, Michael, and Jens Röhrkasten, eds. *Franciscans in Medieval En-
    gland*. Canterbury: JEM, 2008.

Röckelein, Hedwig. "Die Auswirkung der Kanonikerreform des 12. Jahrhun-
    derts auf Kanonissen, Augustinerchorfrauen und Benediktinerinnen." In
    *Institution und Charisma. Festschrift für Gert Melville zum 65. Geburts-
    tag*, edited by Franz J. Felten, Annette Kehnel, and Stefan Weinfurter.
    Cologne: Böhlau, 2009. 55–72.

———."Frauen im Umkreis der benediktinischen Reformen des 10. bis
    12. Jahrhunderts. Gorze, Cluny, Hirsau, St. Blasien und Siegburg." In
    Female vita religiosa *between Late Antiquity and the High Middle Ages:
    Structures, Developments and Spatial Contexts*, edited by Gert Melville
    and Anne Müller. Berlin: LIT, 2011. 275–327.

Roest, Bert. *A History of Franciscan Education (c. 1210–1517)*. Leiden:
    Brill, 2000.

———. *Order and Disorder. The Poor Clares Between Foundation and
    Reform*. Leiden: Brill, 2013.

Röhrkasten, Jens. "The Early Franciscans and the Towns and Cities." In *The
    Cambridge Companion to Francis of Assisi*, edited by Michael Robson.
    Cambridge, UK: Cambridge University Press, 2012. 178–92.

———. The *Mendicant Houses of Medieval London 1221–1539*. Münster:
    LIT, 2004.

Rösener, Werner. "Die Agrarwirtschaft der Zisterzienser. Innovation und Anpassung." In *Norm und Realität. Kontinuität und Wandel der Zisterzienser im Mittelalter*, edited by Franz Felten and Werner Rösener. Berlin: LIT, 2009. 67–95.

Rosenwein, Barbara. "Cluny's Immunities in the Tenth and Eleventh Centuries. Images and Narratives." In *Die Cluniazenser in ihrem politisch-sozialen Umfeld*, edited by Giles Constable, Gert Melville, and Jörg Oberste. Münster: LIT, 1998. 133–63.

———. *To Be the Neighbor of Saint Peter. The Social Meaning of Cluny's Property 909–1049*. Ithaca, NY: Cornell University Press, 1989.

Rousseau, Phillip. *Basil of Caesarea*. Berkeley: University of California Press, 1994.

———. *Pachomius. The Making of a Community in Fourth-Century Egypt*. Berkeley: University of California Press, 1985.

Ruh, Kurt. *Geschichte der abendländischen Mystik*. 4 vols. Munich: C. H. Beck, 1990–1999.

Rusconi, Roberto. "Celestiniana: dal santo eremita al santo papa." *Sanctorum* 7 (2010): 109–29.

———. *Francis of Assisi in the Sources and Writings*. Saint Bonaventure, NY: Franciscan Institute Publications, 2008.

Rüther, Andreas. *Bettelorden in Stadt und Land. Die Straßburger Mendikantenkonvente und das Elsaß im Spätmittelalter*. Berlin: Duncker & Humblot, 1997.

Rüthing, Heinrich. "Die Kartäuser und die spätmittelalterlichen Ordensreformen." In *Reformbemühungen und Observanzbestrebungen im spätmittelalterlichen Ordenswesen*, edited by Kaspar Elm. Berlin: Duncker & Humblot, 1989. 35–58.

Ryan, John. *Irish Monasticism: Origins and Early Development. New Introduction and Bibliography*. Dublin: Four Courts Press, 1986.

Rychterová, Pavlína. *Die Offenbarungen der heiligen Birgitta von Schweden. Eine Untersuchung zur alttschechischen Übersetzung des Thomas von Štítné (um 1330–um 1409)*. Cologne: Böhlau, 2004.

Saak, Eric. *High Way to Heaven: The Augustinian Platform Between Reform and Reformation, 1292–1524*. Leiden: Brill, 2002.

Sabatier, Paul. *Life of St. Francis of Assisi*. New York: Scribner, 1930.

San Romualdo. Storia, agiografia e spiritualità, Atti del XXIII convegno del Centro di studi avellaniti (Fonte Avellana, 23–26 agosto 2000). Negarine di San Pietro in Cariano (Verona): Il Segno dei Gabrielli Ed., 2002.

Sarbak, Gabor. "Entstehung und Frühgeschichte des Ordens der Pauliner." *Zeitschrift für Kirchengeschichte* 99 (1988): 93–103.

Sarbak, Gabor, ed. *Der Paulinerorden. Geschichte—Geist—Kultur*. Budapest: S. István Társulat, 2010.

Sarnowsky, Jürgen. *Der deutsche Orden*. Munich: C. H. Beck, 2007.

————. *Die Johanniter. Ein geistlicher Ritterorden in Mittelalter und Neuzeit*. Munich: C. H. Beck, 2011.

Schäferdiek, Knut. "Columbans Wirken im Frankenreich (591–612)." In *Die Iren und Europa im früheren Mittelalter*. Vol. 1, edited by Heinz Löwe. Stuttgart: Klett-Cotta, 1982. 171–201.

Schieffer, Theodor. "Cluny und der Investiturstreit." In *Cluny, Beiträge zu Gestalt und Wirkung der Cluniazensischen Reform*, edited by Helmut Richter. Darmstadt: Wissenschaftliche Buchgesellschaft, 1975. 226–54.

Schindele, Maria Pia. "'Rectitudo' und 'puritas.' Die Bedeutung beider Begriffe in den Gründungsdokumenten von Cîteaux und ihre Auswirkungen in der Lehre des hl. Bernhard von Clairvaux." In *Zisterziensische Spiritualität. Theologische Grundlagen, funktionale Voraussetzungen und bildhafte Ausprägungen im Mittelalter*, edited by Clemens M. Kasper and Klaus Schreiner. Studien und Mitteilungen zur Geschichte des Benediktiner-Ordens und seiner Zweige. Ergänzungsband 34. St. Ottilien: EOS, 1994. 53–73.

Schiwy, Günther. *Birgitta von Schweden. Mystikerin und Visionärin des späten Mittelalters. Eine Biographie*. Munich: C. H. Beck, 2003.

Schlotheuber, Eva. *Klostereintritt und Bildung. Die Lebenswelt der Nonnen im späten Mittelalter. Mit einer Edition des "Konventstagebuchs" einer Zisterzienserin von Heilig-Kreuz bei Braunschweig (1484–1507)*. Tübingen: Mohr Siebeck, 2004.

————. "Sprachkompetenz und Lateinvermittlung. Die intellektuelle Ausbildung der Nonnen im Spätmittelalter." In *Kloster und Bildung im Mittelalter*, edited by Nathalie Kruppa and Jürgen Wilke. Göttingen: Vandenhoeck & Ruprecht, 2006. 61–87.

Schmidt, Hans-Joachim. "Klosterleben ohne Legitimität. Kritik und Verurteilung im Mittelalter." In *Institutionen und Geschichte. Festschrift für Gert Melville zum 65. Geburtstag*, edited by Franz J. Felten, Annette Kehnel, and Stefan Weinfurter. Cologne: Böhlau, 2009. 377–400.

————. "Legitimität von Innovation. Geschichte, Kirche und neue Orden im 13. Jahrhundert." In *Vita religiosa im Mittelalter. Festschrift für Kaspar Elm zum 70. Geburtstag*, edited by Franz J. Felten and Nikolas Jaspert. Berlin: Duncker & Humblot, 1999. 371–91.

————. "Vogt, Vogtei." In *Lexikon des Mittelalters*. Munich and Zurich: Artemis & Winkler, 1997. 8:1811–14.

Schmitz, Philibert. "La liturgie de Cluny." In *Spiritualità Cluniacense, 12–15 ottobre 1958*. Todi: Presso l'Accademia tudertina, 1960. 85–99.

Schmitz, Timothy J. "The Spanish Jeronymites and the Reformed Texts of the Council of Trent." *Sixteenth Century Journal* 37 (2006): 375–99.

Schmucki, Oktavian. "Schrittweise Entdeckung der evangeliumsgemäßen Lebensform durch den heiligen Franziskus von Assisi." In *Oktavian*

Schmucki OFMCap. Beiträge zur Franziskusforschung, edited by Ulrich Köpf and Leonhard Lehmann. Kevelaer: Butzon und Bercker, 2007. 305–58.

Schreiber, Georg. *Kurie und Kloster im 12. Jahrhundert: Studien zur Privilegierung, Verfassung und besonders zum Eigenkirchenwesen der vorfranziskanischen Orden vornehmlich auf Grund der Papsturkunden von Paschalis II. bis auf Lucius III. (1099–1181).* 2 vols. Stuttgart: Enke, 1910.

Schreiner, Klaus. "'Brot der Mühsal.' Körperliche Arbeit im Mönchtum des hohen und späten Mittelalters. Theologisch motivierte Einstellungen, regelgebundene Normen, geschichtliche Praxis." In *Arbeit im Mittelalter: Vorstellungen und Wirklichkeiten*, edited by Verena Postel. Berlin: Akademie, 2006. 133–70.

———. "Dauer, Niedergang und Erneuerung klösterlicher Observanz im hoch- und spätmittelalterlichen Mönchtum. Krisen, Reform- und Institutionalisierungsprobleme in der Sicht und Deutung betroffener Zeitgenossen." In *Institutionen und Geschichte. Theoretische Aspekte und mittelalterliche Befunde*, edited by Gert Melville. Cologne: Böhlau, 1992. 295–341.

———. "Ein Herz und eine Seele. Eine urchristliche Lebensform und ihre Institutionalisierung im augustinisch geprägten Mönchtum des hohen und späten Mittelalters." In *Regula Sancti Augustini. Normative Grundlage differenter Verbände im Mittelalter*, edited by Gert Melville and Anne Muller. Paring: Augustiner-Chorherren-Verlag, 2002. 1–47.

———. "Hirsau und die Hirsauer Reform. Lebens- und Verfassungsformen einer Reformbewegung." In *Die Reformverbände und Kongregationen der Benediktiner im deutschen Sprachraum*, edited by Ulrich Faust and Franz Quarthal. St. Ottilien: EOS, 1999. 89–124.

———. "Hirsau und die Hirsauer Reform. Spiritualität, Lebensform und Sozialprofil einer benediktinischen Erneuerungsbewegung im 11. und 12. Jahrhundert." In *Hirsau St. Peter und Paul 1091–1991*. Vol. 2, *Geschichte, Lebens- und Verfassungsformen eines Reformklosters*, edited by Klaus Schreiner. Stuttgart: Konrad Thiess, 1991. 59–84.

———. "Kirchen- und Klosterpolitik des Adels im Mittelalter als Mittel der Herrschaftssicherung." In *17. Congreso International de Ciencias Historicas: Madrid 1990*. Madrid: Comité international des sciences historiques, 1992. 2:676–83.

———. *Mönchsein in der Adelsgesellschaft des hohen und späten Mittelalters: Klösterliche Gemeinschaftsbildung zwischen spiritueller Selbstbehauptung und sozialer Anpassung*. Munich: Stiftung Historisches Kolleg, 1989.

———. "Observantia regularis—Normbildung, Normkontrolle und Normwandel im Mönchtum des frühen und späten Mittelalters." In *Prozesse der*

Normbildung und Normveränderung im mittelalterlichen Europa, edited by Doris Ruhe and Karl-Heinz Spiess. Stuttgart: Steiner, 2000. 275–313.

―――. "Verschriftlichung als Faktor monastischer Reform. Funktionen von Schriftlichkeit im Ordenswesen des hohen und späten Mittelalters." In *Pragmatische Schriftlichkeit im Mittelalter. Erscheinungsformen und Entwicklungsstufen*, edited by Hagen Keller, Klaus Grubmüller, and Nikolaus Staubach. Munich: Wihelm Fink, 1992. 37–75.

Schürer, Markus. "Das 'propositum' in religiös-asketischen Diskursen. Historisch-semantische Erkundungen zu einem zentralen Begriff der mittelalterlichen 'vita religiosa.'" In *Oboedientia. Zu Formen und Grenzen von Macht und Unterordnung im mittelalterlichen Religiosentum*, edited by Sebastien Barret and Gert Melville. Münster: LIT, 2006. 99–128.

―――. "Innovation und Variabilität als Instrumente göttlicher Pädagogik: Anselm von Havelberg und seine Position in den Diskursen um die Legitimität religioser Lebensformen." *Mittellateinisches Jahrbuch* 42 (2007): 373–96.

Schwaiger, Georg, ed. *Mönchtum, Orden, Klöster. Von den Anfängen bis zur Gegenwart. Ein Lexikon*. Munich: C. H. Beck, 2003.

Secondin, Bruno. *La regola del Carmelo. Per una nuova interpretazione*. Rome: Edizioni IC, 1982.

Seibert, Hubertus. "Libertas und Reichsabtei. Zur Klosterpolitik der salischen Herrscher." In *Die Salier und das Reich*. Vol. 2, *Die Reichskirche in der Salierzeit*, edited by Stefan Weinfurter. Sigmaringen: Thorbecke, 1991. 503–69.

Semmler, Josef. "Benedictus II. Una regula—una consuetudo." In *Benedictine Culture 750–1050*, edited by Willem Lourdaux. Leuven: Leuven University Press, 1983. 1–49.

―――. "Benediktinische Reform und kaiserliches Privileg. Zur Frage des institutionellen Zusammenschlusses der Klöster um Benedikt von Aniane." In *Institutionen und Geschichte. Theoretische Aspekte und mittelalterliche Befunde*, edited by Gert Melville. Cologne: Böhlau, 1992. 259–93.

―――. "Das Erbe der karolingischen Klosterreform im 10. Jahrhundert." In *Monastische Reformen im 9. und 10. Jahrhundert*, edited by Raymund Kottje and Helmut Maurer. Sigmaringen: Thorbecke, 1989. 22–77.

―――. "Die Klosterreform von Siegburg (11. und 12. Jahrhundert)." In *Die Reformverbände und Kongregationen der Benediktiner im deutschen Sprachraum*, edited by Ulrich Faust and Franz Quarthal. St. Ottilien: EOS, 1999. 141–51.

―――. *Die Klosterreform von Siegburg. Ihre Ausbreitung und ihr Reformprogramm im 11. und 12. Jahrhundert*. Bonn: Röhrscheid, 1959.

―――. "Traditio und Königsschutz." *Zeitschrift der Savigny-Stiftung für Rechtsgeschichte: Kanonistische Abteilung* 45 (1959): 1–34.

Sereno, Cristina. "La 'crisi del cenobitismo': un problema storiografico." *Bullettino dell'Istituto storico italiano per il Medio Evo* 104 (2002): 32–83.

Sickert, Ramona. "'Difficile tamen est iudicare alieni cordis occulta . . . .' Persönlichkeit oder Typus? Elias von Cortona im Urteil seiner Zeitgenossen." In *Das Eigene und das Ganze. Zum Individuellen im mittelalterlichen Religiosentum*, edited by Gert Melville and Markus Schürer. Münster: LIT, 2002. 303–38.

———. *Wenn Klosterbrüder zu Jahrmarktsbrüdern werden. Studien zur zeitgenössischen Wahrnehmung der Franziskaner und Dominikaner im 13. Jahrhundert*. Münster: LIT, 2006.

Signori, Gabriella. "Zelle oder Dormitorium? Klösterliche Raumvisionen im Widerstreit der Ideale." *In Situ. Zeitschrift für Architekturgeschichte* 4 (2012): 55–68.

Silanos, Pietro. "'In sede apostolica specula constituti.' Procedure curiali per l'approvazione di regole e testi normativi all'alba del IV concilio lateranense." *Quellen und Forschungen aus italienischen Archiven und Bibliotheken* 94 (2014): 33–93.

Simons, Walter. *Cities of Ladies: Beguine Communities in the Medieval Low Countries 1200–1565*. Philadelphia: University of Pennsylvania Press, 2001.

Sinderhauf, Monica. "Die Reform von St. Blasien." In *Die Reformverbände und Kongregationen der Benediktiner im deutschen Sprachraum*, edited by Ulrich Faust and Franz Quarthal. St. Ottilien: EOS, 1999. 125–40.

Smet, Joachim. *The Carmelites. A History of the Brothers of our Lady of Mount Carmel*. 2nd ed. Vol. 1. Darien, IL: Carmelite Spiritual Center, 1988.

Smet, Joachim, and Ulrich Dobhan. *Die Karmeliten. Eine Geschichte der Brüder Unserer Lieben Frau vom Berge Karmel von den Anfangen (ca. 1200) bis zum Konzil von Trient*. Freiburg im Breisgau: Herder, 1981.

Sonntag, Jörg. *Klosterleben im Spiegel des Zeichenhaften. Symbolisches Denken und Handeln hochmittelalterlicher Mönche zwischen Dauer und Wandel, Regel und Gewohnheit*. Berlin: LIT, 2008.

———. "Le rôle de la vie regulière dans l'invention et la diffusion de divertissements sociaux au Moyen Âge." *Revue Mabillon* 83 (2011): 79–98.

———. "Tempus fugit. La circolarità del tempo monastica nello specchio del potenziale di rappresentazione simbolica." In *Religiosità e civiltà. Le comunicazioni simboliche (secoli IX–XIII)*, edited by Giancarlo Andenna. Milan: Vita e pensiero, 2009. 221–42.

———. "Welcoming High Guests to the Paradise of the Monks—Social Interactions and Symbolic Moments of Monastic Self-Representation According to Lanfranc's Constitutions." In *Self-Representation of Medieval Religious Communities. The British Isles in Context*, edited by Anne Müller and Karen Stöber. Berlin: LIT, 2009. 45–65.

Sot, Michel. *Gesta episcoporum, gesta abbatum*. 2 vols. Turnhout: Brepols, 1981, 1985.

Staubach, Nikolaus, ed. *Kirchenreform von unten. Gerhard Zerbolt von Zutphen und die Brüder vom gemeinsamen Leben*. Frankfurt am Main: Peter Lang, 2005.

Steckel, Sita. "Ein brennendes Feuer in meiner Brust. Prophetische Autorschaft und polemische Autorisierungsstrategien Guillaumes de Saint-Amour im Pariser Bettelordenstreit (1256)." In *Prophetie und Autorschaft. Charisma, Heilsversprechen und Gefährdung*, edited by Christel Meier and Martina Wagner-Egelhaaf. Berlin: de Gruyter, 2014. 129–68.

Stewart, Columba. *Cassian the Monk*. New York: Oxford University Press, 1998.

Stüdeli, Bernhard. *Minoritenniederlassungen und mittelalterliche Stadt. Beiträge zur Bedeutung von Minoriten und anderen Mendikantenanlagen im öffentlichen Leben der mittelalterlichen Stadtgemeinde, insbesondere der deutschen Schweiz*. Werl: Dietrich-Coelde, 1969.

Studio e studia. Le scuole degli ordini mendicanti tra XIII e XIV secolo. Atti del XXIX Convegno internazionale. Assisi, 11–13 ottobre 2001. Spoleto: Presso l'Accademia tudertina, 2002.

Sykes, Katharine. *Inventing Sempringham. Gilbert of Sempringham and the Origins of the Role of the Master*. Berlin: LIT, 2011.

Symons, Thomas. "Regularis Concordia: History and Derivation." In *Tenth-Century Studies. Essays in Commemoration of the Millennium of the Council of Winchester and Regularis Concordia*, edited by David Parsons. London: Phillimore, 1975. 37–59, 214–17.

Thom, Catherine. *Early Irish Monasticism. An Understanding of Its Cultural Roots*. London: T & T Clark, 2006.

Thompson, Augustine. *Francis of Assisi: A New Biography*. Ithaca, NY: Cornell University Press, 2012.

Tolan, John Victor. *Saint Francis and the Sultan: The Curious History of a Christian-Muslim Encounter*. Oxford: Oxford University Press, 2009.

Torrell, Jean-Pierre. *Pierre le Vénérable et sa vision du monde. Sa vie, son œuvre, l'homme et le démon*. Leuven: Spicilegium Sacrum Lovaniense, 1986.

———. *Saint Thomas Aquinas*. Vol. 1, *The Person and His Work*. Revised ed. Washington, DC: The Catholic University of America Press, 2005.

Toussaert, Jacques. *Antonius von Padua. Versuch einer kritischen Biographie*. Cologne: J. P. Bachem, 1967.

Troncarelli, Fabio. *Vivarium. I libri, il destino*. Turnhout: Brepols, 1998.

Tugwell, Simon. "Notes on the Life of St. Dominic." *Archivum Fratrum Praedicatorum* 65 (1995): 5–169; 66 (1996): 5–200; 67 (1997): 27–59; 68 (1998): 5–116; 73 (2003): 5–141.

Tutsch, Burkhardt. *Studien zur Rezeptionsgeschichte der Consuetudines Ulrichs von Cluny*. Münster: LIT, 1998.

Ulpts, Ingo. "Die Mendikanten als Konkurrenz zum Weltklerus zwischen Gehorsamsgebot und päpstlicher Exemption." *Wissenschaft und Weisheit* 66 (2003): 190–227.

Untermann, Matthias. "Gebaute 'Unanimitas': Zu den Bauvorschriften der Zisterzienser." In *Zisterzienser. Norm, Kultur, Reform. 900 Jahre Zisterzienser*, edited by Ulrich Knefelkamp. Berlin: Springer, 2001. 239–66.

Vanderputten, Steven. "Gérard de Brogne en Flandre. État de la question sur les réformes monastiques du Xe siècle." *Revue du Nord* 92 (2010): 271–97.

Vanderputten, Steven. *Reform, Conflict, and the Shaping of Corporate Identities: Collected Studies on Benedictine Monasticism in Medieval Flanders, c. 1050–c. 1150*. Berlin: LIT, 2013.

———, ed. *Understanding Monastic Practices of Oral Communication (Western Europe, Tenth–Thirteenth Centuries)*. Turnhout: Brepols, 2011.

Van Engen, John. "The 'Crisis of Cenobitism' Reconsidered. Benedictine Monasticism in the Years 1050–1150." *Speculum* 61 (1986): 269–304.

———. "Multiple Options: The World of the Fifteenth-Century Church," *Church History* 77 (2008): 257–84.

———. *Sisters and Brothers of the Common Life. The Devotio Moderna and the World of the Later Middle Ages*. Philadelphia: Pennsylvania University Press, 2008.

van Moolenbroek, Jaap J. *Vital l'ermite, prédicateur itinérant, fondateur de l'abbaye normande de Savigny*. Assen: Van Gorcum, 1990.

van 't Spijker, Ineke. *Fictions of the Inner Life. Religious Literature and Formation of the Self in the Eleventh and Twelfth Centuries*. Turnhout: Brepols, 2004.

Vauchez, André. *Francis of Assisi: The Life and Afterlife of a Medieval Saint*. New Haven, CT: Yale University Press, 2012.

Vauchez, André, ed. *Ermites de France et d'Italie (XIe–XIIe siècle). Actes du colloque de la Chartreuse de Pontignano, 5–7 mai 2000*. Rome: École française de Rome, 2003.

Vauchez, André, and Cécile Caby, eds. *L'histoire des moines, chanoines et religieux au Moyen Âge: Guide de recherche et documents*. Turnhout: Brepols, 2003.

Vedovato, Giuseppe. *Camaldoli e la sua congregazione dalle origini al 1184. Storia e documentazione*. Cesena: Badia di S. Maria del Monte, 1994.

Veilleux, Armand, ed. *Pachomian koinonia. The Lives, Rules, and Other Writings of Saint Pachomius and his Disciples*. 3 vols. CS 8. Kalamazoo, MI: Cistercian Publications, 1980–1982.

Venarde, Bruce L. "Robert of Arbrissel and Women's *vita religiosa*. Looking Back and Ahead." In Gert Melville and Anne Muller, eds., *Female* vita religiosa *between Late Antiquity and the High Middle Ages: Structures, Developments and Spatial Contexts*. Berlin: LIT, 2011. 329–40.

Verheijen, Luc. *La regle de saint Augustin*. Vol. 2, *Recherches historiques*. Paris: Études augustiniennes, 1967.

Viallet, Ludovic. *Les sens de l'observance. Enquête sur les réformes franciscaines.* Berlin: LIT, 2014.

Vicaire, Marie Humbert. *Histoire de Saint Dominique.* 2 vols. 2nd ed. Paris: Études augustiniennes, 1982.

Violante, Cinzio. "Monasteri e canoniche nello sviluppo dell'economia monetaria (secoli XI–XIII)." In *Istituzioni monastiche e istituzioni canonicali in Occidente (1123–1215). Atti della settima Settimana internazionale di studio. Mendola, 28 agosto–3 settembre 1977.* Milan: Vita e pensiero, 1980. 369–416.

Vogel, Christian. *Das Recht der Templer. Ausgewählte Aspekte des Templerrechts unter besonderer Berücksichtigung der Statutenhandschriften aus Paris, Rom, Baltimore und Barcelona.* Berlin: LIT, 2007.

Voigt, Jörg. *Beginen im Spätmittelalter. Frauenfrömmigkeit in Thüringen und im Reich.* Cologne, Weimar, Vienna: Böhlau, 2012.

Vones-Liebenstein, Ursula. "Der Verband der Regularkanoniker von Saint-Ruf. Entstehung, Struktur und normative Grundlagen." In *Regula Sancti Augustini. Normative Grundlage differenter Verbände im Mittelalter*, edited by Gert Melville and Anne Müller. Paring: Augustiner-Chorherren-Verlag, 2002. 49–103.

————."Hadrian IV. *regularis inter primos disciplinae aemulator* und die Regularkanoniker." In *Päpstliche Herrschaft im Mittelalter. Funktionsweisen—Strategien—Darstellungsformen*, edited by Stefan Weinfurter. Ostfildern: Thorbecke, 2012. 97–126.

von Falkenhausen, Vera. "Il monachesimo italo-greco e i suoi rapporti con il monachesimo benedettino." In *L'esperienza monastica benedettina e la Puglia.* Vol. 1, edited by Cosimo Damiano Fonseca. Galatina: Congedo Ed., 1983. 119–35.

von Moos, Peter. "Abaelard, Heloise und ihr Paraklet. Ein Kloster nach Maß, zugleich eine Streitschrift gegen die ewige Wiederkehr hermeneutischer Naivität." In Peter von Moos, *Abaelard und Heloise. Gesammelte Studien zum Mittelalter*, edited by Gert Melville. Münster: LIT, 2005. 1:233–301.

————. "Krise und Kritik der Institutionalität. Die mittelalterliche Kirche als 'Anstalt' und 'Himmelreich auf Erden.'" In *Institutionalität und Symbolisierung. Verstetigungen kultureller Ordnungsmuster in Vergangenheit und Gegenwart*, edited by Gert Melville. Cologne, Weimar, and Vienna: Böhlau, 2001. 293–340.

————. "Le vêtement identificateur. L'habit fait-il ou ne fait-il pas le moine?" In *Le corps et sa parure. The Body and Its Adornment*, edited by Thalia Brero. Firenze: Edizioni del Galluzzo, 2007. 41–60.

von Pföstl, Markus Karl. *Pueri oblati.* 2 vols. Kiel: Solivagus, 2011.

von Severus, Emmanuel. "Benedikt von Aniane." In *Theologische Realenzyklopädie.* Berlin: de Gruyter, 1980. 5:535–38.

Waddell, Chrysogonus, ed. *Narrative and Legislative Texts from Early Cî-teaux. Latin Text in Dual Edition with English Translation and Notes.* Cîteaux: Abbaye de Cîteaux, 1999.

Walter, Johannes von. *Die ersten Wanderprediger Frankreichs. Studien zur Geschichte des Mönchtums.* 2 vols. Aalen: Scientia, 1903, 1906.

Weber, Max. *Economy and Society. An Outline of Interpretive Sociology,* edited by Guenther Roth and Claus Wittich. Berkeley: University of California Press, 1978.

Wehrli-Johns, Martina. "Das mittelalterliche Beginentum. Religiöse Frauenbewegung oder Sozialidee der Scholastik." In *Fromme Frauen oder Ketzerinnen? Leben und Verfolgung der Beginen im Mittelalter,* edited by Martina Wehrli-Johns and Claudia Opitz. Freiburg im Breisgau: Herder, 1998. 25–51.

Weinfurter, Stefan. "Norbert von Xanten als Reformkanoniker und Stifter des Prämonstratenserordens." In *Norbert von Xanten. Adliger, Ordensstifter, Kirchenfürst,* edited by Kaspar Elm. Cologne: Wienand, 1984. 159–88.

———. "Norbert von Xanten und die Entstehung des Prämonstratenserordens." In *Barbarossa und die Prämonstratenser.* Göppingen: Gesellschaft für staufische Geschichte, 1989. 67–100.

———. "Reformkanoniker und Reichsepiskopat im Hochmittelalter." *Historisches Jahrbuch* 97/98 (1978): 158–93.

———. "St. Blasien—seine Frühzeit und das Aufblühen in der jungcluniazensischen Klosterreform." In *Macht des Wortes: Benediktinisches Mönchtum im Spiegel Europas,* edited by Holger Kempkens, Gerfried Sitar, and Martin Kroker. Regensburg: Schnell & Steiner, 2009. 1:195–202.

———. *Salzburger Bistumsreform und Bischofpolitik im 12. Jahrhundert. Der Erzbischof Konrad I. von Salzburg (1106–1147) und die Regularkanoniker.* Cologne and Vienna: Böhlau, 1975.

Weinfurter, Stefan, ed. *Die Salier und das Reich.* Vol. 2, *Die Reichskirche in der Salierzeit.* Sigmaringen: Thorbecke, 1991.

Werckmeister, Otto Karl. *Irisch-northumbrische Buchmalerei des 8. Jahrhunderts und monastische Spiritualität.* Berlin: de Gruyter, 1967.

Wernicke, Michael Klaus. "Die Augustiner-Eremiten im Deutschland des 13. Jahrhunderts." *Analecta Augustiniana* 70 (2007): 119–32.

Wesjohann, Achim. "Flüchtigkeit und Bewahrung des Charisma oder: War der heilige Dominikus etwa auch ein Charismatiker?" In *Charisma und religiöse Gemeinschaften im Mittelalter,* edited by Giancarlo Andenna, Mirko Breitenstein, and Gert Melville. Münster: LIT, 2005. 227–60.

———. *Mendikantische Gründungserzählungen im 13. und 14. Jahrhundert. Mythen als Element institutioneller Eigengeschichtsschreibung der mittelalterlichen Franziskaner, Dominikaner und Augustiner-Eremiten.* Berlin: LIT, 2012.

————. "Simplicitas als franziskanisches Ideal und der Prozeß der Institutionalisierung des Minoritenordens." In *Die Bettelorden im Aufbau. Beiträge zu Institutionalisierungsprozessen im mittelalterlichen Religiosentum*, edited by Gert Melville and Jörg Oberste. Münster: LIT, 1999. 107–67.

————. "Überschüsse an Armut. Mythische Grundlagen mendikantischer Armutsauffassungen." In *In proposito paupertatis. Studien zum Armutsverständnis bei den mittelalterlichen Bettelorden*, edited by Gert Melville and Annette Kehnel. Münster: LIT, 2001. 169–201.

Wiener, Jürgen. "Kritik an Elias von Cortona und Kritik von Elias von Cortona: Armutsideal und Architektur in den frühen franziskanischen Quellen." In *Frömmigkeitsformen in Mittelalter und Renaissance*, edited by Johannes Laudage. Düsseldorf: Droste, 2004. 207–46.

Wischermann, Else Maria. *Marcigny-Sur-Loire. Gründungs- und Frühgeschichte des 1. Cluniacenserinnenpriorates (1055–1150)*. Munich: Wilhelm Fink, 1986.

Wollasch, Joachim. "Benedictus abbas Romensis. Das römische Element in der frühen benediktinischen Tradition." In *Tradition als historische Kraft. Interdisziplinäre Forschungen zur Geschichte des früheren Mittelalters. Festschrift Karl Hauck*, edited by Joachim Wollasch. Berlin: de Gruyter, 1982. 119–37.

————. "Benedikt von Nursia. Person der Geschichte oder fiktive Idealgestalt?" *Studien und Mitteilungen zur Geschichte des Benediktinerordens und seiner Zweige* 118 (2007): 7–30.

————. *Cluny—"Licht der Welt." Aufstieg und Niedergang der klösterlichen Gemeinschaft*. Düsseldorf and Zürich: Artemis & Winkler, 1996.

————. "Das Schisma des Abtes Pontius von Cluny." *Francia* 23 (1996): 31–52.

————. "Die mittelalterliche Lebensform der Verbrüderung." In *Memoria. Der geschichtliche Zeugniswert des liturgischen Gedenkens im Mittelalter*, edited by Karl Schmid and Joachim Wollasch. Munich: Wilhelm Fink, 1984. 215–32.

————. "Eleemosynarius. Eine Skizze." In *Sprache und Recht. Beiträge zur Kulturgeschichte des Mittelalters. Festschrift für Ruth Schmidt-Wiegand zum 60. Geburtstag*, edited by Karl Hauck and Karl A. Kroeschell. Berlin: de Gruyter, 1986. 972–95.

————. *Mönchtum des Mittelalters zwischen Kirche und Welt*. Munich: Wilhelm Fink, 1973.

————. "Mönchtum, Königtum, Adel und Klöster im Berry während des 10. Jahrhunderts." In *Neue Forschungen über Cluny und die Cluniacenser*, edited by Gerd Tellenbach. Freiburg im Breisgau: Herder, 1959. 17–165.

————. "Totengedenken im Reformmönchtum." In *Monastische Reformen im 9. und 10. Jahrhundert*, edited by Raymund Kottje and Helmut Maurer. Sigmaringen: Thorbecke, 1989. 147–66.

————. "Zur Verschriftlichung der klösterlichen Lebensgewohnheiten unter Abt Hugo von Cluny." *Frühmittelalterliche Studien* 27 (1993): 317–49.

Wortley, John, ed. *The Anonymous Sayings of the Desert Fathers: A Select Edition and Complete English Translation.* Cambridge, UK: Cambridge University Press, 2013.

Zelzer, Michaela. "Die 'Regula Donati,' der älteste Textzeuge der Regula 'Benedicti.'" *Regulae Benedicti Studia* 16 (1987): 23–36.

Zerner, Monique. "L'hérétique Henri dans les sources de son temps (1135–1145)." *Revue Mabillon*, n.s. 25 (2014): 79–134.

Ziegler, Walter. "Die Bursfelder Kongregation." In *Die Reformverbände und Kongregationen der Benediktiner im deutschen Sprachraum*, edited by Ulrich Faust and Franz Quarthal. St. Ottilien: EOS, 1999. 315–407.

Image Credits

Page 5: © akg-images | page 11: From W. Geerlings and C. Schulze, eds., *Der Kommentar in Antike und Mittelalter.* Vol. 2, *Neue Beiträge zu seiner Erforschung* (Leiden, 2004), pl. 6 | page 25: © akg-images / Elizabeth Disney | page 46: © akg-images | page 76: © Yvan Travert / akg-images | page 79: © picture-alliance / United Archives / TopFoto | page 81: © akg-images | page 102: © bpk / RMN /Jean-Gilles Berizzi | page 104: © Paolo Airenti / Shutterstock images | page 119: © akg-images | page 143: © Herve Champollion / akg-images | page 152: © akg-images / Erich Lessing | page 208: © akg-images | page 226: © Archivi Alinari | page 241: © Iberfoto / Archivi Alinari | page 285: © picture alliance / dpa | page 325: © Iberfoto/ Archivi Alinari | page 327, from *Die Concordantiae caritatis des Ulrich von Lilienfeld. Edition des Codex Campiliensis 151 (um 1355)*, ed. Herbert Douteil, Rudolf Suntrup, Arnold Angenendt, and Volker Honemann (Münster, 2010), 621 | page 330: Drawing: Peter Palm, Berlin | page 331: © akg-images / Catherine Bibollet | page 360: Foundation altarpiece (left wing, outside) from Maulbronn 1450, from M. Untermann: *Forma Ordinis* (Munich/Berlin, 2001), 216 | page 369: © akg-images | pages 382–83: Map: Peter Palm, Berlin.

Index of People and Places

Abelard, Peter, 78, 153, 339
Adalbert, bishop of Laon, 65
Adalbert, bishop of Würzburg, 130
Adalbert II, bishop of Metz, 53
Adalbert II, count of Calw, 85
Adalbert II, count of Ebersberg, 85
Adam, founder of Mortara, 128
Aelred of Rievaulx, 188
Aethelbert, king of Kent, 20
Aethelward, bishop of Winchester, 54
Agnes, daughter of King Ottokar I Premysl, 228
Agnes of Rome, martyr and saint, 86
Ailbert, hermit, 115
Alberic, prior of Molesme, abbot of Cîteaux, 140
Albert V, duke of Austria, 308
Albert, bishop of Vercelli, patriarch of Jerusalem, 250
Alexander III, pope, 180
Alexander IV, pope, 229
Alighieri, Dante, 152
Altmann of Passau, bishop, 129, 130, 143, 376
Alypius, bishop of Thagaste, 10, 12
Ambrose of Milan, 316
Angelo Clareno, 294
Anno II, archbishop of Cologne, 84
Anonymus (from Normandy), 201

Anonymus (regular canon of Lauterberg near Halle), 200, 202, 221
Anselm, bishop of Lucca, 128
Anselm of Canterbury (of Bec), 371
Anselm of Havelberg, 182
Anthony, hermit, desert father, 3–5, 88, 90, 138, 176, 373
Anthony of Padua, 224
Aquinas, Thomas, 290, 372, 379
Arduin of Ivrea, king of Italy, 71
Arno of Reichersberg, 319
Arnold, abbot of Cîteaux, 192
Athanasius, patriarch of Alexandria, 3
Augustine, archbishop of Canterbury, 20–21
Augustine, bishop of Hippo, doctor of the church, 10–12
Aymardus, abbot of Cluny, 57, 58

Balthild, Frankish queen, 34
Barnabas, disciple of Christ, 263
Bartholomew, bishop of Laon, 118, 123
Bartholomew, bishop of Pécs, 268
Basil the Great, archbishop of Caeserea, 9–10, 89
Benedict VII, pope, 62
Benedict VIII, pope, 63
Benedict XII, pope, 267, 300–306, 307, 309, 335, 379

Benedict Biscop, 33
Benedict of Aniane (born as
    Witiza, son of the Count of
    Maguelonne), 39
Benedict of Nursia, 24–27, 352,
    374
Bernard, author of *Consuetudines
    Cluniacenses*, 68
Bernard of Clairvaux, 152–54, 155,
    156, 169, 170, 188, 191, 321,
    326, 361, 377
Bernard of Tiron, 110, 111, 145
Bernardino of Siena, 297, 312
Bernardo Tolomei, founder of
    Monte Oliveto, 274
Berno, abbot of Cluny, 57–58
Berthold of Regensburg, 287
Birgitta of Sweden, 280–85, 286,
    289, 304, 339, 340, 379
Bonaventure, minister general,
    230, 289, 290, 292, 293, 350,
    379
Boniface VIII, pope, 177, 292, 294
Boniface IX, pope, 279
Boniface (Winfrid), missionary
    bishop, 37, 44
Bridget of Kildare, 18
Bruno of Cologne, founder of the
    Carthusian Order, 103–6, 110,
    121, 123, 139–40, 153, 273,
    344, 376
Bruno of Schauenburg, bishop of
    Olmütz, 291
Busch, John, 311

Caesaria, sister of Caesarius of
    Arles, 16
Caesarius of Arles, 13, 16, 35, 374
Caesarius of Heisterbach, 358
Calixtus II, pope, 77, 114, 118
Canterbury, 20
Carloman, brother of King Pippin,
    37

Carpini. *See* John de Piano Carpini
Cassian, John, 17–18, 373
Cassiodorus, Roman senator, 365,
    374
Catherine, daughter of Saint
    Birgitta, 284
Celestine V, pope. *See* Peter of
    Morrone
Charlemagne, emperor, 29, 37–38,
    39, 41, 43, 44, 45, 374
Charles II, king of Naples (Sicily),
    272
Charles V, emperor, 274
Charles of Anjou, king of Sicily,
    272
Chrodegang, bishop of Metz, 41
Chrysostom, John, 1, 4
Ciaran of Clonmacnois, 18
Clare of Assisi, 225–31, 379
Clement IV, pope, 299
Clement V, pope, 172, 294
Clement VI, pope, 274
Clovis, Frankish king, 15, 374
Columban the Elder, 19
Columban the Younger, 21–22, 35,
    374
Comgall, founder of Bangor, 18
Conrad I, archbishop of Salzburg,
    133, 377
Constantine, Roman emperor, 8,
    373

Daire Calcaic (Londonderry), 19
Damian, Peter, cardinal, 73, 74, 92
Daniel, prophet, 316
David, king of Judah, 352
Decius, Roman emperor, 3
Desiderius, Lombard king, 34
Diego, bishop of Osma, 233–34,
    238
Dominic Guzman, founder of the
    Dominican Order, 202, 232,
    234–38, 327, 378

Donatus, bishop of Besançon, 35

Dunstan, archbishop of
Canterbury, 54

Eckhart (Master), Dominican
mystic, 368

Edgar, Anglo-Saxon king, 54

Elias of Cortona, minister general,
224

Elijah, prophet, 250, 255, 292, 352

Elisabeth of Thüringia, 359

Elisha, prophet and disciple of
Elijah, 255, 352

Eugene III, pope, 132, 150

Eugene IV, pope, 294

Eusebius, bishop of Vercelli, 13

Eusebius, cathedral canon of
Esztergom, 267

Felix of Valois, founder of the
Trinitarian Order, 178

Ferreolus of Uzes, 13

Finnian of Clonard, 18

Francis of Assisi, founder of the
Franciscan Order, 202–5,
206–16, 344, 378

Franz of Paola, founder of the
Paulines, 275

Frederick I, archbishop of Cologne,
115

Frederick I Barbarossa, emperor,
377

Frederick II, emperor, 229, 251

Fulbert, abbot of Maria Laach, 363

Fulco, bishop of Toulouse, 234

Galvaneus Flamma, Dominican
historian, 302

Gebhard, archbishop of Salzburg,
130

Gelasius II, pope, 77, 117

Gerard de Arvernia, historian, 355,
358

Gerard of Brogne, 52

Gerardus de Fracheto, Dominican
historian, 248

Gerhoh, prior of Reichersberg, 129

Gilbert of Poitiers, 153

Gilbert, founder of the congregation of Sempringham, 164, 377

Giovanni Battista Bernadone,
father of Francis of Assisi, 209

Giselbert, duke of Lotharingia, 52

Glaber, Rodulf, historian, 73

Godehard, abbot of Niederaltaich,
bishop of Hildesheim, 83

Goffredus da Trani, canonist, 299,
317 n. 5

Gozelinus, bishop of Toul, 52

Gratian, canonist, 187, 336

Gregory (I) the Great, pope, 20, 24–
29, 32, 43, 101, 306, 374, 400

Gregory II, pope, 36, 37

Gregory V, pope, 63

Gregory VII, pope, 75, 77, 103,
126, 127, 129, 376

Gregory IX, pope (first Cardinal
Hugolino), 176, 195, 213, 221,
222, 228, 229, 232, 252, 258,
260, 299, 300, 337, 378

Gregory XI, pope, 268

Groote, Geert, founder of the
Devotio moderna, 276–79, 379

Guerin, bishop of Sion, 140

Gui (Viard), founder of the Caulites,
270

Guibert of Nogent, historian, 104

Guibert of Tournai, theologian, 291

Guido II, bishop of Assisi, 210

Guido, founder of a hospital in
Montpellier, 175–76

Gunther of Niederaltaich, hermit,
94, 110

Harding, Stephen, abbot of Cîteaux,
146–47, 156

Henry I, king of England and duke of Normandy, 112
Henry II, emperor, 77, 81, 83
Henry III, emperor, 77, 82
Henry IV, emperor, 77, 81, 82, 87, 130, 133, 376
Henry V, emperor, 115
Henry, abbot of Clairvaux, 192
Henry Eger of Kalkar, mystic, 277
Henry of Friemar, historian, 261–62
Henry of Lausanne, wandering preacher, 116–17
Henry Suso, mystic, 368
Herman of Tournai, Benedictine abbot, 161
Herrad of Landsberg, abbesss, 369, 370
Hersendis of Champagne, first prioress of Fontevraud, 114
Hieronymus Bosch, painter, 4, 5
Hildegard of Bingen, *magistra* and visionary, 370
Honoratus of Aries, founder of the monastery at Lérins, 15
Honorius III, pope, 180, 213, 215, 220, 235, 236, 252, 270
Honorius IV, pope, 260
Hugh I, abbot of Cluny, 57, 63, 65, 68, 74, 77, 78, 81, 376
Hugh II, abbot of Cluny, 78
Hugh V, abbot of Cluny, 167
Hugh, archbishop of Rouen, 145
Hugh, bishop of Grenoble, 104, 123
Hugh Capet, West Frankish king, 375
Hugh de Lacerta, companion of Stephen of Thiers, 102
Hugh of Die, archbishop of Lyon, 140
Hugh of Fosses, organizer of the Praemonstratensian Order, 117, 159, 377

Hugh of Fouilly, 188, 190, 328, 329
Hugh of Payns, founder of the Templars, 168
Hugh of Saint-Victor, 370
Hugolino, cardinal and protector of the Franciscan Order. *See* Gregory IX
Humbert of Romans, master general, 242, 243, 246, 248, 291, 334

Innocent II, pope, 106, 160, 171
Innocent III, pope, 142, 175, 176, 180, 192, 198, 199, 201, 209, 212, 214, 233, 257, 260, 270, 298, 306, 378
Innocent IV, pope, 177, 207, 229, 253, 255, 258, 259, 260, 269, 292, 296, 359
Ivo, bishop of Chartres, 96–97, 109, 111, 116, 128, 137, 138

James I, king of Aragon, 178
James, apostle, 116
James of Vitry, bishop of Acre, cardinal, 156, 194, 203, 248, 250
Jan van Ruysbroeck, mystic, 276, 279
Jerome, church father, 3, 14, 105, 269, 274, 373
Joachim of Fiore, visionary, 264, 378
Job, prophet, 108, 316
John XI, pope, 60, 61, 62
John XVIII, pope, 71
John XIX, pope, 62
John XXII, pope, 196
John Bonus, founder of the John Bonites, 258, 259
John, cardinal of St. Paul, 212, 218
John Cassian. *See* Cassian, John

John Chrysostom. *See* Chrysostom, John
John de Piano Carpini, traveler to Asia, 207
John, disciple of Romuald, 64
John Gualbert, founder of Vallombrosa, 94
John Nider. *See* Nider, John
John of Matha, founder of the Trinitarian Order, 178
John Olivi. *See* Olivi, John
John Tauler. *See* Tauler, John
John the Baptist, 116, 352
Jordan of Saxony, master general, 239, 243
Joshua, prophet, 263
Judas Iscariot, 56

Kunigunde of Luxembourg, wife of Emperor Henry II, 83

Landuin, successor of Bruno in the Grande Chartreuse, 106
Lanfranc of Bec, archbishop of Canterbury, 70, 98
Leidrad, archbishop of Lyon, 39
Leo IX, pope, 170
Lietbert, abbot of St. Rufus, 352
Lindisfarne, 20, 33
Liudolf, hermit, 115
Lothar III, emperor, 80
Louis IX (Saint), king of France, 207, 378
Louis the Pious, emperor, 39, 43, 45
Lucius II, pope, 161
Lucius III, pope, 197, 420
Ludwig the Bavarian, emperor, 296, 379

Macarius, hermit, 138
Maiolus, abbot of Cluny, 57, 59, 67, 69, 92
Marbod, bishop of Rennes, 112, 113

Marcella, prominent Roman, 14
Martha of Bethany, 319 n. 11
Martin of Tours, 14, 72, 373
Mary, mother of Jesus, 72, 75, 248, 256, 286, 319
Mary of Bethany, 319 n. 11
Mary, sister of Pachomius, 8
Michael of Cesena, minister general, 295, 296
Moses, leader of the Israelites, 263, 352

Nicholas II, pope, 127
Nicholas III, pope, 293, 294, 299
Nicholas V, pope, 310
Nicholas of Cusa, 310, 311
Nicholas of Dinkelsbühl, 308
Nicholas of Narbonne, general-prior of the Carmelite Order, 253
Nicholas Seyringer. *See* Seyringer, Nicholas
Nider, John, theologian, 312
Noah, 71, 316
Norbert of Xanten, 110, 115, 119, 121, 123, 125, 128, 132, 156, 158, 160, 276, 314, 339, 344, 377

Odilo, abbot of Cluny, 57, 63, 65, 68, 73, 74
Odo III, duke of Burgundy, 270
Odo, abbot of Cluny, 57, 58, 60, 61
Odo, West Frankish king, 55
Oliba, bishop of Vic, 91
Olivi, Peter John, 293, 294
Orderic Vitalis, chronicler, 95, 98, 138, 139, 141, 144
Oswald, bishop of Worcester, 54
Oswald, king of Northumbria, 20
Otto I, bishop of Bamberg, 87
Otto I, emperor, 50, 52, 77, 80, 375
Otto III, emperor, 89, 92, 375

Otto, duke of Brunswick-
Göttingen, 310
Otto of Freising, bishop, 186, 190,
248, 263, 316

Pachomius, monastic founder, 7, 8,
9, 15, 39, 373
Paolucci Trinci. *See* Trinci,
Paolucci
Paschal II, pope, 65, 66, 114, 141
Patrick, Irish missionary, 18
Paul, apostle, 72, 187, 263
Paul, bishop of Veszprem, 268
Paul of Thebes, desert father, 3,
14, 269
Paul the Deacon, historian, 28, 37
Peter II, bishop of Poitiers, 114
Peter, abbot of Moutier-la-Celle,
188, 320, 322
Peter, apostle, 71, 72, 177, 284
Peter Abelard. *See* Abelard, Peter
Peter Catanii, minister general, 214
Peter John Olivi. *See* Olivi, Peter
John
Peter of Bruis, wandering preacher,
116
Peter of Morrone (Celestine V),
271, 273, 294
Peter the Venerable, abbot of
Cluny, 78, 153, 182, 188, 190,
342, 377
Petronax, second founder of
Montecassino, 36, 37
Petronilla of Chemillé, abbess of
Fontevraud, 114
Petrus Ferrandi, hagiographer, 238
Petrus Nolascus, founder of the
Mercederian Order, 178
Petrus Olavi, prior, 282
Philip IV, king of France, 172
Philip of Harvengt, 188
Pietro Gambacorta, founder of the
Poor Hermits of St. Jerome, 274

Pippin, Frankish king, 37
Pirmin, missionary bishop, 34
Pius II, pope, 310
Pontius of Melgueil, abbot of
Cluny, 78
Poverello. *See* Francis of Assisi

Radegundis, Frankish queen, 16,
51
Radewijns, Florens, 279
Rainald, hermit, 97, 98, 138
Rambold, abbot of St. Emmeram,
83
Raymond V, count of Toulouse,
192
Raymond Athenulfi, founder of the
Sack Brothers, 291
Raymond Gaufridi, minister
general, 294
Raymond of Capua, master
general, 312
Raymond of Peñaforte, master
general, 178, 244, 337
Richard Annibaldi, cardinal, 257,
258, 260
Richer of Sens, historian, 288
Robert II, West Frankish king, 65
Robert Curthose, duke of
Normandy, 112
Robert of Arbrissel, founder of the
congregation of Fontevraud,
110, 112–15, 117, 121, 123,
125, 198, 220, 341, 344, 376
Robert of Mortain, brother of
William the Conqueror, 111
Romuald, founder of the
Camaldolese, 68, 92, 109, 110,
270, 352, 375
Rubruk, William, 207
Rudolf I, general prior of the
Camaldolese, 93
Rudolf I, West Frankish king, 60,
63

Rudolf, founder of the Magdalens, 178

Rupert II, count palatine, 310

Saladin, sultan, 172

Seyringer, Nicholas, leader of the Melk reform, 307, 308, 380

Siegfried I, count of Luxemburg, 83

Silvester Guzzolini, founder of the Silvestrines, 269

Sixtus IV, pope, 275

Stephen de Liciaco, prior of Grandmont, 103

Stephen of Obazine, abbot, 107–9

Stephen of Thiers (Muret), founder of the Grandmontines, 99, 102, 103, 105, 108, 118, 142, 184, 198, 344, 345, 376

Tauler, John, mystic, 368

Theoderic the Great, king of the Ostrogoths, 365

Theodomarus, abbot of Montecas-sino, 73

Theodoric, count of Autun, 37

Thomas of Cantimpré, encyclope-dist, 235

Thomas of Celano, hagiographer, 224

Thomas of Kempen, mystic of the *Devotio moderna*, 280

Trinci, Paolucci, 312

Ubertino of Casale, 294

Ulrich of Zell, author of the *Consuetudines Cluniacenses*, 341

Urban II, pope, 55, 72, 75, 77, 79, 105, 113, 130, 140, 187, 376

Urban IV, pope, 230, 272

Urban V, pope, 281, 284

Urban VI, pope, 284

Venerandus, abbot of Hauterive, 29, 32

Viard. *See* Gui

Victor II, pope, 94

Victor, Saint, 17

Vincent of Beauvais, encyclopedist, 263, 264, 265, 286, 292, 368

Vitalis, abbot of Savigny, 98, 110, 111, 155

Waldebert, abbot of Luxeuil, 35

William I (the Conqueror), king of England, 70

William, abbot of Hirsau, 69

William, abbot of Saint-Thierry, 188

William, duke of Aquitaine, foun-der of Cluny, 55

William of Malavalle, founding figure of the Williamites, 257, 258

William of Ockham, theologian and philosopher, 296

William of Saint-Amour, Parisian theologian, 290

William of Volpiano, abbot of Saint-Benigne (Dijon), 71, 83, 375

William Rubruk, traveler to Asia, 207

Willibald, bishop of Eichstätt, 37

Willibrord, missionary to Frisia, 29

Winfried Boniface *see* Boniface, Winfried

Wolfgang, bishop of Regensburg, 83

Zachary, pope, 36, 37, 38

Index of Monasteries, Congregations, and Orders

The main passages for congregations and orders are in boldface. All forms of Saint, Sainte, Sankt, San, Sant', Santa, Santo, and St. have been simplified to S.

Alvastra, 281, 282

Annegrey, 21

Antonite Order (Order of S. Anthony), 176–78, 376

Arrouaise (congregation), 163, 166, 280, 299

Au, 134

Augsburg, Franciscan convent, 206

Augustinian Canons. *See* Regular Canons

Augustinian Hermits, 204, 243, 249, **256–62**, 267, 268, 269, 270, 287, 292, 334, 335, 379

Aulps, 140, 149

Aylesford (Carmelite monastery), 250, 252, 253

Balerne, 149

Bangor, 18, 21

Basilian monasteries (in southern Italy), 52

Baume, 58

Bec, 70

Beguines, **193–96**, 227, 276, 278, 359, 372, 378

Benedictines, **24–49**, **50–88**, 92, 93, 94, 95, 97, 99, 111, 134,

144, 145, 266, 267, 270–71, 280, 282, 300–302, 306, 308–11, 321, 323, 328, 329, 346, 357, 360, 361

Benediktbeuern, 82

Berchtesgaden, 364

Birgittines (Order of the Holy Savior), 265, 266, 285, 304

Bobbio, 22, 23, 35, 334

Bologna, Dominican monastery, 236

Brogne, 52

Bursfelde (reform congregation), 310, 311, 380

Caen, 70, 98

Camaldoli, Camaldolese (congregation), 68, **92–93**, 104, 109, 250, 335, 339, 352, 353, 375

Canons (not regular canons), 5, 39, 43, 126

Canonesses, 39, 42, 43, 51, 127, 132–33, 311, 357, 372

Cappenberg, 158

Carmel, Carmelites, 204, **250–56**, 269, 287, 292, 378

Carthusians, 106, 124, 151, 156, 158, **164–66**, 249, 266, 302,

329, 332, 336, 338, 341, 342, 347, 348, 354

Caulites (congregation), 270

Celestines, **273**, 362, 363

Châtillon, 270

Chelles, 34

Cîteaux, Cistercians, 103, 132, **136–57**, 164, 165, 301

Clairvaux, 146, 155, 363

Clonard, 18

Clonmacnois, 18

Cluny, Cluniacs, **54–80**, 82, 83, 84, 86, 87, 88, 90, 92, 128, 132, 137, 139, 166, 167–68, 186, 302, 307, 314, 323, 334, 342, 347, 354, 357, 375, 376, 377

Coburg, 85

Collan (hermit colony), 139

Conventuals, 297

Corbie, 34, 38

Corvey, 44, 50, 311

Coulombs, 96, 137

Craon (hermit colony), 98, 111, 112, 267

Cuissy, 162

Cuxa, 92

Dalon, 109

Damianites (Order of S. Damian), 229

Deols, 58

Disibodenberg, 48

Doire, 18

Dominicans (Order of Preachers), 185, 195, 204, **232–48**, 249, 251, 252, 253, 254, 258, 259, 261, 262, 263, 264, 265, 268, 287, 288, 289, 290, 291, 292, 302, 312, 314, 329, 332, 334, 335, 337, 339, 341, 346, 347, 348, 349, 368, 372, 378

Ecclesia Mortariensis. See Mortara

Essen, 42, 51

Evreux, 70

Farfa, 44, 61, 68, 307

Fécamp, 69, 70

Fleury, 35, 36, 37, 52, 53, 54, 61

Floreffe, 158, 162

Fons Evraldi. *See* Fontevraud

Fontaines (Dijon), 21

Fonte Avellana, 92

Fontevraud (congregation), **114**, **115**, 121, 123, 156, 341, 349

Franciscans (Order of Friars Minor), 100, 151, 200, 204, **206–31**, 232, 236, 237, 246, 248, 249, 252, 254, 255, 258, 260, 262, 264, 265, 274, 286, 287, 288, 289, 290, 291, 292, 293, 295, 296, 298, 299, 301, 302, 312, 317, 332, 335, 359, 378, 379

Fraticelli, 294

Friars of the Sack, **291**

Fruttuaria, 71, 83, 84, 354, 375

Fulda, 37, 43, 82

Gandersheim, 42, 51

Gars, 134

Gembloux, 311

Gigny, 58

Glastonbury, 70

Gorze, 52, 71, 83, 87, 88, 354, 375

Gottweig, 130

Grande Chartreuse, 103, 106, 164, 165, 344, 376

Grandmontines, **101**, **106**, 124, 142, 151, 156, 248, 249, 252, 266, 299, 317, 338, 339, 354, 359

Groenendaal, 277, 279

Gurk (regular cathedral chapter), 134

Hamersleben, 131
Hauterive (Alta Ripa), 29
Heidenfeld, 130
Herford, 42
Hermits of Brettino (congregation), 259
Hermits of Monte Favale, 260
Hermits of S. Jerome. *See* Poor Hermits
Herrenchiemsee, 134
Hersfeld, 94
Hirsau (reform circle), 53, 69, **85–87**, 88, 151, 307, 309, 311, 341, 351, 354, 376
Hospitalers (Order of St. John), 173
Hulne (Carmelite monastery), 252
Humiliati, **196–200**, 202, 212, 250, 265, 378

Ilbenstadt, 161
Inden (Kornelimünster), 39, 40, 354

Jeronimites, 274
John Bonites, **258**
Jully, 156
Jumieges, 70

Kastl (reform circle), 307, 309, 310, 358, 380
Kentheim, 86
Kildare, 18
Klosterrath, 115, 132, 341
Kornelimünster. *See* Inden
Kremsmünster, 83

La Chaise-Dieu, 104, 106
La Charité-sur-Loire, 64
La Ferté, 146
Laon (regular canonry), 118, 162
La Roe, 112, 125
Lauterberg, 200, 202, 203

Lazarites (Order of Lazarus), 173
Lérins, 15, 16, 22, 33, 35, 357, 373
Les Aygalades (Carmelite monastery), 252
Lesser Brothers. *See* Franciscans
Le Tart, 156
Lippoldsberg, 86
Lugny, 270
Luxeuil, 21, 23, 35

Magdalens, **178**
Maiella. *See* S. Spirito a Maiella
Marbach, 132
Maria Laach, 363
Maria Saal, 134
Marmoutier, 14, 373
Massay, 58
Maursmünster, 39
Melk (reform circle), **307–10**, 358, 380
Mercedarians, **178**
Messina (Carmelite monastery), 252
Michelsberg (Bamberg), 310
Minims, 275
Minorites. *See* Franciscans
Moissac, 64, 65
Molesme, 103–4, 136–42, 145, 146, 156
Monnikhuizen, 277
Monte Cassino, 24, 26–28, 36–38, 48, 52, 55, 61, 374
Monte Fano (congregation), 259
Monte Favale (congregation), **260**
Monte Oliveto (congregation), **274**
Montpellier (Hospital), 175, 176
Montserrat, 91
Morimond, 146, 155
Mortara (congregation), **128**, 199, 200, 250, 334
Moutier-la-Celle, 139, 320
Moyenmoutier, 53
Münsterschwarzach, 310

Neumünster (near Ottweiler), 53
Niederaltaich, 83, 94
Nivelles, 39
Nonantola, 44

Obazine (today Aubazine, congre-
gation), 107, **108**, 109, 110, 124
Observants, 297, 306, 312
Odilienberg, 43
Olivetaner. *See* Monte Oliveto
Order of Friars Minor. *See*
Franciscans
Order of Preachers. *See*
Dominicans
Order of the Holy Spirit, **176**
Order of the Savior. *See* Birgittines

Paisley, 64
Paraclete, 78, 339
Paris (Dominican convent), 236,
239
Paulines, **268–70**, 379
Patacs, 268
Petershausen, 307, 351
Polirone, 64
Pombeiro, 64
Pomposa, 44
Pontigny, 146
Poor Clares, **230**
Poor Hermits of St. Jerome, 274
Portiuncula, 211, 213, 214
Premontré, Premonstratensians,
118, **120**, 124, 132, **158–63**,
165, 167, 207, 235, 237, 242,
243, 246, 266, 280, 298, 299,
314, 335, 336, 342, 347, 348,
377, 383
Premy (congregation), **348**
Prouille, 234

Quedlinburg, 42, 51

Regular canons, 7, **125–35**, 163,
166, 170, 180, 191, 199, 203,
204, 266, 301, 302, 314, 319,
328, 340, 341, 360, 375, 376,
377
Reichenau, 34, 38, 43, 44, 46
Reichersberg am Inn, 134
Remiremont, 35, 53
Reuerinnen. *See* Magdalens
Rinchnach, 94
Roggenburg, 161
Romainmôtier, 61
Rottenbuch, 129, 130, 131, 132

S. Agnes (Schaffhausen), 86
S. Anna (Rocca di Mondragone),
307
S. Antoine-l'Abbaye, 176
S. Apollinare (near Ravenna), 92
S. Arnoul (Metz), 53
S. Ayoul de Provins, 139
S. Benedetto. *See* Subiaco
S. Benigne (Dijon), 39, 69, 363,
375
S. Benoit-sur-Loire. *See* Fleury, 35,
36, 37, 52, 53, 54, 61
S. Bertin, 356
S. Blaise, 71, 87
S. Croix (Poitiers), 16
S. Cyprian (Poitiers), 66, 111
S. Damiano (Assisi), 210, 213,
216, 225, 227, 228, 229
S. Denis (near Paris), 39, 332, 363
S. Didier-de-la-Motte. *See*
S. Antoine-l'Abbaye
S. Emmeram (Regensburg), 81, 83,
85, 310
S. Etienne (Caen), 70
S. Evre (Toul), 52
S. Evroul, 111
S. Florian (near Linz), 129
S. Gall, 38, 44, 46, 48, 310
S. Gilles, 66, 117
S. Giustina (Padua), 311
S. Goeric (Epinal), 53

S. James (Mainz), 311
S. Jean (Arles), 16
S. Maria degli Angeli. *See*
    Portiuncula
S. Maria in Saxia, 175
S. Maria Novella (Florence), 241,
    289
S. Marie-aux-Nonnaines, 53
S. Martial (Limoges), 64
S. Martin (Laon), 162
S. Martin-des-Champs, 64
S. Martin in Lucca (regular
    cathedral chapter), 126
S. Maurice (Geneva), 48
S. Maurice (Magdeburg), 50
S. Maximin (Trier), 52, 83
S. Michel de Tonnerre, 139
S. Miniato (Florence), 94
S. Nicholas (Passau), 129
S. Peter (Erfurt), 311
S. Peter (Montmajour), 177
S. Peter (Salzburg), 309
S. Pierre-en-Nonnains, 53
S. Polten, 130
S. Romain (Toulouse), 234, 235,
    236
S. Rufus (near Avignon), 126, 132
S. Sabina (Rome), 236
S. Salvatore (Brescia), 34
S. Salvatore in Laterano
    (congregation), **311**
S. Savin-sur-Gartempe, 111
S. Spirito, Hospital Order. *See*
    Order of the Holy Spirit
S. Spirito a Maiella, 271, 272
S. Ulrich und Afra (Augsburg), 309
S. Victor (Marseille), 17, 39
S. Victor (Paris), 131
S. Victor (Xanten), 115
Sarabaites, 96, 137, 212

Savigny (congregation), 112, 164
Schottenkloster (Vienna), 309
Seche-Fontaine, 104
Segovia, Dominican friary, 236
Siegburg (congregation), **84, 87,
    88,** 115, 117, 376
Speyer (Franciscan friary), 206
Spirituals, 273, 294, 295, 312
Springiersbach, 131, 132, 166, 341
Subiaco, 25, 26, 27, 36, 208, 306,
    307, 308, 310

Tabennisi, 7
Tart. *See* Le Tart
Tegernsee, 43, 309
Templars, 166, **168–73**, 295, 339,
    377
Teutonic Order, **173**, 377
Thagaste, 10, 12
Tiron (congregation), 111
Trinitarians, **178**
Tuscan Hermits, 258

Urbanites, 287

Valenciennes (Carmelite friary),
    252
Vallombrosa (congregation), **94,**
    147
Val-Saint-Lambert, 364
Varlar, 161
Vercelli (regular clerical commu-
    nity), 13
Vivarium, 365, 374

Whitby, 34, 35
Williamites, 257, 258, 260
Windesheim (near Zwolle, congre-
    gation), **279–80**, 311, 380
Worms, Franciscan friary, 206